Peter Ehlers, Marian Paschke (Eds.)

Maritime Law – Current Developments and Perspectives

Veröffentlichungen des Instituts für Seerecht
und Seehandelsrecht der Universität Hamburg

Herausgegeben von

Rolf Herber, Rainer Lagoni und Marian Paschke

Band 24

LIT

Maritime Law –
Current Developments and Perspectives

Publication on the occasion
of the 35th anniversary
of the Institute for the Law of the Sea
and Maritime Law (Hamburg)

edited by

Peter Ehlers and Marian Paschke

LIT

This book is printed on acid-free paper.

Bibliographic information published by the Deutsche Nationalbibliothek
The Deutsche Nationalbibliothek lists this publication in the Deutsche Nationalbibliografie; detailed bibliographic data are available on the Internet at http://dnb.d-nb.de.

ISBN 978-3-643-91072-1 (hc)
ISBN 978-3-643-96072-6 (PDF)

A catalogue record for this book is available from the British Library.

Klosbachstr. 107
CH-8032 Zürich
Tel. +41 (0) 44-251 75 05
E-Mail: zuerich@lit-verlag.ch http://www.lit-verlag.ch
Distribution:
In the UK: Global Book Marketing, e-mail: mo@centralbooks.com
In North America: Independent Publishers Group, e-mail: orders@ipgbook.com
In Germany: LIT Verlag Fresnostr. 2, D-48159 Münster
Tel. +49 (0) 2 51-620 32 22, Fax +49 (0) 2 51-922 60 99, e-mail: vertrieb@lit-verlag.de
e-books are available at www.litwebshop.de

OUTLINE CONTENTS

Contents

Preface

35 years ago, the Institute for Law of the Sea and Maritime Law was founded at the University of Hamburg, taking into account that Hamburg is one of the maritime centers worldwide. Ten years later, the Maritime Law Foundation was established with the dual aim to support the work of the Institute and to promote the active teaching of and research in maritime law. These anniversaries therefore provide the perfect opportunity to reflect on the achievements and current activities as well as future priorities of the Institute and the Foundation. The broad thematic scope of this dual-anniversary publication demonstrates the wide-ranging reach that modern maritime law possess in the various fields of public and private law at the national as well as international levels.

Looking back at the Institute's evolution into a center of excellence in the maritime field, it is with gratitude to recall and honor the foresight and efforts of the founding fathers, Rolf Herber and Rainer Lagoni. Their vision and leadership have borne many fruits and it is to them that we dedicate this publication. We also recognize the profound contributions of the Institute's scientific associates, lecturers, colleagues and staff members over the years. Today, the professors and scholars of the Institute offer a wide-array of courses, activities and publications on maritime law and the law of the sea to law students and practitioners. The Institute also enjoys the cooperation of numerous partners all over the world.

The contributions of the publication should give all those who are interested in maritime law an insight into the activities of the Institute and significant current legal issues that face the maritime industry. For the students of the Hamburg University degree program in Maritime Business Law, the articles may provide some teaching and study material. The members of the general public will hopefully also find interest in the contributions

The articles are written by scholars and legal practioners who are particularly linked to the work of the Institute and have supported its activities over the years in many ways. We want to thank all the authors for their contributions, without which this publication could not have succeeded. Our special gratitude goes to the Edmund Siemers Foundation for their generous financial support.

Hamburg, September 2018
Marian Paschke and Peter Ehlers

Chapter I

The International Tribunal for the Law of the Sea and New Challenges Lying Ahead

Vladimir Golitsyn

A. Introduction

The 1982 United Nations Convention on the Law (hereinafter "the Convention") is one of the most complex international treaties that have ever been negotiated. While the Convention confirmed many provisions of customary international law codified in the 1958 Geneva Conventions, its main achievement was the progressive development of international law. In this regard, the Convention declares the Area (the seabed, ocean floor and subsoil thereof beyond limits of national jurisdiction) and its mineral resources the common heritage of mankind and establishes an international regime governing activities of exploration for and exploitation of the mineral resources of the Area. It introduces the concepts of the exclusive economic zone and archipelagic waters, clarifies the regime governing passage through straits used for international navigation, defines the legal regime of the continental shelf and sets up the criteria to be used by a coastal state in establishing the outer limits of its continental shelf. The Convention also contains extensive provisions concerning the protection and preservation of the marine environment, and provides for a mechanism, in the form of compulsory procedures entailing binding decisions, which aims at ensuring compliance with the provisions of the Convention.

The Convention also represents a major step forward with respect to the matters of dispute settlement and compulsory adjudication. It first echoes the duty imposed on states by the United Nations Charter to settle disputes by peaceful means.[1] In addition, the Convention obliges States Parties to submit disputes for which no such settlement has been reached to binding international adjudication or – in the words of the Convention – to "compulsory procedures entailing binding decisions".[2]

Of the adjudicatory bodies referred to in the Convention, the International Tribunal for the Law of the Sea (hereinafter "the Tribunal") is the central judicial body entrusted under the Convention to deal with disputes concerning its application and interpretation.

The Tribunal's jurisdiction encompasses, in the first place, the adjudication of contentious cases between States Parties in disputes concerning the application or interpretation of the Convention. In addition, the Tribunal enjoys specific competencies with regard to provisional measures and the prompt release of arrested vessels and their crews. Moreover, both the full Tribunal and one of its specialized chambers, the Seabed Disputes Chamber, have the power to issue advisory opinions in specific cases.

B. Contribution of the Tribunal to the peaceful settlement of disputes under UNCLOS

Although the Tribunal has not been in existence for long, it has developed substantial jurisprudence in the cases submitted to it. This article is aimed at synthesizing some of the conclusions reached by the Tribunal in its decisions.

In exercising its jurisdiction, the Tribunal, by dealing with various issues which relate to the interpretation or application of the Convention, has not only made a major contribution to the peaceful settlement of international disputes – a function which has aptly been referred to as the "archetypical role"[3] of international courts and tribunals, but also contributed to the progressive development of the international law of the sea.

Procedurally a dispute may be submitted to the Tribunal on the basis either of declarations made under article 287 of the United Nations Convention on the Law of the Sea (which I will refer to simply as "the Convention") or of a special agreement concluded between the parties to the dispute.

Recently, Ghana and Côte d'Ivoire concluded a special agreement to submit to a special chamber of the Tribunal the dispute concerning delimitation of their maritime boundary in the Atlantic Ocean. The special agreement was entered into further to consultations which I, as President of the Tribunal, held with the representatives of those States in December 2014. By Order of 12 January 2015, the Tribunal, acting at the request of the parties, formed a special chamber composed of five members, including one judge ad hoc chosen by Ghana and one chosen by Côte d'Ivoire.

This is not the first time that the procedure for an ad hoc special chamber has been used. Such an option was exercised by Chile and the European Community in the *Case concerning the Conservation and Sustainable Exploitation of Swordfish Stocks in the South-Eastern Pacific Ocean*. This special chamber system has proven to be a flexible mechanism combining the advantages of a permanent court with those of an arbitral body, while avoiding the significant expenses parties often incur in arbitral proceedings.

I. CONTENTIOUS JURISDICTION

In one of its earliest judgments, in the *M/V "SAIGA"* case, the Tribunal in 1997 provided clarification regarding the meaning of the term "ship" or "vessel" under the Convention; it has relied on this clarification in a number of its subsequent judgments. The Tribunal concluded in that case that:

> *"... the Convention considers a ship as a unit, as regards the obligations of the flag State with respect to the ship and the right of a flag State to seek reparation for loss or damage caused to the ship by acts of other States and to institute proceedings under article 292 of the Convention. Thus the ship, everything on it, and every person involved or interested in its operations are treated as an entity linked to the flag State. The nationalities of these persons are not relevant".*[4]

With reference to the question of whether the fact that the vessel's owner and its crew are not nationals of the flag State has any bearing on the issue of the existence of a genuine link between the flag State concerned and the ship flying its flag, the Tribunal concluded in the *M/V "Virginia G"* case that "the Convention provides in article 91, paragraph 1, that 'every State shall fix the conditions for the grant of its nationality to ships' and does not impose in this regard any limitations on the nationality of ship-owners or crew".[5]

Since a significant number of cases considered by the Tribunal have related to the arrest and detention of vessels and their crews, which frequently involved use of force, the Tribunal has found it necessary in those cases to highlight the importance of humanitarian considerations and respect for human rights. In the *M/V "Louisa"* case the Tribunal reiterated its view, expressed in various forms in several of its previous judgments,[6] "that States are required to fulfil their obligations under international law, in particular human rights law, and that considerations of due process of law must be applied in all circumstances".[7]

In the *M/V "SAIGA"* case the Tribunal stated:

"Although the Convention does not contain express provisions on the use of force in the arrest of ships, international law, which is applicable by virtue of article 293 of the Convention, requires that the use of force must be avoided as far as possible and, where force is unavoidable, it must not go beyond what is reasonable and necessary in the circumstances. Considerations of humanity must apply in the law of the sea, as they do in other areas of international law".[8]

In one recent case the Tribunal had to provide what I would call a progressive interpretation of the Convention on the issue of bunkering and its regulation within the exclusive economic zone of the coastal State. In the *M/V "Virginia G"* case the Tribunal came to a conclusion that "the regulation by a coastal State of bunkering of foreign vessels fishing in its exclusive economic zone is among those measures which the coastal State may take in its exclusive economic zone to conserve and manage its living resources under article 56 of the Convention read together with article 62, paragraph 4, of the Convention" and noted that "this view is also confirmed by State practice which has developed after the adoption of the Convention".[9]

The Tribunal thus concluded that "the bunkering of foreign vessels engaged in fishing in the exclusive economic zone is an activity which may be regulated by the coastal State concerned". At the same time the Tribunal emphasized that "the coastal State, however, does not have such competence with regard to other bunkering activities, unless otherwise determined in accordance with the Convention".[10]

Another provision of the Convention, the proper understanding and interpretation of which has required clarification by the Tribunal, is article 300 on "good faith and abuse of rights", which provides:

"States Parties shall fulfil in good faith the obligations assumed under this Convention and shall exercise the rights, jurisdiction and freedoms recognized in this Convention in a manner which would not constitute an abuse of right."

It was in the *M/V "Louisa"* case that the provisions of this article were invoked before the Tribunal for the first time. The Tribunal found in that case "that it is apparent from the language of article 300 of the Convention that article 300 cannot be invoked on its own. It becomes relevant only when 'the rights, jurisdiction and freedoms recognised' in the Convention are exercised in an abusive manner".[11]

Subsequently, in the *M/V "Virginia G"* case the Tribunal provided further clarification regarding the application of article 300 of the Convention.

"In the view of the Tribunal, it is not sufficient for an applicant to make a general statement that a respondent by undertaking certain actions did not act in good faith and acted in a manner which constitutes an abuse of rights without invoking particular provisions of the Convention that were violated in this respect".[12]

"The Tribunal considers that it is not for it to make assumptions and that it is the duty of an applicant when invoking article 300 of the Convention to specify the concrete obligations and rights under the Convention, with reference to a particular article, that may not have been fulfilled by a respondent in good faith or were exercised in a manner which constituted an abuse of right."[13]

The Tribunal has received two cases involving the delimitation of maritime areas between States. One concerned delimitation of the maritime boundary between Bangladesh and Myanmar in the Bay of Bengal (Bangladesh/Myanmar).

In the *Bay of Bengal* case, the Tribunal capitalized, in great measure, on the existing jurisprudence of other international courts and tribunals in delimitation cases. It should be emphasized, in this respect, that this jurisprudence should not be seen as a straitjacket immobilizing courts and tribunals in future cases. While the applicable law and pertinent jurisprudence will constitute the basis on which decisions will have to be reached in maritime delimitation cases, each case will always be unique and will have to be considered in light of its particular circumstances.

While integrating its judgment into the framework developed in the international decisions, the Tribunal also made a number of contributions to the advancement of this jurisprudence.

The *Bay of Bengal* is a unique case because the Tribunal was confronted with a wholly unprecedented issue, one never previously decided or even faced by any judicial body, namely, the delimitation of the continental shelf extending beyond 200 nautical miles. The most significant elements of this case are highlighted below.

The first important clarification provided by the Tribunal concerned the role of the notion of "natural prolongation" under article 76 of the Convention. The Tribunal stated in this regard that:

"... one of the principal objects and purposes of article 76 of the Convention is to define the precise outer limits of the continental shelf, beyond which lies the Area. The Tribunal therefore finds it difficult to accept that natural prolongation referred to in article 76, paragraph 1, constitutes a separate and independent criterion a coastal State must satisfy in order to be entitled to a continental shelf beyond 200 nm".[14]

"For these reasons, the Tribunal is of the view that the reference to natural prolongation in article 76, paragraph 1, of the Convention, should be understood in light of the subsequent provisions of the article defining the continental shelf and the continental margin. Entitlement to a continental shelf beyond 200 nm should thus be determined by reference to the outer edge of the continental margin, to be ascertained in accordance with article 76, paragraph 4. To interpret otherwise is warranted neither by the text of article 76 nor by its object and purpose".[15]

The second important clarification provided by the Tribunal was on the interrelationship between delimitation and delineation, entitlement and delimitation.

The Tribunal observed that:

"There is a clear distinction between the delimitation of the continental shelf under article 83 and the delineation of its outer limits under article 76. Under the latter article, the Commission (this refers to the Commission on the Limits of the Continental Shelf) is assigned the function of making recommendations to coastal States on matters relating to the establishment of the outer limits of the continental shelf, but it does so without prejudice to delimitation of maritime boundaries. The function of settling disputes with respect to delimitation of maritime boundaries is entrusted to dispute settlement procedures under article 83 and Part XV of the Convention, which include international courts and tribunals".[16]

The Tribunal concluded in this regard that:

"There is nothing in the Convention or in the Rules of Procedure of the Commission or in its practice to indicate that delimitation of the continental shelf constitutes an impediment to the performance by the Commission of its function".[17]

"Just as the functions of the Commission are without prejudice to the question of delimitation of the continental shelf between States with opposite or adjacent coasts, so the exercise by international courts and tribunals of their jurisdiction regarding the delimitation of maritime boundaries, including that of the continental shelf, is without prejudice to the exercise by the Commission of its functions on matters related to the delineation of the outer limits of the continental shelf".[18]

The Tribunal further observed that delimitation does of course presuppose an area of overlapping entitlements and the first step in any delimitation is therefore to determine whether there are entitlements and whether they overlap[19] and noted in this regard that "[n]ot every coast generates entitlements to a continental shelf extending beyond 200 nm".[20]

In the *Bangladesh/Myanmar* case the Tribunal initiated an innovative approach to dealing with the so-called grey zone in delimitation cases. A grey zone area results "when a delimitation line which is not an equidistance line reaches the outer limit of one State's exclusive economic zone and continues beyond it in the same direction, until it reaches the outer limit of the other State's exclusive economic zone".[21]

The Tribunal observed "in this respect that the legal regime of the continental shelf has always coexisted with another legal regime in the same area. Initially that other regime was that of the high seas and the other States concerned were those exercising high seas freedoms. Under the Convention, as a result of maritime delimitation, there may also be concurrent exclusive economic zone rights of another coastal State. In such a situation, pursuant to the principle reflected in the provisions of articles 56, 58, 78 and 79 and in other provisions of the Convention, each coastal State must exercise its rights and perform its duties with due regard to the rights and duties of the other".[22]

In the view of the Tribunal "there are many ways in which the Parties may ensure the discharge of their obligations in this respect, including the conclusion of specific agreements or the establishment of appropriate cooperative arrangements. It is for the Parties to determine the measures that they consider appropriate for this purpose".[23]

Another maritime boundary delimitation dispute, this one between Ghana and Côte d'Ivoire, is now being considered by a special chamber of the Tribunal. This will offer another opportunity to provide any further clarifications necessary on the application of the Convention with regard to this important issue.

II. PROVISIONAL MEASURES

The Tribunal has dealt with a number of requests for provisional measures. When the Tribunal is seized of a contentious case on the merits, it has the power to prescribe, pending its final decision, any provisional measures to preserve the respective rights of the parties to the dispute or to prevent serious harm to the marine environment (article 290, paragraph 1, of the Convention). Even if the case on the merits is not submitted to the Tribunal but to arbitration, the Tribunal may prescribe provisional measures, pending the constitution of the arbitral tribunal, if it considers that *prima facie* the arbitral tribunal would have jurisdiction and that the urgency of the situation so requires (article 290, paragraph 5, of the Convention). In fact, the Tribunal has ordered provisional measures in several cases of this kind.

In deciding on provisional measures the Tribunal has also provided a number of important clarifications regarding the obligations of States under the Convention.

Starting with the *Southern Bluefin Tuna* cases the Tribunal has consistently held the view that parties should "act with prudence and caution" to prevent serious harm to the marine environment, demanding in effect, though not in these precise terms, application of the precautionary approach.[24]

It was in the case of a request for the prescription of provisional measures that the Tribunal gave clarification regarding the application of article 32 of the Convention concerning the immunities of warships in internal maritime waters. In the "*ARA Libertad*" case the Tribunal noted that article 32 of the Convention states that "nothing in this Convention affects the immunities of warships" without specifying the geographical scope of its application[25] and further observed that "although article 32 is included in Part II of the Convention entitled 'Territorial Sea and Contiguous Zone', and most of the provisions in this Part relate to the territorial sea, some of the provisions in this Part may be applicable to all maritime areas, as in the case of the definition of warships provided for in article 29 of the Convention".[26]

In its Order adopted on 25 April 2015, the Special Chamber formed to deal with the delimitation case between Ghana and Côte d'Ivoire elaborated on the conditions for the exercise of the power to prescribe provisional measures under article 290, paragraph 1, of the Convention. The Chamber stated that it may not prescribe provisional measures unless it finds that there is a real and imminent risk that irreparable prejudice may be caused to the rights of the parties in dispute,[27] underlining, in this regard, that urgency was required.[28] As to the existence of the parties' rights, the Chamber observed that, before prescribing provisional measures, it need only satisfy itself that the rights which the requesting party claims on the merits and seeks to protect are "at least plausible".[29] Concerning the risk of irreparable prejudice, the Chamber was of the view that such risk exists "where, in particular, activities result in significant and permanent modification of the physical character of the area in dispute and where such modification cannot be fully compensated by financial reparations".[30] As noted above, the case remains pending on the merits before the Chamber.

III. PROMPT RELEASE OF VESSELS AND CREWS

The Tribunal has heard nine applications for the prompt release of vessels and their crews, in accordance with the procedure established in article 292 of the Convention.

Article 292 of the Convention provides for an independent remedy which enables the flag State to seek the release of its vessel and crew before the Tribunal, without prejudice to the merits of the case in the appropriate domestic forum. In specific cases, States Parties to the Convention having detained a vessel flying the flag of another State Party are required under the Convention to release the vessel and its crew promptly upon the posting of reasonable bond or other financial security. When it is alleged that the detaining State has not complied with this obligation, the flag State may, under conditions specified in the Convention, submit the question of release from detention to the Tribunal. In such cases, the Tribunal deals only with the question of release, without prejudice to the merits of any case in the appropriate domestic forum.

In considering prompt release cases the Tribunal has provided clarification on a number of points regarding the application of article 292 of the Convention. This article highlights several of them, namely the determination of the reasonableness of a bond or other financial security, the financial nature of the bond or other financial security, the effects of the confiscation of the vessel, and the relationship of the provisions of article 292 to domestic procedures.

On the first issue the Tribunal has pointed out that "a number of factors are relevant in an assessment of the reasonableness of bonds or other financial security. They include the gravity of the alleged offences, the penalties imposed or imposable under the laws of the detaining State, the value of the detained vessel and of the cargo seized, the amount of the bond imposed by the detaining State and its form".[31] At the same time the Tribunal stated that "this is by no means a complete list of factors. Nor does the Tribunal intend to lay down rigid rules as to the exact weight to be attached to each of them … ".[32] In this respect, the Tribunal has added that "the amount of a bond should be proportionate to the gravity of the alleged offences".[33]

In elucidating the meaning of the expression "bond or other security" as used in article 73, paragraph 2, the Tribunal has stated that the phrase must be seen in its context and in light of its object and purpose. According to the Tribunal, the relevant context includes the Convention provisions concerning prompt release of vessels and crews upon the posting of a bond or security, namely: article 292; article 220, paragraph 7; and article 226, paragraph 1(b). In view of these provisions, the Tribunal came to the conclusion that the expression "bond or other security" in article 73, paragraph 2, "should ... be interpreted as referring to a bond or security of a financial nature" and therefore "non-financial conditions cannot be considered components of a bond or other financial security".[34]

As to the question of the effects of the confiscation of a vessel, the Tribunal has observed that "[a] decision to confiscate eliminates the provisional character of the detention of the vessel rendering the procedure for its prompt release without object".[35] The Tribunal emphasized, however, that "considering the object and purpose of the prompt release procedure, a decision to confiscate a vessel does not prevent the Tribunal from considering an application for prompt release of such vessel while proceedings are still before the domestic courts of the detaining State".[36]

On the issue of the relationship to domestic proceedings the Tribunal has pointed out that "when determining whether the assessment made by the detaining State in fixing the bond or other security is reasonable, the Tribunal will treat the laws of the detaining State and the decisions of its courts as relevant facts." The Tribunal, however, has made it clear that, "under article 292 of the Convention, it is not an appellate forum against a decision of a national court".[37] The Tribunal pointed out in this regard that "it is not logical to read the requirement of exhaustion of local remedies or any other analogous rule into article 292"[38] and that "article 292 provides for an independent remedy and not an appeal against a decision of a national court".[39]

IV. ADVISORY OPINIONS

Under the Convention the Seabed Disputes Chamber, which is established pursuant to the Convention within the framework of the Tribunal, has the competence to issue advisory opinions upon the request of either the Assembly or the Council of the International Seabed Authority. In addition, the full Tribunal may give an advisory opinion on a legal question if an international agreement related to the purposes of the Convention specifically provides for the submission to the Tribunal of a request for such an opinion. A request for an advisory opinion was submitted to the full Tribunal in 2013 by the Sub-Regional Fisheries Commission (hereinafter "the SRFC"), established by a group of West African States. The questions submitted concerned illegal, unreported and unregulated (IUU) fishing within the exclusive economic zones of those States. The Tribunal rendered its response on 2 April 2015.

1. Advisory Opinion given by the Seabed Disputes Chamber

In response to a request received from the International Seabed Authority, the Seabed Disputes Chamber in 2011 delivered – by unanimous decision, it is important to note – an advisory opinion on the "Responsibilities and obligations of States with respect to activities in the Area".[40] As this opinion has received much attention, there is no need to describe it in detail and this article highlights only a number of the most important points clarified by the Chamber in its opinion.

The questions on which the opinion of the Chamber was sought were submitted to it by the International Seabed Authority, an international organization established by the Convention and mandated to organize and control activities in the Area. The Chamber was asked by the International Seabed Authority to explain what would be the obligations of the sponsoring State in respect of activities in the Area. In its reply, the Chamber specified that the sponsoring State had two kinds of obligations.

According to the Chamber, under the first obligation the sponsoring State is required to ensure compliance by sponsored contractors with the terms of the relevant contract and the obligations set out in the Convention and other instruments. This obligation, termed "responsibility to ensure", was described by the Chamber as follows:

"The sponsoring State's obligation 'to ensure' is not an obligation to achieve, in each and every case, the result that the sponsored contractor complies with the aforementioned obligations. Rather, it is an obligation to deploy adequate means, to exercise best possible efforts, to do the utmost, to obtain this result. To utilize the terminology current in international law, this obligation may be characterized as an obligation 'of conduct' and not 'of result', and as an obligation of 'due diligence'".[41]

This prompted the Chamber to give details about the concept of "due diligence". The Chamber observed that the content of the "due diligence" obligation "may not easily be described in precise terms" and that "among the factors that make such a description difficult is the fact that 'due diligence' is a variable concept" which "may change over time as measures considered sufficiently diligent at a certain moment may become not diligent enough in light, for instance, of new scientific or technological knowledge. It may also change in relation to the risks involved in the activity".[42]

According to the Chamber the second type of obligations of the sponsoring State encompasses direct obligations with which the sponsoring State must comply of its own accord. These include, among others, the obligation to assist the Authority, the obligation to apply a precautionary approach, and the obligation to apply the best environmental practices.[43]

In its Advisory Opinion, the Chamber also clarified the question of the liability of a State which sponsors private entities conducting activities in the Area.

The Chamber observed that failure of the sponsored contractor to comply with its obligations does not in itself give rise to liability on the part of the sponsoring State. The sponsoring State is absolved from liability if it has taken "all necessary and appropriate measures to secure effective compliance" by the sponsored contractor with its obligations. This exemption from liability does not apply to a failure by the sponsoring State to carry out its direct obligations to which I have referred to earlier.

On the basis of the wording of article 139, paragraph 2, of the Convention the Chamber clarified that "the liability of the sponsoring State arises from its failure to carry out its own responsibilities" and when such failure results in damage. This requires a causal link between the failure and the damage. The Chamber also explained "the sponsoring State is not, however, liable for the failure of the sponsored contractor to meet its obligations"[44]. In the view of the Chamber, this also rules out the application of a standard of liability based on strict liability, i.e. liability without fault.[45] Thus, according to the Chamber, the liability of the sponsoring State and that of the sponsored contractor exist in parallel and are not joint and several; and, therefore, the sponsoring State bears no residual liability.

Two conditions need to be met, in the view of the Chamber, for the liability of the sponsoring State to arise: failure to carry out its own responsibilities and occurrence of damage.[46] For that a causal link need to be established between such failure and damage and a causal link cannot be presumed and must be proven.[47]

On the widely debated issue of application of the notion of "common but differentiated responsibilities" under the Convention to deep seabed mining activities, the Chamber pointed out that "none of the general provisions of the Convention concerning the responsibilities (or the liability) of the sponsoring State 'specifically provides' for according preferential treatment to sponsoring States that are developing States" and that "there is no provision requiring the consideration of such interests and needs beyond what is specifically stated in Part XI". The Chamber, therefore, concluded that "the general provisions concerning the responsibilities and liability of the sponsoring State apply equally to all sponsoring States, whether developing or developed".[48]

And finally, with reference to an important issue, that of the precautionary approach, the Chamber observed that "the precautionary approach has been incorporated into a growing number of international treaties and other instruments, many of which reflect the formulation of Principle 15 of the Rio Declaration" and therefore concluded that "this has initiated a trend towards making this approach part of customary international law".[49]

2. Advisory Opinion given by the Tribunal

a) Scope of the advisory jurisdiction of the Tribunal

In its Advisory Opinion, the Tribunal provided clarifications on the scope of its jurisdiction to give the advisory opinion requested by the SRFC. On this point, the Tribunal explained that the expression "all matters specifically provided for in any other agreement which confers jurisdiction on the Tribunal", which is contained in article 21 of its Statute, "does not by itself establish the advisory jurisdiction of the Tribunal". It stated that "[i]n terms of article 21 of the Statute, it is the "other agreement" which confers such jurisdiction on the Tribunal" and that "[w]hen the 'other agreement' confers advisory jurisdiction on the Tribunal, the Tribunal then is rendered competent to exercise such jurisdiction with regard to 'all matters' specifically provided for in the 'other agreement'". The Tribunal concluded that "[a]rticle 21 and the 'other agreement' conferring jurisdiction on the Tribunal are interconnected and constitute the substantive legal basis of the advisory jurisdiction of the Tribunal".[50]

On the other hand, according to the Tribunal, article 138 of the Rules "does not establish the advisory jurisdiction of the Tribunal" as "[i]t only furnishes the prerequisites that need to be satisfied before the Tribunal can exercise its advisory jurisdiction".[51] With reference to article 138 of the Rules, the Tribunal enumerated the following prerequisites: an international agreement related to the purposes of the Convention must specifically provide for the submission to the Tribunal of a request for an advisory opinion; the request must be transmitted to the Tribunal by a body authorized by or in accordance with the agreement mentioned above; and the matter on which such an opinion is requested must be "a legal question".[52]

b) Obligations and liability of the flag State as regards the IUU fishing in the exclusive economic zones of the SRFC Member States

On the issue of flag State obligations, the Tribunal first underlined that under the Convention "responsibility for the conservation and management of living resources in the exclusive economic zone rests with the coastal State". It is namely the coastal State which has in that zone "sovereign rights for the purpose of exploring and exploiting, conserving and managing the natural resources, whether living or non-living".[53]

The Tribunal then identified a number of obligations of flag States in the exclusive economic zone (hereinafter "the EZZ") of the coastal State, including among others:

"the obligation to take necessary measures, including those of enforcement, to ensure compliance by vessels flying its flag with the laws and regulations enacted by the SRFC Member States concerning marine living resources within their exclusive economic zones for purposes of conservation and management of these resources".[54]

According to the Tribunal, in fulfilment of its obligation to effectively exercise jurisdiction and control in administrative matters under article 94 of the Convention, the flag State is also required to adopt "the necessary administrative measures to ensure that fishing vessels flying its flag are not involved in activities in the exclusive economic zones of the SRFC Member States which undermine the flag State's responsibility under article 192 of the Convention for protecting and preserving the marine environment and conserving the marine living resources which are an integral element of the marine environment".[55] The Tribunal specified that these are obligations of "due diligence".[56] In addition, the Tribunal referred to the obligation of the flag State and the SRFC Member States to cooperate in cases involving IUU fishing in the EEZ of the SRFC Member States.

With regard to the issue of the liability of the flag State for IUU fishing activities conducted by vessels under its flag, the Tribunal pointed out that:

"The liability of the flag State does not arise from a failure of vessels flying its flag to comply with the laws and regulations of the SRFC Member States concerning IUU fishing activities in their exclusive economic zones, as the violation of such laws and regulations by vessels is not per se attributable to the flag State."[57]

The Tribunal explained that the liability of the flag State "arises from its failure to comply with its 'due diligence' obligations concerning IUU fishing activities conducted by vessels flying its flag in the exclusive economic zones of the SRFC Member States." Hence, "[t]he flag State is not liable if it has taken all necessary and appropriate measures to meet its 'due diligence' obligations to ensure that vessels flying its flag do not conduct IUU fishing activities in the exclusive economic zones of the SRFC Member States".[58]

c) RESPONSIBILITY AND LIABILITY OF AN INTERNATIONAL ORGANIZATION TO WHICH ITS MEMBER STATES HAVE TRANSFERRED COMPETENCE IN MATTERS CONCERNING FISHERIES

In its advisory opinion the Tribunal also examined the question of the responsibility and liability of an international organization, to which its member States have transferred competence in matters concerning fisheries, in cases of IUU fishing by vessels of its Member States. The Tribunal observed that in the case before it, such organization was the European Union, which had concluded fisheries agreements with SRFC Member States to allow European Union fishing vessels access to their exclusive economic zones. In this regard, the Tribunal stated that:

"In cases where an international organization, in the exercise of its exclusive competence in fisheries matters, concludes a fisheries access agreement with an SRFC Member State, which provides for access by vessels flying the flag of its member States to fish in the exclusive economic zone of that State, the obligations of the flag State become the obligations of the international orga-nization."[59]

According to the Tribunal, "only the international organization may be held liable for any breach of its obligations arising from the fisheries access agreement, and not its member States". The Tribunal was of the view that "if the international organization does not meet its 'due diligence' obligations, the SFRC Member States may hold the international organization liable for the violation of their fisheries laws and regulations by a vessel flying the flag of a member State of that organization and fishing in the exclusive economic zones of the SRFC Member States within the framework of a fisheries access agreement between that organization and such Member States".[60]

d) RIGHTS AND OBLIGATIONS OF THE SRFC MEMBER STATES IN MANAGING CERTAIN FISH STOCKS

In its Advisory Opinion the Tribunal also dealt with the issue of the rights and obligations of the SRFC Member States in ensuring the sustainable management of shared stocks and tuna. The Tribunal noted that the term "shared stocks" had been defined by the SRFC Member States and therefore applied to both situations described in paragraphs 1 and 2 of article 63 of the Convention.[61] It also observed that the ultimate goal of "sustainable management" of fish stocks was "to conserve and develop them as a viable and sustainable resource",[62] construing this concept as meaning "conservation and development", as referred to in article 63, paragraph 1, of the Convention.[63]

The Tribunal identified a number of obligations of the coastal State to ensure the sustainable management of shared stocks. These included, among others: the obligation to cooperate with the competent international organizations to ensure through proper conservation and management measures that the maintenance of the shared stocks in the exclusive economic zone was not endangered by over-exploitation; the obligation to "seek ... to agree upon the measures necessary to coordinate and ensure the conservation and development of such stocks"; and, in relation to tuna species, the obligation to cooperate directly or through the SRFC with a view to ensuring conservation and promoting the objective of optimum utilization of such species in their exclusive economic zones.[64]

C. THE 20TH ANNIVERSARY OF THE TRIBUNAL

2016 was a very special year for the Tribunal since it commemorated the 20th anniversary of its establishment. On that occasion, a special event, namely a round table discussion on "The role of the Tribunal in settlement of law of the sea disputes" was organized in New York in June during a Meeting of States Parties to the Convention.

On 7 October 2016 a commemorative ceremony took place in the City Hall of Hamburg. On that occasion, statements were made by the then Secretary-General of the United Nations Mr Ban Ki-moon, the President of the Federal Republic of Germany, the First Mayor of the Hanseatic City of Hamburg and myself. More than 500 guests attended this event.

The commemorative ceremony was preceded by a two-day international symposium dedicated to the "The contribution of the Tribunal to the rule of law", which was held on 5 and 6 October 2016. The symposium was attended by over 150 participants, among them Judges of the Tribunal, of the International Court of Justice and of other judicial institutions, academics, lawyers and counsel who have appeared before international courts and tribunals.

D. NEW CHALLENGES

The negotiations on the Convention in the 1970s and early 1980s took place in a prevailing spirit of appreciation of international law and cooperation between states. The Convention is clearly influenced by the notion of rule of law. In its preamble, States Parties to the Convention declare that what they desire to establish through the Convention is nothing less than "a legal order for the seas and oceans".

While the Convention represents the best effort on the part of the international community of states to address governance issues which required solution at the time of its conclusion, the Convention did not resolve all of them in detail. Consequently, while the Convention quite rightly is being called "a constitution for the oceans" – and there is no doubt that the conclusion of the Convention constituted a remarkable achievement – it should also be acknowledged that the regime for the governance of oceans, that it contributed to create, still has gaps which need to be addressed. That was clearly demonstrated by the fact that shortly after the conclusion of the Convention two implementing agreements had to be negotiated to supplement its provisions, namely the 1994 Agreement Relating to the Implementation of Part XI of the United Nations Convention on the Law of the Sea of 10 December 1982 and the 1995 Agreement for the Implementation of the Provisions of the United Nations Convention on the Law of the Sea of 10 December 1982 Relating to the Conservation and Management of Straddling Fish Stocks and Highly Migratory Fish Stocks.

It should be acknowledged that the Convention does not provide and has never been intended to provide an answer to every problem that arises in sea-related matters. It is a framework convention and, as a framework convention which enjoys almost universal acceptance, it has proved to be a flexible instrument serving as a solid legal foundation for the further progressive development of the international law of the sea. The Convention therefore should be viewed as providing a solid foundation for the international governance of maritime activities; as a platform on which new emerging issues relating to the international governance of activities in the oceans are to be addressed.

Although the Convention, as already noted, addresses issues relating to the management of marine resources in a somewhat comprehensive way, it does not cover a number of emerging issues such as the conservation of marine biodiversity, CO2 sequestration, the use of marine genetic resources; issues arising in connection with global warming and rapidly increasing demand for energy sources. So, new issues continue to arise and need to be addressed. The most recent – and most noteworthy – development in this regard is the decision by the United Nations General Assembly, taken last year, "to develop an international legally binding instrument under the United Nations Convention on the Law of the Sea on the conservation and sustainable use of marine biological diversity of areas beyond national jurisdiction".[65] The work of the preparatory commission set up by the General Assembly to this end will be followed closely by all those interested in the development of the international law of the sea.

The international community of states should seek solution to these emerging issues through the process of international governance within the framework of relevant existing institutions, first of all the United Nations, its agencies and related organizations that provide fora where states and other actors can engage in a dialogue and negotiations which, if successful, should result in additional norms and regulatory regimes supplementary to those established by the Convention and facilitating its implementation.

In this context, reference needs to be made to the conservation and sustainable use of ocean resources, which in our days should be viewed as a matter of common concern. As noted by Patricia Birnie, Alan Boyle and Catherine Redgwell, in their book on "International Law and the Environment", the concept of "common concern" implies that the international community of states as a whole has a legitimate interest in such resources of global significance. It follows from the above that the international community of states has a common responsibility to ensure conservation and sustainable use of these resources and that individual states have a legal obligation in this regard vis-a-vis the whole international community of states regarding the conservation and sustainable use of these resources and that such obligation can be enforced by or on behalf of that community of states.[66]

It goes without saying, for example, that marine living resources of the high seas constitute a matter of common concern for the international community of states as a whole. Consequently, any State Party to the Convention or a group of such states have the right to invoke the responsibility of a state or states not complying with their obligations under Section 2 of Part VII of the Convention by breaching those obligations owed to the international community of states. If such invocation of responsibility is contested by the state or states concerned, the matter must be resolved through the compulsory procedures entailing binding decisions contained in Part XV, section 2 of the Convention.

As the oceans offer a vast and powerful source of energy that has so far not been utilized on a significant scale, another emerging issues concerns oceans energy resources.

I. METHANE HYDRATES

One of the issues that arise relates to the potential use of methane hydrates, white, ice-like solids that consist of methane and water. Methane hydrates are only stable under certain pressures (in excess of 35 bar) and at low temperatures. Methane hydrates may therefore primarily be found on the continental slopes, those areas where the continental plates meet the deep-sea regions.

Methane hydrates constitute a natural non-living resource and their mining in all likelihood will take place in the exclusive economic zone or on the continental shelf of a coastal state. Thus, pursuant to the Convention their exploration and exploitation will be governed by the applicable laws and regulations of coastal States. However, as it is unclear to what extent it would be possible to mine the ocean floor for such resources without inflicting significant harm to the marine environment and negatively affecting climate on our planet in general, this type of activities should be a matter of concern for the entire world community. Consequently, in the context of marine governance of energy resources the question arises as to whether the regulation of the potential use of methane hydrates should be left to the discretion of coastal states or should be subject to some form of international regulations as well.

Furthermore, the vast spaces of the open ocean make it an intriguing location for extracting renewable energy. Wind, waves and currents together contain 300 times more energy than humans are currently consuming. It is hoped that wind, waves and ocean currents will meet a substantial share of the world's electricity need.

II. OCEAN ENERGY

The production of environmentally friendly energy from the oceans is now being promoted worldwide. The broad suite of technologies collectively known as ocean energy is also beginning to emerge as a viable base-load source of renewable energy. Ocean energy involves a wide range of engineering technologies which permit to obtain energy from the ocean using a variety of conversion mechanisms.

It appears that most of the offshore renewable energy installations, at least in the near future, will be constructed in the internal waters, territorial sea and the EEZ of coastal states, and, in the case of archipelagic states, also in the archipelagic waters.

Despite some uncertainties the Convention provides guidance with regard to marine governance of renewable ocean energy resources in areas under national jurisdiction.

In this regard the Convention recognizes that a balance must be struck in the EEZ and on the continental shelf between the rights and duties of the coastal State and the rights and duties of other states and that the rights of the coastal state in the EEZ and over the continental are to be exercised with due regard to the rights and duties of other states and in a manner compatible with the provisions of the Convention.

It may be assumed, however, that on some occasions it will be difficult to find such a delicate balance of interests and therefore a dispute may arise between the states concerned. It should be observed in this connection that one of the most important achievements of the Convention is the inclusion of provisions on compulsory procedures for the resolution of disputes concerning its interpretation or application. The Convention provides that, should all efforts to strike a due balance between the rights and duties of the coastal state and those of other states be unsuccessful and should a dispute arises regarding the interpretation or application of the Convention, then such a dispute should be submitted to the compulsory procedures entailing binding decisions. These procedures are contained in Part XV, section 2, of the Convention. In this regard, article 297, paragraph 1, stipulates that disputes concerning the interpretation or application of the Convention with regard to the exercise by as coastal state of its sovereign rights or jurisdiction are subject to the procedures provided for in the aforementioned section 2, *inter alia,* in the following cases:

"(a) when it is alleged that a coastal State has acted in contravention of the provisions of this Convention in regard to the freedoms and rights of navigation, overflight or the laying of submarine cables and pipelines, or in regard to other internationally lawful uses of the sea specified in article 58" ("Rights and duties of other States in the EEZ");

"(b) when it is alleged that a State in exercising the aforementioned freedoms, rights or uses has acted in contravention of this Convention or of laws or regulations adopted by the coastal State in conformity with this Convention and other rules of international law not incompatible with this Convention";

"(c) when it is alleged that a coastal State has acted in contravention of specified international rules and standards for the protection and preservation of the marine environment which are applicable to the coastal State and which have been established by this Convention or through a competent international organization or diplomatic conference in accordance with this Convention".

It may sound too optimistic in our days to talk about a potential use of renewable ocean energy resources of the high seas. However, at least theoretically wind and wave energy of the high seas could be a source of renewable energy in the future. While at first glance the high seas may seem an endless expanse, suitable areas for renewable energy development shrink when factors such as shipping lanes, fishing interests, and proximity to onshore demand and infrastructure are taken into account.

The Convention is much less clear on governance of such resources on the high seas. According to article 87, paragraph 1, of the Convention the high seas are open to all States and freedom of the high seas listed in the Convention comprise, *inter alia,* freedom to construct artificial islands and other installations permitted under international law, subject to Part VI on the continental shelf. The Convention emphasizes in paragraph 2 of that article that "these freedoms of the high seas must be exercised by all States with due regard for the interests of other States in their exercise of the freedom of the high seas, and also with due regard for the rights under the Convention with respect to activities in the Area".

Once the technology exists to do so, a state can construct renewable ocean energy installations in an area on the high seas and lay, if necessary, cables for the transmission of energy back to shore, in accordance with article 87, paragraph 1(c) concerning freedom of laying submarine cables on the high seas. The state that will exercise exclusive jurisdiction over such installations, will also be responsible for providing warning of their presence, and removing them when disused.

As pursuant to article 87, paragraph 2, of the Convention freedoms of the high seas are to be exercised by states with due regard for the interests of other states in their exercise of the freedom of high seas, the construction of large installations of renewable ocean energy generators on the high seas will inevitably raise a question of marine governance. For this reason, the development of a special regulatory regime for high seas renewable energy installations would seem to be prudent. This regime should supplement the current regime established by the Convention and provide a fair balance between the freedom to construct renewable ocean energy installations and other freedoms of the high seas and it should be governed by the settlement of disputes mechanism established by Part XV of the Convention.

III. TRANSBOUNDARY RESOURCES

Another issue that has not yet been the object of international adjudication but which seems to be of growing importance is that of the management of transboundary resources shared by adjacent or opposite States. With an increasing number of exploration and exploitation activities taking place on the ocean floor, it is only a matter of time before an ever-increasing number of oil and gas fields straddling maritime boundaries will be discovered.

This issue has yet to be addressed in any delimitation judgment by an international court or tribunal. Jurisprudence has so far relied almost entirely on factors of coastal geography[67] and considerations of proportionality. Also, States parties to such disputes have not made any specific requests in this regard. However, the question arises whether the requirement of an equitable solution is really achieved by this approach, in which the future use of transboundary resources is not given due consideration.

In respect of how to treat transboundary resources, there is considerable state practice to be found in bilateral treaties. Practice is not uniform, of course, and I will not venture into an in-depth analysis of it here. What emerges from several such treaties is the idea of unitization, i.e. the joint development of transboundary deposits as a unit.[68] More generally, treaties regularly stress the importance of cooperation between the States concerned, including information-sharing. Another recurrent element of such agreements is the laying down of procedures for the parties to follow in case transboundary deposits are discovered.[69]

It remains to be seen to what extent international judicial bodies will be confronted with disputes involving the management of transboundary resources. When agreeing to submit a boundary dispute to international adjudication, states may find it necessary to request the court or tribunal to take into account the existence of transboundary resources.

It will be for the judicial body seized in a dispute to decide whether and to what extent its decision on the course of the boundary line needs to be informed by the location of such resource deposits so that an equitable solution can be achieved. I wish to emphasize that a decision of that kind can only be made with on a case-by-case basis, taking into account all the particularities of each case. Parties may request an international court or tribunal to decide how they should arrange for the exploitation of shared resources straddling the boundary line. Inspiration may be taken from bilateral treaty practice to which I previously referred. If requested by the parties to the case, a judicial body may, again if the specifics of the case so warrant, give indications on how the parties should organize the necessary cooperation between them. This could include unitization, if appropriate.

IV. DEEP SEABED MINING

Another issue which undoubtedly counts among those receiving the most attention in the current international law of the sea is the exploration and exploitation of the resources of the deep seabed beyond the limits of national jurisdiction.

These areas of the world's oceans may contain deposits of key strategic metals and minerals such as copper, cobalt, nickel and manganese. While the demand for these continues to grow, including to meet the needs of the green economy, land resources are increasingly stretched, causing the economic, social and environmental costs of mining to rise.

Current global supply of these metals and minerals is distributed unevenly around the world. For example: the Democratic Republic of the Congo controls 47% of global cobalt reserves and Chile 30% of global copper reserves; South Africa possesses 80% of global manganese reserves, while China controls 95% of the global market in rare earth elements.

Deposits of these resources in the deep seabed by far exceed those on land. The economic situation will therefore change drastically once exploitation of them commences.

States and private-sector mining interests are keen to explore the potential of marine minerals both within and beyond national jurisdiction. Thanks to technological advances and a stable regulatory regime, both in national jurisdictions and in the Area, deep seabed mining is an increasingly attractive option for investment in mineral development.

Twenty-five private companies and public entities, including from Japan, China, India, and Russia, have concluded contracts with the International Seabed Authority under the Convention's regime for the exploration of the deep seabed mineral resources. Depending on the development of market prices for the minerals concerned, exploitation of the deep seabed may actually start in the next two, three years.

As activity in the Area will increase in the future, the likelihood of new disputes will grow in proportion. In particular, it is to be expected that, when the various activities enter the exploitation phase, the potential for conflict among the actors will increase and disputes may arise, for instance between the Authority and contractors. Given the comprehensive mandate of the Seabed Disputes Chamber of the Tribunal in this regard, a significant amount of work would appear to lie ahead for the Chamber.

1. MARINE SCIENTIFIC RESEARCH AND ACTIVITIES IN THE AREA

In this regard, mention may be also made of an emerging issue which is currently discussed at the International Seabed Authority; namely the carrying out of marine scientific research in exploration areas.

Article 87, paragraph 1(f), of the Convention, concerning freedom of the high seas, stipulates that freedom of high seas includes, *inter alia,* freedom of marine scientific research, subject to Parts VI and XIII of the Convention. In accordance with paragraph 2 of that article, freedoms of the high seas must be exercised by all States with due regard, inter alia, for the rights under the Convention with respect to activities in the Area.

However, the Convention does not have any specific provisions which address a situation where the conduct of marine scientific research affects the exercise of the rights of an entity that has signed a contract with the Authority authorizing it to conduct exploration activities in a particular part of the Area. It follows from the discussions that took place at the last session of the International Seabed Authority that there appear to be situations where the conduct of marine scientific research may allegedly interfere with the full implementation by a contractor of its plan of work approved by the Authority.

2. SUBMARINE CABLES AND PIPELINES

Another issue is the interrelationship between the exercise of the freedom of the high seas, such as of the laying of submarine cables, and activities in the Area. Some of these cables may be laid on parts of the ocean floor that the International Seabed Authority has designated for exploration and subsequent exploitation activities.

It should be noted in this regard that article 139 of Part XI of the Convention provides that States Parties shall have the responsibility to ensure that activities in the Area, whether carried out by States Parties or state enterprises or natural or juridical persons which possess the nationality of States Parties or are effectively controlled by them or their nationals, are carried out in conformity with Part XI of the Convention.

3. STRADDLING RESOURCES

Another potential source of conflict is the issue of transboundary resources straddling the line dividing national jurisdiction and the Area. Article 142, paragraph 2, of the Convention provides that "in cases where activities in the Area may result in the exploitation of resources lying within national jurisdiction, the prior consent of the coastal State concerned shall be required." A dispute may arise between the Authority, or entities that are given contracts by it, and the coastal state concerned in the context of managing such transboundary resources. If such a dispute arises, the issues that need to be addressed are: who are the parties to such a dispute and which judicial body would have the authority under Part XV of the Convention to adjudicate this dispute.

E. CONCLUDING REMARK

This article attempts to give an overview of some of the emerging issues that may arise with regard to potential uses of maritime spaces and their resources. It also attempts to highlight the extent to which the International Tribunal for the Law of the Sea may be involved in settling international disputes arising in this regard. New challenges and problems will continue to come to light and the Tribunal will stand ready to offer its services to States and other actors seeking a peaceful resolution of sea-related disputes.

NOTES

1 Article 279 of the Convention.

2 Article 286 and title of Part XV, Section 2, of the Convention.

3 *Karen J. Alter,* The Multiple Roles of International Courts and Tribunals: Enforcement, Dispute Settlement, Constitutional and Administrative Review, in: Jeffrey L. Dunoff / Mark A. Pollack (eds.), Interdisciplinary Perspectives on International Law and International Relations. The State of the Art, Cambridge: Cambridge University Press, 2013, pp. 345 – 370, at p. 354.

4 M/V "SAIGA" (Saint Vincent and the Grenadines v. Guinea), Judgment, ITLOS Reports 1997, p. 16, para. 106.

5 M/V "Virginia G" (Panama/Guinea-Bissau), Judgment, ITLOS Reports 2014, to be published, para. 323.

6 "Juno Trader" (Saint Vincent and the Grenadines v. Guinea-Bissau), Prompt Release, Judgment, ITLOS Reports 2004, p. 17, at pp. 38–39, para. 77; "Tomimaru"

(Japan v. Russian Federation), Prompt Release, Judgment, ITLOS Reports 2005–2007, p. 74, at p. 96, para. 76.

7 M/V "Louisa" (Saint Vincent and the Grenadines v. Kingdom of Spain), Judgment, ITLOS Reports 2013, to be published, para. 155.

8 M/V "SAIGA"(Saint Vincent and the Grenadines v. Guinea), Judgment, ITLOS Reports 1997, p. 16, para. 155.

9 M/V "Virginia G" (Panama/Guinea-Bissau), Judgment, ITLOS Reports 2014, to be published, para. 217.

10 *Ibid.,* para. 223.

11 M/V "Louisa" (Saint Vincent and the Grenadines v. Kingdom of Spain), Judgment, ITLOS Reports 2013, to be published, para. 137.

12 M/V "Virginia G" (Panama/Guinea-Bissau), Judgment, ITLOS Reports 2014, to be published, para. 398.

13 *Ibid.*, para. 399.

14 Delimitation of the maritime boundary between Bangladesh and Myanmar in the Bay of Bengal (Bangladesh/Myanmar), Judgment, ITLOS Reports 2012, para. 435.

15 *Ibid.,* para. 437.

16 *Ibid.,* para. 376.

17 *Ibid.,* para. 377.

18 *Ibid.*, para. 379.

19 *Ibid.,* para. 397.

20 *Ibid.,* para. 439.

21 *Ibid.*, para. 464.

22 *Ibid.,* para. 475.

23 *Ibid.,* para. 476.

24 Southern Bluefin Tuna (New Zealand v. Japan; Australia v. Japan), Provisional Measures, Order of 27 August 1999, ITLOS Reports 1999, p. 280; MOX Plant (Ireland v. United Kingdom), Provisional Measures, Order of 3 December 2001, ITLOS Reports 2001, p. 95; Land Reclamation in and around the Straits of Johor (Malaysia v. Singapore), Provisional Measures, Order of 8 October 2003, ITLOS Reports 2003, p. 10; M/V "Louisa" (Saint Vincent and the Grenadines v. Kingdom of Spain),Provisional Measures, Order of 23 December 2010, ITLOS Reports 2008–2010, p. 58.

25 "ARA Libertad" (Argentina v. Ghana), Provisional Measures, Order of 15 December 2012, ITLOS Reports 2012, p. 326, para. 63.

26 *Ibid.,* para. 64.

27 Dispute concerning Delimitation of the Maritime Boundary between Ghana and Côte d'Ivoire in the Atlantic Ocean (Ghana/Côte d'Ivoire), Request for the prescription of provisional measures, Order of the Special Chamber dated 25 April 2015, para. 41.

28 *Ibid.,* para. 42.

29 *Ibid.,* para. 58.

30 *Ibid.,* para. 89.

31 "Camouco" (Panama v. France), Prompt Release, Judgment, ITLOS Reports 2000, p. 10, para. 67.
32 "Monte Confurco" (Seychelles v. France), Prompt Release, Judgment, ITLOS Reports 2000, p. 86, para. 76.
33 "Hoshinmaru" (Japan v. Russian Federation), Prompt Release, Judgment, ITLOS Reports 2005–2007, p. 18, para. 88.
34 "Volga" (Russian Federation v. Australia), Prompt Release, Judgment, ITLOS Reports 2002), p. 10, para. 77.
35 "Tomimaru" (Japan v. Russian Federation), Prompt Release, Judgment, ITLOS Reports 2005–2007, p. 74, para. 76.
36 *Ibid.,* para. 78.
37 "Monte Confurco" (Seychelles v. France), Prompt Release, Judgment, ITLOS Reports 2000, p. 86, para. 72.
38 "Camouco" (Panama v. France), Prompt Release, Judgment, ITLOS Reports 2000, p. 10, para. 57.
39 *Ibid.,* para. 58.
40 ITLOS Reports 2011, p. 10.
41 *Ibid.*, para. 110.
42 *Ibid.*, para. 117.
43 *Ibid.*, para. 131.
44 *Ibid.*, para. 172.
45 *Ibid.*, para. 189.
46 *Ibid.*, para. 176.
47 *Ibid.*, para. 182.
48 *Ibid.*, para. 158.
49 *Ibid.*, para. 135.
50 Request for an Advisory Opinion submitted by the Sub-Regional Fisheries Commissions (SRFC), Advisory Opinion of the Tribunal of 2 April 2015, para. 58.
51 *Ibid.*, para. 59.
52 *Ibid.*, para. 60.
53 *Ibid.*, para. 104.
54 *Ibid.*, para. 219 (3).
55 *Ibid.*, para. 219 (3).
56 *Ibid.*, para. 219 (3).
57 *Ibid.*, para. 219 (4).
58 *Ibid.*, para. 219 (4).
59 *Ibid.*, para. 219 (5).
60 *Ibid.*, para. 219 (6).
61 *Ibid.*, para. 186.
62 *Ibid.*, para. 190.
63 *Ibid.*, para. 191.
64 *Ibid.*, para. 207.
65 "Development of an international legally binding instrument under the United Nations Convention on the Law of the Sea on the conservation and sustainable use

of marine biological diversity of areas beyond national jurisdiction", Resolution adopted by the General Assembly on 19 June 2015, A/RES/69/292, para. 1.

66 *Patricia Birnie, Alan Boyle, Catherine Redgwell,* International Law and the Environment, Third Edition, Oxford University Press, 2009.

67 Cf. *Y. Tanaka,* Predictability and Flexibility in the Law of Maritime Delimitation, Oxford/Portland 2006, p. 323/324.

68 Treaty between the Kingdom of Norway and the Russian Federation concerning Maritime Delimitation and Cooperation in the Barents Sea and the Arctic Ocean (2010), Annex II; Treaty between the Republic of Trinidad and Tobago and Grenada on Delimitation of Marine and Submarine Areas (2010), Article VII; Agreement between the Government of the State of Israel and the Government of the Republic of Cyprus on the delimitation of the exclusive economic zone (2010), Article 2; Unitisation Agreement for the exploitation and development of hydrocarbon reservoirs of the Loran-Manatee field that extends across the delimitation line between the Republic of Trinidad and Tobago and the Bolivarian Republic of Venezuela (2010).

69 Such clauses may, more generally, provide for the parties to engage in further negotiations (Treaty between the Republic of Trinidad and Tobago and Grenada on Delimitation of Marine and Submarine Areas (2010), Article VII) or may establish more detailed procedures to be followed (Treaty between the Kingdom of Norway and the Russian Federation concerning Maritime Delimitation and Cooperation in the Barents Sea and the Arctic Ocean (2010), Annex II).

CHAPTER II

THE CONTRIBUTIONS OF ITLOS TO THE LAW ON MARITIME DELIMITATION

Suzette V. SUAREZ

A. INTRODUCTION

Maritime delimitation disputes constitute the most popular types of cases before international courts and tribunals. Most of the maritime delimitation cases have been submitted to the International Court of Justice (ICJ) and to arbitral tribunals. This is not surprising since the ICJ has been an established judicial institute since 1946 while international arbitration has a much longer history dating back to the Jay Treaty of 1794 between the United States and Great Britain. In comparison, the International Tribunal for the Law of the Sea (ITLOS), established in 1996 following the entry into force of the treaty that created it, the United Nations Convention on the Law of the Sea (1982 LOS Convention),[1] has so far considered two delimitation disputes in its docket during its twenty years of existence: Bangladesh/Myanmar decided in 2012 and the Ghana/Cote d'Ivoire cases decided in 2016.

This article reflects on the jurisprudence of the ITLOS on maritime delimitation as it celebrates its twentieth year in 2017. In doing so, I hope to contribute to the discussion of the Hamburg court's contributions to the continuing development of the law on maritime delimitation. Following the introduction, part II will provide an overview of the law on maritime delimitation relating to three maritime zones under the 1982 LOS Convention: the territorial sea, the exclusive economic zone and the continental shelf. Part III will discuss the law-making role of courts and tribunals on maritime delimitation. Part IV and V will highlight the contributions of ITLOS. Part IV will make an assessment of the maritime delimitation method applied by ITLOs in the context of predictability and stability. Part V will focus on the approach taken by ITLOS in dealing with novel issues. Finally, conclusions will be made in Part VI.

B. OVERVIEW OF THE HISTORY OF THE LAW ON MARITIME DELIMITATION

The evolution and development of the law on maritime delimitation can be divided into three phases.[2] The first phase was the phase prior to the four 1958 Conventions on Law of the Sea which were products of the First UN Conference on the Law of the Sea. During that time, the law on maritime delimitation was not codified. Maritime delimitation as a legal and political activity was hardly in existence. This was because the maritime entitlement under national jurisdiction at that time was insignificant in terms of area size. There was only one maritime zone within national jurisdiction and this was the territorial sea which for any coastal States was at most 4 nautical miles from the baselines. Beyond the narrow belt of territorial sea were the high seas. Given the narrow territorial seas the maritime entitlements of coastal States did not overlap.

The second phase is from 1958 to 1982, or the period after the four Conventions on the Law of the Sea were adopted at the First United Nations Conference on the Law of the Sea (UNCLOS I) but before the 1982 Convention on the Law of the Sea was adopted at the Third United Nations Conference on the Law of the Sea (UNCLOS III). The four Conventions adopted in 1958 were: the Convention on the Territorial Sea and the Contiguous Zone;[3] the Convention on the High Seas;[4] the Convention on Fishing and Conservation of the Living Resources of the High Seas;[5] and the Convention on the Continental Shelf.[6]

During this phase, the relevant maritime zones that could be subject of maritime delimitation were the territorial sea and the newly established continental shelf. However, there were no uniform limits to the territorial sea. The delegates to UNCLOS I failed to agree on the limits at UNCLOS I. Hence, a second UN Law of the Sea Conference in 1960 specifically aimed to fix the limit of the territorial sea was organized.[7] But the delegates at UNCLOS II also failed to arrive at a fixed limit for the territorial sea.[8]

Despite the lack of uniform limits, the Convention on the Territorial Sea and the Contiguous Zone provides on how to delimit in case of overlaps. Article 12 of the Convention on the Territorial Sea and the Contiguous Zone which has two paragraphs, requires adjacent or opposite States not to extend their territorial seas beyond the median line equidistant from the nearest points on the baselines from which the breadth of the territorial seas of each of the two States is measured.

As for the continental shelf, the 1958 Convention on the Continental Shelf also does not provide any clear fixed limits. Article 1 of the 1958 Convention on the Continental Shelf places the limits to the depth of 200 meters or beyond such depth up to where technology allows the exploitation of the resources of that area.

In case of overlaps, the 1958 Convention on the Continental Shelf provides for the method of maritime delimitation in the case of a continental shelf shared by two or more States, which has coasts that are adjacent to each other or opposite each other. The boundary of the continental shelf of States whose coasts are opposite each other shall be determined by agreement. "In the absence of agreement, and unless another boundary line is justified by special circumstances, the boundary is the median line, every point of which is equidistant from the nearest points of the baselines from which the breadth of the territorial sea of each State is measured."

For States whose coasts are adjacent to each other, the boundary of their shared continental shelf shall also be determined by agreement. "In the absence of agreement, and unless another boundary line is justified by special circumstances, the boundary shall be determined by application of the principle of equidistance from the nearest points of the baselines from which the breadth of the territorial sea of each State is measured."

Since the maritime entitlements became broader, overlaps as well as disputes concerning these overlaps became inevitable. The jurisprudence on the law on maritime delimitation started to be developed during this phase. The landmark cases were the 1969 ICJ judgments on the North Sea Continental Shelf. In these joint cases, Germany, Denmark and the Netherlands requested the International Court of Justice (ICJ) to state the principles of law applicable to enable the three States to delimit the continental shelf in the North Sea.

The other notable case during this period was the Continental Shelf Arbitration between France and United Kingdom which was decided on 30 June 1977).[9] In this case, the Parties disagreed, among others, as to the applicable law of delimitation of the continental shelf. Both are Parties to the 1958 Convention on the Continental Shelf but France argued that it did not enter into force between the two of them because of the U.K.'s refusal to accept France's reservations.[10] The Parties also disagreed on the interpretation of article 6 of the 1958 Convention on the Continental Shelf, including as to whether the median line as a method could be applied right away or only in the absence of an agreed solution, and as to whether the two States were adjacent or opposite or neither with respect to the dispute area.[11]

Complicating the issues arising out of the 1958 Convention on the Continental Shelf, was the consideration whether it had become obsolete in light of the upcoming new law of the sea convention which was being negotiated at the Third United Nations Conference on the Law o the Sea (UNCLOS III) during the proceedings of the case.[12] In the draft convention on the law of the sea, the state practice on the then-new exclusive economic zone of up to 200 nm was emerging and was set to be codified in the new convention.[13]

The Arbitral Court took cognizance of the continuing dynamism of the law of the sea, noting of " the importance of the evolution of the law of the sea which is now in progress and the possibility that a development in customary law may, under certain conditions, evidence the assent of the States concerned to the modification, or even termination, of previously existing treaty rights and obligations."[14] The Arbitral Court also considered the role of the equidistance as a method and concluded that in both the 1958 Convention and the draft Revised Negotiating text of the upcoming treaty, the equidistance method was not conclusive and the choice of method depended on the relevant geographical circumstances.[15]

The third and current phase starts from the end of 1982, when the current 1982 LOS Convention was adopted by the delegates to UNCLOS III in December 1982 up to the present time. Although the 1982 LOS Convention did not enter into force until 1996, its provisions were cited and their consequences were considered by international courts in cases decided even before its entry into force.

In the 1982 LOS Convention, the provisions on maritime delimitation are contained in article 15 for the territorial sea, article 74 for the exclusive economic zone (EEZ) and article 83 for the continental shelf.

The provision on maritime delimitation of the territorial sea in the 1982 LOS Convention is basically a reiteration or *in toto* adoption of the provision on maritime delimitation of the territorial sea in the 1958 Convention on the Territorial Sea and Contiguous Zone. When parties fail to reach an agreement, the method of delimitation under both treaties is the median line, "which is every point of which is equidistant from the nearest points on the baselines from which the territorial seas of both States is measured."

With respect to the continental shelf however, the delimitation method provided in the 1958 Convention is different from that provided in the 1982 LOS Convention. The latter treaty also requires parties to resolve any dispute by agreement under article 83. Failing agreement, however, no delimitation method for overlapping continental shelves is provided under the 1982 LOS Convention. Instead, parties are under a duty to resort to Part XV procedures to resolve the dispute concerning overlapping maritime zones under paragraph 2 of article 83.

As for the EEZ, it is a maritime zone created under the 1982 LOS Convention. Therefore, there is no comparable provision of the delimitation of overlapping EEZs in the 1958 Convention. The formulation used in the 1982 UNCLOS for the delimitation of the EEZ is notable as it is identical to the formulation of the delimitation of the continental shelf in article 83. This means that for the EEZ, no particular delimitation method has been assigned. Parties are required to first resolve the dispute by agreement under paragraph 1 of article 74. In case of a failure to agree, parties are required to pursue compulsory procedures under paragraph 2 of article 74.

Since the 1982 LOS Convention was adopted, the cases that have been submitted to international courts and tribunals involved the delimitation of all three maritime zones; the territorial sea, the exclusive economic zone and the continental shelf.

C. THE RULE-MAKING ROLE OF INTERNATIONAL COURTS AND TRIBUNALS IN THE LAW ON MARITIME DELIMITATION

There are three sources of international law as outlined in article 38.1 a, b, and c of the Statute of the International Court of Justice.[16] Under article 38.1.d, judicial decisions are subsidiary means of determining international law. An international court of tribunal does not make the law, it either interprets or applies the law. Hence it is a subsidiary means of determining what the law is.

As was underscored in the last section, the 1982 LOS Convention did not prescribe a delimitation method for the EEZ and the continental shelf. Judge Wolfrum, in his Declaration to the Judgment of ITLOS in the Bay of Bengal case, expanded on the majority's statement concerning the significant role of courts and tribunals in maritime delimitation. According to Wolfrum, courts and tribunals have a law-making function in the delimitation of the EEZ and the continental shelf and this decisive role was by design. Since the delegates at UNCLOS III could not agree on the method of delimitation of the EEZ and the continental shelf, they included paragraph 2 in both articles 73 and 84 which require the Parties who fail to agree, to refer the dispute to courts or tribunals referred in Part XV of the 1982 LOS Convention. Courts and tribunals, according to Wolfrum, therefore, are not only subsidiary means but are *acquis judiciare*, to be read as source of international law on the delimitation of the EEZ and the continental shelf.

It must be underscored however that even before the 1982 LOS Convention, international courts and tribunals went beyond mere interpretation or application of the law on maritime delimitation. Following the 1958 Convention on the Continental Shelf, disputes concerning overlaps of the continental shelf increased and gave courts and tribunals the opportunity to contribute to the development of the law on maritime delimitation, and in particular, developing the methods of delimitation. The first of such cases were the 1969 ICJ Judgments on the *North Sea Continental Shelf*. In that case, the contribution of the ICJ to the law on maritime delimitation is among others, the method of delimitation that is applicable. The 1958 Convention on the Continental Shelf was applicable to Denmark and the Netherlands as parties. However, Germany was not a party but only a signatory. In that case, the ICJ ruled that the 1958 Convention, which prescribed the equidistance method, did not apply. Rather, the ICJ stated that delimitation was to be achieved through the application of equitable principles, taking account of the relevant circumstances. The ICJ based its ruling on relevant state practice at that time, in particular, on the concept of natural prolongation as well as the equitable principles-relevant circumstances method as encompassed in the 1945 Truman Proclamation.[17] In the 1945 Truman Proclamation, equitable principles and factors " were to include: the general configuration of the coasts of the Parties, as well as the presence of any special or unusual features; so far as known or readily ascertainable, the physical and geological structure and natural resources of the continental shelf areas involved; the element of a reasonable degree of proportionality between the extent of the continental shelf areas appertaining to each State and the length of its coast measured in the general direction of the coastline, taking into account the effects, actual or prospective, of any other continental shelf delimitations in the same region."

Following the 1969 *North Sea Continental Shelf* cases, the equidistance/median line method has since been paired with the equitable-relevant circumstance method, becoming the most relied upon combination of methods by courts and tribunals to delimit overlapping maritime entitlements. This particular method has assumed a "substantial authority" and "easily exceeds all the other methods of maritime boundary de limitation in frequency of use."[18]

In its current version, the equidistance-relevant circumstances method consists of three stages of delimitation as developed by the ICJ in the *Black*

Sea case. The ITLOS describes the three-stage equidistance-relevant circumstance method as developed by the ICJ in the *Black Sea* case[19] in its Judgement in the Bay of Bengal case as follows:

233. In the Black Sea case, the ICJ built on the evolution of the jurisprudence on maritime delimitation. In that case, the ICJ gave a description of the three-stage methodology which it applied. At the first stage, it established a provisional equidistance line, using methods that are geometrically objective and also appropriate for the geography of the area to be delimited. "So far as delimitation between adjacent coasts is concerned, an equidistance line will be drawn unless there are compelling reasons that make this unfeasible in the particular case" (Maritime Delimitation in the Black Sea (Romania v. Ukraine), Judgment, I.C.J. Reports 2009, p. 61, at p. 101, para. 116). At the second stage, the ICJ ascertained whether "there are factors calling for the adjustment or shifting of the provisional equidistance line in order to achieve an equitable result" (ibid., at pp. 101, para. 120). At the third stage, it verified that the delimitation line did not lead to "an inequitable result by reason of any marked disproportion between the ratio of the respective coastal lengths and the ratio between the relevant maritime area of each State by reference to the delimitation line" (ibid., at p. 103, para. 122).[20]

The reasons why the equidistance-relevant circumstances method is popular among courts and tribunals to delimit overlapping maritime entitlements are because it provides predictability/stability and flexibility to Parties.[21] Theorists have stated that "legal certainty requires a balance between stability and flexibility."[22] Predictability of judicial decisions in any given area is particularly important as it enables Parties to "calculate the legal consequences of their actions as well as the outcomes of legal proceedings."[23] The application of the equidistance/median line method in a provisional manner contributes to the predictability of the process of delimitation for the Parties. The equidistance/median line is a method that is "geometrically objective" according to courts, therefore predictable by nature.[24] However, each case is different and in cases where issues are novel, the rigid application of the same method could lead to inequitable results, hence in such a situation predictability will not serve the goals of the rule of law. The consideration of relevant circumstances following the establishment of the equidistant line on a provisional basis provides Parties the sense that the law though predictable and stable is also flexible as it considers their particular circumstances relevant.[25]

Notwithstanding the overwhelming popularity of the equidistance-relevant circumstances method, courts and tribunals have declined to confer on it the status of customary law, binding and applicable on all delimitation disputes. Indeed, the notion of methods alternative to the equidistance-relevant circumstances method has remained to be accepted. The most common of the so-called alternative delimitation method is the angle-bisector method which has been applied in a number of cases.[26]

As will be seen in the next section, ITLOS preferred to apply the equidistance-relevant circumstances method in its two delimitation cases. Did these two recent delimitation cases finally hammer the last nail on the coffin of other alternative methods, in particular, the angle bisector method?

D. THE ITLOS JURISPRUDENCE ON MARITIME DELIMITATION METHODOLOGY – THE TRIUMPH OF PREDICTABILITY AND STABILITY IN THE LAW ON MARITIME DELIMITATION?

In the Bay of Bengal case, Bangladesh argued against the equidistance/median and relevant circumstance method on account of the concavity of the Bangladesh coast.[27] Myanmar advocated for the application of the equidistance-relevant circumstances method.[28] In its case against Ghana, Cote D'Ivoire also argued for the application of the angle-bisector method on account of what it described as "macro-geography and the coastal micro-geography ... of the two States' coastlines ... which are unstable in nature."[29] Ghana disagreed, describing the geographical situation of the two adjacent States as a "textbook" case for the application of the equidistance-relevant circumstances method.[30]

In both cases, the ITLOS relied on the equidistance-relevant circumstances as delimitation method. In the Bay of Bengal case, the ITLOS disagreed with Bangladesh, pointing out that the angle-bisector method was applied in previous case law only when "it has not been possible or appropriate" to apply the equidistance/relevant circumstances rule."[31] ITLOS stated that the angle-bisector method was not appropriate as it led to several "directions, depending on the angles and bisectors."[32] The ITLOS also was not convinced of the angle bisector method as it "failed to give adequate effect to the southward projection of the coast of Bangladesh."[33] For ITLOS, the equidistance-relevant circumstances method was most convincing as it "reduce(d) the elements of subjectivity and uncertainty" and at the same time, was "flexible enough to accommodate the different circumstances of each delimitation dispute."

In the Ghana/Cote D'Ivoire case, the ITLOS Special Chamber carefully addressed Cote D'Ivoire's arguments in support of the angle-bisector method, pointing out however that the geographical situation in the coasts of Ghana and Cote D'Ivoire is rather straight-forward and lacked the geographical complexity of the cases where the courts were compelled to apply the angle-bisector method.[34] The Special Chamber therefore concluded that "international jurisprudence confirms that, in the absence of any compelling reasons that make it impossible or inappropriate to draw a provisional equidistance line, the equidistance/relevant circumstances methodology should be chosen for maritime delimitation."[35]

In the Bay of Bengal case, the Parties disagreed on the role of St. Martin's Island in the delimitation of the territorial sea. Myanmar argued since St. Martin lies immediately off its coast, opposite the mainland of Myanmar, it was a special circumstance which called for the disapplication of the median line.[36] Myanmar acknowledged that St. Martin is an island in accordance with article 121 LOS Convention[37] but its legal effects should be ignored in accordance with State practice, or given very little effect.[38] ITLOS acknowledged that previous case law gives less than full effect to islands in the delimitation of territorial sea but these were rather "insignificant maritime features" such as Qit'at Jaradah, a very small island, uninhabited and without any vegetation in the case between Qatar and Bahrain.[39] In contrast, St. Martin is an island that has "a large permanent population" with fishing and tourism as its main economic activities.[40] The ITLOS therefore found no compelling reasons to treat St. Martin Island as a special circumstance or give it less than full effect in the delimitation of the territorial sea.[41]

No special circumstances were raised in the delimitation of the territorial sea between Ghana and Cote D'Ivoire.

Bangladesh argued three factors as relevant circumstances that could affect or change the application of the provisional equidistance line in the delimitation of the EEZ and the continental shelf: concavity, instability of the coast and the presence of St. Martin's island.[42] Of the three circumstances, the ITLOS accepted concavity as relevant circumstance that warranted the adjustment of the provisional equidistance line.[43] Concavity of the coast is not *per se* relevant, according to ITLOS.[44] "However, when an equidistance line drawn between two States produces a cut-off effect on the maritime entitlement of one of those States, as a result of the concavity of the coast, then an adjustment of that line may be necessary in order to reach an equitable result."[45] The ITLOS found that due to the concavity of the Bangladeshi coast, the provisional equidistance line produced a cut-off effect, essentially depriving Bangladesh of its maximum coastal projection, and in particular, preventing Bangladesh from its continental shelf beyond 200 nm.[46]

The provisional equidistance line was therefore adjusted in the Bay of Bengal case on account of the cut-off effect that resulted because of the concavity of the Bangladeshi coast. In adjusting the provisional equidistance line, the ITLOS had difficulty finding an objective method. The ITLOS noted that in previous rulings, three approaches of adjusting the provisional equidistance line were undertaken.[47] In one, the court changed the position of the line but not the direction (*Continental Shelf between Libyan Arab Jamahiriya/ Malta*), in another case, the court adjusted the position and direction of the line (*Maritime Delimitation in the Area between Greenland and Jan Mayen*), and in a third case, the court deflected the line at a certain point based on the relevant circumstance (*Arbitration between Barbados and the Republic of Trinidad and Tobago*).[48] The ITLOS found the approach taken in the Barbados and Trinidad and Tobago case suitable.[49] The ITLOS ruled that the "provisional equidistance line is to be deflected at the point where it begins to cut off the seaward projection of the Bangladesh coat." Locating the point where deflection had to be done did not appear complicated but the deciding on the actual direction of the adjusted line did not appear simple.

ITLOS had a vague formula in mind, which was that "direction of the adjustment is to be determined in the light of those circumstances."[50] As for the actual direction of the deflected equidistance line, the ITLOS settled on a geodetic line starting at an azimuth of 215°. It has to be recalled that the angle-bisector method advocated by Bangladesh, which was rejected by the ITLOS as unsuitable, also started at 215°azimuth line.[51] A comparison of the delimitation line proposed by Bangladesh based on an angle-bisector method and the adjusted line of the ITLOS in Table 1 reveals the similarity of the direction and angle of the two lines.

In Ghana/Cote D'Ivoire case, both Parties invoked relevant circumstances to argue the adjustment of the provisional equidistance line. Ghana invoked the conduct of parties as a relevant circumstance to adjust the provisional equidistance line. According to Ghana, the Parties had a tacit agreement or a modus vivendi on a delimitation line which existed for 50 years; Ghana was therefore advocating the provisional line be adjusted to coincide with the tacitly agreed line.[52] Cote D'Ivoire invoked concavity, the slight protrusion of a Ghanaian land mass, and the location of the mineral resources, all of which were considered but subsequently rejected by the Special Chamber as justifiable to adjust the provisional equidistance line. Unlike the concavity

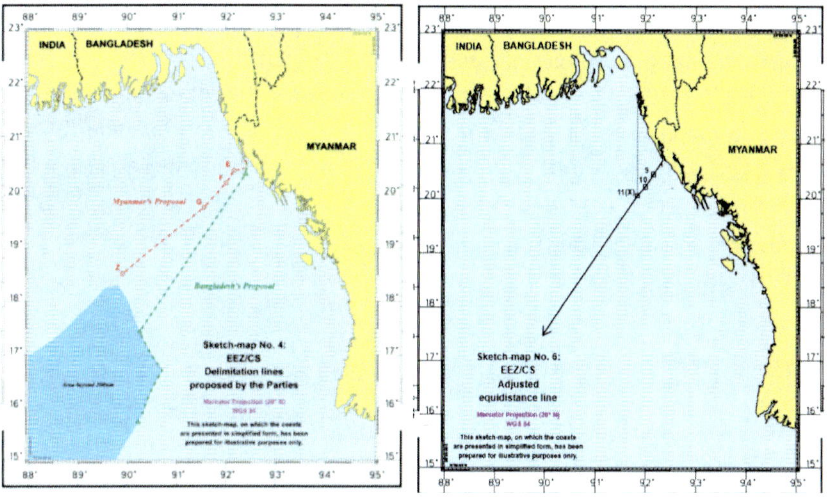

Table 1. Comparison of the Parties' proposed delimitation lines and the adjusted equidistance line of ITLOS in the Bay of Bengal case.

in the Bangladeshi coast, the concavity in the coast of Cote D'Ivoire did not produce a significant cut-off effect for Cote D'Ivoire as it is still able to claim entitlements beyond 200 nm and as such was not a relevant circumstance.[53] The Special Chamber also rejected Cote D'Ivoire's argument that the location of the natural resources in the disputed area according to Cote D'Ivoire was exceptional as it would deprive one party completely from accessing the resources.[54] The Special Chamber agreed with Ghana that there was no evidence that the hydrocarbon resources were highly concentrated on the Ghana side of the delimitation line.[55] And even if that were the case, the ITLOS Special Chamber underscored that the process of delimitation is not meant to "refashion nature"[56] nor is it a "means for distributing justice."[57] Rather, the ITLOS Special Chamber underscored that "(a)ccording to international jurisprudence, delimitation of maritime areas is to be decided objectively on the basis of the geographic configuration of the relevant coasts."[58] The Special Chamber rejected the tacit agreement or the modus vivendi argument, recalling that there was no sufficient evidence of the same.[59]

Following the judgments in these two cases, the status of the equidistance-relevant circumstances method has been further strengthened. Are these two cases the equivalent of the death knell of delimitation methods other than the equidistance-relevant circumstances method? In the Bay of Bengal case, though the ITLOS applied the equidistance-relevant circumstances method, it tempered its approach when it underscored that the issue of delimitation method should always depend on the circumstances of the case and the prevailing geographic realities which could lead to an equitable result.[60] In the Ghana/Cote D'Ivoire case, on the other hand, the Special Chamber had been more firm in its regard of the equidistance-relevant circumstances method, underlining the fact of its almost universal application, especially in recent decisions. The Special Chamber underscored that only the most compelling of reasons would be acceptable in turning to an alternative method.[61]

E. The ITLOS and the Delimitation of the Area of the Continental Shelf beyond 200 NM – A Bold, Initial Exploration of the Final Frontiers of the Law on Maritime Delimitation?

While the previous section focused on the aspects of predictability and stability in the ITLOS decisions on its two maritime delimitation cases, this section will look at the approach ITLOS took on the novel issues of these two cases. The Bay of Bengal case was a novel case as it was the first to delimit the claims of overlapping continental shelf beyond 200 nm. The Ghana/Cote D'Ivoire case, on the other hand, was the third case that delimited overlapping areas of the continental shelf beyond 200 nm. The ITLOS Special Chamber had the fortune of being able to refer to the ITLOS rulings in the Bay of Bengal case on issues relating to the delimitation of the continental shelf beyond 200 nm. The focus in this section will therefore be mainly on the novel issues dealt with by the ITLOS in the Bay of Bengal case.

The Bay of Bengal case posed very particular, fundamental challenges to the ITLOS because both Parties have not yet received recommendations from their submissions on their outer limits to the Commission on the Limits of the Continental Shelf (CLCS) at the time the case was on-going. In two past cases dealing with the delimitation of the continental shelf beyond 200 nm, the court and tribunal refrained from delimiting any overlaps of the extended continental shelf because the entitlements have not yet been considered by the CLCS.[62] A fundamental issue therefore before ITLOS was whether it had jurisdiction to delimit the area beyond 200 nm before the CLCS had made its recommendations. ITLOS answered this issue in the affirmative.[63] Article 83 of the LOS Convention speaks of delimitation of the continental shelf, without making any distinction between the area up to 200 nm and beyond. ITLOS being one of the courts or tribunals referred to in Section of Part XV may exercise jurisdiction over a maritime delimitation dispute submitted to it for resolution.[64]

ITLOS, however, asked whether it was proper to delimit the extended continental shelf before the CLCS had made a determination of the entitlement to a continental shelf beyond 200 nm. Myanmar did not deny that the ITLOS had jurisdiction to interpret article 76 but underscored that delimitation should not be undertaken before the CLCS had made its recommendations on the entitlement of both Parties to a continental shelf beyond 200 nm.[65] The resolution of the issue of entitlement was especially critical because both Myanmar and Bangladesh rejected each other's entitlement of an area of the continental shelf beyond 200 nm. In determining whether it should exercise jurisdiction, the ITLOS therefore dealt with several sub-issues, including, "what is the meaning of natural prolongation and its connection with continental margin", and "whether Parties have entitlements to the continental shelf beyond 200 nm and whether they overlap?"[66]

On the sub-issue of natural prolongation and its relationship to the outer limits of the continental margin, Bangladesh argued that it alone is entitled to the continental shelf beyond 200 nm because it has an uninterrupted natural prolongation or continuity by virtue of the "uninterrupted seabed geology and geomorphology, including specifically the extensive sedimentary rock deposited by the Ganges-Brahmaputra river system."[67] In addition to geological evidence, Bangladesh also provided evidence that the extent of its continental margin is beyond the 200 nm by applying the Gardiner formula or the sedimentary thickness formula.[68] Myanmar, according to Bangladesh, does not have a natural prolongation in the Bay of Bengal because of the "fundamental discontinuity beyond the landmass of Myanmar from the seabed beyond 200 nm." This is because Myanmar sits on the Burma plate, while the continental margin on the Bay of Bengal sits on the Indian plate, indicating "two separate continental shelves, or two separate natural prolongations."[69]

Myanmar did not contradict Bangladesh' evidence on the two separate tectonic plates but disagreed that natural prolongation can only be proven based on geology. Myanmar provided evidence that it has such natural prolongation by applying the Gardiner formula on sedimentary thickness in article 76 paragraph 4 (a)(i). Myanmar, on the other hand, rejected Bangladesh's contention that it had a continental shelf beyond 200 nm because the delimitation line for Bangladesh "stops well before reaching the 200 nm limit measured from the baselines of both Sates."[70]

The term "natural prolongation" of a coastal State's land territory has not always been associated with the concept of the legal continental shelf. The 1945 Truman Declaration, which was the first written document which contains a claim for the legal continental shelf, did not use the term "natural prolongation." When the US made the first claim for a continental shelf, it referred to the area "beneath the high seas but contiguous to the coasts of the United States." The first and only other global treaty on the continental shelf, other than the 1982 LOS Convention, is the 1958 Convention on the Continental Shelf and it also does not contain the term "natural prolongation" in describing the legal continental shelf. Article 1 thereof refers to the "submarine areas adjacent to the coast but outside of the territorial sea, to a depth of 200 metres or, beyond that limit, to where the depth of the superjacent waters admits of the exploitation of the natural resources of said areas."

The term "natural prolongation" of the land territory of a coastal State can be traced from the ICJ's judgement in the *North Sea Continental Shelf* cases in 1969, and since then, its exact definition and scope have been much debated. The ICJ's introduction of the term which gave the legal concept of continental shelf a quasi-territorial nature, a continuation of the land territory of a coastal State, was therefore unfortunate as it inadvertently set-off a debate so difficult that it could never be concluded.

During the debate at UNCLOS III, the idea that the continental shelf was a submerged physical or geological continuation of the coastal State's land territory clearly did not sit well with all delegates, especially those without broad continental margins or those without any geological continental shelves. Nevertheless, the delegates at UNCLOS III included the term "natural prolongation" in paragraph 1 of article 76 but its inclusion was more a result of a political compromise rather than an indication of a common accepted understanding of its scope and meaning.

In its 1999 Scientific and Technical Guidelines, the CLCS rather than defining the term "natural prolongation" put the focus on explaining the formulas and constraints on establishing the outer limits of the continental margin which effectively neutralized or reduced the effect of the term "natural prolongation" on the legal continental shelf.[71] The formulas and constraints are rules developed by the delegates at UNCLOS III based not only on geological but geomorphological considerations as well.

The CLCS position is supported by the International Law Association's Committee on the Legal Issues of the Outer Continental Shelf. (ILA)[72] According to the ILA, paragraphs, 3, 4 and 9 1 of Article 76 itself are the bases for the reference to both geology and geomorphology in the term "natural prolongation." Paragraph 3 of article 76 refers to the submerged prolongation of the land mass of the coastal State which has no reference to the nature of that landmass.[73]

ITLOS' ruling in the Bay of Bengal concurs with the position of the CLCS and the ILA that that the basis of natural prolongation, can be either or both geology and geomorphology. ITLOS rejected Bangladesh's position that there was a legal divide between the Parties' continental shelves, observing that the "notion of natural prolongation and that of continental margin ... refer to the same area."[74] While there are indeed two tectonic plates, ITLOS noted the uncontested scientific evidence that the "sea floor of the Bay of Bengal is covered by thick layer of sediments" including in areas appertaining to Bangladesh and Myanmar.[75] Neither Party contested this scientific evidence relating to the seafloor of the Bay of Bengal.[76] Indeed ITLOS noted that both Parties calculated their outer limits based on the sediment thickness formula and submitted this information to the CLCS.[77] The ITLOS concluded that both Parties have proof that their continental margins extend beyond 200 nm and that they overlap.[78]

In addition to the fundamental issues of jurisdiction, another development to the law which the ITLOS contributed was the delimitation method that is appropriate to the overlapping areas of the continental shelf beyond 200 nm. The ITLOS took the position that article 83 applies equally to the continental shelf beyond 200 nm and therefore, the method of delimitation should not be different from that employed for the overlapping areas within 200 nm.[79] Thus, equidistance adjusted up to the 200 nm mark, could be continued in the area beyond 200 nm.

Before the adjusted equidistance line was continued in the area beyond 200 nm, the ITLOS however considered Bangladesh's argument that relevant circumstances of geology and geomorphology and its coastal concavity were justified to adjust the line and make it equitable. Bangladesh repeated its argument that it "has the most natural prolongation", whereas, Myanmar has little or no natural prolongation beyond 200 nm."[80] Given its position that the basis of natural prolongation can either be geologic or geomorphologic, the ITLOS did not accept Bangladesh's argument on natural prolongation.[81] Its argument on concavity was accepted as the cut-off effect if the provisional equidistance line was not adjusted continued even beyond 200 nm.[82] The direction of the adjusted equidistance line was therefore continued until it reached "the area where the rights of third States may be affected."[83]

F. CONCLUSIONS

In these two cases, the ITLOS contributed in strengthening and consolidating the case law on maritime delimitation by choosing to apply the equidistance-relevant circumstances method of delimitation. ITLOS' embrace of the equidistance-relevant circumstances method is understandable as it ensures predictability and stability on one hand. On the other hand, it provides flexibility in case relevant circumstances exist that warrant adjustment of the equidistance line.

However, this paper has shown that the equidistance-relevant circumstances method is not immune from subjectivity. This was evident in the Bay of Bengal case when the ITLOS adjusted the provisional equidistance line without any objective method, thereby ending up drawing a line that closely resembled the line proposed by Bangladesh which it had rejected in the first place. No court or tribunal in past cases has successfully developed an objective method of adjusting the equidistance line. Whether an objective robust method to adjust equidistance line is feasible remains to be seen. The Special Chamber rejected arguments that relevant circumstances existed and therefore did not have to adjust the equidistance line.

The most remarkable aspects of the ITLOS jurisprudence lie without doubt on its rulings and exposition on the novel issues relating to the delimitation of the continental shelf beyond 200 nm in the Bay of Bengal case. The ITLOS ruling in the Bay of Bengal is significant as it marked a shift away from focusing on a geologic only-basis of natural prolongation to both geologic and geomorphologic considerations, concurring with the position taken by the CLCS since 1999.

The ITLOS ruling on the propriety of exercising jurisdiction to delimit the continental shelf beyond 200 nm before the CLCS had made its recommendation is a step in the right direction. The LOS Convention does not require that delimitation precedes the delineation, or vice versa. Further, the ITLOS ruling in the Bay of Bengal is to be welcomed as it clarifies that a judicial or arbitral remedy under Part XV of the LOS Convention is available to ensure that Parties who have maritime delimitation disputes over an area beyond 200 nm do not get stuck in a legal limbo.

Considering that the areas beyond 200 nm are being delineated in accordance with article 76, an increase in the number of disputes on issues relating to the extended continental shelf can be expected. The rulings of the ITLOS on these issues though only binding on the Parties are therefore welcomed as they will provide clarity and guidance to States who are confronted with similar issues.

NOTES

[1] United Nations Convention on the Law of the Sea, adopted 10 December 1982, entered into force 16 November 1994, 1833 UNTS 3. (hereinafter "1982 LOS Convention").
[2] Shi Jiuyong, "Maritime Delimitation in the Jurisprudence of the International Court of Justice", 9 Chinese Journal of International Law (2010), pp. 271–291.
[3] 15 UST 1606; 516 UNTS 205.
[4] 13 UST 2312; 450 UNTS 11.
[5] 17 UST 138; 559 UNTS 285.
[6] 15 UST 471; 499 UNTS 311.
[7] UNGA Resolution 1307 (XIII) of 10 December 1958, https://documents-dds-ny.un.org/doc/RESOLUTION/GEN/NR0/747/51/IMG/NR074751.pdf?OpenElement
[8] See the Final Act of the Second United Nations Conference on the Law of the Sea, DOCUMENT A/CONF.19/L.15, 26 April 1960. http://legal.un.org/docs/?path=../diplomaticconferences/1960_los/docs/english/vol_1/a_conf19_l15.pdf&lang=E
[9] Arbitral Decision of 30 June 1977, reprinted in 18 LL.M. 397 (1979).
[10] *Ibid*, paragraph 30.
[11] *Ibid*, paragraph 35.
[12] *Ibid*, paragraphs 45 and 46.
[13] *Ibid.*
[14] *Ibid*, paragraph 47.
[15] *Ibid*, paragraph 96.
[16] 33 U.N.T.S. 993
[17] Proclamation 2667–Policy of the United States With Respect to the Natural Resources of the Subsoil and Sea Bed of the Continental Shelf, September 28, 1945.
[18] Jonathan I. Charney, "Progress in International Maritime Boundary Delimitation Law, The American Journal of International Law (1994), Vol. 88, No. 2, pp. 227–256, at 245.
[19] *Maritime Delimitation in the Black Sea (Romania v. Ukraine), Judgment, I.C.J. Reports 2009*, p. 61. ("*Black Sea*" case)
[20] *Delimitation of the maritime boundary in the Bay of Bengal (Bangladesh/ Myanmar), Judgment, ITLOS Reports 2012*, p. 4, at p. 66. ("*Bay of Bengal*" case)
[21] Yoshifumi Tanaka, *The International Law of the Sea,* (Cambridge University Press, 2012), at 197.
[22] Elina Paunio, "Beyond Predictability – Reflections on Legal Certainty and the Discourse Theory of Law in the EU Legal Order", in German Law Journal, Vol. 10 No. 11 (2009), pp. 1469–1493, at 1469.
[23] *Ibid.*
[24] *Black Sea* Case, at 101, paragraph 116.
[25] Tanaka, *supra* note 20, at 197.
[26] *Continental Shelf (Tunisia/Libyan Arab Jamahiriya) Judgment, I.C.J. Reports 1982*, p. 18; *Delimitation of the Maritime Boundary in the Gulf of Maine Area,*

Judgment, I.C.J. Reports 1984, p. 246; *Delimitation of the Maritime Boundary between Guinea and Guinea-Bissau, Decision of 14 February 1985*, ILR, Vol. 77, p. 635; *Territorial and Maritime Dispute between Nicaragua and Honduras in the Caribbean Sea (Nicaragua v. Honduras) Judgment, I.C.J. Reports 2007*, p. 659, at p. 741.

27 *Bay of Bengal* case, p. 62, paragraph 213.

28 *Ibid*, p. 63, paragraph 219.

29 *Delimitation of the maritime boundary in the Atlantic Ocean (Ghana/Côte d'Ivoire), Judgment, ITLOS Reports 2017*, to be published, (Ghana/ Cote D'Ivoire), pp. 80–81, paragraph 272.

30 *Ibid*, p. 79, paragraph 266.

31 *Bay of Bengal* case, p. 66, paragraph 234.

32 *ibid*, p. 67, paragraph 236.

33 *Ibid*, p. 67, paragraph 237.

34 Ghana/Cote D'Ivoire, p. 85, paragraph 287.

35 *Ibid*, p. 86, paragraph 289.

36 Bay of Bengal case, p. 43, paragraphs 131–134.

37 *Ibid*, p. 44, paragraph 135.

38 *Ibid*, p. 44, paragraph 136.

39 *Case concerning Maritime Delimitation and Territorial Questions between Qatar and Bahrain (Merits, Judgment, I.C.J. Report 2001*, p. 40, at p. 104, paragraph 219.

40 Bay of Bengal case, p. 46, paragraphs 143 and 145.

41 *Ibid*, p. 47, paragraph 152.

42 *Ibid,* p. 78, paragraph 276.

43 *Ibid*, p. 86, paragraph 318, p. 87, paragraph 322, p. 82, paragraph 297.

44 *Ibid*, p. 81, paragraphs 292, 293.

45 *Ibid.*

46 *Ibid.*

47 *Ibid*, p. 88, paragraph 328.

48 *Ibid.*

49 *Ibid.*

50 *Ibid.*

51 *Ibid,* p. 63 paragraph 217.

52 Ghana/Cote D'Ivoire, p. 128, paragraph 457.

53 *Ibid*, p. 120, paragraph 424.

54 *Ibid*, p. 125, paragraph 439.

55 *Ibid*, p. 127, paragraph 451.

56 *Ibid.*

57 *Ibid,* p. 128, paragraph 451.

58 *Ibid.*

59 *Ibid,* p. 134, paragraph 478.

60 Bay of Bengal, p. 67, paragraph 235.

61 Ghana/Cote D'Ivoire, p. 86, paragraph 289.

[62] *Arbitration between Barbados and the Republic of Trinidad and Tobago, Decision of 11 April 2006*, RIAA, Vol. XXVII, p. 147, at p. 242, paragraph 368. *Nicaragua v. Honduras, supra* note 25, p. 759, paragraph 319.
[63] *Bay of Bengal* case, p. 97, paragraph 363.
[64] Decision of 11 April 2006, *supra* note 63, at pp. 208–209, paragraph 213.
[65] *Bay of Bengal* case, p. 106, paragraph 405.
[66] *Ibid*, p. 105, paragraph 401.
[67] *Ibid*, p. 108, paragraph 415.
[68] *Ibid.*
[69] *Ibid*, p. 109, paragraph 417.
[70] *Ibid*, p. 110, paragraph 423.
[71] CLCS, Rules of Procedure, CLCS/11, 11 May 1999.
[72] International Law Association, Toronto Conference Report (2006).
[73] *Ibid.*
[74] *Ibid,* p. 112, paragraph 434.
[75] *Ibid,* p. 115, paragraphs 44–445.
[76] *Ibid,* paragraph 446.
[77] *Ibid,* paragraph 445.
[78] *Ibid,* p. 116, paragraph 449.
[79] *Ibid,* p. 117, paragraphs 45 and 455.
[80] *Ibid,* p. 117, paragraph 457.
[81] *Ibid,* p. 118, paragraph 460.
[82] *Ibid,* p. 118, paragraph 461.
[83] *Ibid,* p. 118, paragraph 462.

CHAPTER III

MARITIME TRANSPORT LAW AND THE EUROPEAN UNION IN THE 21ST CENTURY

Henning JESSEN

A. INTRODUCTION

In January 2009, the European Commission presented a Communication on the strategic objectives and recommendations for the European Union's (EU) maritime transport policy until 2018.[1] This Communication was placed in the broader context of the general EU Transport Policy,[2] which covers all modes of transportation, and also took into account the broader objectives of the EU Integrated Maritime Policy.[3] The six key action areas for maritime transport as identified by the 2009 Communication were:

- European shipping in globalized markets;
- human resources;
- quality shipping;
- international scene;
- short sea shipping;
- research and innovation.

However, the decade that followed the 2009 Communication was largely characterized by one of the longest financial and economic crises that had ever hit the global shipping sector. Political crisis followed later for the EU, most prominently symbolized by the buzzword "*Brexit*" and the associated challenges. Nevertheless, focussing specifically on the maritime sector, there was also intensified regulatory activity, both on the international and on the regional level. Furthermore, the timespan between 2009 and 2018 witnessed enormous developments in technological advancements. Above all, digitalisation and more autonomous procedures (both onshore and offshore) are at the forefront of the new inevitable challenges for all stakeholders. As a result, the six broadly phrased key areas as mentioned above have, of course, not lost their general relevance. However, they are subject to a continuously and rapidly changing environment. Nevertheless, in the 21st century, it is safe to say that two major regulatory areas will never lose their priority rank for any modern maritime regulator, be it an international Organisation (like the International Maritime Organisation, IMO), a supranational institution (like the EU) or a nation State: These two selected priority areas are: First, safety and security in maritime affairs and, second, environmental sustainability and the decarbonisation of the maritime sector. Both of these major regulatory areas are closely interlinked with a variety of other cross-cutting challenges (social, economic, financial and technological). For reasons of both space and thematic complexity, this paper shall concentrate on the core elements and latest EU developments in the two major maritime regulatory areas as identified above.

B. Safety and Security – A Short Primer on the EU's Regulatory Activity

Already by 1998, the EU had adopted a total of three Regulations, 35 Directives and three Council decisions in relation to maritime policy.[4] But while this development was still under way, further major accidents involving the disastrous casualties of the "*Erika*" in 1999 and the "*Prestige*" in 2002 led to an acceleration, strengthening and amplification of EU regulatory activity, via the so-called "*Erika Packages I – III*".[5] *Inter alia*, the relevant measures included:

- A reinforcement of the EU rules on port State control;[6]
- a reinforcement of the EU rules on classification societies;[7]
- an accelerated phase-out of single hull tankers within the EU;[8]
- improvements in intra-EU vessel traffic monitoring,[9] including also ongoing work to achieve a more coherent places of refuge concept;[10]
- the creation of the European Maritime Safety Agency (EMSA);[11] and
- a revision and introduction of stricter EU rules on compensation and liability, including criminal responsibility.[12]

Generally, the maritime sector has been influenced heavily by broader EU environmental and security policies. In the area of maritime security, following the events of 11 September 2001 and subsequent terrorist activity, the security aspects of maritime transport inevitably assumed greater importance with a series of new initiatives being taken at EU and international level. These are:

- An effective implementation of the International Ship and Port Facility Security Code (ISPS Code);[13]
- action on advanced cargo declaration;[14] and
- intensified cooperation with the authorities of third countries, especially with the United States.[15]

As a result, SOLAS Chapter XI-2 and part A as well as certain parts of part B of the ISPS Code have been added to the EU's '*acquis communautaire*'. The regime is complemented by Directive 2005/65/EC on enhancing port security[16] which addresses elements of port security not covered by the ISPS-related EU Regulation. The Commission was given powers to perform inspections, to verify the effectiveness of national quality control systems and maritime security measures, procedures and structures. More than 870 maritime security inspections have been conducted by the European Commission since 2005, with the technical assistance of EMSA, in order to ensure a harmonised implementation throughout the EU of the maritime security provisions, whilst also contributing to keeping the level of vigilance high in this domain.[17]

In the area of maritime safety, regulatory action has been taken, based on existing global standards as agreed under the IMO's MARPOL Convention, Annex VI, to limit the sulphur in marine diesel[18] or the IMO's Anti-Fouling Convention to phase out the use of certain marine paints containing biocides.[19] One of the latest regulatory activities of the EU addresses the disposal of hazardous waste which can include ship breaking/ship recycling.[20] Some more focus shall be attached to this topic in the sustainability section of this paper.

In general, the 2009 Communication highlighted the need to give priority to the enforcement of existing EU and international rules and to speedy implementation of measures introduced with the (latest) Third Maritime Safety Package. Almost a decade later, the EU explicitly claims that it has established one of the world's most stringent legislative frameworks covering the entire chain of responsibility in the maritime sector.[21] The 2009 Communication also aimed at the revision of the mandate and functioning of the EMSA to further enhance its technical and scientific assistance capability. This has been achieved since 2013; however, it is also a continuous policy process. It should also be highlighted that EU has established a comprehensive Maritime Information and Exchange System (*SafeSeaNet*).[22] Step by step, this system has gradually phased into full operational capability and now covers all European coastal waters, tracks 12.000 ships/day and receives and records 100.000.000 ship (AIS) positions per month.[23] This enables the EU to identify high-risk vessels earlier as well as to take more efficient and coordinated precautionary actions. It also provides for improved emergency response to incidents or marine pollution, including search and rescue operations and places of refuges for ships in need of assistance.

In sum, the EU has established an operational integrated information management system operated. It is operated by EMSA and it is also used by other EU Agencies. The future establishment of a "European Coastguard and Maritime Border Control" represents the latest institutional challenge for the EU but this development cannot be analysed in more detail in this paper.[24]

C. ENVIRONMENTAL SUSTAINABILITY AND DECARBONISATION – A SHORT PRIMER ON THE EU'S REGULATORY ACTIVITY

Improving the general environmental record of all modes of transportation is among the prime aims of the EU for years. In maritime transport, this materialises as a long term EU objective to achieve "*zero waste, zero emission*".[25] This is despite the fact that maritime transport is recognised as the most environmentally sustainable and energy efficient way of moving large quantities of cargo. Nevertheless, shipping has not been exempted from public demands to achieve a substantial reduction of the amount of emissions that are harmful for human health and the environment. The need for cleaner shipping has thus come into focus in relation to both emissions having a global impact – namely greenhouse gas (GHG) (2.5% of global CO2 emissions) – and emissions of substances that are particularly harmful at regional level and notably close to coastal areas and port cities (for example, sulphur, particulate matter and nitrogen-oxides).[26] Already in October 2008, the IMO had adopted amendments to MARPOL Annex VI with the aim to strengthen restrictions on emissions of sulphurous and nitrous oxides. The threshold for sulphur emission levels was to be reduced progressively from the former global level of 4.5% to 3.5% by 2012 and to 0.5% by 2020.

Stricter regional standards are already included for Sulphur Emission Control Areas (SECAs) within the EU, like the Baltic Sea, the English Channel and the North Sea. Following a European Commission proposal in 2011,[27] the EU has adopted legislation to implement the latest amendments to MARPOL Annex VI adopted by the IMO: By 2015, the allowed sulphur content in fuel has been reduced to 0.1% in the European SECAs and by 2020 for passenger ships generally. Some regional discussions are focussing on the fair enforcement of the SECA provisions and the need to avoid negative effects on short sea shipping and passenger transportation possibly leading to a shift of traffic to road haulage. The shipping industry's contribution to carbon dioxide emissions has attracted increasing attention and other sectors have been subjected to new disciplines in the context of policy to address global warming already since 2007.[28] First, in December 2008, the European Council and Parliament reached an agreement on the European Commission's proposed climate change package, including so-called "*effort sharing*". This package set binding targets for each Member State to reduce GHG emissions from sources not subject to the EU's emission trading system, including therefore those from shipping. The relevant emissions are to be reduced by 20% between 2013 and 2020.

The European Commission had also launched a consultation on how the EU might adopt measures to reduce GHG from ships in the absence of an adequate international agreement on the subject. In 2015, the EU unilaterally passed its "MRV Regulation", i.e. Regulation EU/757/2015 on the monitoring, reporting and verification of carbon dioxide emissions from maritime transport.[29] The EU's MRV Regulation marks the first of three consecutive steps. As a second step, based on the evaluation of the MRV Regulation, the EU intends to set up GHG reduction targets for the maritime transport sector. However, priority might be given to globally applicable reduction targets as negotiated within the realm of the IMO. As a potential third step, further measures (including market based measures, MBM) might be introduced by the EU in the medium to long term.

D. How Far May the EU's Regulatory Arm Extend? The Example of Ship Recycling

As stated above, one of the core objectives of the EU is to achieve a good environmental status of "*zero waste, zero emission*". In the following, this paper shall draw some attention to the objective of "*zero waste*" and related legal challenges. At the IMO level, via MARPOL Annex V, stringent and updated global requirements have been established for operational waste generated on vessels. There is also existing EU legislation on port reception facilities for ship-generated waste and cargo residues where changes from the related MARPOL provisions have been incorporated.[30] With the assistance of EMSA, the Commission has facilitated and streamlined the relevant electronic reporting and works on the implementation of an information and monitoring system set up under Directive 2000/59/EC[31] which will expedite port handling and facilitate enforcement by the competent authorities.[32]

However, are vessels hazardous wastes as well? There are some inadequacies and practical weaknesses of generally applicable international legal instruments, like the Basel Convention[33] or the relevant general waste management legislation of the EU[34] in relation to ship recycling. The practical realities of the global ship recycling business reflect that these broader legal instruments, in particular the Basel Convention, have been largely circumvented by the maritime industry in the past. The practical result has been, among others, a large spread of environmentally unsustainable ship recycling practices which are generally associated with the term "beaching" and with a major geographical share of ships being demolished and scrapped at "beaching yards" along the shallow coastlines of India, Pakistan and Bangladesh.[35] It has also led to a significant dependence of those national economies on a steady influx of steel as generated from the scrapping activities.[36] In 2012, the European Commission proposed the adoption of a specific Regulation to give binding legal effect to the IMO's 2009 Hong Kong Convention for the Safe and Environmentally Sound Recycling of Ships.[37] This policy area has been subject to some heated discussions[38] but the work on the EU Regulation on Ship Recycling – resulting in Regulation EU/1257/2013 – was finally completed at the end of 2013 and imposed some more stringent requirements on European-flagged vessels and shipowners.[39] Though more limited in relation to its geographical scope (enforceable in EU ports, also in relation to third parties) as well as its substantive coverage (vessels flying the flag of an EU Member), the EU Regulation gradually brings forward some of the requirements of the applicable IMO Convention and shall contribute to accelerating its global entry into force.[40]

In this regard, an interesting question has arisen after 2013 which addressed the question of potential extra-territorial measures to achieve the goal of generating "*zero waste*". Between 2013 and 2017, the EU had been evaluating various policy approaches on how to implement, in particular, Article 29 of the Ship Recycling Regulation. This provision explicitly states that "*[The European] Commission shall, by 31 December 2016, submit to the European Parliament and to the Council a report on the feasibility of a financial instrument that would facilitate safe and sound ship recycling and shall, if appropriate, accompany it by a legislative proposal.*" A number of different policy options for possible legislative action, ranging from a passive approach to different, more pro-active concepts (e.g., a ship recycling guarantee, an escrow account, an insurance model or a port levy) were prepared by external consultants and had been submitted to the European Commission.[41]

Assessing the practical impact of different approaches and considering all legal problems and challenges associated with Article 29 of the EU's Ship Recycling Regulation, the introduction of a time-based ship recycling license (i.e. an EU Ship Recycling License Scheme) emerged to be a possible "technical" approach for the EU, to be advocated, at least from a more ambitious policy perspective.[42] However, an EU Ship Recycling License Scheme has not been implemented yet. This is also for good reasons. The legality of the most ambitious ideas on ship recycling could be seriously challenged from various legal perspectives. In 2017, the Commission concluded that a number of issues "*deserve further analysis, including with regard to the compatibility of such a potential financial instrument with EU and international law.*"[43] As a result, the need for additional measures on financial incentives will be reassessed at a later stage, based on an analysis of the use and effects of the "*European List of Ship Recycling Facilities*" which has been created since the end of 2016, in accordance with Article 16 of the EU's Ship Recycling Regulation.[44]

Both the IMO and the EU establish operational requirements for ship recycling facilities. For example, both the IMO and the EU demand from recycling facilities to prepare and implement a specific ship recycling facility plan which is generally defined as "*a plan prepared by the operator of the ship recycling facility and adopted by the board or the appropriate governing body of the ship recycling company that describes the operational processes and procedures involved in ship recycling at the ship recycling facility and that covers in particular workers' safety and training, protection of human health and the environment, roles and responsibilities of personnel, emergency preparedness and response, and systems for monitoring, reporting and record-keeping, taking into account the relevant IMO guidelines and resolutions*" (see Article 3(1)(17) of the EU Ship Recycling Regulation).

However, the list approach differs considerably: The first version of 2016 of the "*European List of Ship Recycling Facilities*" included 18 approved facilities, situated exclusively in the EU. From 2017, only those ship recycling facilities on the EU list have exclusive "legal access" to EU-flagged vessels destined to be recycled. Thus, it is unlawful for a ship owner which flies an EU flag to disregard the recycling facilities listed by the European Commission and to send a vessel to an "un-listed" recycling yard, be it within or outside the EU. Remarkably, none of the 18 approved facilities within the EU have a track-record of being able to recycle only one "big" ocean-going vessel. Rather, these European yards specialize in the recycling of small boats, domestic shipping and inland waterway craft, which is all outside the scope of the EU Ship Recycling Regulation and the IMO's Hong Kong Convention. In sum, the current gap between law and reality cannot be overseen. Moreover, it is quite easy for ship owners to circumvent this legal requirement anyway, i.e., by changing to a non EU-flag for recycling purposes. Ship owners might not even arrange for the re-flagging themselves but they might simply sell the vessel while it is still operational. By all means, it is hard to prove the subjective intention of the seller to dispose of the vessel as hazardous waste while it could – technically – still continue to trade.

In 2017, the European Commission had received 22 applications from ship recycling yards located in third (non-EU) countries.[45] While nine out of those 22 applications were from India, conspicuously absent among these petitioners to the Commission were recycling facilities from Bangladesh and Pakistan. The European Commission started to review these applications since 2017. Its representatives will make technical visits to these non-EU recycling sites to decide on their future inclusion in the list. Until mid-2018, however, no decisions on a further expansion of the "European List" had been taken.

In this context, it is important to note that the IMO Hong Kong Convention defines the term "*ship recycling facility*" to mean "*a defined area that is a site, yard or facility used for the recycling of ships*" (Article 2(11) Hong Kong Convention). However, the respective EU definition omits the term "*site*" and defines a "*ship recycling facility*" to mean "*a defined area that is a yard or facility located in a member State or in a third country and used for the recycling of ships*" (Article 3(1)(7) Regulation EU/1257/2013). As a result, the practical effects of the omission of the term "*site*" works against the inclusion of certain ship recycling companies situated in Bangladesh, India or Pakistan (or other third countries) into the "European List".[46] By obviously demanding a concrete structure (or other form of "*defined area*" which is not a "*site*") the EU thus sets out stricter standards as compared to the international accord. From a standard-based approach, it is still an open question whether environmentally sound and sustainable ship recycling depends decisively on the factor whether a facility is a "*site*" or whether it should operate as a "*yard*" or "*facility*" from "*built structures*" (see Article 13(1)(f) of the EU Ship Recycling Regulation and Regulation 3 of the Annex to the Hong Kong Convention).[47]

In any case, a number of ship recycling yards – situated both within and outside the EU – seek inclusion into the "*European List*" as a quality seal for environmental sustainability. They also seek private and/or public certification according to the standards of the IMO Hong Kong Convention. Interesting cases of doubt may potentially arise if a non-EU recycling yard is actually certified according to the IMO standards but is denied to be included in the relevant "*European List*". The potential result could be that a recycling facility adheres to the global standards of the IMO but could be in violation of the more stringent regional standards of the EU at the same time.

Thus, one could argue that ambitious policy goals, like the EU's "*zero waste*" objective have both and negative effects. One positive effect is a legally-induced "race to the top". But this race also has the potential to create some dislocations between practice and reality. Nevertheless, the EU's "ship recycling gold standard" is generally legitimate under international law: The local introduction of stricter requirements is lawful because Article 1(2) of the IMO Hong Kong Convention establishes that "*no provision of this Convention shall be interpreted as preventing a Party from taking, individually or jointly, more stringent measures consistent with international law, [. . .]*". This consistency requirement might, however, be challenged in the future in another area – should the EU decide to re-visit the issue of a ship recycling-related financial incentive scheme in some years.

E. GENERAL CONCLUSIONS

Between 2009 and 2018, the on-going implementation of the EU Maritime Transport Strategy has been marked by a rapid evolution of the challenges and by evidence that interaction and cross-dependencies between the different areas of work become ever more relevant.[48] Nevertheless, the EU continues to regionally promote safe, secure and efficient intra-European and international shipping on clean oceans. This development has started long before 2009 and it is both driven by the jurisprudence of the Court of Justice of the EU (CJEU) and the dynamic regulatory reaction to some disastrous shipping accidents in EU waters, most prominently the "Erika" (1999) and the "Prestige" (2002). The result is that EU maritime law has emerged to become an integral part of the EU's internal market and its regulation. As a separate area of law, EU maritime law has hardened and deepened to cover various aspects of competition law and transport law in general as well as all relevant maritime-related safety and security issues. This development has occurred despite the important position of the IMO as the globally competent regulator for – in the words of the IMO itself – "safe, secure and efficient shipping on clean oceans".

All EU member States are active members and participants in all IMO matters. Their individual position as sovereign IMO members is carefully coordinated in Brussels – under active leadership of the European Commission – mostly resulting in a common policy position of the "EU block" at the IMO. Generally, EU maritime law now covers a wide array of both public law and even private law aspects of shipping as well. It is inextricably interlinked with the work of the IMO and, ultimately, both regulators cannot globally succeed without the other. Even the EU's regional rules for the regulation of international shipping affect the rest of the world, for example, by introducing stricter regional environmental standards to be adhered to both by EU-flagged vessels and non-EU flags when entering EU waters and, in particular, EU ports.

The rise of EU maritime law as a separate source of law is also the result of shipping being one of the key factors for economic growth and prosperity throughout Europe's history. About half of the EU's population lives less than 50 km from the sea. Waterborne freight transport has proved to be a vital instrument for the development of the EU's trade whether national, intra-EU or external. Today, the maritime industry is an important source of revenues and jobs in Europe. But there are also dangers and risks inherent to maritime transport. The EU's reliance on maritime transport means that it is as surrounded and penetrated by the risk of pollution from shipping, both chronic and catastrophic, as it is by the sea itself. The words of the European Commission are both true in a positive and in a negative way: "*Maritime transport has a direct impact on the quality of life of citizens.*" As a result, the EU has the strongest interests in promoting safe, secure and efficient intra-European and international shipping on clean oceans and seas, assuring the long-term competitiveness of European shipping and related maritime industries in world markets, and assisting the entire seaborne transport system to continuously adapt to new challenges of the 21st century.

LITERATURE

Anyanova, The EC and Enhancing Ship and Port Facility Security, pp. 101, in: Ehlers/Lagoni (eds.), Maritime Policy of the European Union and Law of the Sea (2008)

Begines, The EU Law on Classification Societies, Journal of Maritime Law & Commerce 2005
Christodoulou-Varotsi, Maritime Safety Law and Policies of the European Union and the United States of America, 2008
Chuah, The Third Maritime Safety Package – Objectives and Challenges, Journal of International Maritime Law 2009, p. 271
Ecorys et al., Financial instrument to facilitate safe and sound ship recycling, 2nd Interim Report (30 October 2015)
Ehlers/Lagoni (eds.), Maritime Policy of the European Union and Law of the Sea (2008)
G. Samiotis et al., SPOUDAI Journal of Economics and Business, Vol. 63 (2013), Issue 3–4, pp. 158–171
Jessen/Werner, EU Maritime Transport Law, Brussels Commentary, 2016
König, The EU Directive on Ship-Source Pollution and on the Introduction of Penalties for Infringements, pp. 767, in: Ndiaye/Wolfrum (eds.), Law of the Sea, Environmental Law and Settlement of Disputes (2007)
Mandaraka-Sheppard, Modern Maritime Law – Vol. 2: Managing Risks and Liabilities, 3rd Edition 2013
Molenaar, The EC Directive on Port State Control in Context, International Journal of Marine and Coastal Law 1996, pp. 241
Ringbom, The EU Maritime Safety Policy and International Law, 2008
Salvarani, The EC Directive on Port State Control: A Policy Statement, International Journal of Marine and Coastal Law 1996, pp. 225
Schoenbaum/Langston, An All Hands Evolution: Port security in the wake of September 11th, Tulane Law Review (6) 2003, pp. 1345–56
Tsimplis, Recycling of EU Ships: From Prohibition to Regulation?, Lloyd's Maritime and Commercial Law Quarterly 2014, pp. 415 (433)
Vatankhah, The Contribution of the EC to Maritime Safety in View of the "Third Maritime Safety Package" of the European Commission, pp. 41, in: Ehlers/Lagoni (eds.), Maritime Policy of the European Union and Law of the Sea (2008)

NOTES

1 COM(2009) 8 final, 21.01.2009.
2 COM(2006) 314, 22.06.2006.
3 COM(2007) 575, 10.10.2007.
4 See *Ehlers/Lagoni* (eds.), Preface (p. VI), in: Maritime Policy of the European Union and Law of the Sea (2008), for detailed commentaries on selected EU legislation see *Jessen/Werner*, EU Maritime Transport Law (Brussels Commentary, 2016).
5 See, e.g., *Chuah*, The Third Maritime Safety Package – Objectives and Challenges, Journal of International Maritime Law 2009, p. 271;*Mandaraka-*

Sheppard, Modern Maritime Law – Vol. 2: Managing Risks and Liabilities (3rd ed. 2013), pp. 29; *Ringbom*, The EU Maritime Safety Policy and International Law (2008), pp. 49; *Vatankhah*, The Contribution of the EC to Maritime Safety in View of the "Third Maritime Safety Package" of the European Commission, pp. 41, in: *Ehlers/Lagoni* (eds.), Maritime Policy of the European Union and Law of the Sea (2008); *Christodoulou-Varotsi*, Maritime Safety Law and Policies of the European Union and the United States of America (2008), pp. 34.

6 See Directive 2009/16/EC of 23.04.2009 on port State control (Recast), OJ L131/57 of 28.05.2009; see generally *Molenaar*, The EC Directive on Port State Control in Context, International Journal of Marine and Coastal Law 1996, pp. 241; *Salvarani*, The EC Directive on Port State Control: A Policy Statement, International Journal of Marine and Coastal Law 1996, pp. 225.

7 See Regulation (EC) 391/2009 of 23.04.2009 on common rules and standards for ship inspection and survey organisations (Recast), OJ L131/11 of 28.05.2009 and Directive 2009/15/EC of 23.04.2009 on common rules and standards for ship inspection and survey organisations and for the relevant activities of maritime administrations (Recast), OJ L131/47 of 28.05.2009. Besides clarifying existing provisions, the new texts have strengthened the inspection procedures of recognised organisations, introduced an independent body to certify the organisations' quality management and have empowered the Commission to be more effective in its supervisory role by fining organisations in breach of their obligations; see generally *Begines*, The EU Law on Classification Societies, Journal of Maritime Law & Commerce 2005, pp. 487.

8 See Regulation (EC) No 1726/2003 of the European Parliament and of the Council of 22.07.2003 amending Regulation (EC) No 417/2002 on the accelerated phasing-in of double-hull or equivalent design requirements for single-hull oil tankers, OJ 2003 L 249/1.

9 See Directive 2009/17/EC of the European Parliament and of the Council of 23.04.2009 amending Directive 2002/59/EC establishing a Community vessel traffic monitoring and information system, OJ 2009 L 131/101.

10 The EU is currently (2018) still working on a more coordinated and legally-binding intra-EU concept in relation to places of refuge for vessels in distress.

11 See generally: http://www.emsa.europa.eu/.

12 See Directive 2005/35/EC of 07.09.2005 on ship-source pollution and on the introduction of penalties for infringements, OJ L255/11 of 30.09.2005 and Directive 2009/123/EC of the European Parliament and of the Council of 21.10.2009 amending Directive 2005/35/EC on ship-source pollution and on the introduction of penalties for infringements, OJ L 280/52 of 27.10.2009; see also *König*, The EU Directive on Ship-Source Pollution and on the Introduction of Penalties for Infringements, pp. 767, in: *Ndiaye/Wolfrum* (eds.), Law of the Sea, Environmental Law and Settlement of Disputes (2007).

13 Regulation (EC) 725/2004 on enhancing ship and port facility security, OJ L129/6 of 29.04.2004; see generally *Anyanova*, The EC and Enhancing Ship and Port Fa-

cility Security, pp. 101, in: *Ehlers/Lagoni* (eds.), Maritime Policy of the European Union and Law of the Sea (2008).

14 As already envisioned by Directive 2002/6/EC, OJ L67/31 of 09.03.2002 and later advanced by Directive 2010/65/EU of the European Parliament and of the Council of 20.10.2010 on reporting formalities for ships arriving in and/or departing from ports of the Member States.

15 Quite evidently, after 2002, the US has been extremely active and progressive in the area of maritime security, e.g., via the "Container Security Initiative" (CSI) as part of the United States' Bureau of Customs and Border Protection's Cargo Security Strategy which was first announced in January 2002 (US Code, Title 6 Chapter 3IIA§945); see *Schoenbaum/Langston*, An All Hands Evolution: Port security in the wake of September 11th, Tulane Law Review (6) 2003, pp. 1345–56.

16 Directive 2005/65/EC of the European Parliament and of the Council of 26.10.2005 on enhancing port security – OJ L 310, 25.11.2005.

17 European Commission Staff Working Document on the implementation of the EU Maritime Transport Strategy 2009–2018: SWD(2016) 326 final, 30.09.2016, p. 7.

18 See Directive 2005/33/EC as regards the sulphur content of marine fuels, OJ L191/59 of 22.07.2005, as amended by Directive 2012/33/EC, OJ L327/1 of 21.11.2012. The relevant act after 2016 is now Directive (EU) 2016/802 of the European Parliament and of the Council of 11.05.2016 relating to a reduction in the sulphur content of certain liquid fuels, OJ L 132, 21.05.2016.

19 Regulation (EC) No 782/2003 of the European Parliament and of the Council of 14.04.2003 on the prohibition of organotin compounds on ships, OJ L 115, 09.05.2003.

20 See generally Regulation (EU) No 1257/2013 of the European Parliament and of the Council of 20.11.2013 on ship recycling (and amending Regulation (EC) No 1013/2006 and Directive 2009/16/EC)OJ L330/1 of 10.12.2013; see more specifically the EMSA Study of two hazardous substances (PFOS and HBCDD) included in the annexes of regulation (EU) 1257/2013 on ship recycling, available online at: http://emsa.europa.eu/emsa-documents/latest/item/3168-emsa-study-of-two-hazardous-substances-pfos-and-hbcdd-included-in-the-annexes-of-regulation-eu-1257--2013-on-ship-recycling.html.

21 See the European Commission Staff Working Document on the implementation of the EU Maritime Transport Strategy 2009–2018: SWD(2016) 326 final, 30.09.2016.

22 See Commission Directive 2014/100/EU and Directive 2009/17/EC of 23 April 2009 amending Directive 2002/59/EC establishing a Community vessel traffic monitoring and information system, OJ L131/101 of 28.05.2009. The main features of the system and its most recent amendments have been to ensure that *SafeSeaNet* is gradually upgraded to become the exclusive standard system for maritime data exchange throughout the EU; to establish a European LRIT centre at EMSA for collecting and distributing long range information on the identity

and position ships; to equip progressively all fishing vessels over 15 metres long with automatic identification systems (AIS); to establish detailed rules concerning the accommodation of ships in need of assistance in places of refuge, notably, by the designation of an independent authority for evaluating the situation of ships in difficulty and deciding whether and where the ship can be sheltered; and to ensure the adoption of information and prevention measures concerning ice formation creating a serious risk for shipping.

23 See the European Commission Staff Working Document on the implementation of the EU Maritime Transport Strategy 2009–2018: SWD(2016) 326 final, 30.09.2016, p. 5.

24 See generally Regulation (EU) 2016/1624 of the European Parliament and of the Council of 14.09.2016 on the European Border and Coast Guard and amending Regulation (EU) 2016/399 of the European Parliament and of the Council and repealing Regulation (EC) No 863/2007 of the European Parliament and of the Council, Council Regulation (EC) No 2007/2004 and Council Decision 2005/267/EC.

25 COM(2009) 8 final, 21.01.2009, p. 7.

26 European Commission Staff Working Document on the implementation of the EU Maritime Transport Strategy 2009–2018: SWD(2016) 326 final, 30.09.2016, p. 13.

27 Proposal for a Directive amending Directive 1999/32/EC as regards the sulphur content of marine fuels, COM(2011)439 final of 15 July 2011.

28 See Commission Communication 'Greening of Transport', COM(2008)433 final of 8 July 2007.

29 Regulation (EU) 2015/757 on the monitoring, reporting and verification of carbon dioxide emissions from maritime transport, OJ L123/55 of 19.05.2015.

30 Commission Directive (EU) 2015/2087 of 18 November 2015 amending Annex II to Directive 2000/59/EC of the European Parliament and the Council on port reception facilities for ship-generated waste and cargo residues, OJ L 302, 19.11.2015, p. 99–102.

31 Directive 2000/59/EC of the European Parliament and of the Council of 27 November 2000 on port reception facilities for ship-generated waste and cargo residues, OJ L 332, 28.12.2000, p. 81–90.

32 European Commission Staff Working Document on the implementation of the EU Maritime Transport Strategy 2009–2018: SWD(2016) 326 final, 30.09.2016, p. 14.

33 "*Basel Convention on the Control of Transboundary Movements of Hazardous Wastes and Their Disposal 1989*", 22 March 1989, U.N.T.S. 126, 28 I.L.M. 657 (entered into force 5 May 1992), for further information see www.basel.int and the Basel Action Network ("Ban") Amendment 1995 (the "*Ban Protocol*").

34 See in particular Regulation (EC) No 1013/2006 of the European Parliament and of the Council of 14 June 2006 on shipments of waste, OJ L190/1 of 12 July 2006.

[35] See in general *G. Samiotis et al.*, SPOUDAI Journal of Economics and Business, Vol. 63 (2013), Issue 3–4, pp. 158–171; for a long time, beaching practices in ship recycling have been monitored and criticised, in particular, by environmental NGOs like Greenpeace (in cooperation with the International Federation of Human Rights Leagues) or the "*NGO Shipbreaking platform*", see e.g.: http://www.greenpeace.org/international/en/publications/reports/end-of-life-the-human-cost-of/; in addition, the IMO continuously updates its openly accessible list of bibliography on various regulatory topics of international shipping, for the area of ship recycling see: http://www.imo.org/en/KnowledgeCentre/InformationResourcesOnCurrentTopics/RecyclingOfShips/Pages/default.aspx (last update May 2013).

[36] See e.g. a Lloyd's List report of 07 February 2017 ("*Government ban stifles Pakistan's recycling market*") which referred to the fact that "*the absence of recycling activity at local yards has created a shortage of supply of steel plates to domestic steel mills, which in turn is pushing demand and local steel prices higher.*".

[37] COM(2012)118 final, 23 March 2012; see generally *Mandaraka-Sheppard*, Modern Maritime Law – Vol. 2: Managing Risks and Liabilities (3rd ed. 2013), p. 52

[38] See, e.g., the front page of Lloyd's List of 13 May 2013 "*EU beaching ban could cost owners millions*"; generally and with more details on the EU's political objectives in this policy area:*Engels*, European Ship Recycling Regulation (2013), pp. 62.

[39] Regulation (EU) No 1257/2013 of 20 November 2013 on ship recycling and amending Regulation (EC) No 1013/2006 and Directive 2009/16/EC, OJ L330/1 of 10 December 2013.

[40] The EU Ship Recycling Regulation has widened the existing list of prohibited hazardous substances and, in particular, the EU has also introduced stricter requirements for ship recycling facilities, demanding from them to operate "*from built structures*", see Article 13(1)(f) EU Ship Recycling Regulation. In practice, this requirement effectively outlaws beaching practices in ship recycling without explicitly prohibiting the practice itself.

[41] See Ecorys et al., Financial instrument to facilitate safe and sound ship recycling, 2nd Interim Report (30 October 2015), hereinafter Ecorys Interim Report.

[42] Ecorys Interim Report, pp. 35.

[43] Report from The Commission to the European Parliament and to the Council on the feasibility of a financial instrument that would facilitate safe and sound ship recycling, Brussels, COM(2017) 420 final, 08.08.2017.

[44] See http://ec.europa.eu/environment/waste/ships/list.htm.

[45] According to public reports, 22 non-EU facilities have applied (nine from India, seven from Turkey, four from China, two from the US) "*none of which are expected to make the list before the end of 2017*", see Lloyd's List (online edition of 27 Oct 2017).

[46] See generally *Tsimplis*, Recycling of EU Ships: From Prohibition to Regulation?, Lloyd's Maritime and Commercial Law Quarterly 2014, pp. 415 (433).

[47] The provision states that: "*Parties shall take measures to implement the requirements of the regulations of this Annex, taking into account relevant and applicable standards, recommendations and guidance developed by the International Labour Organization and the relevant and applicable technical standards, recommendations and guidance developed under the Basel Convention on the Control of Transboundary Movements of Hazardous Wastes and their Disposal.*".

[48] European Commission Staff Working Document on the implementation of the EU Maritime Transport Strategy 2009–2018: SWD(2016) 326 final, 30.09.2016, p. 21.

CHAPTER IV

50 YEARS MARINE ENVIRONMENT PROTECTION – ACHIEVEMENTS AND UNSOLVED ISSUES

Peter EHLERS

A. THE DEVELOPMENT OF MARINE ENVIRONMENTAL LAW

Half a century has passed since the accident of the *Torrey Canyon* has given a major impetus for the protection of the marine environment, at least as far as shipping is concerned. However, this was by no means the beginning of efforts to prevent pollution from ships. Already in 1954 OILPOL[1] was adopted, which prohibited the discharge of oil near the coast and introduced the designation of special areas. The Geneva Convention on the High Seas[2] contained a corresponding obligation of states to prevent pollution by the discharge of oil from ships. [3] In 1959, the Intergovernmental Maritime Consultative Organization, today named the International Maritime Organization,[4] began its work, which since then has included the protection of the sea from pollution from ships.[5]

I. THE TORREY CANYON IMPETUS

On 18 March 1967 the Liberian tanker *Torrey Canyon* struck a rock between Land's End and the Isles of Scilly. Large quantities of oil were spilled, causing massive pollution in the south west of England and in the Channel Islands as well as in Brittany in France.[6] This was a wake-up call for the international community to strengthen efforts to prevent marine pollution from ships.

1. INTERVENTION POWER

The accident made it clear that both important public-law and private-law issues had to be solved. States had to be empowered to take measures even beyond their territorial waters in case of an accident; there was also the need to regulate more clearly the compensation for pollution damage. This led to the adoption of the Intervention Convention in 1969.[7] It authorizes the coastal states to take all necessary measures on the high seas, in order to prevent dangers to the coasts when a ship accident occurs, which may cause a serious threat to the coast, to fishing, to the health of the coastal population, to the animal and plant life, or to the preservation of the living marine resources. In this context the term "high seas" covers all marine areas seaward of territorial waters.[8] Restricting the principle of freedom of navigation the convention applies to seagoing vessels of all kinds flying the flag of a contracting state. In 1973, the convention was supplemented by a protocol, which includes measures in cases of marine pollution by substances other than oil.[9]

2. POLLUTION RESPONSE

The *Torrey Canyon* accident in 1969 also led to the conclusion of an Agreement for Cooperation in Dealing with the Pollution of the North Sea by Oil[10] by the North Sea states. It became the firm basis for joint response measures to pollution incidents and was replaced in 1983 by a new agreement, covering also other harmful substances, which since then has been amended several times.[11]

3. LIABILITY AND COMPENSATION

In the same year the 1969 CLC[12] was adopted. The convention applies to pollution damage resulting from oil spills from tankers caused in the territory, including the territorial sea of the states parties. It lays down the principle of strict liability of the ship owner, and creates a system of compulsory liability insurance with the right for claimants to take direct action against the insurer. Under certain conditions the ship owner is entitled to limit his liability to an amount linked to the tonnage of the vessel.[13] The 1969 CLC is supplemented by the Fund Convention[14], which was adopted in 1971. Its purpose is the establishment of an International Oil Pollution Compensation Fund for providing additional compensation to victims of tanker oil spills when the compensation available under the 1969 CLC is inadequate to provide full compensation.[15] In 1992 the 1969 CLC and the Fund Convention were amended by two protocols, in particular extending the area of application also to the EEZ[16] and increasing the maximum compensation to be paid by the Fund.[17] An additional protocol was adopted in 2003, which introduces an International Supplementary Fund to ensure full compensation in cases where the amount under the Fund Convention is insufficient.[18]

4. MARPOL

A little later, MARPOL[19] was adopted in 1973 to replace OILPOL, but entered into force only in 1983 after a modification by the 1978 Protocol.[20] The aim is to achieve the complete elimination of intentional pollution of the marine environment by oil and other harmful substances and the minimization of accidental discharge of such substances.[21] The regulations mainly focus on pollution caused by the discharge of operational and cargo-related residues. As concerns accidents with an impact on the marine environment, MARPOL establishes structural and operational requirements for ships in order to prevent or limit the release of pollutants in the event of an accident. MARPOL is divided into the convention itself, including the protocol adopted for this purpose in 1978, two protocols on reporting obligations and arbitration proceedings, and originally five annexes, which specify requirements for the different pollutants, i.e. oil, noxious liquid substances, harmful substances carried in packaged form, sewage and garbage.[22] In 1997 an additional Annex VI on air pollution was added, which since then has been amended several times and also includes measures for the reduction of greenhouse gas emissions from ships.[23]

5. SOLAS

The prevention of ship accidents, though they might have an impact on the marine environment is not regulated by MARPOL, but is the subject of SOLAS.[24] This convention, the first version of which was already adopted in 1914, has been revised several times.[25] It aims at ensuring maritime safety and accident prevention and in this context has also become increasingly important for preventive marine environmental protection.[26] SOLAS consists of the convention itself and an Annex, nowadays comprising 14 Chapters, which contain specific technical and operational safety standards and requirements for different types of ships.

II. General protection approaches

In the years following the *Torrey Canyon* accident marine environmental protection did not gain importance in the shipping sector only. It became more and more clear that the seas were not primarily threatened by maritime shipping, but that other pollution sources, such as land-based inputs and offshore activities were of much greater significance. The voices, warning of a degradation of the marine quality status, increased and demanded reductions of the manifold polluting inputs. The Stockholm Environmental Conference in 1972 took this into account by stating the common conviction that States shall take all possible steps to prevent pollution of the seas by substances that are liable to create hazards to human health, to harm living resources and marine life, to damage amenities or to interfere with other legitimate uses of the sea.[27] This led to several marine environment protection conventions on regional level. The Oslo Convention[28] and the Paris Convention[29] for the North Atlantic area, the Helsinki Convention[30] for the Baltic Sea area and the Barcelona Convention[31] for the Mediterranean Sea were adopted between 1972 and 1976. Whereas the Oslo and Paris Conventions were restricted to dumping and land-based inputs respectively, the Helsinki and Barcelona Conventions covered various sources of marine pollution. In addition to the regional Oslo Convention dumping of harmful substances at sea was regulated by the global London Convention,[32] which was also adopted in 1972.

III. UNCLOS

A fundamental review of the law of the sea started in 1973 by the work of the third United Nations Conference on the Law of the Sea, and finally resulted in the adoption of UNCLOS[33] in 1982. This convention, which is quite rightly called the constitution of the seas, does not only define the rights of states with regard to the use of the seas, but also creates corresponding duties. In particular it establishes the obligation of states to protect and preserve the marine environment.[34] States have to cooperate in formulating and elaborating international rules and standards[35] as well as in promoting scientific research and the exchange of relevant information.[36] Furthermore they shall monitor the effects of pollution and assess the potential effects of planned activities, which may cause significant and harmful changes to the marine environment.[37] States are asked to establish global and regional rules to prevent pollution from land-based sources, by dumping, or through the atmosphere.[38] However, this duty is weakened as states are only obliged to "endeavour" to come to agreement on these issues,[39] whereas with regard to seabed activities and maritime shipping UNCLOS creates a binding obligation for establishing international regulations.[40] States shall adopt and enforce corresponding national law.[41] The jurisdiction area of coastal states also covers the EEZ.[42] In view of the international nature of shipping, UNCLOS does not only determine the powers of the responsible flag state, but also of coastal and port states, as concerns the prevention and control of pollution from ships.[43] Quite remarkable is the provision that generally accepted international rules and standards are to be applied by all ships,[44] irrespective of the flag they are flying, even if it is still unclear under which conditions general acceptance can be assumed.[45] Though UNCLOS is mainly focussing on marine pollution, States also have the duty to take measures necessary for the conservation of living resources.[46] With respect to activities in the Area concerning the recovery of mineral resources the ISA[47] shall adopt appropriate protection rules[48] and exercise the necessary control with the assistance of affected states.[49]

IV. INCREASING INTERNATIONAL ENDEAVOURS

While the entry in force of UNCLOS took another 12 years, the early 1980s were the time when the marine environment protection conventions entered into force.

1. REGIONAL COOPERATION

In implementing the regional conventions, the Oslo and Paris Commissions and the Helsinki Commission were established leading to a close cooperation of the states bordering the respective sea area. Primarily the Commissions had to elaborate concrete measures to implement the more general obligations of the conventions, and started joint programmes for monitoring the seas and assessing their environmental status, and for combatting pollution incidents. The cooperation in the North Sea area was strongly advanced by ministerial conferences, the first of which took place in Bremen, Germany, in 1984.[50] Comparable approaches were undertaken in the Baltic Sea area by ministerial meetings of the Helsinki Commission.[51] These gatherings of ministers resulted in ministerial declarations highlighting still existing environmental problems and deciding on a variety of protection measures. Though the declarations have been criticized as non-binding political commitments only, they laid a fruitful basis for further joint activities and tighter regulations. Similar agreements and programmes since then have been adopted for other sea areas differing, however, in objectives, regulatory scope and institutional organisation.[52]

2. IMPLEMENTATION AND ENFORCEMENT OF IMO CONVENTIONS

As concerns maritime shipping the entry into force of SOLAS (1980) and MARPOL (1983) were quite important milestones for improving maritime safety and the reduction of pollution from ships. Since then, both the Annexes to MARPOL and SOLAS have been continuously amended to take account of experience gained, new insights and technical developments, and increased protection requirements. Owing to the tacit acceptance procedure, which is provided by the conventions,[53] amendments of the technical regulations in the annexes can be realized within rather short time. For further substantiating and concretizing the regulations, they have been complemented by various codes, guidelines, and other IMO recommendations.[54]

Both conventions are also to be applied to vessels flying the flag of a non-contracting state in order to ensure that no more favourable treatment is granted to them.[55] As some states do not sufficiently survey ships under their flag, inspections of foreign ships in ports play an important role.[56] To intensify and harmonize these inspections a number of European States agreed in 1982 on the Paris Memorandum of Understanding on Port State Control,[57] which was followed by several other Memoranda of Understanding for different regions and aims at the elimination of "substandard" ships.[58]

3. REVIEW AND EXTENSION OF MARINE ENVIRONMENTAL LEGISLATION

While the protection efforts initially concentrated on pollution sources, since the end of the 1980s it has become increasingly clear that the protection of habitats and species also has to be taken into account. First approaches, which had been made by the Ramsar Convention,[59] the Convention on the Conservation of Migratory Species of Wild Animals,[60] and the European Birds Directive,[61] were taken up e.g. by the Third North Sea Protection Conference in 1990.[62] At the same time, environmental policy principles were highlighted, including the precautionary principle, the use of best available technology and best environmental practise, and the polluter-pays principle. This led to a revision of the Helsinki Convention[63] and a new OSPAR Convention,[64] which replaced the Oslo and Paris Conventions. In their basic message, the conventions are broadly consistent, although they differ considerably in detail. Both these conventions define fundamental environmental principles[65] and constitute obligations to prevent and eliminate pollution from land-based sources, and from exploration and exploitation of the seabed and its subsoil; subject to some minor exemptions dumping and incineration of wastes at sea is prohibited. Subsequently the London Dumping Convention was amended correspondingly in 1996.[66] The Helsinki Convention additionally includes measures to prevent pollution from ships and introduces principles of cooperation to respond to pollution incidents, whereas for the North Sea area the Bonn Agreement covers combatting issues.[67] Furthermore, for the first time measures to conserve natural habitats and biodiversity, to protect ecological processes and to ensure the sustainable use of natural resources are integrated into marine environment conventions. The cooperation between the bordering states is institutionalized by the Helsinki and the OSPAR Commissions, each supported by a secretariat.[68] The Commissions and subordinated expert bodies develop measures to concretize the obligations of the conventions, observe their implementation and recommend amendments. Whereas the Helsinki Commission can only make recommendations, which are legally not binding, the OSPAR Commission, however, is empowered to adopt either recommendations or binding decisions.[69]

4. Rio 1992

A very important milestone for marine environment protection was the Earth Summit held in Rio de Janeiro, Brazil, in 1992, which resulted in the Rio Declaration on Environment and Development.[70] The declaration clarifies that the environmental and the economic and social development cannot be regarded as isolated fields, but must be components of a comprehensive sustainable development. It is complemented by a detailed action plan Agenda 21, which under Chapter 17 includes measures for the protection of the oceans and seas.[71] Though the Rio Conference only produced soft law, the political commitments to implement Agenda 21 got specific weight, as they were affirmed at following conferences.[72] At the occasion of the Rio Conference also the CBD[73] was concluded. The objectives are the conservation of biological diversity and the sustainable use of its components.[74] The CBD applies in the territory of contracting states, including the marine areas of their national jurisdiction, whereas the high seas and the Area are only covered to quite a limited extent.[75] Influenced by the Rio Conference and the CBD, protection measures since then have been increasingly guided by the ecosystem approach, which is defined as a strategy for the integrated management of land, water and living resources that promotes conservation and sustainable use in an equitable way.[76]

5. GPA

Also as a follow-up of the Rio Conference 108 Governments declared their commitment to protect and preserve the marine environment from the impacts of land-based activities[77] in 1995 by adopting the Washington Declaration[78] and agreed on a GPA.[79] The GPA was preceded by the Montreal Guidelines for the Protection of the Marine Environment against Pollution from Land-Based Sources,[80] which were already adopted in 1985 and include detailed measures to prevent, reduce and control pollution from land-based sources.[81] The GPA has become an important basis for international cooperation in this field, which is coordinated by UNEP. The implementation of the GPA is accompanied by international review meetings to provide additional impetus. This led to the 2001 Montreal Declaration on the Protection of the Marine Environment from Land-based Activities (2001),[82] the Beijing Declaration on Furthering the Implementation of the GPA (2006)[83] and the Manila Declaration (2012).[84] However, all global attempts to regulate land-based marine pollution until now have only led to non-binding instruments.[85]

6. Additional regulations for maritime shipping

Though maritime shipping is by no means the largest "environmental villain", the most comprehensive regulatory work has been provided by IMO. The organization has not only been responsible for supplementing and amending the existing regulations, but has also initiated numerous additional conventions. This includes the HNS Convention,[86] adopted in 1996, which aims at the compensation of damage caused by accidents at sea, involving hazardous and noxious substances. It is superseded by a Protocol to the Convention,[87] which was adopted in 2010 to overcome some practical problems that had prevented many States from ratifying the Convention, but is not yet in force. In addition, in 2001 the Bunker Convention[88] was concluded to ensure compensation for damage caused by spills of oil, when carried as fuel in ships' bunker. Also in 2001 the AFS Convention[89] was adopted. It prohibits the use of harmful organotins in anti-fouling paints used on ships and establishes a mechanism to prevent the potential future use of other harmful substances in anti-fouling systems. Just recently the Ballast Water Management Convention, which was already concluded in 2004, entered in force.[90] As invasive aquatic species present a major threat to the marine ecosystems, and shipping has been identified as a major pathway for introducing species to new environments, the convention aims to prevent the spread of harmful organisms from one region to another, by establishing standards and procedures for the management and control of ships' ballast water and sediments. For providing international rules to ensure the prompt and effective removal of wrecks located beyond the territorial sea, which may affect maritime safety as well as the marine environment, in 2007 the Wreck Removal Convention[91] was adopted.

V. EUROPEAN ENDEAVOURS

In addition to global and regional regulations for specific sea areas, measures to protect the marine environment have also been taken on the European level.[92]

1. GENERAL MARINE ENVIRONMENTAL LEGISLATION

Already in 1979 the Bern Convention[93] was concluded, which aims at the protection of habitats and endangered species and covers Europe and some African countries. In connection with and in response to this convention, the EU[94] adopted the Birds Directive[95] in 1979 and the Habitats Directive[96] in 1992. These directives set up a network of Special Protection Areas and Special Areas of Conservation.[97] Although the directives are not directly aimed at the marine area, they also cover the European waters, i. e. the waters of jurisdiction of the EU member states.[98] Achieving good qualitative and quantitative status of all water bodies including coastal waters up to one nautical mile from shore is the objective of the Water Framework Directive[99], adopted in 2000, which is of special importance for land-based pollution. It is followed by the Marine Strategy Framework Directive,[100] adopted in 2008. This directive is based on the ecosystem approach and the principle of sustainable development, and aims at reaching good state of the marine environment by 2020. That requires that ecologically divers and dynamic oceans and seas are clean, healthy and productive within their intrinsic conditions, and the use of the marine environment is at a level that is sustainable, thus safeguarding the potential for uses and activities by current and future generations.[101] Several directives deal with pollution prevention with regard to specific industrial, urban and agriculture activities, including among others air emissions, waste incinerators, waste waters and nitrate inputs.[102]

2. OIL AND GAS

The *Deep Sea Horizon* accident in 2010 has made it clear that global regulations for offshore oil and gas operations are still lacking. At least at the European level, the Offshore Directive shall tackle this.[103] The objective is to reduce as far as possible the occurrence of major accidents relating to offshore oil and gas operations and to limit their consequences, thus increasing the protection of the marine environment and coastal economies against pollution.

3. MARITIME SHIPPING

Based on the principles of the Paris Memorandum of Understanding, already in 1995 the then EC introduced legally binding port state control procedures by a directive,[104], which was replaced by the Port State Control Directive 2009.[105] Since the late 1990s the EU has, in particular in response to the *Erika* and *Prestige* ship accidents, adopted a number of regulations and directives on the prevention of pollution from ships.[106] They partly serve the effective and harmonized implementation of international requirements, but in part they also go beyond them, and include the following legal acts: The Directive on port reception facilities[107] aims at the avoidance of illegal discharges of ship-generated waste and cargo residues and obliges ports to ensure the availability of adequate reception facilities in ports, and ships to deliver all waste before leaving the port.[108] The Sanctions Directive[109] serves for incorporating international standards for ship-source pollution into Community law and for ensuring that persons responsible for discharges are subject to adequate penalties.[110] The purpose of the Sulphur Directive[111] is to reduce the emissions of sulphur dioxide resulting from the combustion of certain types of liquid fuels and thereby to reduce the harmful effects of such emissions on man and the environment.[112] In anticipation of appropriate IMO measures the MRV Regulation[113] lays down rules for the accurate monitoring, reporting and verification of CO_2 emissions from ships arriving at, within or departing from ports under the jurisdiction of a EU member state, in order to promote the reduction of CO_2 emissions from maritime transport in a cost effective manner.[114]

European legal acts supplementing international maritime safety regulations concern the safety of passenger ships, technical safety requirements, traffic control and reporting obligations, the qualification of seafarers and the fulfilment of flag state obligations.[115] The prevention of marine pollution caused by ship accidents is in particular the subject of the Vessel Traffic

Information Directive,[116] which aims at the establishment of a vessel traffic monitoring and information system with a view to enhancing the safety and efficiency of maritime traffic, improving the response of authorities to accidents and dangerous situations at sea, and contributing to a better prevention and detection of pollution by ships.[117]

B. UNSOLVED ISSUES

All in all, over the past 50 years, a comprehensive set of rules for protecting the marine environment has emerged at a global, regional and European level[118] albeit with a quite unbalanced regulatory density. While initially marine environmental protection was concentrated almost single-sidedly on the protection against pollution, the much more broader ecosystem approach, including the preservation of biodiversity, has increasingly gained in importance. This requires a balance between the use and the protection of the oceans, as is reflected in the UN Agenda 2030 on Sustainable Development,[119] which was adopted in 2015 and calls for conserving and sustainably using the oceans, seas and marine resources.[120] However, it would be wrong to assume that the problems of marine environmental protection are solved now.[121] As the findings of the First World Ocean Assessment, which was initiated by the UN and completed in 2014, indicate, the oceans' carrying capacity is near or at its limit and urgent action on a global scale is needed to protect the world's oceans from the many pressures they face.[122] Climate change, which causes ocean warming and acidification, leads to additional threats for marine ecosystems.[123] The serious situation became apparent from the results of the Ocean Conference, which took place in June 2017 as the first UN conference of its kind on this issue. The 193 participating states and organizations expressed the need and their commitment to halt and reverse the decline in the health and productivity of the ocean and its ecosystems and to protect and restore its resilience and ecological integrity. They agreed on a Declaration "Our ocean, our future: call for action",[124] and on more than 1400 voluntary commitments to reverse the challenges the ocean is facing.[125] As the outcome of the conference shows, it is obvious that there is a compelling need for additional marine protection measures. That is also true for the regulatory frame. Though marine environment law has become quite extensive and is continuously further developed and concretised, in particular as concerns shipping, there still exist many gaps, deficits, weaknesses and ambiguities,[126] which require closer examination.

I. ENVIRONMENTAL PRINCIPLES

Though UNCLOS provides an extremely important basis for marine environmental law, the convention reflects the state of discussion of the early 1980s, so that more recent findings, insights and developments have not been taken into account. Still existing regulatory gaps and weaknesses must be remedied.[127]

1. PRECAUTIONARY PRINCIPLE

An unambiguous obligation to apply modern environmental policy principles is still missing. This includes, first and foremost, the precautionary principle. It is true that some provisions can be found in UNCLOS, which at least indirectly reflect the precautionary principle, for example, in the definition of the term "pollution".[128] There are indications that this principle is becoming gradually consolidated into international customary law.[129] Nonetheless it remains unclear what exactly is to be understood by this term.[130] On a global scale, it has been adopted for the first time in the Rio Declaration, which stipulates that lack of full scientific certainty shall not be used as a reason for postponing cost-effective measures to prevent environmental degradation, where there are threats of serious or irreversible damage.[131] However, the declaration refers to the "precautionary approach", so it remains open, whether it can be fully equated with the term "precautionary principle", used above all in European legislation, and regional marine environment conventions.[132] Whereas the Rio Declaration is not legally binding, the precautionary approach has explicitly been enshrined in the ISA regulations for the prospecting and exploration of minerals[133] as well as in the FSA.[134] An unambiguous and binding anchoring of the precautionary principle into international marine environmental legislation in general would be desirable.

2. POLLUTER-PAYS PRINCIPLE, BEST AVAILABLE TECHNOLOGY

The world-wide introduction of the polluter-pays principle, which again can be found in European law and in regional marine environmental conventions[135] is no less desirable as an essential tool to make the users and perpetrators responsible for the environmental impacts of their activities. The same goes for the global mandatory application of the use of best environmental practice and the best available technology, as they are already provided for in regional marine environment conventions.[136]

3. MONITORING

Art. 204 UNCLOS calls upon states that they shall endeavour to monitor the risks or effects of marine pollution. However, it is necessary to make this duty much more concrete and to fill it with life. Especially the first World Ocean Assessment has made it evident that much better knowledge about the oceans is needed as an indispensable basis for responsible decision-making.[137] Comprehensive monitoring programs, such as, for example, initiated by the Helsinki and the OSPAR Commission, are required worldwide. They should not be restricted to specific environmental issues, but must be extended to a comprehensive and sustainable ocean observation system, covering all relevant variables, as it has been introduced at least partially by the Intergovernmental Commission of UNESCO and WMO[138] under the name GOOS.[139] So far, however, the willingness of many states for a reliable long-term commitment for participation in such a system is still lacking.

4. ENVIRONMENT IMPACT ASSESSMENT

Article 206 UNCLOS in principle, sets out the duty to conduct environmental impact assessments.[140] However, there is a need for greater clarity and more detailed regulations concerning the planned activities as well as the content and the procedural requirements of an assessment,[141] in particular by taking into account the ESPOO Convention[142]. The EU Directive on the assessment of environmental effects[143] could serve as a model.

5. MANAGEMENT TOOLS

Effective and appropriate area-based management tools, including marine protected areas and other integrated, cross-sectoral approaches, in particular marine spatial planning and integrated coastal zone management,[144] are needed to find a sound balance between the different uses of the seas and marine environment protection.[145] Currently the designation of marine protected areas quickly comes up against legal limits within the EEZ, in particular with regard to shipping, and is inadmissible on the high seas.[146] Appropriate possibilities for designating marine protected areas could be introduced in the context of new regulations on marine biodiversity issues.[147] More and more, states are applying marine spatial planning not only for their territorial waters, but also within the EEZ. Even if scholars agree that marine spatial planning in this zone is in line with UNCLOS as far as it is directly connected to the sovereign rights and jurisdiction of the coastal states,[148] it could be helpful, if this instrument were firmly enshrined in international law. A first step has already been taken on the European level.[149]

II. SPECIFIC PROTECTION STANDARDS

Significant deficits exist with respect to specific sources of pollution. UNCLOS itself is a framework convention and does not lay down any substantive standards, but only calls on states to establish the necessary international rules.[150] Whereas for maritime shipping a worldwide, very comprehensive regime is in force, which is continuously further developed by IMO and which also includes the prohibition of dumping and incineration at sea, there is still a need for global regulations concerning pollution from other sources.

1. LAND-BASED POLLUTION

In particular land-based inputs, which are by far the major marine pollution source,[151] are only regulated fragmentarily by regional conventions.[152] As these regulations are more or less restricted to general principles, the marine environment commissions must fill them by concrete decisions, which, however, in most cases are not legally binding. Global regulatory approaches, on the other hand, have not gone beyond the non-binding GPA, as much as it is to be welcomed that this program is taken care of and further developed by UNEP.[153] One of the recent issues, having gained utmost attention, is marine litter,[154] which is becoming more and more a global problem, mostly caused by land-based inputs. However, it must not be overlooked that marine litter has not least become a general focus because it is particularly visible and therefore suitable for TV prime time news. At the same time other harmful substances, such as pesticides, residues from medicines and innumerable organic compounds lead to invisible, creeping pollution, when discharged into rivers or directly into the sea.[155] In this context one should not even forget the impacts of the inputs from the ever-expanding coastal tourism infrastructure or the growing use of seawater desalination plants, which also cause additional marine threats.[156]

2. SEABED ACTIVITIES

Whereas UNCLOS only calls on states, to "endeavour" to establish global and regional rules and standards to prevent and reduce pollution from land-based sources, a clear obligation has been introduced to conclude international regulations for seabed activities.[157] But despite this obligation, no global rules exist for the protection of the marine environment with respect to seabed activities within waters of coastal states' jurisdiction including the EEZ and the continental shelf.[158] So far, this matter has been left to coastal states, which have, at most, accepted common standards for oil and gas operations in regional agreements,[159] but not for minerals. The European Offshore Directive,[160] too, is restricted to oil and gas operations only. It looks a bit different for deep seabed mining beyond waters of national jurisdiction in the Area, where environmental requirements are set by the ISA.[161] After having already established regulations on prospecting and exploration,[162] the ISA is currently working on regulations governing exploitation of minerals, which in Part IV include environmental matters.[163] It is to be hoped that these regulations will not only become applicable in the Area, but will also be taken into account as minimum standards by coastal states, when approving mining activities within their EEZ and on their continental shelf.[164] In addition, international environmental standards for seabed-related activities should not only include the exploitation of all mineral resources, but also the environmental impacts of submarine cables and pipelines, which, though dealt with by UNCLOS,[165] also lack more concrete regulations.

3. OTHER OFFSHORE ACTIVITIES

Neither UNCLOS nor the regional marine environment conventions contain provisions on other offshore activities, in particular, the operation of offshore wind power plants.[166] More and more, wind energy replaces fossil energy and thus contributes to CO_2 reduction. In the longer run, energy, generated from the sea will also be gain in importance. Tidal, current and wave power plants are tested as well as thermal and osmosis systems.[167] Until now, it is up to the coastal states to take the necessary protective measures in exercising their responsibilities for the marine environment.[168] It also has to be noted that there are other economic activities at sea, which may affect the marine environment and are not explicitly covered by international regulations. That includes aquaculture, the world's fastest growing sector in the food producing industry. Though in many cases still pond culture, aquaculture is more and more spread to marine areas.[169] In the future many other new projects are imaginable, ranging from installations, structures and artificial islands for hotel and housing complexes and airports to factories at sea, which use the energy generated at sea on site. All this speaks in favour of elaborating international environmental standards for offshore activities in general, not only restricted to oil and gas operations.

4. Marine biotechnology

Already today, biotechnological projects are carried out on the use of marine genetic resources,[170] which have impact on the marine environment, but are not adequately covered by international regulations.[171] Marine organisms attract more and more attention in order to develop new products, in particular for pharmaceuticals and cosmetics, but also for food, feed and the chemical industry. Research has focused on marine microorganisms as a nearly inexhaustible source of novel biological agents, also including the production of bio-energy. The deep sea, in particular hydrothermal vents, the so-called black smokers, and Polar Regions have become areas of special interest.

5. Marine biodiversity

The activities at sea make it increasingly clear that the marine environment is not only threatened by pollution, but that it is equally important to protect habitats and species. UNCLOS is largely limited to protecting the oceans from pollution.[172] Only Art. 194 para. 5 UNCLOS offers a first approach towards a comprehensive ecosystem protection.[173] As the CBD is not in all aspects applicable on the high seas, it is quite important that the UN General Assembly decided to develop an international legally binding instrument under UNCLOS on the conservation and sustainable use of marine biological diversity of areas beyond national jurisdiction and to convene an intergovernmental conference, the first session of which shall take place in the second half of 2018.[174] The recent work progress of a Preparatory Committee, established by the UN, is prompting the expectation that important environmental policy principles and management tools such as the designation of marine protection areas will be anchored in the proposed agreement and that also the prerequisites for the use of genetic resources will be defined.[175] Such an instrument offers the opportunity to close gaps and eliminate weaknesses left in UNCLOS as concerns marine environmental protection,[176] without the need for a presumably barely feasible amendment of UNCLOS itself. It will therefore be of paramount importance not only for biodiversity issues, but for marine environmental protection as a whole.

6. Fisheries

Not least in the context of biodiversity, it becomes evident that the marine environmental conventions are lacking regulations on fisheries.[177] It is true that Art. 61 and 117 UNCLOS establish the duty of states to ensure the conservation of living resources. These regulations, however, primarily aim at the maintenance of fish population for producing the maximum sustainable yield.[178] But they do not really focus on environmental impacts from fishing on the ecosystem, e.g. from the use of harmful fishing techniques. It would be beneficial, if a closer link could be established between environmental protection and fisheries management.[179] In this regard the FSA offers a valuable approach.[180] Although the long-term sustainability of the fish stocks and their optimum utilization,[181] seem to be the focus, the agreement explicitly emphasizes the application of the precautionary approach in order to protect the living marine resources and to preserve the marine environment, as well as the minimisation of pollution and the protection of biodiversity.[182] However, this agreement only applies to straddling and highly migratory fish stocks, and in principle covers stocks beyond areas of national jurisdiction only. It would be a great advance, if the agreement were also extended to other fish stocks and marine biological resources[183] and to the EEZ either. In this context existing problems concerning the global application and enforcement of the rules, in particular with regard to unreported, illegal and unregulated fishing should also be addressed,[184] taking into account i. a. the Agreement to Promote Compliance with International Conservation and Management Measures by Fishing Vessels on the High Seas[185] and the Code of Conduct for Responsible Fisheries.[186] It seems important to develop ways to ensure that the rules in force apply to all fishing vessels, regardless of the flag they are flying. For this purpose, port state control should be further strengthened, based on the FAO Agreement on Port State Measures to Prevent, Deter and Eliminate Illegal, Unreported and Unregulated Fishing.[187] A compulsory licensing and registration system for all vessels is also conceivable.[188]

III. LIABILITY AND COMPENSATION

In the end preventive protection and control regulations alone are not sufficient. They must be supplemented by a firm liability regime for compensation of damage caused by activities, which affect the marine environment, including the high seas.[189] Art. 235 UNCLOS creates corresponding obligations of states, but is rather embryonic in nature.[190] As concerns seabed activities in the Area, Art. 22 Annex III to UNCLOS establishes the liability of the contractor for any damage arising out of wrongful acts. This also covers environmental damage, as is clarified in the ISA regulations on prospecting and exploration[191] and the draft Regulations on the Exploitation of Mineral Resources in the Area.[192] However, as concerns environmental damage the question arises whether strict liability would be preferable. Some guidance could be drawn e.g. from the existing liability conventions for maritime shipping.[193] In addition, the European directive on environmental liability[194] could be taken into account.[195] With regard to the preparation of a legal instrument on biodiversity on the high seas it is currently under discussion to take the seabed mining regulations as a model.[196] In any case it has to be discussed how to define environmental damage and how compensation for residual ecological damage that cannot be eliminated by reinstatement measures could be achieved.[197]

IV. COMPLIANCE

1. BINDING LAW

For further advancing marine environmental protection it is not enough only to agree on regulations, but it is much more crucial that they are effectively implemented by all states. This is often still lacking.[198] States are only obliged to comply with those environmental standards that are binding international law. In principle, this is the case only, if the individual state has consented to be bound, especially by accepting an agreement.[199] In particular conventions have to be formally ratified by the contracting states, though more and more at least the annexes of marine environment conventions, containing the substantive technical rules, can by amended by a tacit acceptance procedure, which allows a considerable simplification and acceleration. But even in case of no explicit or tacit acceptance of a regulation, UNCLOS has established a pioneering provision, though only as far as shipping is concerned, by obliging states to conform to generally accepted international regulations, procedures and practices.[200] It could trigger a remarkable advancement, if such a principle were also introduced for other fields of marine protection law. In association therewith a progressive interpretation should be promoted, by considering environmental standards, consensually adopted by a competent international organization, to be recognized as generally accepted, at least if they aim at complementing or concretising existing agreements.

2. INTERNATIONAL COMPLIANCE CONTROL

Usually it is quite difficult to get clarity whether states comply with their implementation duties. Even if international conventions provide for an obligation to report to the competent international organization on the relevant national legislation and other implementing measures,[201] that alone is not enough. It is more important that the organization can, on its own initiative, control the activities of states for fulfilling their implementation duties. Some major steps forward may be attributed to IMO. To ensure the consistent and effective implementation of IMO instruments, already in 1995 IMO has introduced a Member State Audit Scheme, which at the beginning was voluntary[202] and, following an amendment of the respective regulations,[203] has become mandatory in 2017. Under this audit scheme the states are subject to periodic audits by IMO in accordance with an audit standard[204] to verify compliance with the conventions. Such an audit is a systematic, independent and documented process for obtaining audit evidence and evaluating it objectively to determine the extent to which audit criteria are fulfilled,[205] taking into account specific guidelines developed by IMO.[206] The audit scheme enables a structured and transparent substantive dialogue with the relevant state on the implementation measures taken. As a result, existing deficits can be identified and remedial measures proposed. While preserving anonymity, a feedback is made available to the IMO member states and considered in the IMO with a view to verifying the effectiveness and suitability of the respective international regulations.[207] The question arises whether an audit scheme could also be helpful for the effective implementation of marine environmental conventions in general.[208] In particular for the regional marine environment commissions such a scheme could serve as a tool for getting more precise information about the activities of the member states. Similarly, it could apply to global agreements, provided that there is an international institution that can be entrusted with audit services. It is also conceivable to extend the system to fields where there is still a lack of comprehensive international regulation, in particular land-based pollution. For example, a procedure could be developed within the framework of the UNEP to identify, as a first step, more clearly, which protective measures have already been taken by the individual states, what deficits exist and how these can be remedied by cooperation and the elaboration of appropriate international law. An audit system could also be considered for other regulations, concerning e.g. the exploitation of oil and gas from the sea and fisheries. By providing greater clarity as to whether and how a state has implemented regulations, additional pressure is indirectly exerted on states to fulfil their duties and may help states to eliminate remaining deficits. Other states can benefit from the lessons learned as concerns their own implementation measures. A further step could be to announce insufficient audit results by name. However, this would amount to a “name and blame” culture, which the states have so far resisted. An even greater interference with the current self-conception of states' sovereignty could be the introduction of a system of sanctions for insufficient implementation measures.[209] Such a system, however, is applied e.g. in the context of the European Union, where financial penalties may be imposed on a member state that does not comply with an obligation to implement an EU directive.[210]

V. INTERNATIONAL COOPERATION

The reflection on stronger control powers for international organizations leads to the related question whether the international cooperation of states for marine environmental protection is properly organized.

1. INTERGOVERNMENTAL NETWORK

So far, mainly marine environment protection commissions are established as regional bodies, supported by the Regional Seas Programme of UNEP.[211] Furthermore there exist marine fisheries management organizations with regional competencies,[212] supported by FAO.[213] In addition, numerous global organizations perform specific tasks that are relevant for marine environment protection. These include UNEP, IMO, IOC,[214] ISA, IAE0,[215] FAO and IHO[216]. To a certain extent coordination efforts are undertaken by UN-Oceans, which is an inter-agency mechanism that seeks to enhance the coordination, coherence and effectiveness of competent organizations of the United Nations system.[217] Whether it makes sense to merge these organizations or parts of them by establishing one overarching marine environment or ocean organization,[218] seems doubtful because many new interfaces and problems of competence could arise.[219] In any case there is a need to strengthen cross-sectoral cooperation, policy coherence and coordination among the existing international institutions at all levels.[220] A close functional, horizontal and vertical cooperation between the different organizations should ensured by a network as dense as possible.[221]

2. INVOLVEMENT OF CIVIL SOCIETY

As far as international cooperation is concerned, the question arises, how civil society can best be incorporated. Although, due to the intergovernmental character of organizations and the principle of states' sovereignty, final decisions have to be made by the states themselves, NGOs, however, should closely be involved and given the opportunity to contribute their ideas and expertise.[222] This applies to environmental groups as well as to industry associations and science organizations. The practise of granting observer status to NGOs should be further advanced. In addition, specific civic engagement, as reflected e.g. in private certification initiatives, such as Marine Stewardship Council, Friend of the Sea, Aquaculture Stewardship Council,[223] should be strongly promoted.

VI. FINANCIAL RESOURCES

An indispensable precondition for marine environment protection is the availability of sufficient financial resources. They are needed in order to enable international bodies to perform their tasks efficiently, but also to promote environmental projects and studies and to finance protection programs. It seems conceivable to make more and better use of the already existing finance institutions, in particular GEF,[224] for this purpose. However, it would be even more desirable to set up a separate marine environment fund.[225] In applying the polluter-pays principle levies to be paid by those using the seas and their resources[226] as well as monetary penalties in case of environmental damage[227] could serve as a source of funding. However, at the moment it seems unlikely that the international community would come to agreement on such a fund.

VII. CAPACITY BUILDING

Not least in the context of financial considerations, it becomes clear that globally efficient marine environmental protection ultimately depends on the capacity of states for active and substantive activities and participation on the international level. All considerations must take into account that, in particular, many long-coast and small island states still are developing countries. It is indispensable to intensify capacity building activities by focussing special attention on marine environment protection and ocean policy and management in general.[228] But also marine scientific research[229] and the transfer of marine environment technology are to be intensified.[230] That requires targeted support for these states to establish an effective administrative and science infrastructure as a basis for the responsible use of the seas and their protection. The mobilisation of financial means is also needed for investment in environmentally friendly production and waste management projects for reducing land-based pollution, as well as for the development of sustainable ocean-related activities.[231] How urgent that is, becomes clear from the example of marine litter.

C. CONCLUSION

In summary, the protection of the seas and oceans has been pushed forward over the past 50 years. Since long it has become clear that this is not just about pollution, but the conservation of marine ecosystems as a whole must be sought. It is not enough to decide on reasonable and feasible measures and on the necessary agreements once and for all. Rather, a permanent process of continuous improvement is needed to eliminate still remaining deficits and to counter new developments and challenges, not the least caused by climate change. The overall objective to be pursued is sustainable maritime development. Accordingly, marine environmental protection cannot be considered in isolation. Rather, it is only one, albeit extremely important element of sustainable development, in which economic and social impacts also play an equal role. The necessary measures in the context of effective international cooperation are increasingly labelled as ocean governance.[232] This term may be understood as the efforts to steer, control and manage marine activities in accordance with the aims of sustainable development. Hopefully, good ocean governance will lead to striking the right balance between protection and use of the oceans.

LITERATURE

Biermann, Frank, Internationale Meeresumweltpolitik, Europäische Hochschulschriften, series XXXI, vol. 248, 1994

Brusendorff, Anne Christine, HELCOM's Contribution to the Prevention of Marine Pollution, in: Jürgen Basedow/Ulrich Magnus (eds.), Pollution of the Sea – Prevention and Compensation, Hamburg Studies on Maritime Affairs, vol. 10, 2007, p. 85–94Churchill, R. R./Lowe, A. V., The law of the sea, 3rd Edition, eighth impression, 2010

Churchill, Robin, Compliance Mechanisms in the International Law of the Sea: from the Individual to the Collective, in: Holger Hestermeyer et al. (eds.), Coexistence, Cooperation and Solidarity, 2012, p. 777–806

Ehlers, Peter, Die Tätigkeit der Zwischenstaatlichen Beratenden Seeschifffahrts-Organisation (IMCO) von 1958 bis zum 31.3.1969, JIR 1970, p. 706–722

Ehlers, Peter/Kunig, Philip, Abfallbeseitigung auf Hoher See, Werkhefte des Instituts für Internationale Angelegenheiten der Universität Hamburg, vol. 31, 1978

Ehlers, Peter, The History of the International North Sea Conferences, in: David Freestone/Tom Ijlstra (eds.); The North Sea: Perspectives on Regional Environmental Cooperation, 1990, p. 3–14

Ehlers, Peter, The Helsinki Convention, 1992 – Improving the Baltic Sea Environment, IJMCL 1993, 191–243

Ehlers, Peter, Origins and Compensation of Marine Pollution – A Survey, in: Jürgen Basedow/Ulrich Magnus (eds.), Pollution of the Sea – Prevention and Compensation, Hamburg Studies on Maritime Affairs, vol. 10, 2007, p. 113–127

Ehlers, Peter, The Governance of the Global Ocean Observing System (GOOS), in: Holger Hestermeyer et al. (eds.), Coexistence, Cooperation and Solidarity, 2012, p. 1413–1437

Ehlers, Peter, Blue growth and ocean governance – how to balance the use and the protection of the seas, WMU Journal of Maritime Affairs (WMU J Marit. Affairs), vol. 15, no. 2 (2016), p. 183–203

Ehlers, Peter, Übersicht über die die Meeresverschmutzung betreffenden Vorschriften, in: Das Deutsche Bundesrecht, I L 60, 1283rd issuance, 2018, p. 1–35

Friedland, Julia Christine, Der Schutz der biologischen Vielfalt der Tiefseehydrothermalquellen, Rostocker Schriften zum Seerecht und Umweltrecht, vol. 41, 2007

Güner-Özbek, Meltem Deniz, Paris Memorandum of Understanding – an Example of International Cooperation and its Perspectives, in: Peter Ehlers/Rainer Lagoni (eds.), International Maritime Organisations and their Contribution towards a Sustainable Marine Development, Schriften zum See- und Hafenrecht, vol. 12, 2006, p. 105–134

Hafner, Gerhard, in: Vitzthum et al., Handbuch des Seerechts, 2006, Chapter 5 note 11 et seq.

Hassan, Daud, Land-Based Sources of Marine Pollution – The Global Framework for Control, Australian International Law Journal (AILJ), 2003, p. 61 et seq

Heintschel v. Heinegg, Wulf, Ökologisierung des Schadensbegriffs und Rückführung der Haftungsbeschränkungen im Seerecht, in: Peter Ehlers/Wilfried Erbguth (eds.), Aktuelle Entwicklungen im Seerecht, Rostocker Schriften zum Seerecht und Umweltrecht, vol. 13, 2000, p. 83–106

Höltmann, Michael, Schiffssicherheit und Meeresumweltschutz in der EU nach Erika und Prestige, Studies in International Law of the Sea and Maritime Law, vol. 4, 2012

Huang, Yuna, Compensation of Damage to the Marine Environment, in: Peter Ehlers/Rainer Lagoni (eds.), Responsibility and Liability in the Maritime Context, Schriften zum See- und Hafenrecht, vol. 16, 2009, p. 11–43

Jacobsson, Mans, The Torrey Canyon fifty years on: the legal legacy, Journal of International Maritime Law (JIML), vol. 23 (2017), p. 20 et seq.

Jessen, Henning/Werner, Michael Jürgen (eds.), EU Maritime Transport Law, 2016

Kateka, James L., Protection and Preservation of the Marine Environment in the Area under UNCLOS, in: Holger Hestermeyer et al. (eds.), Coexistence, Cooperation and Solidarity, 2012, p. 919–931

Krämer, Ludwig, The Contribution of the European Union to Marine Pollution Prevention, in: Jürgen Basedow/Ulrich Magnus (eds.), Pollution of the Sea –

Prevention and Compensation, Hamburg Studies on Maritime Affairs, vol. 10, 2007, p. 63–83

De La Fayette, Louise, The Concept of Environmental Damage in International Liability Regimes, in: Michael Bowman/Alan Boyle (eds.), Environmental Damage in International and Comparative Law, 2002, p. 149–191

Lagoni, Rainer, Das OSPAR-Übereinkommen von 1992 und der Schutz der Nordsee: Einwirkungen auf das deutsche Umweltrecht, in: Hans-Joachim Koch/Rainer Lagoni (eds.), Meeresumweltschutz für Nord- und Ostsee, Forum Umweltrecht, vol. 19, 1996, p. 79–101

Lagoni, Rainer, Die Internationale Seeschiffahrts-Organisation (IMO) als Rechtsetzungsorgan, in: Peter Ehlers/Wilfried Erbguth (eds.), 50 Jahre Vereinte Nationen – Tätigkeit und Wirken der Internationalen Seeschiffahrts-Organisation (IMO), Rostocker Schriften zum Seerecht und Umweltrecht, vol. 2, 1997, p. 45–56

Lagoni, Rainer, Völkerrechtliche Vorgaben für die Anwendung des Umweltschadensgesetzes in der Ausschließlichen Wirtschaftszone und auf dem Festlandsockel, Rostocker Schriften zum Seerecht und Umweltrecht, vol. 40, 2007.

Lamers, Verena, The 2007 Nairobi International Convention on the Removal of Wrecks, in: Peter Ehlers/Rainer Lagoni (eds.), Enforcement of International and EU Law in Maritime Affairs, Schriften zum See- und Hafenrecht, vol. 15, 2008, p. 149–180

Mensah, Thomas A., Prevention of Marine Pollution: The Contribution of IMO, in: Jürgen Basedow/Ulrich Magnus (eds.), Pollution of the Sea – Prevention and Compensation, Hamburg Studies on Maritime Affairs, vol. 10, 2007, p. 41–61

Proelß, Alexander, Meeresschutz im Völker- und Europarecht, Tübinger Schriften zum internationalen und europäischen Recht, vol. 71, 2004

Proelss, Alexander (ed.), United Nations Convention on the Law of the Sea, 2017

Schubert, Mathias, Maritimes Infrastrukturrecht, Jus Publicum, vol. 243, 2015

Starre, Mario, Der Meeresboden – Haftungsregime des Tiefseebergbaus, Studies in International Law of the Sea and Maritime Law, vol. 10, 2016

Suarez, Suzette V., Towards Sustainable Ocean Development: The Participation and Contribution of Non-Governmental Organisations to the Work of International Organisations in the Ocean Sector, in: Peter Ehlers/Rainer Lagoni (eds.), International Maritime Organisations and their Contribution towards a Sustainable Marine Development, Schriften zum See- und Hafenrecht, vol. 12, 2006, p. 53–75

Tanaka, Yoshifumi, Regulation of Land-Based Marine Pollution in International Law: A Comparative Analysis between Global and Regional Legal Frameworks, ZaöRV 66 (2006), p. 535 et seq.

Vitzthum (ed.), Wolfgang Graf, Handbuch des Seerechts, 2006

Wacht, Frank, in: Proelss (ed.), United Nations Convention on the Law of the Sea, 2017

Wissenschaftlicher Beirat der Bundesregierung Globale Umweltveränderungen (WBGU), World in Transition – Governing the Marine Heritage, Flagship

Report, Berlin, 2013, (http://www.wbgu.de/en/flagship-reports/fr-2013-oceans, last retrieved 13.1.2018)

Witt, Jörn-Ahrend, Obligations and Control of Flag States, Schriften zum See- und Hafenrecht, vol. 14, 2007

Wolfrum, Rüdiger, Maritime Pollution – Compensation or Enforcement, in: Jürgen Basedow/Ulrich Magnus (eds.), Pollution of the Sea – Prevention and Compensation, Hamburg Studies on Maritime Affairs, vol. 10, 2007, p. 129–136

Zhu, Ling, Do we need a Global Organisation for the Protection of the Marine Environment?, in: Peter Ehlers/Rainer Lagoni (eds.), International Maritime Organisations and their Contribution towards a Sustainable Marine Development, Schriften zum See- und Hafenrecht, vol. 12, 2006, p. 157–180

Zhu, Ling, International Convention on Civil Liability for Bunker Oil Pollution Damage, 2001 – Liability and Insurance Aspects, in: Jürgen Basedow/Ulrich Magnus (eds.), Pollution of the Sea – Prevention and Compensation, Hamburg Studies on Maritime Affairs, vol. 10, 2007, p. 171–180

NOTES

1 International Convention for the Protection of Pollution of the Sea by Oil; cf. Churchill/Lowe (2010), p. 339; Hafner, in: Vitzthum (ed.), Handbuch des Seerechts (2006), Chapter 5 note 11 et seq.

2 The Geneva Convention on the High Seas 1958.

3 Art. 24.

4 The Organization was renamed in 1982.

5 For details see Mensah, Prevention of Marine Pollution: The Contribution of IMO, in: Basedow/Magnus (eds.), Pollution of the Sea – Prevention and Compensation (2007); cf. Ehlers, JIR 1970.

6 Jacobsson, JIML 23 (2013), p. 20; Mensah, Prevention of Marine Pollution: The Contribution of IMO, in: Basedow/Magnus (eds.), Pollution of the Sea – Prevention and Compensation (2007), p. 44.

7 See Churchill/Lowe (2010), p. 353 et seq.; Hafner, in: Vitzthum (ed.), Handbuch des Seerechts (2006), Chapter 5 note 192.

8 In the context of the convention "high seas" include the exclusive economic zone (EEZ).

9 The Protocol Relating to the Intervention on the High Seas in Cases of Pollution by Substances Other Than Oil, 1973, has been amended subsequently to update the list of substances attached to it; cf. Mensah, Prevention of Marine Pollution: The Contribution of IMO, in: Basedow/Magnus (eds.), Pollution of the Sea – Prevention and Compensation (2007), p. 49 et seq.

10 Agreement for Cooperation in Dealing with Pollution of the North Sea by Oil, 1969.

[11] Agreement for cooperation in dealing with the pollution of the North Sea by oil and other harmful substances, 1983; for details see http://www.bonnagreement.or g (last retrieved 9.1.2018); Churchill/Lowe (2010), p. 357.

[12] 1969 International Convention on Civil Liability for Oil Pollution Damage.

[13] Cf. Jacobsson, JIML 23 (2013), p. 23; Churchill/Lowe (2010), p. 359 et seq.; Höltmann (2012), p. 204 et seq.

[14] International Convention on the Establishment of an International Fund for Compensation for Oil Pollution Damage 1971.

[15] Cf. Jacobsson, JIML 23 (2013), p. 24.

[16] Exclusive economic zone.

[17] Protocol of 1992 to amend the International Convention on Civil Liability for Oil Pollution Damage, 1969, Protocol of 1992 to amend the International Convention on the Establishment of an International Fund for Compensation for Oil Pollution Damage, 1971; for details see Jacobsson, JIML 23 (2013), p. 26 et seq.; Churchill/Lowe (2010), p. 361.

[18] Protocol of 2003 to the International Convention on the Establishment of an International Fund for Compensation for Oil Pollution Damage, 1992; for details see Jacobsson, JIML 23 (2013), p. 28 et seq.; Höltmann (2012), p. 211.

[19] International Convention for the Prevention of Pollution from Ships, 1973.

[20] Protocol of 1978 Relating to the International Convention for the Prevention of Pollution from Ships; Annex II and the optional Annexes III, IV and V to MARPOL entered into force only at later dates.

[21] Cf. WBGU (2013), p. 86.

[22] For details see Churchill/Lowe (2010), p. 339 et seq.; Mensah, Prevention of Marine Pollution: The Contribution of IMO, in: Basedow/Magnus (eds.), Pollution of the Sea – Prevention and Compensation (2007), p. 47, 50 et seq.; Proelß (2004), p. 136 et seq.

[23] For additional future measures cf. the IMO strategic plan for the six-year period 2018–2013 (IMO/Res. A 1110(30)).

[24] International Convention for the Safety of Life at Sea.

[25] The latest version was adopted in 1974.

[26] For details see Churchill/Lowe (2010), p. 265 et seq., 342; Proelß (2004), p. 139 et seq.

[27] For details see the Report of the United Nations Conference on the Human Environment (A/CONF.48/14/Rev.1), Chapter I (Declaration of the United Nations Conference on the Human Environment), Principle 7; Chapter II (Action Plan for the Human Environment) Rec. 86–94, Annex III (General Principles for Assessment and Control of Marine Pollution); Hassan, AILJ (2003), p. 84.

[28] Convention for the Prevention of Marine Pollution by Dumping from Ships and Aircraft, 1972; for details see Ehlers/Kunig (1978), p. 10 et seq.

[29] Convention on the Prevention of Marine Pollution from Land-Based Sources, 1974; cf. Ehlers/Kunig (1978), p. 43 et seq.

[30] Convention on the Protection of the Marine Environment of the Baltic Sea Area; cf. Ehlers/Kunig (1978), p. 40 et seq.

[31] Convention for Protection of the Mediterranean Sea against Pollution 1976, cf. WBGU (2013), p. 89.
[32] Convention on the Prevention of Marine Pollution by Dumping of Wastes and other Matters; cf. WBGU (2013), p. 86; for details see Ehlers/Kunig (1978), p. 28 et seq.; Proelß (2004), p. 141 et seq.
[33] United Nations Convention on the Law of the Sea.
[34] Art. 192.
[35] Art. 197.
[36] Art. 200.
[37] Art. 204, 206; for the significance of environmental monitoring see WBGU (2013), p. 98.
[38] Art. 207, 210, 212.
[39] Cf. Wacht, in: Proelss (ed.), United Nations Convention on the Law of the Sea (2017), Art. 207 note 16, Art. 210 note 15, Art. 212 note 11; Tanaka, ZaöRV 66 (2006), p. 543; Hassan, AILJ (2003), p. 76.
[40] Art. 208, 211; cf. Wacht, ibid., Art. 208 note 15, Bartenstein in: Proelss (ed.), United Nations Convention on the Law of the Sea (2017), Art. 211 note 11.
[41] Art. 213 et seq.
[42] Art. 56 para. 1 (b) (iii), 210 para. 5.
[43] Art. 211 para. 5, 6, 217 et seq.
[44] Art. 94 para. 5, 211 para. 2.
[45] See Guilfoyle in: Proelss (ed.), United Nations Convention on the Law of the Sea (2017), Art. 91 note 11, Bartenstein in: Proelss (ed.), United Nations Convention on the Law of the Sea (2017), Art. 211 note 33 et seq.; Höltmann (2012), p 30 et seq.; Vitzthum, Handbuch des Seerechts (2006), Chapter 2 note 91, 175; Witt (2007), p. 59 et seq.
[46] Art. 61, 117 et seq.
[47] International Seabed Authority.
[48] Art. 145, 209.
[49] Art. 153.
[50] Cf. Ehlers, The History of the International North Sea Conferences, in: Freestone/Ijlstra (eds.); The North Sea: Perspectives on Regional Environmental Cooperation (1990), p. 3 et seq.
[51] Cf. Ehlers, IJMCL 1993, p. 193 et seq.
[52] For details cf. the UNEP regional seas programme, http://web.unep.org/regionalseas (last retrieved 9.1.2018); WBGU (2013), p. 89.
[53] Art. 16 MARPOL, Art. VIII SOLAS; cf. Mensah, Prevention of Marine Pollution: The Contribution of IMO, in: Basedow/Magnus (eds.), Pollution of the Sea – Prevention and Compensation (2007), p. 58 et seq.
[54] For details cf. Lagoni, Die Internationale Seeschiffahrts-Organisation (IMO) als Rechtsetzungsorgan, in: Ehlers/Erbguth (eds.), 50 Jahre Vereinte Nationen – Tätigkeit und Wirken der Internationalen Seeschiffahrts-Organisation (IMO) (1997), p. 50 et seq.; Mensah, Prevention of Marine Pollution: The Contribution

of IMO, in: Basedow/Magnus (eds.), Pollution of the Sea – Prevention and Compensation (2007), p. 48.

55 Art. 5 para. 4 MARPOL, Art. II para. 3 Protocol of 1978 relating to the International Convention for Safety of Life at Sea of 1 November 1978; cf. Proelß (2004), p. 129 et seq., who qualifies this competence as a generally accepted international regulation.

56 Cf. Höltmann (2012), p. 73 et seq.; Churchill/Lowe (2010), p. 274 et seq.

57 http://seafarersrights.org/wp/wp-content/uploads/2014/11/INTERNATIONAL_TREATY_PARIS-MOU-ON-PORT-CONTROL_1982_ENG.pdf (last retrieved 9.1.2018).

58 For details cf. Paris MoU (https://www.parismou.org, last retrieved 9.1.2018); Güner-Özbek, Paris Memorandum of Understanding – an Example of International Cooperation and its Perspectives, in: Ehlers/Lagoni (eds.), International Maritime Organisations and their Contribution towards a Sustainable Marine Development (2006), p. 121 et seq.; WBGU (2013), p. 80 et seq.; Churchill, Compliance Mechanisms in the International Law of the Sea: from the Individual to the Collective, in: Hestermeyer et al. (eds.), Coexistence, Cooperation and Solidarity (2012), p. 792 et seq.

59 Convention on Wetlands of International Importance Especially as Waterfoul Habitat, Ramsar 2.2.1971 (https://www.ramsar.org/document/copy-of-the-convention-copy-certified-by-unesco, last retrieved 9.1.2018).

60 For details see http://www.cms.int/en/legalinstrument/cms (last retrieved 9.1.2018).

61 Council Directive 79/409/EEC of 2 April 1979 on the conservation of wild birds (OJ L 103, 25.4.1079, p. 1).

62 See no. 39 Ministerial Declaration of the Third International Conference on the Protection of the North Sea, The Hague, 8 March 1990; cf. Churchill/Lowe (2010), p. 393 et seq.

63 For details see Ehlers, IJMCL 1993; Brusendorff, HELCOM's Contribution to the Prevention of Marine Pollution, in: Basedow/Magnus (eds.), Pollution of the Sea – Prevention and Compensation (2007).

64 For details see Lagoni, Das OSPAR-Übereinkommen von 1992 und der Schutz der Nordsee: Einwirkungen auf das deutsche Umweltrecht, in: Koch/Kagoni (eds.), Meeresumweltschutz für Nord- und Ostsee (1996); Proelß (2004), p. 192 et seq.

65 Churchill/Lowe (2010), p. 337.

66 1996 Protocol to the Convention on the Prevention of Pollution by Dumping of Wastes and Other Matter, 1972; for details see Proelß (2004), p. 146 et seq.

67 Supra part A I 2.

68 The OSPAR secretariat also performs secretarial functions for the Bonn Agreement.

69 Art. 20 Helsinki Convention, Art. 13 OSPAR Convention.

70 UNGA A/CONF.151/26 (Vol.I).

71 Report of the United Nations Conference on Environment and Development, Chapter 17, UNGA A/CONF.151/26 (Vol.II); see Hassan, AILJ (2003), p. 87 et seq.

72 Rio+5 – 19th special session of the United Nations General Assembly, 1997; World Summit on Sustainable Development, WSSD, Johannesburg, South Africa, 2002; The United Nations Conference on Sustainable Development (UNCSD), 2012; cf. WBGU (2013), p. 83.

73 Convention on Biological Diversity.

74 Art. 1; cf. Churchill/Lowe (2010), p. 336, 394.

75 Art. 4; cf. Friedland (2007), p. 144; WBGU (2013), p. 84, 263.

76 So defined by Decision V of the 5th Conference of CBD Parties (COP 5).

77 An overview about land-based inputs is provided by WBGU (2013), p. 31 et seq.

78 Washington Declaration on Protection of the Marine Environment from Land-Based Activities.

79 Global Programme of Action; see Tanaka, ZaöRV 66 (2006), p. 544; Hassan, AILJ (2003), p. 83, 89 et seq.

80 UNEP/WG.120/3 (Part IV).

81 See Tanaka, ibid.; Hassan, AILJ (2003), p. 85 et seq.

82 UNEP/GPA/IGR.1/9 Annex I.

83 UNEP(DEPI)/RS.9/INF11.

84 UNEP/WBRS.18/INF10; a fourth review meeting scheduled for October 2017 in Bali was postponed.

85 Tanaka, ZaöRV 66 (2006), p. 547; Hassan, AILJ (2003), p. 92.

86 International Convention on Liability and Compensation for Damage in Connection with the Carriage of Hazardous and Noxious Substances by Sea, 1996 (http://www.hnsconvention.org/the-convention, last retrieved 11.1.2018); for details see Höltmann (2012), p. 213 et seq.

87 Protocol of 2010 to the International Convention on Liability and Compensation for Damage in Connection with the Carriage of Hazardous and Noxious Substances by Sea, 1996 (http://www.hnsconvention.org/the-convention, last retrieved 11.1.2018).

88 International Convention on Civil Liability for Bunker Oil Pollution Damage; for details see Höltmann (2012), p. 211 et seq.; Zhu, International Convention on Civil Liability for Bunker Oil Pollution Damage, 2001 – Liability and Insurance Aspects, in: Basedow/Magnus (eds.), Pollution of the Sea – Prevention and Compensation (2007).

89 International Convention on the Control of Harmful Anti-fouling Systems on Ships.

90 International Convention on the Control and Management of Ships' Ballast Water and Sediments; entry into force 8 September 2017.

91 Nairobi International Convention on the Removal of Wrecks; for details see Lamers, The 2007 Nairobi International Convention on the Removal of Wrecks, in: Ehlers/Lagoni (eds.), Enforcement of International and EU Law in Maritime Affairs (2008), p. 158 et seq.

[92] An overview of the European marine environment policy is given by WBGU (2013), p. 90 et seq.; cf. Krämer, The Contribution of the European Union to Marine Pollution Prevention, in: Basedow/Magnus (eds.), Pollution of the Sea – Prevention and Compensation (2007).

[93] Convention on the Conservation of European Wildlife and Natural Habitats.

[94] Then EEC (1979) or EC (1992).

[95] See supra footnote 61, replaced by Directive 2009/147/EC of the European Parliament and of the Council of 30 November 2009 on the conservation of wild birds (OJ L 20, 28.1.2010, p. 7); for details see Proelß (2004), p. 369 et seq.

[96] Council Directive 92/43/EEC of 21 May 1992 on the conservation of natural habitats and of wild fauna and flora (OJ L 206, 22.7.1992, p. 7); for details see Proelß (2004), p. 357 et seq.

[97] For details see Schubert (2015), p. 116 et seq.

[98] This includes the EEZ; see ECJ Case C-6/04 (http://curia.europa.eu/juris/liste.jsf?language=en&jur=C,T,F&num=C-6/04&td=ALL, last retrieved 8.1.2018).

[99] Directive 2000/60/EC of the European Parliament and of the Council of 23 October 2000 establishing a framework for Community action in the field of water policy (OJ L 327, 22.12.2000, p. 1); Krämer, The Contribution of the European Union to Marine Pollution Prevention, in: Basedow/Magnus (eds.), Pollution of the Sea – Prevention and Compensation (2007), p. 70 et seq.; Proelß (2004), p. 349 et seq.

[100] Directive 2008/56/EC of the European Parliament and of the Council of 17 June 2008 establishing a framework for community action in the field of marine environmental policy (OJ L 164, 25.6.2008, p. 19).

[101] Art. 3 no. 5.

[102] See Krämer, The Contribution of the European Union to Marine Pollution Prevention, in: Basedow/Magnus (eds.), Pollution of the Sea – Prevention and Compensation (2007), p. 73 et seq.

[103] Directive 2013/30/EU of the European Parliament and of the Council of 12 June 2013 on safety of offshore oil and gas operations and amending Directive 2004/35/EC (OJ L 178, 28.6.2013, p. 66).

[104] Council Directive 95/21/EC of 19 June 1995 concerning the enforcement, in respect of shipping using Community ports and sailing in the waters under the jurisdiction of the Member States, of international standards for ship safety, pollution prevention and shipboard living and working conditions (OJ L 157, 07.07.1995, p. 1).

[105] Directive 2009/16/EC of the European Parliament and of the Council of 23 April 2009 on port State control (OJ L 131, 28.5.2009, p. 57), as amended by Regulation (EU) 2015, 757 (OJ 123, 19.5.2015, p. 55); for details see Pimm, Commentary on Directive 2009/16/EC of the European Parliament and of the Council of 23 April 2009 on Port State Control, in: Jessen/Werner (eds.), EU Maritime Transport Law (2016), p. 856 et seq.; Höltmann (2012), p. 84 et seq.

[106] See the overview by Coleman/Jessen, in: Jessen/Werner (eds.), EU Maritime Transport Law (2016), p. 566 et seq.

[107] Directive 2000/59/EC of the European Parliament and of the Council of 27 November 2000 on port reception facilities for ship-generated waste and cargo residues (OJ L 332, 28.12.2000, p. 81).

[108] For details see Brinkmann, Commentary on Directive 2000/59/EC of 27 November 2000 on Port Reception Facilities for Ship-Generated Waste and Cargo Residues, in: Jessen/Werner (eds.), EU Maritime Transport Law (2016), p. 635 et seq.

[109] Directive 2005/35/EC of the European Parliament and of the Council of 7 September 2005 on ship-source pollution and on the introduction of penalties for infringements (OJ L 255, 30.9.2005, p. 11), as amended by Directive 2009/123/EC (OJ L 280, 27.10.2009, p. 52); for details see Höltmann (2012), p. 136 et seq.

[110] For details see Jessen, Commentary on Directive 2005/35/EC on ship-source pollution and on the introduction of penalties, including criminal penalties, for pollution offences (as amended by Directive 2009/123/EC), in: Jessen/Werner (eds.), EU Maritime Transport Law (2016), p. 667 et seq.

[111] Directive (EU) 2016/802 of the European Parliament and of the Council of 11 May 2016 relating to a reduction in the sulphur content of certain liquid fuels (OJ L 132, 21.5.16, p. 58), which replaced Council Directive 1999/32/EC of 26 April 1999 (OJ L 121, 11.5. 1999, p. 13).

[112] For details see Schinas, Commentary on Directive 1999/32/EC as regards the sulphur content of marine fuels, as amended by Directive 2012/33/EC, in: Jessen/Werner (eds.), EU Maritime Transport Law (2016), p. 589 et seq.; Höltmann (2012), p. 173 et seq.

[113] Regulation (EU) 2015/757 of the European Parliament and of the Council of 29 April 2015 on the monitoring, reporting and verification of carbon dioxide emissions from maritime transport, and amending Directive 2009/16/EC (OJ L 123, 19.5.2015, p. 55).

[114] For details see Jessen, Commentary on Regulation (EU) 2015/757 on the Monitoring, Reporting and Verification of Carbon Dioxide Emissions from Maritime Transport, in: Jessen/Werner (eds.), EU Maritime Transport Law (2016), p. 1060 et seq.

[115] For further information see the overview by Coleman/Jessen, in: Jessen/Werner (eds.), EU Maritime Transport Law (2016), p. 566 et seq; Krämer, The Contribution of the European Union to Marine Pollution Prevention, in: Basedow/Magnus (eds.), Pollution of the Sea – Prevention and Compensation (2007), p. 71 et seq.

[116] Directive 2002/59/EC of the European Parliament and of the Council of 27 June 2002 establishing a Community vessel traffic monitoring and information system and repealing Council Directive 93/75/EEC (OJ L 208, 5.8.2002, p. 10).

[117] See in detail Werner, Directive 2002/59/EC establishing a Community vessel traffic monitoring and information system and repealing Council Directive 93/75/EEC, in: Jessen/Werner (eds.), EU Maritime Transport Law (2016), p. 902 et seq.; Höltmann (2012), p. 157 et seq.

[118] For the domestic German legislation on marine pollution cf. Ehlers (2018).

119 UNGA A/RES/70/1.

120 Goal no. 14 of the Agenda 2030.

121 For details see WBGU (2013), p. 36 et seq.

122 See in detail First Global Integrated Marine Assessment (First World Ocean Assessment) (http://www.un.org/Depts/los/global_reporting/WOA_RegProcess.htm, last retrieved 12.1.2018).

123 For details see The Ocean Foundation, Ocean and Climate Change (https://www.oceanfdn.org/resources/ocean-and-climate-change, last retrieved 12.1.2018); WBGU (2013), p. 85, 175, 280.

124 Endorsed by the UN General Assembly (UNGA A/RES/71/312).

125 For details see https://oceanconference.un.org/commitments/ (last retrieved 12.1.2018).

126 Cf. WBGU (2013), p. 104 et seq.

127 Cf. WBGU (2013), p. 106, 250.

128 Art. 1 para. 1 no. 4 UNCLOS; cf. Tanaka in: Proelss (ed.), United Nations Convention on the Law of the Sea (2017), Art. 1 note 13.

129 ITLOS/Case No. 17, note 135; cf. Harrison/Morgera in: Proelss (ed.), United Nations Convention on the Law of the Sea (2017), Art. 61 note 22; WBGU (2013), p. 78.

130 See Kateka, Protection and Preservation of the Marine Environment in the Area under UNCLOS, in Hestermeyer et al. (eds.), Coexistence, Cooperation and Solidarity (2012), p. 926 et seq.

131 Rio Declaration on Environment and Development (1992), Principle 15.

132 Cf. Art. 191 para. 2 Treaty of the Functioning of the European Union (OJ C 2016/202/47); Art. 3 para. 2 Helsinki Convention; Art. 2 para. 2 (a) OSPAR Convention; Tanaka, ZaöRV 66 (2006), p. 559 et seq.; Churchill/Lowe (2010), p. 336; Proelß (2004), p. 106.

133 Reg. 33 para. 2, 5 Regulations on Prospecting and Exploration for Polymetallic Sulphides in the Area (ISA Doc. ISBA/16/A/12/Rev. 1, Annex); Reg. 31 para. 1, 5 Regulations on Prospecting and Exploration for Polymetallic Nodules in the Area (ISA Doc. ISBA/19/C/17, Annex, ISBA/20/A/9); Reg. 33 para. 2, 5 Regulations on Prospecting and Exploration for Cobalt-rich Ferromanganese Crusts in the Area (ISA Doc. ISBA/18/A/11, Annex); cf. Starre (2016), p. 185.

134 Art. 5 lit. c), 6 Agreement for the Implementation of the Provisions of the United Nations Convention on the Law of the Sea of 10 December 1982 relating to the Conservation and Management of Straddling Fish Stocks and Highly Migratory Fish Stocks.

135 Cf. Art. 191 para. 2 Treaty of the Functioning of the European Union; Art. 3 para. 4 Helsinki Convention; Art. 2 para. 2 (b) OSPAR Convention.

136 Cf. Art. 3 para. 3 Helsinki Convention, Art. 2 para. 3 OSPAR Convention; Tanaka, ZaöRV 66 (2006), p. 563 et seq.

137 Cf. UNGA A/RES/71/312 Annex, no. 13 f.; WBGU (2013), p. 259.

138 World Meteorological Organization.

[139] Gobal Ocean Observing System; for details see http://www.goosocean.org (last retrieved 12.1.2018); cf. Ehlers, The Governance of the Global Ocean Observing System (GOOS), in: Hestermeyer et al. (eds.), Coexistence, Cooperation and Solidarity (2012).
[140] Cf. Blitza in: Proelss (ed.), United Nations Convention on the Law of the Sea (2017), Art. 206 note 1.
[141] For regulations in regional conventions see Tanaka, ZaöRV 66 (2006), p. 566 et seq.
[142] Convention on Environmental Impact Assessment in a Transboundary Context.
[143] Directive 2011/92/EU of the European Parliament and of the Council of 13 December 2011 on the assessment of the effects of certain public and private projects on the environment (OJ L 26, 28.1.2012, p. 1); for details see Schubert (2015), p. 120 et seq.
[144] Cf. WBGU (2013), p. 99 et seq., 273 et seq., 291 et seq.
[145] Cf. UNGA A/RES/71/312 Annex No. 13 j.
[146] Cf. Czybulka in: Proelss (ed.), United Nations Convention on the Law of the Sea (2017), Art. 194 note 34 et seq.
[147] See infra part 2.2.5.
[148] Cf Proelss, in: Proelss (ed.), United Nations Convention on the Law of the Sea (2017), Art. 56 note 27; Schubert (2015), p. 59 et seq.
[149] See Directive 2014/89/EU of the European Parliament and of the Council of 23 July 2014 establishing a framework for maritime spatial planning (OJ L 257, 28.8.2014, p. 135); for details see Schubert (2015), p. 140 et seq.
[150] Cf. Czybulka in: Proelss (ed.), United Nations Convention on the Law of the Sea (2017), Art. 192 note 8 et seq.; Tanaka, ZaöRV 66 (2006), p. 543.
[151] Cf. Wacht, in: Proelss (ed.), United Nations Convention on the Law of the Sea (2017), Art. 207 note 2.
[152] For details see Tanaka, ZaöRV 66 (2006), p. 550 et seq.
[153] Cf. Wacht, ibid., Art. 207 note 17; Churchill/Lowe (2010), p. 380 et seq.; for details concerning the problems of a global legal framework and regional conventions see Tanaka, ZaöRV 66 (2006), p. 547 et seq., 572 et seq.
[154] Cf. WBGU (2013), p. 32 et seq.
[155] Cf. UNGA A/RES/71/312 Annex no. 13 g et seq.; A/RES/71/257, no. 182.
[156] Cf. Ehlers, WMU J Marit. Affairs (2016), p. 195.
[157] Art. 208, 209.
[158] Cf. Churchill/Lowe (2010), p. 371.
[159] Cf. Churchill/ Lowe (2010), p. 372 et seq.; an overview about marine mining activities is given by WBGU (2013), p. 34 et seq.; Ehlers, WMU J Marit. Affairs (2016), p. 192.
[160] See supra footnote 103.
[161] Cf. Starre (2016), p. 107 et seq.
[162] See supra footnote 133.
[163] See Draft Regulations on Exploitation of Mineral Resources in the Area, ISBA/23/LTC/CRP.3*.

164 An overview about the use of marine mineral resources is given by WBGU (2013), p. 49 et seq.

165 Art. 79, 208.

166 Cf. WBGU (2013), p. 205 et seq.

167 Cf. WBGU (2013), p. 207 et seq.; Ehlers, WMU J Marit. Affairs (2016), p. 191 et seq.

168 Potential environmental impacts are described by WBGU (2013), p. 215 et seq.

169 For details see WBGU (2013), p. 54, 153 et seq., 284 et seq.; Ehlers, WMU J Marit. Affairs (2016), p. 190.

170 For details cf. WBGU (2013), p. 53; Ehlers, WMU J Marit. Affairs (2016), p. 190 et seq.

171 For a comprehensive analysis of the legal situation see Friedland (2007).

172 WBGU (2013), p. 77.

173 Cf. Czybulka in: Proelss (ed.), United Nations Convention on the Law of the Sea (2017), Art. 194 note 30 et seq.; Proelß (2004), p. 105 et seq.

174 UNGA A/RES/69/262, A/RES/72/249; cf. WBGU (2013), p. 85, 263.

175 See the Chair's streamlined non-paper on?elements of a draft text of an international legally-binding instrument under the United Nations Convention on the Law of the Sea on?the conservation and sustainable use of marine biological diversity of areas beyond national jurisdiction; for further information about the work progress of the Committee see http://www.un.org/depts/los/biodiversity/prepcom.htm (last retrieved 12.1.2018).

176 Cf. supra part B I.

177 WBGU (2013), p. 89.

178 Cf. WBGU (2013), p. 78, 131 et seq.; Proelß (2004), p. 108.

179 For the importance and effects of fisheries in general see WBGU (2013), p. 114 et seq.

180 See WBGU (2013), p. 137 et seq.; Proelß (2004), p. 149 et seq.

181 Art. 5 lit. a.

182 Art. 5 lit. c, f, g, Art. 6.

183 WBGU (2013), p. 257, 264.

184 Cf. UNGA A/RES/71/312 Annex, no. 13 l et seq.; WBGU (2013), p. 142 et seq., 262 et seq., 280; cf. Churchill/Lowe (2010), p. 323.

185 http://www.fao.org/docrep/MEETING/003/X3130m/X3130E00.HTM (last retrieved 13.1.2018).

186 http://www.fao.org/docrep/005/v9878e/v9878e00.HTM (last retrieved 13.1.2018); see WBGU (2013), p. 136.

187 OJ L 191, 22.7.2011, p. 3.

188 WBGU (2013), ibid.

189 Cf. WBGU (2013), p. 102, 275.

190 Wolfrum, Maritime Pollution – Compensation or Enforcement, in: Basedow/Magnus (eds.), Pollution of the Sea – Prevention and Compensation (2007), p. 130; Lagoni, (2007), p. 26 et seq.

191 Reg. 32 Regulations on Polymetallic Sulphides, Reg. 32 Regulations on Crusts.

[192] Annex 10, Section 8 Draft Regulations on the Exploitation of Mineral Resources in the Area (footnote 163).

[193] Cf. supra part A I 3, A IV 6.

[194] Directive 2004/35/EC of the European Parliament and of the Council of 21 April 2004 on environmental liability with regard to the prevention and remedying of environmental damage (OJ L 143, 30.4.2004, p. 56).

[195] Cf. Ehlers, Origins and Compensation of Marine Pollution – A Survey, in: Basedow/Magnus (eds.), Pollution of the Sea – Prevention and Compensation (2007), p. 122 et seq.

[196] See Part X (p. 55) of the Chair's streamlined non-paper (supra footnote 175).

[197] Cf. Wolfrum, Maritime Pollution – Compensation or Enforcement, in: Basedow/Magnus (eds.), Pollution of the Sea – Prevention and Compensation (2007), p. 135 et seq.; for details about the term of ecological damage cf. Heintschel v. Heinegg, Ökologisierung des Schadensbegriffs und Rückführung der Haftungsbeschränkungen im Seerecht, in: Ehlers/Erbguth (eds.), Aktuelle Entwicklungen im Seerecht (2000); Ehlers, Origins and Compensation of Marine Pollution – A Survey, in: Basedow/Magnus (eds.), Pollution of the Sea – Prevention and Compensation (2007), p. 116.

[198] For shipping cf. Churchill/Lowe (2010), p. 273.

[199] Cf. Art. 11 et seq. Vienna Convention on the Law of Treaties.

[200] Supra part A III.

[201] E.g. Art. 11 MARPOL, Art. 16 Helsinki Convention, Art. 23 OSPAR Convention; cf. Churchill, Compliance Mechanisms in the International Law of the Sea: from the Individual to the Collective, in: Hestermeyer et al. (eds.), Coexistence, Cooperation and Solidarity (2012), p. 803.

[202] Cf. Churchill, Compliance Mechanisms in the International Law of the Sea: from the Individual to the Collective, in: Hestermeyer et al. (eds.), Coexistence, Cooperation and Solidarity (2012), p. 796 et seq.

[203] E.g. MARPOL Annex I Reg. 44 et seq.

[204] IMO Instruments Implementation Code (IMO Res. A.1070(28)).

[205] E.g. MARPOL Annex I Reg. 1 no. 44 et seq.

[206] Framework and Procedures for the IMO Member States Audit Scheme (IMO Res. 1067(28)).

[207] For details see no. 5 of the Framework and Procedures.

[208] Cf. Churchill, Compliance Mechanisms in the International Law of the Sea: from the Individual to the Collective, in: Holger Hestermeyer et al. (eds.), Coexistence, Cooperation and Solidarity (2012), p. 806, who favours the introduction and growing use of collective compliance mechanisms in the law of the sea.

[209] Cf. WBGU (2013), p. 103.

[210] Art. 260 Treaty on the Functioning of the European Union.

[211] Cf. Zhu, Do we need a Global Organisation for the Protection of the Marine Environment?, in: Ehlers/Lagoni (eds.), International Maritime Organisations and their Contribution towards a Sustainable Marine Development (2006), p. 165 et seq.; WBGU (2013), p. 83.

212 Cf. WBGU (2013), p. 139 et seq.

213 Food and Agriculture Organization.

214 Intergovernmental Oceanographic Commission of UNESCO.

215 International Atomic Energy Organization.

216 International Hydrographic Organization; IHO is an intergovernmental organization, but not a specialised ageny of the UN system.

217 For details see http://www.unoceans.org; cf. WBGU (2013), p. 84, 87 (last retrieved 13.1.2018); cf. UNGA A/72/70/Add.1, no. 73 et seq., 92.

218 WBGU (2013), p. 253, proposes the supplementary establishment of a World Oceans Organization; see also Biermann (1994), p. 269 et seq.

219 See Zhu, Do we need a Global Organisation for the Protection of the Marine Environment?, in: Ehlers/Lagoni (eds.), International Maritime Organisations and their Contribution towards a Sustainable Marine Development (2006), p. 175 et seq.

220 Cf. UNGA A/72/70/Add.1, no. 72.

221 Cf. WBGU (2013), p. 265 et seq.

222 For information about the participation of NGOs cf. Suarez, Towards Sustainable Ocean Development: The Participation and Contribution of Non-Governmental Organisations to the Work of International Organisations in the Ocean Sector, in: Ehlers/Lagoni (eds.), International Maritime Organisations and their Contribution towards a Sustainable Marine Development (2006), p. 65 et seq.

223 Cf. WBGU (2013), p. 91 et seq., 272 et seq.; Churchill/Lowe (2010), p. 323.

224 Global Environment Facility, for details see https://www.thegef.org (last retrieved 13.1.2018); cf. WBGU (2013), p. 84.

225 Cf. WBGU (2013), p. 269 et seq.; Biermann (1994), p. 267.

226 Cf WBGU (2013), p. 104.

227 De La Fayette, The Concept of Environmental Damage in International Liability Regimes, in: Bowman/Boyle (eds.), Environmental Damage in International and Comparative Law (2002), p. 186 et seq.; Huang, Compensation of Damage to the Marine Environment, in: Ehlers/Lagoni (eds.), Responsibility and Liability in the Maritime Context (2009), p. 42, 43.

228 Cf. Churchill/Lowe (2010), p. 396; cf. UNGA A/RES/71/257, 10 et seq.

229 For the need of gaining sufficient knowledge about the seas cf. Ehlers, WMU J Marit. Affairs (2016), p. 201.

230 Cf UNGA A/RES/71/312 Annex, no 15.

231 Cf. UNGA A/RES/71/312 Annex, no 13 q et seq.

232 Cf. WBGU (2013), p. 71 et seq., 248; Ehlers, WMU J Marit. Affairs (2016), p. 197.

Chapter V

The Progressive Development of the Law of the Sea in Light of Current Environmental Concerns

Katharina Reiling

A. UNCLOS: An Extraordinary Framework Convention

The UN Convention on the Law of the Sea (UNCLOS)[1] does not provide an answer to every problem that arises in sea related matters, as the text and the development of the convention imply[2]. Thus, UNCLOS is often described as a framework convention[3]. A framework convention largely abstains from substantive provisions; rather, it creates a legal basis, which requires the subsequent regulation with further details and new aspects to be agreed on in the future[4]. The overall goal to be achieved by a framework convention is the possibility to flexibly cope with increasing challenges of a regulatory nature by using the technique of 'slicing the salami thinly'[5]; therefore, framework conventions are considered to build an essential part of global governance[6]. While containing substantial provisions on, inter alia, maritime zones, such a framework structure is particularly attributed to the provisions of UNCLOS that are concerned with the protection and preservation of the marine environment[7], so that UNCLOS follows a mixed strategy by combining concrete provisions with framework provisions[8].

However, UNCLOS is not a typical framework convention[9] in the sense applied to many international environmental treaties[10], since it is neither termed framework[11] nor contains formal provisions for the adoption of further protocols and annexes as a means of developing the legal regime to meet new concerns[12] nor is amendment made easy[13]. Moreover, UNCLOS does not formally establish a Conference of the Parties (COP)[14], while a COP is said to be a common arrangement of framework conventions[15].

Rather, the widely used description of UNCLOS as a 'comprehensive constitution for the oceans which will stand the test of time'[16] implies a certain inflexibility, particularly as constitutions are usually difficult to amend[17]. Despite its roots in the nation state, constitution is not an inappropriate term to describe UNCLOS, since the convention emphasizes the importance of a firm legal framework, in order to preserve the consensus decision making process, on which UNCLOS is based on[18]. This crucial concern of balancing the further development and the prevalence of UNCLOS is reflected, for instance, by article 311[19].

Against this backdrop, the objective of this contribution is to explore the specific means that have emerged, in order to seek solutions to new issues within the framework of UNCLOS (B.) and – in a further step – to point out its respective legal challenges (C.). Hence, as distinguished from Harrison's comprehensive case study[20], the particular interest of this contribution is not mainly the institutional aspect of law making, but the legal toolbox and the legal follow-up problems of the progressive development of UNCLOS. Furthermore, the focus is on 'hard' instruments by contrast to the instruments of interpretation of international treaties, such as soft law or the so-called dynamic or living interpretation[21]. For the in such a manner outlined purpose, this contribution studies three fundamental issues of the current marine environmental law: the environmental protection regarding the deep seabed mining, the conservation of marine biological biodiversity in areas beyond national jurisdiction and, finally, the preventing, the deterring and the eliminating of illegal, unreported and unregulated fishing.

B. Current Concerns in the Area of Marine Environmental Law

I. Environmental Protection in the Deep Seabed Mining Regime

1. Implementing the Common Heritage of Mankind Principle by the ISA

The deep seabed beyond the outer limits of the continental shelf, referred to as as 'the Area' in UNCLOS (article 1), which compromises about sixty percent of the whole seabed[22], has a unique legal status, since, in 1970, the UN General Assembly declared the Area and its resources to be the 'common heritage of mankind'[23], now incorporated into article 136 UNCLOS. The common heritage of mankind principle does not dictate specific measures; rather, its key element is that the Area is managed on behalf of the international community as a whole by an international organization, called the International Seabed Authority (ISA)[24]. Accordingly, the ISA is tasked with operationalizing the common heritage of mankind principle in the context of deep seabed mining, in order to fill gaps in the framework left by UNCLOS[25]. This task particularly applies to the protection of the marine environment, an environment about which little was known at the time of the negotiations of UNCLOS; therefore, it was intended that the legal regime should develop gradually, as knowledge of the deep seabed expands[26]. Hence, in what is referred to as an instance of 'institutionalized precaution', the ISA was established to ensure effective protection over the time[27]. How the ISA fulfills this function is objective of the following.

2. Environmental Risks of the Deep Seabed Mining

Deep seabed mining involves extracting submerged minerals and deposits from the ocean floor in water depths between about 800–6000 meters[28]. All proposed seabed minerals mining operations are based on using a seabed resource collector, a lifting system and support vessels; many proposed seabed collection systems envisage the use of remotely operated vehicles, which extract deposits from the seabed using mechanical or pressurized water drills[29]. The three main targets for deep seabed mining are polymetallic sulphides, manganese nodules and cobalt-rich ferromanganese crusts, primarily in the Pacific Ocean[30].

The potentially vast mineral wealth of the ocean, which formed the starting point for the common heritage of mankind principle, has not yet been materialized, however, spurred by the increased demand for copper, cobalt, nickel, silver and rare earth and specialty metals, inter alia driven by the growth of renewable energy technologies and, on the supply side, by the evolution of technical capabilities, the prospect of deep seabed mining has renewed attention. The exploitable resources of the deep seabed could be worth $20 trillion to $30 trillion, considering current metal prices[31]. At the same time, the growing understanding of the deep seabed has increased the awareness for the environmental risks of mining activities. Once considered an empty expanse, we now know that the deep ocean contains one of the largest reservoirs of biodiversity left on Earth, while, at the same time, deep seabed habitats show high vulnerability to human activities[32].

Although the commercial exploitation has not yet occurred and the proponents of seabed mining consider the risks to be minimal compared to the land-based counterpart[33], the conclusion of seabed disturbance experiments – namely the German project DISCOL (Disturbance and Recolonization Experiment)[34], the MiningImpact project of the JPI initiative (Joint Programming Initiative Healthy and Productive Seas and Oceans)[35] and the EU-funded project MIDAS (Managing Impacts of Deep Sea Resource Exploitation)[36] – are worrying. The key conclusions of these projects were: The impact of offshore mining is expected to be on the form of sediment 'plumes' of an as yet unknown size, turbidity in the water column and addition of bottom sediments to the surface. Mining at sea may result in the emission of toxic materials into the ocean or the discharge of fine particulate material that can smother benthic communities. Another concern is, whether mining will harm or sever genetic links between different populations of deep sea animals. With regard to the longevity of impacts following the cessation of mining, it was found that seafloor habitats did not recover for decades following disturbance and concluded that it was likely that the effects of commercial mining would be evident for a longer timeframe. Against this background, the exploitation causes much greater environmental concerns than the exploration work.

a) Fulfilling the ISA's Mandate by Environmental Standard Setting

When UNCLOS was negotiated, the focus was on establishing a regime to regulate access to seabed minerals and the sharing of benefits from their exploitation[37]. Nevertheless, it was recognized that uncontrolled seabed mining could have adverse effects on the marine environment – as article 209 illustrates that requires the adoption of measures to prevent, produce and control pollution of the marine environment in the Area –, while the content of such measures was left to the future elaboration by the ISA: Article 145 expressly foresees the adoption of 'appropriate rules, regulations and procedures', in order to 'ensure effective protection for the marine environment from harmful effects which may arise from such activities', and article 17(2)(f) Annex III says that 'the rules, regulations and procedures shall be drawn up in order to secure effective protection of the marine environment from harmful effects directly resulting from activities in the Area or from shipboard processing immediately above a mine site of minerals derived from that mine site, taking into account the extent to which such harmful effects may directly result from drilling, dredging, coring and excavation and from disposal, dumping and discharge into the marine environment of sediment, wastes or other effluents'. These powers were complemented by the ISA's mandate regarding marine scientific research in the Area (article 143).

After an examination of the legal competences of the ISA (i.), the substance of its environmental standards regarding the exploitation of deep seabed minerals will be outlined (ii.).

aa) LAW MAKING AS THE ISA'S CORE COMPETENCE

Article 157(1) provides that the ISA is 'the organization through which States Parties shall, in accordance with this Part, organize and control activities in the Area, particularly with a view to administering the resources of the Area'. The ISA, which formally came into existence in 1994, has three principal organs and is served by two specialized bodies consisting of individual experts[38]. All states parties of UNCLOS are 'ipso facto members of the Authority' (article 156(2)). The principal organs are the Assembly – 'the supreme organ' (article 160(1)), composed of all members –, which elects the 36 members of the Council as the executive organ (article 162(1)) according to a complex formula (article 161), and finally the Secretariat (article 166). Furthermore, there are specialized bodies, such as the Legal and Technical Commission (article 165).

The function of the ISA is to regulate the way in which activities in the Area may be carried out. Activities in the Area are 'all activities of exploration for, and exploitation of, the resources of the Area' (article 1(3)). Prospecting only requires a notification to the ISA in respect of the sites, in which prospecting is to be conducted, while exploration and exploitation require specific authorization[39], since they shall be carried out by a qualified entity in accordance with a formal written plan of work drawn up in accordance with Annex III and approved by the Council after review by the Legal and Technical Commission; the plan of work shall be in the form of a contract between the ISA and the relevant entity (article 153(3)).

One of the primary competences of the ISA is its law making power[40]. UNCLOS requires the ISA to adopt 'rules, regulations, and procedures' for all activities in the Area (article 137(2)), which concretize the legal framework provided by UNCLOS. The ISA adopts two types of standards: regulations and recommendations[41]. The ISA regulations are significant, since they are legally binding on all member states, regardless of individual consent and without the possibility to opt out[42]; this binding status is provided for by article 137 and article 153(2). Furthermore, the ISA regulations are not only relevant to states but also to contractors. The application of the regulations to contractors is done by the way of the above mentioned contracts (article 153(3) and article 3(5) Annex III), respectively in the case of prospecting, the investor must provide a written undertaking that it will comply with UNCLOS and relevant rules, regulations and procedures of the ISA (article 2 Annex III). Thus, the ISA regulations become directly binding on investors, regardless of their integration into domestic law[43].

bb) THE MINING CODE

The ISA's standards that develop the legal framework of UNCLOS are commonly referred to as the 'Mining Code'. After the introduction of three sets of regulations for prospecting and exploration for polymetallic nodules, polymetallic sulphides and cobalt-rich ferromanganese crusts in 2000, 2010 and 2012 ('Exploration Regulations')[44], the current regulatory step, which started in 2014, lies in drafting regulations to govern the exploitation of the seabed mineral resources. From the outset it was clear that environmental protection will be amongst the most important elements[45]. In 2018, the Legal and Technical Committee issued the 'Revised Draft Regulations on Exploitation of Mineral Resources in the Area'[46], which aim at reducing the likelihood of environmental damage and provide compensatory measures:

The Draft Regulations identify applicable principles, particularly the need to apply the precautionary approach (Draft Regulation 2(5)(b)). Furthermore, they extend the environmental obligations of the states and the ISA to the contractors (Draft Regulations 46 and 47). However, referring to a standard of 'as far as reasonably practicable' Draft Regulation 47 introduces a more moderate approach with respect to the contractor. The general obligation of the contractor to protect the marine environment is specified by the obligation to generate environmental knowledge by submitting specific 'environmental plans' reflecting 'good industry practice' and 'best available techniques' (Draft Regulation 11 (1)(a)) – namely an 'environmental impact statement' (Draft Regulation 7 (3)(d) and Annex IV) and an 'environmental management and monitoring plan' (Draft Regulation 7 (3)(h) and Annex VII). In the post-authorization phase the contractor is obliged to monitor and report on the environmental effects of its activities on the marine environment and manage all such effects, implement all applicable mitigation and management measures to protect the marine environment and maintain the currency and adequacy of the environmental management and monitoring plan during the term of its exploitation contract in accordance with 'good industry practice' (Draft Regulation 49).

Lastly, the Draft Regulations introduce provisions regarding the ISA's compliance and enforcement competences and the liability of the contractor. For instance, in order to ensure credibility of the procedure of knowledge generating by the contractor, the Draft Regulations arrange different stages, at which the information is continuously subject to an external scrutiny ('performance assessment') by the ISA itself (Draft Regulation 50(3)-(5)) or by an independent competent person appointed by the ISA (Draft Regulation 50(5) and (6)) and the provision for publication and consultation with interest persons before key decision making stages (Draft Regulations 11 and 50(4)). When the Legal and Technical Commission concludes that the contractor has failed to comply, the ISA can issue a 'compliance notice' (Draft Regulation 8(a)) requiring remedial action or other steps. If the contractor fails to implement these measures, the ISA may suspend or terminate the exploitation contract (Draft Regulation 101(5)). Draft Regulation 49 foresees the establishment of an 'Environmental Liability Trust Fund'. The concept of a Fund was mooted by the International Tribunal for the Law of the Sea (ITLOS) Seabed Disputes Chamber in order to cover any environmental liability gap in cases where the sponsoring state cannot be held responsible[47]. Accordingly, a purpose of the Fund is the 'implementation of any necessary measures designed to prevent, limit or remediate any damage to the Area arising from activities in the Area, the costs of which cannot be recovered from a Contractor or sponsoring State, as the case may be' (Draft Regulation 53(a)). However, due to the limited knowledge a precise determination of a compensation amount seems to be difficult, and a further concern of compensatory measures is that, unlike land-based mining, restoration and rehabilitation might not be realistically feasible in the context of deep seabed mining[48]. Hence, a further purpose of the Fund is 'the funding of research into Best Available Techniques for the restoration and rehabilitation of the Area' (Draft Regulation 53(d)). Against this background, the term Environmental Liability Trust Fund seems to be misleading, since the Fund is not only addressed to close the liability gap.

b) CONCLUSION

In a nutshell, the ISA tries to draw an appropriate balance between economic development and environmental protection by using a 'flexible approach'[49], respectively an 'incremental approach'[50], which allows the continuous enhancement of the legal regime when better information is gained about the precise impacts of mining on the deep sea environment[51]. This is particularly reflected by the application of the precautionary principle[52]. Its application is an evolution since the conclusion of UNCLOS, as the precautionary principle was not an accepted principle of international law at that time, albeit taking into account that prominent international institutions, namely the ITLOS Seabed Disputes Chamber[53], have provided support for the adoption of the precautionary approach to seabed mining[54].

3. Conservation and Sustainable Use of the Marine Biological Diversity in Areas Beyond National Jurisdiction

a) Growing Threats for the Marine Ecosystems in ABNJ

Marine areas beyond national jurisdiction (ABNJ) are those areas of the oceans, for which no nation has the sole responsibility for management; these are the high seas and the Area[55]. In recent years, the international community has become increasingly aware of the growing and expanding threats to marine biological diversity in ABNJ, such as overfishing, overexploitation, pollution and also unintended impacts of anthropogenic activities, which lead to ocean degradation[56]. These threats are due to the fact that oceans are more and more a source of human, particularly economic activity[57]: Besides new activities such as bottom trawling on seamount ecosystems, there is an increased intensity of existing activities such as global shipping and traditional fishing techniques; furthermore, technological advance provides more opportunities to access new resources of the high seas and the Area as well as the use of geoengineering activities[58]. At the same time, an increased use of the marine environment might be expected as a result of the growing world population. However, the current regulatory regime is perceived not to be able to cope with this double challenge[59]:

b) Multiple Gaps of the ABNJ Governance Regime

In UNCLOS, there is no explicit reference regarding the conservation and the sustainable use of the marine biological diversity in ABNJ as such. However, it establishes an expansive framework for the protection and preservation of the marine environment in Part XII, which aims to cover all areas of ocean space including ABNJ[60]. Especially, pursuant to article 192 the states have the general obligation to protect and preserve the marine environment; this obligation is unlimited in geographical scope. Part XII is complemented and expanded by specific provisions referring to the ABNJ, for instance by the articles 117–120 regarding marine living resources and by article 145 regarding the Area. Hence, UNCLOS does not contain jurisdiction gaps in a strict sense, but the implementing and enforcing of the UNCLOS framework provisions regarding the marine environment of ABNJ remains difficult due to the multitude of actors involved in its governance as well as to interpretive problems[61]:

The existing international conventions regarding the marine environment – such as the International Convention for the Prevention of Pollution from Ships and its Protocol (MARPOL), the Convention on the Prevention of Marine Pollution by Dumping of Wastes and Other Matter and the 1996 London Protocol and recently the International Convention for the Control and Management of Ships' Ballast Water and Sediments – refer to areas in as well as areas beyond national jurisdiction, but they pursue a sectoral scheme, which is inadequate for addressing matters that fall outside or between the sectors[62]. An example for this problem is the discussion whether marine genetic resources in ABNJ are subject to the freedom of the high seas or whether they should be categorized as part of the Area and therefore part of the common heritage of mankind with the consequence that all states could benefit from the economic returns due to benefit sharing obligations. Marine genetic resources, which are a potential source for drug and medicinal use, consist of the genetic material of deep sea marine sponges, krill, corals, seaweeds etc. UNCLOS is silent on marine genetic resources, since, when the negations of the regime for the Area started, it was generally considered that the deep seabed was rich only in mineral resources[63].

Substantive gaps also exist in a geographical sense[64]: In contrast to UNCLOS, which is of universal coverage, the existing regional regimes regarding the marine environment, for instance regional fisheries management organizations, have a more limited geographical scope and leave large parts of the oceans uncovered, depending on the activity or species concerned.

UNCLOS recognizes the developments in international marine environmental law taking place in other international marine environmental regimes, as article 237 illustrates. Of most importance for the conservation of the marine biological biodiversity is the Convention on Biological Diversity (CBD). However, the CBD does not include a direct obligation of the contracting parties to conserve or sustainably use the components of the marine biological biodiversity in ABNJ[65].

An example for the difficulties that might arise from the abovementioned gaps is the issue of the so-called Marine Protected Areas (MPAs). MPAs are a feature of marine spatial planning and can be used to deal with multiple threats to biodiversity[66]. Hence, they are considered to prove an effective instrument regarding ABNJ by managing the different environmental concerns, such as overfishing, protecting species, conserving and protecting particularly valuable ecological marine areas or avoiding shipping-related disturbances[67]. However, unlike MPAs established under national jurisdiction, there is no authority that could provide oversight of a MPA in ABNJ; rather, their establishment demands multilateral cooperation, at global or regional level. This cooperation proves to be difficult: Establishing MPAs in ABNJ has been on the political agenda since the beginning of the 1990s. The international community has committed itself to establishing a representative network of MPAs by 2012[68]. However, this objective could not be achieved; there are only a couple of successful examples: In 2014, under the Convention for the Protection of the Marine Environment of the North-East Atlantic (OSPAR), together with the North-East Atlantic Fisheries Commission (NEAFC), a collective arrangement on cooperation and coordination on selected areas in the North-East Atlantic was adopted[69]. In 2017, the world's largest MPA in the Ross Sea entered into force[70]; a joint proposal by New Zealand and the United States, advanced through the Commission for the Conservation of Antarctic Marine Living Resources (CCAMLR), led to an agreement amongst the 24 state parties and the EU after more than five years of negotiations.

In a nutshell: Current discussions relating to the governance gaps of ABNJ concern two intertwined subjects: In particular, they concern a regime for genetic resources beyond the limits of national jurisdiction and, in general, the idea of a more integrated regime of environmental protection in ABNJ[71]. Hence, the main criticism is the patchwork of legal provisions as well as the regulatory and institutional gaps, since they seem to make the governance of ABNJ less effective than the governance of areas within national jurisdiction.

c) THE IDEA OF A NEW INTERNATIONAL LEGALLY BINDING INSTRUMENT

In 2004, the UN General Assembly created an 'Ad-Hoc Open-ended Informal Working Group' (BBNJ Working Group) to discuss the conservation and sustainable use of marine biological diversity in ABNJ[72]. In 2015, states took the historic step of agreeing to open negotiations for a new international legally binding instrument under UNCLOS[73]. For this purpose, a Preparatory Committee was established[74] and convened during 2016 and 2017 in order to prepare substantive recommendations on the elements of a draft text. The UN General Assembly decided that the negotiations were to focus on a package of issues[75], particularly marine genetic resources, measures such as area-based management tools including MPAs, environmental impact assessments and capacity building and the transfer of marine technologies. The process was not to undermine existing legal instruments and regulatory actors[76]; hence, the Preparatory Committee was open to all member states of the UN, members of specialized agencies, parties of UNCLOS and others as invited observers[77]. The Preparatory Commission reported to the UN General Assembly in 2017[78]. The UN General Assembly decided to convene an intergovernmental conference under the auspices of the UN that shall meet for four sessions, the fourth session taking place in 2020[79].

d) CONCLUSION

The effective conservation and sustainable use of marine biological diversity in ABNJ will remain a challenge. This underlines section B of the report of the Preparatory Committee that highlights all the elements, on which there is a divergence of views[80]. This refers not only to the from the beginning controversially discussed issue of the marine genetic resources[81], but also to the objective of an integrated governance regime for the ABNJ.

4. ILLEGAL, UNREPORTED AND UNREGULATED FISHING

a) IMPACTS AND DRIVERS

Approximately 75 percent of the world's fisheries are either over or fully exploited, mainly due to the so-called illegal, unreported, and unregulated fishing (IUU fishing)[82]. IUU fishing consists of a broad concept that encompasses numerous wrongful and illicit fishing capture activities[83].

IUU fishing has significant environmental, but also economic and social impacts worldwide. Namely, it is a threat to the health of fish stocks, and thus to food security for countries, which depend on fishing resources, and represents a source of damage to the biological diversity. Furthermore, it creates unfair competition with the consequences of the impoverishment of legal fishers, whose profits are harmed by the activities of IUU fishing, and of local traditional fishing communities. Studies conducted by the UN Office on Drugs and Crime identify the fisheries industry as vulnerable to international organized crime[84]. Furthermore, the International Labour Organization has expressed concerns about poor and forced labor conditions on board of fishing vessels[85]. Although IUU fishing is conducted everywhere around the world, its effects vary region by region, particularly affected are developing countries[86].

The Committee for Fisheries of the Organisation for Economic Co-operation and Development (OECD) recently completed a major study, making sure that all underlying causes of IUU fishing have been correctly identified, in order to select the most appropriate solutions to the problem[87]. According to the OECD report, people engage in IUU activities primarily due to economic incentives: 'IUU fishing persists because it pays'. On a deeper analysis, the report identifies two major forces that drive IUU fishing[88]: Firstly, overcapacity, ineffective management, poor living conditions as well as subsidies are identified as four of the economic and social causes of IUU fishing. Secondly, the international regulatory framework is incomplete and inadequately applied, so that certain fishing activities are beyond the reach of effective regulations. However, when the risk of getting caught is low, and the proceeds from the crime exceed the consequence of the unlawful act, the offender is more likely to engage in non-compliant behavior[89]. This second, institutional factor of IUU fishing will be dealt with in the following:

b) International Framework for the Exploitation and Conservation of Marine Living Resources

aa) Institutional Weakness of the UNCLOS's Fisheries Regime

In its preamble, UNCLOS recognizes the aim of promoting the conservation of marine living resources[90]. An important component is the establishment of 200 mile economic zones (EEZs), articles 55–75. The regime of the EEZs recognizes the sovereign rights of coastal states in conserving and managing the living resources in the zone (Part V). Coastal states are subject to the basic duties of ensuring that their fisheries resources therein are not endangered by overexploitation, article 61(2), and promoting the objective of optimum utilization of such resources, article 62(2). Pursuant to article 73(1), they can arrest ships and crews for breaches of national conservation and management standards in the EEZ. A key principle of UNCLOS regarding the high seas is that nationalists of all states have the right to fish there, article 116. However, flag states are required to fulfill three general obligations: to adopt measures for the conservation of the living resources of the high seas, to ensure that the nationals of the states adhere to those measures and the third is to cooperate with other states (article 117 and article 118). Further significant provisions relate to the cooperation of states in order to manage transboundary stocks (articles 63, 63, 66 and 118).

The traditional approach of UNCLOS to the conservation of marine living resources comprises limitations in several aspects[91]. A crucial weak point is that it is primarily based upon the 'nationality orientated approach'[92], since it is for the flag states and as a result of the concept of an extended EEZ for the coastal states to take measures falling under their jurisdiction[93]. Therefore, the effectiveness of this international regime depends on the degree to which states comply with it. A central root causing IUU fishing is a lack of effective flag state control; vessels flying a so-called flag of convenience are prone to be engaged in IUU fishing, as this enables them to circumvent regulations[94]. Furthermore, the IUU fishing takes advantage of corrupt administrations and exploits weak management regimes, in particular those of developing countries, which lack the capacity and resources for effective monitoring, control and surveillance[95]; as a consequence, there are are different levels of fisheries regulations, which may limit the detection of IUU activities, increase revenue and lower cost for perpetrators[96].

bb) INTERNATIONAL FISHERIES INSTRUMENTS

The resulting overfishing prompted the development of legal and voluntary instruments. The Food and Agriculture Organization of the United Nations has been at the forefront of these international efforts to address IUU fishing:

Regarding binding instruments, of particular relevance are the Fish Stocks Agreement, the Agreement to Promote Compliance with International Conservation and Management Measures by Fishing Vessels on the High Seas and the Agreement on Port State Measures to Prevent, Deter, and Eliminate Illegal, Unreported, and Unregulated Fishing. They all attempt to strengthen the exercise of flag state jurisdiction while imposing a variety of obligations on the flag state to actually exercise its rights respectively they include port state inspections of third state vessels in order to reduce the incentives to engage in IUU fishing. However, their conventional nature means that they are not binding on states, which do not consent to be bound by them[97], or – with regard to port state control – their effectiveness depend on the number and the force of the respective port states.

The International Plan of Action to Prevent, Deter and Eliminate Illegal, Unreported and Unregulated Fishing (IPOA-IUU), adopted in 2001, addresses IUU fishing by giving guidance on the implementation of the UNCLOS and the Fish Stock Agreement provisions. The IPOA-IUU is considered a comprehensive 'toolbox'[98], which contains a range of measures that can be used by states to address various manifestations of IUU fishing as well as a number of general responsibilities of states[99]. The IPOA-IUU is a voluntary instrument, which can give wider acceptance among states, but it might not have effects at the national level if it is not adopted by states, and not many states have effectively provided for the prevention, deterrence and elimination of IUU fishing in national laws[100].

In sum, the international fisheries instruments per se are not able to compensate the institutional weakness of UNCLOS and, therefore, they will not solve the problem of IUU fishing.

c) Market Related Measures: the Example of the EU IUU Regulation

A current development in the implementation of domestic measures against IUU fishing demonstrates a shift towards controlling IUU fishing at the points of market entry, including the imposition of import restrictions against fish and fisheries products obtained through IUU fishing[101]. This tendency shall be illustrated by the EU Regulation to combat IUU fishing, since the EU has not only made the most far reaching legislative efforts in this issue[102], but also the EU is the world's largest market for and leading importer of fisheries products[103], so that its regulation is considered to be an example par excellence. In contrast, the regional fisheries management organizations (RFMOs) have in place market related measures for some time, but it is not possible for them to act alone and to ensure that unlawful harvests are not laundered through non-RFMO states[104].

The EU IUU Regulation[105], which entered into force in 2010, applies to all landings and transshipments of EU and third country fishing vessels in EU ports and all trade of marine fisheries products to and from the EU (articles 1(3), 2 (5) and (8)). Its three core market related elements are examined in the following:

aa) Catch Certification Scheme

According to chapter III, the 'importation into the Community of fishery products obtained from IUU fishing shall be prohibited' (article 12(1)). The importation is only allowed regarding to fisheries products accompanied by a catch certification, which has been validated by the competent flag state and verified by the EU member states (article 12(2) and article 17). A valid catch document may also be issued by a RFMO (article 13(1)). It certifies that such catches have been made 'in accordance with applicable laws, regulations and international conservation and management measures' (article 12 (2)). The verification by the EU member states consists of 'examining the products, verifying declaration data and the existence and authenticity of documents, examining the accounts of operators and other records, inspecting means of transport, including containers and storage places of the products and carrying out official enquiries and other similar acts, in addition to the inspection of fishing vessels at port under the port states control' (article 17(2)). Only importers, who have been granted the status of approved economic operator, may advise the competent authorities of the member state of the arrival of the products and keep the validated catch certificate available to the competent authorities (article 16(2)). Criteria for granting the status of approved economic operator include, inter alia, the establishment of the importer on the territory of that member state, an appropriate record of compliance with the requirements of conservation and management measures and financial solvency (article 16(3)). However, port measures alone cannot effectively close off markets, since IUU products may circumvent port and first landing measures by passing through third party states[106]. Therefore, the EU IUU Regulation requires that indirect importation is also subject to the validation of a catch certificate (articles 14 and 15).

bb) THIRD COUNTRY CARDING PROCESS

Furthermore, the EU IUU Regulation aims at bringing third states to comply with their 'duties incumbent upon it under international law as flag, port coastal or market State, to take action to prevent, deter and eliminate IUU fishing' (article 31(3)). For this reason, the EU establishes a list of 'non-cooperating third countries', which is published (articles 33 and 35). On the basis of this list, the EU IUU Regulation has established the so-called third country carding process: Countries identified as having inadequate measures in place to combat IUU fishing may be issued with a formal warning, article 33(2) (pre-identification or 'yellow card'). If they fail to do so, they face different measures, particularly having their fish banned from the EU market, article 38 (identification and listing or 'red card'). If they make the required improvements, they are delisted, article 34 (lifting the pre-identification or 'green card'). In order to assess, whether the national systems are in place to combat IUU fishing, the Commission enters into dialogue with third-country authorities considering the following criteria (article 31(4)-(6)): the ratification of international instruments and participation in regional and multilateral cooperation, including membership of RFMOs and compliance with RFMO conservation and management measures, cooperation with the EU regarding IUU fishing, the specific constraints of developing countries and existing capacity of their competent authorities.

To date, twenty-five countries have received 'yellow cards' to improve their fisheries management, of which several have undertaken robust reforms and been delisted, while six countries have been issued with a 'red card'[107].

cc) IUU VESSEL LISTING

Pursuant to article 27 an IUU vessel list shall be established, which includes information on fishing vessels that have engaged in IUU fishing. It also includes IUU vessels listed by RFMOs (article 30). The IUU list shall be published (article 29(2)) in the spirit of 'naming and shaming'; furthermore, a range of measures shall be applied to vessels included in the IUU vessel list that aim to sanction IUU fishing. These measures encompass economic sanctions such as confiscation of catches and fishing gear, prohibition of the exportation and re-exportation of fishery products, denial of port access and provisioning (article 37).

d) CONCLUSION

Since the international regulatory framework regarding sustainable fishing is inadequately applied, certain fishing activities are beyond the reach of regulation. The difficulties of reinforcing the obligations of the states under UNCLOS to fight against IUU fishing have generated increasing interest in the exploration of other compliance measures, most notably market related measures, which are beginning to supplant flag state implementation in the pursuit of eliminating IUU fishing. The EU IUU Regulation seems to be particularly important, since the catch certification and verification requirements together with the threat of economic sanctions under this regulation are considered to have significant impacts on IUU fishing due to the economic power of the EU; especially, it is acknowledged that one of its greatest achievements has been to encourage improvements in fisheries management standards in third countries by its carding system; the countries themselves have stated that the carding process is a strong incentive to align their national policies and legislation with international law and to ensure best possible performance[108], even if potential for further improvements remains[109]. Furthermore, the EU IUU Regulation can support the measures of RFMOs against IUU fishing[110].

C. ELABORATING THE LEGAL FRAMEWORK OF UNCLOS

I. TECHNIQUES OF UNCLOS

UNCLOS does not know formal provisions for the adoption of further protocols and annexes[111]; instead, it influences the further regulatory process by compensating for the lack of substantive rules in a twofold way[112]:

1. DELEGATION TO INTERNATIONAL ORGANIZATIONS

Firstly, it provides for norms, which determine who is competent to issuing substantive standards and enforcing them. This technique is applied in the deep seabed mining regime that delegates the task of standard setting to the ISA (article 145).

2. OBLIGATION OF STATES TO COOPERATE

Secondly, UNCLOS imposes on all state parties the duty to cooperate. Regarding the protection and preservation of the marine environment article 197 includes the general obligation to cooperate. This cooperative approach underlies the idea of a new legally binding instrument regarding the conservation and the sustainable use of the marine biological diversity in ABNJ. In this sense, article 311 even foresees that state parties continue to regulate their relations through subsequent treaties. Notwithstanding its unilateral character, the EU expressively refers to international cooperation regarding its actions against IUU fishing[113]. Particularly, it addresses 'non-cooperating third countries' (article 31), which are states with poor records of compliance, and subjects them to process of notification and persuasion. Furthermore, it supports the measures of RFMOs against IUU fishing, for instance by including IUU vessels listed by RFMOs in the EU IUU list (article 30). By this means, the EU IUU Regulation stimulates international cooperation.

II. VARIETY OF INSTRUMENTS

1. STANDARD SETTING

Regarding the deep seabed mining regime the primary function of the common heritage of mankind principle is the development of environmental standards by the ISA that concretize the UNCLOS framework provisions. Secondary law making by international organizations is a common means to continuously enhance an international legal regime[114]. The reason for the importance of standard setting by the ISA lies in the lack of experience with deep seabed mining at the time of the negotiations of UNCLOS. However, due to the still existing knowledge gaps concrete standards for exploitation are hardly possible; instead and in the light of the precautionary approach, the so-called Mining Code of the ISA prioritizes the establishment of regulatory structures enabling knowledge generation over the time.

2. IMPLEMENTATION AGREEMENTS

The initiative to negotiate a new legally binding instrument regarding the conservation and sustainable use of the marine biological diversity in ABNJ has to been seen in the context of the so-called implementation or implementing agreements[115]. The notion of implementation agreement is generally used in academic literature and in state practice to describe methods that enhance the effectiveness of an international treaty, particularly when the original international treaty needs evolution over time[116]. Similar to protocols to a framework convention these implementation agreements interpret, amplify and develop the existing framework provisions; however, they remain open to signature, whereas traditional amendments and revisions are normally confined to the parties of the original treaty[117]. Accordingly, the importance of implementation agreements lies in their ability to offer comprehensive solutions for problems that are identified within a framework convention. It is for this reason why the UN is an appropriate forum for the conclusion of implementation agreements[118]. The implementation agreements that have been concluded on the law of the sea since the adoption of UNCLOS are the 1994 Agreement Relating to Part XI, which main objective was to achieve as wide a participation in UNCLOS as possible, and the 1995 UN Fish Stocks Agreement, which is intended to enhance the implementation of UNCLOS provisions in particular regarding the managing and conservation of straddling and highly migratory fish stocks by arranging a mechanism for cooperation, especially through regional and sub regional fisheries organizations[119]. Typical for the intended new legally binding instrument regarding the ABNJ is that it does not only refer to a separable element, such as the Area or the managing and conservation of straddling and highly migratory fish stocks, but addresses a number of cross-cutting issues.

3. COMPLIANCE MECHANISMS

In respect to the IUU fishing, elaborating the legal framework means dealing with non-compliance of states with its UNCLOS obligations[120]. Since UNCLOS leaves out the fundamental concern of non-compliance, defining adequate compliance tools is the major challenge. In general, the trends in means and techniques to induce compliance with international agreements show a very complicated picture; in international environmental law, 'economic instruments' are popular, that is to say instruments, which create economic advantages or disadvantages as a consequence of compliance or non-compliance[121]. The international fisheries law follows this approach by using market related measures, such as the EU IUU Regulation.

III. LEGAL CHALLENGES

1. DEMOCRATIC LEGITIMACY

The ISA has unusual far-reaching law making powers by adopting standards, which are legally binding to states as well as to individuals. However, the more power an international institution has and the more its decisions refer to important areas of policy, the greater the reservations regarding its democratic legitimacy are[122].

The legally binding nature of the ISA regulations exists despite the fact that – although the law making power is formally vested in the Council (article 162(2)(o)(ii)) – the Council does not act alone in formulating the Mining Code. Instead, the environmental regulations are drafted by the Legal and Technical Commission and are adopted by the Council, in which only 36 member states have a vote[123]. Moreover, there is an option to adopt the regulations by a two-thirds majority (article 159(8)). Transparency and public opinion are initially not reflected in the current institutional architecture of the ISA[124]; for instance, the Legal and Technical Commission's meetings are closed in general. However, transparency and public opinion seem to be important in all levels of the ISA's decision making process, especially with respect to determining what levels of risk and harm may be deemed acceptable. Therefore, the ISA's law making power has been described as 'an unprecedented experiment in international law-making', which, particularly with the transition from mineral exploration to exploitation, raises concerns regarding its legitimacy[125].

However, although in comparison to the practices of other international maritime-related institutions the ISA's practices have been considered to be expandable[126], there is much to be optimistic, since the process of drafting the Mining Code demonstrates the ISA's efforts to fill the gap by including elements of transparency and public participation[127]. For instance, the ISA has initiated 'stakeholder surveys' concerning the development of regulations for the exploitation of seabed minerals[128]. In 2017, the ISA's Internal Review Committee recommended that the ISA should adopt a policy of transparency, particularly in respect of the Legal and Technical Commission, which should be encouraged to hold more open meetings in order to allow for greater transparency in its work[129]. These efforts illustrate that in the process of the implementation of the common heritage of mankind principle the time for legitimacy concerns has clearly arrived.

2. META GOVERNANCE

A key challenge of implementation agreements is how they can be conceived of within the original international treaty and the wider landscape of international law[130]. In article 311, UNCLOS only regulates its prevalence in relation to other international treaties in a general fashion by, inter alia, procedural provisions and the safeguarding of its main principles.

The special feature of the 1994 Agreement Relating to Part XI is that it is intended to modify UNCLOS (article 2) and therefore 'disapplies' several UNCLOS provisions[131]; however, the respective negotiations began before the entry into force of UNCLOS and contributed to form a common interest of the international community, which in turn brought acceleration of the ratification and accession to the convention. The 1995 UN Fish Stocks Agreement only complemented the general rules in UNCLOS by providing specific rules regarding the management of straddling fish stocks (article 2)[132].

According to the mandate of the UN General Assembly, the new legally binding instrument regarding the ABNJ should be 'fully consistent with the provisions of the United Nations Convention on the Law of the Sea' (paragraph 6) and the new legal instrument should not 'undermine existing relevant legal instruments and frameworks and relevant global, regional and sectoral bodies' (paragraph 7)[133]. However, the governance of the ABNJ is not about simple normative conflicts, but goes beyond it, since the promoting of an enhanced coordination between a multitude of actors and legal instruments is needed. Therefore, the key issue to be faced in the upcoming negotiations is how this new instrument can be situated within a highly fragmented legal and institutional landscape[134]. It seems to be essential that the future agreement builds upon existing experiences, for example the OSPAR initiative regarding MPAs[135], and, in this sense, focuses on providing a global platform for ensuring coherence, cooperation and compliance.

3. UNILATERALISM

By putting international guidelines into action and sharpening them, the EU IUU Regulation is considered to provide an effective instrument that subjects the world's main fisheries product consumer bloc to its provision[136]. Hence, the example of the EU IUU Regulation illustrates that instead of consensus negotiations unilateral action can provide an adequate way to fill regulatory gaps. Accordingly, unilateral actions do not necessarily mean revolution, but they can contribute to evolution[137]. Therefore, the EU IUU Regulation clearly shows that the effective further development of UNCLOS depends not primarily on the formal status of actors, but is related to their ability to regulate.

However, the EU IUU Regulation raises questions regarding the legitimacy of the EU's extraterritoriality[138]. Though the consistency of the EU IUU Regulation with existing international instruments and measures combating fishing as well its compatibility with trade law agreements have been examined elsewhere and could mostly be confirmed[139], significant concerns remain, particularly with respect to the rights and obligations to the respective third states and to the respective individuals[140]. To give an example for the latter problem: The inclusion of a fishing vessel on the EU IUU list has been subject to challenge on the basis that, inter alia, there were infringements of the principle of 'audi alteram partem', as the vessel was included automatically in the EU IUU list following its inclusion in the IUU list of the Inter-American Tropical Tuna Commission without procedural requirements being observed to ensure that the party concerned was heard and although the Inter-American Tropical Tuna Commission would have exceeded its powers[141].

However, the question what should and could be done against such forms of unilateralism from a legal point of view remains unclear. The problem is that such forms of unilateralism do not offer exclusive benefits for the regulating state, but are motivated by global concerns, as for instance the sustainable managing of fishing; since they can act as an impetus for action at the international level, they can even appear welcome as a contribution to the solution of global problems. Furthermore, on a strictly formal level such unilateral activity is legally unobjectionable, as the consensual process provided for under international law for cross-border cooperation is complied with.

According to one approach, national states that act 'as trustees of humanity' are under an obligation to take into account the negative effects of their internal decisions on those outside the boundaries of the state[142]. It remains doubtful, whether such a general obligation to take account is an appropriate means to protect the interests of third states and foreigners. Instead, one should consider an obligation to establish provisions that effectively compensate for the negative consequences for third states and foreigners[143].

D. CONCLUSION

It could be illustrated that UNCLOS acknowledges the value of global governance by forming a stable, but at the same time flexible framework, which allows the different actors to put their aims into concrete terms, in order to address emerging environmental issues relating to the oceans. Furthermore, international standards, implementing agreements and compliance mechanisms could be identified as three important instruments, which fill the voids of UNCLOS. However, these instruments in turn leave legal voids, such as the lack of democratic legitimacy, coordination problems and threats for the rights of states and foreigners by unilateral actions. Therefore, specific attention should be paid to progressively fill these legal voids.

NOTES

1 United Nations Convention on the Law of the Sea adopted on 10 December 1982 and entered into force on 16 November 1994, 1833 UNTS. 397.

2 See the preamble of UNCLOS, last paragraph ('Affirming that matters not regulated by this Convention continue to be governed by the rules and principles of general international law') and International Legal Materials 1261 (1982).

3 UN General Assembly, A/RES/64/71, preamble.

4 Aust, Modern Treaty Law and Practice, third edition, 2013, p. 111.

5 Palmer, New ways to make international environmental law, American Journal of International Law 86 (1992), pp. 259, 274.

6 Tietje, The Changing Legal Structure of International Treaties as an Aspect of an Emerging Global Governance Architecture, German Yearbook of International Law 42 (2000), pp. 26, 38. Gehring, Dynamic International Regimes, 1994.

7 Beyerlin/Marauhn, International Environmental Law, 2011, p. 119.

8 Similar to the WTO system, see for the WTO agreements, Tietje, The Changing Legal Structure of International Treaties as an Aspect of an Emerging Global

Governance Architecture, German Yearbook of International Law 42 (2000), pp. 26, 37, 47.

9 Boyle, Further Development of the Law of the Sea Convention: Mechanisms for Change, The International and Comparative Law Quarterly 54 (2005), pp. 563, 564; Kojima/Vereshchetin, Implementation Agreements, in: Max Planck Encyclopedia of Public International Law [MPEPIL]; March 2013, para. 9.

10 Cassese, International Law, 2nd edition, 2005, p. 493; Ott, Umweltregime im Völkerrecht, 1998, pp. 286–287; Palmer, New ways to make international environmental law, American Journal of International Law 86 (1992), pp. 259, 274.

11 See in particular the 1992 Framework Convention on Climate Change.

12 Regarding the framework-protocol model: Beyerlin/Marauhn, Law-Making and Law-Enforcement in International Environmental Law after the 1992 Rio Conference, 1997, pp. 28–33; in general Matz-Lück, Framework Agreements, in: Max Planck Encyclopedia of Public International Law [MPEPIL], February 2011, para. 2. The 1992 Framework Convention on Climate Change, for instance, requires further negotiations of more detailed provisions by the adoption of protocols (article 17), for instance the 1987 Montreal Protocol and the 1995 Kyoto Protocol. The Convention on Biological Diversity makes no explicit reference to its framework character, however according to its article 28 it provides for the adoption of protocols to achieve the convention's objectives.

13 The simplified amendment procedure of article 313 UNCLOS is not considered to be time-saving, Harrison, Making of the Law of the Sea, 2011, pp. 67.

14 Harrison, Making of the Law of the Sea, 2011, p. 70; in contrast, see for amendments regarding international environmental conventions for example article 21 Kyoto Protocol.

15 For instance article 7 1992 Framework Convention on Climate Change; in general Brunnée, Reweaving the Fabric of International Law? Patterns of Consent in Environmental Framework Agreements, in: Wolfrum, Developments of International Law in Treaty Making, 2005, p. 101, 102; Beyerlin/Marauhn, International Environmental Law, 2011, pp. 258, 259, 272.

16 The term is attributed to Tommy T.B. Koh, President of the Third United Nations Conference on the Law of the Sea, available under: http://www.un.org/Depts/los/convention_agreements/convention_overview_convention.htm.

17 Regarding the German constitution: article 79 Grundgesetz.

18 Harrison, Making of the Law of the Sea, 2011, pp. 284–292.

19 Article 311 goes further than a mere conflict clause, see Matz-Lück, in: Proelss, United Nations Convention on the Law of the Sea, article 311, paras. 1–3.

20 Harrison, Making of the Law of the Sea, 2011. He describes the international organizations and their specific role in the development of the law of the sea.

21 In this regard Boyle, Further Development of the Law of the Sea Convention: Mechanisms for Change, The International and Comparative Law Quarterly 54 (2005), pp. 563, 567.

22 Thistle, The deep-sea floor: an overview, in: Tyler; Ecosystems of the World, 28 (2003), p. 5.

23 Resolution 25/2749; the term is attributed to the Maltese Ambassador to the UN, Dr. Avid Pardo, see UN Doc A/C.1/PV1515.

24 Wolfrum, The Principle oft he Common Heritage of Mankind, Zeitschrift für ausländisches öffentliches Recht und Völkerrecht 43 (1983), pp. 312, 324. 332.

25 Bourrel/Thiele/Currie, The common heritage of mankind as a means to assess and advance equity in deep seas mining, Marine Policy 95 (2018), pp. 311, 314.

26 Fritz, Deep Sea Anarchy, International Journal of marine and costal law 30 (2015), pp. 445–453.

27 Rayfuse, Precaution and the Protection of Marine Biodiversity in Areas Beyond National Jurisdiction, International Journal of Marine and Coastal Law, 27 (2012), pp. 773, 778.

28 EU-MIDAS, Deep-Sea Mining: An introduction, available under: http://www.eu-midas.net/sites/default/files/downloads/Briefs/MIDAS_brief_Introduction_lowres.pdf.

29 Miller/Thompson/Johnston/Santillo, An overview of seabed mining, Frontiers in Marine Science 4 (2018), Article 148, available under: https://www.frontiersin.org/articles/10.3389/fmars.2017.00418/full.

30 https://www.isa.org.jm/mineral-resources/55. The manganese nodules are of economic interest due to their relatively high copper, nickel and cobalt content. In the case of massive sulphides the precious metals gold and silver and trace metals such as cobalt and selenium are of particular interest in addition to the non-ferrous metals, Wiedicke/Kuhn/Rühlemann/VinkSchwarz-Schampera, Deep-sea Mining – a Future Source of Raw Materials, in: Mining Report 151 (2015), pp. 318–332.

31 Boetius/Haeckel, Mind the seafloor, Science 359 (2018), p. 34.

32 With further references Jaeckel/Rayfuse, Conceptions of Risks in an Institutionalized Context, in: Ambrus/Rayfuse/Werner, Risks and the Regulation of Risks in international law, 2017, p. 163; Craig, Protecting the Oceanic Gardens of Eden, Georgetown International Environmental Law Review 13 (2001), p. 563.

33 See Nautilus chief executive Johnson, available under: https://www.theguardian.com/sustainable-business/2017/jun/28/deep-sea-mining-environmental-mistakes.

34 https://www.discol.de/de.

35 http://www.jpi-oceans.eu/ecological-aspects-deep-sea-mining.

36 http://www.eu-midas.net/science.

37 Fritz, Deep Sea Anarchy, International Journal of marine and costal law 30 (2015), pp. 445, 447.

38 The ISA also compromises the Enterprise. The Enterprise was intended to buy the mining technology from commercial operators or to enter into joint ventures with them. However, with the 1994 Implementing Agreement its role has been revised, see Schatz, in: Proelss, United Nations Convention on the Law of the Sea, 2017, article 159, paras. 8–10.

39 Tuerk, The International Seabed Area, in: The IMLI Manual on International Maritime Law, Volume I, 2015, pp. 276, 292.

[40] Harrison, Making the Law of the Sea, 2011, p. 122.
[41] Jaeckel, The International Seabed Authority and the Precautionary Principle, 2017, p. 145.
[42] Jaeckel, The International Seabed Authority and the Precautionary Principle, 2017, pp. 145–147.
[43] Harrison, Making the Law of the Sea, 2011, p. 123.
[44] Cai, Role of the International Seabed Authority in Global Ocean Governance, in: The IMLI Treatise on Global Ocean Governance, Volume I, 2018, 2.1.
[45] In detail Jaeckel, The International Seabed Authority and the Precautionary Principle, 2017, pp. 152.
[46] ISBA/24/LTC/WP.1, available under: https://www.isa.org.jm/document/isba24ltcwp1.
[47] Advisory Opinion on the Responsibilities and Obligations of states Sponsoring Persons and Entities with Respect to activities in the Area, Case No. 17, 1 February 2011, para. 205.
[48] Lodge, Sharing and preserving the resources in the deep sea, International Journal of marine and coastal law 32 (2017), pp. 427, 443.
[49] Harrison, Saving the Oceans Through Law, 2017, p. 246.
[50] Jaeckel/Rayfuse, Conceptions of risk in an Institutional Context, in: Ambrus/Rayfuse/Werner, Risks and the Regulation of Risks in international law, 2017, pp. 161, 168.
[51] See for detailed analyses the workshop related to the development of the Exploitation Regulations, available under: https://www.isa.org.jm/legal-instruments/ongoing-development-regulations-exploitation-mineral-resources-area; furthermore, Jessen, Advancing the Deep Seabed 'Mining Code', in: The IMLI Treatise on Global Ocean Governance, Volume I, 2018, 3.4. and 3.5.
[52] In detail Jaeckel, The International Seabed Authority and the Precautionary Principle, 2017.
[53] Advisory Opinion, Responsibilities and obligations of states sponsoring persons and entities with respect to activities in the area, Case No. 17, 1 February 2011, paras. 125–135. The Chamber extended its application even to activities outside the ISA mining regime by considering the precautionary principle as part of the general obligation of due diligence of the sponsoring states, ibid para. 131.
[54] See also UN General Assembly, UN Doc A/RES/58/240, 23 December 2003, para. 52.
[55] Warner, Conserving Marine Biodiversity in Areas Beyond National Jurisdiction, in: The Oxford Handbook of the Law of the Sea, 2015, p. 752.
[56] Scheiber, Economic uses of the oceans and the impacts on marine environments: past trends and challenges ahead, in: Vidas/Schei, The World Ocean in Globalisation, 2011, pp. 65, 66.
[57] Freestone, Sustainable Management of Ocean Ecosystems, in: Kotur/Matz-Lück/Proelss/Verheyen/Sanden, Sustainable Ocean Resource Governance, 2018, pp. 134.
[58] Du, An International Legal Framework for Geoengineering, 2016.

59 Ardron/Rayfuse/Gjerde/Warner, The sustainable use and conservation of biodiversity in ABNJ: What can be achieved using existing international agreements?, Marine Policy 49 (2014), pp. 98.

60 Warner, Conserving Marine Biodiversity in Areas Beyond National Jurisdiction, in: The Oxford Handbook of the Law of the Sea, 2015, pp. 752, 753.

61 Ringbom/Henriksen, Governance Challenges, Gaps and Management Opportunities in Areas Beyond National Jurisdiction, 2017, p. 90.

62 Mißling/Unger, Schutz und nachhaltige Nutzung der marinen Biodiversität in Gebieten jenseits nationaler Hoheitsgewalt, Zeitschrift für Umweltrecht 2017, pp. 338, 340.

63 See with further references Mossop, Marine Bioprospecting, in: The Oxford Handbook of the Law of the Sea, 2017, pp. 825, 836–839; Chiarolla, The Work of WIPO, in: The IMLI Treatise on Global Ocean Governance, Volume II, 2018, p. 10.

64 Ringbom/Henriksen, Governance Challenges, Gaps and Management Opportunities in Areas Beyond National Jurisdiction, 2017, p. 90.

65 Narula, Ocean Governance, Maritime Affairs 2016, pp. 65, 68–69.

66 OECD, Marine Protected Areas, 2017.

67 Wolf/Bischoff, Marine Protected Areas, in: Max Planck Encyclopedia of Public International Law [MPEPIL], November 2013, para. 4.

68 Agenda 21, adopted at the 1992 Rio Summit, (UN Doc. A/CONF.151/26 (Vol. II)) calls upon states to 'identify marine ecosystems exhibiting high levels of biodiversity and productivity and other critical habitat areas and to provide necessary limitations on use in these areas, through, inter alia, the designation of protected areas' (para. 17.85).

69 See Jakobsen, Marine Protected Areas in International Law, 2016, pp. 228–232.

70 https://www.ccamlr.org/en/organisation/ccamlr-create-worlds-largest-marine-protected-area.

71 Treves, Principles and Objectives of the Legal Regime Governing Areas Beyond National Jurisdiction, in: Molenaar/Elferink, The International Legal Regime of Areas Beyond National Jurisdiction, 2010, pp. 7, 16–26.

72 A/RS/59/24, para. 73.

73 A/RES/69/292.

74 A/RES/69/292, para. 1(a).

75 A/RES/69/292, para. 2.

76 A/RES/69/292, para. 3.

77 A/RES/69/292, para. 1(a).

78 A/AC.287/2017/PC.4/2.

79 A/72/249.

80 A/AC.287/2017/PC.4/2, para. 38(a).

81 According to Section B further discussions are required on whether the instrument should regulate access to marine genetic resources; the nature of these resources; what benefits should be shared; whether to address intellectual property

rights; and whether to provide for the monitoring of the utilization of marine genetic resources of areas beyond national jurisdiction.

82 FAO Fisheries and Agriculture Report No. 932, FIRF/R932, 2010, p. 12.

83 In detail Fuchs, Marine Living resources, International Protection, in: Max Planck Encyclopedia of Public International Law [MPEPIL], February 2015, para. 56. There is no generally accepted definition of IUU fishing, but paragraph 3 of the FAO International Plan of Action to Prevent, Deter, and Eliminate Illegal, Unreported and Unregulated Fishing (IPOA-IUU) can assist in identifying the relevant activities.

84 http://www.unodc.org/documents/human-trafficking/Issue_Paper_-_TOC_in_the_Fishing_Industry.pdf.

85 See https://www.ilo.org/wcmsp5/groups/public/--ed_norm/--declaration/documents/publication/wcms_214472.pdf; http://www.ilo.org/wcmsp5/groups/public/@ed_norm/@declaration/documents/publication/wcms_429048.pdf.

86 Agnew/Pearce/Pramod/Peatman/Watson/Beddington/Pitcher, Estimating the worldwide extent of illegal fishing, PLoS ONE 4 (2009), pp. 1–8.

87 OECD, Why fish piracy persists: the economics of illegal, unreported and unregulated fishing, 2005; see Le Gallic, An economic analysis of illegal, unreported and unregulated (IUU) fishing, Marine Policy 30 (2006), p. 689.

88 OECD, Why fish piracy persists: the economics of illegal, unreported and unregulated fishing, 2005, pp. 37. 79.

89 EU DG for Internal Policies, Illegal, Unreported and Unregulated Fishing: Sanctions in the EU, July 2014, p. 24, available under http://www.europarl.europa.eu/RegData/etudes/STUD/2014/529069/IPOL_STU(2014)529069_EN.pdf.

90 In detail Matz-Lück/Fuchs, Marine Living Resources, in: The Oxford Handbook of the Law of the Sea, 2015, pp. 491, 497.

91 Tanaka, The Changing Approaches to Conservation of Marine Living Resources in International Law, Zeitschrift für ausländisches öffentliches Recht und Völkerrecht 71 (2011), pp. 291–330.

92 Harrison, Making the Law of the Sea, 2011, p. 200.

93 Metuzals/Baird/Pitcher/Sunaila/Ganapathiraju, Handbook of Marine Fisheries Conservation and Management, pp. 165, 167.

94 EU DG for Internal Policies, Illegal, Unreported and Unregulated Fishing, July 2014, p. 25.

95 FAO, Report of the Expert Workshop to estimate the magnitude of illegal, unreported and unregulated fishing globally, February 2015, FIRO/R1106, p. 15, available under: http://www.fao.org/3/a-i5028e.pdf.

96 EU DG for Internal Policies, Illegal, Unreported and Unregulated Fishing, July 2014, p. 25.

97 See Harrison, Making the Law of the Sea, 2011, pp. 99, 208.

98 http://www.fao.org/iuu-fishing/international-framework/ipoa-iuu/en/.

99 FAO, Technical Guidelines for Responsible Fisheries, 2002, para. 16, available under: http://www.fao.org/3/a-y3536e.pdf; Palma/Tsamenyi/Edeson, Promoting Sustainable Fishing, 2010, p. 16.

[100] See the review of the FAO Committee on Fisheries on the progress of implementing the FAO Code of Conduct, paras. 9–29, ONLY 65 percent of FAO members responded to the questionnaire, para. 5, available under: http://www.fao.org/3/MX205EN/mx205en.pdf; see for new initiatives against IUU fishing: OECD, Review of Fisheries, 2017, pp. 26, 27.

[101] Calley, Market Denial and International Fisheries Regulation, 2012, pp. 103–160, in general Cooreman, Global Environmental Protection through Trade, 2017, regarding IUU fishing, part III. 6.3.

[102] Palma/Tsamenyi/Edeson, Promoting Sustainable Fisheries, 2010, p. 246.

[103] Recital 9 EU IUU Regulation in value terms: http://www.eumofa.eu/documents/20178/30530/The+EU+fish+market_EN.pdf; in general Damro, Market Power Europe, Journal of European Public Policy, 19 (2012), p. 682.

[104] Calley, Market Denial and International Fisheries Regulation, 2012, 125–159, 231.

[105] Council Regulation 1005/2008 of 29 September 2008 establishing a Community system to prevent, deter and eliminate illegal, unreported and unregulated fishing, OJ L 286, p. 1.

[106] Calley, Market Denial and International Fisheries Regulation, 2012, p. 225.

[107] https://ec.europa.eu/fisheries/sites/fisheries/files/illegal-fishing-overview-of-existing-procedures-third-countries_en.pdf.

[108] https://oceana.org/publications/reports/eu-iuu-regulation.

[109] DG for Internal Policies, Illegal, Unreported and Unregulated Fishing: Sanctions in the EU, July 2014, available under http://www.europarl.europa.eu/RegData/etudes/STUD/2014/529069/IPOL_STU(2014)529069_EN.pdf; Mundy, The impact of the EU IUU Regulation on seafood trade flows: Identification of intra-EU shifts in import trends related to the catch certification scheme and third country carding process. February 2018; EJF/OCEANA/PEW/WWF, The EU IUU Regulation, February 2016, pp. 12, available under: https://wwf.be/assets/RAPPORT-POLICY/OCEANS/UK/IUU-report-01--02--16-web.pdf.

[110] Calley, Market Denial and International Fisheries Regulation, 2012, pp. 227–228, 231–232.

[111] See above under I.

[112] See Beyerlin/Marauhn, International Environmental Law, 2011, p. 119.

[113] EU IUU Regulation, recitals 18 and 38.

[114] Ruffert/Walter, Institutionalised International Law, 2015, pp. 33–38.

[115] Matz-Lück, in: Proelss, United Nations Convention on the Law of the Sea, A Commentary, 2017, article 311 para. 1.

[116] Kojima/Vereshchetin, Implementation Agreements, in: Max Planck Encyclopedia of Public International Law, March 213, paras. 1, 2.

[117] Ibid, para. 9.

[118] Harrison, Making the Law of the Sea, 2011, p. 113.

[119] Part III of the Agreement, see Rothwell/Stephens, The International Law of the Sea, 2016, p. 343.

[120] As the terms 'illegal' and 'unreported' indicate, IUU fishing primarily refers to problems regarding compliance with existing regimes, effective control over a vessel's actions and enforcement jurisdiction or the lack of either, while the term 'unregulated' rather refers to a failure to install a regulatory framework by the respective state, as well as the question of how to deal with vessels without a nationality or non-party vessels under a regional scheme, see Fuchs, Marine Living resources, International Protection, in: Max Planck Encyclopedia of Public International Law [MPEPIL], February 2015, paras. 56, 57.

[121] 'Carrot and sticks': Bothe, The Evolution of Enforcement Mechanisms in International Environmental Law, in: Wolfrum, Enforcing Environmental Standards, 1996, pp. 13, 17–22.

[122] Wouters/De Man, International organizations as law-makers, in: Klabbers/Wallendahl, Research Handbook on the Law of International Organizations, 2011, pp. 190, 208–210.

[123] See article 165(2) (f-g).

[124] Jaeckel/Rayfuse, Conceptions of Risk in an Institutional Context, in: Ambrus/Rayfuse/Werner, Risk and Regulation of Uncertainty in International Law, 2017, pp. 161, 175.

[125] Bourrel/Thiele/Currie, The common heritage of mankind as a means to assess and advance equity in deep sea mining, Marine Policy 95 (2018), pp. 311, 316; regarding all levels of ISA's decision making: Christiansen/Ardon/Jaeckel/Singh/Unger, Towards Transparent Governance of Deep Seabed Mining, IASS Policy Brief 2/2016; Jaeckel, The International Seabed Authority and the Precautionary Principle, pp. 266.

[126] Ardron, Transparency in the operations of the International Seabed Authority: An initial assessment; Marine Policy 95 (2016), p. 324; Ardron/Ruhl/Jones, Incorporating transparency into the governance of deep-seabed mining in the Area beyond national jurisdiction, Marine Policy 89 (2018), pp. 58.

[127] See ISA, Developing a Regulatory Framework for Mineral Exploitation in the Area, July 2016, pp. 5, 7, Available under: https://www.isa.org.jm/files/documents/EN/Regs/DraftExpl/Draft_ExplReg_SCT.pdf; and Draft Regulation 2(5) (d), ISBA/24/LTC/WP.1.

[128] See https://www.isa.org.jm/legal-instruments/ongoing-development-regulations-exploitation-mineral-resources-area.

[129] ISBA/23/A/3, para. 26, recommendation 16.

[130] Kojima/Vereshchetin, Implementation Agreements, in: Max Planck Encyclopedia of Public International Law, March 2013, paras. 9–12, 17–19.

[131] Harrison, Making the Law of the Sea, 2011, p. 91.

[132] Edeson, Towards long-term sustainable use, in: Boyle/Freestone, International Law and Sustainable Development, 1999, p. 173.

[133] A/RES/69/292.

[134] Sceptical Treves, Principles and Objectives of the Legal Regime Governing Areas Beyond National Jurisdiction, in: Molenaar/Elferink, The International Legal Regime of Areas Beyond National Jurisdiction, 2010, pp. 7, 20–25.

[135] Molenaar/Oude Elferink, Marine protected areas in areas beyond national jurisdiction. The pioneering efforts under the OSPAR Convention, Utrecht Law Review 5 (2009), p. 5.

[136] Calley, Market Denial and International Fisheries Regulation, 2012, p. 228; OECD Review of Fisheries, 2013, pp. 119, 126: 'enormous potential'.

[137] Differently Boyle, Further Development of the law of the Sea Convention: Mechanisms For Change, The International and Comparative Law Quarterly 54 (205), pp. 563, 584.

[138] He, The EU Illegal, Unreported, and Unregulated Fishing Regulation Based on trade and Market related Measures: Unilateralism or a Model Law?, Journal of International Wildlife Law & Policy 20 (2017), pp. 168; Meunier/Nicolaidis, The European Union as a Conflicted Trade Power, Journal of European Public Policy, 13 (2006), p. 906. In general: Benvenisti, The Law of Global governance (2014), p. 72; Bodandsky, What's so bad about unilateral action to protect the environment?, European Journal of International Law 11 (2000), p. 339.

[139] Auld, Trade Measures to prevent illegal fishing and the WTO, World Trade Review 2017, pp. 1; Leroy/Galletti/Chaboud, The EU restrictive trade measures against IUU fishing, Marine Policy 64 (2016), pp. 82; Young, International trade law compatibility of market-related measures to combat illegal, unreported and unregulated (IUU) fishing, Marine Policy 69 (2916), pp. 209; Tsamenyi/Palma/Miligan/Mfodwo, Fairer Fishing?: The Impact on Developing Countries of the European Community Regulation on Illegal, Unreported and Unregulated Fisheries, 2009, Chapter 10; Tsamenyi/Palma/Milligan/Mfodwa, The European Council regulation on illegal, unreported and unregulated fishing, The International Journal of Marine and Coastal Law 25 (2010), p. 5; skeptical for states who have not agreed to relevant conventional cooperation obligations: Rosello, Cooperation and unregulated fishing: interactions between customary international law, and the European Union IUU fishing regulation, Marine Policy 84 (2017), p. 306.

[140] Tsamenyi/Palma/Milligan/Mfodwa, The European Council regulation on illegal, unreported and unregulated fishing, The International Journal of Marine and Coastal Law 25 (2010), pp. 5, 31; critical with regard to a potential proliferation of unilateral approaches Hosch, Trade Measures to combat IUU Fishing, 2016, p. 54.

[141] Seatech International and others v. Council and Commission, Case T-337/10.

[142] Benvenisti, Sovereigns as Trustees of Humanity, The American Journal of International Law 107 (2013), p. 295.

[143] See Meyer/Reiling, Extraterritoriale Inspektionen der EU, Archiv des Völkerrechts 55 (2017), pp. 414–443.

CHAPTER VI

THE DOMESTIC LAW OF THE SEA – AN OVERVIEW

Peter EHLERS, Nico NOLTE

A. INTRODUCTION

Discussions on the law of the sea usually refer to international law, while national law tends to be neglected. Completely wrongly, because the international law, as it is mainly characterized by UNCLOS[1], wins in practice its real meaning only through the implementation in domestic law and its enforcement.

I. DEFINITION AND SCOPE OF APPLICATION

Overall, law of the sea can be defined as the part of public law that concerns order, use and protection of the sea, whereas maritime law is part of private law regulating the relations between natural persons and private entities. In particular, the law of the sea covers maritime shipping, fishing and other uses of the sea, marine research and technology, and marine environmental protection. The law of naval warfare and the military use of the sea are conceptually part of the law of the sea, but here they are not taken into consideration. The domestic law of the sea deals with the organization, tasks and powers of the state and public administrations in the maritime sector.

From a spatial perspective the domestic law of the sea covers the area of the sea including the ocean. Also the so-called national maritime aquitorium[2] belongs to the sea area. According to the WaStrG[3] this is true for the German sea waterways, which cover the area between the coastline at mid-flood or the seaward boundary of the inland waterways and the seaward boundary of the territorial sea.[4] A similar, but not identical inward delimitation of the sea is contained in the FlRG[5] and the FlRV.[6] The WHG[7] distinguishes between coastal waters and surface waters. Coastal waters cover the sea between the coastline during medium high tide or the seaward limitation of surface waters and the seaward limitation of the coastal sea. As many important German seaports are not situated at the sea the spatial definition of the term "law of the sea" must be supplemented by functional elements. Accordingly the SeeAufgG[8] and the SeeSchStrO[9], when dealing with traffic rules and shipping police, do not differentiate between sea and inland waterways, but whether a waterway is navigated by sea-going vessels or inland waterway vessels. The navigable maritime waterways therefore also include the Kiel Canal and the river sections leading to the German seaports. For marine environment protection it becomes evident that necessary protective measures must not only be taken at sea. As marine pollution is crucially affected by land-based inputs, regulations are required that are primarily assigned to inland areas and cover other fields of law, such as immission control law, water law, waste disposal law, but have an impact on marine environmental law.

II. International and European legal basis

The domestic law of the sea is above all influenced by UNCLOS and the maritime conventions developed within the IMO[10] and the ILO[11] as well as by the marine environment conventions, and has in particular to take account of the rights and competences of states in the various maritime zones. According to UNCLOS the German territorial sea, in principle, has a width of 12 nautical miles, measured from the baseline or the low water line.[12] In the North and the Baltic Sea, an EEZ[13] has been designated,[14] which coincides with the limits of the German share of the continental shelf. To contribute to adequate international regulations Germany closely collaborates with other States in the IMO, the ILO, the OSPAR and Helsinki Commission[15] and other international maritime organizations.[16] Furthermore the national law takes account of numerous directives and regulations the European Union has adopted in particular with regard to maritime shipping[17] and marine environment protection.[18]

III. Basics of constitutional law

The GG[19] contains only very few regulations with a maritime reference. According to Article 27 GG, all German merchant vessels form one merchant fleet. The purpose of this historically substantiated regulation is to make it clear that the merchant fleets are not allocated to the individual Länder[20] and that it is the responsibility of the Federation to take care of the external affairs of the merchant fleet.[21] Article 73 (1) no. 5 GG assigns to the Federation exclusive legislation on treaties of commerce and navigation. In the area of concurrent legislation, the Federation has the right to legislate under Article 74 (1) GG for the following matters:

- the law relating to economic matters (no. 11), which also includes mining and, therefore, marine mining, as well as the energy industry,
- labour law (no. 12), i. e. also maritime labour law, as well as social security,
- deep-sea and coastal fishing and coastal protection (no. 17),
- maritime and coastal shipping as well as aids to navigation, sea routes and waterways (no. 21),
- waste disposal and air pollution control (no. 24), which is also relevant for marine environmental protection,
- protection of nature (no. 29), which also includes marine nature conservation,
- management of water resources (no. 32).

Administrative competence in law of the sea matters is based on the basic decision of Article 83 GG, which states that the Länder shall execute federal laws in their own right, unless the GG does not provide or permit otherwise. According to Article 87 (1) in conjunction with Article 89 GG the Federation administers the federal waterways through its own authorities and carries out those functions of maritime shipping, which are conferred on it by law. Article 87 (3) GG offers the possibility of establishing higher Federal authorities for matters on which the Federation has legislative power. As far as international law of the sea assigns certain rights and powers to coastal states, even outside their state territory, in particular with regard to the EEZ and the continental shelf, the GG is also applicable in these areas.[22] The application of specific laws can be taken for granted in the case of an explicit extension clause and otherwise if a corresponding legislative will can be assumed.[23]

B. MARITIME TRANSPORT LAW

I. GENERAL OVERVIEW

Maritime transport law is that part of the law of the sea that addresses shipping. A connecting factor for maritime transport regulations may be seen in the territorial principle, i.e., the provisions are applicable within the area of national jurisdiction for all ships irrespective of the flag they fly. This applies in particular to traffic rules. In other cases provisions are based on the flag state principle, i. e., they only apply to vessels flying the German flag. This is true in particular to ship-related requirements such as construction, design, equipment, manning and labour conditions. The right and the duty to fly the German flag are regulated in the FlRG and the FlRV. Proof that the conditions for flying the German flag are met is provided by the ship's certificate, the issuing of which is regulated in the SchRegO.[24] All ships flying the German flag are recorded in a flag register which is managed by the BSH[25] as the national flag authority. In addition, the size of ships is another important criterion for ship-related regulations. It is defined by means of tonnage measurement, which is tasked to the BSH[26] and based on the International Convention on Tonnage Measurement of Ships, 1969,[27] and is determined as a non-dimensional gross and net tonnage (GT/NT).

Basic maritime transport regulations are contained in the SeeAufgG, FlRG, SchSG,[28] SLG,[29] and the SeeUG[30] as well as in the port laws of the Länder. The SeeAufgG aims at conferring maritime functions on the Federation following the principle of facultative Federal power under Article 89 GG. The act mainly includes the conferment of functions, the assignment of responsibilities and competencies of Federal authorities, the authorisation for issuing ordinances, principles for levying fees, dues and charges and for the administrative prosecution of violations of maritime transport regulations. Though the SeeArbG, [31] which implements the Maritime Labour Convention,[32] in principle is to be assigned to private labour law, it also contains elements under public law. This includes i.a. the suitability for service at sea, the need of a crew list, powers of the master to maintain order and safety,[33] complaints of crewmembers, maritime labour certificates and flag state control by the BG Verkehr.[34] The German inland and sea waterways up to the outward limit of the territorial sea are administered and maintained by the WSV as part of the Federal administration.[35] The most important statutory source is the WaStrG, which regulates the transport function of the waterways. Everybody is allowed to navigate on the waterways in compliance with the relevant shipping and waterways regulations.[36] Waterways police functions for averting hazards for the navigable state of the waterways (Strompolizei) are assigned to the WSV.[37]

Only a few maritime transport responsibilities remain with the Länder. In particular, they are responsible for vocational training at school.[38] As part of the special ex parte jurisdiction, managing the ship register is the responsibility of the Länder by courts. The most important task of the Länder is the management of the ports, unless they are federal-owned ports of refuge. The tasks include economic issues, provision of infrastructure and port safety. In addition to the Länder, the Federation is also responsible for safeguarding of the seaports capabilities.[39]

II. MARITIME SAFETY AND SHIP-RELATED ENVIRONMENT PROTECTION

1. SHIPPING POLICE LAW

Shipping police, which is assigned as a federal task to be executed by the WSV, is defined as averting of dangers for the safety and easy flow of maritime traffic as well as the prevention of dangers and harmful environmental impacts emanating from maritime shipping.[40] Safety and easy flow of traffic comprises all measures enabling a vessel to participate in traffic without endangering herself or others and without any delay and interference. The term must be interpreted broadly, including the safety of the ship, cargo and crew in so far as it relates to traffic-related hazards, covering as well external hazards to the safety and security of shipping. As concerns the prevention of dangers and harmful environmental impacts measures can only be directed against ships in order to prevent dangers, whereas cleanup measures in case of a pollution incident in the territorial waters are part of the responsibilities of the Länder for water management.[41] In terms of space, the area of Federal responsibility for shipping police covers the sea waterways and the maritime navigable waterways, including some Federal ports.[42] Despite of the responsibility of the Länder shipping police measures can also be taken in ports, in particular in exercising port state control, with the aim to avert hazards outside the port area. Beyond the territorial sea a Federal responsibility for shipping police only exists, if permitted or required by international law.[43] In this area, shipping police measures are particularly relevant for ships flying the German flag. They can be directed against ships under foreign flag, if international law, in particular UNCLOS permits so.[44] In addition, the Federal police functions beyond the territorial sea also include the prevention of dangers and the removal of disturbances to public safety and order in other cases, when related to maritime traffic.[45]

In the event of a concrete danger, the responsible authorities of the WSV can take individual shipping police measures.[46] The most important measure is the shipping police order, which is an administrative act that is addressed to specific persons or to a specific group of persons and consists of commands or prohibitions.[47] If a responsible person can not be reached on time, measures can be executed directly by the police.[48] Under certain conditions, orders can also be directed against non-responsible persons.[49] Certain behaviours and situations abstractly harbour in themselves a hazard for the safety and easy flow of the traffic or the environment. In these cases, reporting requirements and the need for specific permits are set up.[50] If the navigable state of a Federal waterway or the safety or ease of traffic on a Federal waterway are affected by helplessly driving, stuck, stranded or sunken vessels or floating installations or by other driving or grounded objects, the authorities of the WSV can remove the obstacle themselves; the prerequisite is that an immediate intervention is required and a responsible person can not be called in time or will not effectively remove the obstacle.[51]

2. Maritime traffic regulations

To ensure proper behavior in maritime traffic, the KVR[52] has been issued to implement the International Regulations for Preventing Collisions at Sea, 1972.[53] These global regulations are supplemented by the SeeSchStrO, which applies on the German maritime navigable waterways and precedes the KVR. Another regulation is the SeeFSichV,[54] which sets out the duties of conduct in specific critical situations. Additional requirements are established in accordance with the relevant European legislation by the AnlBV[55] for vessels bound for, leaving, or operating in the internal German waters.

3. Ship safety law

Maintaining ship safety is in particular a matter of regulations governing the design, construction, equipment and operation of the ships, also including specific load line rules. The safety standards are set internationally by the IMO through conventions, such as SOLAS and LLC,[56] and supplementary codes and guidelines. Insofar as they are international generally accepted rules, they must be observed by ships under all flags.[57] The consistent and effective implementation of the international regulations is provided for by the SchSG, which aims at ensuring maritime safety, including labour protection, as far as related to safety, and environmental protection.[58] In particular, it clarifies which international, European and national ship safety regulations apply in detail. In Germany applicable generally accepted international rules and standards, other multilateral agreed rules, international guidelines and standards that must be taken into account when applying generally accepted rules and standards, European legal acts, and international safety standards, which are applicable as generally accepted rules of technology or good seamanship, are listed in the Annex to the SchSG. The act regulates the scope of application for ships under German and foreign flags,[59] obligations and responsibilities of the ship-owner, the master and other persons in charge,[60] and enforcement powers, including measures for controlling ships flying foreign flags.[61]

The SchSG is in detail complemented by the SchSV.[62] I. a. it sets up additional specifications for applying European and international safety standards,[63] and determines requirements for ships that are not subject to the international maritime safety regulations.[64] Competent authorities for the implementation and enforcement of the regulations are the Maritime Safety Department of BG Verkehr and the BSH.[65] In performing their duties they can use the assistance of recognised organisations.

In implementing European legislation[66] additional regulations for mandatory ship equipment are set up by the SchAusrV.[67] Items of marine equipment may only be placed on the market if, following a conformity assessment procedure, they are confirmed in a declaration of conformity that they comply with the product safety requirements. The procedure is carried out by notified bodies. The supervision of the notified bodies and market surveillance, i.e. the supervision of the placing on the market, installation, maintenance and use of the marine equipment, are the responsibility of the BSH.[68]

4. Dangerous goods law

In implementing the relevant international regulations,[69] requirements for the transport of dangerous goods are dealt with separately as part of the maritime safety measures because special regulations exist under the GGBefG[70] and the GGVSee[71] based thereon. Dangerous goods may only be carried on seagoing vessels if the relevant IMO standards and additional provisions relating to stowage and securing of packaged dangerous goods, transport documents and reporting duties are complied with. This also applies to seagoing vessels flying a foreign flag, insofar as they are within waters of German jurisdiction.

5. Safety requirements relating to seafarers

To ensure maritime safety, it is necessary that the ship's crew is sufficiently qualified and the manning is sufficient in qualification and numbers. Internationally, the qualification issue is regulated by STCW.[72] In implementing

STCW the training and education requirements are provided by the See-BAV.[73] The supervision of vocational training on board ships and the assessment of seafarers are the responsibility of the Berufsbildungsstelle Seeschifffahrt, [74] a private association, which is entrusted to perform sovereign functions. The competencies, proficiencies and other requirements for the issuing and withdrawal of certificates of competency, certificates of proficiency and other certificates for masters, officers and ratings are governed by the See-BV.[75] It specifies the types of certificates, which are issued by the BSH, and the requirements for their acquisition. The ordinance recognises the constitutional distribution of the Federal competencies for qualification of seafarers and the competences of the Länder for school education by accepting final school examinations as vocational aptitude tests, if specific requirements laid down in the See-BV are met. [76] The manning of a ship, as concerns master, officers and ratings is regulated by the SchBesV.[77] It no longer stipulates the manning in detail, as did earlier regulations. Rather, it determines that it is the ship-owner's duty to man the ship in such a way that with due regard to the number, competence and qualification of the crew members maritime safety, occupational safety, and the maintenance of public safety and order on board are ensured. The BG Verkehr issues a safe manning certificate, if these requirements are fulfilled.

Specific regulations exist for sport boats. According to the SpFV[78] a driving licence is required. After an exam the licence is issued by Deutscher Motoryachtverband[79] or Deutscher Segler-Verband,[80] which are entrusted to perform sovereign functions.[81] Additional qualification certificates for skippers are provided by the SpSeeSchV.[82]

6. Ship security regulations

In response to the events of 9/11/2001, SOLAS has been extended to include regulations to enhance security against external threats to ships and port facilities.[83] As far as ship-related measures are concerned, the regulations are implemented by the national implementation Act[84] and the SeeeigensichV.[85] The competent authority is essentially the BSH, assisted by BG Verkehr and recognised organisations. Security measures in the ports are determined by legislation of the Länder.[86]

As concerns measures against pirate attacks, the responsibility primarily lies with the Federal Police and the WSV,[87] in the context of international operations the Federal Navy is also involved. The use of armed private security services on board German ships is governed, in particular, by the Seeschiffsbewachungsverordnung,[88] the implementing ordinance issued thereto[89] and the SeeeigensichV.

7. CONTROL AND ENFORCEMENT EXECUTION OF MARITIME SAFETY REGULATIONS

In order to ensure that the maritime safety regulations are complied with, government officials are authorised to enter seagoing ships and equipment manufacturers' plants, and carry out inspections.[90] By an agreement between the Federal Government and the Länder[91] enforcement measures on the federal waterways are executed by the water police authorities of the Länder, acting as a "borrowed administration." This includes identifying imminent dangers to maritime safety and dangers arising from ships, monitoring compliance with the relevant rules, and controlling ship documents and certificates. The execution of shipping police enforcement tasks seaward the limitation of the territorial sea is assigned to the Federal Police and the Federal Customs Administration.[92] The compliance with ship safety, manning, occupational safety and environment protection regulations is essentially controlled in the ports by inspectors of BG Verkehr.[93] Port state control measures with regard to ships flying foreign flags are permissible according to international law of the sea. In numerous cases violations of maritime police regulations can be punished as administrative[94] or criminal offences.[95]

8. MARITIME SERVICES

The SeeAufgG assigns specific maritime services to the Federation, which are not of direct police character, but contribute significantly to maritime safety. This includes the provision of a search and rescue service required in distress,[96] based on the Convention on Search and Rescue Services.[97] This task since long has been performed by the DGzRS.[98] Quite important are the nautical-hydrographic services of BSH.[99] The German territorial waters and the exclusive economic zone are regularly surveyed in order to determine the available water depths, and searched for wrecks and underwater obstacles. The BSH publishes nautical charts and pilots, which contain important information for safe navigation in the respective area. The information is continuously updated by weekly notices to mariners. The tidal, water level and storm surge warning services, the ice information service and the geomagnetic service of the BSH are other important sources of information for shipping.

III. Marine Casualty Investigation

An obligation for marine casualty investigation is internationally established in the relevant conventions with the aim of ensuring maritime safety and counteracting marine pollution hazards.[100] These obligations are implemented by the SUG,[101] which takes account of supplementary IMO rules[102] and a relevant EU Directive.[103] The SUG provides for a clear separation between the actual finding of the causes of a casualty and the revocation of certificates as an administrative procedure against those being responsible.

1. Safety investigation

In the interest of maritime safety, including ship-related environmental protection and occupational safety insofar as it is inextricably linked to maritime safety, marine casualties and marine incidents are officially investigated.[104] The purpose of the safety investigation is to uncover any safety deficiencies in order to prevent future casualties by reviewing and improving existing national and international safety regulations, but not to apportion blame or determine liability. An investigation is carried out in the case of casualties or other marine incidents, when vessels flying the German flag are involved, the casualty site is in German territorial waters or the EEZ, or there is any other justified interest.[105] The official investigation is the responsibility of the BSU,[106] which is a higher Federal authority under the supervision of the Federal Ministry for Transport and Digital Infrastructure. It is free from any instructions regarding the initiation of an investigation, its content and scope, as well as the investigation report and the safety recommendations. In addition to its own staff, the BSU can use suitable private persons and experts as authorized auxiliary organs.[107]

The carrying out of an investigation follows the applicable international standards.[108] It takes precedence over all other technical investigations; the powers of the law enforcement authorities remain unaffected.[109] Authorized representatives of other states may participate in the proceedings.[110] The investigative powers include all necessary measures, in particular unimpeded access to the location of the casualty, seizure of evidence, inspection of documents, request of information, as well as hearing of witnesses and experts.[111] The results of the investigation lead to an investigation report, which must be elaborated while maintaining the anonymity of those involved in the casualty.[112] If possible safety recommendations should be made.[113] A safety recommendation must not lead to a presumption of guilt or liability for a marine casualty. The BSU should publish the report not later than 12 months after the marine casualty.[114] If urgently needed, the safety recommendations are issued even before the finalisation of the investigation. Where applicable, the IMO and the European Commission have to be informed. In case of marine casualties of particular significance and seriousness, an investigation chamber may be established to draw up the definite investigation report.[115]

2. ADMINSTRATIVE PROCEDURE AGAINST RESPONSIBLE PERSONS

In addition to the safety investigation the SUG provides for administrative measures against persons responsible on board with regard to their certificates.[116] For this purpose, a separate administrative procedure is foreseen, which is carried out by an investigation committee. A total of five committees, which have retained the traditional name of "Seeamt", have been set up as legally not independent parts of the GDWS[117] in Kiel, Hamburg, Rostock, Bremerhaven and Emden.[118] After a preliminary examination by the GDWS, whether there is an investigation interest,[119] the Seeamt decides as a panel with four members[120] after a hearing, whether a faulty behavior exists and whether a navigation suspension must be imposed or a certificate must be withdrawn.[121] A navigation ban shall be issued for a maximum of 30 months, if such a measure is necessary for the safety of navigation, because the person concerned does not possess the aptitude or the necessary sense of responsibility required to act as master or other responsible person. If this is not sufficient, a certificate can also be revoked permanently.[122] An appeal may be lodged against the decision and, if rejected, an action may be brought before the administrative court.[123]

IV. MARITIME PILOTAGE

The task of the maritime pilot is to support the ship's command in safe navigation with his special local and expert knowledge, especially in coastal areas with difficult fairway conditions and congested traffic situations. Efficient pilotage services are an important element of the maritime traffic safety system and of great public interest. This is taken into account by the SeeLG,[124] which is made up of a mixture of public-law and private-law provisions, and is supplemented by the ALV[125] and five District Pilotage Ordinances.[126] The establishment and maintenance of maritime pilotage, including supervision functions, are responsibilities of the Federal government, carried out by the GDWS.[127] Seven maritime pilotage districts have been set up to provide consistent, continuous pilotage services. The district ordinances oblige shipping to take a pilot when navigating in the district. In the districts, the self-government of pilotage is the responsibility of the LB[128] and the BLK,[129] which are corporations under public law.[130] The GDWS is responsible for the pilot stations and transfer vessels required to carry out the pilotage services, but has entrusted the BLK with the task, on which behalf the non-profit Lotsbetriebsverein[131] as a private entity carries out the task.

District pilots need a formal appointment by the GDWS. The number of candidates to be selected depends on the volume of traffic and the need for personnel. Candidates, fulfilling specific professional qualification requirements in addition to their physical and mental aptitude, must pass the training prescribed for the district and a final exam.[132] Pilots do not perform public functions, but exercise a freelance, non-commercial job.[133] The pilot gives advice to the captain, with whom the ultimate responsibility for the ship's command remains, but does not belong to the ship's crew.[134] The pilotage service is performed on the basis of a private contract concluded with the owner of the ship or another contracting entity. The district pilot, however, is not directly involved in the conclusion of the contract and has no influence on which ship he advises next. Rather, in this respect, the LB acts on his behalf with legal power of representation.[135] Liability to the ship-owner or another client for damages in the exercise of the pilotage activities is limited to intent and gross negligence. If claims of third parties are also subject to liability for damages of the ship-owner or any other contracting party, then the pilot is internally obliged to compensation only in cases of intent or gross negligence.[136] In the interest of traffic safety, the pilot must immediately inform the WSV of any observation concerning the safety of shipping or pollution and must report on every accident of a vessel which he has piloted.[137]

All pilots of a district are compulsory members of the LB. As a public corporation, it must, as part of its self-government, uphold and promote the interests of the pilot district. The extensive tasks include among others the internal operation of the pilotage services, and in particular the determination of the sequence of pilots for providing their services, the supervision of the professional duties of the pilots, the reception of the pilot remuneration for the account of the pilots, and the care for pension and illness provision.[138] All LB form the BLK, which is responsible for matters concerning the entirety of the fraternities.[139]

For the provision of the pilotage facilities[140], "pilotage fees" are levied from all ships navigating in a district, whereas for the service of the pilot a "pilot remuneration" is to be paid. The pilotage fees have to be calculated in such a way that their revenue does not exceed the public expenditure for the public tasks with regard to maritime pilotage. The pilot remuneration is to be sized so that the pilots have an income in accordance with their educational background and the responsibility of their profession. Fees and remunerations are collected by the GDWS in accordance with administrative enforcement law regulations.[141]

Pilotage services can also be offered outside the districts. This includes above all deep sea pilotage on routes outside the territorial waters of or to a foreign port. Pilots outside the districts require a licence to be issued by the GDWS.[142]

V. PROMOTION OF SHIPPING

Germany relies on extensive maritime trade and, therefore, needs an adequate, high-quality and efficient merchant fleet that is operated on a private-sector basis by economically sound companies. According to SeeAufgG[143] the Federal government is responsible for the promotion of the German merchant fleet, which is in the general German interest.[144]

For shipping to be operated successfully by private companies, it is necessary to generate sufficient income. This means that shipping under the German flag must be possible at comparable costs with regard to other flags. Since Germany is a high-wage country, in particular the wages on German ships are much higher than under other flags, amounting to disadvantages up to 65%. Above all, cost reductions are possible if only so-called "home wages"[145] are paid to foreign seafarers. The prerequisites for this have been created by establishing an International Shipping Register. In accordance with FlRG[146], ships under German flag operating in international transport can be listed in this register, which is run by the BSH as the German flag authority.[147] As a result, home wages can be agreed with foreign seafarers who are not resident in Germany.[148]

As an essential relief the taxable profit in the operation of merchant ships can be determined according to the ship's tonnage instead of the usual income tax principles.[149] The tax is based on the respective net tonnage, regardless of the actual income. In addition, shipowners may withhold 100% of the income tax to be paid by seafarers. The tonnage tax and the exemption from income tax serve to strengthen the international competitiveness of German shipowners in accordance with the comparable regulations in other countries. Additionally, ships under German flag are granted financial contributions by the BSH to mitigate their higher operating costs. The amount of the contributions is determined annually on the basis of the available public budget. At present, financial contributions are provided for non-wage labour costs for the employment of German and European seafarers on German-flagged ships[150] and for training subsidies on ships under German or another EU member state flag.[151]

Under certain conditions, the obligation to fly the German flag may be temporarily waived. If a ship is given to an operator (bare boat charterer), who is not German or does not have a German domicile or seat, for managing the ship in his own name, the use of a foreign flag may be temporarily permitted instead of the German flag, if this is allowed under the relevant foreign law.[152] The change of the flag is limited in time for a maximum of two years and can be repeated. During the temporary flagging-out the ship remains in the German shipping register and enjoys the privilege of the tonnage tax system.The approval of a temporary flagging-out depends on the condition that the disadvantages for Germany as an important shipping location, caused by the flag change, are compensated. This compensation can be achieved either through providing trainee positions for ship mechanics or officer assistants on the respective ship or by paying a compensation fee to the Stiftung Schifffahrtsstandort Deutschland,[153] which in turn supports training measures.

C. ECONOMIC ACTIVITIES AT SEA

In addition to maritime transport the seas, and in particular their living and non-living resources, are used for many other economic purposes. According to UNCLOS the right for using the seas depends on the different maritime zones.

I. MINING

The mining of marine mineral resources from the seabed or its subsoil, in particular oil, gas, sand and gravel play an important role as concerns the supply with raw materials. The main legal basis for mining is the BBergG.[154] It aims at managing and promoting the exploration, extraction and processing of mineral resources ensuring the safety of mining and strengthening precautions against risks arising from mining activities for life, health and property of third parties. The BBergG also covers the territorial sea and the German part of the continental shelf. Mineral resources in the area of the continental shelf are freely mineable resources.[155] A permit is required for exploration, and a license or mining propertyship for the extraction of mineral resources.[156] Permits, licenses and mining propertyship are subject to annual royalties, to be paid to the Land in which the field of a permit, license or mining propertyship is located, within the area of the continental shelf to the Land on whose coastal waters the field borders.[157] Exploration of the continental shelf and the territorial sea is inadmissible if it impairs nautical installations or signs, underwater cables, pipelines and marine research more than is unavoidable under the circumstances, or if it unreasonably impairs the use of shipping routes, shipping or fishing, or excessively endangers flora and fauna and water bodies as integral part of ecology.[158] For exploration and extraction of mineral resources, operation plans must be drawn up and approved by the competent authority. In the closure plan required for the termination of an operation, it is necessary to ensure the complete removal of the operational structures and facilities down to the seabed.[159] The establishment and operation of drilling and production platforms in the territorial sea and on the continental shelf require an environmental impact assessment.[160] The examination is to be carried out within the framework of a plan approval procedure.[161] Additional necessary protective measures are in particular regulated by the ABBergV.[162] The administrative tasks are the responsibility of the mining authorities of the Länder. This also applies to the continental shelf area.[163]

Mining in the Area, which means the seabed and ocean floor and subsoil thereof beyond the limit of national jurisdiction[164] is subject to a specific regime under UNCLOS.[165] Domestic regulations, which complement the rules and responsibilities of the International Seabed Authority, are set up by the MBergG.[166] The act particular contains access conditions, regulations on responsibilities, mining supervision activities as well as penalties and penal provisions. The administrative responsibility lies with the Landesamt für Bergbau, Energie und Geologie,[167] which acts, albeit an authority of the State of Lower Saxony, on behalf of the Federation as a "borrowed administration".[168]

II. PIPELINES AND CABLES

The laying and operation of pipelines and underwater cables on the continental shelf is also regulated by BBergG. For transit pipelines and underwater cables two licenses are required. Construction and operation of a transit pipeline needs approval from the competent Land mining authority[169] and additionally, as concerns the order of the use of the water above the continental shelf and the airspace above these waters, a further license from

BSH.[170] The reasons for refusal include the impairment of prevailing public interests, which shall be presumed to exist if nautical installations and signs, shipping, fishing, flora and fauna would be unjustifiably impaired, or underwater cables and pipelines as well as scientific research would be impaired more than is unavoidable under the circumstances, or if marine pollution is to be worried about or if the safety of the Federal Republic of Germany is endangered.

In accordance with the International Treaty for the Protection of Subsea Telegraph Cables[171] damage to subsea telegraph cables is prosecuted as an administrative offence, if masters and fishermen do not keep a certain minimum distance from laid cables.[172]

III. INSTALLATIONS AT SEA

Renewable energy generated especially by offshore wind power contributes increasingly to meet the energy demands and to reduce greenhouse emissions. According to UNCLOS coastal States are entitled to the right of energy production from water, current and wind in their EEZ.[173] Furthermore, they have the jurisdiction with regard to the establishment and use of artificial islands, installations and structures.[174]

The construction and operation of installations for the production or transmission of energy from wind requires a planning approval in accordance with WindSeeG.[175] BSH is the consultation and plan approval authority.[176] The procedure is governed by VwVfG[177] and thus also by the concentration effect, according to which the approval of the plan determines the admissibility of the project with regard to all relevant public interests. On the basis of the documents to be submitted, such as technical plans, analyses of the risk of collision between ship and wind turbine and an environmental impact study in accordance with WindSeeG in connection with UVPG[178], a plan may in particular only be approved, if the safety and easy flow of traffic and the security of national and alliance defense are not impaired, and if the marine environment is not endangered, in particular with regard to pollution and the migration of birds. Furthermore the plan must be compatible with existing and planned cables, offshore grid connections, pipelines and other lines, converter platforms and transformer substations.[179] In accordance with SeeAnlG[180] a planning approval is also required for installations for the production of energy from water or current as well as the transmission of energy from water or current.[181] For installations regarding other economic purposes or scientific research[182], a license is necessary.[183] BSH may establish safety zones in the EEZ around installations as far as this is necessary to guarantee the safety of shipping or of the installations.[184] Once the plan or license has expired, the installations must be disposed of; in this context a security deposit for the dismantling can be demanded.[185]

IV. SEA FISHERIES

The domestic sea fishing legislation is largely shaped by the Common Fisheries Policy of the European Union, which was already foreseen in the EEC Treaty of 1957. Under this fisheries policy, a large number of EU rules cover, in particular, sustainable management, equal access, permissible catch, technical catch limits, fisheries control, fleet structure, common market organization and international relations.[186] In the light of and in implementing EU law, the German maritime fisheries law is governed in particular by SeeFischG[187] and the SeefiV[188]. The spatial scope of application is the area seaward the delimitation of maritime shipping as defined by the FlRG and the FlRV. Including the EEZ the regulations also apply to fishing by vessels flying a foreign flag.[189]

If fishing at sea is restricted according to EU or domestic law, a fishing permit is required, which may be denied, if the available catch quotas have been distributed already, a foregoing permit has been significantly exceeded or facts justify the assumption that the applicant will not use the fishing permit himself. Furthermore the permit will only be issued if specific requirements for the fishing vessels are met.[190] A special permission is required, if fishing is carried out in the EEZ and in the territorial sea by fishing vessels not flying the flag of an EU member state, or carried out in the territorial sea by vessels flying a flag of a EU member state, unless they may claim a legal right according to EU fisheries law. In implementing and supplementing EU law, SeeFischV regulates further details on catch limits, fishing gear, the obligations of the captain of a fishing vessel and control measures.

The granting of permits and special permissions as well as the monitoring and the support of fishing activities seaward of the territorial sea are assigned to the Federation, executed by the BLE,[191] which also carries out the tasks of the fisheries monitoring center provided for in the EU fisheries law.

D. Marine Environmental Protection

I. Introduction

Marine environmental protection concerns above all so-called anthropogenic influences. On the one hand, these are pollutant inputs caused by human activities. However, besides pollution adverse ecological effects can also occur, for example, as a result of fishing (overfishing, bottom trawl fishing), aquaculture (fish farming) and mining as well as climate warming. The protection of the marine environment is dealt with here primarily from the point of view of pollution prevention, whereas nature conservation including biodiversity issues is only mentioned marginally. Marine pollution may be caused by land-based inputs either by direct discharges or via rivers and via the atmosphere, disposal of onshore waste and dredged material at sea, activities at sea, such as mining and energy generation, and by shipping. For most of the discharges the data is very incomplete. There are only rough estimates. It is clear, however, that land-based discharges are the most important source of pollution by far. In contrast, all other types of pollution are considerably less significant. Measures on the national level alone are not enough to prevent marine pollution, but international regulations are required,[192] which have to be effectively implemented and enforced by domestic law.[193] Depending on the source of pollution, the relevant law is assigned to different areas of law (water law, waste disposal law, mining law, shipping police law).

II. General protection obligations

In particular, the WHG contains comprehensive provisions for protecting the environment. Inter alia, they are designed to implement the WFD[194] as a most important regulatory framework for water protection, which also covers some marine waters, and the MSFD,[195] which aims directly at marine environmental protection. The WHG defines marine waters as coastal waters and waters in the area of the German EEZ and continental shelf, including the seabed and the subsoil thereof.[196] The waters must be managed in such a way that deterioration of the condition is avoided and good status is achieved by 2020.[197] The terms “condition” and “good condition” are defined in more detail. A “good status” of marine waters exists where they are ecologically diverse and dynamic, clean, healthy and productive, and used at a sustainable level.[198] Starting from an initial assessment, environmental targets have to be established and a monitoring program for ongoing assessment as well as a program of measures has to be developed.[199] Competent authorities for executing the measures are the Länder authorities as concerns the area of territorial waters, while for the EEZ the competence of Federal authorities can be regulated by ordinance, which has not yet been done.[200]

III. LAND-BASED POLLUTION

The WHG is the most important national legal basis for avoiding inputs in rivers and direct discharges into the sea. Accordingly, using a water body, including the introduction and discharge of substances, requires specific permission,[201] which must be refused if damaging changes are to be expected; moreover, the granting of permissions is subject to due discretion.[202] Banning of the marketing and the use of hazardous substances is regulated by the ChemG.[203] Further important legal bases are provided by the AbwAG,[204] the BImSchG,[205] the PflSchG[206] and the DüngG.[207] A reduction of atmospheric emissions is achieved in particular by the BImSchG and the 13. BImschV.[208]

IV. WASTE DISPOSAL AT SEA

Waste disposal at sea means that industrial waste, sewage sludge and dredged material produced on land is transported by ships to sea and discharged there or incinerated on combustion vessels. Since the end of 1989, the disposal of waste at sea in Germany has completely been stopped. In the meantime, this attitude has become widely accepted internationally. Pursuant to the Hohe-SeeEinbrG[209] the introduction and incineration of waste and other substances into the high seas is generally prohibited. According to this law, the term "high seas" also includes the EEZ. Exemptions are possible for dredged material and urns for burial at sea. An exemption permit shall be refused if there is a risk of pollution, and in the case of dredged material if appropriate possibilities exist to dispose of the dredged material ashore. Within the territorial sea the WHG applies to the discharge of waste and other substances.

V. MINING AT SEA AND OTHER MARITIME USES

In accordance with the relevant marine environmental conventions permits, licenses or mining propertyships under the BBergG are not granted, if the activities excessively endanger the marine environment.[210] As concerns deep seabed mining, the administrative measures in accordance with the MBergG take account of the environment protection standards, established by the International Seabed Authority. According to the WindSeeG and the SeeAnlG installations at sea are only approved, if the marine environment is not endangered.[211] Adverse environmental impacts from fisheries have to be taken into account by applying the SeeFischG and the SeeFischV.

VI. Maritime Shipping

The prevention of pollution from ships is covered by the maritime shipping police law,[212] in particular by the SeeAufgG, the SchSG and the SchSV.[213] The requirements for environmentally correct behavior in compliance with MARPOL,[214] the AFS Convention[215] and the Ballast Water Management Convention[216] are defined and specified by the SeeUmwVerhV.[217] The provision of reception facilities in ports and the determination of terms of use are the task of the Länder within the scope of their responsibilities for waste disposal and ports.[218]

VII. Marine Nature Conservation

Promoted by relevant international conventions and EU law, marine nature conservation is becoming increasingly important. The decisive domestic legal basis is the BNatSchG.[219] On this basis, national parks and nature reserves have been established in the German territorial sea, where navigation is restricted by specific ordinance.[220] Nature reserves have also been designated in the German EEZ.[221] In these areas in the EEZ all actions for the purpose of exploration, exploitation and management, which may lead to destruction, damage or modification of the nature reserve or to a lasting disturbance are prohibited.[222] This does do not apply to air traffic, shipping, military use insofar as permitted under international law, scientific marine research and professional sea fishing.[223] Certain projects, such as the construction of wind farms or pipelines, have to be checked for their admissibility with regard to conservation purpose of the nature reserve[224] before they can be approved.[225] The competent administrative authority is the BfN,[226] which has to develop the relevant management plans for these nature conservation areas.

E. Maritime Spatial Planning

The different uses of sea areas off the German coasts are steadily increasing, especially because of offshore wind energy. In order to enable an appropriate balance between individual uses and other interests as well as between uses and marine environment protection, the tool of spatial planning, which was previously used primarily on land, is also applied at sea. For that reason the ROG[227] as the legal basis is extended to the EEZ, as far as UNCLOS grants rights and jurisdiction to coastal states.[228] After some preparatory work by the BSH, including in particular the drafting of spatial plans and a strategic environmental assessment with public participation, spatial planning in the German EEZ in the North and the Baltic Sea is now regulated in two ordinances.[229] The guiding principle is a sustainable spatial development by harmonizing the social and economic demands for space with its ecological functions and aiming at a lasting, large-scale balanced order.[230] The spatial plans for the EEZ, annexed to the ordinances, set out legally binding objectives and general principles of spatial planning with regard to economic and scientific use, the safety and easy flow of traffic and the protection of the marine environment. They lay down coordinated specifications for the individual uses and functions of shipping, raw material extraction, pipelines and submarine cables, scientific marine research, wind energy production, fishing and mariculture as well as for the protection of the marine environment. In particular, priority areas are defined for shipping, pipelines and submarine cables as well as for offshore wind farms, where other uses are excluded, provided that they are incompatible with the priority uses. Reservation areas are designated for shipping, pipelines and scientific research, which are given specific emphasis in balancing competing spatially significant uses. The legally binding effect of the objectives of spatial planning for subsequent decisions by public authorities applies for example to licensing procedures according to BBergG, WindSeeG and SeeAnlG.[231]

The limits of spatial planning in the EEZ under international law can be seen in the fact that the freedoms of the high seas have to be observed.[232] This applies to navigation, overflight and submarine cables and pipelines.[233] Hence, artificial islands, installations and structures and the safety zones around them may not be established where interference may be caused to the use of recognized sea lanes essential for international navigation.[234] Therefore, the main shipping routes, which consist of traffic separation schemes and other heavily used routes, constitute the basic structure for the overall planning. The other uses in the German EEZ must fit into this system. This approach contributes to an increase in safety and easy flow of traffic by minimizing barrier effects for shipping.[235] With regard to the marine environment the strategic environmental assessments conclude that the specifications of the spatial plans do not result in significant adverse effects.[236]

F. MARINE OBSERVATIONS AND RESEARCH

Thorough marine knowledge is an indispensable prerequisite for managing the sustainable use of the seas and for protecting the marine environment. The SeeAufgG creates the responsibility of the Federation to carry out marine observations including the monitoring of changes in the marine environment and assigns this task to the BSH.[237] In contrast to specific research activities, which are project oriented and restricted in time, marine observations are a permanent task and have to be performed on a regular basis to provide analyses, predictions and other information products, which are needed by decision makers.

Specific research activities by scientific institutions or third parties are partly subject to certain conditions. Research activities relating to the continental shelf for discovery or identification of mineral resources require an exploration permit.[238] For other marine scientific research activities relating to the continental shelf, which are obviously unsuitable for discovery or identification of resources, a permit issued by BSH is required with regard to the order and use of waters above the continental shelf and airspace above these waters.[239] The permit may only be refused for specific reasons, especially if there are overriding public interests, such as shipping, fishing or flora and fauna. For research activities that only concern the water column no similar restrictions exist. However, in accordance with the sovereign rights and jurisdiction of coastal States in the territorial sea and the EEZ, as attributed by UNCLOS,[240] the MForschG[241] authorizes the issuance of an ordinance to make scientific marine research in the German territorial sea or EEZ by vessels flying a foreign flag subject to prior notification or approval by the BSH. To date, no such ordinance has been issued.

LITERATURE

Beckert, Erwin/ Breuer, Gerhard, Öffentliches Seerecht, 1991

Breuch-Moritz, Monika/ Nolte, Nico, Wind Energy and Maritime Spatial Planning, in: Koch, Hans- Joachim (Ed.), Climate Change and Environmental Hazards related to Shipping, 2013, p. 223–225

Bundesministerium für Umwelt, Naturschutz, Bau und Reaktorsicherheit (BMUB), MSRL-Maßnahmenprogramm zum Meeresschutz der deutschen Nord- und Ostsee, 2016

Dahlke, Christian/ Nolte, Nico, Die neuen Raumordnungspläne für die deutsche AWZ in Nord- und Ostsee, in: Erbguth, Wilfried/ Breuch-Moritz, Monika (Eds.), Landes- und Wirtschaftsentwicklung zu Wasser, Rostocker Schriften zum Seerecht und Umweltrecht, vol. 49, 2011, p. 13 – 25

Ehlers, Peter, Nutzungsregime in der Ausschließlichen Wirtschaftszone, in: Ehlers, Peter/ Erbguth, Wilfried (Eds.), Nutzungs- und Schutzkonflikte in der Ausschließlichen Wirtschaftszone, Rostocker Schriften zum Seerecht und Umweltrecht, vol. 31, 2005, p. 13–29

Ehlers, Peter, Meeresfreiheit und aquitoriale Ordnung – zur Entwicklung des Seerechts, in: Erbguth, Wilfried (Ed.), Stand und Entwicklung im Seerecht, Umweltrecht, Städtebaurecht, Raumordnungs- und Fachplanungsrecht, Rostocker Schriften zum Seerecht und Umweltrecht, vol. 51, 2013, p. 15 – 36

Ehlers, Peter, Recht des Seeverkehrs, Handkommentar, 2017

Ehlers, Peter, Der Kapitän als Hilfssheriff, RdTW 2017, p. 361 – 367

Ehlers, Peter, Übersicht über die die Meeresverschmutzung betreffenden Vorschriften, in: Das Deutsche Bundesrecht, I L 60, 1281. EL – January 2018

Erbguth, Wilfried, Maritime Raumordnung, Die öffentliche Verwaltung 2011, p. 373 – 382

Jessen, Henning/ Werner, Michael Jürgen (Eds.), EU Maritime Transport Law, 2016

Krämer, Ludwig, The Contribution of the European Union to Marine Pollution Prevention, in: Basedow, Jürgen/ Magnus, Ulrich (Eds.), Pollution of the Sea – Prevention and Compensation, Hamburg Studies on Maritime Affairs, vol. 10, 2007, p. 63 – 83

Lagoni, Rainer, Sicherheitszonen um künstliche Inseln, Anlagen und Bauwerke im Meer, in Delbrück, Jost/ Heinz, Ursula et al. (Eds.), Aus Kiel in die Welt, Festschrift zum 100-jährigen Bestehen des Walther-Schücking-Instituts für Internationales Recht, 2014, p. 491 – 519

Marinekommando, Jahresbericht 2017 – Fakten und Zahlen zur maritimen Abhängigkeit der Bundesrepublik Deutschland

Proelß, Alexander (Ed.), United Nations Convention on the Law of the Sea, 2017

Schubert, Mathias, Maritimes Infrastrukturrecht, 2015

Vitzthum (Ed.), Wolfgang Graf, Handbuch des Seerechts, 2006

NOTES

[1] United Nations Convention on the Law of the Sea.

[2] See Vitzthum (2006), chpt. 2 note1, who has coined this term.

[3] Wasserstraßengesetz (Federal Waterways Act, revised version of 23 May 2007, last amended by Act of 23 December 2016).

[4] §1 (2); the seaward boundary of the inland waterways is defined in detail in Annex 1 to the WaStrG.

[5] Flaggenrechtsgesetz (Flag Act, last amended by Act of 18 July 2016).

6 Flaggenrechtsverordnung (Flag Ordinance, last amended by Act of 29 March 2017), see §1 FlRV.

7 Wasserhaushaltsgesetz (Water Management Act, last amended by Act of 29 March 2017).

8 Seeaufgabengesetz (Maritime Responsibilities Act, revised version of 17 June 2016, last amended by Act of 13 October 2016).

9 Seeschifffahrtsstraßen-Ordnung (Regulations on Navigable Maritime Waterways, last amended by Ordinance of 29 November 2016).

10 International Maritime Organization.

11 International Labour Organization.

12 Proclamation of 19 October 1994.

13 Exclusive economic zone; for details about the application of domestic law in the EEZ see Ehlers, in: Erbguth (2013), p. 25 et seq.

14 Proclamation of 25 November 1994; the designation of an EEZ is a precondition for a state to lawfully exercise its sovereign rights therein, cf. Proelß (2017), Art. 55 note 3.

15 Cf. Art. 10 Convention for the Protection of the Marine Environment of the North-East Atlantic; Art. 19 Convention on the Protection of the Marine Environment of the Baltic Sea Area, 1992.

16 Such as World Trade Organization, International Telecommunications Union, International Hydrographic Organization, World Meteorological Organization, Food and Agricultural Organization and Intergovernmental Commission of UNESCO.

17 For details see Jessen/Werner (2016).

18 For details see Krämer, in: Basedow/Magnus (2007); Ehlers (2018), note 20, 23, 61 et seq.

19 Grundgesetz (Basic Law).

20 Federal states.

21 Cf. Ehlers (2017), FlRG, Einl. note 6 et seq. with further references.

22 See Ehlers, in: Erbguth (2013), p. 25.

23 Ehlers, ibid., p. 28.

24 Schiffsregisterordnung (Ship's Register Regulations, last amended by Act of 28 April 2017).

25 Bundesamt für Seeschifffahrt und Hydrographie (Federal Maritime and Hydrographic Agency).

26 §1 no. 5, §5 SeeAufgG.

27 International Convention on Tonnage Measurement of Ships, 1969.

28 Schiffssicherheitsgesetz (Maritime Safety Act), see infra Part 2.2.3.

29 Seelotsgesetz (Sea Pilotage Act), see infra Part 2.4.

30 Seesicherheits-Untersuchungs-Gesetz (Maritime Safety Investigation Act), see infra Part 2.3.

31 Seearbeitsgesetz (Maritime Labour Act, last amended by Act of 22 December 2015).

32 Maritime Labour Convention, 2006.

[33] For details see Ehlers, RdTW (2017), p. 361 – 367.
[34] Berufsgenossenschaft für Verkehr Postlogistik Telekommunikation (Occupational Insurance Association for Transport Post-Logistics Telecommunication).
[35] Wasserstraßen- und Schifffahrtsverwaltung (Waterways and Shipping Administration), see Art. 89 GG.
[36] §5 WaStrG.
[37] §24 WaStrG.
[38] See infra Part 2.2.5.
[39] §1 no. 1 SeeAufgG; see Ehlers (2017), SeeAufgG, §1 note 11 et seq.
[40] §1 no. 2 SeeAufgG; for details see Ehlers, ibid., note 15 et seq.
[41] Cf. Ehlers, ibid. note 18.
[42] §1 no. 2 in conjunction with §9 (1) no. 1 SeeAufgG; cf. Ehlers, ibid., note 20 et seq.
[43] §1 no. 3 a SeeAufgG; for details see Ehlers, ibid., note 23 et seq.
[44] E. g. Art. 211, 220 UNCLOS.
[45] §1 no. 3b SeeAufgG; cf. Ehlers, ibid., note 25.
[46] §§3 SeeAufgG, 55 SeeSchStrO; for details see Ehlers (2017), SeeAufgG, §3 note 1 et seq.
[47] Details of requirements for issuing a maritime police order are regulated in §§3a et seq. SeeAufgG.
[48] §3b SeeAufgG.
[49] §3c SeeAufgG.
[50] See §§57, 58 SeeSchStrO.
[51] §30 WaStrG, cf. Beckert/Breuer (1991), note 234 et seq.
[52] Verordnung zu den Internationalen Regeln von 1972 zur Verhütung von Kollisionen auf See (Ordinance Relating to the International Regulations for Preventing Collisions at Sea, 1972, last amended by Act of 13 October 2016).
[53] last amended by Ordinance of 18 March 2009.
[54] Verordnung über die Sicherung der Seefahrt (Ordinance on the Safety of Navigation, last amended by Ordinance of 31 August 2015).
[55] Anlaufbedingungsverordnung (Internal Waters Entering Requirements Ordinance, last amended by Ordinance of 28 June 2016; English version http://www.bsh.de/de/Schifffahrt/Sportschifffahrt/Berichtigungsservice_NfS/Schifffahrtsvorschriften/2015/Beilage01--2015.pdf; last retrieved 4.2.2018).
[56] International Convention for the Safety of Life at Sea (last amended by Ordinance of 17 June 2016); International Convention on Load Lines (last amended by Ordinance of 15 April 2016).
[57] Art. 94, 211 UNCLOS.
[58] For details see Ehlers (2017), SchSG, Einleitung, note 1 et seq., §1 note 1 et seq.
[59] §2 SchSG.
[60] §§3 et seq. SchSG.
[61] §§10 et seq. SchSG.
[62] Schiffssicherheitsverordnung (Ship Safety Ordinance, last amended by Art. 1 of the Ordinance of 7 March 2018).

[63] §5 SchSV.
[64] §6 SchSV.
[65] §§5, 6 SeeAufgG, for details see Ehlers (2017), SeeAufgG, §1 note 29 et seq., §5 note 1, 116 et seq., §6 note 2 et seq., note 8 et seq.
[66] Directive 2014/90/EU of the European Parliament and of the Council of 23 July 2014 on marine equipment and repealing Council Directive 96/98/EC (OJ 2014 L 257/146).
[67] Schiffsausrüstungsverordnung (Ship Equipment Ordinance, last amended by Ordinance of 2 July 2017).
[68] §5 (1) no. 1a SeeAufgG; for details see Ehlers (2017), SeeAufgG, §1 note 35 et seq., §5 note 4, §7a note 1 et seq.
[69] Dangerous goods are in particular regulated in Chapter VII of the Annex to SOLAS.
[70] Gefahrgutbeförderungsgesetz (Act on the Carriage of Dangerous Goods, last amended by Act of 26 July 2016).
[71] Gefahrgutverordnung See (Ordinance on Maritime Dangerous Goods).
[72] International Convention on Standards of Training, Certification and Watchkeeping for Seafarers (last amended by Ordinance of 30 March 2017).
[73] See-Berufsausbildungsverordnung (Maritime Vocational Training Ordinance, last amended by Ordinance of 31 August 2015).
[74] Responsible Body for Maritime Vocational Training, see §7 SeeAufgG, §3 See-BAV; cf. Ehlers (2017), SeeAufgG, §7 note 2.
[75] Seeleute-Befähigungsverordnung (Seafarers' Competencies and Proficiencies Ordinance, last amended by Ordinance of 2 June 2016).
[76] See Art. 2 SeeAufgG, §10 (3) See-BV; cf. Ehlers (2017), SeeAufgG, §2 note 3.
[77] Schiffsbesetzungsverordnung (Safe Manning Ordinance, last amended by Ordinance of 9 June 2016); cf. Ehlers (2017), SeeAufgG, §1 note 40.
[78] Sportbootführerscheinverordnung (Sport Boat Driving Licence Ordinance).
[79] German Motor Yacht Association.
[80] German Sailing Association.
[81] §7 SeeAufgG, §16 SpFV.
[82] Sportseeschifferscheinverordnung (Skipper Licence Ordinance, last amended by Ordinance of 3 May 2017).
[83] Chapter V, Reg. 19, Chapter XI-2 of the Annex to SOLAS, International Code for the Security of Ships and of Port Facilities.
[84] Gesetz zur Ausführung der im Dezember 2002 vorgenommenen Änderungen des Internationalen Übereinkommens zum Schutz des menschlichen Lebens auf See und des Internationalen Codes für die Gefahrenabwehr auf Schiffen und in Hafenanlagen (Act for Implementing the Amendments of the International Convention for the Safety of Life at Sea, adopted in December 2002).
[85] See-Eigensicherungsverordnung (Maritime Self Protection Ordinance, last amended by Ordinance of 1 March 2016).
[86] For details see Ehlers (2017), SeeAufgG, §1 note 55 et seq.

[87] Cf. §6 Bundespolizeigesetz (Federal Police Act), §3 SeeAufgG, §1 Nr. 2a Zuständigkeitsbezeichnungs-Verordnung See (Maritime Responsibilities Ordinance, last amended by Ordinance of 2 June 2016).

[88] Maritime Vessel Guard Ordinance.

[89] Maritime Vessel Guard Implementation Ordinance.

[90] §8 SeeAufgG; for details see Ehlers (2017), SeeAufgG, §8 note 1 et seq.

[91] Agreement on the execution of shipping police enforcement tasks; cf. §20 (1) no. 5 SeeAufgG; Ehlers, ibid., §3 note 7, §20 note 1.

[92] §3 (2) SeeAufgG in conjunction with Seeschifffahrtsaufgaben-Übertragungsverordnung (Maritime Responsibilities Delegation Ordinance, last amended by Act of 21 June 2005); see Ehlers, ibid., §3 note 8.

[93] Cf. Ehlers (2017), SchSG, §14 note 1 et seq.

[94] Cf. §15 SeeAufgG, for details see Ehlers (2017), SeeAufgG, §15 note 1 et seq.

[95] In particular §§315 et seq., §324 StGB (German Penal Code).

[96] §1 no. 7 SeeAufgG; for details see Ehlers (2017), SeeAufgG, §1 note 43.

[97] International Convention on Maritime Search and Rescue, 1979.

[98] Deutsche Gesellschaft zur Rettung Schiffbrüchiger (German Lifeboat Association); cf. Beckert/Breuer (1991), note 775 et seq.

[99] §1 no. 9, 10 SeeAufgG; for details see Ehlers, ibid., note 46 et seq.

[100] These are mainly UNCLOS, ILO-Agreement No. 147 on minimum standards on merchant vessels, SOLAS, MARPOL and the Convention on Load Lines (see Annex A to the SUG).

[101] Seesicherheits-Untersuchungsgesetz (Marine Casualty Investigation Act, last amended by Act of 18 July 2016).

[102] Code of the international standards and recommended practices for a safety investigation into a marine casualty or marine incident (IMO Res. MSC.255(84), Guidelines to assist investigators in the implementation of the casualty investigation code (IMO Res. A.1075(28).

[103] Directive 2009/18/EC of the European Parliament and of the Council of 23 April 2009 (OJ 2009 L 131/114).

[104] §9 SUG.

[105] §11 SUG.

[106] Bundesstelle für Seeunfalluntersuchung (Federal Bureau of Maritime Casualty Investigation).

[107] §12 SUG; for details see Ehlers (2017), SUG, §12 note 1 et seq.

[108] §1 (1) SUG.

[109] §19 SUG.

[110] §24 SUG.

[111] §§22, 26 SUG.

[112] §27 SUG.

[113] §29 SUG.

[114] §28 SUG.

[115] §32 SUG.

[116] See §39 SUG.

[117] Generaldirektion Wasserstraßen und Schifffahrt (Directorate General for Waterways and Shipping), which is the intermediate authority of the WSV.
[118] §43 SUG.
[119] §41 SUG.
[120] §44 SUG.
[121] §48 et seq. SUG.
[122] §50 SUG.
[123] §52 SUG; for details see Ehlers, SUG, §52 note 1 et seq.
[124] Seelotsgesetz (Maritime Pilotage Act, last amended by Act of 18 July 2016).
[125] Allgemeine Lotsverordnung (General Pilotage Ordinance, last amended by Ordinance of 27 February 2004).
[126] For details see Ehlers (2017), SeeLG, §5 note 1.
[127] See §3 SeeLG; pilotage in ports is a task of the Länder.
[128] Lotsenbrüderschaften (Pilots Fraternies).
[129] Bundeslotsenkammer (Federal Chamber of Pilotage).
[130] For details see Ehlers, ibid., §3 note 1 et seq.
[131] Association for operating pilotage facilities; see §6 SeeLG; cf Ehlers, ibid., §6 note 2.
[132] §7 et seq. SeeLG; details are regulated by ordinance.
[133] §21 (1) SeeLG.
[134] §23 SeeLG; for details see Ehlers, ibid., §23 note 1 et seq.
[135] See Ehlers, ibid., §21 note 5.
[136] §21 (3) SeeLG.
[137] §26 SeeLG; for details see Ehlers, ibid., §26 note 2 et seq.
[138] §27 et seq. SeeLG.
[139] §34 et seq. SeeLG.
[140] In particular pilot stations and transfer vessels; cf. §6 SeeLG.
[141] §45 SeeLG; further provisions are set up by the Lotstarifverordnung (Pilotage Tariffs Ordinance); for details see Ehlers, ibid., §45 note 1 et seq.
[142] §42 SeeLG; for details see Ehlers, ibid., §42 note 1 et seq.
[143] §1 (1) SeeAufgG.
[144] In December 2017, 326 merchant ships with more than 100 GT flew the German flag totaling a tonnage of 9.15 million GT; additionally 2,017 ships with 51.4 million GT were registered in the German shipping register, while temporarily flying a foreign flag (http://www.bsh.de/en/Maritime_shipping/Commercial_shipping/German_ merchant_fleet/index.jsp, last retrieved 28.02.2018); as at 01.01.2017 the world merchant fleet totaled 52183 ships with more than 300 GT, see Marinekommando, p. 118.
[145] Wages which are comparable to those that are paid in the home countries of seafarers.
[146] §12 FlRG; for details see Ehlers (2017), FlRG, §12 note 1 et seq.
[147] §§23, 27 FlRV.

148 §21 (4) FlRG; for details see Ehlers, ibid., §21 note 9 et seq.; in December 2017, 183 ships with 8.6 million GT were registered in the ISR (http://www.bsh.de/en/Maritime_shipping/Commercial_shipping/German_merchant_fleet/index.jsp; last retrieved 28.02.2018).

149 §5a Einkommenssteuergesetz (Act on Income Tax, amended by Act of 14 August 2017).

150 Richtlinie zur Senkung der Lohnnebenkosten in der Seeschifffahrt vom 28. Oktober 2016 (Guideline on reducing non-wage labour costs in shipping of 28 October 2016).

151 Richtlinie zur Ausbildungsplatzförderung in der Seeschifffahrt vom 6. Oktober 2015 (Guideline on training subsidies in shipping of 6 October 2015). In total, BSH granted support totaling just under €60 million in 2016, of which around €3.6 million were for the promotion of training places.

152 §7 FlRG; for details see Ehlers, ibid., §7 note 2 et seq.

153 German Shipping Foundation, founded by Verband Deutscher Reeder (German Ship-owners Association).

154 Bundesberggesetz (Federal Mining Act (last amended by Act of 20 July 2017).

155 §3 BBergG.

156 §6 BBergG.

157 §§30 et seq., 137 BBergG.

158 §49 BBergG.

159 §51 et seq. BBergG.

160 Verordnung über die Umweltverträglichkeitsprüfung bergbaulicher Vorhaben (Ordinance on Environmental Impact Assessment of Mining Projects of 13 July 1990, last amended by Act of 20 July 2017).

161 Planfeststellungsverfahren, see §57a BBergG.

162 Allgemeine Bundesbergverordnung (General Federal Mining Ordinance, last amended by Ordinance of 18 October 2017).

163 §136 BBergG.

164 Art. 1 (1) no. 1 UNCLOS.

165 Part XI UNCLOS.

166 Meeresbodenbergbaugesetz (Seabed Mining Act of 6 June 1995, last amended by Art. 4 (69) of the Act of 18 July 2016).

167 Land Office for Mining, Energy and Geology.

168 §3 MBergG.

169 §133 (1) no. 1 BBergG.

170 §133 (1) no. 2 BBergG.

171 *Convention* for the *Protection* of *Submarine Telegraph Cables, 1884.*

172 Gesetz zur Ausführung des internationalen Vertrages zum Schutz der unterseeischen Telegraphenkabel vom 14. März 1884 (Act on the Implementation of the International Agreement for the Protection of Subsea Telegraph Cables of 14 March 1884, last amended by Act of 23 May 2017).

173 Art. 56 sec. 1 lit. a UNCLOS; cf. Proelß, in: Vitzthum (2006), chpt. 3 note 254 et seq.

174 Art. 60 UNCLOS.

175 §45 Windenergie-auf-See-Gesetz (Windenergy at Sea Act, last amended by Act of 20 July 2017).

176 §45 (2) WindSeeG; consent of the GDWS is needed.

177 §§72 to 78 Verwaltungsverfahrensgesetz (Act on Administrative Procedure, last amended by Act of 18 July 2017).

178 §47 WindSeeG in connection with Umweltverträglichkeitsprüfungsgesetz (Environmental Impact Assessment Act, last amended by Act of 8 September 2017).

179 §48 (4) WindSeeG.

180 §1 (2) no. 1, 2 SeeAnlG (Seeanlagengesetz, Maritime Installations Act).

181 §2 SeeAnlG.

182 §1 (2) no. 3, 4 SeeAnlG.

183 §6 SeeAnlG.

184 §53 WindSeeG, §10 SeeAnlG; consent of the GDWS is needed. Cf. Lagoni, in: Delbrück/Heinz (2014), p. 504 et seq.

185 §58 WindSeeG, §15 SeeAnlG.

186 Based on Regulation (EU) No 1380/2013 of the European Parliament and of the Council of 11 December 2013 (OJ 2013 L 354/22) and Regulation No 1379/2013 of the European Parliament and of the Council of 11 December 2013 (OJ 2013 L 354/1).

187 Seefischereigesetz (Sea Fisheries Act, last amended by Act of 23 December 2016); as concerns the implementation of EU law see §1 (1) no. 2 SeeFischG.

188 Seefischereiverordnung (Sea Fisheries Ordinance, last amended by Ordinance of 2 March 2016).

189 §1 (2) SeeFischG.

190 §3 SeeFischG.

191 Bundesanstalt für Landwirtschaft und Ernährung, a higher Federal authority under the supervision of Federal Ministry for Agriculture and Food. The administrative competence of the Federation arises from the facultative Federal competence under Art. 87 (3) GG; see in detail §2 SeeFischG.

192 As concerns the international marine environment protection law see the contribution by Ehlers, 50 Years Marine Environment Protection – Achievements and Unsolved Issues, p. xxx.

193 For details see Ehlers (2018) with further references.

194 Water Framework Directive (Directive 2000/60/EC of the European Parliament and of the Council of 23 October 2000 establishing a framework for Community action in the field of water policy, OJ 2000 L 327/1).

195 Marine Strategy Framework Directive (Directive 2008/56/EC of the European Parliament and of the Council of 17 June 2008 establishing a framework for community action in the field of marine environmental policy, OJ 2008 L 164/19).

196 §§2 (2) no. 2a, 3 WHG.

197 §45a WHG.

198 §45b WHG.

[199] §45d et seq. WHG; for details of the German program according §45 h WHG see BMUB (2016). General information available under www.meeresschutz.info.

[200] §45 l WHG.

[201] §§8, 9 (1) no. 4 WHG.

[202] §12 WHG.

[203] Chemikaliengesetz (Chemicals Act, amended by Act of 18 July 2017).

[204] Abwasserabgabengesetz (Waste Water Levy Act, last amended by Act of 1 June 2016).

[205] Bundes-Immissionsschutzgesetz (Federal Immission Control Act, last amended by Act of 18 July 2017).

[206] Pflanzenschutzgesetz (Plant Protection Act, last amended by Act of 18 July 2016).

[207] Düngegesetz (Fertilisers Act, last amended by Act of 5 May 2017).

[208] Verordnung über Großfeuerungs-, Gasturbinen- und Verbrennungsmotoranlagen (Ordinance on Large Combustion, Gas Turbine and Combustion Engine Plants, last amended by Ordinance of 19 December 21017).

[209] Hohe-See-Einbringungsgesetz (Act on Dumping at High Seas, last amended by Act of 24 May 2016).

[210] See supra Part 3.1.; for details see Ehlers (2018), note 34.

[211] See supra Part 3.3.

[212] For details see Ehlers, ibid., note 75 et seq.

[213] See supra Part 2.2.1., 2.2.3.

[214] International Convention for the Prevention of Pollution from Ships, 1973.

[215] International Convention on the Control of Harmful Anti-fouling Systems on Ships.

[216] International Convention on the Control and Management of Ships' Ballast Water and Sediments.

[217] See-Umweltverhaltensverordnung (Maritime Environmental Behaviour Ordinance, last amended by Ordinance of 20 February 2018); for details see Ehlers (2018), note 69.

[218] See Ehlers (2018), note 74, with further references.

[219] Bundesnaturschutzgesetz (Federal Nature Conservation Act, last amended by Act of 15 September 2017).

[220] Verordnung über das Befahren des Naturschutzgebietes "Helgoländer Felssockel" (Ordinance concerning sailing in the nature conservation area "Helgoländer Felssockel); Verordnung über das Befahren der Bundeswasserstraßen in Nationalparken im Bereich der Nordsee (Ordinance concerning sailing on the Federal waterways in national parks in the North Sea area); Befahrensregelungsverordnung Küstenbereich Mecklenburg-Vorpommern (Ordinance concerning the coastal area of Mecklenburg- West Pommerania).

[221] The following nature reserves have been established by ordinance: "Borkum Riffgrund", "Doggerbank" and "Sylter Außenriff – Östliche Deutsche Bucht in the North Sea EEZ, and "Fehmarnbelt", "Kadetrinne" and "Pommersche Bucht – Rönnebank" in the Baltic Sea EEZ.

[222] Cf. §4 Ordinance Borkum Riffgrund as an example for all ordinances.
[223] Cf. §4 (3) Ordinance Borkum Riffgrund as an example for all ordinances.
[224] §34 BNatSchG.
[225] Cf. §5 Ordinance Borkum Riffgrund as an example for all ordinances.
[226] Bundesamt für Naturschutz (Federal Agency for Nature Conservation).
[227] Raumordnungsgesetz (Spatial Planning Act, last amended by Act of 20 July 2017); see §1 (4) ROG.
[228] Cf. Proelß (2017), Art. 56 note 27.
[229] Verordnung über die Raumordnung in der deutschen AWZ in der Nordsee (Ordinance on Spatial Planning in the German EEZ in the North Sea); Verordnung über die Raumordnung in der deutschen AWZ in der Ostsee (Ordinance on Spatial Planning in the German EEZ in the Baltic Sea); cf. Schubert (2015), p. 227.
[230] Cf. Erbguth (2011), p. 378, referring to spatial coordination.
[231] §4 ROG.
[232] Art. 58 (1) in conjunction with Article 87 UNCLOS; cf. Schubert (2015), p. 228.
[233] Cf. Beckert/Breuer (1991), notes 303 et seq. (navigation), 1388 et seq. (overflight), 1462 et seq. (submarine cables and pipelines); Proelß (2017), Art. 58 note 11 et seq.
[234] Art. 60 (7) UNCLOS.
[235] See Breuch-Moritz/Nolte, in: Koch (2013), p. 223; Dahlke/Nolte, in: Erbguth/Breuch-Moritz (2011), p. 25.
[236] See Dahlke/Nolte, in: Erbguth/Breuch-Moritz (2011), p. 21; the increased importance of maritime spatial planning is recognised by Directive 2014/89/EU of the European Parliament and of the Council of 23 July 2014 establishing a framework for maritime spatial planning (OJ 2014 L 257/135), as each member state shall establish and implement maritime spatial planning and set up maritime spatial plans the latest by 31 March 2021; member states bordering marine waters shall cooperate with the aim of ensuring that maritime spatial plans are coherent and coordinated across the marine region concerned.
[237] §1 no. 11, §5 (2a) SeeAufgG; see also Ehlers (2017), SeeAufgG, §1 note 53, §5 note 15; international obligations are in particular created by Art. 200 UNCLOS and the monitoring requirements laid down in the marine environmental conventions.
[238] See supra Part 3.1.
[239] §132 BBergG.
[240] Art. 245 et seq. UNCLOS.
[241] Gesetz über die Durchführung wissenschaftlicher Meeresforschung (Act on Scientific Marine Research, last amended by Ordinance of 31 August 2015).

CHAPTER VII

SHIPPING LAW

Klaus RAMMING

A. INTRODUCTION

Over the last decades, the international trade of goods increased to a level not seen before. This concerns both the amount of goods and their diversity, ranging from bulk cargo such as oil, ore or grain, shipped in large quantities, to sophisticated electronic devices. Also, there are complex supply chains feeding customers, which rely on regular and reliable deliveries. Goods produced all over the world are available nearly everywhere, and all of us have become used to be able to effortlessly shop products manufactured at the other end of the world. This is made possible by a complex and worldwide transport and logistics industry which provides an amazing selection of individual transport services and which is constantly and quietly in operation in the background. Within that system, shipping plays a major role, as ships are able to carry big amounts of goods over long distances at relatively low cost.

B. THE SHIPPING INDUSTRY

As one of the pillars of the international transport system, which facilitates the worldwide trade of goods, the shipping industry offers a variety of services. One very visible group of stakeholders are the shipping lines, which provide liner services with regular departures on a number of routes (see below). Typically, a multitude of consignments of smaller amounts of containerised cargo are shipped and handled uniformly. Other players offer more tailor-made transport services to customers who need to ship cargo unsuitable for containers, such as heavy lift or project cargo or large amounts of e.g. bulk cargo. These shipments normally are made on the basis of voyage charter parties (for details, see the chapter on Charter Parties).

C. THE UNDERLYING SALES CONTRACT

The driving force behind shipping is the international trade. Both of them are closely related. If an international sales contract is concluded, transport services are required to execute the contract, as the goods need to be shipped from the seller to the buyer. The sales contract defines where, when and how the goods are delivered to the buyer and which party is supposed to arrange for the carriage of the goods. The sales contract may be subject to the Incoterms and the familiar abbreviations provided by them, such as CIF (cost, insurance, freight), FOB (free on board) and many others. The seller may have the duty to deliver the goods alongside the vessel or in the vessel at a named port of loading or in the vessel or alongside the vessel at the port of destination. Also, the sales contract would specify whether it is the seller or the buyer who bears the risk of the goods being lost or damaged underway. The contract of carriage with the carrier may be concluded by the seller or by the buyer. Further, transport documents issued by the carrier, in particular a bill of lading or a sea waybill, may be required to perform the sales contract, namely in respect of the payment of the purchase price, e.g. if payment is to be made against presentation of documents. However, the shipping of goods not in all cases serves to perform a contract of carriage. This is not so if the party ships its own goods to use them at the port of destination, e.g. if a contractor requires materials and machines for a particular project, or if a person moves to another home overseas and it needs to transport its household goods.

D. THE PLAYERS

The most distinctive players in the shipping industry are the shipping lines, some of them with familiar names. Their counterparts are the shippers who need to have their goods shipped. The list would not be complete without another relevant group of service providers, i.e. the forwarders who render important assistance when it comes to shipping goods.

I. THE SHIPPING LINES

The players most visible in shipping are the shipping lines. Often, their ships are of a uniform appearance with identical paintwork, easily recognisable all over the world. If containerised goods are shipped, the containers themselves often also bear the well-known marks of shipping companies. Typically, they provide liner services on one or more defined routes with regular departures in the respective ports of call. Liner services normally are for containerised cargo only, although a few general cargo services have survived.

The shipping lines act as carriers and conclude contracts of carriage with the shippers, for the goods to be delivered to the consignee at the port of destination. Normally, the shipping line would issue a bill of lading or sea waybill. Also, the vessels used by the shipping lines are not owned or bareboat chartered by them. Usually, the respective vessels are on time charter to the line.

II. THE SHIPPERS

The customers of the shipping lines are the shippers. In a sale context, it is either the seller or the buyer who concludes the contract of carriage with the shipping line as carrier, depending on the terms of the sales contract. The carrier is instructed to deliver the goods to the buyer, normally the consignee under the contract of carriage. Traditionally, the shipping lines are dominating and have superior bargaining power over the shippers. The Hague Rules[1] sought to rectify this imbalance (see E I.1 below). However, this does not apply to all shippers. Some of them require the shipment of large quantities of cargo, say some hundreds of containers per year. Here, the balance of powers has shifted in favour of the shippers, who in some cases are able to dictate the conditions of the contracts of carriage.

III. THE FORWARDERS

Between the shippers and the shipping lines, there are further service providers assisting the shippers. These are the freight forwarders, involved by the shippers as well as the consignees. The forwarders render all kinds of services in relation to the transport of goods. They arrange for the packing, the stowing and the transport of the goods to the port of destination as well as the pickup of the goods at the port of destination and the final carriage to the consignee. Beyond that, the forwarder is concerned with export, import and related customs issues. Basically, the forwarder is not himself a carrier but merely, as an intermediate, arranges for the transport of the goods on behalf and for the account of the customer. The forwarder concludes the contract with the carrier as an agent of his customer. As a result, if there is cargo damage, it is not the forwarder who is responsible, as he did not undertake to carry the goods. He may, however, be liable if he breached his contractual duties as a forwarder, e.g. to carefully select a carrier. In some cases, on the other hand, the forwarder himself, vis-à-vis the shipper, acts as carrier and thus is liable accordingly. Here, the forwarder sub-contracts the carriage owed by him to the shipping line. In the circumstances, it can be difficult to determine whether the forwarder accepted to carry the goods or whether he merely undertook to arrange for their transferred by a carrier.

In some legislations, freight forwarders, who are contractually bound to arrange for the transport of goods by a third party carrier, are by law considered to be carriers themselves. The trigger for that may be that a fixed price was agreed for the carriage including all related services rendered by the forwarder. Normally, when the freight forwarder settles accounts with the customer, the forwarder would charge the payments made to the various service providers including the shipping line plus a remuneration for the forwarder's services. If the forwarder agrees on a fixed price for all services including the carriage, he would seek to obtain the carriage at the lowest possible price in order for him to increase his profit. In such a situation, the respective legislation may put the forwarder on par with a regular carrier as far as the carriage of the goods is concerned.

E. The International Legal Framework

There are four international conventions, which deal with contracts of carriage and bills of lading in a shipping context. The mother of all maritime conventions are the Hague Rules of 1924 which until today are the basis of the international industry standard. The Hague Rules were amended by a Protocol of 1968, adopted in the city of Visby (the Hague/Visby Rules[2]). There was an entirely new approach with the Hamburg Rules[3] of 1978. The latest and perhaps most prominent attempt to unify the law on contracts of carriage and bills of lading are the Rotterdam Rules[4] of 2008.

I. The Hague Rules

1. The Development of the Hague Rules

The trigger for the Hague Rules to evolve was the situation in shipping in the late 18th century. The industrialisation in shipping already had reached a considerable level, following the availability of ships built of iron and steel as well as reliable means of mechanic propulsion instead of wind. Liner services with regular departures were common on a number of routes. At the time, the typical situation was that the shipping lines had substantial bargaining power over the shippers and often were able to dictate the terms of the carriage. This resulted in clauses by which the lines sought to limit or exclude, respectively, the liability for cargo damage to a great extent. This met the resistance of the shippers. The first piece of national legislation which sought to restrict the lines' practice regarding the limitation of liability in their clauses was the US Harter Act of 1897, which was followed by corresponding legislations in New Zealand, Australia, Canada and Japan. On an international scale, the respective interest groups lobbied for an international convention, which addressed, inter alia, the carriers' liability clauses. After many years of discussions, the Hague Rules were finally adopted in 1924. They entered into force on 2 June 1931.

The Hague Rules were the first international convention on the carriage of goods, and others were to follow in respect of the other modes of transport. However, compared to the modern standards observed in international conventions on the carriage of goods, the Hague Rules make a somewhat incomplete impression. One of the reasons for this is that originally the Hague Rules were meant to be directly incorporated in bills of lading as bill of lading terms. In the wake of the Hague Rules, international conventions and the carriage of goods by air, railway, inland waterway shipping and multimodal transport emerged.

2. The Scope of Application

The Hague Rules apply, in principle, to bills of lading, as the title of the Convention confirms. The bill of lading must be issued in a contracting state of the Hague Rules. Live animals are excepted, just as cargo carried on deck. Neither do the Hague rules apply to the period prior to loading and after discharging of the goods (if they already or still are in the custody of the carrier). This concept is generally referred to as the Hague Rules' "tackle to tackle" Clause. Within the aforementioned exceptions, the carrier is not bound by the Hague Rules and may thus seek to exclude liability, if the law otherwise applicable to the bill of lading or the contract of carriage allows so. In particular, clauses excluding the carrier's liability for deck cargo are common. The same applies to clauses in which the carrier seeks to exclude liability for damage occurring prior to loading and after discharging the goods.

3. THE PROVISIONS OF THE HAGUE RULES

Three main issues are addressed in the Hague Rules, i.e. the issuance of a bill of lading, the shippers' liability vis-à-vis the carrier and, the main focus of the Rules, the carrier's liability for loss of or damage to the goods. In particular, the Hague Rules deal with, as their title confirms, bills of lading. Compared to the modern international conventions on the carriage of goods, this is a somewhat narrow approach. However, the Hague Rules remain the pioneer of the international transport conventions. The provisions of the Convention apply mandatorily against the carrier. He is unable to deviate from the Convention's liability system, in particular in the bill of lading terms. This is one of the principal purposes of the Hague Rules.

The Hague Rules provide for an obligation of the carrier to issue a bill of lading to the shipper. And so far, the Convention distinguishes between bills of lading issued after the goods were accepted for carriage and shipped bills of lading issued after the goods have been loaded on the ship. Bills already issued after the acceptance of the goods may be transformed into shipped bills of lading by an additional shipped on board clause added after loading. The bill of lading is *prima facie* evidence that the goods have been received by the carrier and that they correspond to what is stated in the bill.

The heart of the Hague Rules' provisions are the regulations concerning the carrier's liability for loss of damage to the goods (delay in delivery is not at all addressed in the Hague Rules). They reflect the compromise reached between the interest groups involved at the time. The respective regulations until today are the model for corresponding provisions in the modern conventions in the carriage of goods. The underlying principle is that the carrier's liability is limited to a certain defined extent, but that the relevant provisions are mandatory to the effect that the parties are unable to deviate from them. In particular, the carrier's general terms are void so far as they seek to limit or exclude liability in a way that exceeds the scheme provided by the Hague Rules.

The impact of some of the traditional provisions of the Hague Rules is still felt today. They introduced the concept that the carrier is responsible for the vessel's seaworthiness. Also, the Convention provides for an exclusion of liability if the damage to the goods was caused by an error in navigation or by fire. Further, the Hague Rules introduced a fixed limitation amount at 100 pounds sterling per package or unit. It is, however, uncertain how this amount should be calculated today. Finally, the Hague Rules provide for a one year time limit which begins when the goods are delivered or on the day when they (in case of loss) should have been delivered.

II. THE HAGUE/VISBY RULES

In 1968, the Hague rules were amended by a protocol adopted in Visby. The so called Hague/Visby Rules are today's industry standard. The amendments made by the Visby Protocol concern the carrier's liability. The Protocol introduced a number of features which since then have found their way into other international conventions on the carriage of goods. Compared to the Hague Rules, the Hague/Visby Rules have a broader scope of application relating to international carriages between ports of two different states, if, alternatively, the bill of lading has been issued in a contracting state; or the goods are loaded in a port of a contracting state; or if the bill provides that the contract of carriage is subject to the Hague Rules or a Hague Rules legislation.

One amendment made by this protocol concerns the effects of the bill of lading. While the Hague Rules say that the bill is *prima facie* evidence as to the amount and condition of the goods as described in the bill, the Hague/Visby Rules provide that in respect of these assumptions proof of the contrary is excluded in relation to third parties who have acquired the bill in good faith. It would seem that thereby an entirely new concept of liability was introduced, similar to the issuance of a false bill of lading.

While the Hague Rules did not specify what damages the carrier is responsible for, the Hague Rules verify that the carrier's liability is based on the value of the goods (in case of loss) or on the balance of the good's value in damaged and sound condition, at the time and the place when the goods actually were or should have been delivered. Secondly, the Visby Protocol introduced a new way of calculating the limitation amount in an alternative and more practical way. The aforementioned limitations do not apply in cases of a particularly severe, qualified personal fault of the carrier. The Hague/Visby Rules confirm that the liability exclusions and limitations in favour of the carrier not only apply to contractual claims, in particular under the contract of carriage and/or the bill of lading, but also in respect of corresponding non-contractual claims. Finally, the Visby Protocol introduced a statutory Himalaya Provision in favour of the carrier's servants, who may rely on the liability exclusions and limitations provided in the Hague/Visby Rules if they are being held responsible for loss of or damage to the goods.

III. THE HAMBURG RULES

While the Visby Protocol amended the old Hague Rules, the Hamburg Rules, adopted in 1978, are a completely new convention applicable to both contracts of carriage and bills of lading (but not to charter parties). As the Hague and the Hague/Visby rules, the Hamburg Rules feature regulations on the issuance and the effects of a bill of lading as well as the shipper's liability vis-à-vis the carrier. Further, the Hamburg Rules include the familiar set of provisions concerning the carrier's liability for loss of any damage to the goods. While the Hamburg Rules still have the fire exception, the error in navigation defence has been removed. The carrier's liability is limited to 835 Special Drawing Rights (SDR) per package or unit or 2.5 SDR per kilogram, whichever is the higher. The SDR is an artificial currency used by the International Monetary Fund (IMF) in respect of its internal transactions. The exchange rate of the SDR in relation to a number of "real" currencies is daily published by the IMF. The SDR is the accepted unit used in all international transport and maritime conventions.

The carrier is not protected by the Hamburg Rules' limitations if the damage was caused by his personal qualified fault. The liability exclusions and limitations apply to non-contractual claims against the carrier. Also, the Hamburg Rules features a Himalaya Clause in favour of the carrier's servants. One of the new features introduced by the Hamburg Rules is the actual carrier's responsibility (see below G VI.8). Both the contractual and the actual carrier are responsible not only for loss of and damage to the goods but also for a delay in delivery. Insofar, the carriers' liability is limited to an amount corresponding to 2.5 times the freight. Under the Hamburg Rules, time expires within a period of two years (instead of one year as provided for in the Hague and Hague/Visby Rules). Also, the Hamburg Rules are concerned with jurisdiction issues in relation to claims under the Convention. The parties are, in principle, not entitled to agree on terms deviating from the Hamburg Rules in the contract of carriage or the bill of lading. The Hamburg Rules entered into force on 1 November 1992. While technically they are considered to be well made and evenly balanced, they have not been widely accepted and ultimately were only ratified by a limited number of states.

IV. THE ROTTERDAM RULES

The latest attempt to develop an internationally recognised and modern liability system relating to the carriage of goods at sea are the Rotterdam Rules, which were adopted on 11 December 2008. That convention features an approach different from the Hague and Hague/Visby Rules as well as the Hamburg Rules. The Rotterdam Rules are more detailed than the previous conventions and consist of not less than 96 articles. For the first time, the Rotterdam Rules seek to extend their scope of application not only to carriage by sea, but also to land transport prior to or following a sea lay (the "maritime +" concept). The Rotterdam Rules apply to contracts of carriage (but not to charter parties) as well as shipping documents. The term "Bill of Lading" does not at all appear in the Convention.

In principle, the provisions of the Rotterdam Rules follow the familiar pattern set by the previous conventions. The Rotterdam Rules deal with the carrier's obligations in relation to the transport and the delivery of the goods; the issuance and the effects of shipping documents; the shipper's obligations and responsibilities vis-à-vis the carrier; and, of course, the carrier's liability in case of loss of or damage to the goods and delay in delivery. The Rotterdam Rules apply mandatorily; the parties are, in principle, not entitled to agree on deviating terms. There are, however, a number of exceptions.

As the Hamburg Rules, the Rotterdam Rules exclude the carrier's liability in case of fire but do not allow him to rely on an error in navigation as a defence. The carrier's liability is limited to 875 SDR the package or unit or 3 SDR per kilogram, whichever is the higher. If there is a delay in delivery, the carrier's liability is, as in the Hamburg Rules, limited to 2.5 times the freight. The Rotterdam Rules' liability exclusions and limitations also apply to parallel non-contractual cargo claims against the carrier. He is not entitled to limit liability if the damage was caused by qualified fault. As opposed to the previous conventions, it is sufficient to break limitation that there is qualified fault by the carrier's servants and sub-contractors. The Rotterdam Rules concern the contractual carrier's liability as well as the liability of what is described as the "maritime performing party", i.e. the equivalent to the actual carrier.

Finally, the Rotterdam Rules feature provisions on time bars, on jurisdiction and jurisdiction clauses, on proceedings against the maritime performing party, on the recognition and enforcement of judgements on issues covered in the Convention handed down by the courts in one contracting state in any other contracting state, and on arbitration.

F. THE CONTAINER TRADE

Most of today's shipping industry relies on the goods being in standard containers, to the effect that vessels and terminals with corresponding standard cargo facilities may be used. As a result, transport services based on standard containers are very cost effective. Normally, containers are provided by the lines to the shippers. In some cases, producers which need large amounts of their product to be shipped, may maintain a fleet of owned or leased containers, often with their own marks.

The standard procedure is that the shipper requests the line to provide a container and to present it at an agreed time and place for it to be stuffed by or on behalf of the shipper. The line would arrange for the container to be carried from a depot to the shipper. Once stuffing is completed, the shipping line would collect the container and haul it to the port of loading. At the port of destination, the container would be stored at the terminal to await delivery to the consignee. If there are delays, the carrier may charge for the storage of the container. In the normal course of events, the consignee would collect the container at the terminal and transport it to his facilities for unloading. Subsequently, the container would be returned to a depot or the terminal. Normally, the consignee would be allowed some days to return the container. In case of a late redelivery, container demurrage would accrue.

If the carrier receives a container stuffed by the shipper for shipment, the term FCL would be used ("full container load"). However, the carrier may accept that the shipper delivers the goods at the carrier's terminal. The goods are then loaded by the carrier into a container. If the amount of goods is not sufficient to fill the entire container, the carrier may also load further goods received from other shippers into the very container (consolidated cargo or container). The abbreviation LCL ("less than a full container load") is used to describe this procedure. The same concepts would apply at the port of destination. The carrier may deliver the container to the consignee (FCL delivery). Or the container would be unloaded at the terminal and to allow the carrier to deliver only the goods to the consignee (LCL delivery). This would necessarily occur in case of consolidated containers. In the circumstances, goods shipped FCL may be delivered on LCL terms, just as LCL goods may be delivered on FCL terms.

If the consignee, duly notified by the carrier that the container is available, fails to collect the container at the terminal, the carrier is unable to deliver the container as promised to the shipper. The carrier would then turn to the shipper for instructions. If no instructions are forthcoming, the carrier may ultimately be entitled, based on his lien on the goods, to sell the goods and to deduct any freight costs still owed as well as storage fees from the proceeds of sale (if these are sufficient).

G. CONTRACTS OF CARRIAGE

The basic type of contract relating to the transport of goods is the contract of carriage. The contracts considered in this chapter are for the carriage of goods by sea. Typically, they concern containers or general cargo. The goods are received by the carrier at the port of loading and carried by him to the port of discharge to be delivered to the consignee. Shipping lines often provide overall transport solutions, which may include land carriage from the place of receipt of the goods to the port of loading and/or from the port of destination to the place of delivery, typically by road haulage or train. Here, there would be one contract of carriage, which covers a land, a sea and yet another land leg, i.e. a multimodal transport. These type of contracts are not covered in this chapter. The focus of the contract of carriage by sea is on the goods. It may need to be distinguished from a charter, in particular the voyage charter, by which a ship or a part of the ship is put at the disposal of the charterer to perform the carriage (for details, see the chapter on Charter Parties, B II.1).

In many instances, there will be a chain of contracts of carriage. The carrier instructed by the (original) shipper would not perform the transport himself, but would involve a sub-carrier. This may be repeated in the circumstances. Further sub-contracts may be a time charter (usually not a voyage charter) and ultimately a bareboat charter contract (for details, see the chapter on charter parties, A.10).

I. THE TERMS OF THE CONTRACT

The contract of carriage is subject to the relevant national law, which in turn is determined by the international private law principles (below VII.). The national law may feature more or less detailed provisions on aspects relevant for the conclusion and performance of the contract. Moreover, the national law may apply mandatorily to the effect that the parties are unable to agree on deviating terms. However, in many cases the national law may be mandatory in certain respects only to the effect that the parties are free to agree on their own terms otherwise. Normally, the regulations applying mandatorily are those in line with the relevant maritime conventions, in particular with the Hague and Hague/Visby Rules. Thus, it would often be the national law's provisions on the carrier's liability for loss of or damage to the goods to which the parties remain bound, whilst all other issues are dealt with in the contractual agreements.

The contract of carriage is subject to the terms negotiated between the parties. In many cases however, in particular if a shipping line is involved, the contract of carriage is based on the carrier's general terms. After the goods are received for shipment or loaded on the vessel, the carrier may issue a sea waybill (or a bill of lading, see below H.), which evidences the contract of carriage, i.e. the details agreed between the parties, and reproduces the carrier's general terms on its reverse side in small print. Typically, they would, inter alia, include a choice of law and jurisdiction clause. BIMCO,[5] the most prominent provider of a large variety of forms for all kinds of contracts relating to shipping, offers e.g. the Linewaybill, the most recent edition being of 2016. However, there may be cases where the shipper is able to dictate the terms of the contract of carriage to the effect that shipper's general terms prevail. Today, most sea waybills are still issued on paper, although it would seem that the considerable efforts are made to introduce electronic sea waybills.

In some legislations, the contract may be subject to judicial review if and in so far as the contract is based on one party's general terms. Normally, the judicial review of contracts is a facility found in consumer law. However, some jurisdictions apply the respective principles, perhaps in a less strict form, also to contracts between merchants and thus to contracts of carriage. As a result, if the contract is subject to the carrier's general terms, a provision may be void because it is not in line with mandatory national law or, even if there is no mandatory law, because it does not withstand judicial review.

II. THE BOOKING

Normally, contracts of carriage are concluded somewhat informally by booking the goods for a particular departure. Some shipping lines have developed sophisticated electronic booking systems. The shipper may book the goods in his own name and on his own account, or maybe through a freight forwarder acting on behalf of the shipper. Typically, the carrier sends a booking confirmation to the shipper, which summarizes the details of the contemplated transport. Also, the carrier may issue a sea waybill or a bill of lading (below H.) once the goods are received for shipment or loaded on the vessel.

III. THE CARRIER'S DUTY TO CARRY AND DELIVER THE GOODS

Under a contract of carriage, the carrier's principal duty is twofold, i.e. to carry the goods to the port of destination and to deliver them to the consignee.

1. CARRIAGE OF THE GOODS

The carrier is under the obligation to carry the goods from the port of loading to the port of destination. In principle, the goods must be carried in the particular ship and on a direct route. However, under the respective law applicable to the contract of carriage or under the terms of the contract, the carrier may be entitled to tranship the goods to another vessel on one or more occasions or to discharge and reload the goods onto the same vessel at intermediate ports (which may be necessary for stowage purposes). The carrier may even be entitled to use other means of transport to carry the goods to their destination. In the circumstances, the carrier may not be able to carry out the transport in the way originally contemplated by the parties, e.g. if a certain route the vessel was supposed to take is blocked. The parties' rights in these cases are determined by the law applicable to the contract of carriage and the terms of the contract and may range from the right to cancel the contract to an obligation of the carrier to seek instructions from the shipper.

2. DELIVERY OF THE GOODS

The second principal obligation of the carrier under the contract of carriage following the transport to the port of destination is to deliver the goods to the consignee. The applicable national law and the terms of the contract of carriage may specify what amounts to a delivery of the goods. Delivery may occur after the goods have been discharged and positioned alongside the vessel where they may be collected by the consignee. If the carriage is on *free out* terms, it may be sufficient if the carrier allows the consignee to discharge the goods. In effect, delivery occurs when the goods still are in the vessel. In many cases and in particular in the container trade, the goods are discharged by the carrier and then stored on the terminal until they are delivered to the consignee by the terminal on behalf of the carrier. Problems may arise if the carrier is bound, by the local law, to hand over the goods to the port authorities, normally for customs purposes, who then release the goods to the consignee. In case the carrier is unable to deliver the goods to the consignee, e.g. for the lack of response from him, the parties' rights are determined by the law applicable to the contract of carriage and its terms. The carrier may be required to turn to the shipper for instructions. If none are forthcoming, the carrier may be entitled to rely on his lien over the goods and to sell them.

3. Amending the Contract

In the circumstances, it may be necessary to amend the contract of carriage after it was concluded. The shipper may require the carrier to return the goods to him already at the port of loading, at an intermediate port or at the port of destination, or it may be necessary to deliver the goods to a new consignee. For the carrier, it may be necessary to tranship the goods to another vessel en route or two reload the goods at an intermediate port. In order to redefine the carrier's obligations, the parties may enter into an agreement which amends the original contract of carriage. However, the parties may be entitled to amend the contract, within certain limits, by a mere one-sided declaration which the other party is bound to accept. The applicable national law and the terms of the contract of carriage, respectively, may allow the shipper (or the consignee) to give instructions to the carrier as to the carriage and the delivery of the goods. Also, the respective national law and, in particular, the terms of the contract may allow the carrier to effect the carriage and the delivery of the goods in a way not contemplated in the original agreement.

IV. The Shipper's Obligations

Under the contract of carriage, the shipper's foremost duty is to pay the agreed amount of freight. Also, there are a number of obligations relating to the goods prior to shipment.

1. The Pre-Shipment Obligations

In order to allow the carrier to perform the carriage, the shipper must provide information on the goods to the carrier, e.g. its dimensions, weight, and marks. This applies, in particular, if dangerous goods are shipped. Here, the shipper is required to give the necessary information to the carrier and to observe any international regulations as well as the national regulations applicable in the port of loading. Further, the shipper must sufficiently pack goods to ensure that they are not damaged during transport, and that neither the persons handling the goods nor the ship nor other goods loaded are affected. This applies, in particular, to the stuffing of containers and the securing of the goods in closed containers or on flat racks. Both the law applicable to the contract of carriage as well as the terms of the contract may provide that the shipper is liable for all damages suffered by the carrier rising from the non-observance of the aforementioned obligations, even to the extent that the shipper is responsible regardless of fault. All the international conventions referred to above, particular the Hague and the Hague/Visby Rules feature provisions on the shipper's liability, with strict liability in relation to dangerous goods.

Also, the shipper must deliver the goods to the carrier in time for the contemplated departure. It is for the national law and the terms of the contract to determine the carrier's rights in case the goods are not provided in a timely manner. In particular, the carrier may be entitled to cancel the contract and/or to claim damages. If the shipper fails to supply the goods, the carrier may have a claim for deadfreight, i.e. the freight originally agreed, perhaps with deductions in respect of costs saved.

2. The Obligation to Pay Freight

The shipper's primary obligation under the contract of carriage is to pay the agreed freight. The national law applicable or the terms of the contract will specify when the freight is payable. It may be due right after the goods have been accepted for carriage, upon shipment, upon the issuance of a bill of lading (see below H.) or on delivery of the goods. In many instances, the carrier accepts a credit period.

The law applicable to the contract of carriage as well as its terms determine the effects of a loss of the goods prior to shipment or upon shipment on the carrier's freight claim and whether the freight is reduced in case of loss of or damage to the goods. The freight may be increased if, on the shipper's instructions, the carrier is bound to transport the goods further than originally agreed. The respective legislation may prohibit, in favour of the carrier, any set-off of counter-claims against the carrier's claim for freight. If the shipper fails to deliver the goods to the carrier at the port of loading, the carrier is able to claim deadfreight.

Beyond the freight, the carrier may be entitled to claim for reimbursement of extraordinary expenses incurred for the transport and the delivery of the goods. It is for the law applicable to the contract to decide what circumstances the carrier may claim the freight and expenses from the consignee. Normally, the carrier's claim for freight and expenses against the shipper and/or the consignee is secured by a lien on the goods.

V. The Consignee

Under a contract of carriage, the carrier must deliver the goods, at the port of destination, to the consignee. Normally, the consignee is a third party not identical with the shipper, in particular in a sales contract situation where the goods need to be shipped from the seller to the buyer. However, situations may occur where the consignee and the shipper is one and the same person, i.e. if the shipper needs to transport his own goods to the port of destination, e.g. if a contractor ships material and machines to an overseas construction site or in case household goods are moved.

In some legislations, the contractual relation to a party who has not concluded the contract may give rise to problems. The applicable national law and the terms of the contract of carriage determine the consignee's position in relation to the carrier and in what circumstances rights against the carrier arise. In particular, the consignee may obtain the right to claim delivery of the goods from the carrier, either at the moment the contract is concluded, when the goods are shipped, or at a later stage, e.g. only when the goods arrive at the port of destination. Moreover, it may be relevant whether and in what circumstances the shipper, by giving the appropriate instructions to the carrier, may determine that the goods are delivered to another consignee, thus terminating the first consignee's rights.

Another issue may be whether and in what circumstances the carrier may actually bring claims against the consignee. The claims may, e.g. be for freight and expenses arising under the contract, or for container demurrage in case of a late delivery of a container to the carrier. Also, it may be necessary to clarify whether the shipper remains responsible for these amounts once the consignee's liability arises.

VI. The Carrier's Liability for Cargo Damage

By far the most disputes in shipping concern the carrier's liability for loss of or damage to the goods or for delay in delivery. These issues are extensively dealt with in the relevant maritime conventions, in particular the Hague and the Hague/Visby Rules. Normally, the respective national law in relation to the carrier's liability for cargo damage applies mandatorily, to the effect that any deviating terms in the contract are void. The provisions on the carrier's liability for cargo damage included in the maritime conventions and the corresponding national law are in line with the accepted standard which today can be found, in principle, in all other international transport conventions.

1. THE BASIS OF LIABILITY

The carrier's liability is established if the claimant is able to prove that the (partial) loss of or damage to the goods occurred in the period between the carrier's acceptance of the goods at the port of loading and their delivery. In case of a total loss of the goods, there is of course no delivery. The acceptance of the goods in their full amount and in undamaged condition by the carrier often is evidenced by a receipt issued by the carrier, normally contained in the bill of lading or a sea waybill. Insofar, problems may arise in respect of goods delivered to the carrier in closed transport units such as containers. The partial loss of or damage to the goods at the time of delivery often are investigated with the assistance of experts who determine the extent of the loss and the damage.

2. THE DEFENCES

If the claimant succeeded in proving that the loss of or damage to the goods occurred while they were in the carrier's custody, he may come forward with the defences available to him. Insofar, the burden of proof is fully on the carrier. He may raise one or more of the available defences. The Hague Rules' traditional catalogue of defences can, in principle, be found, in a modernised form, in any of the international transport conventions as well as in a number of national legislations.

The carrier may prove that the damage resulted from perils of the sea, force majeure, war, terrorist acts, arrest proceedings, government interference, quarantine restrictions, acts and omissions of the shipper or his servants and sub-contractors, labour disputes such as strikes and lockouts, riots and civil commotions, saving or attempting to save life or property at sea, an inherent vice of the goods, insufficiency of packing, insufficiency and inadequacy of marks, and latent defects. The most prominent and much discussed defences are the exclusion of liability in case of fire (not necessarily on the ship) and, in particular, the unique error in navigation defence. Here, the carrier's liability is excluded if the damage to the goods was caused by any act or omission of the crew in the navigation or in the management of the ship.

If the carrier is not able to rely on one of these special defences, he may still escape liability if he proves that the damage was not caused by negligence on the part of the carrier or any of his servants and sub-contractors or the vessel's crew. If the carrier is unable to raise a defence, he remains liable for the damage as proven by the claimant.

3. Title to Sue

It is for the law otherwise applicable to the contract of carriage to determine who is entitled to claim, in case of loss of damage to the goods, from the carrier. Normally, it is the consignee who may bring corresponding claims against the carrier. The respective damage claims compensate for the lost value of the consignee's claim for delivery of the goods. The relevant legislation may also provide that, alternatively, it is only the shipper who may claim or that both the shipper and the consignee are entitled to bring claims against the carrier. In case a cargo insurer is involved and compensation is paid to the consignee or the shipper as insured under the insurance contract, the insurance claim against the carrier may be transferred to the insurer allowing him to directly reclaim from the carrier. Such a transfer of rights may be based on the respective law applicable to the insurance contract or to corresponding agreements in the contract. Another alternative is that there is only a subrogation of rights to the insurer. This leaves the insured's claims against the carrier intact. In case a bill of lading is issued it is normally only the holder of the document who may claim against the carrier to the exclusion of shipper.

4. The Value of the Goods

The carrier's liability for loss of or damage to the goods, once it is established, is subject to the specific characteristics of the transport law. In particular, the carrier the only needs to compensate the value of the goods lost or damaged. In case of a loss, the carrier must reimburse the value of the goods lost. If the goods are damaged, the carrier is liable for the balance of the good's value in sound and in damaged condition. The value of the goods and any balance of value is determined in relation to the time and place where the goods actually were delivered or should have been delivered. The CIF-price of the goods as specified in a commercial invoice may serve as an indication as to the value of the goods. If the invoice only states the FOB-price, the agreed freight may be added to obtain an indication of the good's value at the port of destination. However, in the circumstances the good's actual value at the port of destination, ultimately established e.g. by expert evidence, may differ from the amount stated in the commercial invoice.

The fact that the carrier's liability is tied to the value of the goods implies a limitation of liability, as the carrier is not responsible for any consequential damages such as, in particular, loss of profit, e.g. where a plant operated by the consignee needs to be shut down temporarily due to the non-delivery of or the damaged condition of material. Also, the focus on the value of the dates to the exclusion of any other heads of claim would also apply in respect of costs incurred for expert evidence to establish the amount and the reason for the damage, which thus may not be recoverable. On the other hand, the concept that the carrier's liability is based on the value of the goods is also applied in cases where the damage suffered by the shipper and/or consignee in fact is less than the value of the goods, e.g. in cases were goods are shipped for humanitarian purposes with no underlying sales contract. Here, the carrier may not refer the claimant to the fact that the consignee in fact did not suffer any loss because he obtained or would have obtained the goods without having to pay for them.

5. LIMITED LIABILITY

The carrier's liability relating to the value of the reduction of the value of the goods is subject to a further limitation. His liability is capped at a particular amount to the effect that he, in principle, does not need to compensate the claimant beyond that amount. The capped liability is part of the compromise reached in respect of the Hague Rules (see E I. above) which can be found in all of today's international transport conventions. The Hague/Visby Rules, which are the industry standard of today, limit the carrier's liability to 2 SDR per kilogram of the goods lost or damaged or to an amount of 666.67 SDR per package or unit, whichever is the higher. This awkward alternative way of calculating the limitation amount is the result of the negotiations concerning the Visby Protocol. The cap is not relevant if the damages recoverable from the carrier do not reach the respective limitation amount.

If e.g. one vehicle weighing 2,000 kg is shipped, the kilogram alternative would lead to 4,000 SDR whilst the package alternative would allow only 666.67 SDR. Here, the kilogram alternative would be relevant. Generally, it prevails in cases where the respective package or unit weighs less than 333.33 kg. The provisions for the calculation of the limitation amount clearly have general cargo in mind. In cases of bulk cargo, it is doubtful whether the package alternative is applicable at all. There are no packages. It is unclear whether the term "unit" includes units relating to the amount of the cargo, i.e. normally its weight in tons. If so understood, the package alternative would determine the cap at 666.67 SDR per ton, whilst the kilogram alternative would arrive at 2.000 SDR. In any event, the value of the bulk cargo in most cases is less than 666.67 SDR per ton, so that the cap would be irrelevant anyway.

Difficulties may arise when containers are shipped. If the loaded container weighs 10 tons, the kilogram alternative would cap the carrier's liability at 20,000 SDR. If the respective container is stuffed with 10 pallets each loaded with 100 cartons, it would need to be determined whether, for the purpose of applying the package alternative, the relevant package is the (one) container or whether one would need to consider the (10) pallets or the (1,000) cartons. Here, the package alternative would arrive at 666.67 SDR (one container), 6,666.7 SDR (10 pallets) or 666,670 SDR (1,000 cartons). As a result, the kilogram alternative would be relevant if the container or the pallets are considered to be the respective packages, while the package alternative would prevail if it is assumed that the cartons are the yardstick. In fact, the amount of 666,670 SDR in most cases would exceed the damages recoverable from the carrier, to the effect that there would in fact be no limitation.

The Visby Protocol introduced a regulation generally referred to as the "Container Clause" (although it is not a contractual clause but a statutory provision) which addresses the problem. It provides that the number of packages noted in the bill of lading as being stowed in the container shall be deemed the number of packages for the purposes of the package alternative. Otherwise, the container is considered to be the relevant package. The national law applicable to the contract of carriage may verify that the Container Clause also applies in cases were no bill of lading but a sea waybill is issued. However, the Container Clause is not of immediate assistance if the carrier does not issue a transport document at all or if a bill of lading or a sea waybill is issued by a sub-carrier.

6. Unlimited Liability

In certain cases, the carrier is not entitled to rely on the limitations of liability. This is so where the damage resulted from an act or omission of the carrier done with intent to cause damage, or recklessly and with knowledge that damage would probably result. This proviso and its somewhat bulky wording was introduced by the Visby Rules first, but meanwhile has found its way into all international transport conventions as well as all international maritime liability conventions. Both alternatives are addressed here as "qualified fault". In practice, they may be difficult to apply as both of them refer to the state of mind of the respective person. Normally, the court must rely on the facts of the case to conclude that the respective acts or omissions were intended or the result of recklessness. In any event, it is important to note that it is only the carrier's personal "qualified fault" which deprives him of the limitations. They are left untouched in cases of qualified fault of his servant's and sub-contractor's or the vessel's crew. This may not be so in other international transport law conventions, where the servants' and subcontractors' qualified fault is not sufficient to break limitation.

7. Delay in Delivery

The carrier may be responsible for any delay in the delivery of the goods. International maritime law traditionaly was slow to introduce a corresponding liability of the carrier. Neither the Hague Rules nor the Hague/Visby Rules address that issue. Only the Hamburg and the Rotterdam Rules feature regulations on the carrier's liability for delay delivery. As a result, the carrier's corresponding liability normally is subject to the national law applicable to the contract of carriage. The respective regulations determine whether the carrier is liable at all, whether the carrier may escape liability by proving that he acted diligently, whether liability is limited in some way, and whether the parties may agree on deviating terms in the contract of carriage. Both the Hamburg and the Rotterdam Rules provide for a cap at 2.5 times the freight.

8. The Actual Carrier's Liability

In principle, it is only the (contractual) carrier who is responsible for the loss of the damage to the goods vis-à-vis the shipper and/or consignee. However, it has become common also to involve the actual carrier, who is liable for the damage in the same way as the contractual carrier. Neither the Hague nor the Hague/Visby Rules refer to the actual carrier. Only the Hamburg and the Rotterdam Rules feature corresponding provisions which address the actual carrier or, as he is referred to in the Rotterdam Rules, the maritime performing party. In principle, the actual carrier is liable for the loss of and the damage to the goods as well as the delay in delivery, respectively, in the same way as the contractual carrier. The purpose is to allow the shipper and/or consignee to proceed either against the contractual or against the actual carrier or against both. The actual and the contractual carrier's liabilities for cargo damage are identical in many respects. However, if the contractual carrier agreed on more generous terms in respect of his liability for cargo damage, this would only affect the actual carrier if he agreed to it. The actual carrier is the party who performs the services owed by the contractual carrier. Normally, this would be the owner of the respective vessel on which the damage occurred.

VII. INTERNATIONAL PRIVATE LAW ISSUES

In most cases, the circumstances concerning contracts of carriage are linked to more than one jurisdiction. Here, the legislation applicable to the contract of carriage needs to be determined. The court will readily apply its own international private law principles, i.e. those of the state where the court is located. European courts would refer to the Rome I Regulation.[6]

Traditionally, international private law would accept agreements in the contract on the law to be applied. The parties thus are free to choose the legislation the contract is subject to. This is also the approach favoured by Article 3 of the Rome I Regulation. It would depend on the respective international private law whether any formalities need to be observed or whether an oral or even an implied choice of law is acceptable. Also, the agreements on the relevant legislation often are found in one party's general terms. Shipping lines acting as carriers would routinely include choice of law clauses in their general terms. The respective international private law principles also would decide whether the parties may agree on the law applicable after the conclusion of the contract of carriage, e.g. when a dispute arises.

The parties may be entitled to include a partial choice of law agreement in the contract of carriage, limited to certain aspects. Often, it is the carrier's liability for loss of or damage to the goods which may be subject to one legislation, while the contract otherwise is governed by the law determined by the general choice of law clause or by the principles relevant in the absence of such a clause. This may in particular be the case if the contract includes a Paramount Clause (see below H XI.). A partial choice of law may refer to all legal provisions of the respective law relating to the particular issue. However, in particular Paramount Clauses, which qualify as partial choice of law clauses, reference may be made to a set of regulations only and not to the full body of the respective law. Here, it is the law otherwise applicable to the contract of carriage, which remains relevant in case the regulations referred to are incomplete.

If there is no choice of law agreement in the contract of carriage, the general international private law principles to determine the applicable law in the absence of a choice of law need to be considered. In Europe, Article 5.1 of the Rome I Regulation is relevant. It offers two alternatives. The law of the state where the carrier has his habitual place of residence is to be applied if either the port of loading or the port of destination or the habitual residence of the shipper is located in that same state. If this does not lead to any results, contract of carriage is subject to the law of the state of the port of destination.

H. BILLS OF LADING

Since centuries, bills of lading have been the most important shipping documents. They are issued by the carrier and in certain respects can be considered to replace the goods loaded on the ship and under way to the port of destination, thus facilitating the performance of the underlying sales contract and allowing the buyer's to re-sell the floating goods to another buyer. The bills of lading considered here refer to a voyage from the port of loading to the port of destination, where the goods are delivered to the holder of the bill. Similar documents are used in multimodal transport (considered elsewhere in this book).

I. THE CONCEPT

The purpose of a bill of lading is to assist in the performance of the underlying sales contract, in particular in relation to the payment of the purchase price. In an international sales contract requiring transport of the goods overseas, the buyer normally would not wish to pay for the goods before they are delivered to and inspected by him and the seller would hesitate to ship goods before he received the agreed price. There are a number of tools available which seek to protect the interests of both parties to the sales contract. One of them traditionally was and today still is the bill of lading. The seller delivers the goods to the carrier and receives the bill, which he then passes on to the buyer for payment while the goods are still underway. Also, the buyer may be interested to re-sell the goods to yet another buyer while they are still on their way to the port of destination. Therefore, it is necessary that the bill of lading can be transferred to another party, which obtains all the rights in the goods. In some trades, the goods are sold a number of times before they arrive at the port of destination.

In these situations, the bill of lading in a particular way represents goods. The buyer effectively buys the bill of lading and must pay the full price for it. As a result, it is of paramount importance that the bill of lading protects the interests of its holder in the goods and their delivery, as the buyer relies on the position conveyed by the bill of lading. To that effect, the bill of lading has a number of features, which seek to protect its holder. E.g., the bill of lading is a receipt which confirms that the carrier has received the goods, it may confirm that the goods have been loaded onto the vessel, it provides for certain statutory assumptions as to the correctness relating to the details of the goods stated in the document, and the carrier is under the obligation to deliver the goods only against presentation of the bill (see below VIII.).

The basis for the various functions of a bill of lading as described in the preceding paragraphs is the relevant legislation governing the bill. Some issues already are addressed in the respective maritime conventions, in particular in the Hague and the Hague/Visby Rules as well as in the Hamburg and Rotterdam Rules. Other aspects are covered in the national law applicable to the bill. The overall concept in all cases is to protect the position of the holder of the bill of lading and his rights in the goods. The respective national laws may vary, however, in their approach how to achieve this. The Anglo-Saxon system understands the bill of lading to be a document of title which by itself conveys the rights in the goods to the holder. Other systems do not rely on that concept, but achieve corresponding results by other means.

II. Bills of Lading and Contracts of Carriage

The relation between bills of lading and contracts of carriage is determined by the respective national law. Again, there may be different approaches. The Anglo-Saxon system, in principle, does not distinguish between the two and assumes that the bill of lading evidences the bill of lading contract. Only in cases where the bill of lading is issued by the owner under a voyage or time charter, the bill of lading and the relation between its holder and the owner is separate from the charter concluded between the owner and the charterer. Another approach is to assume that bills of lading and the contract of carriage (as well as voyage and time charters) are to be distinguished and independent from each other. Obviously, a number of issues may arise here, e.g. whether the terms of the bill of lading may be different from the terms of the contract of carriage or whether the carrier may find himself in a situation where the holder of the bill of lading is not the same as the consignee under the contract of carriage, both claiming for delivery of the goods. It may even be that the bill of lading and the contract of carriage are governed by two different legislations (perhaps with only one of them accepting the separation between the bill and the contract of carriage).

III. The Issuance of the Bill

The carrier may be under the obligation to issue a bill of lading to the shipper. It is for the respective legislation to decide whether the shipper's claim arises automatically or whether an agreement to that effect is required. Under the Hague and the Hague/Visby Rules, there is a statutory obligation of the carrier to issue a bill of lading. Normally, in particular in the liner trade, the shipper would prepare the document based on a form provided by the carrier. In particular, the shipper would insert the relevant data, including details as to the goods and their amount and condition. The carrier is bound to issue the bill with the details relating to the goods as supplied by the shipper. However, the carrier is entitled to make reservations in the bill. As these in many cases are unacceptable for the shipper, because they would render the bill of lading useless for the purposes of the sales contract, quite a number of disputes have arisen on this point.

The carrier may issue the bill after he received the goods from the shipper. However, the bill of lading would offer more value if the carrier confirmed that the goods already have been loaded, as the bill would indicate that an interference by the shipper now is less likely. Therefore, in practice the carrier issues shipped bills of lading confirming that the goods are on the vessel. If the carrier issued the bill of lading after he received them for shipment, the shipper may present the bill of lading to the carrier for him to add a "shipped on board" remark.

IV. THE BILL OF LADING LAYOUT AND TERMS

Today, bills of lading feature a typical layout. On the front page there are a number of boxes where e.g. the names of the shipper and the consignee, the port of loading at the port of destination, the name of the vessel and details regarding the goods, i.e. the type of goods, the amount and their condition may be entered. At bottom right, there is a box in which the date and place of the bill of lading may be stated and where the carrier or a person acting on his behalf signs the document. The signature is crucial, as it is, in most legislations, one of the fundamental requirements that convert a document into a bill of lading with its particular effects.

On the reverse side, the carrier's bill of lading terms are reproduced, usually in small print. Normally, the bill of lading terms include jurisdiction and choice of law clauses. Quite a number of Bill of Lading forms are available, many of them provided by BIMCO. One recognized form is the Conlinebill, its latest edition being of 2016, which is designed to be used by shipping lines. Today, most bills of lading are paper documents. However, it is likely that electronic bills of lading are introduced on a broad scale in the near future.

The bill of lading is subject to the applicable national law determined by the relevant principles of international private law (see below X.). Often, the national law is based on the Hague or Hague/Visby Rules (see E I. and II. above). As far as the national law applies mandatorily, any deviating terms in the bill of lading are void. Also, the respective legislation may provide that general terms used by one party are subject to judicial review. This would also apply to the carrier's bill of lading terms.

V. Three Types of Bills of Lading

There are three types of bills of lading, which are distinguished by the way the party entitled to claim under the bill is identified. Traditionally, the prototype is the order bill of lading. It is issued "to the order" of a particular person. Alternatively, if no such person is named, it is normally issued to the order of the shipper. The second type is the bearer bill of lading. It is the party in whose possession the bill is who is entitled to claim. In practice, bearer bills are normally not issued as such. However, an order bill of lading may be transformed, by way of a blank endorsement, into a bearer bill (see below VI.). The last type is the named bill of lading. Here, the person entitled to claim is identified by name in the document. Some legislations do not recognise named bills as proper bills of lading, but consider them to be mere sea waybills (see below XII.).

VI. The Transfer of the Bill

One of the important functions of the bill of lading is that it is transferable, thus allowing to on-sell the goods whilst they are loaded on the vessel and on their way to the port of destination. Once issued, the first holder, may transfer the bill to another party. It is that party who is then entitled to claim from the carrier while the previous holder's position in relation to the carrier ends. It is the law governing the bill of lading, which determines whether and by what means the bill of lading can be transferred.

The most prominent way to achieve this is when order bills of lading are transferred to another party by way of a formal endorsement. Normally, this is merely a notification on the reverse side of the bill of lading, signed by the previous holder, clarifying that the bill is transferred to a certain named party. Alternatively, the previous holder may add a blank endorsement to the bill, which clarifies that it is transferred without specifying to whom. This will have the effect that any holder who has the bill of lading in his possession is entitled to claim from the carrier. Such a bill of lading may then be transferred to the next holder by simply handing the document over to him to the effect that it is now in his possession.

One way of transferring named bills of lading, if they are recognised as proper bills of lading, to the next holder is to transfer the claim for delivery of the goods against the carrier evidenced by the bill. The new holder would then be entitled to the bill, which he requires to claim the goods from the carrier. Insofar, it could be said that the document follows the title.

VII. THE EFFECTS OF A BILL OF LADING

The bill of lading has a number of functions, which serve to reinforce the position of the holder of the bill in relation to the carrier. In the bill of lading, the carrier confirms that he has received the goods. Insofar, the bill of lading is a receipt. Also, in case of a shipped bill of lading, the carrier further confirms that the goods have been loaded on the vessel. Therefore, the holder may assume that the seller of the goods now is less likely to interfere and that it would be difficult for him to retrieve the goods from the carrier. Further, there is a statutory assumption that the declarations in the bill concerning the goods, their amount and their condition are correct, which shifts, in case of a dispute, the burden of proof to the carrier. In certain circumstances, the assumption may even be binding on the carrier who is thus barred from proving otherwise. It would seem that here the focus of the carrier's liability is not any more on the compensation of a loss of or damage to the goods but the issuance of a bill of lading with incorrect declarations as to the goods. The most important tool, however, to protect the holder's interest in the goods is that the carrier may only deliver the goods if the original of the bill of lading is physically presented to him (see below VIII.).

VIII. DELIVERY OF THE GOODS UNDER A BILL OF LADING

The holder's principal claim under a bill of lading against the carrier is for the delivery of the goods. In order to obtain the goods, the holder must physically present the original of the bill of lading to the carrier. Normally, if more than one original has been issued, it is sufficient that one original is presented. This is confirmed by the phrase "... one [of the originals] to be accomplished the others to stand void ... ". These words also clarify that the bill of lading needs to be presented to the carrier in order to raise the claim for delivery of the goods. It is not sufficient that a copy is submitted or sent by fax or email to the carrier. The requirement of a presentation of the original seeks to ensure that the carrier delivers the goods to the holder of the bill and no other. This principle, at the same time, confirms that the carrier is entitled to deliver the goods to the party presenting the bill. If the carrier delivers the goods to a third party which is not the holder of the bill, the carrier is responsible, vis-à-vis the holder, for the total loss of the goods. Also, delivering the goods to third party who is not identified in the bill normally would amount to a criminal offence.

The somewhat archaic principle that an original document needs to be presented serves to protect the holder and his position in relation to the carrier, but is also one of the drawbacks of the system, because the bill of lading must be available when the holder wishes the goods to be delivered. It is not uncommon that the original bills of lading have not yet arrived, to the effect that the holder is not entitled to claim. In practice, the carrier may agree to deliver the goods to the holder without presentation of the bill, but against a security to be provided by the person claiming to be the holder. This is obviously against the principles relating to the function of the bill of lading. Any carrier should be aware that delivering the goods without presentation of the bill of lading would expose him to a number of risks including liability for loss of the goods, criminal liability and perhaps the loss of insurance cover.

IX. THE CARRIER'S LIABILITY FOR CARGO DAMAGE UNDER THE BILL OF LADING

The case of loss of or damage to the goods or if there is a delay in delivery, the carrier of the bill of lading would be liable for the damages suffered by the holder of the bill just as a carrier would be under a contract of carriage (for details, see G VI. above). The holder of the bill would need to demonstrate that the damage occurred while the goods were in the custody of the carrier. Insofar, the holder would be supported by the assumptions as to the details of the goods provided in the bill of lading. In the circumstances, these assumptions may even be binding on the carrier to the effect that he would be unable to rebut them. All relevant defences are available to the carrier. He is only liable for the value of the goods lost and the difference in the value of the goods in undamaged and damaged condition. Also, the carrier's liability may be limited to the relevant limitation amount.

X. INTERNATIONAL PRIVATE LAW ISSUES

The bill of lading is subject to the national law determined by the relevant principles of the international private law on bills of lading. So far, the Rome I Regulation in many cases will not be applicable, as claims arising under bill of lading would be subject to the exceptions clause in Article 1.2 (d), which excludes, from the scope of the regulations, obligations arising under a number of enumerated and other negotiable documents, which would include bills of lading, to the extent that the respective obligations arise out of the negotiable character of the document.

As a result, if the Rome I Regulation is not applied, it would be the international private law found in the respective national legislations of the court seized which determines the law applicable to the bill of lading. In legislations, which assume that the relationship flowing from the bill of lading is separate and independent from the underlying contract of carriage, the contract and the bill of lading may be subject to different laws. The relevant international private law principles will often refer to a choice of law clause routinely included in the bill of lading terms. Also, there may be a partial choice of law, in particular in Paramount Clauses (see below XI.).

In case there is no choice of law, it may be determined that the bill of lading is subject to the law of the state in which the carrier has his habitual residence or the law of the state of the port of destination named in the bill of lading. The fact that Article 5.1 Rome I Regulation provides likewise in respect of a contract of carriage does not exclude corresponding principles in the relevant international private law concerning bills of lading.

XI. PARAMOUNT CLAUSES

Most bills of lading feature Paramount Clauses. They may also be found in contracts of carriage as well as in voyage and time charters. The purpose of a Paramount Clause is to ensure that the bill of lading is subject to the Hague or the Hague/Visby Rules or a legislation based on the Hague or the Hague/Visby Rules. There may be also Paramount Clauses relating to the Hamburg and, in the future, to the Rotterdam Rules and the corresponding legislations. Often, Paramount Clauses are not easy to understand and may include a number of applications arranged in a hierarchy. In some cases, Paramount Clauses may be understood to be partial choice of law agreements relating to a national legislation adopting the Hague or the Hague/Visby Rules. More often, however, Paramount Clauses would only serve to include the Hague or the Hague/Visby Rules or the provisions of the identified legislation based these conventions into the bill of lading terms as further conditions. As the term "paramount" suggests, the Hague and Hague/Visby Rules and the provisions of the relevant legislation would have priority over the written terms. The bill of lading would still be subject to the respective law. If that law applies mandatorily, any of the incorporated Hague or Hague/Visby Rules or the provisions of the corresponding legislation, which deviate from the law applicable are disregarded.

XII. Bills of Lading and Sea Waybills

At the outset, bills of lading are very similar to sea waybills. Both documents feature the same layout, in particular identical boxes on the front page and often identical terms on the reverse side. However, bills of lading are documents of title and may be the basis of a separate legal relation between the holder and the carrier, while sea waybills merely evidence the contract of carriage. It is for the respective national legislation to qualify the document as being a bill of lading or a sea waybill. If the document features the proviso "... one to be accomplished, the others to stand void ... " (see VIII. above), this may be an indication that it is a Bill of Lading.

I. Contracts of Affreightment; Frame Agreements

Both contracts of carriage and bills of lading refer to one shipment of goods from the port of loading to the port of destination. The contract of carriage relating to each consignment needs to be negotiated individually (often concluded by way of an informal booking). However, a shipper may have larger quantities of goods that need to be shipped on a regular basis. Here, he may enter into a contract of affreightment with a carrier. This type of contract refers to a number of uniform shipments. The parties would, in particular, agree on the amounts of cargo to be shipped and the relevant times, e.g. 50 containers per month. The shipper is be able to negotiate more competitive freight rates if the contract concerns larger amounts of cargo. Also, the parties would agree on the terms for the performance of individual shipments. Under a contract of affreightment, the carrier is bound to carry the goods received from the shipper in performance of the contract. Insofar, the contract of affreightment has the characteristics of a special contract of carriage.

Moreover, the shipper is under the obligation to ship the contracted amount of cargo with the carrier. The individual shipments under a contract of affreightment would be subject to separate contracts of carriage (or voyage charters), the terms of which already are determined in the contract of affreightment. The formalities for the conclusion of the separate contracts of carriage are laid out in the contract of affreightment. In the circumstances, it may be sufficient that the shipper merely delivers the goods to the carrier at the agreed times. In the circumstances, the carrier may be bound, under the contract of affreightment, to issue bills of lading relating to each shipment.

Another type of "overall" contract is the frame agreement. The parties would agree on the rates for shipments as well as their terms. However, the shipper is not bound to ship a particular amount of cargo with the carrier. The frame agreement would only become relevant if cargo is shipped. In a frame agreement, the shipper may also bind himself to the effect that he is under the obligation to ship all cargo to which the agreement relates with the carrier (to the exclusion of other carriers). This, however, may in the circumstances give rise to antitrust issues.

NOTES

1 International Convention for the Unification of Certain Rules of Law relating to Bills of Lading, 1924.
2 Hague Rules as amended by the Protocol of 1968.
3 United Nations International Convention on the Carriage of Goods by Sea, 1978.
4 United Nations Convention on Contracts for the International Carriage of Goods Wholly or Partly by Sea, 2008.
5 www.bimco.org.
6 Regulation (EC) No 593/2008 of the European Parliament and of the Council of 17 June 2008 on the law applicable to contractual obligations.

CHAPTER VIII

CHARTER PARTIES

Klaus RAMMING

In the maritime industry charter parties are a type of contract widely used for a number of purposes. The principal concept is that the vessel owner lets the ship or perhaps a part of it to the charterer who may then makes use of the vessel. Again, the focus is on the carriage of goods. In that respect, charter parties need to be distinguished from contracts of carriage. However, time and bareboat charters may also relate to vessels not involved in the transport of goods. In practice, the term "charter party" is used in two different ways. Firstly, it refers to the contract entered into by the parties. Further, the word "charter party" concerns the document in which the terms of the charter are evidenced.

A. INTRODUCTION

I. TYPES OF CHARTER PARTIES

There are three traditional types of internationally recognised charter parties. The voyage charter basically is concerned with one voyage with cargo from the port of loading to the port of destination. The owner provides a vessel, which is fully operational. He shoulders all ship related costs e.g. for the crew, fuel and insurance. A time charter refers to a manned vessel and normally is concluded for a particular period of time, in which the time charterer may employ the vessel as he sees fit and within the limits provided for in the charter. While the crew costs are borne by the owner, the time charterer is responsible for the fuel. The vessel may be used for the transport of goods or for other functions such as the carriage of passengers or further purposes. A bareboat charter in some respects is similar to a time charter, with the excep tion, however, that the vessel is provided to the charterer without a crew. As a result, it is upon the charterer to man the vessel to enable him to operate it.

II. THE PARTIES OF THE CHARTER

A charter party is concluded between the owner, who provides the vessel, and the (voyage, time or bareboat) charterer. Traditionally, the term "owner" is used, even if that particular person does not in fact own the vessel. If a distinction needs to be made, reference would be made to the "registered owner". In order to clarify that the owner in a charter is only the (head) charterer of the vessel, he may be addressed as "disponent owner". The counter party of the owner under the charter is the charterer, who has a position similar to the shipper in a contract of carriage. In jurisdictions where a distinction is made between the contractual and the non-contractual shipper (who initiates the shipment of the goods), the latter may also be relevant in a voyage charter context. Also, the voyage or time charter owner may be under the obligation to deliver the goods carried at the port of destination to a consignee not identical with the charterer/shipper.

III. THE CHARTERING OF SHIPS

The common feature of the various types of charter parties is that they are concerned with the letting of the ship to the charterer for the respective purpose. The voyage charter usually relates to the carriage of goods from the port of loading to the port of discharge. In that respect, the voyage charter is a particular form of contract of carriage. The latter focuses on the relevant goods, such as e.g. containers, whilst the vessel used to perform the carriage is generally of minor relevance. Under a voyage charter, the focus is on the vessel (or a part of it), which is used to carry the goods. The function of the time charter is to provide a manned ship to the time charterer. If the vessel is used to carry goods, there are some typical situations where time charters are preferred (instead of voyage charters). The ship may be time chartered to the charterer to allow him to offer a liner service with regular departures on certain routes. Another occasion where the parties would refer to a time charter may be where the time charter is for one laden voyage only (trip time charter, see below C VIII.) and thus replaces a voyage charter. Furthermore, the ship may be time chartered for other purposes than the carriage of goods. The bareboat charter is a particular contract for the purpose of leasing the unmanned "bare" ship to the charterer.

IV. THE BALANCE OF POWER

Often, the parties involved in negotiating a voyage charter, depending on the market situation, have a more balanced bargaining power than a shipper in relation to a shipping line (for details, see the chapter on Shipping Law). As a result, both would be able to ensure that their interests are protected. And in many instances, it would even be the charterer who would be in the dominating position. Correspondingly, the provisions of the national law applicable to charters normally do not apply mandatorily. Also, neither the Hague Rules[1] nor the Hague/Visby Rules[2] or the Hamburg[3] and Rotterdam Rules[4] apply to charter parties (for details on these conventions, see the chapter on Shipping Law).

V. THE LEGAL BASIS

Charter parties are subject to the relevant law applicable to the respective type of contract. Within the European Union, the provisions of the Rome I Regulation[5] are relevant to determine what state's law must be applied to the contract. Usually, a charter party would include a choice of law clause, which normally would be accepted under Article 3 Rome I Regulation. The provisions of Article 4 and 5 paragraph 1 Rome I Regulation would assist to determine the applicable law in cases where the charter does not feature a choice of law clause.

The relevant national law may then provide a legal framework for the particular type of charter party. It is for the national law to decide whether the parties may deviate from the statutory provisions in the respective charter. Normally, the national law on charter parties is not mandatory so that the parties are free to agree on any terms. Typically, the regulations on charter parties in the national law are less specific and assume that the parties are able to negotiate and agree on the details of the charter between themselves.

It also depends on the respective national law whether and to what extent the parties may rely on general terms and conditions. In some jurisdictions, general terms are subject to judicial review. This may also apply to charter parties.

The international conventions on the carriage of goods, in particular the Hague or Hague/Visby Rules and the Hamburg Rules traditionally refrain from extending their scope of application to charter parties. One of the functions of the international conventions on the carriage of goods is to overcome the traditionally limited bargaining power of shippers vis-a-vis carriers, in particular liner services (for details, see the chapter on Shipping Law, see D I.). Contrary to that, in the charter market there are usually stakeholders of approximately equal strength, sometimes even with the shippers/charterers in the stronger position. As a result, it is not necessary to improve the position of the shipper or charterer, respectively.

VI. The Charter Party Forms

If a charter party is concluded, the parties frequently refer to standard forms provided by the industry as a basis for the contract. Quite a number of forms are available in the market, for different types of charters, for different vessels such as dry cargo vessels or tankers, or for different cargoes such as general cargo, containers, and various dry and wet bulk cargoes. One of the most important providers for standard charter party forms is BIMCO,[6] an organisation located in Copenhagen who acts as a shipping advisor to its customers and renders various services to the maritime industry. The standard forms submitted by BIMCO are available on their homepage and are regularly reviewed and updated.

Modern standard forms normally consist of two parts. The front page, normally referred to as "Part I", features a number of labelled boxes in which the parties are expected to make certain entries concerning the characteristics of the charter, such as the identity of the parties, the name of the vessel, the cargo to be carried or trading limits, respectively, the freight or hire payable, as well as further details. Part II of the form features, often in small print, the further terms of the contract. These may, depending on the form, be quite detailed. It is normally intended that the clauses in Part II remain unaltered. However, in practice this does not always happen. Words, sentences, paragraphs and full clauses may be deleted or amended as the parties may agree. Also, so called "Rider Clauses" can be added to the charter complementing the pre-printed text of the form. As the parties in the heat of the negotiations may have a tendency to overact, it sometimes can be difficult to reconcile all the agreements made. As a result, regular courts and tribunals dealing with charter party disputes often are faced with a difficult job when it comes to construing the contents of a charter.

VII. Concluding the Contract

Charter parties are contracts entered into by the vessel owner and the (voyage, time or bareboat) charterer. Whether the contract in the circumstances was validly concluded is normally, in particular as per Article 10.1 Rome I Regulation, determined by the law applicable to the contract (assuming that it in fact has been concluded between the parties).

In the chartering industry, it is usual that one or more brokers are involved in the negotiations. They may be appointed by and act for either the owner or the charterer or in certain circumstances for both parties, which may give rise to a conflict of interest. In practice, the parties, with the broker's assistance, seek to agree on the main terms of the charter whilst leaving the details to the agreed standard form and perhaps rider clauses. Often, the parties will just refer to the terms of a previously concluded charter (not necessarily between the parties now negotiating) "with logical alterations". As a result, the terms ultimately agreed are perhaps found in a series of documents with cross-references.

In practice, the negotiations are made by exchanging emails. Here, the parties traditionally use abbreviations, which may give rise to communication problems. One of the mechanisms is that the contract terms suggested by one party are accepted with the exception of the details the other party refers to in the counter email. This may be indicated by the abbreviation "a/e" ("accepted except"). Once the negotiations are finalised, either party or the broker may summarise the terms of the charter in a "fixture recap".

VIII. ARBITRATION AGREEMENTS

In many instances, charter parties feature an arbitration agreement. The parties wish to have their disputes determined not by the regular courts but by an arbitration tribunal. London and New York are the places of arbitration most frequently chosen. There are, however, other places such as Singapore, the Scandinavian States and Germany.

IX. THE CHARTER PARTY

Once the terms of the charter are successfully negotiated and the contract concluded, a charter party may be drawn up. This document includes all the agreed terms and thus evidences the contents of the charter. In some jurisdictions, there is a statutory assumption that the charter party reflects the agreed terms, i.e. that the provisions of the charter party correspond to the agreements reached and that there are no further agreements beyond the contents of the document. Normally, preparing the charter party is the job of the broker or brokers involved.

The relevant national law applicable to the charter may require, in order for the charter to be valid, that a charter party is drawn up. Mostly, the parties are free to decide whether a formal charter party is prepared. Also, the national law may give either party the right to produce a charter party. Sometimes there may be no charter party at all or it may be produced at a later stage, perhaps only when a dispute has arisen between the parties and evidence as to the contents of the charter is required.

The charter party standard forms provide boxes for the parties' signature. However, in practice a number of charter parties, in particular those drawn up at a later stage, remain unsigned or carry the signature of one party only. This normally would not impair the validity of the contract, but may affect any statutory assumptions, which would apply to a duly signed charter party.

X. CHAINS OF CONTRACTS

Typically, there is not only one charter, concluded directly between the registered owner and the charterer, but a chain of head and sub-charters. Often, the registered owner, in particular for flag purposes (see below D I.1), has bareboat-chartered out the vessel to a bareboat charterer. There may be further sub-bareboat charters. The bareboat charterer may then, as dispondent owner, let the vessel to a time charterer. In the circumstances, there may be one or more sub-time charters. The bareboat charterer or the (sub-) time charterer may further make use of the vessel at their disposal and enter into a voyage charter. Again, the voyage charterer may appear as an owner in a sub-voyage charter. It is not unusual that the chain of charters involves three, four or more sub-contracts. Every owner under the respective charters seeks to make profit. As a result, the hire or freight owed under any sub-charter would increase with each upstream link.

The same scenario can be considered from the opposite downstream perspective. The party who wishes to have its cargo carried may enter into a voyage charter and agree on a certain amount of freight. The owner will then seek to purchase the necessary services required to perform the voyage charter in the market and may conclude, as charterer, another voyage charter, with a lower freight. The balance between the rates of freight agreed is the owner's profit. Also, the owner may already have the vessel in time charter and will now use it to perform the sub voyage charter. Alternatively, the owner may time charter the vessel solely for the purpose of performing the sub-charter, perhaps on the basis of a corresponding trip time charter (see below C VIII.). The head owner who time chartered the vessel to the (voyage charter) owner may in turn time charter the vessel from another owner (who may be the bareboat charterer or the registered owner of the vessel). Normally, the hire payable under the head time charter would be less than the hire owed under the sub time charter.

The amounts of freight owed under the (head and sub-) voyage charters and the daily hire owed under the (head and sub-) time charter can be easily compared. In a chain of charter parties, however, the transition from a time to a voyage charter needs careful consideration. This applies to an intermediate owner who time charters the vessel and owes hire to the head owner and, as disponent owner, enters into a voyage charter against payment of freight. The time based hire and the voyage related freight cannot be directly compared. In order to make the business profitable, the intermediate owner would need to ensure that the freight earned under the sub voyage charter covers the hire payable to the head owner and, beyond that, the fuel and all other costs, which would fall upon the intermediate owner. In order to assist with the required comparison, the "time charter equivalent" may be calculated. The intermediate owner would need to define the costs based on the costs the time chartered owner would incur if he performed the voyage charter, e.g. the costs for fuel and other services not covered under the time charter, such as perhaps in relation to loading and discharging. Further, based on the calculated cost and the (expected) duration of the voyage, the owner would be able to calculate a (hypothetical) daily hire, which would allow him to perform the contemplated voyage under the sub voyage charter. Generally, a (sub) voyage charter is more profitable to the owner than a (sub) time charter.

The party acting as an intermediate (sub-)charterer/(head-)owner in a chain of charter parties faces particular risks. It would be in his immediate interest to ensure that the risks and liabilities under the head charter correspond to those under the sub charter. Ideally, the intermediate owner would seek to contract back-to-back, i.e. with identical terms (except for the hire or freight, respectively) in both the head- and the sub-contract. In particular, the intermediate owner would wish to be able to easily pass on any claims brought against him by his head owner to his sub-charterer. In practice, however, this may be difficult to achieve. As a result, some risks and liabilities may remain with the intermediate owner. One of the typical issues is that there are identical limitation periods for claims under the head and the sub charter. Thus, if the claim against the intermediate owner is brought right at the end of the limitation period, he may not be able to protect time in relation to his sub-charterer. Corresponding problems may in particular occur if the intermediate owner has time chartered the vessel to perform a sub-voyage-charter.

XI. Brokers

Charter parties are often concluded with the assistance of brokers. Their principal job is to bring together the parties to allow them to negotiate a charter. Often, brokers have specialised on particular trades such as container vessels or tankers. The broker may be involved by an owner seeking an employment for his vessel. Also, the party who needs to have cargo shipped to a particular destination would turn to a broker to find a suitable vessel. In the circumstances, the broker may act as an agent for both parties. Brokers constantly collect data on vessels and employment opportunities and thus have a particularly good overview over the market. Networking is essential for a broker. During the negotiations, the communication between the parties is channelled through the broker, who also assists by suggesting to use forms or certain terms to be included in the charter. If the broker is successful and the charter finally is concluded, he may be required to draw up a document evidencing the agreement is reached, i.e. a charter party.

For his services, the broker earns a commission, which usually is expressed as a certain percentage of the hire or freight and the demurrage, respectively. A commission is only due if the charter is finally concluded. An early termination of the charter likewise affects the brokers' claim for a commission. Normally, the commission is paid by the charterer. However, the parties may agree otherwise in the charter and e.g. split the commission between themselves. While the charter is performed, the broker would remain available to facilitate the performance of the charter and assist the parties.

XII. Port Agents

Another important figure, which appears in the charter business, is the port agent. He is familiar with its particulars of the port, renders a wide range of services to the vessel and generally is of assistance. The services may include the communication with the port authorities, with the pilots, tugs and linesmen as well as the local terminal and stevedores. The port agent will assist the vessel if a supply of bunkers, spare parts, groceries, freshwater or other items is required. He will also arrange for the transfer of crewmembers or assist them if they require medical help. It may also be the agent's job to give notices of readiness (on behalf of the vessel) or to accept them (on behalf of the charterer) and to prepare the statements of fact (see below B V.). Also, the port agent may, on behalf of the owner, issue bills of lading. He is normally appointed by the charterer, who also owes the fees for the agent's services. However, the agent may, as a so called "husbanding agent", render services relating only to the vessel and its operation which do not fall into the realm of the charterer. In so far, the owner may appoint his own (husbanding) agent who would attend to the vessel. Alternatively, the agent appointed by the charterer would at the same time render services to the vessel for which the owner would be charged separately.

B. VOYAGE CHARTERS

One of the three principal types of charter parties is the voyage charter. The owner undertakes to carry the goods from the port of loading to the port of destination and to deliver them to the consignee. For these services, the charterer owes the agreed freight. The relevant voyage charter may be a sub-charter in a chain of one or more sub-charter parties (see A X. above).

I. WHEN VOYAGE CHARTERS ARE USED

Typically, the parties would conclude a voyage charter in cases where a larger amount of uniform goods needs to be lifted, such as bulk cargo, e.g. grain or ore, or perhaps empty containers. As a result, in most instances the cargo would require the full capacity of the vessel; as to part charters, see below VII. Also, voyage charter parties would be entered into if a contract of affreightment is performed (see below X.). Voyage charters are not suitable in relation to vessels involved in a liner service.

II. INTRODUCTION

1. VOYAGE CHARTERS AND CONTRACTS OF CARRIAGE

Voyage charters may need to be distinguished from mere contracts of carriage (as to those, see the chapter on Shipping Law). The latter concern the transport of particular goods, often containers, from the port of loading to the port of destination by sea. Here, the focus of the contract is on goods and less so on the vessel. The voyage charter is a contract under which the owner provides the vessel to the charterer for the carriage of goods. These two types of contracts may need to be distinguished because they would be subject to diverting provisions in the respective national law applicable. Typically, the voyage charterer is afforded more rights in relation to the vessel and the execution of the voyage as compared to a mere shipper under a contract of carriage, as it is assumed that there is only one charterer or perhaps just a few charterers as opposed to numerous shippers. The parties may clarify in the contract whether they intend it to be a charter or a contract of carriage. Otherwise, a clear separation between the two types of contract may be difficult, because one would need to ascertain whether the agreements relate primarily to the goods with the vessel being of less relevance or rather focus on the vessel used to execute the transport of the goods. It is possible that under a contract of carriage the amount of goods to be carried reaches the vessel's full capacity. Also, there may be part charters relating to a particular part of the vessel. As a general rule, however, one may assume that the contract has the character of a voyage charter if the amount of goods the agreements referred to corresponds approximately to the vessels full capacity or to the capacity of a specified part of the vessel, e.g. one particular hold or tank.

2. The Parties

The voyage charter is concluded between the owner who provides the vessel to carry the goods and to deliver them at the port of destination and the charterer who owes the freight. Corresponding to a contract of carriage, the parties of a voyage charter may agree that the owner delivers the goods to a consignee not identical with the charterer. As a result, the voyage charter may be a contract in favour of the consignee who is entitled to claim the delivery of the goods from the owner at the port of destination (for details as to the consignee's position, see the chapter on Shipping Law). In many cases, the owner under a voyage charter is not the registered owner of the vessel but merely a disponent owner who himself has (time or voyage) chartered the vessel (see A X. above).

3. The Legal Framework

The principles of international private law determine the law applicable to a voyage charter (see below 5). Typically, the national law would deal with the presentation of the vessel to the charterer at the port of loading, the performance of the carriage and delivery of the goods, freight as well as laytime and the demurrage issues, the parties' right to terminate the charter and breaches of contract. Also, the national law may apply the Hague or Hague

Visby scheme on the carrier's liability for loss of or damage to the goods to the owner under the voyage charter. Typically, the provisions taken from the Hague or Hague/Visby Rules do not apply mandatorily to voyage charters. The parties are free to agree on deviating terms, either expressly or perhaps by way of a Himalaya Clause, which incorporates the Hague or Hague/Visby Rules into the voyage charter.

4. STANDARD FORMS

A voyage charter will often be concluded on the basis of a standard contract form. There are numerous forms available on the market, for a number of types of ships, for specific cargoes and for different trades. The most widely used general form for voyage charters is the Gencon 1994 provided by BIMCO.

5. INTERNATIONAL PRIVATE LAW ISSUES

In order to determine the national law applicable for the voyage charter, the first step is to consider a choice of law agreement (see Article 3 Rome I Regulation). If the voyage charter features a Paramount Clause in favour of the Hague or Hague/Visby Rules (for details, see the chapter on Shipping Law, H XI.), it may in the circumstances be recognized to amount to a part choice of law referring, in particular, to the owner's liability for loss of or damage to the cargo. However, normally it will not be possible to understand the Paramount Clause in this way, but rather as a tool to incorporate the provisions of the Hague or Hague/Visby Rules into the charter. If there is no choice of law agreement, the law applicable would, within the European Union, be determined by Article 5.1 Rome I Regulation. As a result, the relevant law would be the law of the state in which the owner has his habitual residence or, alternatively, where the agreed place of delivery is located.

III. THE OWNER'S OBLIGATIONS

1. PRESENTATION OF THE VESSEL; LAYCAN

The owner must present the vessel at the agreed time and place for loading. The vessel must be in the condition as described in the charterer or as is required by the applicable law. In relation to the presentation of the vessel, the parties often agree on a "laycan" period. This is an abbreviation for the combined terms "laytime" and "cancelling". The charterer is not under the obligation to accept the vessel before the date the laycan period begins (but the owner may present the vessel prior to the laycan period). If the vessel is not presented by the end of the laycan period, the charterer is entitled to terminate the charter.

2. LOADING OF THE GOODS

It would then depend on the agreements in the charter and the applicable law whether it is the owner or the charterer, who must load, stow and secure the goods. Often, loading would be the charterer's job, so that the owner's sole duty in that respect is to present the vessel and allow the loading operations to be carried out. In other instances, in particular if the vessel is equipped with loading facilities, the owner may be required to load, stow and secure the goods. The charter may be on "free in" or "fio" ("free in and out") terms. Although this in principle refers to cost issues, it is widely understood to clarify that it is the charterer who must load the goods.

3. THE VOYAGE

Once loading is completed, the owner is bound to carry the goods to the agreed port of destination. The voyage must be commenced and performed without delay. Otherwise, the owner may be liable for damages arising from a late delivery of the goods. The risk of delay in the course of the voyage is upon the owner (as opposed to a time charter, see below), who earns the agreed amount of freight irrespective of the duration of the voyage. Once the vessel has arrived at the port of destination there may be delays due to port congestion or the unavailability of the berth. In the circumstances, the risk of delay may shift to the charterer, as laytime may start running to the effect that, once laytime has expired, the vessel will be on demurrage.

4. DISCHARGING OF THE GOODS

In relation to the discharging of the goods, it is once more the agreed terms of the contract or the law applicable to the charter, which decide whether discharging of the goods is the duty of the owner or the charterer. The latter would be responsible for the discharging if the charterer was on "free out" or "FIO" terms. The party's obligations need not be the same in relation to loading and discharging. Often, goods may be loaded by the charterer and discharged by the vessel's crew, i.e. the owner. Whether discharging of the goods is the charterer's or the owner's responsibility is relevant for the question as to when and in what circumstances the goods are delivered (see below).

5. DELIVERY OF THE GOODS

The owner's final principal duty is to deliver the goods to the consignee (for details, see the chapter on Shipping Law). He may in the circumstances be identical with the charterer. Depending on the law applicable, the consignee may have a direct claim against the owner for the goods to be delivered to him, the consignee. Also, the owner may have issued a bill of lading. As a result, the holder of the bill is entitled to claim delivery of the goods. The owner's duty to deliver the goods depends on whether discharging is to be performed by the owner or not.

If discharging is the duty of the charterer, the goods are delivered when on the vessel's side all necessary steps have been taken to allow the stevedores to commence discharging. In this case, the goods are delivered to the consignee. However, under the charter, discharging of the goods, although in fact performed by the consignee, remains the charterer's responsibility. Here, the consignee is the charterer's agent. If the goods for some reason are not discharged, the owner has a claim against the charterer (and not the consignee) to have the goods discharged.

On the other hand, if it is agreed or prescribed by the law applicable to the charter that the owner is to discharge the goods, delivery occurs when the discharging of the goods is completed. The goods are delivered at the ship's side on the pier, where they are accepted by the consignee.

In the circumstances, the owner may have a lien on the goods which would allow him to refuse to deliver them if he has outstanding claims against the charterer and/or the consignee, e.g. for freight and demurrage (see below). The extent of the lien depends on the agreed terms of the charter and the law applicable to the contract, i.e. whether only claims rising directly from the charter are secured or whether the owner is entitled to rely on the lien also in respect of other claims against the charterer or consignee, respectively. It is the national law otherwise applicable to the charter, which determines whether the owner also is entitled to a forced sale of goods.

IV. PAYMENT OF FREIGHT

The charterer's principal duty under the charter is to pay the agreed freight. Often, in particular if the charter concerns bulk cargo, the freight is determined by a particular rate per ton of cargo. The relevant amount of cargo normally is determined by the quantity actually loaded by the vessel. The date on which the agreed freight is payable is subject to individual agreements. The freight may be payable immediately after the contract is concluded or, more often, when loading is completed and bills of lading have been issued, or only when the goods are delivered at the port of destination. In some legislations, the owner's claim for freight is protected from the set-off of counterclaims by the charterer. Also, the respective legislation may allow the owner to claim the freight from the consignee or at least to withhold delivery of the goods to the consignee until the freight is settled.

If the charterer fails to deliver the agreed amount of cargo to the vessel, to the effect that the owner would earn less than the full amount of the agreed freight, the owner may have a claim against the charterer for deadfreight, which would cover the balance. It depends on the law applicable whether the deadfreight claim is an additional claim for freight or a claim for breach of contract.

V. Laytime and Demurrage

The agreed freight covers the owner's services in respect of the carriage of the goods and their delivery. This would include a reasonable time for loading and discharging of the goods, either by the charterer or consignee, respectively, or the owner. However, there may be delays, e.g. because the vessel is prevented from berthing immediately, because the cargo is not yet available, because the loading or discharging rate, respectively, is slower than expected, or for other reasons. Normally, the operation of a voyage charter implies that these risks would be borne by the owner.

However, according to the agreements of the charter or the law applicable to it, there may be regulations concerning laytime, i.e. the time available for loading and discharging, and demurrage payable to the owner in case more than the agreed laytime is spent on loading and/or discharging. The underlying data for the calculation of laytime and demurrage normally is summarized by the port agent in a schedule known as "Statement of Facts" (SOF). Questions of laytime and demurrage are typical for voyage charters, but not in respect of time charters, due to the fact that hire is paid on the basis of time and that, as a result, the risk of delay already is on the time charterer.

Usually, the beginning of the agreed laytime requires a valid notice given by the owner to the charterer. The notice triggers the beginning of the laytime, i.e. the time available for loading or discharging. If these operations take longer than the agreed laytime, the owner may have a claim for demurrage. Laytime and demurrage issues often give rise to disputes between the parties. At the outset, there is a claim by the owner against the charterer for demurrage. Usually, the point in time when the time on the demurrage ends is clear, i.e. when the loading or discharging operations are finalised. However, laytime and demurrage disputes often focus on the question on when laytime expired and the time on demurrage commenced. The disputes may concern the question whether the notice of readiness was valid, when laytime commenced to run, how the laytime available would be calculated, the running of the laytime, the point in time when the vessel would be on demurrage, and the running of the time on demurrage.

1. NOTICE OF READINESS

Under a voyage charter, the vessel as a matter routine issues a notice of readiness after the arrival at the port of loading or discharging, respectively. The notice is only valid if in fact the vessel is ready to load or discharge. Also, the notice can only be given if the vessel has reached the port, if she is an "arrived" ship. Obviously, a notice given while the vessel still is on the voyage would serve no purpose. In principle, this requires that the vessel proceeded as far as possible in the circumstances towards the respective port. It may thus be sufficient that vessel arrived at the normal anchorage to allow her to give a valid notice. Further, the agreements of the charter may require that notice is given during office hours, to a particular party such as e.g. the owner or a port agent, or in a particular form. Further, the charter may provide for a certain period of time to expire after the notice has been given before laytime actually starts to run.

2. LAYTIME

The term "laytime" refers to the time allowed for loading and discharging the vessel. The loading and discharging time may be individually agreed in the charter. It may also provide a period of time relating to both loading and discharging so that both may be counted against each other. Often, the laytime is not determined by a fixed period of time for loading and discharging or both, but is related to the amount of cargo loaded or discharged, e.g. one day per thousand tons of cargo. In so far, different rates may be agreed for loading and discharging.

The beginning of a laytime requires that a valid notice of readiness has been given by the vessel (see before) and that the waiting time has expired. One issue, which has given rise to quite a number of disputes, is whether laytime commences if no notice or only an invalid notice was rendered.

Once laytime has commenced, another issue may be the running of the laytime, i.e. whether or not there are excepted periods. E.g. the charter may provide that Saturdays, Sundays and holidays are excluded (abbreviated "shex"), and it may be added that they remain excluded even if loading or discharging in fact occurs ("even if used", abbreviated "eiu"). Also, the charter may expressly confirm that Saturdays, Sundays and holidays are included and do not interrupt the running of the laytime (abbreviated "shinc"). When the laytime expires, the vessel is on demurrage.

3. TIME ON DEMURRAGE

When the agreed laytime is exhausted, the time on demurrage will automatically begin. No further formalities such as e.g. another notice are required. The time of demurrage normally runs without interruption, as the exceptions provided in relation to the laytime do not apply to the time on demurrage. Here, the traditional principle "once on demurrage, always on demurrage" applies. Demurrage accrues at the daily rate agreed in the charter. That rate is only subject to negotiation and thus to the market situation and it cannot be assumed that the agreed rate in any way reflects the actual running costs of the vessel.

4. DETENTION OF THE VESSEL

The provisions on laytime and demurrage concern a situation where loading or discharging takes longer than the parties anticipated. The vessel, however, may be detained by other reasons the charterer is responsible for. Here, the owner may have a damage claim against the charterer for detention based on breach of contract. The claim is for loss of profit and the charterer, in principle, needs to prove his damages by calculating the lost earnings and giving credit for costs saved. Strictly speaking, the agreed demurrage rate is not applicable, as it is normally not based on the vessels daily cost. However, some arbitration tribunals have applied the demurrage rate agreed to calculate the owner's damages for detention.

5. DESPATCH

Demurrage is due if the time required for loading or discharging exceeds the agreed laytime. But there may be situations where in fact the loading or discharging of the goods is completed earlier so that the charterer does not use the full laytime. As a result, the vessel at an earlier point in time is again at the disposal of the owner, allowing him to trade the vessel otherwise. Here, it may be justified to allow the charterer to claim "negative demurrage", in practice called "despatch". In order for the charterer to be able to claim despatch, an express agreement in the charter is required. The typical phrase often used is "despatch half demurrage". Thereby the parties confirm that despatch may be payable. At the same time the despatch rate is determined to be half the demurrage rate.

VI. LIABILITY FOR CARGO DAMAGE

If loss of or damage to the goods occurs under a voyage charter, the owner may be liable for damages. His liability is determined by the terms of the charter and the law applicable. In principle, the Hague/Hague Visby Rules do not apply to charter parties in general and thus not to voyage charters. However, the relevant national law may provide that the Hague/Hague Visby Rules liability scheme is applicable to voyage charters. Normally, however, the respective provisions do not apply mandatorily, to the effect that the parties are free to agree on deviating terms in the charter. Clause 2 of the Gencon 1994 form is a prominent example for a term seeking to limit the owner's liability for cargo damage.

Another set of deviating clauses relating to liability would be introduced by way of a Paramount Clause; as to these types of clauses, see the chapter on Shipping Law, H XI. In a voyage charter context, Paramount Clauses are normally not a (part) choice of law agreement, but rather incorporate the provisions of the Hague/Hague Visby Rules as further terms of the charter, leaving the legal framework provided by the applicable national law untouched. As deviating provisions in the charter are normally allowed, the paramount clause introduces the Hague/Hague Visby Rules liability scheme into the charter. As a result, all exclusions and limitations of liability for cargo damage provided for in the Rules apply in favour of the owner. His liability is limited and he may rely on the error in navigation and the fire defence.

VII. PART CHARTER PARTIES

In many cases, the voyage charter concerns the full vessel, to the effect that there is one owner and one charterer. It is also possible, however, that a voyage charter is concluded in respect of a part of the vessel. The contract may refer to one or more holds or to one or more tanks; as to slot charters, see below VIII. In particular, the carriage of chemicals in product tankers is often done on the basis of part charter parties. Here, one owner would be facing two or more part charterers. It is implied, when a part charter is concluded, that the owner is entitled to accept and carry goods for other charterers on the same voyage. Part charter parties may give rise to difficult disputes, e.g. whether delays caused by one cargo may lead to demurrage claims against other charterers.

VIII. Slot Charter Parties

The container trade, in particular of shipping lines, has developed a particular form of a part charter party, i.e. the slot charter. It concerns a certain amount of TEUs, which are "reserved" for the charterer on particular departures of the line. The containers provided by the charterer may be stored anywhere on the vessel, on or under deck. So far, the slot charter is distinct from the traditional part voyage charter, which often refers to a particular hold or tank.

IX. Bills of Lading

Under a voyage charter, a bill of lading may be issued by or on behalf of the owner. As to the functions and the effects of a bill of lading, see the Shipping Law section (H). The voyage charter may specify by whom the bill is issued on behalf of the owner and provide for the authority of the respective person to act on behalf for the owner. This could be the master of the vessel, or the vessel's port agent, or the port agent on behalf of the master. There are a variety of forms available for bills of lading to be issued under a voyage charter, relating to all types of trades and commodities. One recognised document is the Congenbill form issued by BIMCO, the latest edition of which is from 2016.

Often, bills of lading issued under a voyage charter only feature a limited number of basic terms, whilst an incorporation clause refers to the terms of the voyage charter. The purpose of this is to ensure that the terms of the bill of lading correspond to those of the voyage charter (i.e. charter party bills of lading), to the effect that the owner's liability under the charter and under the bill are in line. However, in practice a number of problems may arise. The identification of the respective charter may be difficult, in particular if there is a chain of sub charters. If it turns out that the charter referred to actually is a time charter, its terms normally are not applied easily in a bill of lading context. Also, the respective charter, once identified, may not be available; so that the holder of the bill of lading is unable to determine the terms the bill is subject to. This refers, in particular, to a jurisdiction or an arbitration clause, which is part of the voyage charter and by way of the incorporation clause is incorporated into the bill of lading terms. If the holder of the bill must commence proceedings against the carrier under the bill in order to protect time, it is of highest relevance whether the holder would need to refer the dispute to arbitration or whether a suit must be brought, and, in the latter case, which state's courts would have jurisdiction. Although charter party bills of lading, despite all the problems that may arise, have been recognised in shipping for decades, some legislations today do not accept incorporation clauses, to ensure that the holder of the bill only needs to rely on the terms reproduced on the bill's reverse side.

X. CONTRACTS OF AFFREIGHTMENT

As to contracts of affreightment, see the remarks in the Shipping Law section (I). Shipments under the overriding contract of affreightment may be made on the basis of separate contracts of carriage. In the circumstances, however, the individual shipments may be performed based on voyage charters. Contracts of this type are often found in respect of bulk cargoes to secure a long-term supply of large amounts of cargo to the customer, e.g. one million tons per year of coal to a power plant or of iron ore to a steel mill. The owner undertakes to provide a vessel of a certain type and size at the dates and ports laid down in the charter. Each shipment then is based on a voyage charter, often on the agreed standard form and further terms.

C. TIME CHARTERS

The other type of traditional charter party often encountered, besides the voyage charter (above B), is the time charter. The owner lets the manned vessel to the charterer for a period of time, who is entitled to use the vessel for his own purpose. The charterer may give direct instructions concerning the (commercial) employment of the vessel to her master. While a voyage charter normally only is concerned with the transport of goods, a time chartered vessel may be used for other purposes, i.e. in respect of the carriage of passengers, for scientific and research services or for leisure. The time charter owes hire for the time the vessel is on hire. The respective time charter contract may be part of a chain of sub charters. The time charterer could enter into a sub time or a sub voyage charter (see above A X.). Time charters typically concern the full vessel, there are no part time charters.

I. WHEN TIME CHARTERS ARE USED

Under a time charter, the charterer may use the vessel for a period of time. In relation to the carriage of goods, the vessel normally would perform a number of voyages for the charterer, both laden and in ballast. One typical situation where time charters are concluded is when the charterer operates a liner service and requires vessels to perform the regular departures. As a result, although the ships used by the lines for their services often feature the same corporate appearance (funnel marks, paintwork), these vessels are not owned by the shipping line but only on time charter. Also, a time charterer may wish to have a vessel available because he expects to be able to trade her in the market. Finally, the time charter may be concluded for one voyage only (trip time charter) and thus would replace the voyage charter that would normally be agreed (see below VIII.).

II. INTRODUCTION

1. TIME AND VOYAGE CHARTERS

One of the features of a time charter is that the vessel is placed at the charter's disposal for a period of time, irrespective, in principle, of the amount of voyages performed for the charterer. It is the element of time, which is characteristic for this type of contract. Contrary to that, the focus of a voyage charter is on the relevant voyage to be carried out.

Also, the owner's duty under a time charter is limited to operate the vessel as required by the charterer, whilst it is the charterer's job to provide the further services to actually perform the voyages, such as the loading and securing as well as the discharging of cargo, the provision of tugs, pilots and linesmen. Also, in a time charter, the fuel would be the charterer's responsibility. All told, the services rendered by the owner under a time charter are less extensive than those provided by an owner under a voyage charter. As a result, voyage charters normally are more profitable for the owner than time charterers.

Further, the most important issue in relation to time and voyage charters is that in a time charter, the risk of delay lies on the charterer. In principle, he is bound to pay hire continuously even if there are delays. However, in the circumstances the vessel may go off-hire for a limited period of time, in which the charterer's obligation to pay hire is suspended (see below VI.2). Contrary to that, the owner under a voyage charter is entitled to the fixed amount of freight, irrespective of any delays en route.

2. THE PARTIES

Under a time charter, it is the owner's duty to provide the vessel to the charterer while the charterer must pay hire for the time the vessel is on hire. As opposed to a voyage charter, there normally is no consignee to whom the goods must be delivered by the owner. However, the owner may issue the bill of lading under which the party entitled to claim may require delivery of the goods to him (see below IX.).

3. THE LEGAL FRAMEWORK

The law applicable to a time charter is determined on the basis of the relevant international private law principles (see below 5). In many instances, the respective national law does not feature any particular regulations relating to time charters, or they may be limited to just some basic provisions. These may concern presentation of the vessel at the agreed time and place, the maintenance and the employment of the vessel, loading and discharging of goods, the vessel's costs, the payment of hire, off-hire issues, the owner's lien on e.g. sub-freights, and the re-delivery of the vessel. Normally, the national law on time charterers does not apply mandatorily so that the parties are free to agree on deviating terms in the charter.

4. STANDARD FORMS

Like voyage charters, time charterers are often concluded on the basis of standard forms. There are quite a number of forms available for time charters, most of them relating to particular trades. Many of them are provided by BIMCO. There are two particularly well known general standard forms, i.e. the New York Produce Exchange form, which was first issued in 1946, with the latest issue of 2015 (NYPE 2015), and the Baltime form from 1939, revised 2001.

5. INTERNATIONAL PRIVATE LAW ISSUES

If the law applicable to a time charter needs to be determined, the principles of international private law of the state where the issue is decided by the courts is relevant. Within the EU member states, the provisions of the Rome I Regulation will be relevant. Normally, a time charter would feature a choice of law provision, which would specify which law the charter would be subject to (see Article 3 Rome I Regulation). However, if there is no choice of law agreement, the respective national law is, it is submitted, identified by

Article 4.1 (b) or 4.2 Rome I Regulation. In that case, the law applicable to the contract would be subject to the law of the state where the owner has his habitual residence. As time charters do not qualify as contracts of carriage, Article 5.1 Rome I Regulation remains inapplicable.

III. The Charter Period

Normally, the period of time for which the vessel is chartered to the time charterer is determined in the contract. This may vary between a few days and many years, sometimes the entire lifespan of the vessel. In case of a trip time charter (below VIII.), the relevant period is determined by the duration of the voyage for which the vessel is chartered. The charter may provide for an option of the charterer to add an additional charter period, or it is extended automatically for a period of time, unless either party cancels the charter. Different hire rates may apply to the extension periods. Also, the parties may decide not to agree on a fixed period, but to allow both parties to cancel the charter any time, after the expiry of a minimum period, normally with an agreed period of time between the cancellation and the actual termination of the contract.

IV. Delivery and Redelivery of the Vessel

Under a time charter, the owner lets the vessel to the charterer for a period of time. That period commences when the vessel is delivered to the charterer and ends with its redelivery to the owner. When a vessel is about to be delivered, in many cases a survey of the vessel is carried out by experts appointed by both parties. They consider the condition of the vessel and, in particular, whether it fulfils the requirements of the charter. The experts also determine the amount of fuel on board. Finally, they agree on the date and time the vessel is delivered to the charterer. The vessel goes on hire and the charter's obligation to pay the agreed hire commences. There is a corresponding procedure at the end of the charter when the vessel is redelivered to the owner. Again, the condition of the vessel is examined and the amount of fuel on board determined.

Sometimes, the delivery and the redelivery of the vessel is less formal, in particular if the charter is not for an extended period of time of time. The parties are free to agree on the circumstances in which the vessel is automatically delivered or redelivered, respectively, e.g. when the vessel at sea has reached a particular position. Quite often, the term "dlop" with a reference to a port would be used. The abbreviation stands for "dropping last outbound pilot". In relation to the delivery under the time charter, the port referred to normally would be the last discharging port under the previous charter. Here, the time charter would commence immediately after the vessel left the previous port, with a ballast voyage to the first loading port. If the redelivery is subject to *dlop* terms, the time charter would end immediately after the vessel left the last discharging port.

V. THE OWNER'S OBLIGATIONS

1. DELIVERY OF THE VESSEL; LAYCAN

The owner must present the vessel at the agreed time and place for the delivery to the charterer and in a condition in line with the terms of the charter. In particular, the vessel needs to correspond to the ship's particulars listed in the charter and to be in a condition to perform the charter, in particular in respect of the vessel's seaworthiness. When delivery occurs, the owner sells the fuel on board to the charterer, who also becomes the owner of the fuel. As with voyage charter parties, a *laycan* period of time may be agreed in relation to the delivery under the time charter (see above B III.1).

2. RENDERING THE REQUIRED SERVICES

In the course of the time charter, between the delivery and the redelivery of the vessel, it is the owner's obligation to ensure that the vessel is at the charterer's disposal and that all services agreed under the charter are rendered. One of the traditional terms regularly found in time charters is the requirement that the owner must carry out all voyages with utmost dispatch, subject to possible instructions by the charterer in respect of slow steaming (for the purpose of saving fuel). The utmost dispatch requirement results from the fact that the risk of delay in a time charter lies on the charterer (see above II.1). In the circumstances, the owner may be bound to render further services, such as loading, storing, securing and discharging the goods.

3. REDELIVERY OF THE VESSEL

At the end of the charter period, when the vessel is redelivered by the charterer, the owner is bound to accept the vessel. Also, he must purchase the fuel on board from the charterer and agree that property in the fuel passes to him, the owner.

VI. The Charterer's Obligations

1. Payment of Hire

The charterer's principal obligation is to pay hire throughout the period between the delivery and the redelivery of the vessel at the daily rate agreed in the charter. The duty to pay hire may be suspended when the vessel is off-hire (see below 2). Typically, hire payments are to be made in advance every 15 days. In some legislations, the owner's claim for hire is protected from set-offs by the charterer, who may not rely on possible counterclaims against the owner to reduce hire payments. Due to the fact that the risk of delay (see II.1 above) is on the charterer, time charters, unlike voyage charters, do not feature provisions on laytime and demurrage.

2. Off-Hire

In principle, the charterer's duty to pay hire runs uninterrupted in the period between the delivery and the redelivery of vessel. However, there are exceptions in cases where the vessel for some reason is not at the disposal of the charterer. Here, the vessel goes off-hire for a period of time to the effect that the charterer is not bound to pay hire. As the off-hire of the vessel is an exception to the principal duty to pay hire, any terms in the charter dealing with off-hire must be construed narrowly. Off-hire disputes between owner and time charterer are common. Time charterers normally feature one or more off-hire clauses covering a variety of situations, the off-hire events, which may trigger a suspension of the duty to pay hire. Typical off-hire events are defects of the vessel, including the cargo gear, an arrest of the vessel, accidents, the outbreak of hostilities, or actions taken by local authorities against the vessel. Whether a situation qualifies as an off-hire event as well as the point in time when the event began and when it ended needs to be carefully investigated. In some cases, the catalogue of off-hire events is qualified by the requirement that they must prevent the full working of the vessel. Off-hire clauses may provide that the vessel is off-hire for the full period in which the off-hire event is in effect. Other clauses may put the vessel off-hire only for the time actually lost by the off-hire event. E.g. if there is a breakdown of one of the ship's cranes which serves holds already loaded, loading of the other holds by the remaining cranes is not disturbed. Finally, it depends on the respective off-hire clause whether the vessel is fully off-hire in all cases or whether there may be a partial off-hire for the fact that a share of the hire still is payable.

3. The Fuel

Under a time charter, the charterer is under the obligation to provide the necessary fuel to the vessel. When the vessel is delivered, the fuel on board is sold to the charterer. Also, the charterer becomes the owner of the fuel. In the course of the charter, the charterer purchases the required fuel to be delivered to the vessel. At the vessel's redelivery, the fuel on board is sold to the owner, who also becomes the owner of the fuel. The charter may provide for fixed prices in respect of the fuel applicable on delivery and redelivery, or it may set out how the prices are calculated in relation to the market. Also, the charter may provide for a particular (minimum) amount of fuel on board when the vessel is redelivered.

4. Loading and Discharging

Normally, the owner's duty under a charter is to put the vessel at the disposal of the charterer. As a result, it is his job to carry out the loading and discharging of the goods. This may even be so in cases where the vessel is in fact equipped with cargo handling gear. However, if the charter concerns a heavy lift vessel, loading and discharging of the goods by the vessel's own heavy lift gear may be carried out by the vessel on behalf of the charterer. This may also apply in the tanker trade, where discharging of the cargo by the vessel's pumps may be the duty of the owner. The charterer's principal duty to load and discharge may be qualified in a certain way in the terms of the charter. E.g. the charter may provide that the loading of the goods is carried out under the supervision of the master or even in his responsibility. Moreover, it remains the vessel's duty to ensure that the loading of the cargo by the charterer does not affect the vessel's seaworthiness. The various responsibilities of the charterer, the owner and the vessel have given rise to quite a number of disputes.

5. Redelivery of the Vessel

At the end of the charter, the vessel is redelivered by the charterer to the owner. It is the charterer's duty to ensure that redelivery occurs at the agreed date and place. This may need careful planning at the end of a long term charter. Sometimes, allowances are made in the contract in relation to the time of redelivery when the last voyage under the time charter is not yet completed. When the vessel is redelivered, the fuel on board is purchased by and property in the fuel is transferred to the owner. The owner may refuse a premature redelivery prior to the agreed time.

VII. Liability for Cargo Damage

If cargo carried on the vessel is lost or damaged in the course of the charter, the question may arise whether the charterer may bring damage claims against the owner. The familiar Hague or Hague/Visby liability scheme is not by itself applicable to time charters. The applicable legal framework may feature provisions on the owner's liability. In the first place, however, the owner's liability would be subject to the terms of the charter.

In that respect, Paramount Clauses (for details, see the chapter on Shipping Law, H CI.) included in the charter and their reference to the Hague or Hague/Visby liability scheme for cargo loss or damage may be relevant and applicable against the owner. In a time charter context, Paramount Clauses serve to include the respective provisions of the Hague or Hague/Visby Rules into the charter, as if they were further written terms which apply with priority. As a result, the familiar Hague or Hague/Visby liability scheme is imported into the time charter although at the rules by themselves do not apply to time charters. The owner is responsible for the cargo damage as if he was a carrier under the Hague or Hague/Visby Rules. In particular, the owner may rely on the limited liability, the error in navigation defence and the one-year time bar. A Paramount Clause in a time charter thus may have far reaching effects not obvious at first glance.

For a number of years, another liability régime in respect of loss of or damage to cargo has become common in relation to time charters. Triggered by the large amount of disputes, the P&I Clubs (which cover the underlying risks) have developed an agreement which allows for a swift settlement of cargo disputes in time charters. Originally, that agreement was concluded between the P&I Clubs. The latest version of the Inter-Club Agreement is from 2011 (ICA 2011). The P&I Clubs in turn encourage their members to include the ICA 2011 directly in the time charter and to settle disputes based on that Agreement directly with the respective other party. The ICA 2011 provides a rough and ready yardstick to determine the charter's and the owner's liability in cases of cargo damages. The liability is either 100 % or 50 % on either the charterer or the owner, respectively. This depends, inter alia, on whether the damage was caused by the vessel's unseaworthiness, during loading or discharging, respectively, and whether the charter features terms shifting the responsibility, such as clauses providing that loading is carried out under the supervision or responsibility of the master.

VIII. TRIP TIME CHARTERS

One particular form of time charter is the trip time charter, which is concluded for one sole voyage. So far, the time charter actually replaces the voyage charter to the effect that the time charters particular mechanisms apply. There may be a number of reasons why the parties choose a time charter instead of a voyage charter. One of the effects of using a time charter is that the risk of delays in the performance of the voyage shifts from the owner to the charterer, as the obligation to pay hire will run, in principle, uninterrupted until the vessel is redelivered to the owner (see II.1 above). Also, the charter period is determined by the duration of the voyage.

IX. BILLS OF LADING

Although the focus of a time charter is not directly on the carriage of goods, the owner under a time charter may agree to issue bills of lading in respect of the goods loaded on the vessel. As to bills of lading in general, see the remarks in the chapter Shipping Law (H), and in respect of bills of lading issued under a voyage charter see B IX. above. The terms of the charter will specify by whom the bill of lading is issued on behalf of the owner. This may be the master of the vessel or her port agent. Although the particular charter party bill of lading forms are not specifically designed to be used under a time charter, this occasionally happens in practice. If the vessel is time chartered for the purpose of the charterer's liner service, the bills of lading are normally issued by the charterer (as the line operator) and based on a regular bill of lading form with a full set of terms.

D. BAREBOAT CHARTERS

In addition to voyage and time charters, the bareboat charter is another common type of charter party used in practise. The bareboat charter is a contract for the lease of the vessel.

I. INTRODUCTION

By way of a bareboat charter, the vessel owner lets the unmanned "bare" ship to the charterer, thencc thc labcl "barcboat charter". If the vessel does not require a crew to be operated, such as barges or floating platforms or storages, the parties would normally not enter into a time charter but bareboat charter. In case the vessel needs to be manned, the owner lets the vessel to the bareboat charterer who provides a crew and furnishes the vessel with fuel etc. to use it for his own account. The vessel may be used for the carriage of goods or passengers or, as the case may be, other purposes.

1. Flag Issues

Often, the bareboat charter is not required as a device to facilitate transport or other services but rather serves as a tool within the organisation of the vessel's operation. The ship may be entered in the ship register of one state for the purpose of evidencing the property in the vessel and perhaps mortgages. The owner may wish to fly the flag of another state, e.g. to reduce the costs for the operation of the vessel. It may now be necessary to "bareboat charter out" the vessel to a party with a place of business in that other state. In some instances, the bareboat charterer re-charters the vessel, under a sub bareboat charter, back to the registered owner or an affiliated company.

2. The Bareboat Charterer as Owner pro hac vice

A vessel that is bareboat chartered out normally is operated by the bareboat charterer whilst the registered owner's function is reduced to hold the property in the vessel. In some jurisdictions, the bareboat charterer is considered to be the owner *pro hac vice*. As such, the bareboat charterer assumes the role of an owner in relation to third parties. As a result, if a third party suffers damages, it is the bareboat charterer (and not the registered owner) who is considered to be the vessel owner and thus liable vis-à-vis the damaged third party.

3. The Barecon 2017 Form

As with most other types of charter parties, bareboat charter parties typically are concluded on the basis of standard forms. Again, BIMCO provides a number of forms, of which the Barecon form, recently updated in 2017, is the one, which is most widely in use. The Barecon 2017 form, inter alia, features special provisions on newbuilding vessels, on purchase options in favour of the charter, and on vessels entered in a bareboat charter register.

II. The Charter Period

The performance of the bareboat charter begins with the vessel to being delivered to the charterer and ends with her redelivery to the owner. If the bareboat charter is used for flag etc. purposes (see I.1 above), the contract is normally concluded for a longer period of time, perhaps many years, decades or even the entire life span of the vessel. A bareboat charter may begin when the new built vessel is delivered to the owner by the shipyard. In other circumstances, the agreed charter period may be anything between days and years. Normally, the relevant period is defined in the charter. However, the parties are free to agree on a bareboat charter for an unlimited period of time, which may be terminated by either party any time.

III. THE OWNER'S OBLIGATIONS

The concept of a bareboat charter is to lease the vessel to the charterer to allow him to use it for his own purposes. The principal obligation of the owner is to let vessel to the charterer, i.e. to make the vessel available to him and to allow him to use it as he requires. Often, the charter party expressly specifies for what purposes and in what circumstances the vessel may be used by the charterer. The charterer is entitled to use the vessel undisturbed by the owner.

It is the owner's obligation to present the vessel to the charterer at the time and place agreed in the contract. Also, at that point in time, the vessel must be in the condition as specified in the charter. In particular, the vessel must correspond with its description in the contract. The law applicable to the charter may assist by providing a yardstick as to the vessel's condition upon delivery. E.g., the law may require that the vessel is fit for the mutually intended use by the charterer. Here, the concept of the seaworthiness of the vessel may become relevant. If the vessel is chartered for the purpose of carrying goods, the issue of cargoworthiness may arise.

The condition of the vessel at the time of her delivery to the charterer is often determined with the assistance of surveyors appointed by owners and/or charterers. If the vessel at the time of delivery is not in the condition provided for in the charter, the charterer may, according to the terms of the contract and the law applicable to the charter, be entitled to refuse to accept the vessel, to require the owner to rectify the deficiencies, to reduce the hire owed, to claim for damages, or ultimately to terminate the contract. If the vessel was delivered to the charterer in proper condition, it is the charterer's duty to maintain the vessel in that condition. This does not refer to normal wear and tear.

IV. The Performance of the Charter

Once the vessel is delivered to the charterer, he is entitled to make use of it as provided for in and subject to the limits of the bareboat charter. Normally, if the vessel needs to be manned by a crew, the charterer would provide it and equip her as is required by the intended services. The owner's obligation is not to interfere with the operation of the vessel by the bareboat charterer. It is the duty of the bareboat charterer to maintain the vessel in an efficient state, however subject to normal wear and tear.

V. The Charterer's Obligations

Under a bareboat charterer, the charterer's principal obligation is to pay the agreed hire. Also, while the vessel is in the charterer's possession, he must maintain the condition of the vessel, subject to normal wear and tear. Finally, it is the charterer's duty to redeliver the vessel as agreed in the charter.

1. Payment of Hire

The bareboat charterer must pay the hire, in principle without interruption, in the time between the delivery and the redelivery of the vessel. As in a time charter, payment of hire normally must be made every 15 days in advance. Under a bareboat charter, the vessel may go off-hire, to the effect that the duty to pay hire is suspended. In practice this rarely occurs, as in a bareboat-charter there are only very limited reasons for the vessel to be off-hire.

2. The Redelivery of the Vessel

At the end of the bareboat charter, the charterer must redeliver the vessel to the owner. Redelivery must occur at the agreed timev and in the agreed place. The Charterer needs to make sure that he uses the vessel in a way that he is able to meet the contractual requirements as to her redelivery. The owner is entitled to refuse a premature redelivery prior to the agreed time. If the vessel is redelivered late, the charterer's obligation to pay hire normally would continue until the actual redelivery. Further, as a delayed delivery may amount to a breach of contract, the owner may be entitled to claim damages from the charterer. If the vessel is not presented for redelivery at the place agreed in the charter, the owner in the circumstances may be allowed to refuse to accept the vessel or to claim damages from the charter.

NOTES

[1] International Convention for the Unification of Certain Rules of Law relating to Bills of Lading, 1924.
[2] Hague Rules as amended by the Protocol of 1968.
[3] United Nations International Convention on the Carriage of Goods by Sea, 1978.
[4] United Nations Convention on Contracts for the International Carriage of Goods Wholly or Partly by Sea, 2008.
[5] Regulation (EC) No 593/2008 of the European Parliament and of the Council of 17 June 2008 on the law applicable to contractual obligations.
[6] www.bimco.org.

CHAPTER IX

UNMANNED SHIPPING

Carina LUTTER

A. INTRODUCTION

Digitalization is currently increasing in all business areas, putting forth innovative technologies and creating possibilities never expected before. The shipping industry is now confronted with the idea of unmanned ships sailing the oceans without even one human soul on board. Instead, those ships shall be controlled remotely from ashore or by autonomous computer systems able to navigate the ship on their own.

Remote controlled and autonomous ships have already become a vision of leading developers. Technical components are currently being tested.[1] It is no longer the question *whether* but rather *when* such crewless vessels will conquer the oceans. The use of unmanned vessel technology is probably the most challenging development in shipping industry of recent years. This article aims to give an overview on the future use of unmanned ships and the manifold regulatory challenges associated.

B. DEVELOPMENTS TOWARDS THE UNMANNED SHIP

Digital technology has made an enormous progress in recent years. Already today, modern ships are highly dependent on computers and software technology. Systems like the Electronic Chart Display and Information System (ECDIS), the Automatic Identification System (AIS) or the Global Positioning Systems (GPS) and others are part of the ship's bridge and support masters and officers in navigating the vessel safely. However, unmanned shipping technology brings the digitalisation of shipping to a whole new level.

Unmanned ships are currently subject to several research projects that focus on technical, economic and legal issues. Components and even models of remotely controlled and autonomous vessels are being tested.

The project MUNIN (Maritime Unmanned Navigation through Intelligence in Networks) is a collaborative research project, co-funded by the European Commission, which aims to develop and verify a concept for an autonomous ship.[2] MUNIN's topic to explore is a dry bulk carrier operating in intercontinental tramp trades that is primarily controlled by an autonomous computer system but still operated by a remote controller from a shore-based control station. In 2016 the project was completed and, as an outcome, a technical concept for the operation of unmanned ships was developed. It basically consists of an Advanced Sensor Module, an Autonomous Navigation System, an Autonomous Engine and Monitoring Control System as well as a Shore Control Centre.[3] While the Advanced Sensor Module collects data from various sensors like radars or cameras to perform the ship's outlook, the Autonomous Navigation System independently navigates the vessel.[4] The Autonomous Engine and Monitoring Control System surveys the ship's functionalities for efficiency and failure-pre-detection purposes.[5] During its autonomous voyage, the ship is monitored by the Shore Control Centre and may be controlled remotely if necessary.[6] As for the legal feasibility of unmanned ships, the project concluded that adaptions of the legal framework are necessary and feasible, provided that unmanned ships can operate at least as safely as manned ships.[7]

The Advanced Autonomous Waterborne Applications (AAWA) Initiative is a project funded by Tekes (Finnish Funding Agency for Technology and Innovation) in cooperation with universities and maritime players like e.g. Rolls-Royce and DNV GL. It comes from the point that the technology to remotely or autonomously operate ships does already exist and focuses on the reliable and cost-effective implementation of such technologies.[8] The AAWA Autonomous Navigation System consists of different modules dealing with route planning, situation awareness, collision avoidance and ship state definition.[9] Together, the components shall be able to autonomously navigate the ship. However, the project estimates the future of unmanned shipping in hybrid forms of remotely controlled ships and autonomously navigated ships.[10]

The DNV GL has even built a 1:20 scaled model of an autonomous short-sea vessel, called the ReVolt.[11] The ReVolt shall be 60 metres long, fully battery powered and able to navigate autonomously without any crew on board.[12] The vessel shall operate within a range of 100 nautical miles and be able to carry 100 twenty-foot containers.[13] The said model is currently being tested.[14]

The probably first autonomous container ship in real size, with a capacity of 120 TEU, is already under construction.[15] The Yara Birkeland shall operate within 12 nautical miles from the coast, calling at three ports in southern Norway.[16] The ship is expected to be ready for testing in the first quarter of 2018 and shall then be operated with a captain and a reduced crew on board.[17] In 2019, the autonomous navigation shall be tested and in 2020 the vessel shall finally be fully autonomous.[18]

Based on the above-mentioned findings and the ongoing research, unmanned ships are likely to be introduced within the next few decades.

C. BENEFITS OF CREWLESS SHIPS

The advantages of the implementation of unmanned ships are very diverse. First, the use of advanced technologies offers the opportunity to increase the safety of shipping by reducing incidents caused by human error.[19] 75 % to 96 % of all marine accidents are due to human fault, e.g. fatigue is one major cause.[20] By shifting tasks to technical devices and computers, it is anticipated to reduce these risks.

Moreover, unmanned shipping allows savings by reducing the costs for the ship's crew as well as for fuel. It is very likely that fewer personnel will be needed in the shore control centres to navigate or survey unmanned ships as compared to an onboard crew. Possibly, even more than one ship at a time may be controlled and/or surveyed by the land-based "crew". Without a crew on board ships may further on proceed at slow steam and thus reduce fuel consumption. Today, the simultaneously increasing costs for the crew counteract this effect.[21] The absence of a crew, furthermore, enables new ship designs as the bridge, cabins and other crew facilities become dispensable. This can also lead to further fuel savings. At the same time, the ship's environmental performance can be improved and support sustainable shipping.[22] Additionally, those new designs allow using a lot more space for cargo. This can be relevant when coping with the continuous growth in transport volumes.[23]

Further opportunities in respect of efficiency result from voyage planning and just-in-time delivery. Crewless ships may change the route or adjust speed more easily and can thus react better to changing demands during the transport. Especially for cargo subject to high price fluctuations, this may be of interest.

Finally, unmanned shipping creates social benefits. As work is shifted from the seas to shore, working conditions improve and become more family-friendly. Seafaring develops into an ordinary office job with regulated working hours and returning home after work every day.

In summary, unmanned ships come along with a high amount of advantages with regard to safety, economic, ecological and social aspects but still, there are challenges to consider. Can those ships be operated legally under the current framework? How to deal with the increasing risk of technical failure and cyber risks?

D. ARE UNMANNED VESSELS CONSIDERED "SHIPS"?

The first question to be raised is whether unmanned vessels are "ships" in legal terms. The answer is not as simple as one may think at first sight and moreover, it is highly important for determining the legal basis for unmanned ships' operation. International shipping conventions are applicable to ships only. Hence, unmanned vessels may be obliged under their rules or claim the rights granted by them only if their status as ships is recognized.

International law does not provide a uniform definition of the term ship.[24] Each convention defines its scope of application in a different manner, taking into account its respective purposes.[25] Some conventions do not at all define the term ship. The United Nations Convention on the Law of the Sea (UNCLOS), for example, does not contain a definition and uses the terms "ship" and "vessel" interchangeably.[26] The travaux préparatoires to the preceding Convention on the High Seas show that a definition was once discussed in context of article 6 of the convention. It was suggested that a ship should be "a device capable of traversing the sea but not the air space, with equipment and crew appropriate to the purpose for which it is used."[27] In the end, it was unanimously agreed to delete the article.[28] Nevertheless, the proposed definition demonstrates that the understanding of the term ship was very wide as the convention aims to cover ship operations comprehensively. It is noteworthy that the crew forms a part of the definition. It is therefore arguable that unmanned craft may not be regarded as ships, at least as far as UNCLOS is concerned. However, including the crew in the definition might be due the factual circumstances at the time the definition was discussed. The rather descriptive character of the whole definition is noticeable, and nobody would have thought of unmanned ships, even in the mid-20th century.

Other conventions with an equal approach likewise provide wide-ranging definitions and do not expressly indicate that a crew is essentially needed. The International Regulations for Preventing Collisions at Sea (COLREGs), for example, state in Rule 3 a) "the word "vessel" includes every description of water craft, including non-displacement craft, WIG craft and seaplanes, used or capable of being used as a means of transportation on water". The International Convention for the Prevention of Pollution from Ships (MARPOL) defines the term ship as "a vessel of any type whatsoever operating in the marine environment and includes hydrofoil boats, air-cushion, submersibles, floating craft and fixed or floating platforms", article 2 no. 4. After the plain reading of those conventions, it might be concluded that the definitions can also refer to unmanned ships.

However, no international convention does expressly address unmanned vessels. Moreover, one should take into consideration that all the international conventions are clearly drafted with manned ships in mind. Hence, different views on the convention's application to unmanned ships are possible, each with striking arguments.[29]

However, denying unmanned craft the status of a ship would risk the fragmentation of law. In that case, no convention would apply, and unmanned ships would operate in a legal vacuum. Therefore, it is necessary to clarify whether unmanned vessels are considered ships in legal terms for each convention. It is essential to reach an international consensus to operate unmanned ships with legal certainty.

E. CROSS-BORDER OPERATION OF UNMANNED SHIPS

As soon as technical conditions will allow, unmanned ships are going to be used in cross-border shipping. Assuming that they will be considered ships, they need to comply with several rules set out in international law. The question whether they can meet the requirements is still unsolved. The following examples shall outline the basic problems.

I. FLAG STATE JURISDICTION

One major issue to consider in the context of unmanned shipping is related to the ship's flag. The ship's flag is its outer sign of nationality and of fundamental relevance for the legal conditions of the ship's operation. Rights as well as duties are connected to the flag. Ships may only claim freedoms of the sea, like e.g. the freedoms of the high sea or the right of innocent passage, when flying the flag of a state. Consequently, flying a flag is inevitable in the cross-border operation of ships. In return, the states may only exercise jurisdiction over ships flying their flag. It is therefore to be questioned, whether unmanned ships would be entitled to fly a flag and under what conditions.

International law almost does not set out provisions with respect to the conditions for the right to fly a flag. UNCLOS leaves it up to the states to fix the conditions under which they entitle ships this right. Article 91 I UNCLOS just requires that there must exist a "genuine link" between the ship and the state. The reason behind this is to ensure that the state is able to effectively exercise jurisdiction over ships flying its flag.[30] In their national conditions, the states often refer to the nationality of the ship's owner. Ships at least partly owned by a national of the flag state may be registered in the national ship registers.[31] Jurisdiction over the ship may thus be exercised via its owner. As for unmanned ships, a genuine link between the ship and the state may still be established by the nationality of its owner. Other criteria found in the practise of states, like e.g. the nationality of the ship's master, officers or crew[32], obviously face more difficulties as those persons do no longer exist on unmanned ships. Anyway, it can be considered whether the remote controller or others in charge of the ship from ashore may constitute the master, officers or crew and thus a genuine link can be established.

Eventually, it is up to every single state whether and in which factors it sees a genuine link and is convinced to be capable to effectively exercise jurisdiction. The so called "Roboship", a craft of eight metres in length that is operated by the German Ministry of Defence, is a first example of a remotely controlled vessel entitled to fly the German flag.[33]

II. Crewing requirements

Undeniably, the most important difference between unmanned and conventional ships is the absence of any onboard crew. Even though the presence of a crew on board is not necessarily required by the term ship, crewing requirements are subject to several regulations in international as well as in national law.

UNCLOS mainly requires the flag states to fix own provisions with respect to manning, article 94 III b). These shall ensure "that each ship is in the charge of a master and officers who possess appropriate qualifications, in particular in seamanship, navigation, communications and marine engineering, and that the crew is appropriate in qualification and numbers for the type, size, machinery and equipment of the ship", article 94 IV b UNCLOS. What is noticeable is that the number of crew does not only depend on the ships size but its equipment as well. This leads to the conclusion, that it is internationally accepted to reduce the crew depending on the level of technical support and, where appropriate, to even replace crew members.[34] Still, it cannot be said with certainty that a number of zero would be accepted. In addition, it is highly questionable whether the master and officers are dispensable.

Besides, Article 94 V b UNCLOS obliges the states to act in accordance with generally accepted international regulations, procedures and practices related to manning. Those may be found e.g. in the International Convention for the Safety of Life at Sea (SOLAS) and the International Convention on Standards of Training, Certification and Watchkeeping for Seafarers (STCW). The SOLAS Chapter V Regulation 14 states that the contracting governments shall ensure that all ships are sufficiently and efficiently manned and thereby refers to the IMO Principles of Safe Manning.[35] Those neither set out a minimum number of crew required for safe manning, but they establish some criteria to take into consideration when determining the minimum safe manning. As for unmanned ships, attention should be drawn to points 1.1.3 and 1.1.10 of the Principles. When determining the minimum safe manning, the level of ship automation and the degree of shore side support provided to the ship by the company should be taken into account. Again, the relevance of technical equipment for the number of the crew is internationally recognised. However, it remains unclear whether a number of zero could be established.

As for the STCW convention it is highly questionable whether the provisions would at all apply to unmanned ships. Pursuant to its article III, the convention is applicable to "seafarers serving on board seagoing ships", hence persons in charge of the ship from ashore are most likely not included.[36]

In summary, international law only sets out few criteria with respect to manning but does not categorically exclude unmanned ships.[37] It is mainly up to the national governments to set out specific provisions or even minimum manning requirements. As for German law, neither a minimum nor an explicit prohibition of unmanned ships can be found. Like international law, German law makes reference to the degree of ship's automation when it comes to manning. The German Safe Manning Regulation recognises the degree of automation as a relevant factor in determining the manning requirements. Whether or not a high degree of automation e.g. a fully autonomous ship, can reduce the crew to a number of zero under German law, however, is hard to predict. The provisions were clearly drafted with manned ships in mind but are frank in their wording and open to automation. At least, the German administration has issued a "flag attestation" for the "Roboship", referred to above, and obviously accepted its operation without any onboard crew. Merchant ships, however, give a whole new dimension to unmanned shipping operations.

In conclusion, there are indications in international as well as in German national law, that ships could be operated legally without a crew on board. Nonetheless, unmanned ships are not explicitly subject to the provisions, so that differing interpretation is possible. In the interests of legal certainty, this should be clarified.

III. Proper Lookout

To ensure the safe operation and navigation of ships it is necessary to maintain a proper lookout. Technical support, e.g. radar, has long played an important role in fulfilling lookout duties. Especially for autonomous ships a significant question is whether a proper lookout can be maintained by the autonomous system and without any human influence.

The COLREGs constitute the legal bases for collision avoidance and therefore contain lookout duties. According to rule 5 "every vessel shall at all times maintain a proper look-out by sight and hearing as well as by all available means appropriate in the prevailing circumstances and conditions so as to make a full appraisal of the situation and of the risk of collision". The wording clearly refers to the human abilities of seeing and hearing.[38] This indicates that lookout duties cannot be fulfilled without human participation. Instead, expressions like "optical and acoustical lookout" could have been used to make clear that the traditional human watch can be replaced by technical means. This view is supported by the case of "The Anneliese", brought before the court of Appeal.[39] Lord Justice Karminski came to the conclusion that "the use of radar is by no means to be despised, especially in fog, where it has been described as an extra eye; but the human eye can sometimes see more quickly than radar even in fog, and so is able to appreciate the position in less time than is needed to examine the recordings of a radar"[40] and that "the Arietta should have had a good visual look-out in addition to the radar"[41]. This suggests that a human lookout is required by the COLREGs.

However, rule 5 of the COLREGs does not explicitly say that the human lookout needs to be on board of the ship. One may argue that it is sufficient when the human participation takes place ashore in the monitoring centre.[42]

At least as far as remotely controlled ships are concerned, it is quite likely the control room ashore resembles the bridge of current ships. Recordings from cameras, microphones, radar data and other information about the ship's surrounding could run together in those centres and be available for human perception. Thus, an indirect human lookout could be established. However, it should be clarified whether this is sufficient to comply with rule 5 of the COLREGs.[43]

Autonomous ships, on the other hand, are most likely not monitored to the same extend. Possibly, not every information and not every single camera perspective would be shown to the surveying person the whole time. This could be due to the fact that more than one ship is monitored at a time by the person in charge. Images would only be brought to the attention of a human being if the image recognition software detected anything unusual. In this event, not even an indirect human lookout is continuously assured.

Finally, delay in signal transmission, technical failures as well as sudden disconnection need to be considered. In these events, unmanned ships would be in breach of the duty to maintain a proper lookout at all times.

Further duties with respect to watchkeeping are set out in chapter IV of the SOLAS convention. Regulation 12 requires every ship, while at sea, to maintain a continuous watch on VHF and MF/HF radio installation as well as on distress and safety DSC frequencies, if fitted with the respective installations. Additionally, ships shall maintain a radio watch for broadcasts of maritime safety information. The wording does not explicitly require that those duties are exercised on board of the ship; hence unmanned ships could comply with the rule by transmitting the relevant signals to shore. However, problems may arise in the event of malfunctions or disconnection. Of course, those may as well occur on manned ships. Still, as far as the connection to the land side is concerned, unmanned ships create a new venture in transmitting the signals. For this reason, it is likely that unmanned vessels would be in breach of the watchkeeping duties in the event of disturbances.

F. LIABILITY FOR UNMANNED SHIPS

Unmanned shipping technology offers the opportunity to reduce events of loss or damage caused by human error. Nevertheless, crewless vessels are not free of failure either. But who is liable in the event of an accident caused by an unmanned ship? The scenarios leading to loss or damage are multiple. Accidents might still be caused by human fault, e.g. by the ship's remote controller or the responsible person that monitors the autonomous ship from ashore. They might as well be due to the fault of the programmer who developed the relevant software. In addition, technical defects may cause damage without any human interference. To fulfil the highly sophisticated tasks of navigation and collision avoidance, the software of autonomous ships cannot be pre-programmed for every single situation but needs to be capable of making decisions on its own to some extent. Programming can be de lege artis, mistakes will be made anyway. The following part shall outline the major challenges unmanned vessels impose on liability law.

I. Liability for Collision caused by an Unmanned Ship

Ship collisions represent a considerable risk for shipping. In the future collisions may take place between an unmanned and a manned vessel as well as between two unmanned vessels. The most urgent issue, however, remains the same. Who is liable for collision damage caused by unmanned ships?

Ship collisions are governed by the Convention for the Unification of Certain Rules of Law with respect to Collisions between Vessels (Collision Convention). Basically, the rules oblige the vessel which caused the collision by its fault to make good the damage caused to other vessels or to any things or persons on board thereof. If two or more vessels are in fault, liability shall be shared proportionally, article 4. In its article 3, the convention refers to the vessel's fault, nevertheless the category of fault implies characteristics commonly awarded to human beings. The German implementation of the convention therefore refers to the ship owner's fault and the fault of persons attributable to the owner.[44]

Whether the fault of persons involved in the unmanned ship's operation from ashore is attributable to the ship, may be answered differently in international and national law. As for international law, no certain statement is made. The Collision Convention only refers to the vessel's fault but does not say anything in respect of the persons committing these faults. This question is left up to national regulation.[45] German collision liability law, in contrast, names several persons whose fault shall be attributable to the owner, like the ship's crew and the pilot operating on board, §§570 S. 1, 480 S. 1 German Commercial Code (HGB). So, for German law, it needs to be questioned whether persons engaged in the unmanned ship's navigation from ashore may constitute its crew. A definition of the ship's crew is given in §478 HGB. Accordingly, the crew consists of the master, the ship's officers, other crew members and further persons employed in the ship's operation. As for the other persons involved in the ship's operation, it cannot necessarily be said that the crew must only act on board of the ship. However, problems may arise as the definition does not include independent contractors.[46] Crew members need to be employed either by the ship's owner or they need to have been put at the disposal of the owner by a third party for the purpose of performing work in the context of the ship's operation while being subject to the orders of the master. Depending on the specific business relations to be developed in unmanned shipping, it is unclear whether these requirements can be met. Unmanned shipping technology allows to control and to survey more than one ship at once, which is why it is conceivable that those tasks are going to be concentrated in specialized centers. At least as far as German collision law is concerned, the ship owner could not be held responsible for the fault of persons employed in independent monitoring centers. As for international law, the Collision Convention is less restrictive and may allow holding the owner responsible for faults committed in such centers.

However, the most relevant question is probably who will be liable for technical defects when no human fault was involved. The Collision Convention is quite clear in that point as liability is fault-based. As already mentioned above, the convention refers to the ship's fault. Though, the travaux préparatoire explain that the convention had human actions in mind. It refers to the liability of "[...] the vessel on board of which the said fault was committed"[47] and not to the ship' s fault itself. This view is underlined by the meaning of fault which indicates either action with intent or negligence. Liability based on fault refers to holding someone responsible when acting blameworthy. It can hardly be imagined how computer systems could act in such a way as the decision-making ability of software is not comparable to human decision-making. Thus, no fault can be attributed to the owner. Consequently, it is most likely that the owner would not at all be liable in the event of technical defects or misleading decisions of autonomously acting computer systems.[48]

In summary, two major gaps in respect of collisions caused by unmanned ships can be identified. As for German national law, the owner's liability for faults committed in independent monitoring centers is in doubt. Overall, the fault based liability set out in the Collision Convention is not able to deal with technical defects and software-based decision-making.

II. PRODUCT LIABILITY FOR UNMANNED SHIPS

As the owner's liability in respect of unmanned ships is afflicted with difficulties, one might try to hold the manufacturer responsible instead. Product liability law is not internationally unified, but the European Union has harmonized the regulations to some extent. The Council Directive 85/374/EEC of 25 July 1985 on the approximation of the laws, regulations and administrative provisions of the Member States concerning liability for defective products (Product Liability Directive) is the basis for product liability in the European Union. The Member States are encouraged to implement the provisions in their national laws.

According to article 1 of the directive, liability attaches to the producer who shall be responsible for damage caused by a defect in his product. Producers are mainly the manufacturer of a finished product, the producer of any raw material and the manufacturer of a component part. So, for ships, the producer is the shipyard as well as everyone who produces parts of the ship like the ship's engine, the steering gear or even single screws. The question of whether the manufacturer of unmanned ship's software is liable for defects in programming needs further consideration; it is linked to the understanding of the term product.

At first, it should be clarified that ships in general are products in the sense of the product liability directive. Although no one might have had ships in mind when drafting the directive, it is commonly agreed that ships are included.[49] Software and other "digital products" were also not considered. Problems arise out of the definition of the term product in article 2 of the directive that refers to "movables". Movables are not defined in the laws of the European Union; hence, it is necessary to refer to national law. As for German law, §90 of the German Civil Code (BGB) only considers corporeal objects as things as defined by law. Though, in the prevailing view, computer programs are regarded as things, movables and even products for the purpose of product liability, provided that they are stored on an electronic device.[50] The European Commission shares this view. In an official statement it declared that the directive applies to software in the same way.[51]

However, with respect to unmanned ships, the directive has one major weakness. According to article 9, the directive only covers damage to or destruction of any item of property, provided that the item of property is of a type ordinarily intended for private use or consumption and that it was used by the injured person mainly for the own private use or consumption. As most damages to items of property caused by an unmanned ship, e.g. in case of a collision, would probably be designated to commercial use, the practical significance is limited.[52] At least as far as the European Union is concerned, the producer of an unmanned ship would not be liable for many claims.

However, the Product Liability Directive applies to damages caused to e.g. yachts in private use or private relocation goods. Another case of application arises out of personal injuries. An unmanned ship' s producer would be liable for damage caused by death or by personal injuries that is caused by a defect of the ship. As liability is strict, no fault on part of the producer is required. Therefore, he will be liable even for damage caused by technical defects or software malfunctions of an autonomously acting ship.

III. LIABILITY OF THE CARRIER

Unmanned shipping is also likely to affect the liability of the carrier. Carrier liability is subject to several conventions in international law, such as the Hague Rules and the protocol thereto, the Hague-Visby Rules, the Rotterdam Rules and the Hamburg Rules. All conventions focus on liability of the carrier for loss of or damage to the goods carried under contracts of carriage by sea or under bills of lading. The Rotterdam Rules and the Hamburg Rules additionally deal with delay.

What they all have in common is fault-based liability. Under the Hague Rules and the Hague-Visby Rules, neither the carrier nor the ship shall be responsible for loss or damage caused by unseaworthiness, provided that the carrier exercised due diligence to make the ship seaworthy, article 4 I. Besides, special exclusion clauses, the so called "catch-all"[53] exclusion clause in article 4 II q), exempts the carrier from liability in case the damages result from any other cause arising without the actual fault or privity of the carrier, or without the actual fault or neglect of his agents or servants. Pursuant to article 17.2 of the Rotterdam Rules, the carrier is entirely or partly relieved of liability if the cause of loss, damage or delay is not attributable to his fault or to the fault of any person named in article 18 of the convention. Under the Hamburg Rules, the carrier is liable for loss of or damage to the goods, unless he proves that he, his servants or agents took all measures that could reasonably be required to avoid the occurrence and its consequences, art. 5 I.

In the first instance, this means that carriers will need to draw more attention to maintaining, monitoring and updating technical equipment and software in the future to prevent malfunctions as well as cyber-attacks. Otherwise they would at least act negligently as they would not have taken all measures reasonably required to prevent damage. Risks arising from the use of unmanned shipping technology will need to be reduced as far as possible by exercising due diligence.

The most urgent question to be answered is, again, how the software of autonomous ships could act with intent or negligently so that a malfunction attributable to the carrier could be established. Most likely, this is not possible as the decision-making of human beings is not comparable with possible decisions made by software. Consequently, the carrier would not at all be liable provided that the software's malfunction was the sole cause of loss or damage.

Remotely controlled ships on the other hand, are possibly easier to deal with. Decision-making will still be in human hands so that the category of fault is applicable. The persons in charge will act from ashore but liability is quite flexible as it does not only attribute the master, officers or the crew who commonly serve on board of the ship to the carrier but also his servants and agents. Those may also act from ashore. Thus, e.g. the remote controller can easily be regarded as the carrier's servant so that his fault is still attributable to the carrier.

IV. Liability for Environmental Damages and Shipping Hazards

As opposed to the regulations mentioned above, marine environmental liability is better suited for unmanned, especially autonomous ships. As far as environmental damages or shipping hazards are concerned, liability is not based on fault.[54] Liability attaches to the ship's operation only, which is why there are no problems holding the owner responsible without any actual fault. Problems in attributing other people's fault to the owner or in establishing an autonomous system's fault do not occur in this context.

G. Unmanned Ships in Marine Insurance

Unmanned Shipping is last but not least an important issue of marine insurance. Besides the uncertainties regarding the regulatory framework for unmanned ship's operation and the difficulties in liability law, which are problems for insurance as well, the use of advanced digital technology makes those ships vulnerable to cyber-attacks. Thus, cyber risks are expected to increase by the introduction of unmanned ships. Insurers fear that hackers may take charge of a ship by exploiting the ship's data link to the shore and thereby may cause high losses. Hacker's motivations are various and reach from terroristic backgrounds to theft of the cargo up to the demand of ransom for releasing the vessel. In the past, several cyber-attacks have already attracted attention. In June 2017, even the world's largest container shipper Maersk Line was affected.[55]

Cyber risks matter at all levels of marine insurance such as hull and machinery insurance, cargo insurance as well as protection and indemnity insurance. Those are not governed by internationally unified rules but traditionally characterized by terms and conditions. The insurance market provides different types of cover which may roughly be categorized in all risks cover and limited cover. As for all risks cover, all risks are included unless explicitly excluded. Thus, cyber risks would be covered in the absence of an exclusion clause. Limited cover, in contrast, only provides cover for named perils, which is why cyber risks would alike need to be named. Besides, the type of damage covered should be considered carefully. Marine hull and marine cargo insurance for example focus on property damages and would not cover delay or ransom attributable to a cyber-attack or technical malfunctions.

With respect to cyber-attacks, attention should be drawn to the Institute Cyber Attack Exclusion Clause – Cl. 380. The clause can be incorporated in existing policies like marine hull and marine cargo policies. It says: "[...] in no case shall this insurance cover loss, damage, liability or expense directly or indirectly caused by or contributed to by or arising from the use or operation, as a means for inflicting harm, of any computer, computer system, computer software programme, malicious code, computer virus or process or any other electronic system." By incorporating this clause, criminal acts of hackers would no longer be covered. However, the insurance market has also responded to the occurrence of cyber risks by providing new solutions. Insurers offer buy-backs for the Clause 380[56] or overarching marine cyber insurance that encompasses different insurances.[57] In any case, cyber risks should be taken seriously in shipping, including the insurance market.

H. SUGGESTIONS FOR A FUTURE LEGISLATIVE FRAMEWORK FOR UNMANNED SHIPS

The above findings show that the current legal framework is not ready to deal with unmanned ships yet. Maritime law was not drafted with crewless ships in mind; hence there is a lack of specific regulations. However, technical progress makes it more and more important to provide a reliable legislative framework for unmanned ships in the near future to ensure that those ships can be operated safely and with legal certainty.

First, it should be clarified whether unmanned vessels are ships in the sense of the numerous conventions governing international shipping and thus subject to the regulations set out therein. Provided that unmanned ships are subject to the same legal provisions as their manned counterpart, further clarification is needed to make sure that they meet the requirements. It should, inter alia, be clarified whether or not the manning requirements set out in UNCLOS, SOLAS and the IMO Principles of Safe Manning would allow a number of zero crew members. With respect to lookout duties, an amendment is possibly needed to ensure that unmanned and especially autonomous ships comply with these rules. Manning requirements and lookout duties are only two examples of challenging aspects with respect to unmanned ships. Further examination of the legislative framework is necessary to identify other critical aspects and to decide whether unmanned ships can meet the requirements or if amendments would be needed.[58] In a second step, it should be discussed how clarifications or amendments could be incorporated into the legal framework most practically. The procedures for amending conventions are complicated and of protracted nature. Depending on how many conventions and provisions would need to be modified, this could be a challenging task. Thus, consideration could also be given to whether it could be reasonable to create an encompassing "Unmanned Shipping Code".

As for liability law, new solutions are primarily required to cope with autonomous ships. Fault-based liability fails to handle technical defects or software-based decisions properly, leaving gaps as compared to the situation of manned ships. Thus, it is obvious to consider strict liability for the operation of unmanned ships. Regulations found in liability law for environmental damage could serve as a model for future regulations. Liability attaches to the owner of the vessel in these regulations, though another opportunity would be to extend the liability of the producer.

Besides, it needs to be discussed who should bear the risks of autonomous ships under contracts of carriage. As the liability of the carrier is fault-based under the current rules, the carrier would not at all be liable for damage caused by technical defects or malfunctions of software provided that there was no fault on his part. The implementation of a strict liability could turn this result around.

I. FINAL CONSIDERATIONS

Unmanned shipping is not only revolutionizing the shipping industry but also going to affect every part of maritime law. International cooperation on this topic is urgently needed to avoid hindering the developments in progress.[59] First steps have been made by the IMO Maritime Safety Committee which put unmanned ships on the agenda for its ninety-ninth session in May 2018.[60] The Comité Maritime International is engaged as well and even initiated an international working group on "Maritime Law for Unmanned Craft".[61]

Those activities are important and necessary to pave the way towards the unmanned ship and to ensure that it can be operated safely and within a reliable legal framework.

LITERATURE

Allianz Global Corporate & Specialty (ed.), Safety and Shipping 1912–2012. From Titanic to Costa Concordia, 2012

Allianz Global Corporate & Specialty (ed.), Safety and Shipping Review 2017. An annual review of trends and developments in shipping losses and safety

CMI Working Group "Maritime Law for Unmanned Craft", CMI International Working Group Position Paper on Unmanned Ships and the International Regulatory Framework, 2017

Comité Maritime International, The Travaux Préparatoires of the 1910 Collision Convention and of the 1952 Arrest Convention, 1997

Deketelaere, Pol, The legal challenges of unmanned vessels, Master Thesis, 2017

Deutscher Verein für Internationales Seerecht, Reply by the German Maritime Law Association to the CMI IWG Questionnaire of 29 March 2017 "Unmanned Ships", 2017

Florio, Franco, Nazionalità della Nave e Legge della Bandiera, 1957

Gidel, Gilbert, Le droit international public de la mer, Tome 1, La haute mer, 1932

Herber, Rolf, Seehandelsrecht, 2016

International Tribunal for the Law of the Sea, Case No. 2 M/V Saiga, Judgement of 01.07.1999, 1999

Jahn, Carlos, Autonome Schifffahrt – Zum Stand der Entwicklung/Forschung, in: Deutscher Verkehrsgerichtstag (ed.), Veröffentlichung der auf dem 55. Deutscher Verkehrsgerichtstag vom 25. bis 27. Januar 2017 in Goslar gehaltenen Vorträge, Referate und erarbeiteten Empfehlungen 2017, p. 249–263

Jessen, Henning, Autonome Schiffe als zukünftige Herausforderung für das Seevölkerrecht und für den Rechtsrahmen der IMO, in: Deutscher Verkehrsgerichtstag (ed.), Veröffentlichung der auf dem 55. Deutscher Verkehrsgerichtstag vom 25. bis 27. Januar 2017 in Goslar gehaltenen Vorträge, Referate und erarbeiteten Empfehlungen, 2017, p. 265–273

Jokioinen, Esa, Introduction, in: Rolls-Royce (ed.), AAWA Position Paper– Remote and Autonomous Ships – The Next Steps 2016, p. 3–14

Lazaratos, George, The definition of ship in national and international law, in: Revue Hellénique de Droit International (RHDI) 1969, S. 57–99

Lucchini, Laurent, Le Navire et les Navires, in: Dupuy, René-Jean (ed.), Le navire en droit international, 1992, p. 11–42

Lutter, Carina, Fragen der Produkthaftung im Hinblick auf den Betrieb unbemannter Schiffe, RdTW 2017, p. 281–286

Nadan, Satya N./Rosenne, Shabtai, United Nations Convention on the Law of the Sea 1982. A Commentary, Vol. III, Art. 86–132, 1995

Norris, Andrew, Legal Issues Relating to Unmanned Maritime Systems, 2013

O'Connell, D. P./Shearer, I. A., The international law of the sea, 1984

Poikonen,Jonne/Hyvönen, Mika/Kolu, Antti/Jokela, Tero/Tissari, Jari/Paasio, Ari, Technology, in: Rolls-Royce (ed.), AAWA Position Paper– Remote and Autonomous Ships – The Next Steps 2016, p. 15–34

Ramming, Klaus, Die Haftung aus Zusammenstößen unter Beteiligung unbemannter Schiffe, RdTW 2017, p. 286–292

Ringbom, Henrik/Collin, Felix/Viljanen, Mika, Legalities, in: Rolls-Royce (ed.), AAWA Position Paper– Remote and Autonomous Ships – The Next Steps, 2016, p. 35–55

Rødseth, Ørnulf Jan/Burmeister, Hans-Christpoh, Developments toward the unmanned ship, 2012

Schmidt-Salzer, Joachim, Kommentar EG-Richtlinie Produkthaftung, Band 1, 1986.

Schwampe, Dieter, Zivilrecht und Versicherungsrecht, in: Deutscher Verkehrsgerichtstag (ed.), Veröffentlichung der auf dem 55. Deutscher Verkehrsgerichtstag vom 25. bis 27. Januar 2017 in Goslar gehaltenen Vorträge, Referate und erarbeiteten Empfehlungen, 2017, p. 275–295

Singh, Lachmi, The Law of Carriage of Goods by Sea, 2011

Sohn, Louis B./Gustafson, J.D., The Law of the Sea, 1984

Tüngler, Grit/tho Pesch, Sebastian, Seevölkerrechtliche Anforderungen an unbemannte Schiffe, RdTW 2017, p. 121–127

United Nations (ed.), Yearbook of the International Law Commission, Vol. 2, 1951

United Nations (ed.), Yearbook of the International Law Commission, Vol. 1, 1955

van Hooydonk, Eric, The law of unmanned merchant shipping – an exploration, in: The Journal of International Maritime Law (JIML) 2014, p. 403–423

Veal, Robert/Tsimplis, Michael, The integration of unmanned ships into the lex maritima, in: LMCLQ 2017, p. 303–335

von Ziegler, Alexander, Haftungsgrundlage im internationalen Seefrachtrecht, Evolution der Haftungsgrundlage von den Haager Regeln zu den Hamburg Regeln unter Berücksichtigung des nationalen und internationalen Seerechts von Großbritannien, den Vereinigten Staaten von Amerika, Kanada, Frankreich, Deutschland und der Schweiz, 2002

Wagner, Gerhard, Kommentar zum Produkthaftungsgesetz, in: Säcker et al., Münchener Kommentar zum Bürgerlichen Gesetzbuch, 2017

Walker, George K., Definitions for the Law of the Sea, Terms Not Defined by the 1982 Convention, 2012
Westphalen, Friedrich Graf von (ed.), Produkthaftungshandbuch, Band 2, 1999

NOTES

1 Jahn, in: Deutscher Verkehrsgerichtstag (2017), pp. 249.
2 For detailed information on the project and its results see MUNIN's website http://www.unmanned-ship.org/munin/.
3 http://www.unmanned-ship.org/munin/about/munin-results-2/.
4 http://www.unmanned-ship.org/munin/about/munin-results-2/.
5 http://www.unmanned-ship.org/munin/about/munin-results-2/.
6 http://www.unmanned-ship.org/munin/about/munin-results-2/.
7 http://www.unmanned-ship.org/munin/about/munin-results-2/.
8 Poikonen et al., in: Rolls-Royce (2016), p. 16.
9 Poikonen et al., in: Rolls-Royce (2016), p. 20.
10 Jokioinen, in: Rolls-Royce (2016), p. 13.
11 https://www.dnvgl.com/technology-innovation/revolt/index.html.
12 https://www.dnvgl.com/technology-innovation/revolt/index.html.
13 https://www.dnvgl.com/technology-innovation/revolt/index.html.
14 https://www.dnvgl.com/technology-innovation/revolt/index.html.
15 http://www.ship-technology.com/projects/yara-birkeland-autonomous-container-vessel/.
16 https://www.km.kongsberg.com/ks/web/nokbg0240.nsf/AllWeb/4B8113B707A50A4FC125811D00407045?OpenDocument.
17 https://www.km.kongsberg.com/ks/web/nokbg0240.nsf/AllWeb/4B8113B707A50A4FC125811D00407045?OpenDocument.
18 https://www.km.kongsberg.com/ks/web/nokbg0240.nsf/AllWeb/4B8113B707A50A4FC125811D00407045?OpenDocument.
19 http://www.unmanned-ship.org/munin/wp-content/uploads/2016/02/MUNIN-final-brochure.pdf, p. 3.
20 Allianz (2012), p. 41; Allianz (2017), p. 32.
21 Rødseth/Burmeister (2012), p. 9.
22 For a calculation see Rødseth/Burmeister (2012), p. 7.
23 Rødseth/Burmeister (2012), p. 2.
24 van Hooydonk, JIML 2014, p. 406; O' Connell/Shearer (1984), p. 747 f.; Walker (2012), p. 60; Deketelaere (2017), p. 25.
25 Sohn/Gustafson (1984), p. 13; Lazaratos, RHDI 1969, p. 57; O'Connell/Shearer (1984), p. 748.
26 Van Hooydonk, JIML 2014, p. 406; Walker (2012), p. 56.
27 Yearbook of the International Law Commission (1955 Vol. 1), p. 10.
28 Yearbook of the International Law Commission (1955 Vol. 1), p. 10.

29 In favour: van Hooydonk, JIML 2014, p. 409; Veal/Tsimplis, LMCLQ 2017, p. 314; Schwampe, in: Deutscher Verkehrsgerichtstag (2017), p. 278; Jessen, in: Deutscher Verkehrsgerichtstag (2017), p. 268 f.; Deketelaere (2017), p. 28.

30 Nadan/Rosenne (1995), article 91.9 (c); International Tribunal for the Law of the Sea (1999), para 83.

31 See §1 of the German Flag Act, article 219 of the French Code des douanes, article 7 of the Great Britain Merchant Shipping (Registration of Ships) Regulations. As for member states of the European Union, it is considered satisfying if the owner is a national of a member state of the European Union.

32 Sohn/Gustafson (1984), p. 5; Florio (1957), p. 38, 39; Lucchini, in: Dupuy (1992), p. 34; Gidel (1932), p. 82; Yearbook of the International Law Commission (1951 Vol. 2), p. 76; O'Connell/Shearer (1984), p. 751 f., 760.

33 Deutscher Verein für Internationales Seerecht (2017), p. 3; Ramming, RdTW 2017, p. 287.

34 Tüngler/tho Pesch, RdTW 2017, p. 123.

35 Resolution A.1047(27) adopted on 30 November 2011.

36 Norris (2013), p. 54; Ringbom/Collin/Viljanen, in: Rolls-Royce (2016), p. 47; CMI Working Group (2017), p. 16; Deutscher Verein für Internationales Seerecht (2017), p. 12.

37 Veal/Tsimplis, LMCLQ 2017, p. 320; CMI Working Group (2017), p. 10.

38 CMI Working Group (2017), p. 14; Tüngler/tho Pesch, RdTW 2017, p. 125.

39 Lloyd's Rep. 1970 Vol. 1, p. 355–364.

40 Lloyd's Rep. 1970 Vol. 1, p. 359.

41 Lloyd's Rep. 1970 Vol. 1, p. 359.

42 Veal/Tsimplis, LMCLQ 2017, p. 326; CMI Working Group (2017), p. 14; Deutscher Verein für Internationales Seerecht (2017), p. 11.

43 CMI Working Group (2017), p. 14.

44 Schwampe, in: Deutscher Verkehrsgerichtstag (2017), p. 284.

45 Comité Maritime International (1997), p. 54.

46 BT-Drucks. 17/10309, S. 63.

47 [...] le navire à bord duquel cette faute a été commise", Comité Maritime International (1997), p. 52 f.

48 Deutscher Verein für Internationales Seerecht (2017), p. 14; Ramming, RdTW 2017, p. 291.

49 Herber (2016), p. 184; Westphalen (1999), §47, para 35; Wagner, in: Säcker et al. (2017), §2 ProdHaftG, para 9; Schmidt-Salzer (1986), Art. 2, para 50.

50 Wagner, in: Säcker et al. (2017), §2 ProdHaftG, para 17; Westphalen (1999), §73, para 39.

51 Official Journal 1989, C 114, p. 42.

52 Deutscher Verein für Internationales Seerecht (2017), p. 14, 15; Lutter, RdTW 2017, p. 285.

53 Singh (2011), p. 238; von Ziegler (2002), p. 322.

54 See e.g. article 10 of the Nairobi International Convention on the Removal of Wrecks, article III of the International Convention on Civil Liability for Oil Pol-

lution Damage, article 3 of the International Convention on Civil Liability for Bunker Oil Pollution Damage.

55 https://www.reuters.com/article/us-cyber-attack-maersk/cyber-attack-hits-shipper-maersk-causes-cargo-delays-idUSKBN19J0QB.

56 https://www.norclub.no/products/special-risks/cyber-clause-380-buy-back-/.

57 http://edgegroup.com/portfolio/cyber-attack-exclusion-buyback-insurance/.

58 E.g. provisions concerning design and construction of vessels or the obligation to render assistance at sea.

59 https://www.porttechnology.org/news/lack_of_regulation_hindering_unmanned_ships.

60 MSC 99/1/Rev.1.

61 Further information on the working group's activities can be found under http://www.comitemaritime.org/Maritime-Law-for-Unmanned-Craft/0,27153,115332,00.html.

Chapter X

Shipping in Polar Waters – Institutional Challenges and Perspectives on International Arctic Policy

Marilena Mross

A. Introduction

The melting of ice in consequence of global warming provides access to different Arctic resources and offers new opportunities, which were not conceived. Most relevant are the new sea routes through the Polar Sea, which will now become accessible[1], mineral resources like ores and energy resources under the seabed as well as rich fishing grounds in the polar waters.

Against this background the Arctic States try to make respective territorial claims. The increased interest for the Arctic region has found, in particular, symbolic expression by the planting of a Russian flag on the seabed below the North Pole in 2007.

When considered superficially, it appears possible that North and South Pole constitute substantially similar regions of the earth's surface, which for their part are subject to similar rules. Due to climatic conditions both Poles presented a surface difficult to control effectively – a *terra incognita*. This leads to the hypothesis that both areas have to take similar governance-structures as a basis. But this is not the case. In fact, a distinction must be made between both Polar Regions. The North Polar Region – the Arctic – consists majorly of water and ice masses, while there is a continent below the Antarctic region in the South. Furthermore, Antarctica is a "*global common*", thus a sovereignty-free "common room of states", whereas there is no comparable communitarisation in the Arctic region. For the purpose of an international Antarctic policy an international treaty regime in the form of the Antarctic Treaty was concluded. For the Arctic a final, coherent and comprehensive governance-strategy is still missing. This is due to the absence of a comprehensive agreement – perhaps on the model of the Antarctic Treaty – as well as due to institutional redundancies. The overlapping of international and national actors leads to collisions of interest and legal uncertainty. Finally, there is the question whether *Arctic-Governance* should remain the task of a few Arctic riparian states alone. However, there are reasons to be hopeful because the institutional actors are moving towards each other: A development from the concept of an excluding *exclusive Governance* to an including *inclusive Governance* raises the question of possible extensive cooperation or even merger.

In the absence of a comprehensive Arctic treaty regime this article will state relevant abstract legal issues of fragmentary public international law and highlight some solution models.

B. ANTARCTICA – COUNTERPART OF THE ARCTIC

The Antarctic Treaty, which is regulating the political and legal status of Antarctica in its 14 Articles, came into force in 1961. It is applicable to the area South Latitude, including all ice shelves.[2] In light of the partially overlapping of territorial claims of some of the riparian states, the aim of freezing territorial claims was to guarantee the peaceful use of the continent.[3] Accordingly, Article 4 of the Antarctic Treaty stipulates that riparian states with potential rights do not lose their previously asserted rights of or claims to territorial sovereignty but neither will existing claims be admitted nor new claims be justified. The states agreed in the preamble, that it is in the interest of all mankind that Antarctica shall continue forever to be used exclusively for peaceful purposes. Thus, any form of military action is prohibited.[4] The principle of exclusively peaceful uses is complemented by the explicit enshrining of the freedom of scientific investigation, the principle of cooperation research and the exchange of scientific information.[5] The Protocol on Environmental Protection of 1991 contains regulations concerning marine protection, waste disposal, protection of Antarctic flora and fauna as well as the introduction of a scheme for the environmental screening for activities in Antarctica. This protocol prohibits any activity relating to mineral resources, other than scientific research.[6] This results to a prohibition of any commercial excavating of natural resources within Antarctica.

C. ARCTIC'S ALLOCATION UNDER INTERNATIONAL LAW

If one looks at the international Arctic policy one notes that there is a lack of uniform governance – there is no completed international agreement or regime. The derivation of the competences is closely related to the territorial belonging and the rights of use.

I. ARCTIC AS NO GLOBAL COMMON – WHOM DOES THE REGION BELONG TO?

"Global commons" are characterized by sovereignty-free areas that cannot be appropriated by any state, since their usage is equally open to the whole international community.[7] In addition to the high sea as a *locus classicus*, also Antarctica became – among others – a global common due to the Antarctic Treaty.[8] The traditional regulation model of the priority principle was suppressed by the concept of *fair and equitable use* that finds its basics in the idea of equality.[9] In contrast to Antarctica, the Arctic is, however, not a global common. The usage rights broadly belong to the riparian states.[10]

1. THE SECTOR THEORY

The Sector Theory is based on a suggestion of the Canadian Senator *Poirier* from 1907.[11] According to this theory riparian states of the Arctic Ocean are entitled to claim the sector that results from an extension of the national border to the North Pole. *Böhmert* defines it as a triangle: "The line between the outermost point of the northern boundary of the respective riparian state's mainland coast is forming the basis; the North Pole is forming the peak of the triangle, from which the sidelines run to the outermost points of the basis."[12] Although especially Canada and the then Soviet Union understood the theory as a version of the Geographic contiguity after which the rights of the coastal state apply *ipso iure* and *ab initio*, and thus do not require any further enforcement to claim it, Norway and the US, quite rightly, opposed it constantly.[13] Contiguity alone, hence spatial proximity as such cannot establish any entitlement to sovereign rights over extended sectors.[14]

2. UNCLOS AS A LEGAL BASIS AND BASIS OF CLAIMS

Despite its climatic and geographical parameters, the Arctic Ocean is in all its parts subject to the UNCLOS[15].[16] All eight states bordering on the polar circle have ratified the UNCLOS, the sole exception is the US. However, the US mainly accepts its proviso as customary international law.[17] So all of the five riparian states have the right to a territorial sea (with an extension up to 12 nautical miles from baseline, cf. Art. 3 UNCLOS), to a contiguous zone (further 12 nautical miles, cf. Art. 33 UNCLOS) and to an exclusive economic zone (EEZ) with a maximum extension of 200 nautical miles (Art. 57 UNCLOS).

The territorial sea belongs to the state's territory, thus coastal states are capable of enforcing its sovereign rights in this region. On the contrary, in the contiguous zone the coastal states may merely exercise rights of control. In the EEZ the coastal states have sovereign rights for the purpose of exploring and exploiting natural resources, whether living or non-living, of the waters superjacent to the seabed and of the seabed and its subsoil (Art. 56 UNCLOS). Since all five riparian states proclaimed an EEZ, nearly 50 % of the Arctic Ocean is subject to such zones with sovereign rights or sovereign usage rights.[18]

3. The continental shelf

Furthermore, a continental shelf is granted: According to Art. 77 (1) UNCLOS, a coastal state exercises sovereign rights over the continental shelf for the purpose of exploring it and exploiting its nature resources. The UNCLOS defines the continental shelf in Art. 76 (1) UNCLOS as followed: "The continental shelf of a coastal State comprises the seabed and subsoil of the submarine areas that extend beyond its territorial sea throughout the natural prolongation of its land territory to the outer edge of the continental margin, or to a distance of 200 nautical miles from the baselines, (…) where the outer edge of the continental margin does not extend up to that distance."

According to Art. 77 (4) UNCLOS the sovereign rights cover all "mineral and other non-living resources of the seabed and subsoil". Hence, the importance of the continental shelf question as to the Arctic oil and gas deposits for the Arctic States is obvious.[19]

Riparian states that want to exploit mineral resources outside the 200 nautical mile zone, have to claim an extended continental shelf. All the Arctic riparian states strive for the maximum possible extension of their particular continental shelf. Partly, the claims raised are even overlapping, which leads to a certain conflict potential.[20] However, the maximum outer limit may not exceed 350 nautical miles from the baseline or, alternatively, 100 nautical miles seawards from the 2500 metre isobath (cf. Art. 76 (5) UNCLOS).

Art. 76 (8) UNCLOS provides a procedure for the determination of the outer limit of an extended continental shelf. According to that rule, the coastal state has to submit the information on the extended continental shelf to the Commission on the Limits of the Continental Shelf (CLCS), which then makes a non-binding recommendation concerning the establishment of the outer limits. Coastal states' applications to the CLCS have to be submitted within a period of 10 years, starting with the entry into force of the UNCLOS, but no earlier than 13 May 1999 for the respective state. Except for the US, since they have not yet ratified the UNCLOS, all riparian states, in other words Norway, Russia, Canada and Denmark, have already submitted such an application for an extension of their continental shelf. The maritime boundaries have not been finally clarified yet. This is not least attributable to the fact that Art. 76 UNCLOS, dealing with the outer limits of the continental shelf, belongs to the most complicated legal norms within the realm of the law of the sea, because it refers to a multitude of non-legal, namely geological and/or hydrographical, and difficult-to-interpret criteria.[21] But it can already be assumed that only few regions of the Arctic will not be part of the nationalization of the seabed.

D. PLURALITY OF ACTORS AS A PROBLEM

I. VARIOUS ACTORS AND THEIR INTERESTS

As well as the Arctic riparian states also other actors act as stakeholders with interests in the Arctic.

The main level is constituted by the participating states and the states interested in participation. These are primarily the five riparian states with direct access to the Arctic Ocean, thus, Russia, Canada, the US, Norway and Denmark due to the Greenlandic sovereign territory (the so-called "Arctic 5"). Furthermore the three Nordic states on the polar circle, Sweden, Iceland and Finland are also participating. Together with the Arctic 5 they build the so-called Arctic 8.

Their behaviour is aiming the exploitation of the resources and an economic-commercial exploitation of the Arctic, what they have already expressed with making territorial claims.

But many other states that – at first glance – are not connected in any way with the Arctic are also interested in shaping Arctic's policy and legal system. While some of the states' interests and motives to get involved in the Arctic are very similar, others are opposing.[22] Polar research for example is of outstanding interest to the international community and to numerous research countries – not least because the Arctic is an early indicator of climate change.[23] But there are also other possible motivations: Dependencies on energy supply from abroad, interest in the development of new sea routes, interest in external security in the Arctic region, concerns about the fragile environment, the willingness to share experiences for example in the field of environmental issues, interest in preserving the Arctic and its ecosystem...

Beyond the nation states there are a series of international organizations. The highest body – which all involved states are members of – is the UN. Parts of the participating states are also members of the EU or NATO. As a special regional institution there is the Arctic Council (AC), whose structure will be explained in detail in the following.

Below the national level there is a third group of relevant stakeholders, who – even though they do not have an immediate voice in foreign policy – can in different ways also have large influence on the development of the Arctic.[24]

Besides large companies in the energy and raw materials industry (e.g. Statoil, Gazprom and Rosneft, where the national states hold large shares anyway, so that there is a smooth transition from national to subnational level) there are also important stakeholder groups like NGOs (e.g. Greenpeace, WWF) and other interest groups such as the representations of indigenous peoples of the region as well as the group of scientific researchers, that study the Arctic environment.[25] While the indigenous peoples' and NGOs' key concerns are environment protection and social issues, the companies are chiefly concerned about the exploitation of resources.

II. ARCTIC COUNCIL

The Arctic Council is the most important Arctic institution. It was formed through the merger of several regional collaborations as from 1987, until it was finally formally established with the Ottawa-Declaration in 1996. The Arctic 8 are the member states of the AC. Six NGOs that represent indigenous interests are permanent participants.[26] In this respect, the Council is constructed *inclusively*: With the integration of indigenous peoples it connects national with subnational governance-level.[27]

Even though the AC presents itself as inclusive in a way, the Council's handling with interests approached from the outside is more restrictive: A number of nations and organizations do have an observer status but without being entitled to vote. By now there are 39 observers – among them also economic power China.[28] Also, the EU obtained the status as an ad-hoc-observer.[29] All Arctic Council decisions and statements require consensus of the eight Arctic States. The Permanent Participants, however, participate actively and are fully consulted in all deliberations and activities of the Arctic Council.

Thus, the Arctic states together dominate the shaping of Arctic Governance within the AC *exclusively*. Chairmanship of the Council rotates every two years among the eight member states; currently Finland is serving as Chair of the AC until 2019.

Tasks of the Council are the promotion of environmental protection and nature conservation as well as the sustainable development of the region. Firstly, the AC functions as a forum of periodic high-level consultations between the member states' Arctic Ministers. Secondly, six permanent working groups develop scientific advice in the areas of nature and marine protection, disaster control, environmental monitoring and sustainable development and control of environmental toxicants.[30] These presented advices of the working groups, however, are not legal binding. This is somehow a deficiency of the AC.

The AC has actually not the status of an international organization. Rather, it is a cooperation forum *sui generis*, thus, an intergovernmental cooperation institution.[31] On the downside, the non-binding nature of their work allows them a certain degree of flexibility, because possible political conflicts of interests do not constitute massive barriers for their work.[32]

The AC has also achieved progressing successes in their role as a forum of regular intergovernmental consultation: By now, several agreements that are fully legally binding were negotiated during the Ministerial meetings to plug regulatory gaps identified.[33]

III. UN/International Maritime Organization

The highest body is the UN, which all Arctic 8 are members of. The UN is manifested by the CLCS, the International Maritime Organization (IMO) as a specialized agency of the UN and by the numerous conventions that are also relevant for shipping in the Arctic.

E. LEGAL FRAMEWORK OF THE ARCTIC

Since large parts of the Arctic fall within the sovereignty of the riparian states, the national legal systems of the Arctic 5 as riparian states build an integral part of the Arctic's legal framework. In addition, public international law serves as an organizational framework for the regulation of the Arctic region. International law in turn affects the national jurisdictions. Also, the European law is relevant for parts of the Arctic, since Finland and Sweden as AC members are also member states of the European Union.[34]

Apart from a few exceptions, the relevant treaties do not address the Arctic in particular. Instead, global or regional agreements are applicable to the Arctic or parts of the Arctic quasi incidentally and reflexively.[35] Thus, these agreements differ in regard to the initiator, the norm quality as well as to the scope of application.[36]

The UNCLOS, the so-called constitution for the oceans[37], is primarily providing a broader legal framework. Regarding many aspects the UNCLOS is an "umbrella treaty".[38] When it comes to substantial management issues, e.g. about sea rescue or the joint use of resources, it often remains general. It even suggests its member states to regulate further details in appropriate multilateral agreements.[39] The elimination of regulatory loopholes regarding the Arctic with the help of newly developed regional agreements has already started under the lead of the AC (e.g. the Arctic Search and Rescue Agreement).

Other relevant international conventions are, besides the UNCLOS, also IMO's more concrete conventions concerning shipping traffic, especially the MARPOL-Convention[40] with its protocols, the SOLAS-Convention[41], the STCW-Convention[42], as well as the Polar Code[43]. The Polar Code is an additional specification of the three other conventions considering the characteristics of shipping in polar waters. It entered into force in 2017 and is a collection of binding regulations and recommendatory provisions that are applicable to IMO's member states. According to Introduction 1 of the Polar Code the goal of the Polar Code is *"to provide for safe ship operation and the protection of the polar environment by addressing risks present in polar waters and not adequately mitigated by other instruments of the Organization"*. The establishment of the Polar Code is an important step towards more environmentally friendly shipping in the Arctic. The Code, however, suffers from a few weaknesses, such as the lack of a ban of heavy fuel oil as engine fuel[44], a limited scope of its application for certain ships, an inadequate regulation concerning soot emissions and the handling of ballast water, as well as the lack of regulations concerning the reduction of greenhouse gases, and air and noise pollution.

The Arctic Council also develops important soft law instruments. But, also the AC as *the* Arctic institution is confronted with other bodies, like e.g. the Barents Euro-Arctic Council, the Nordic Council or the Arctic Economic Council.

As you can see, there is a governance potpourri of various legal sources that can partly be read from Art. 38 (1) of the ICJ Statute. Alongside various national jurisdictions there are regulations and agreements of global, regional or bilateral nature. These seem to be an uncoordinated patchwork rug of different, partly even overlapping regulatory approaches with varying memberships.[45]

F. POLITICAL OBJECTIVE AND INTERNATIONAL CREDO

I. CHALLENGES AND TASKS OF ARCTIC GOVERNANCE

"It is vitally important [. . .] to implement governance structures for the Arctic region based on international law, aiming at a cooperative and peaceful management of resources and preserving the ecological heritage of mankind"[46]

Peace, freedom and self-determination as well as sustainable development are the three ambitious governance aims for the Arctic.[47]

Main tasks, arising from these general governance aims are regulations concerning the protection and use of living resources and biodiversity in the Arctic, the reducing of emissions into the Arctic, the adapting to climate change, the sustainable access to fossil and raw mineral resources in the Arctic[48], regulations concerning the shipping in Arctic waters and the construction/expansion of maritime infrastructure, the militarization and the safeguarding of security in the region, as well as the improvement of living conditions of indigenous peoples and their possibilities to participate in shaping the Arctic's future. Due to the fact that all of these issues have a cross-border character, there is a need for a cross-bordered international governance to tackle these many main tasks. Profession of our time is to create a suitable governance.

II. NEED FOR AN INSTITUTIONAL SOLUTION?

Although the Arctic region is not subject of *one* comprehensive treaty regime, the Arctic is far away from being the under-regulated area as it is sometimes described. As demonstrated above, the legal structure of the Arctic is characterised by complexity and confusion.

Considering this melange, the partly demanded and proposed creation of an Arctic Treaty along the lines of the Antarctic Treaty appears quite understandable.[49]

III. INTERNATIONAL CONTRADICTION

Tragedy of the general science of public international law is that the concept of establishing a homogeneous "global legal order" rapidly turns out to be utopian. Moreover, a tendency away from international organizations towards the creation of regional and bilateral cooperation agreements has developed especially in the last three decades. This idea of exclusive institutionalization goes against the wishful thought of a "global law community" or "value community".

Against the background of elementary environmental and climate policy tasks, a solution concept allocated on as many shoulders as possible seems, however, most appropriate. With this thought in mind, it is important to preserve the balance between competence and responsibility.

According to the commitment of other actors, especially on the part of the EU and UN it seems unfair that only eight states in the Arctic, themselves all members of the UN, shall have the competence through their membership in the AC to refuse the observer status to other UN-members.

This is especially incomprehensible in the case of the EU when one remembers that three Arctic countries are EU member states (Denmark, Sweden and Finland) and the EU maintains close relations with Iceland and Norway through the European Economic Area. Canada, Russia and the US are also strategic partners of the EU.[50] It is true, that none of the EU member states are coastal states of the Arctic Ocean (both the Faroe Islands and Greenland, as self-governing entities of Denmark, are not part of the EU). The EU, however, does have competences to deal with issues in the Arctic, such as shipping.[51] The EU declared as a condition to join the UNCLOS that maritime transport, safety of shipping and the prevention of marine pollution contained inter alia in UNCLOS Parts II, III, V, VII and XII are considered to be areas of shared competences between the EU and the Member States, but also subject to continuous development.[52] Moreover, Art. 191 (1) TFEU provides that Union policy on the environment shall contribute to the pursuit of promoting measures at the international level to deal with regional or worldwide environmental problems, in particular combating climate change. Therefore, the EU is competent to develop both internal and external legislation with respect to shipping in the Arctic.[53]

Furthermore, Sweden, Finland and Denmark have transferred sovereign rights to the supranational organization in some areas of environmental policy. Especially the shared competence for environmental and fisheries-related issues (cf. Art. 4 (2) lit. d and e TFEU) and the even exclusive competence of the EU concerning the preservation of marine biological resources in the context of a common fisheries policy following from Art. 3 (1) lit. d TFEU clarify that these states are subject to European interdependencies.

Against this backdrop, it is irritating that the EU did not obtain an observer status with voting rights in the AC – the Arctic 8 are the only states with voting rights.

It should, furthermore, not be forgotten the principle of sovereign equality contained in the Charter of the UN, Art. 2 (1) and the preamble to that Charter, in which the peoples of the United Nations undertake: "to practice tolerance and live together in peace with one another as good neighbours, and to unite our strength to maintain international peace and security, and to ensure, by the acceptance of principles and the institution of methods, that armed force shall not be used, save in the common interest, and to employ international machinery for the promotion of the economic and social advancement of all peoples."

Even if this may initiate an almost boundless and at this point not goal-oriented debate about the validity of duties under international law laid down by the UN-Charter also outside the UN regime, the general legal principle of *Bona fides* and the related provisions which have been regulated in the *friendly-relations-declaration* for the purpose of intergovernmental collaboration, allow the perception, that one member state of the UN should be able to rely on having the participation competency in a special policy area, here due to the existence of the IMO even integrated in the institutional regime of the UN. The member states should be able to rely on their participation competency and it should not be possible to undermine or nullify the participation competence by creating a regional cooperation agreement with exclusive rights; because then cooperative exchange could become impossible.[54]

Admittedly, the so-called Arctic clause – Art. 234 UNCLOS, thus part of the UN regime – determines the competence of the riparian states to adopt and enforce regulations for environmental protection within the limits of the EEZ in ice-covered waters. However, the UNCLOS does not provide them an authority to exclude others from having an observer status and does certainly not at all give them a carte blanche for the creation of exclusive conditions. The Polar Regions are key regions for global climate patterns and, hence, also for life on planet Earth. Arctic changes do have worldwide effects, but the other way around, non-arctic developing and industrialized countries also affect the Arctic due to emissions of greenhouse gases and other pollutants. Thus, a duty of basic cooperation is at least already derived from the general principles of international law.

IV. INSTITUTIONAL APPROACHES FOR THE CREATION OF AN ARCTIC REGIME

Arctic Governance is a prime example of fragmentary international law. This can lead to jurisdictional problems, conflict of laws and to contract conflicts. What needs to be done is to create an Arctic Governance as consistent as possible keeping in mind the existing actors and set of rules.

A development from *exclusive governance* to cooperative *inclusive governance* is most likely to prove compatible with elementary principles of international law. However, it remains questionable what degree of inclusion appears enforceable and thus realistic.

1. APPROACH I: ARCTIC TREATY AS A COPY OF THE ANTARCTIC TREATY

The proponents of a single comprehensive convention modelled on the Antarctic Treaty of 1959 explain their opinion, in particular, with three arguments: (1) The apparent success of the Antarctic Treaty, (2) the Polar Regions being similar areas should be treated similarly, (3) the Arctic is a common heritage of humankind.[55] There is, however, one profound and crucial difference between the two Polar Regions: Antarctica is land – the Arctic is sea, where the UNCLOS is applicable. Thus, the Arctic Ocean is, as explained above, subject to the sovereignty and resource-related rights of each individual coastal state.[56] Furthermore, about four million people live in Arctic regions, while Antarctica is uninhabited.[57] These Arctic indigenous inhabitants do have extensive participating opportunities in the existing cooperation, granted by the AC, which are – for the international law, remaining first and foremost a law created of and for states – highly advanced.[58] It is questionable how such rights should be guaranteed under an international law Arctic Treaty.

Moreover, the Arctic 5 explicitly opposed to the creation of an Arctic Treaty.[59] Thus, a willingness of the Arctic States, to get involved in an appropriate negotiation process is not to be expected. Such a process would anyway require considerable investment in time and resources and a convention could be too rigid and inflexible to promote practical and flexible governance in the fast changing Arctic.[60]

2. APPROACH II: ARCTIC TREATY AS A REGIONAL SEAS CONVENTION

The second idea is the creation of a model of an Arctic Treaty parallel to a Regional Seas Convention. This would be a regional version of a treaty regime, limited in the number of participants, functionally exhaustive and could contain shared values of the Arctic States. Model for such a treaty could be the OSPAR-Convention[61]. The OSPAR-Conventions' contract territory even covers a small part of the Arctic. Thus, this convention has already adopted Arctic-relevant regulations.[62]

Even if such a regional treaty is not as utopian as a copy of the Antarctic Treaty it is currently still impossible to reach.[63] The arguments against this treaty model are the same: a regional treaty would also be intergovernmental, thus, it is questionable how indigenous peoples should be included. And again: The Arctic 5 have underlined that they do not see a need for one comprehensive treaty.

3. APPROACH III: FUSION SOLUTION

A strong form of inclusion, with regard to multiple actors, is the fusion of all next to one another standing institutions to *one* institutional unit.

An option worth considering is the incorporation of the Arctic Council into the UN system. This could be viable by setting up the AC as a specialized agency of the UN, along the lines of the IMO.

Specialized agencies are having wide international responsibilities, as defined in their basic instruments, in economic, social, cultural, educational, health, and related fields (cf. Art. 57 (1) of the UN-Charter). They are autonomous organizations, incorporated into the UN system and working with the UN through the coordinating machinery of the United Nations Economic and Social Council at an intergovernmental level. According to Art. 63 of the UN-Charter, the Economic and Social Council may enter into agreements with the agencies defining the terms on which the agency concerned shall be brought into relationship with the UN and may also co-ordinate the activities of the specialized agencies through consultation with and recommendations to such agencies.

Since all voting members of the AC are also members of the UN, none of them would lose the right to vote. But, here would also arise the question of who should become a member or observer within this specialized Arctic agency of the UN. Furthermore, there remains a danger of lowering the value of the Arctic 8 voices also due to their relation to the United Nations Economic and Social Council. From the perspective of the Arctic 8 this is, of course, not desirable. It could also lead to problems with Art. 234 UNCLOS, which is assigning clear competences to the riparian states.

4. APPROACH IV: REGIONAL ARCTIC ORGANISATION ON THE BASIS OF THE ARCTIC COUNCIL OR THE SOLUTION OF SUBSIDIARITY

Another approach is the actor-centred governance. This idea is about an actor-centred cooperation within an Arctic regional organisation on the basis of the Arctic Council. Instead of a regional contract law institution, it could be chosen a governance system that is working over the effective use and coordination of already existing actors' networks.[64] Indigenous peoples, NGOs, scientists, Arctic regions and governments could jointly and rather informally shape Arctic governance in theme-centred networks and committees.[65]

One could even go further and propose that international contract law agreements of the international community shall be subsidiary to special regulations of the Arctic Council.

The idea of subsidiarity is the fundamental principle of the European primary law and enshrined in Art. 5 TEU.[66] Then, the regulations of the AC would be *leges speciales* over other international agreements in the area of Arctic policy.

The result would be that international agreements would only have to be made when the Arctic Council was not able to introduce protection rules or it was otherwise agreed. The topic "Arctic" would therefore mainly remain in the hand of the AC, insofar as it is able to sufficiently achieve regulations.

But the proposal suffers from errors in reasoning from the very beginning.

Firstly, international law applies *inter partes* and not *erga omnes*. If the AC adopts agreements containing the handling of the Arctic, these regulations will not become absolute rights for the whole international community of states.

Furthermore, the science of public international law already knows measures to avoid competition of norms and competition of contracts: According to Art 103 of the UN-Charter, new commitments may not be contrary to the Charter.

The implementation of the principle of subsidiarity would be accompanied by surrender of sovereign rights of individual states, because it constitutes somehow a significant intervention in the international contract autonomy. Thus, the political and social conditions for the realisation of such a concept are missing.

Also, a Council's willingness to make these kinds of changes to its structure or working methods is not recognizable.

5. APPROACH V: COOPERATION SOLUTION

Explicitly recommendable remains the tendency towards inclusive governance in the framework of a cooperation solution. This is ultimately based on general principles of international law as well as on the idea of coherence, which is of particular importance in light of the integration of the EU and its legislative power and institutionalised treaty-making powers. The requirement of inclusion would not lead to institutional alterations, but would only impose a duty of cooperation on the actors. Basis and argument for this is the principle of good faith, which – as a general legal principle according to Art. 38 (I) lit. c of the ICJ Statute – constitutes a legal source of international law.

G. OUTLOOK

I. ON THE WAY FROM EXCLUSIVE TO INCLUSIVE ARCTIC GOVERNANCE?!

The challenges and tasks of the Arctic should be tackled in a cooperative *responsible inclusive Arctic Governance*. In the last ten years a trend towards inclusive governance is quite recognizable:

Both, the Governments of Iceland, Sweden and Finland and the indigenous peoples' representatives were not invited to Ilulissat in 2008. In Ilulissat major decisions about the Arctic region were made, for example the decision that there was no reason to create a new, comprehensive treaty regime for the

Arctic, analogous to the Antarctic Treaty.[67] It were, however, only the Arctic 5 who made these decisions. Hereby, they had given a clear signal of their Arctic primacy and took the path to exclusive governance – this even towards the other Arctic States Iceland, Finland and Sweden with whom together they build the AC (Keyword: Two-class society in the AC).

During the Conference of Nuuk in 2011, the AC adopted with the Arctic Search and Rescue Agreement for the first time a legally binding document. This agreement regulates the joint efforts for the establishment of an efficient and comprehensive sea rescue service in the polar sea[68] and was adopted by all eight Arctic States consensually. This can be interpreted as an indication that the scope of the Arctic 5 alone was, despite all, too small to create comprehensible Arctic policy[69] and, thus, the Arctic 5 began to open at least for the other three Arctic States.

The Agreement on Cooperation on Marine Oil Pollution Preparedness and Response in the Arctic of 2013, which addresses some of the challenges in responding to oil spills, then was the Arctic Council's second binding agreement.[70] It substantially overlaps in scope and wording with IMO's 1990 International Convention on Oil Pollution Preparedness, Response and Cooperation (OPRC), which all members of the AC are parties to.[71] The incorporation of this UN-Convention is a sign of rapprochement towards the UN.

In the beginning of September 2015 US Secretary of State *Kerry* invited to the Glacier-Conference in Anchorage. Surprisingly, he did not only invite the other Arctic States, but also non-arctic states. Also this can be interpreted as a statement that the Arctic 8 had finally realised that Arctic policy is not only the matter of the Arctic States, but instead of global importance.

The Snow, Water, Ice and Permafrost in the Arctic (SWIPA) assessment, a periodic update to the Arctic Climate Impact Assessment, published in 2017 by, inter alia, two of the Arctic Council's working groups[72] contains recommended action steps, which can be seen as another big step towards the UN. On its page 18 the SWIPA Report 2017 states the following:

"The Arctic states, permanent participants, and observers to the Arctic Council should individually and collectively lead global efforts for an early, ambitious, and full implementation of the *Paris COP21 Agreement*, including efforts to reduce emissions of short-lived climate forcers."[73] Thus, the AC adopts the objectives of the UN climate conference in Paris and is obviously willing to cooperate with the UN. This is of great significance, especially in light of the fact that there was no explicit reference to the Arctic, neither in the UN Framework Convention of 1992, nor in the Kyoto Protocol of 1997 or the Paris Agreement of 2015.

This Arctic Council's step towards the UN was then followed by an invitation from the UN to foster the dialogue between both: On 6 November 2017, the AC hosted an official side event at the UNFCCC COP23 in Bonn, Germany.[74]

II. SUMMARY

As has been presented above, there is a confusing multiplicity of regulations and agreements that could be bundled together in one special Arctic treaty regime. Ultimately, however, it needs to be accepted that the Arctic riparian states with territorial claims and special rights concerning the Arctic have explicitly spoken out against the creation of an independent treaty.

The only way to *responsible governance* remains cooperation, which needs to be further encouraged. Fortunately, over recent years willingness to cooperation can be recognized: The AC is on its way from an exclusive to an inclusive Arctic Governance, in which AC and UN operate as cooperation partners. Non-arctic states and the EU, step by step, are integrated to take part of the work as well. The UN should promote further and closer cooperation. Lastly, all actors benefit from knowledge sharing about the region and its specific vulnerability. Even the Arctic states themselves should have a strong interest in a well-functioning cooperation with third states. In the end, also non-arctic countries have an impact on the progression of the melting ice and the development of the Arctic due to their emissions.

LITERATURE

von Arnauld, Andreas, Völkerrecht, 2012

Bartsch, Golo, Die Governance der Arktis – Akteure, Institutionen und politische Perspektiven im tauenden Hohen Norden, 2011

Böhmert, Viktor, Sektorentheorie, in Schlochauer, Hans J. (ed.), Wörterbuch des Völkerrechts (1962), Vol. 3, p. 248 – 250

Dahm, Georg/Delbrück, Jost/Wolfrum, Rüdiger, Völkerrecht, 2. Edition, Vol. 1 (1989), p. 351 et seq.

Gloser, Günter, The Arctic: A Strategic Challenge for the 21th Century, in Witschel, Georg/Wolfrum, Rüdiger (eds.), New Chances and New Responsibilites in the Arctic Region (2010), p. 12

Humrich, Christoph/Wolf, Klaus Dieter, Vom Meltdown zum Showdown?, HSFK-Report 4/2011

Humrich, Christoph, Ressourcenkonflikte, Recht und Regieren in der Arktis, APuZ (5–6/2011), p. 6 – 13

Jenisch, Uwe, Eine Verfassung für die Meere (1995)

Klein, Friedrich, Vertragskonkurrenz, in Schlochauer, Hans J. (ed.), Wörterbuch des Völkerrechts (1962), Vol. 3, p. 555

König, Doris/Neumann, Thilo, Streit um die Arktis, Vereinte Nationen Vol. 56 (1/2008), p. 20 et seq.

Lauta, Kristian Cedervall, A Drop in the Ocean, 5 Arctic Review on Law and Politics, (2/2014), pp. 227 – 249

Liu, Nengye, The European Union's Potential Contribution to Enhanced Governance of Arctic Shipping, ZaöRV (2013), p 705 et seq.

Liu, Nengye/Kirk, Elizabeth A./Henriksen, Tore (eds.), The European Union and the Arctic (2017)

Macnab, Ron et al., Cooperative Preparations for Determining the Outer Limit of the Juridical Continental Shelf in the Arctic Ocean, International Boundaries Research Unit (IBRU), Boundary and Security Bulletin 2001, p. 86 – 96

Pharand, Donat, The Case for an Arctic Council and a Treaty Proposal, Revue générale de droit 23 (1992), p. 163 et seq.

Proelss, Alexander/Müller, Till, The Legal Regime of the Arctic Ocean, ZaöRV 68 (2008), p. 651–687

Roach, Ashley J., Today's Customary International Law of the Sea, 45 Ocean Development and International Law (2014), p. 239 – 259

Schönfeldt, Kristina, Das Völkerrecht als Ordnungsrahmen der Arktis, Leibniz Online, No. 31 (2018)

Schram Stokke, Olav, A Legal Regime for the Arctic?, 31 Marine Policy (4/2007), p. 402 – 408

Stuvøy, Kirsti/Dale, Brigt, Der Arktische Rat – Gesundheit zwischen Wissenschaft und Politik, in Logbuch Arktis, Osteuropa Vol. 61 (2–3/2011), p. 301 et seq.

Freiherr von Welck, Stephan, Die Bundesrepublik Deutschland auf dem Weg in den Antarktischen Klub, Vereinte Nationen Vol. (2/1979), p. 46 et seq.

Verhaag, Melissa A., It is Not Too Late: The Need for a Comprehensive International Treaty to Protect the Arctic Environment, 15 Georgetown International Environmental Law Review, 3, (2002–2003), p. 555 et seq.

Graf Vitzthum, Wolfgang, Schiffssicherheit: Die EG als potentieller Durchsetzungsdegen der IMO, ZaöRV 62 (2002), p. 163 – 182

Graf Vitzthum, Wolfgang (ed.), Völkerrecht, 4. Edition 2007

Watson, Molly, An Arctic Treaty: A Solution To The International Dispute Over The Polar Region, 14 Ocean and Coastal Law Journal 307 (2008–9)

Winkelmann, Ingo, Feste Spielregeln für die Aufteilung des Arktischen Ozeans, SWP-Aktuell 53 (2008), p. 1 et seq.

Winkler, Thomas, An International Governance Framework for the Arctic: Challenges for International Public Law – A Danish Perspective, ZaöRV (2009), p. 643 et seq.

Wolfrum, Rüdiger, Das Rechtsregime der Arktis; available under http://www.mpil.de/files/pdf2/wolfrum_auswaertiges_amt_arktis.pdf (last retrieved: 1.7.2018)

NOTES

1 The Northeast and Northwest Passage become ice-free.
2 Article VI of the Antarctic Treaty.
3 Freiherr von Welck, Die Bundesrepublik Deutschland auf dem Weg in den Antarktischen Klub, Vereinte Nationen (2/1979), p. 46.
4 Article I of the Antarctic Treaty.
5 Article II and III of the Antarctic Treaty.
6 Article 7 of the Protocol on Environmental Protection to the Antarctic Treaty; for details see https://www.ats.aq/documents/recatt/Att006_e.pdf (last retrieved 1.7.2018).
7 Von Arnauld, Völkerrecht (2012), p. 331.
8 Von Arnauld, Völkerrecht (2012), p. 331.
9 Von Arnauld, Völkerrecht (2012), p. 331.
10 Von Arnauld, Völkerrecht (2012), p. 331.
11 Dahm/Delbrück/Wolfrum, Völkerrecht (1989), p. 351 et seq.
12 Böhmert, Sektorentheorie, in Schlochauer (ed.), Wörterbuch des Völkerrechts (1962), Vol. 3, p. 248.
13 Böhmert, Sektorentheorie, in Schlochauer (ed.), Wörterbuch des Völkerrechts (1962), Vol. 3, p. 250.; König/Neumann, Streit um die Arktis, Vereinte Nationen Vol. 56 (1/2008), p. 21.
14 Graf Vitzthum (ed.), Völkerrecht (2007), Note to Section 5 Recital (86).
15 United Nations Convention on the Law of the Sea; for details see http://www.un.org/depts/los/convention_agreements/texts/unclos/unclos_e.pdf (last retrieved 1.7.2018).
16 Only Art. 234 UNCLOS addresses the special characteristics of the Arctic by assigning special competences to the coastal states concerning ice-covered regions within their EEZ.
17 Roach, Today's Customary International Law of the Sea, 45 Ocean Development and International Law (2014), p. 239.
18 König/Neumann, Streit um die Arktis, Vereinte Nationen Vol. 56 (1/2008), p. 21; Macnab et al., Cooperative Preparations for Determining the Outer Limit of the Juridical Continental Shelf in the Arctic Ocean, IBRU, Boundary and Security Bulletin (2001), p. 91.
19 Proelss/Müller, The Legal Regime of the Arctic Ocean, ZaöRV 68 (2008), p. 662.
20 Schönfeldt, Das Völkerrecht als Ordnungsrahmen der Arktis, Leibniz Online, No. 31 (2018), p. 4.
21 Proelss/Müller, The Legal Regime of the Arctic Ocean, ZaöRV 68 (2008), p. 662.

22 For an overview of the political "Arctic strategies" of different states see http://www.arctic-office.de/fileadmin/user_upload/www.arctic-office.de/PDF_uploads/Arktisstrategien_DE_10.11.17.pdf (last retrieved 1.7.2018)

23 Gloser, The Arctic: A Strategic Challenge for the 21th Century, in Witschel/Wolfrum (eds.), New Chances and New Responsibilites in the Arctic Region (2010), p. 12.

24 Bartsch, Klimawandel und Sicherheit in der Arktis (2015), p. 22.

25 See ibid, p. 22 et seq.

26 These permanent participants are: The Aleut International Association (AIA), Arctic Athabaskan Council (AAC), Gwich'in Council International (GCI), Inuit Circumpolar Council (ICC), Russian Association of Indigenous Peoples of the North, Siberia and Far East (RAIPON) and the Saami Council (SC).

27 Bartsch, Klimawandel und Sicherheit in der Arktis (2015), p. 52.

28 A list of the States/Organizations with observer status is available under https://www.arctic-council.org/index.php/en/about-us/arctic-council/observers (last retrieved 1.7.2018).

29 At the Kiruna Ministerial Meeting in 2013, the Arctic Council received the application of the EU for observer status affirmatively, but deferred a final decision. Until such time as Ministers of the Arctic States may reach a final decision, the EU may observe Council proceedings.

30 The six working groups are: Arctic Contaminants Action Program (ACAP), Arctic Monitoring and Assessment Programme (AMAP), Conservation of Arctic Flora and Fauna (CAFF), Emergency Prevention, Preparedness and Response (EPPR), Protection oft he Arctic Marine Environment (PAME) and Sustainable Development Working Group (SDWG).

31 Wolfrum, Das Rechtsregime der Arktis, p. 2.

32 Stuvøy/Dale, Der Arktische Rat, in Logbuch Arktis, p. 308.

33 The Arctic Search and Rescue Agreement 2011, the Agreement on Cooperation on Marine Oil Pollution Preparedness and Response in the Arctic 2013, the Agreement on Enhancing International Arctic Scientific Cooperation 2017 and an agreement banning commercial fishing in the Arctic High Seas also from 2017.

34 The Government of Denmark, itself a member of the EU, only represents the Faroe Islands and Greenland (as parts of the Kingdom of Denmark) as non-EU territories in a number of policy areas.

35 Schönfeldt, Das Völkerrecht als Ordnungsrahmen der Arktis, Leibniz Online, No. 31 (2018), p. 2.

36 See ibid.

37 Jenisch, Eine Verfassung für die Meere (1995).

38 Graf Vitzthum, Schiffssicherheit: Die EG als potentieller Durchsetzungsdegen der IMO, ZaöRV 62 (2002), p. 165.

39 Humrich, Ressourcenkonflikte, Recht und Regieren in der Arktis, APuZ (5–6/2011), p. 9.

40 International Convention for the Prevention of Marine Pollution from Ships, 1973.

[41] International Convention for the Safety of Life at Sea, 1974.

[42] International Convention on Standards of Training, Certification and Watchkeeping for Seafarers, 1978.

[43] International Code for Ships Operating in Polar Waters, 2017.

[44] But from 1 January 2020 the SO_X-value also outside Emission Control Areas shall be reduced from 3.5% to 0.5 % (cf. Regulation 14 1.3 MARPOL Annex VI), so that in any case a changing from heavy fuel over to alternative fuels will take place in the long term.

[45] Humrich/Wolf, Vom Meltdown zum Showdown?, HSFK-Report 4/2011, p. 14.

[46] Steinmeier/Miliband, Europe Has to Face Up to the Security Policy Impact of Climate Change – Joint Contribution by Frank-Walter Steinmeier and his British Counterpart David Miliband, Federal Foreign Office, Press Communication 088/08 (13 March 2008), para. 10.

[47] Humrich/Wolf, Vom Meltdown zum Showdown?, HSFK-Report 4/2011, p. 6.

[48] There have been and still are some attempts to suspend or delay the further exploitation of these resources in the Arctic, but it is certain that further exploitation are going to take place.

[49] For example: Pharand, The Case for an Arctic Region Council and a Treaty Proposal, 23 Rev. Gen. 163 (1992), p. 163 – 195; Watson, An Arctic Treaty: A Solution To The International Dispute Over The Polar Region, 14 Ocean and Costal LJ 307 (2009); Verhaag, It is Not Too Late: The Need for a Comprehensive International Treaty to Protect the Arctic Environment, (2003), 15 Georgetown International Environmental Law Review, Vol. 15(3), p. 555 et seq.

[50] Liu/Kirk/Henriksen, Introduction, in Liu/Kirk/Henriksen (eds.), The European Union and the Arctic (2017), p. 2.

[51] Liu, The European Union's Potential Contribution to Enhanced Governance of Arctic Shipping, ZaöRV (2013), p. 717 et seq.

[52] Declaration Concerning the Competence of the European Community with regard to Matters Governed by the United Nations Convention on the Law of the Sea of ?10 December 1982 and the Agreement of 28 July 1994 Relating to the Implementation of Part XI of the Convention, Council Decision of 23 March 1998, OJ L179 of 23 June 1998, 1.

[53] Liu, The European Union's Potential Contribution to Enhanced Governance of Arctic Shipping, ZaöRV (2013), p. 717 et seq.

[54] This thesis may not be understood too broad. Because, along the same line of reasoning, you could otherwise say that Turkey is under international law entitled to accede to the EU. With regard to the EU's supranational nature, this would take matters too far.

[55] Humrich, Ressourcenkonflikte, Recht und Regieren in der Arktis, APuZ (5–6/2011), p. 11.

[56] Winkler, An International Governance Framework for the Arctic: Challenges for International Public Law – A Danish Perspective, ZaöRV (2009), p. 643 et seq.

[57] Humrich, Ressourcenkonflikte, Recht und Regieren in der Arktis, APuZ (5–6/2011), p. 11.

[58] Schönfeldt, Das Völkerrecht als Ordnungsrahmen der Arktis, Leibniz Online, No. 31 (2018), p. 12.

[59] Winkelmann, Feste Spielregeln für die Aufteilung des Arktischen Ozeans, SWP-Aktuell 53 (2008), p. 2.

[60] Schram Stokke, A Legal Regime for the Arctic?, 31 Marine Policy (4/2007), p. 402 et seq.

[61] Convention for the Protection of the Marine Environment of the North-East-Atlantic (OSPAR), 1992; for details see www.ospar.org (last retrieved 1.7.2018).

[62] Humrich/Wolf, Vom Meltdown zum Showdown?, HSFK-Report 4/2011, p. 25 et seq.

[63] See ibid.

[64] Humrich/Wolf, Vom Meltdown zum Showdown?, HSFK-Report 4/2011, p. 26 et seq.

[65] See ibid.

[66] Art. 5 (3) TEU: "Under the principle of subsidiarity, in areas which do not fall within its exclusive competence, the Union shall act only if and insofar as the objectives of the proposed action cannot be sufficiently achieved by the Member States, either at central level or at regional and local level, but can rather, by reason of the scale or effects of the proposed action, be better achieved at Union level".

[67] For details see http://www.oceanlaw.org/downloads/arctic/Ilulissat_Declaration.pdf (last retrieved 1.7.2018).

[68] Cf. Agreement on Cooperation on Aeronautical and Maritime Search and Resue in the Arctic; for details see https://oaarchive.arctic-council.org/bitstream/handle/11374/531/EDOCS-3661-v1-ACMMDK07_Nuuk_2011_SAR_Search_and_Rescue_Agreement_signed_EN_FR_RU.PDF?sequence=5&isAllowed=y (last retrieved 1.7.2018).

[69] Bartsch, Klimawandel und Sicherheit in der Arktis (2015), p. 66.

[70] For details see https://oaarchive.arctic-council.org/bitstream/handle/11374/529/EDOCS-2068-v1-ACMMSE08_KIRUNA_2013_agreement_on_oil_pollution_preparedness_and_response_signedAppendices_Original_130510.PDF?sequence=6&isAllowed=y (last retrieved 1.7.2018).

[71] Lauta, Kristian Cedervall, A Drop in the Ocean, 5 Arctic Review on Law and Politics (2/2014), p. 238.

[72] The Arctic Monitoring and Assessment Programme (AMAP) and the Conservation of Arctic Flora and Fauna (CAFF).

[73] https://www.google.com/url?sa=t&rct=j&q=&esrc=s&source=web&cd=2&ved=0ahUKEwi83b25ke_bAhUDalAKHWgqBQAQFggvMAE&url=https%3A%2F%2Fwww.amap.no%2Fdocuments%2Fdownload%2F2888&usg=AOvVaw1KDI9LEDrCeqSc1BhchVaE (last retrieved 1.7.2018).

[74] https://www.arctic-council.org/index.php/en/our-work2/8-news-and-events/473-cop23 (last retrieved 1.7.2018).

CHAPTER XI

MARINE HULL AND MACHINERY INSURANCE IN GERMANY

Dieter SCHWAMPE

A. GENERALIA

I. INTRODUCTION

Marine Hull Insurance is one of the oldest class of insurance at all. It was preceded only by risk sharing structures like general average, where sacrifices made or costs incurred to prevent common dangers to ship and cargo from causing loss or damage to ship and cargo are jointly born by all property in peril. The concept of general average is existing in practically all laws of seafaring countries. It provides for basic protection but, compared with insurance, the deficiencies are obvious. As the owners of all property in danger share all sacrifices made in costs incurred, those whose properties have been sacrificed and those who have incurred costs have to bear their shares of the sacrifices and costs. If ship and cargo have the same value, sacrifices to the ship will result in claims for contribution of the ship-owner only for 50 % of the sacrifices made. The other 50 % would have to be borne by the ship-owner. And even more obvious, if all endeavors are in vane and the ship sinks with the cargo, nothing is saved, there are no contributory values and there are no claims for contribution. In such a situation the concept of general average does not provide any protection.

It is no surprise, thus, that other means of securing financial interests in ships were looked for. In ancient times loan constructions were developed which provided for loans given to ship-owners, which were repayable only if the ship had safely reached its destination. If it did not, the ship-owner could keep the loan without having to pay interest. If the ship reached the destination, the loan was repayable with heavy interest. What such loans and the later developed insurance had in common was that obligations were created for the case that the ship was lost at sea. The difference was that the loan was lost free of interest, so that the loss of a loan had to be made good out of interest payable by the owners of all the ships, which safely reached their destinations. Insurance, in contrast, was subject to insurance premium by all assureds, so that also those who were entitled to indemnity in case of loss of their ships contributed with their premium to the funds necessary to fulfill the insurance contracts.

Whilst the first insurance policies on ships were developed in the Italian republics (Venice, Genoa etc.) the first statutory regulation is found in the laws of Barcelona in 1435. The concept of insurance could be spread all over Europe. First policies can be found in the middle of the 15th century in Flanders, and beginning of the 16th century in England, quickly followed by policies issued in the cities of the Hanseatic League. The first German statutory regulation is the *Hamburger Assecuranz- und Havareyordnung of 1738.*

However, in Germany there was no central market place for insurance, comparable with developments in England, but the main market places in Germany were those of the major German cities of the Hanseatic League, in particular Bremen, Hamburg and Lübeck. Over the years Lübeck lost its importance, but the market places in Bremen and Hamburg for a long time kept their independence, including their own policy formats and policy conditions. The insurers active in the Bremen and Hamburg market were organized in the *Verein Bremer Seeversicherer* (VBS) and the *Verein Hamburger Assekuradeure* (VHA), which merged in the year 2000 to become the *Verein Hanseatischer Tansportversicherer* (VHT). The first set of insurance conditions introduced and actually used in all relevant German insurance market places were the *Allgemeine Seeversicherungs-Bedingungen* (ASVB) of 1867. The conditions just had been preceded by the first qualification of commercial law which went beyond the then still existing separate German Kingdoms, namely the *Allgemeines Deutsches Handelsgesetzbuch* (ADHGB) of 1865, which dealt with marine insurance in its chapter 11. As time later should prove, its basic provision in Art. 782 – *jedes in Geld schätzbare Interesse welches jemand daran hat, das Schiff oder Ladung die Gefahren der Seeschifffahrt bestehe, kann Gegenstand der Seeversicherung sein*[1] – was almost identically taken over into § 779 of the *Handelsgesetzbuch* (HGB) of 1900, which was the successor of the ADHGB. It can equally be found in § 1 of the *Allgemeine Deutsche Seeversicherungs-Bedingungen* (ADS) aus 1919, which are the successors of the ASVB. And it can equally be found in clause 1 *DTV-Allgemeine Seeschiffsversicherungs-Bedingungen* (DTV ADS) of 2009. If one were to define what has led to the greatest change in ocean shipping, then one would probably say that it was the introduction of engines on ships. For hundreds, or indeed thousands of years ships had been moved on the ocean by way of sales. The invention of the steam engine led to a revolution not only on land (the industrial revolution), but also on sea. Ships could be built larger, to carry more cargo, at higher speeds and independent from favorable or unfavorable winds. But they created a whole class of different risks, not least fire on ships but also the vulnerability of ships in case of engine failure.

The ASVB of 1867, like all predecessors, was dominated by the risks to and resulting from sailing ships. Wherever steamships had to be insured, the markets reacted with appropriate individual clauses, but the first general set of clauses to address engines on ships were the ADS of 1919. And § 65 ADS gives a good impression on the reliability of engines as well as the readiness of insurers to accept engine risks. For engine damage insurers only provided the so-called stranding cover. Risks covered under the stranding cover were grounding, capsizing, sinking, fire, explosion or collision with other ships. Cover, thus, was for named perils only – a clear distinction from the concept of all risks, which has been governing German statutory insurance law as well as marine insurance conditions since the ADHGB of 1865 and the ASVB of 1867. Obviously the insurers had no problems of accepting the risk of fire and explosion, but they were hesitant enough to avoid cover on an all risk basis.

The ADS were extremely successful and were introduced into practically all policies issued after the release of the conditions. They remained successful for a long time, but the change in commercial realities and the technology demanded alterations and changes. As usual in this line of business, changes were first introduced by insurance brokers, who developed initially individual clauses for their ship-owner customers but then continued using them for all their business. After a number of those clauses had gained such a wide use that they had been common features of practically all policies issued, the then *Deutscher Transportversicherungsverband* (DTV) who was at that time the industry association of the German transport insurers (and who later merged into the *Gesamtverband der Deutschen Versicherungswirtschaft* (GDV); German insurance association), issued what was known on the market as the *DTV-Kaskoklauseln 1960*, which were a collection of clauses developed by brokers.

Whilst the DTV took a closer look on cargo insurance already in the beginning of the 1970s, which led to the deletion of the ADS conditions on cargo insurance and the replacement of those conditions by the *ADS*

Güterversicherung 1973, it took a couple of more years until the DTV released in 1978 the *DTV-Kaskoklauseln 1978*. Different from the concept in cargo insurance, the DTV-Kaskoklauseln did not replace the ADS conditions on hull insurance (§§ 58 – 78 ADS) but, according to clause 1 DTV-Kaskoklauseln only had priority over them. Why the DTV chose a different model for hull insurance than for cargo insurance is unknown nowadays. The result, anyway, was a complicated relationship between ADS and DTV-Kaskoklauseln. Certain areas of ADS remain untouched; others were simply replaced by a clause of the DTV-Kaskoklauseln, and somewhere amended by DTV-Kaskoklauseln. In some cases the DTV-Kaskoklauseln expressly say what they replace or what they amend. But unfortunately in other cases this is not identified, so that careful consideration is required in order to determine what condition of ADS actually remained applicable.

Various versions of the DTV Hull Clauses were released over the time, the latest of 2004. The version which dominates the market, however, is the version of 1992.

After the turn of the millennium the situation grew even more difficult by the fact that relevant changes to the conditions were no more introduced by the insurers association, but by simultaneous action of the insurers in the market. On two occasions so-called *Seekasko-Druckstücke* were introduced to the market, which significantly changed the cover available in the German insurance market.

II. ECONOMIC RELEVANCE

One can look at the economic relevance of hull and machinery insurance by considering the relevance of insurance premium and by considering [the relevance of] ocean shipping as such. Looking on insurance premium, the total estimate of marine premium was USD 27.5 billion[2], whereof 25 %, equivalent to about USD 6.9 billion, relayed to hull and machinery insurance. Looking on regions, about 48 % of this premium is generated in Europe. The German market as such does not even show up in the IUMI statistics because it is too small. This is the more surprising as the German ocean going fleet ranks on the 4th position of the largest fleet in the world. The capacity of the German hull and machinery market has been reducing for years and has reached a size which makes it impossible for larger German fleets to be insured only on the German market. As a consequence, many insurers on the slip of a German fleet meanwhile are residence of foreign insurance markets. It is usual nowadays that where slips are led by a leading German insurer, they are often completed with foreign insurers, with those foreign insurers actually carrying more than 50 % of the risks. As a matter of fact, there is a growing number of German fleets which are insured completely outside the German market. But many of those fleets are insured on basis of German insurance conditions, with German laws applying to those insurance contracts and disputes being subject to the jurisdiction of German courts, mainly the courts in Hamburg. One may, therefore, say that the economic relevance of hull and machinery insurance is very small for the German economy, but that the German marine insurance law and the German marine insurance conditions are of significant relevance for worldwide insurance markets.

And hull and machinery insurance gets an entirely different relevance when considering that ocean transport makes up about 90 % of all transports worldwide. Ocean transport would not be possible without hull and machinery insurance. The simple reason is that ship financing banks, which are nowadays always needed in order to finance new ships, are either bound by law or by their own rules of business to give loans to ship owning companies only if the vessels are insured, and are kept insured, against hull and machinery risks. In so far marine hull and machinery insurance is a mandatory requirement for international transport.

III. STATUTORY PROVISION

German law has traditionally distinguished between marine insurance law and non-marine, or general, insurance law. It has already been mentioned above that marine insurance was the front-runner of insurance business generally, so it is no surprise that marine insurance law was the first to be dealt with by statutes. As regards modern statutes, the AGHGB and the HGB has already been referred to. Since 1900 marine insurance law had been the subject of the 5th book of the HGB, with very detailed provisions in §§ 778–905 HGB. Non-marine insurance law, or general insurance law, in contrast got its first statutory regulation only in 1908 with the *Versicherungsvertragsgesetz (VVG)*, which in its then version stipulated in § 186 VVG, that it did not apply to marine insurance (and to reinsurance).

While the Federal Government set up a commission for a reform of the non-marine insurance law, the recommendations of this commission were to abolish the distinction between marine and non-marine insurance and to make also marine insurance subject to the VVG. This would have obviously also meant to abolish the 5th book of the HGB. The commission was well aware of differences between marine insurance and non-marine insurance, but felt confident that releasing marine insurance from any restrictions which the VVG otherwise might have on freedom of contract would be enough for a continuation of the German marine insurance market. Not surprisingly the industry disagreed, slightly surprisingly that on this occasion both sides of the market – ship-owners as well as insurers – shared their criticism. Not only did they refer to entirely different market practices and market conditions and express their fears that the far reaching effects of the German standard contract legislation would lead to general insurance law stipulations being treated as guidelines for courts to determine the validity of deviating contractual conditions. Hinting to the fact that the German statutory marine insurance law as contained in the HGB since 1900, had been set aside by § 128 ADS and effectively replaced by ADS as such, the industry argued that no statutory legislation would be required. In a rare step of deregulation the government, and eventually the parliament, followed this reasoning with the consequence that the amended VVG 2008 now still stipulates in § 209 VVG that the VVG does not apply to marine insurance (and reinsurance), but that nevertheless the 5th book of the HGB was abolished. As a consequence, Germany may be considered as one of the very few developed insurance markets where there does not exist any special statutory law on marine insurance. Hull and machinery insurance policies, thus, are only subject to the general provisions of the civil code. The German statutory provisions on standard contracts have already been referred to. Their relevance cannot be underestimated. Despite the fact that the courts are expected to take into account trade usage (§ 310 BGB), there is an array of court decisions which show that even undisputed market practice of many years is not safe from being interfered by through the courts. The famous "ILSE" decision of the Hanseatic Court of Appeal of Hamburg is a prime example. This decision will be dealt with in more detail below. Generally one can only hope that courts in the future will be more reluctant, not to say careful, with interfering. Insurance conditions like ADS or DTV Hull Clauses, which are in use since decades, hardly have a "user" in the sense of the German standard contracts legislation. Often it is a matter of chance who introduces those conditions into a contract. From a practical point of view insurers just as ship-owners want to insure on basis of these conditions. The "ILSE" judgment is the best example. The market did not follow the court's reasoning of the proper construction of clause 20 DTV Hull Clauses. Shortly after the decision was published, the market moved to reinstate what it had considered to be the proper understanding for more than 20 years.

IV. GENERAL PRINCIPLES OF HULL AND MACHINERY INSURANCE

1. INTEREST INSURED

Insurance is protection against risk. Risks are different for different parties, even if they are linked to the same asset. Looking on a ship, the ship-owner has an ownership interest, which in its purest form means that he wants to be protected against damage to or loss of the ship in a way that the insurer provides the necessary indemnification for paying repairs or buying a new ship. But the owner also has an income interest in the vessel, which means, that he is at risk of not earning money with the ship. This risk can have many reasons, one being that there is no market for the ship because either there is no cargo or there are too many ships, or that the ship is not available for employment because it suffered damage and is still under repair. Other parties may have similar income interests, e.g. a time charterer who does not own the ship, and, thus, may not have an interest in indemnification for damage, but he is entitled to make use of the ship and suffers loss of income if the ship is not at his disposal. Finally, the ship is not always only an asset, but it can also become a burden if the owner, by operation of the ship, incurs liabilities.

Out of this array of interests hull and machinery insurance covers the ownership interest of the ship-owner. There is no need to stipulate this in the insurance conditions. The *Bundesgerichtshof* has held that even without any express stipulation transport insurance always covers the ownership interest of the assured.[3] As a matter of fact, neither ADS nor DTV-Kaskoklauseln address the question what interest and whose interests are insured under the policy. Only clause 1.211 DTV-ADS now contains a stipulation, saying that in the absence of any other agreement under hull and machinery insurance the ownership interest of the registered owner of the ship as well as his liability interest dealt with in clause 65 DTV-ADS are insured. The provision has been introduced for the sake of contract certainty before the background of the widespread practice to add a growing number of co-assureds to the policy. In respect of many of those possible co-assureds – crew managers, technical managers, bareboat charterers, time charterers and ship finance banks – it was not entirely clear how they should be protected by the hull and machinery policy. The purpose of clause 1.2.1 DTV-ADS now is to make the parties to the insurance contract aware that they need to express what they have in mind when adding co-assureds to a hull and machinery policy. Only this can prevent that courts later find that a protection, which co-assureds had assumed for themselves, is not really given by the policy. It is a matter of course that all interests must be legal. If they were not, an insurance policy governing them would be void according to § 134 BGB. In recent times the legality of the interest has come into the focus in the context of sanctions legislation on national and international level. Starting with sanctions against Iran, and based on UN Security Council resolutions, insurance of (simplified) Iranian interests has become illegal. This fact as such would not have required the introduction of a new clause into the insurance conditions, as the very existence of the prohibition of insurance leads to invalidity of any such insurance contract under § 134 BGB. The problem does not arise from the civil law effect of such a policy, but from the criminal law consequences. The reason is that the conclusion of an insurance contract in breach of sanctions legislation is punishable under the German external trade legislation. In order to avoid such consequences, the German insurers association has developed a sanctions clause, which is nowadays incorporated into any insurance contract entered into by a German insurer. It has found its way into DTV-ADS as clauses 1.1.1 and 1.1.2.

2. Scope of cover

As mentioned above, traditionally marine insurance in Germany always has been all risk insurance. Other markets, most notably the important London insurance market, do not work on all risk bases, but on basis of named perils.[4] In practice both concepts can, in many situations will, lead to the same result for cover, if one form of cover was generally beneficial for ship-owners, the other form would not exist anymore. From a technical point of view, all risk covers compared with named peril covers look entirely different. The cover section can be and actually is very short, simply saying that all risks are covered. The cover section of the named perils policy, in contrast, can be and actually is much longer, because all risks, which are covered under the policy, need to be addressed. As a consequence, a named perils policy may only need less and shorter exclusions for tailoring the risks covered, because naming certain risks as covered already means that other risks are not covered. An all risk policy, on the other hand, needs much more details on exclusions to narrow down what the insurer actually is prepared to insure.

The main difference between an all risk policy and a named perils policy, thus, is widely accepted to be a different burden of proof. It is, or better: until very recently, it has been the general view that the only proof which an assured has to bring under an all risk policy is that his ship was damaged by a peril effectively during the duration of the policy. In case of a named peril policy, however, the assured would have to proof that one of the named perils covered under the policy has caused the loss. If a ship sinks for no known reason on a voyage, this difference in burden of proof can be more than relevant for a ship-owner. But there is one area, which recently has caused concern in the market. The background is not at all new. Since the ADHGB of 1865 the law stipulated that marine insurance is insurance against the risks of ocean shipping (*Seeschifffahrt*), but stipulated in respect of perils that all perils are covered. In ADHGB the true relevant provisions were Art. 782 and 824, in the HGB they were § 778 and § 820, in ADS they are § 1 and § 28 and in DTV-ADS they are clause 1 and 27. Already in the early literature the question arose whether "all risks" in the meaning of the aforementioned provisions or clauses actually means "all risks" or only means "all risks arising from ocean shipping". Ritter/Abraham[5], the "bible" of German marine insurance, acknowledged the problem, combined both provisions and held that cover only exists against all risks of ocean shipping. What sounds like narrowing down from "all risks" "to all risks of sea shipping", however, for Ritter/Abraham effectively did not mean any restriction of cover. The reason for Ritter/Abraham stating that the aspect is of little relevance only is that Ritter/Abraham understood the "perils of sea shipping" in a wide meaning. "Indeed only such perils are excluded which have nothing to do with the ocean shipping of the ocean ship (and its cargo) as such, which exist without consideration of the ship as such, without consideration of the cargo as such, which, thus, have no connection with the insured exercise as such"[6].

This understanding, which has been the market understanding since 1865, however, has been challenged by a reasoned decision of the Hanseatic Court of Appeal of Hamburg.[7] Referring to what Ritter/Abraham had written almost a hundred years ago, the court refers to the fact that only perils of sea shipping would be insured under a hull and machinery policy. Under the burden of proof rules, thus, the assured would have to proof that one of those perils has caused the damage. Exclusions in the policy conditions would only become relevant, and the insurer only is under a burden of proof, if the assured had brought this initial proof. The practical implications of this decision are far reaching. In many cases it is difficult to determine the real cause of a marine loss or damage. Demanding that an assured brings proof in such a situation, would take away what is intended to be the main benefit of an all risk cover: the burden of proof situation. One can, and should, therefore be critical in respect of the judgment. Critical not concerning the starting point, but critical on the question how it should be possible that a risk which leads to damage to a ship, can – within the definition of Ritter/Abraham as showed above – be a risk which has, considering this ship as such, nothing to do with a ship. But even if one were to prefer the narrow view of the court of appeal – which did not show any sign of intending to distinguish itself from Ritter/Abraham – then the conclusions for burden of proof are not convincing. Following the reasoning of the court, a "real" all risk cover, i.e. an all risk cover not limited to the risks of ocean shipping, would call for a burden on the insured that the loss or damage was caused by a "risk" – in contrast to something which was not a risk and unavoidable effect. It seems that so far no one has ever taken this position, and it is questionable whether the court of appeal actually would have gone so far.[8]

3. COVER EXTENSIONS

a) ERROR IN CONSTRUCTION, FAULTY MATERIAL AND MANUFACTURING FAULT

Hull and machinery insurance cover is linked to the operation of the peril during the cover period. It is not decisive whether damage occurs during the cover period, but rather whether it was caused during that period. A simple example: if the crew carries out maintenance work improperly shortly before the end of one cover period and damage occurs as a result of that improper maintenance work shortly after the beginning of the second cover period, cover is available under the first policy only but not under the second policy. This system, in principle, allows allocating losses to individual policies. Admittedly, there may be problematic cases in which the continued operation of a peril aggravates the situation and leads to extended damage, which may not even be visible to the eye until a certain point in time. As all policies must be looked at separately (simply for the reason that participating insurers may change from policy year to policy year), for practical considerations insurers and adjusters partly simply allocate loss over time. As ADS as well as DTV-ADS contain a time limit for requesting cover (see in so far below), such an approach may be difficult. This is not the place to go into details, but this is an area, which still needs further attention.

Where the mentioned principle – causation during the cover period – in most cases fails is the area of error in construction, faulty material and faulty workmanship. Looking at the ship as a whole, all of these causes will properly be identified as risks inherent with the operation of a sea ship, but usually they will occur during or, in case of error in construction, even before the building of the ship. At that time no hull and machinery policy exists, so that loss resulting from any of those risks would not be covered under any policy. For a long time this has been considered an unacceptable situation so that standard hull and machinery cover in the German market provides cover. But this scope of cover has changed over time. Cover was introduced for the first time by clause 20.2 DTV-Kaskoklauseln. It was limited to damage to machinery as a consequence of any of the aforementioned risks. The error in construction, the faulty workmanship and the faulty material could, but did not have to be, in connection with machinery itself, but regardless where those mistakes happened, cover was only available for damage to machinery. Damage to the ship's hull resulting from those causes, thus, was not covered. For more than 20 years the market – insurers, brokers, ship-owners – thought that they understood what clause 20.2 DTV-Kaskoklauseln meant in respect of error and construction: the part which was improperly construed would not be covered, but only consequential damage caused to other parts of the machinery. The Hanseatic Court of Appeal of Hamburg disagreed in the famous "ILSE" judgment.[9] The court held that on basis of the very wording of the clause all damage as a consequence of an error in construction is covered. The construction error would manifest itself in a wrong production plan, which then led to the production of an inappropriate part. This alone would not be enough for cover, because clause 20.2 DTV-Kaskoklauseln does not provide cover for inappropriate parts, but for damage. But if such inappropriate part fails and is damaged, then cover is given. Interesting enough, this decision was not rendered in respect of a hull and machinery policy. The claim rather arose under a loss of hire policy, which required a covered hull claim as a trigger for a loss of hire claim.

The hull and machinery insurers were not prepared to bare this increased risk, which led to the simultaneous appearance of the so-called *Seekasko-Druckstück 2002/2* which reinstated the previous market practice by saying that the part which was affected by the error in construction was not covered. Practice shows that difficulties may arise when it has to be determined what the defective part is and whether the part damaged is still the same part or different part.

Since then market standards developed further. The Norwegian market took the lead and introduced error and construction cover, which extended to wrongly constructed part as long as it was the subject of approval of the classification society. The German market did not stand back and meanwhile developed a similar rule in clause 59.2 DTV-ADS. But also here difficulties may arise, because there may be entirely different views when the requirement of approval by the classifications are fulfilled. In the Norwegian market there is some guidance provided by the commentary to the Nordic plan. It remains to be seen whether German courts would be prepared to follow those considerations.

Apart from this extension, DTV-ADS have extended over for the mentioned perils in a much more relevant way by making it available now not only for damage to machinery, but also damage to the hull.

b) THIRD PARTY LIABILITY

Hull insurance is property insurance. As mentioned above, it generally covers ownership interests of the assured in the sense of the costs required to rectify part damage or the costs required to replace the ship itself after a total loss. Liability risks out of the operation of the ship are something different, and there is no other class of insurance (except for inland vessels, the cover of which is modeled after the ocean hull insurance) where property insurer also cover liability risks out of the use of the property. In ocean hull insurance such cover has been available under a hull and machinery policy since ancient times. Under § 78 ADS it was only a limited collision, i.e. contact between two ships. This is also the cover situation in the so called running-down-clause of the institute time clauses in England. On the German market cover was broadened in clause 43 DTV Hull Clauses, which provides cover for statutory liability of the assured for damage to or loss of a thing caused by the movement of the ship or participation in shipping traffic. Under German cover, thus, the assured has cover also for contact damage with piers, terminals, cranes, bridges etc. But cover is only available in case of physical damage. If only financial damage is caused, this does not fall under the hull and machinery policy. Consequential financial losses resulting from physical damage or loss, however, are accepted as part of the physical damage or loss and, thus, covered. A typical example is collision damage to another ship, which leads to loss of earnings of the other ship-owner.

Whilst cover generally requires a statutory liability, clause 34 DTV-Kaskoklauseln provides cover also for contractual liability in two situations, namely under towage contracts and under contracts with shipyards, if this contractual liability is customary where the contracts were concluded. A reason for these extensions is that internationally contracts with shipyards and tug companies provide for very far reaching liabilities of the ship-owner. Ship-owners who operate their ships in the respective areas cannot avoid incurring such contractual liabilities, and the insurers are prepared to accept these circumstances as a fact of life.

Certain risks are excluded from cover. The list starts with liability for death or personal injury. As cover is limited to liability for damage to things, this is actually no exclusion but a clarification only. The first real exclusion is exclusion for liability in respect of damage caused by the release of liquid or gaseous substances or chemicals or other dangerous goods in the sense of the IMDG-code. This exclusion is often referred to as the pollution exclusion. Pollution has always been the domain of P&I insurance, which covers this risk. There is only a small re-inclusion remaining for pollution damage caused by a collision of the ship insured with another ship to that other ship or anything on it. A recent judgment of the Hanseatic Court of Appeal of Hamburg has clarified that this exclusion has to be construed beyond its actual wording not only to exclude damage caused by pollution, but also costs incurred to prevent pollution. Under the new DTV-ADS the problem does not arise, because here an express exclusion of such expenditure exists in clause 65.4.1.5.

Finally, there is the important exclusion that no liability towards the owners of things on board of the vessel insured is covered. This relates predominantly to damage to cargo, which is, again, a peril insured under the P&I insurance of the ship.

4. COVER EXCLUSIONS

Like many all risk covers, also the German hull and machinery cover under ADS/DTV Hull Clauses and DTV-ADS contains a list of exclusions. Some exclusions are not genuine to marine hull insurance, such as war risks, nuclear energy, acts of authorities and causation of the incident insured. Out of those general exclusions, in the following only causation of the incident insured will be addressed, followed by exclusions peculiar for marine hull insurance.

a) CAUSATION OF THE INCIDENT INSURED

ADS deal with this in § 33. They provide for a tough regime, stipulating that the insurer is free from liability if the insured has caused the insured event. The exclusion is not an objective one, but a subjective one, requiring fault. But the requirements are low: ordinary negligence of the assured is sufficient for releasing the insurer from cover.

This low threshold has been raised by DTV-ADS, which require in clause 34 gross negligence of the assured.

b) UNSEAWORTHINESS VS. BREACH OF SECURITY PROVISIONS

The unseaworthiness exclusion has a long tradition in German marine hull and machinery insurance. ADS dealt with it in § 58, which provided for a projective exclusion regardless of any fault of the assured. Loss or damage which was caused only by unseaworthiness of the vessel was not covered, even if the assured had acted with due diligence.

But this was changed to a subjective exclusion already with clause 23 DTV Hull Clauses. The assured could avoid that the insurer is released from cover by proving that he had not been at fault in respect of unseaworthiness upon commencement of the voyage. Just as in § 33 ADS, however, the threshold was low, because the assured had to prove that he did not act with ordinary negligence.

When the DTV-ADS were drafted by the German insurance association, a different concept was developed. Following the model of the (then) Norwegian insurance plan, the first draft of DTV-ADS did not contain unseaworthiness exclusion, but exclusion for breach of safety regulations. These were defined in clause 33.1.1 as any applicable provisions contained in international conventions, laws, directives and rules of classification societies, which served to safeguard the safe operation of the vessel. When this model was suggested to the ship-owning community, the rejection was almost unanimous. This resulted in the rather unique situation that DTV-ADS, since introduction into the market, now contain alternatives in clause 33. If the assured so choose, the old unseaworthiness regime of clause 23 DTV Hull Clauses is available (clause 33.2 DTV-ADS). But if he does not go for this option, the fall back situation under DTV-ADS is released from cover in case of breach of a security provision. The choice between the two alternatives is not made easy due to the fact that the two models differ not only as regards to the degree of fault required for release from cover, but that they also differ as to the burden of proof in respect of causation. If the assured opts for the new concept of safety regulations, breach of any safety regulation releases the insurer from cover. The assured can save cover by proving either that the breach of the safety regulation was not causative for the loss or damage, or by proving that he did not act with gross negligence. The burden of proof in respect of both aspects, thus, is with the assured. As regards unseaworthiness, in contrast, the old rule of clause 23 DTV Hull Clauses was taken over, so that the insurer is released from cover only if he discharges his burden of proof that the unseaworthiness was causative for loss or damage, and only once this proof is brought it is on the assured to proof that there was no negligence on his part. Both options, thus, have their pros and cons. The downside of the unseaworthiness concept is that cover is lost already by ordinary negligence, which at the same time is the upside of the security provision concept, because there ordinary negligence does not lead to release from cover, for which gross negligence is required. As regards causation, however, the seaworthiness concept is more assured friendly, as it puts the burden of proof on the insurer, whilst the safety provision concept puts it on the assured.

c) PIRACY

Under ADS/DTV Hull Clauses piracy was an insured peril. There was no need to refer to § 73 ADS for cover. It is correct that § 73 ADS addresses the piracy peril expressly, but in view of the lack of piracy exclusion in ADS and DTV Hull clauses piracy was an insured peril under § 28 ADS anyhow. The hijacking of cargo ships around the Horn of Africa, however, started the development under which piracy was excluded by way of special agreement in the policy. This is now also the concept of DTV-ADS, which exclude the risk of piracy under clause 35.1.4 and have moved it to war cover, where it is dealt with in clause 84.1.6 DTV-ADS. The reason is not that piracy is the same like war. The reason is that the peculiar premium model of war risk insurance fits much better to the piracy peril than the premium model of marine hull and machinery insurance. As part of war risk insurance, cover for piracy risks is available at a very low premium, but with those areas excluded from cover, where piracy is an issue. Ships that shall trade in such areas need special cover, which is available at substantial premium. This cover structure allows burdening only those ship-owners with premium for piracy cover, who are actually exposed to the risk of piracy.

d) WEAR AND TEAR, AGE, RUST, CORROSION, CAPITATION

Insurance is meant to protect the ship-owner against risks he cannot account for in his ordinary maintenance of his ship. There are certain risks, which every vessel is exposed to and which, usually, proper maintenance can take account of. These risks are dealt with in clause 27 DTV Hull Clauses and clause 55 DTV-ADS. Damage caused by wear and tear, age, rust, corrosion and capitation are excluded. But life is more colorful than insurance conditions. Situations where one of these perils alone lead to loss or damage are probably rare. In most cases there will be a combination of causes, predominantly with perils of the sea. Given the causa proxima rule applicable in German marine insurance, a court might be called to determine whether corroded shell plating or an extraordinary storm was the proximate cause of the damage. Depending on the decision, there would be either no cover or full cover. Already when the DTV Hull Clauses were developed in the middle of the 1970s both industry partners, insurers as well as ship-owners were not satisfied with this situation. This resulted in a new rule which essentially set aside the causa proxima principle saying that if damage is caused by one of the mentioned excluded perils in combination with an insured peril, there is cover available reflecting the contribution in causation.

B. CO-INSURANCE

Ocean hull and machinery risks can involve substantial values. The insurance industry has developed two general concepts to avoid that an insurer is burdened with major loss. One tool is reinsurance (proportional or excess of loss), another tool is co-insurance. In case of reinsurance the direct insurer remains fully responsible towards the assured and only has a right of indemnity by the reinsurer. In case of co-insurance the risk is split up already in relation to assured between a number of insurers. DTV Hull Clauses deal with this concept in clause 9, DTV-ADS in clause 19. Both clauses stipulate that if several insurers' underwrite a policy they are obliged to indemnify severally for their respective shares only. There is, thus, no joint liability of the insurers. The consequence of this separate liability is, that under the law, there exist as many separate insurance contracts as there exist participating insurers. For practical purposes such structure naturally leads to difficulties in case of an incident insured, because every insurer involved might take a different view on cover and a different view on how to properly handle the incident. Without any further provisions the assured would be in the difficult situation that he is obliged to different insurers expressing different views and, potentially, giving different instructions and approvals. This is avoided by the lead clause contained in clause 9.2 DTV Hull Clauses and clause 19.2 DTV-ADS. Under these the leading insurer is deemed to have been authorized by the co-insurers to enter into agreements with the assured and to settle claims and take recourse. The co-insurers are excluded from any involvement to the extent that the leading insurer is authorized. The benefit for the assured is that in case of an incident insured he only has to deal with the leading insurer, only has to make declarations to the leading insurer and only has to follow instructions of the leading insurer. Both clauses are silent on who is the leading insurer. In practice this does not create a problem, however, as it is the general view that the insurer mentioned first in the security list is the leading insurer. Problems can arise if terms and conditions differ between the leading insurer and co-insurers. Such situations may arise where hull insurance brokers believe they act in the benefit of their customers, the assureds, when negotiating what they believe to be better terms with co-insurers. Such better terms can be lower self-retentions, less exclusions or broader extensions of cover. In practice, however, such scenarios can cause nightmares for ship-owners. The simple reason is that a leader can handle an incident insured only under the terms and conditions he has agreed. If he has agreed on self-retention of USD 100,000, he will not touch a damage of USD 80,000. If followers had agreed to a self-retention of USD 50,000, they are on risk, but the leader will not deal with the damage. This is bad enough for the assured, but what is worse is that none of the co-insurers who had agreed to a self-retention of USD 50,000 can lead the others, so that the assured actually has to handle the case with all insurers in parallel. Similar problems, only in a different area, arise where cover with co-insurers is broader than with the leading insurer. Again, the leader will settle the claim only within the limits of his own cover conditions. Any better cover available with the co-insurers will not be addressed with the leader, so that the assured, again, has to handle his case in parallel with all respective co-insurers.

C. CLOSING REMARKS

The German marine insurance conditions for ocean going vessels are an immature product, which offers us highly sophisticated insurance cover. DTV-ADS has picked up many developments in the market, which have developed outside ADS and DTV Hull Clauses. They offer within one set of clauses what is required for modern marine hull and machinery insurance. The market, however, is conservative and it is believed that still clearly more than 90 % of the policies are issued on basis of ADS and DTV Hull Clauses. Bearing in mind that in many, some say most, areas where they differ from ADS/DTV Hull Clauses they are differing to the benefit of the assured, one may wonder why it takes so long for the new conditions to penetrate the market. In any event, brokers are recommended to take care of detailed and comprehensive protocols and notes of advice given to their ship-owner customers. The day will come where a loss or damage would have been insured under DTV-ADS, but is not insured under ADS/DTV Hull Clauses. If the loss or damage is big enough, this may lead to the insolvency of the respective ship-owner. If this happens, control of the ship-owning company will be in the hands of public receivers. Whatever good relationship the respective ship-owner may have had with his broker over many years, all this will be forgotten if a public receiver has to follow his own duties to investigate whether the insolvency estate has a claim for damages against an insurance broker for breach of the obligation to give best advice to his client.

LITERATURE

Ritter, Carl/Abraham, Hans Jürgen, Das Recht der Seeversicherung, ein Kommentar zu den Allgemeinen Deutschen Seeversicherungs-Bedingungen, Vol. 1, 1953, Vol. 2, 1960

Schwampe, Dieter, Seeschiffsversicherung 2017

NOTES

[1] Any monetary interest that a person has that ship and cargo withstand the perils of ocean shipping can be the subject of marine insurance.

[2] All figures as determined by the International Union of Marine Insurance (IUMI).

[3] BGH VersR 2003, 1171.

[4] Cf. Institute time clauses – hulls.

[5] § 28 marginal note 11.

[6] Ritter/Abraham § 28 marginal note 11.

[7] HansOLG Hamburg VRS 2013, 93.

[8] For details see Schwampe, Seeschiffsversicherung, clause 27 note 44.

[9] OLG Hamburg, VersR 2000, 1142.

CHAPTER XII

A BRIEF HISTORY OF GERMAN SHIP FINANCING

Stefan RINDFLEISCH

A. THE BEGINNING OF SHIP FINANCE BANKING IN GERMANY

Ship financing has a long tradition in Germany. This tradition goes back to the times of the Hanseatic League, more than 500 years ago, when financiers began to join forces in order to build and buy a ship and to share the risks and opportunities of its operation. This basic idea has prevailed up to the present day.

The first banks specializing in ship financing were founded in Germany about a hundred years ago. After World War II, five specialized ship financing banks existed in Germany[1]. These banks were called ship mortgage banks ("*Schiffshypothekenbanken*"). They were specialized in financing merchant ships and they were allowed to refinance themselves by issuing ship mortgage bonds ("*Schiffspfandbriefe*"), provided the corresponding requirements of the Ship Mortgage Bank Act were met. The existence of banks being specialized in ship financing and the concept of refinancing through ship mortgage bonds laid the foundation for the growth of the ship finance industry in Germany in the second half of the 20th century.

Over the years, four of the specialized ship financing banks merged and formed Deutsche Schiffsbank AG in 1989. Its shareholders were Commerzbank, Dresdner Bank and Vereins- und Westbank. Since end of 2011, Commerzbank has held all shares in Deutsche Schiffsbank AG. While business operations were to be continued, Commerzbank decided against a continuation of the brand name. The final merger with Commerzbank on 22 May 2012 therefore marked the end of Deutsche Schiffsbank.

The fifth ship financing bank, *Schiffshypothekenbank zu Lübeck AG*, was founded in Kiel as a subsidiary of the former federal state-owned bank (Landesbank Schleswig Holstein). In 1989 it became a wholly-owned subsidiary of Deutsche Bank AG. In 2008 the bank was fully merged onto Deutsche Bank AG. Since then, Deutsche Bank's entire ship financing business has been managed under the new name Deutsche Shipping.

Parallel to the above specialized ship financing banks, a group of federal state-owned banks (*Landesbanken*) and commercial banks started to build up ship finance activity. During the heydays of German ship financing in the years between 1995 and 2008, over 30 German banks had formed ship finance departments and participated actively in ship financing.

B. THE BIRTH OF THE GERMAN KG MARKET

To finance a ship, the shipowner usually needs debt and equity capital. Since the 1970s, German shipowners, who did not have enough of their own equity capital to maintain or grow their fleet, could tap the rapidly growing equity collecting market, the so-called KG Market.

The idea was simple and straightforward: the initiator of the project was very often a shipping company who wanted to manage the ship in the future. The initiator or a sponsor incorporated an entity. The investors became partners or shareholders in the entity and provided the required equity capital. Whilst initially shipping partnerships (*Partenreedereien*) were used as the entities for these shipping investments, later on and even today the commonly used legal form for a shipping entity in Germany is the limited partnership (*Kommanditgesellschaft* or *KG)* in the form of a GmbH & Co. KG.

Shipping partnerships were not regarded attractive because their partners' liability for the debt of the shipping partnership's debt was only limited by their share in the shipping partnership. Moreover, shipping partnerships were not registered in a public register. This caused a lot of practical issues when they had to provide evidence about their existence, signing authority and so on. Since 2013, due to a change to the German Commercial Code (*Handelsgesetzbuch*), it is no longer possible to incorporate new shipping partnerships.

A GmbH & Co. KG is a modified form of a limited partnership in which the unlimited general partner is a company with limited liability (*Gesellschaft mit beschränkter Haftung* or *GmbH*). It combines the tax and corporate law advantages of partnerships with the limited liability and organizational advantages of corporations. The investors become, directly or through a trustee, limited partners of the GmbH & Co. KG whose liability is limited by their liability contribution (*Hafteinlage*). The shareholders of the general partner of the shipping GmbH & Co.KG are typically closely related to the sponsor or initiator of the financing project.

In the early days of the German KG Market, investors were mainly attracted to shipping investments because of the remarkable tax savings they could benefit from. Back in the 1970s, German tax law allowed an investor to set off a multiple of his investment in a shipowner from his taxable income and, hence, reduce his tax duty substantially. In "best" cases, German investors could book losses up to 300% of their shipping investment against their income in the year they invested in a ship. This tax advantage helped to create a ship finance "culture" in Germany. Over the years, it became normal for a wealthy individual to invest part of his/her earnings in shipping. Due to the tax benefits, many investors invested in ships without even being interested in their investment once their money was invested.

The German legislator started to cut the tax benefits since the early 1980s. After the 1990s, the possibility of tax depreciation was increasingly restricted due to changes in the tax law. It was finally abolished completely with the introduction of Section 15b of the German Income Tax Act in November 2005. In return for the omission of the tax depreciation and in response to other European member states introducing a tonnage tax scheme, tonnage tax was introduced into the German income tax law in 1999. Tonnage tax is a method of determining the taxable income of a shipping company. It has proven to be very attractive as it keeps the tax burden on profitable shipping investments low. The introduction of the tonnage tax proved to be an important tax incentive for shipping investments and turned out to be the motor of continued growth of the German KG Market in the new century.

Since the late 1970s, when shipping investments by private individuals became more and more attractive from a tax perspective, entities were founded whose sole purpose it was to set up and structure retail shipping investments and to collect the equity capital required for these projects from private individuals. These entities were called *Emmissionshäuser* or KG Houses. KG Houses earned their money by deducting their fees from the invested equity capital. They shared these fees with their – in many cases independent – investment advisors who were in direct contact with the investors. The total amount consumed for fees in a typical shipping project was on average between 15% and 20% of the capital invested. In some cases, up to 25% of the equity capital invested were consumed by the fees.

More and more shipowners founded their own KG houses. It was a seemingly easy way to fund the growth of the fleet of managed vessels and of earning money as it was not overly complex and difficult to collect equity capital from German investors. It turned out in the years after 2008 that in many cases the market players who were running a KG House or who were relying on equity capital collected by KG Houses underestimated the legal risks related to this business[2].

At the peak of the German KG Market from the late 1990s until 2008, not less than about 60-70 KG Houses existed. In their most active years in 2005 and 2006, they managed to collect more than EUR 3 billion of equity capital per annum. Taking into account the average mix between bank debt and equity capital during these days being 70/30, this meant the German KG Market generates purchase capacity of about EUR 10 billion.

C. Germany becoming the World's Global Hub for Ship Financing

Parallel to the strong growth of the German KG Market in the years between 1990 and 2008, the German banks grew their ship finance activity and became truly global and dominant players in this market.

One can differentiate between three groups of banks during these years: banks specialized and working exclusively on ship finance, the formerly federal state-owned banks (*Landesbanken*) and the other banks.

In the beginning, Deutsche Schiffsbank AG and Schiffshypothekenbank zu Lübeck AG (until being merged onto Deutsche Bank AG) were the leading German ship financing banks. They had a deep knowhow of the shipping markets and close contacts to shipowners all over the world who appreciated their knowhow and understanding of their business model.

The *Landesbanken* started to do ship financing as from the late 1970s onwards. They were able to offer financings at more attractive terms than other German banks as they refinanced themselves at more attractive terms due to a public guarantor's liability (*Gewährträgerhaftung*). The federal state owning the *Landebank* was obliged to provide its bank with the necessary financial resources and to step in to save it from insolvency. Hamburgische Landesbank, the predecessor of HSH Nordbank AG, led the group of the *Landesbanken* which entered the ship financing business. In total, a group of at least six *Landesbanken* granted ship finance loans.

A further ship finance player with a government background was and is the Kreditanstalt für Wiederaufbau, KfW[3], nowadays doing ship finance through its daughter KfW Ipex Bank GmbH.

Additionally, a number of other German banks started to build up ship finance departments, such as Commerzbank AG, Dresdner Bank AG (merged with Commerzbank AG in 2009), DekaBank Deutsche Girozentrale AöR, Vereins- und Westbank AG (merged with HypoVereinsbank in 2004, the latter merged with Unicredit Bank AG in 2005) as well as various cooperative banks (*Volksbanken*).

From 1990 to 2008, Germany became the ship finance hub worldwide. At the beginning of this century, six out of the ten biggest banks ship financing loan books worldwide were German. HSH Nordbank AG was considered the largest provider of ship finance worldwide. Other major banks in this area were Commerzbank AG, KfW and Norddeutsche Landesbank – Girozentrale.

World trade had increased rapidly since the 1980s mainly due to the strong growth of world population, the end of the cold war (formerly isolated countries were now participating in world trade), the strong economic growth of China and the use of containers. Demand for seaward transport had risen faster than supply. This had led to high freight rates, specifically from 2000 to the summer of 2008. Freight rates had reached all-time highs by mid-2005.

Bank debt and equity capital were available and easily accessible during this period. German ship financing banks wanted to grow their shipping loan books as they needed to deploy their funds. HSH Nordbank AG, the biggest ship financing bank worldwide, was known to work on plans to go public and, hence, increased ship finance volumes very actively. The German KG Market ran on full speed and pumped as much equity into the shipping markets as needed. In the years 2005, 2006 and 2007 each year between EUR 2.5 and 3.5 billion equity capital were invested in closed ship funds.

This development had a considerable impact on the ship financing market and led to speculative overheating. Ever more and larger ships were ordered at a rapidly increasing number of shipyards, mainly in Asia. Massive overcapacities were created. Many ships were ordered and financed without charter contracts being entered into for these ships. Ships were ordered or purchased purely on speculative basis, either ordered for the purpose of selling the newbuilding to a third party during its construction at a higher price[4] or ordered/purchased for the sake of creating a new closed end ship fund.

D. THE TURNING POINT IN AUTUMN 2008

The turning point, the event which made the ship finance markets almost collapse, was the breakdown of Lehman Brothers in the autumn of 2008 which was primarily a consequence of the United States housing bubble followed by the subprime mortgage crisis in the United States in 2007.

The banking crisis spread to the real economy. A recession began in most industrialized countries. The worldwide economic downturn caused the freight markets and market values of ships to drop substantially. This was also reflected in falling prices in the market for ship scrap: in mid-2008 it peaked at USD 650 per tonne whereas in early 2009 it was down to USD 200 per tonne. According to Bundesbank statistics, German shipping had revenues of EUR 18.679 billion in 2009, almost 25 % less than in 2008 (EUR 24.514 billion). Hapag Lloyd alone recorded a loss of EUR 350 million from 1 January to 30 September 2009.

Many charterers also encountered financial difficulties during this time, among them some of the major, internationally best reputed charterers. Shipowners who had chartered out their ships to these charterers were faced with the decision to either insist on the performance of a contract with the risk that the charterer would go bankrupt or to accommodate the charterer financially by agreeing to a reduction of charter rates.

With the sharp fall in charter rates and the decline in worldwide transport, hundreds of ships were laid up. Shipowners even agreed on lay-up pools.

Due to the banking crisis in general and the weak shipping market in particular, shipping loans were no longer available from banks from one day to another. In shipping, a credit crunch occurred leaving most shipowners with no access to bank debt whatsoever. Wherever banks could, they withdrew from soft, non-binding commitments and left alone those shipowners who had ordered ships on the basis of their bank's soft, sometimes only oral commitment to finance that ship.

Shipping companies could either no longer distribute dividends to the limited partners or, as a matter of precaution, they started to hold back liquidity instead of distributing it to their shareholders to build up cash reserves. The first shipping companies had to file for insolvency.

The above developments caused the sudden breakdown of the German KG Market. Investors were no longer willing to invest in shipping projects due to the negative developments.

Within a relatively short period of time, the ship finance markets worldwide, first and foremost the German market as the major ship finance market worldwide, were turned upside down. The market rules and mechanics which had reliably worked for decades did no longer work.

E. THE ERA OF STAGNANCY IN 2009

During the months after the turning point in autumn 2008, the breakdown of Lehman Brothers, the German ship finance market was dominated by stagnancy.

The German banks would have been able to terminate loan agreements due to multiple events of default having occurred under their loan agreements. Some shipowners were no longer able to repay instalments because their charterers stopped paying charter hire at all or only paid a fraction of what was owed and payable under the charter contracts. In many cases, shipowners were not even able to pay interest on their loans. These events would have entitled the banks to terminate the loan agreement straight away.

Market values of vessels dropped dramatically so that loan to value or value maintenance clauses were breached in many cases. This would have entitled the German banks to demand prepayments or additional security.

The German banks did, however, not make use of any of their rights during these first months. They simply waited. In those cases where shipowners did not repay their loans or interest thereon or where loan to value breaches became obvious, they entered into standstill agreements with the owners, confirming to owners they would not make use of their rights and accelerate the loans, but wait. The reasons for this "generous" behaviour of the German banks were multiple and differed from bank to bank.

One reason certainly was that the banks just hoped markets would improve as fast as they had deteriorated, and events of default would disappear automatically. During the last severe shipping crisis in the 1980s the German ship financing banks did do nothing, the markets recovered quite quickly, and the banks gained some experience that by doing nothing things would repair itself. The German banks' passivity even improved their standing among shipowners as shipowners saw their German banks supporting them in difficult times and not letting them down.

Another reason for the German banks' reluctance to take action and accelerate loans can be found in the banks' balance sheets and the need for increases of risk related capital allocations. It would have been very expensive for the banks to write off losses in the course of loan accelerations.

When the German banks realized that shipping would not recover from the crisis quickly enough, they started to take action.

F. RESTRUCTURINGS AND INSOLVENCIES

The period between 2010 and 2017 was dominated by hundreds of ship finance transactions being restructured and by hundreds of insolvencies of single shipowning entities.

By the end of 2009, the German ship financing banks started to slowly and carefully clean up their ship finance loan books. In many cases, they restructured existing finance transactions. The two main elements of these restructurings were (i) the amendment of the repayment schedules and (ii) the waiver of the loan to value provisions. Existing repayment schedules were usually replaced with pay-as-you-earn repayment schemes pursuant to which the shipowners had to use for repayment all liquidity after payment of operating expenses. The waiver of the loan to value clause was necessary due to the continuing low market values of the vessels in almost all segments.

A few banks took more drastic steps. Commerzbank, for instance, decided to quit ship financing altogether. When the bank decided to do so, it was among the top ten biggest ship financing banks in the world. The wind down process took them until 2018. They are expected to close their ship finance department by the end of 2018. They achieved this goal by starting early to sell bundles of ship finance loans to institutional investors and by causing their borrowers to sell their ships to third parties. In cases where a shipowner was not cooperative, they cancelled the loan agreement which caused the shipowner to file for insolvency.

In cases where either a bank cancelled the loan agreement due to an event of default or did not regard the restructuring of that loan reasonable or meaningful or in cases where the shipowner's income situation was too stressed otherwise, insolvency proceedings took place.

To a certain extent, the German insolvency law is unique compared to many other insolvency and bankruptcy regimes worldwide. Pursuant to German insolvency law, an entity must file for insolvency latest within three weeks if it is either illiquid (*zahlungsunfähig*) or over-indebted (*überschuldet*) and a positive going concern prognosis for the current and the successive business year cannot be given. In terms of the German Insolvency Act, an entity is regarded illiquid if it is not able to pay 90% of its debts due over the next three weeks. An entity is regarded over-indebted if its debts exceed its assets and a positive going concern prognosis for the current and the next business year cannot be given. If the managing director(s) of an entity do not file for insolvency within latest three weeks from the date either illiquidity or over-indebtedness has occurred, they become personally liable for most of the entity's debt which is incurred in continuation of the ordinary business operation. Moreover, the managing director(s) may be subject to criminal charges.

During the years between 2009 and 2017 hundreds of German single shipowning entities filed for insolvency. Although the pace of new insolvencies slowed down substantially in 2018, there was still a visible number of fresh filings.

It is noteworthy that in almost all cases of shipowners' insolvencies, the legal basis for the filing was illiquidity and not over-indebtedness. Taking into account the strong decline in vessels' market values over the last years, one would have expected that over-indebtedness would be the first and main legal basis for many entities to file for insolvency. In almost all cases, however, the managing directors were able to reach a positive going concern prognosis and hence did not have to file for insolvency due to this reason.

When the first shipping entities filed for insolvency and numbers of insolvencies started to grow, managing directors of distressed shipping entities looked for service providers who would take over the role as managing director from them and manage the entity through the insolvency proceedings and ultimately liquidate it. Over the years, a small shipping insolvency industry grew in this area. It consisted of people who were willing to take over the role of managing director of a distressed shipowner and to manage the entire process. These people knew when and how to file for insolvency and how to organize the process in the best way. Unlike in other jurisdictions such as the United States, German insolvency law is (still) mainly structured to satisfy the insolvent entity's creditors. In shipping the major creditor is the financing bank, leaving aside those creditors who have priority over the bank's claims anyway, namely the holders of maritime liens. This is why the German shipping insolvency proceedings were mainly driven by the financing banks. In some cases, banks even used the insolvency law for a structured and controlled work out.

Insolvencies usually ended with the sale of the vessel by the insolvency administrator to a third-party buyer.

G. PRIVATE EQUITY AND HEDGE FUNDS ENTERING THE MARKET

The longer the ship finance crisis continued over the first years, the more private equity funds and hedge funds showed interest in German shipping situations. Different types of approaches could be observed.

Some funds approached banks and/or distressed shipowners and offered to purchase their ships at current market values. These funds were initially not very successful in getting access to distressed ships. Especially during the first few years of the crisis the German banks were not (yet) ready to realize the losses which would have occurred if a distressed ship would have been sold at then prevailing market rates. Equally, shipowners and their managers were likewise not willing to give up their business and tried everything to keep their ships under their control.

Other funds approached German shipping companies and formed joint ventures with them. The joint goal was to purchase ships at low market rates and to have these ships operated by the German shipping companies. The reputation of German shipping companies was and still is very good. They had, moreover, the best insight in the German shipping market and direct access to distressed assets. Some of these joint ventures became successful entities and are still active in the market.

Another group of funds created shipping entities on their own. They hired individual shipping professionals or entered into close cooperation with them and set up their own structures to purchase ships and to either manage these ships on their own or to manage the ship managers of these ships.

Some funds offered alternative finance solutions to distressed owners. They offered to grant loans to shipowners to enable them to refinance their loans. Given the single asset and non-recourse structure of most ship financings, the new lenders were expecting the financing banks to take haircuts and waive part of the loans in view of the fallen market values of the ships to be refinanced.

Last, but not least, a number private equity and hedge funds purchased performing and non-performing loan portfolios from German ship financing banks. Some of the German banks decided on this method of winding down their loan book. It enabled these banks to wind down their loan books quite rapidly and to transfer the work out risk to the buyers of these loans. On rare occasions, only a single loan was sold. In most cases, the aggregate nominal loan amount of the loans sold was above USD 100 Million or sometimes even above USD 1 billion. The haircut the selling bank was willing to accept upon the sale and transfer of the loans was between zero in cases where the loans sold were performing loans and over 50% in cases where the loans sold were non-performing.

H. OTHER NEW FINANCIERS AND NEW FINANCE STRUCTURES

Parallel to private equity and hedge funds entering the German ship finance market other players started to show interest in this sector.

The first Chinese banks entered the German ship finance market in or around 2012. They offered ship finance loans to German shipowners with a strong balance sheet against corporate guarantees. In many cases, but not in all, these loans had a Chinese element, be it that the vessels financed were newbuildings built in China or that they were chartered out to a Chinese charterer.

A number of leasing companies, in the first instance those belonging to the big state-owned Chinese banks, started to offer ship finance lease solutions to German owners. The lease contracts in the form of bareboat charter contracts usually had a duration of between five and ten years and contained purchase options for the lessees.

Family offices also showed interest in ship finance transactions. During the first years of the crisis they were still reluctant to enter into transactions but as from about 2012–2014 they started to invest. The overall sum invested by family offices is, however, small compared to other pockets of money being invested in German shipping.

The latest to invest in the German shipping market were insurance companies and pensions funds. These investors used structured finance products to invest in German shipping situations. They invested, for instance, in new loans being granted by banks after 2012. In investing, they were taking over the risk from the financing banks who stayed in the picture to administer the loans.

The Norwegian OTC Market played an important role for some German owners who managed to tap this market and finance the growth of their fleet.

Other finance products were offered to German shipping players, such as ship finance based on bond offerings and crowdfunding solutions.

I. CONSOLIDATION

Prior to 2008, consolidation did not play any role in German shipping. The longer the crisis lasted, however, the more consolidation took place.

When German shipowners realized that neither banks nor other capital providers were willing and able to grant non-recourse ship financings (like they had done before the crisis), they experienced increasing pressure to merge their businesses with other shipping companies. This created a wave of mergers and acquisitions which is still ongoing at the end of 2018.

J. CONCLUDING REMARKS

The banking and shipping crisis during the years after 2008 had a dramatic impact on German ship finance banks, shipowners and other market players. The German ship finance market contracted and changed substantially, with many banks deciding to either close their ship finance business altogether or, at least, to shrink it substantially, with many ships owned by German shipowners being sold and with numerous shipowners filing for insolvency.

Many smaller German shipping companies and ship managers closed their businesses. They disappeared after their last ship was sold and they had no chance to get fresh capital for new business. Some of these smaller ship owners and ship managers managed to consolidate their business with other owners' businesses.

Like every other crisis the latest shipping and ship finance crisis did have some positive effects. The German shipping market is more robust than in 2008. The quality of German ship management has improved, especially in terms of reporting and transparency. The variety of finance instruments is much bigger today. An overheating, however, as in the years between 2005 and 2008 is less likely.

NOTES

[1] Deutsche Schiffsbeleihungsbank, Hamburg, founded in 1918, Deutsche Schiffskreditbank AG, Duisburg, founded in 1918, Deutsche Schiffspfandbriefbank AG, Bremen und Berlin, founded in 1918, Neue Deutsche Schiffspfandbriefbank AG, Bremen founded in 1948, Schiffshypothekenbank zu Lübeck AG, Kiel / Hamburg founded in 1949.

[2] Investors who lost money when investing in shipping sued those who were responsible for the contents of the investment prospectus, i.e. the KG House and the ship manager. Some KG Houses and ship managers were sued in 100+ cases.

[3] The Kreditanstalt für Wiederaufbau is owned by the Federal Republic of Germany and by the federal states.

[4] In some instances, newbuildings were sold up to four times during their construction, with each pass-through buyer earning his fair share of profit.

CHAPTER XIII

A BRIEF INTRODUCTION INTO MULTIMODAL TRANSPORT

Kai Holger DREWS

A. THE BASIC IDEA OF MULTIMODAL TRANSPORT

The basic idea behind the concept of multimodal transport is simple: One contract will cover various different transport services – it will put those services between parenthesis. The client just needs one contract, where he would otherwise have to conclude several individual transport contracts under different legislations and in foreign languages. In legal phrasing, the definition of a multimodal transport reads as follows:

§452 HGB (German Commercial Code):

"Contract for the carriage of goods by several modes of transport

If carriage of goods is performed by several modes of transport under a single contract for the carriage of goods, and if, had separate contracts been concluded between the parties for each part of the carriage involving one mode of transport (transport leg), at least two of these contracts would have been subject to different legal provisions (...)"

As we shall see, the resulting legal implications are quite opposite to a seemingly simple concept.

B. INTRODUCTION

A vast percentage of all transport services performed worldwide by the logistics industry can be considered to be a so-called "Multimodal Transport" or "Combined Transport". However, as opposed to numerous International Conventions covering single mode transports (Hague and Hague Visby Rules for sea transport, CMR for road transport, Montreal Convention for air transport and CMNI for transport by railroad, to name just the most important ones), there is until now no convention in place to govern multimodal transport services as such.[1] This text will therefore concentrate on the regulations laid out in the German Commercial Code (HGB), §§452 – 452d HGB. Nevertheless, most principles can be applied globally.

And – before turning to the topic – please permit yet another introducing remark, which will be a response to the question: Why does this book need a contribution dealing with multimodal transport? Is this not on Maritime Law?

The answer must be: Yes, this book deals with Maritime Law. However, for several reasons to be explained, German Maritime Law was very close to be extinguished almost completely. This was a result of a certain interpretation of the German rules for multimodal transport as laid out in the German Commercial Code, §§452 – 452d HGB. Thanks to a decision of the BGH, this did not happen.[2] However, details are still open to discussion.

Furthermore, multimodal transport is and will remain very much attached to the transport of goods by sea. As an estimate, 90 % of all multimodal transports include a sea transport. Consequently, the future development of legal decisions related to multimodal transport must be observed. Surprises are possible. Therefore, please now follow me into the world of multimodal transport.

C. BASIC PRINCIPLES

Whereas multimodal transport has always been offered as a certain kind of service by the logistics industry and has – in return – been accepted by its customers[3], laws regulating this particular institute have been sparse. This may be a consequence of a number of complications coming with a contract covering a multimodal transport. On the other hand, such reserve may also have caused some of these complications as a clear legal regulation was – in Germany – only created in 1998 with the “new” Transport Law.

It might therefore be useful to line out some thoughts on what multimodal transport actually is and – on the contrary – what German Law thinks it is. Of course, in the end no jurist – neither a judge nor a lawyer providing advice to his client – can deviate from the law and the decisions of the courts being based on this law. But please regard the following remarks as useful for a general understanding.

I. SOME SEMANTICS

The institute is named "multimodal (or combined) transport". The term "transport" implies a contract of carriage between a carrier and (usually) a shipper[4]. Very much simplified for our example, the contractual obligations of a transport contract will basically be to pay the freight (the shipper) and to take the goods into custody, transport them to the place of destination and deliver them to the consignee (the carrier). In other words: The main characteristic is the transport – the carriage of goods. The contractual carrier will perform this task – in the original sense – himself, using a truck, ship or an aircraft. As transpires here, of course, such contract was (and is) always related to one single mean of transport. There is – necessarily – no sea carrier who can perform a following road transport from Hamburg to Munich with his ship.

When looking at a contract covering a multimodal transport, we obviously do not at all see a "transport" contract. What it actually is and must be due to its nature, is a freight forwarding contract.[5] In such contract, the freight forwarder does not perform the transport himself. His obligation is not the carriage, but to organize such carriage. The carriage will then be performed by third parties, the carrier, respectively carriers (at least two of them). Those will be subcontractors of the freight forwarder.

Of course, this is one of the big advantages a freight forwarder offers to the industry: A shipper who exports from – say – Munich to Chicago, does not at all want to conclude three different contracts (land transport to a port, sea transport to the USA, land transport from another port to Chicago). Such procedure would require complicated organisational skills and would result into (most certainly) three different applicable laws and corresponding places of jurisdiction. Also, it should be noted that international communication has not always been as easy as today via the Internet and email. As a consequence, all of this has been and still is taken care of by a freight forwarder. He offers complete transport solutions tailor-made for his client.

This being said – the German Commercial Code categorizes a contract covering a multimodal transport as a "transport" contract – which is underlined by its position in the Code itself. The stipulations for multimodal transport are a part of Chapter 4 of the Code, labelled as "freight business" (Frachtgeschäft). Chapter 5, starting – most ironically – in §453 HGB, subsequently covers the freight forwarding business (Speditionsgeschäft). This is where the institute of multimodal transport would actually belong to – according to its sheer nature.

Such differentiation is – at this point – useful for a basic understanding of the institute of multimodal transport. In the end, it may not make a huge difference when dealing with a multimodal transport in real life (at least, under German Law). As a matter of fact, most freight forwarding contracts will – as German Law does, but frequently also under foreign laws – be treated similarly to a "freight contract" or contract of carriage. The reason for this can be found in §459 HGB in particular: A freight forwarder who performs his services at a so called "fixed price" will be treated as a (sea) carrier. A "fixed price" means a lump sum will be agreed upon for the contractual performance of the freight forwarder. The shipper will – in return – not know the particular prices for the services included into the multimodal contract. These will consist of – for instance – the various carriages and sums paid to the subcontractors of the freight forwarder, customs services, organisation of all this and the freight forwarder's fees. As a matter of fact, virtually all (not only multimodal) freight-forwarding contracts are concluded at a fixed price. Otherwise, the freight forwarder would disclose not only his individual profit, but also some of his business secrets. To summarize: A multimodal freight forwarder concluding at a fixed price will be treated like a carrier under German Law. Still, the nature of his business is different.

When dealing with multimodal transports in real life, it is of vital importance to keep in mind: This contract is in fact a freight forwarder's contract. Consequently, any complications will – in the normal course of events and neglecting the very rare occurrence of an actual fault of the freight forwarder himself – most certainly happen during the transport. The goods are under the responsibility of an additional, third, fourth or even fifth party, depending on the contractual chain. Not only will the actual carrier be the only party to be able to provide information in case of losses, damages or any other problem. He will also be the one who must be held responsible and who will – hopefully – ultimately compensate loss or damage.

II. THE CONFLICT OF LAWS QUESTION

In an ordinary legal life, conflict of law questions hardly ever arise. All legal problems can and will be solved under domestic law. Only if a matter will be connected to (at least) two different legal systems, conflicts of law may occur. For instance, a marriage between citizens of different citizenship: Which country's law shall govern the marriage (or – even worse – the divorce)? For such questions, each country offers solutions in a conflict of law section of the domestic law. In Europe, including of course Germany, the so-called ROME I Regulation must now be applied.

In the logistics industry, virtually each and every case requires to decide which law should be applied to solve a legal question. Related to the transport of goods and to multimodal transports in particular: Under a very theoretical approach, one may construct cases in which a multimodal transport has no international implication. The general rule based on experience, however, clearly says: Every multimodal transport is an international undertaking. On a regular basis, there will be parties from different countries: To start with, shipper and consignee will normally be located in different countries. Depending on the sales contract and the INCOTERMS of this contract, either shipper (seller), or consignee (buyer) will conclude a contract with a freight forwarder to organize the transport of the goods. The freight forwarder may also act under a different jurisdiction. Therefore, already at this point (or level), a decision needs to be made as to which law will have to be applied to the complete multimodal contract.[6] Again, as a rule of thumb, according to the regulations on conflict of laws, two options are possible: The parties can either choose which law will be applied or the law of the country with the strongest connection will be applied.

The respective stipulations can be found in the ROME I Regulation of the EC, which is directly applicable under German Law and within Europe as well. Art. 3, I ROME I points out that in any contract, parties are free to choose the applicable law for their contract. In case they fail to do so, Art. 5 ROME I gives a number of possible solutions how to arrive at an applicable law for transport contracts. The basic idea is that the law shall be applied which has the closest relation to the matter. But alas – again, we do not find a freight forwarding contract. Again, not only the freight forwarding contract, but in particular the multimodal transport is disregarded. Still, it is commonly agreed that Art. 5 ROME I will equally be applied on freight forwarding contracts – and on multimodal contracts.

Such– with all given respect – ignorance of the legislative bodies is unfortunate. And so far, we have been operating only on what I would like to call "the first level" of conflict of laws related to a multimodal transport.

There is a second level: Each multimodal transport includes by definition different mode of transport subject to different legal stipulations. Those can either be international conventions (as laid out above), or national laws. Consequently, after having applied a national law on the "complete" contract of multimodal transport as such, a second choice of law is required. The multimodal freight forwarder will have concluded a number of subcontracts with different parties acting under different jurisdictions. Which law shall govern the individual transports within such multimodal or combined transport – the "transport legs"?

It is time for a confession: The author of this contribution did not cite §452 HGB completely at the top of this text. In full, §452 HGB reads as follows:

"If carriage of goods is performed by several modes of transport under a single contract for the carriage of goods, and if, had separate contracts been concluded between the parties for each part of the carriage involving one mode of transport (transport leg), at least two of these contracts would have been subject to different legal provisions, ***then the provisions of the Subchapter 1 shall apply to the contract, unless the following special provisions or applicable international conventions provide otherwise. This shall also apply if part of the carriage is performed by sea.****"*

The omission of the now added part of §452 HGB had a didactic purpose: In the beginning, the definition of what a multimodal transport is, needed to be explained. This has been explained, and by now, we can go one step further:

The – at this point – decisive part of §452 HGB stipulates: the German Commercial Code, Subchaper 1 – will govern every multimodal transport **unless** the following special provisions provide differently. The most important of these special provisions reads as follows:

§452a HGB:

"If it has been established that the loss, damage or event which caused delay in delivery occurred on a specific transport leg, the liability of the Contractual Carrier shall, in derogation from the provisions of subchapter 1, be determined in accordance with the legal provisions governing a contract for the carriage of goods on this transport leg. The burden of proving that the loss, damage or event which caused delay in delivery occurred on a particular transport leg is borne by the person alleging this."

According to this, provided German Law can be applied on the multimodal transport contract as such: In case the (exact) point of time (and corresponding "transport leg") when/where the problem occurred, can not be defined and thus remains unknown, ordinary German transport law will be applicable – regardless of any other possible solution.

However, leaving aside the onus of proof question, the remaining point is complicated enough. When loss or damage can be referred to a particular section of the multimodal transport, the law applicable on this "transport leg" shall be applied. What appears to be needed is a second choice of law:

Having decided which law shall govern the complete multimodal transport as such (and – for our example – having applied German Law), a second conflict of laws situation arises with regard to the applicable law of a single "transport leg". The dilemma reads: Do we need two subsequent choices of law?

In principal, the answer is: Yes. And, having remarked that multimodal transport should not be categorized as a and located in the transport subchapter 4 of the German Commercial Code, but in the freight forwarder's subchapter, the critic goes further:

By definition, multimodal (freight forwarding) contracts are international business. The decisive question in all these contracts is, which law should be applied to individual "legs of transport" covered by such contracts. This is a genuine conflict of law question. Therefore, the complete topic should be dealt with in ROME I in – for instance – Art. 5a, to be named: "Contracts of Freight Forwarding and Multimodal Freight Forwarding". Being located on this level, there would remain one choice of law: Which law shall be applied to an individual "transport leg" of a multimodal transport? Not only German, but equally European legislation has simply failed to comprehend this problem, and the legislative solution we need to apply now as legal advisors is consequently a bit less than perfect.

As it stands, we do indeed need to choose twice: First, which law will be applied on the multimodal transport as such? Second, in case of loss, damage or delay on a defined – specific – "transport leg": Which law will be applicable on that leg? This can be regarded as being contrary to the established principles of conflict of law: Under normal circumstances, Art. 20 ROME I points out that every reference to an applicable national law excludes the conflict of law regulations of such law. As the regulations regarding multimodal transport in the German Commercial Code are neither located in ROME I, nor in the German conflict of law stipulations of the EGBGB (the Introductory Law to the German Civil Code), this requirement is formally met. However, in fact, §452a HGB clearly stipulates a conflict of law decision: Which law shall be applied on a specific "transport leg" in case we know the loss or damage occurred on this part of the multimodal transport. As we shall see, there are two responses to this: As pointed, the formalistic approach is: §452a HGB is not located in the German EGBGB (or ROME I) and thus, this is no second application of the conflict of laws regulations. The second solution lies in the essence of all German court decisions available so far and will be explained within short.

D. MULTIMODAL TRANSPORT TODAY

In the following explanations, I would like to concentrate on two main issues of multimodal transport under – in particular – German jurisdiction. These may indeed illustrate some of the legal obstacles, which can nowadays – resulting from the very principal misunderstandings as outlined above – be of huge impact on parties involved in multimodal transport.

I. MULTIMODAL TRANSPORT AS OPPOSED TO ORDINARY SEA CARRIAGE – OR IN OTHER WORDS, WHY GERMANY STILL MAKES USE OF ITS MARITIME LAW AT ALL

The heading may appear to be a bit overdone, but hits the target. In fact, German Maritime Law was very close to be simply erased by a decision of a court of appeals at Hamburg. What had happened?[7]

A multimodal "transport" from Germany in the US was under discussion. This began with a transport by truck in Germany and was continued with a carriage by sea from Hamburg to a port in the US. From there, a road transport to the final destination in the US was scheduled. The transported goods were damaged during port handling operations in the US. As always, such handling in the port was included in the contract of carriage by sea. Terminal handling operations – until that decision – had unanimously been considered a part of the sea carriage.

Just as a quick sidestep: The main conventions on sea carriage (Hague and Hague Visby) are mandatory only from "tackle to tackle", even though they cover the whole period of carrier's responsibility for the goods (thus, including terminal handling). Therefore, as they are not mandatory when the cargo is at the terminal, at least the liability of the carrier will be excluded on every decent B/L under those rules (and also under the former German Maritime Code). That may have been a factor in the ruling of the Hamburg Court of Appeals. One may like this or not, however, that is – was – how international conventions on Maritime Law in accordance with the maritime industry had solved the question of terminal handling. However, what if we do not have a question of Maritime Law?

The Hamburg Court of Appeals chose a different approach: The handling of the cargo on the terminal was – according to the court – not a subject to Maritime Law. The – indeed – transport of the cargo on the MAFI trailer for some 300 metres or so plus – indeed – quite complicated crane operations was considered to constitute a separate land transport – not just an annex to the sea carriage. Admittedly, as opposed to a simple container movement, this had been a heavy piece of break bulk requiring special care and attention.

What everybody had been regarded as a pure sea transport, suddenly turned into a multimodal transport: Transport from port to port on the ship: sea carriage. Terminal handling: land transport – terminal ground. These two separate parts ("transport legs", as §452 HGB says) were covered under one contract (for this purpose: The B/L, resp. the contract of carriage by sea). Two separate "transport legs" by different modes of transport would constitute a multimodal transport. By pure definition, Hague and Hague Visby Rules must only be applied on sea transports, but not on multimodal transport. The same counts for German Maritime Law. For instance, now §481, I HGB plainly states in "*a contract for carriage for general cargo, the carrier must carry the goods by sea to their destination*". The heading of this section is "*Primary duties; scope of application*". Consequently, German Maritime Law and – by definition also the "classic" conventions – must not be applied on a transport not limited to sea transport. This court decision opened the case for the German Law on multimodal transport.

Individually, the freight forwarder (respectively his liability insurer) responsible for the damage was confronted with a possible liability of zero (in case the exclusion of liability for terminal operations would work) or 2 SDR per kg (under Hague Visby and German Maritime Law) as opposed to 8,33 SDR per kg under German Transport Law. That is a substantial difference. But in more general terms, the implications were far reaching and in fact of dramatic consequences:

Virtually, all standard contracts to carry goods by sea include the handling of cargo by the terminal or port operator. This is simply international practice, based on the history and traditions of the trade. The sea carrier himself will arrange for the handling of the cargo prior to and after the shipment. This is – in the ordinary container and break bulk business – hardly ever done by shipper or consignee. These services are consequently part of the sea transport and included in that contract.

If the handling of cargo on terminal grounds would constitute a separate "transport leg" (as provided for by the definition of §452 HGB), by definition, every sea transport would cease to be a sea transport. It would be a multimodal transport. Under German Law, Maritime Law would come to its end.

This whole argument is actually on categorization: When can any transport service be categorized as a separate "transport leg"? If terminal handling of any cargo (as done in billion movements around the world daily) would –

by German definition – constitute such a "transport leg", every sea transport would automatically turn into a multimodal transport: No application of Maritime Law anymore, at least under German jurisdiction.

Fortunately – from a maritime lawyers point of view – this did not happen, or at least, not for now. The ruling of the German Federal Court of Justice (BGH) following the court of appeals decision said, port-handling operations would "under normal circumstances" not constitute a separate "transport leg". This also counted for the – quite complicated – handling of a MAFI trailer discussed in this particular matter. However, against all odds, the German Federal Court of Justice still arrived in applying German (land) Transport Law on the incident, thus arriving at a liability of 8,33 SDR per kg as opposed to 2 SDR. The reasoning of the German Federal Court of Justice offers a number of surprises. On the other hand, we now face an excellent opportunity to explain certain aspects of the institute of multimodal transport.

1. THE "TRANSPORT LEG" AS DEFINED BY THE GERMAN FEDERAL COURT OF JUSTICE – RELATED TO TERMINAL OPERATIONS

In very short words, the decision omitted a number of questions in the first place. The approach of the German Federal Court of Justice was merely practical, leaving aside virtually all legal arguments which may have been: Who concluded the terminal operation contract (not the multimodal freight forwarder, but the sea carrier)? Is the terminal handling actually a "real" transport covered by a "real" contract of carriage or maybe something different? Under which law would the terminal contract actually be treated? And can there be a multimodal transport (sea transport plus terminal handling) within yet another multimodal transport?

Instead, the German Federal Court of Justice ruled that any terminal operation should be regarded as part of the sea carriage as long as it is not of "extraordinary nature". In the case under discussion, we are looking at a piece of break bulk on a MAFI trailer to be moved – after discharge from the vessel – for about 300 metres across terminal grounds. After that, the cargo had to be loaded on a truck by crane. The weight was 25,940 kg, the break bulk consisted of a printing machine with a very high centre of gravity (which resulted in the damage, as it flipped over at a close turn). Such kind of terminal operation would not – according to the German Federal Court of Justice – be extraordinary enough to constitute a separate "transport leg".

So far, so good. You can thus rest assured and wait, which complication may be required to change a terminal operation into a "transport leg" under German Multimodal Law. It may come around one day. But definitely, any ordinary cargo handling by terminal operators will not constitute a multimodal sea transport.[8]

However, the German Federal Court of Justice still did not apply Maritime Law, but the German Road Transport Law of §§407 – 449 HGB instead. How could that happen?

2. WHEN DOES A "TRANSPORT LEG" IN GENERAL AND TERMINAL HANDLING PROCEDURE IN PARTICULAR END (WHICH WILL CONSEQUENTLY ALSO DEFINE THE BEGINNING OF THE NEXT "TRANSPORT LEG")?

In "our" case, the cargo flipped over when it was still on the MAFI trailer. Just for general information: A MAFI trailer is a very low trailer with small wheels, designed to move heavy pieces of break bulk. The cargo is lashed and secured on that trailer and then pulled on the vessel (which has a ramp for shipments like these). It remains on the MAFI during sea transport and is discharged from the vessel on the MAFI. It remains on that MAFI until it is finally lifted off the MAFI and loaded on the next transport device (truck, railroad wagon or whatever) – or simply discharged to be picked up by someone else.

In our case, the machine was still standing on the MAFI: Only the chains to secure it on the MAFI had been released. Then, the MAFI was turned around and the cargo – still on that MAFI – flipped over and was a total loss.

What we need to look at in the first place is: When will one transport cease and another transport (both being parts of a multimodal "transport" contract) start? This may be relevant for defining from which point on a certain law will be applied. Of course, the question is not at all different, when several individual contracts of carriage have been concluded without a multimodal transport: It is very important to know exactly when and where responsibilities are transferred to the next carrier in order to allocate the corresponding transfer of rights, duties and liabilities.

In the matter discussed here, quite obvious, everybody would expect the sea carriage – including terminal handling operations – to end when the cargo was finally put on the (in our case) truck for the following land transport. The MAFI was part of the sea carriage, being provided for by the ship (which the German Federal Court of Justice did not even bother to check or discuss) and in particular designed for the handling of break bulk on a carriage by sea and the terminal operations attached thereto. Also, it may be assumed (the German Federal Court of Justice not checking this either) that as usual the port handling charges being paid for by the ship included crane operations to lift the cargo off the MAFI and on the truck. And of course, the crane operator who would (but this was equally not discussed by the German Federal Court of Justice) under given circumstances be employed by the terminal operator, had not even started to lift the machine of the MAFI (had he done that or even straightened the tackle, it could not have flipped over). Therefore, it must also be assumed that the machine was still under the responsibility of the terminal operator – as the crane operator had not even started to deliver the machine to the next carrier, which would have only happened if it was put on the truck.[9]

But quite opposite: Instead, the German Federal Court of Justice ruled the land transport succeeding the sea carriage had begun when the lashing chains on the MAFI had been taken off. In complete ignorance of the contractual and factual situation, the German Federal Court of Justice pointed out, with the beginning of the discharge process from the MAFI, the land transport had begun. This opinion is in contrast to the contractual obligations of the involved parties and also to the established procedures of the trade in actual life. We may see how this will work out in the future, but the decision will cause problems. For now, a certainly surprised trucker from the US will find himself liable under German Transport Law. Not only that he has never heard of such law. Even better, he will be liable for cargo, which has not even touched his truck. At least according to the German opinion. This works out only because – for obvious reasons – nobody will extend such a case into the US by a third party intervention.

Anyhow, land transport be it. But which law should be applied on a land transport within the US – when being part of a multimodal transport under German Law?

II. WHICH LAW SHALL BE APPLIED ON A DEFINED "TRANSPORT LEG"?

Having explained how the German Federal Court of Justice – against all odds, as being said – has defined a "transport leg" at least as far as terminal operations are concerned, under a more general perspective, another question needs to be answered: Which law should be applied on a separate "transport leg" of a multimodal transport? I have put this section into a new subchapter, as it is not limited to terminal handling at all.

In first place, the chance to apply foreign law within a multimodal transport appears to be very much limited indeed: Only in cases of loss of, damage to cargo or delay a law other that §§407 – 450 HGB may be applied. In addition, the place of loss etc. must be known. However, of course, such cases are not the rare ones in the legal world. As long as everything works out, nobody seeks legal advice but the contractual obligations have simply been met. Only when something goes wrong, legal expertise will be requested and this will be one of the exceptions mentioned above and in §452a HGB.

In this contribution, conflict of laws was initially mentioned. However, at that point, we only dealt with conflict of laws in principle and on the level of the multimodal transport. Now, we need to go deeper and see, which law should be applied to an individual transport being part of a multimodal transport.

Taken for granted that the exact location of where a loss occurred can be defined, the question is which law can be applied to the respective "transport leg" of the multimodal transport. Even though we may not be allowed to apply ROME I, it is agreed that the technique to solve conflict of laws questions may be used within §452a HGB.[10] The contract under discussion now is a subcontract between the multimodal freight forwarder and one of his subcontractors or carriers (which is – again – yet another argument to not call port handling operations a "transport leg" under a multimodal transport: These are never concluded by the multimodal freight forwarder, but by the sea carrier).

Let us scrutinize the multimodal transport from our MAFI example above: Land transport by truck in Germany to Hamburg, sea transport to a port in the US, land transport by truck to another city in the US. The multimodal transport is concluded between a German freight forwarder and the German shipper. Therefore, German Law is applicable on the multimodal contract. The cargo is totally damaged "on the road" to – say – Chicago. At first sight, the solution could be: The law governing road transport in the US (that may even differ from state to state) plus possibly the applicable conditions for US – road transport might be applied. §452a HGB states: "*The liability of the contractual carrier shall be determined in accordance with the legal provisions governing a contract for the carriage of goods on this transport leg.*"

How do you identify the law that is applicable on "*this transport leg*", as the law puts it? Applying the established conflict of laws principles, the parties' choice will define such law. However, there never is a choice of the parties of a multimodal transport for the law to be applied on a single (unimodal) leg of such transport. This was actually anticipated when the law was created. In the so called "Motives" of the German Transport Law[11], one can find further advice as to how the law should be interpreted and/or what the idea behind it was. The explanation says, a multimodal transport requires "different means of transport" and "different transport laws to be applied on hypothetically concluded transport contracts for the single transport legs".

It is the phrase "hypothetically" which gives much room for speculation. Initially, one may – as indicated above – look at the transport contract which is actually in place for the "transport leg" under discussion: That is the contract of carriage between the multimodal freight forwarder and his subcontractor (to keep our example as simple as possible here). This contract will be under the laws and conditions of such local carrier.

However, this is a "real" contract, not a hypothetic one. This was the main argument to say, what one needed to look at, was a contract between the parties of the multimodal transport – not for the complete enterprise, but this time only for the individual contract.[12]

The German doctrine decided that such law would have to be applied which the parties of the multimodal contract would have chosen if only they had chosen. The doctrine calls this the "hypothetical choice". As both parties of the multimodal contract (as long as export business from Germany) would be German under German Law, the solution was easy. Surprise, surprise: A German road haulier and his German shipper, concluding a road transport anywhere in the world, will always love to act under German Law. Under such perspective, any "transport legs" of any multimodal transport must be governed by German Law. This could be German Maritime Law, "ordinary" German Transport Law or, of course, one of the unimodal conventions – if applicable.

In the end, therefore, a road transport in the US as a part of a multimodal transport under German Law will – according to the German Federal Court of Justice – fall under German Law. This is – in the end – in the first place easy for the one who needs to apply the law. That will be the court.

The shortcomings of this solution are obvious. The freight forwarder, who is just responsible to organize the multimodal transport but who will not have any influence on the carriage itself, will still be liable under German Law as a carrier. In return, he can try to recover any damages he was held liable for from the actual carriers. In most of all cases, he will fail to do so because local carriers under local law frequently act under far reaching exclusions of liability. And it may be doubted whether both parties of a hypothetical contract would actually both be willing to agree on German Law to be applied on a transport from – say – Boston to Chicago. For the freight forwarder, this does actually not make much sense.

E. CONCLUSION

To summarize, this is why the second application of the principles of conflict of laws will not cause that much trouble: As of today, all ways are not leading to Rome, but to German Law.

In addition, please keep in mind: The basic decision of German Law is, that all multimodal transports shall fall under ordinary German Transport Law, that is §§407 – 449 HGB. This is clearly stated in §452, 2 HGB. One may only deviate, if there is a loss, damage or delay and it is known on which part ("transport leg") of the multimodal transport this occurred. In fact, at least when dealing with multimodal transports including a carriage by sea, this solution seems to be a bit less than perfect.[13]

LITERATURE

Bahnsen, Art. 2 CMR und die UND ADRIYATIK, TranspR 2012, p. 400 et seq.

Bartels, Das Teilstreckenrecht beim Multimodal-Vertrag, TranspR 2005, p. 203 et seq.

Basedow, Internationale multimodale Gütertransporte, in "Seehandelsrecht und Seerecht", Festschrift für Rolf Herber, Hamburg 1999, p. 15 et seq.

Drews, Zum anwendbaren Recht beim multimodalen Frachttransport, TranspR 2003, p. 12 et seq.

Drews, Warenumschlag im Seehafen als Teilstrecke, TranspR 2004, p. 450 et seq.

Drews, Der multimodale Transport im historischen Zusammenhang, TranspR 2006, p. 177 et seq.

Drews, Zum Umschlag von Waren in einem Seehafen, TranspR 2008, p. 18 et seq.

Drews, Der multimodale Transport – eine Bestandsaufnahme, TranspR 2010, p. 327 et seq.

Drews, Der Umschlag von Waren unter dem neuen Seehandelsrecht, TranspR 2013, p. 253 et seq.

Drews, Seehandelsrecht (2018), 4th Edition

Erbe/Schlienger, Der Multimodal-Vertrag im schweizerischen Recht, TranspR 2005, p. 421 et seq.

Freise, Unimodale transportrechtliche Übereinkommen und multimodale Beförderungen, TranspR 2012, p. 1 et seq.

Freise, Das internationale Eisenbahnfrachtrecht als Einheitsrecht für bestimmte Multimodalverkehre, TranspR 2013, p. 426 et seq.

Haak/Hoeks, Conflicting Conventions: The UNCITRAL/CMI draft instrument and the CMR on the subject of intermodal contracts, TranspR 2005, p. 89 et seq.

Hartenstein, Die Bestimmung des Teilstreckenrechts im Multimodaltransport, TranspR 2005, p. 9 et seq.

Herber, Zur Berücksichtigung des Teilstreckenrechts bei multimodalem Transportvertrag in: Festschrift für Henning Piper, p. 877 et seq.

Herber, Probleme des Multimodaltransports mit Seestreckeneinschluß nach neuem deutschem Recht, TranspR 2001, p. 102

Herber, Nochmals: Multimodalvertrag, Güterumschlag und anwendbares Recht, TranspR 2005, p. 59 et seq.

Jayme/ Nordmeier, Multimodaler Transport: Zur Anknüpfung an den hypothetischen Teilstreckenvertrag im Internationalen Transportrecht – Ist §452a HGB Kollisions- oder Sachnorm?, IPRax 2008, p. 503 et seq.

Kirchhof, Der Luftfrachtvertrag als multimodaler Vertrag im Rahmen des Montrealer Übereinkommens, TranspR 2007, p. 133 et seq.

Koller, Die Haftung des Multimodalbeförderers beim bekannten Schadenort, VersR 2000, p. 1187 et seq.

Koller, Beweislastverteilung beim multimodalen Luftbeförderungsvertrag, TranspR 2013, p. 14 et seq.

Koller, Transportrecht (2016), 9th Edition

Koller, Der Umschlag beim CMR Transport, RdTW 2013, p. 417 et seq.

Looks, Der multimodale Transportvertrag nach dem TRG, TranspR 1999, p. 31 et seq.

Mankowski, Neues aus Europa zum Internationalen Privatrecht für Transportverträge: Art. 5 ROM I-VO, TranspR 2008, p. 339 et seq.

Münchener Kommentar zum HGB (2014), 3rd Edition (quoted: MüKo HGB, *reviser*)

Müller-Rostin, Multimodalverkehr und Luftrecht, TranspR 2012, p. 14 et seq.

Paschke/Ramming, Reform des deutschen Seehandelsrechts, RdTW 2013, p. 1 et seq.

Rabe/Bahnsen (eds.), Seehandelsrecht (2018), 5th Edition

Rabe, Auswirkungen des neuen Frachtrechts auf das Seefrachtrecht, TranspR 1998, p. 429 et seq.

Rabe, Die Probleme bei einer multimodalen Beförderung unter Einschluss einer Seestrecke, TranspR 2000, p. 189 et seq.

Rabe, Das Mafi-Trailer Urteil des BGH – Ein Fazit, TranspR 2008, p. 186 et seq.

Rabe, Multimodalvertrag mit See- und anschließender Landstrecke – ein Sonderfall?, TranspR 2017, p. 349 et seq.

Ramming, Zur Abdingbarkeit des Höchstbetrages der Haftung des Frachtführers nach neuem Frachtrecht – unter besonderer Berücksichtigung multimodaler Beförderungen, die eine Seeteilstrecke umfassen, VersR 1999, p. 1177 et seq.

Ramming, Probleme der Rechtsanwendung im neuen Recht der multimodalen Beförderung, TranspR 1999, p. 326 et seq.
Ramming, Durchbrechung der Einheitslösung (§452 Satz 1 HGB) im Hinblick auf besondere Durchführungsvorschriften des Rechts der (See-) Teilstrecke, TranspR 2004, p. 201 et seq.
Ramming, Zur Reichweite der Verweisung nach §452a HGB im Hinblick auf die Erstattung der Fracht, TranspR 2004, pp. 336, 337
Ramming, Teilstrecken einer multimodalen Beförderung und ihre Abgrenzung, TranspR 2007, p. 89 et seq.
Ramming, Internationalprivatrechtliche Fragen des Multimodal-Frachtvertrages und des Multimodal-Ladescheines, TranspR 2007, p. 279 et seq.
Ramming, Hamburger Handbuch Multimodaler Transport (2011)
Reithmann/Martiny/Mankowski, Internationales Vertragsrecht (2004), 6th Edition
Spanjaart, GODAVOSS, the applicability of the CMR within multimodal contracts of carriage, TranspR 2012, p. 278 et seq.
Thume, Haftung für Umschlagschäden – wer haftet wem und wie?, TranspR 2014, p. 179 et seq.

NOTES

1 There are some special sections in some conventions dealing with multimodal transport to a limited extend, as for example Art. 2 CMR, Art. 1, §§3, 4 CIM, Art. 18, IV, 1, 2, 3 Montreal Convention, but there is no convention in force for multimodal transport as such.

2 This footnote refers to two decisions, which will be discussed to some extend within short: Higher Regional Court Hamburg (OLG), Judgment of 19.08.2004 (6 U 178/03), cf. TranspR 2004, p. 402 – 404 and Federal Court of Justice (BGH), Judgment of 18.10.2007 (I ZR 138/04), cf. TranspR 2007, p. 473 – 475.

3 Cf. Drews, Der multimodale Transport im historischen Zusammenhang, TranspR 2006, p. 177 et seq.

4 Or let me say: The customer of the carrier.

5 Is there any reason to define this as a "special type of (mixed) contract", as *Koller* does, cf. Koller, Transportrecht (2016), §452 HGB, no. 1, when it is obviously a freight forwarding contract?.

6 Koller, Transportrecht (2016), §452 HGB, no. 1a.

7 In addition to what will be explained: The court of first instance in Hamburg (Landgericht) had decided, that terminal operations should fall under Maritime Law as previously. The court of appeals, the Higher Regional Court (Oberlandesgericht) – which has a high reputation within Germany for expertise in maritime cases as these are frequently located in Hamburg – however overruled that decision. Therefore, revision was brought to the BGH. For the decisions, please be referred to footnote 2.

[8] Cf. Koller, Transportrecht (2016), §452 HGB, no. 15c – 15e; Müko HGB, *Herber*, §452a HGB, no. 30 – 33b.

[9] Cf. Rabe, TranspR 2017, p. 351; Drews, TranspR 2010, p. 329 in particular for the dissection of port handling operations.

[10] Koller, Transportrecht (2016), §452a HGB, no. 8.

[11] BT-Drucksache 13/8445, page 99, left column; the motives of (any) new law are usually delivered with it. They contain short explanations to every section describing the basic ideas behind the regulation and normally give valuable advice how to interpret such law.

[12] Koller, Transportrecht (2016), §452a HGB, no. 5, 6.

[13] Bahnsen, in: Rabe/Bahnsen (eds.), Seehandelsrecht (2018), §486 HGB, no. 6.

CHAPTER XIV

MARINE INSURANCE

Jens JAEGER*

A. INTRODUCTION

The term marine insurance is commonly used to describe a number of insurance types, dealing with the risks of transport. Subject matter is the insurance of the means of transport and the goods carried, against the perils of transport during the time of transportation. If agreed, this can include storage connected to transport before, during or after the voyage.[1] Marine insurance is subdivided in three main types: hull insurance, cargo insurance and carrier's liability insurance.[2]

Hull insurance refers to the protection against loss or damage to the structure and machinery of a vessel from perils such as collision or sinking of the ship, capsizing or stranding, fire, jettisoning (throwing overboard of property to save other property). This type of insurance is mainly purchased by owner or charterer of the vessel and generally covers physical damage incurred either in motion or while in port.

Cargo insurance caters specifically to the transportation of goods or merchandise packed or in bulk and shipped either by sea, air or land. Separate subsectors exist, for example the travel luggage insurance or the so-called specie insurance, which covers the risks of transported valuables of commercial (securities, cash, checks, coin or barley transported precious metals) and private (jewellery and furs) nature. Special insurances such as film insurance, exhibition insurance and fine art insurance are sometimes (e.g. in Germany) also related to marine insurance.

Carrier's liability insurance protects the policyholders against possible claims they may face in respect of unintentional damage suffered by third parties. Due to the severity of the insured individual risk, the liability insurance in the field of maritime business has created a specialized form of mutual cover provided by mutual insurance clubs (protection and indemnity insurance, P&I Insurance). Key marine liability insurance product in Germany is cover for liability exposures of freight forwarders (freight forwarders liability insurance).

Subject to this article are the cargo insurance and the freight forwarders liability insurance and their meaning in cross-border transactions.

B. HISTORICAL BACKGROUND

The origins of marine insurance go back far in time. The first documented cargo policy originates in Genoa and dates back to the 18th of March 1343.[3] Marine insurance spread from Northern Italy to Flanders and reached England and Germany in the mid of the 16th century.[4]

The rapid industrialization of the nineteenth century, especially that of the Western and Central European countries, fundamentally changed the market situation of Marine insurers, which in the preceding centuries were largely settled on the coastal areas, and mostly individual insurers with only limited capital strength. The increase in goods exchange due to the growing economic importance of the overseas continents, the emergence of new national markets, the development of more efficient means of transport and the expansion of widely distributed transport and communications networks led to a considerable increase in the demand for insurance cover in the maritime transport sector. In addition, increasing competition and increasing competitive pressure in the late 19th century caused widespread disruption of marine insurance markets in Europe each providing their own rules and conditions. Several attempts to harmonise the basic issues of marine insurance law failed.[5] Therefore internationally unified rules do not exist until today.

C. ECONOMIC RELEVANCE

Worldwide marine insurance premiums are estimated to approximately USD 30 billion in 2016. This is equivalent to around 2% of global non-life premiums. Even though this percentage appears to be low, marine insurance plays a crucial role in the global economy as international trade is inseparably linked to transport insurance.[6]

Transport is the essential link between supplier and receiver, and the aim is to receive the goods in good condition, when and where they are needed. This necessitates close collaboration between the seller, the buyer and the carrier. The journey involved, whether overland, sea and/or air, may introduce certain costs and risks that can be mitigated by appropriate different methods, including insurance coverage.

Individual traders are unlikely to operate without insurance, given the high value of cargo and the various risks during transport. Instead, it would be necessary for them to retain large sums of money on their own, to cover possible losses in the future. This would tie down a high amount of capital, without a current benefit.

In addition, commercial credits are often only granted with sufficient insurance cover. Credit institutes are neither willing nor able to bear the risks of transport.[7] By protecting against damage, marine insurers make the future more predictable for traders and increase their economic stability. In this sense, the marine insurance industry acts as an important factor of production in an economy or rather as "business enabler"[8].

With globalization, global trade volume is steadily growing. To meet the growing demand for transport, haulage companies adapt their transport capacities and handling speed to the new developments. For insurance companies, this means two things: on the one hand, the share of marine insurance in their portfolio is growing; on the other hand, they expose themselves to new accumulation risks as a result of the greater value concentration. In this context cumulative risks mean that a single incident triggers an avalanche of claims on insurance companies. The payment entitlements cumulate.

If, for example, the increasing transport capacities and the denser shipping traffic lead to a collision between two container ships, marine insurers must pay not only for the loss of the goods and the ships, but also, if necessary, for environmental damage and business interruptions. Especially in the case of goods in transit, the cumulative potential is considered unpredictable, as goods are subject to constant changes during transport (e.g. due to weather conditions). In fact, however, mobile risks are linked to part of the transportation to storage facilities or ports, which means that the cumulative risk can be approximately determined and an assessment of the cumulative potential for transport insurance is possible. As a result, marine insurers ensure that damage to the cargo is covered even in the event of a disaster through increased risk sensitivity and innovative risk models, thus creating a stable framework for global trade.

In some areas carrier's liability insurance is even mandatory. The International Convention on Civil Liability for Oil Pollution Damage, the International Convention on Liability for Bunker Oil Pollution Damage and the Nairobi International Convention on the Removal of Wrecks obligate shipowners to insure against the liability under the named conventions.

D. LEGAL BASIS

The *lex mercatoria* (from the Latin for "merchant law"), often referred to as "the Law Merchant" in English, is the body of commercial law used by merchants throughout Europe during the medieval period taking into account the peculiarities of the subject area and largely outside of state legislative mechanisms. Since the 20s of the 20th century the commercial law has to a large extent constituted autonomous transnational economic law. In this regard, it is considered that international trade by the repeated use of general terms and conditions (eg Institute Clauses of the Institute of London Underwriters (IUA), German General Rules of Marine Insurance), international contract patterns (standard policies such as Lloyd's SG (Ship and Goods) Policy; Lloyds Open Form/LOF) as well as rules of the International Chamber of Commerce in Paris (INCOTERMS) created his own right, a nova lex mercatoria. However, due to the lack of internationally unified rules for marine insurance, the laws that govern this topic are only applicable on the national level.

In Germany as well as in England, Marine insurance is traditionally characterized by general conditions of insurance. The 1919 German General Rules of Marine Insurance (ADS 1919) were created through the cooperation between ship owners, export merchants, insurers, underwriting agents, brokers and the chambers of commerce of Hamburg and Bremen.[9] Since 01.07.1999 the German Insurance Association (GDV) published revised standard conditions for cargo insurance (DTV Cargo 2000) which also summarize the ADS 1919 as well as the ADS Cargo 1973/1984/1994. The essential provisions may be summarized as follows:

- DTV Cargo Insurance Conditions – All Risks 2000/2011
- DTV Cargo Insurance Conditions – Limited Cover 2000/2011
- DTV Cargo Insurance Conditions – Open Policy 2000/2011

Those standard conditions are allowed to deviate from the provisions of the insurance contract law (Versicherungsvertragsgesetz/VVG) as Cargo insurance is classified as a major risk pursuant to §210 (2) no. 1 VVG and Annex 1 no. 7 to the German Insurance Supervision Act. In addition open policies are very common[10] which leads to contractual freedom as well. However, due to that they are regarded as general terms and conditions, they need to meet the requirements set out in §§305 ff. of the German Civil Code (Bürgerliches Gesetzbuch/BGB).[11]

In England marine insurance is governed by the Marine Insurance Act 1906 (MIA1906), but in practise the Institute Cargo Clauses (ICC) of the In-

ternational Underwriting Association (IUA) are commonly used. Three kinds of cover are provided:
- Institute Cargo Clauses (A) – All Risks
- Institute Cargo Clauses (B) – Named Perils
- Institute Cargo Clauses (C) – Named Perils

The clauses are currently available in the edition of 2009.

Freight forwarders liability insurance in contrast has its origin significantly later at the beginning of the 19th century.[12] The operation of e.g. railways was considered highly dangerous; hence the related liability was strict.[13] As a result, the demand for insurance products became present.[14] The German Forwarders' Standard Terms and Conditions (ADSp) formerly obligated the forwarder to cover by liability insurance. Because of considerable losses, this arrangement was abolished in the ADSp of 2002.[15] Simultaneous the GDV started its work on general conditions for freight forwarders liability insurance. As an outcome the DTV Carrier's Liability Conditions for carriers, forwarders and stockist – Open Policy were published in 2003 and are currently available in the edition of 2011. The current edition of the ADSp of 2017 again contains the forwarders duty to cover by liability insurance.

E. CARGO INSURANCE

Since the DTV-Cargo 2000 are applicable for all kinds of transport including associated storage, the ICC are created for carriage by see in the first place but applicable for land transportation as well; carriage by air is subject to the Institute Cargo Clauses (Air) (ICC Air).

I. INSURABLE INTEREST

The principle of insurable interest is fundamental to all insurance contracts. The idea of insurance is to provide protection, not to offer possible benefits. Any type of insurance therefore requires an insurable interest.[16] It is not the object that is covered by insurance but the interest, a person has concerning the object, due to their relationship.

The subject matter of the cargo insurance can be any monetary interest a person has in seeing that the goods survive the perils of transport and associated storage, no. 1.1.1. DTV Cargo 2000. The ICC are less specific but require an insurable interest in the subject matter insured as well, no. 11.1.

According to section 5 (2) MIA 1906 a legal or equitable relation need to be established. In many cases the owner's interest will be affected, if the goods are damaged or get lost during transport.[17] Though, the economic risk may also concern the purchaser of the goods, if the risk has already been transferred.[18] It highly depends on the terms agreed upon in the sales contract, whose interests are affected. In practise, INCOTERMS[19] are used to shift risks and responsibilities relating to transport. The INCOTERM Cost Insurance and Freight (CIF) for example, transfers the risk of loss and damage from seller to buyer once the goods have passed the ship's rail at the port of shipment.

Thus, it is possible that more than one person has an insurable interest in the goods during the voyage. The insured can insure his own interest (insurance for own account) or another ones (insurance for third-party account), no. 1.1.4. DTV Cargo 2000. He does not even need to determine for whose account he concludes the insurance contract. It is then a contract "to whom it may concern", no. 13 DTV Cargo 2000.

Only legal interest may be insured.[20] Otherwise the insurance contract might be null and void for infringing a prohibition in law (§134 German Civil Code) or because of an offence against morality (§138 German Civil Code). In addition to the general rules of contract law, no. 1.2 DTV Cargo 2000 determines that notwithstanding other provisions of the insurance contract, cover shall be granted only insofar as and as long as not in contradiction to economic, trade or financial sanctions or embargoes enacted by the European Union or the Federal Republic of Germany that are directly applicable to the contracting parties. The same applies to economic, trade or financial sanctions or embargoes enacted by the United States of America with regard of the Islamic Republic of Iran, insofar as those are not in contradiction to European or German legislative provisions. Whether violations against foreign law, other than the ones set out in no. 1.2 DTV Cargo 2000, result in invalidity, depends on the particular case.[21] Section 3 and 41 of the Marine insurance Act 1906 stipulates that the adventure insured needs to be a lawful one and that is shall be carried out in a lawful manner as well. The question of illegality is to be answered by the national law.[22] The handling of embargoes is solved by an exclusion clause, like in the German conditions.[23]

Besides the interest in the goods, other insurable interests can be agreed upon. Those may include anticipated profit, increased value, duty, freight, taxes and charges as well as other costs, no. 1.1.3 DTV Cargo 2000.

II. SCOPE OF COVER

The German general conditions for cargo insurance distinguish between two kinds of cover, all risks cover and limited cover. In the English market, the ICC provide three different kinds of cover, Institute Cargo Clauses (A) which cover all risks as well as Institute Cargo Clauses (B) and (C), each with a limited cover.

The main difference between all risks and limited cover, both in the German and the English conditions, is the variation in the scope of cover provided. Therefore, the further explanations include both for the respective conditions, unless emphasised otherwise.

1. ALL RISKS COVER

According to DTV Cargo Insurance Conditions – All Risks 2000/2011 no. 2.1, the insurer covers all risks to which the goods are subject for the duration of the insurance. He makes good loss of or damage to the insured goods arising from an insured peril, irrespective of percentage. This means in general that any peril is insured, unless cover is explicitly not provided.[24] The principle of universality and totality of the cover is neither affected by the expression "perils of transport and associated storage" in no. 1.1.1 DVT Cargo 2000/2011.[25] All risks are included, even commercial ones.[26] The term peril, in the first instance, means the opportunity that damage may arise.[27] It is rather the cause of damage.[28] Those may be accidents involving the means of transport, fire, storm, warfare, civil war or nuclear energy.[29]

According to no. 2.1 DTV Cargo 2000, only loss of or damage to the insured goods arising from an insured peril, are covered. Other damages are not included. The all risks cover does not mean that all damages arising from an insured peril are covered as well.[30]

The Institute Cargo Clauses (A) likewise provide an all risks cover. Pursuant to no. 1 ICC the insurance covers all risks of loss of or damage to the subject-matter insured except as provided in clauses 4, 5, 6 and 7. Other damages than loss of or damage to the insured object are not covered.[31]

2. LIMITED COVER

Contrary to the all risks insurance, only the listed risks are insured by the limited cover. The insurer makes good the damage, just in case the loss of or damage to the goods arises because of one of the named events. According to no. 2.1 DTV Cargo Insurance Conditions – Limited Cover 2000/ 2011, those may be:

- an accident involving the means of transport carrying the goods (including the ship or vessel carrying the goods strands, strikes ground or runs aground, capsizes, sinks, founders, or is damaged by ice);
- collapse of warehouse buildings;
- fire, lightning, explosion, earthquakes, sea-quakes, volcanic eruptions and other natural disasters; strike or crashing of a flying object or parts thereof including its cargo;
- jettison, washing overboard or otherwise being lost overboard as a result of heavy weather;
- general average sacrifice;
- discharging, interim storage and loading of goods at a port or airport of distress entered as a result of an insured event or following an emergency landing;
- total loss of entire packages during loading on-to or unloading from a means of transport, or during transhipment to or from a means of transport.

The ICC (C) only cover loss of or damage to the subject-matter insured in the event of

- fire or explosion;
- vessel or craft being stranded grounded sunk or capsized;
- overturning or derailment of land conveyance;
- collision or contact of vessel craft or conveyance with any external object other than water;
- discharge of cargo at a port of distress;
- general average sacrifice;
- and jettison.

Apart from that the ICC (B) additionally cover

- earthquake volcanic eruption or lightning;
- entry of sea lake or river water into vessel craft hold conveyance container or place of storage;
- and total loss of any package lost overboard or dropped whilst loading on to, or unloading from, vessel or craft.

3. Insured expenses and costs

In addition to the cover of damages due to loss of or damage to the goods, the insurer indemnifies several other expenses and costs, listed in no. 2.3 DTV Cargo 2000 and no. 2, 3 ICC.

The cover of general average contributions is of particular importance. General average is considered to be any extraordinary sacrifice or expenditure that is intentionally and reasonably made or incurred for the common safety for the purpose of preserving from peril the property involved in a common maritime adventure. This definition goes back to rule A of the York-Antwerp-Rules 1994 (YAR) which is the most prominent international legal framework for the rights and obligations of ship and cargo owners in case of general average.[32] These rules apply by agreement e.g. in contracts of carriage or charter parties. In principle the YAR determine that all parties involved in a sea venture must proportionately share any losses or damages that result from sacrifices made to save ship or cargo. First of all, general average requires that the danger is common to ship and cargo.[33] The sacrifice has to be made intentionally and with the purpose to save ship and cargo.[34] Sacrifices may be jettison of cargo to get a stranded vessel free or actions to deliberately strand the vessel to prevent sinking.[35] The contributions scope is then defined by a general average adjuster in accordance with the procedure laid down for that purpose.

In the end the principle of general average, to share all losses proportionately, means, that those who have not suffered damage, e.g. because their cargo was not jettisoned, may have to contribute; hence the interested party should cover by insurance. Consequently cargo insurance is a liability insurance regarding the cover of general average contributions.[36] The DTV Cargo 2000 indemnify the insured person from general average contributions based on an adjustment drawn up in accordance with the law, the YAR, the IVR or any other internationally recognised rules, provided that the measure was intended to avert an insured loss/damage, no. 2.3.1.1. This means that not every contribution is covered but those which arise in respect of general average that has its cause in an insured risk. No. 2 ICC covers general average and salvage charges, adjusted or determined according to the contract of carriage and/or the governing law and practise. The charges must be incurred to avoid or in connection with the avoidance of loss from any cause except those excluded.

Another important aspect is the cover of compensation and expenses arising from the "Both to Blame Collision Clause" (no. 2.3.1.1 DTV Cargo 2000, no. 3 ICC). The "Both to Blame Collision Clause" is part of most charter parties and bills of lading and has its origin in US law.[37] Under US law the owners of ships colliding due to negligence of both, are liable as joint debtors for loss of or damage to the goods carried.[38] Therefore it is possible that one ship has to pay 100% of the damage first and later takes recourse to the second ship to pay its part. In this constellation the second ship is not necessarily liable for the damage to the cargo it carried. Hence, the "Both to Blame Collision Clause" determines that in these cases the injured cargo party has to indemnify the owner from the recourse of the first ship. Cargo insurance, in turn, indemnifies the injured cargo party from this obligation and additionally covers expenses related to legal protection.

Moreover, cargo insurance covers, under certain conditions, expenses for averting, minimizing and ascertaining the scale or extent of damage (no. 3.3.1.2 DTV Cargo 2000, no. 16 ICC). The same applies to costs that properly and reasonably incurred in transshipping, temporarily storing and forwarding the goods after an insured event or an insured accident involving the means of transport has occurred (no. 2.3.1.3 DTV Cargo 2000, no. 12 ICC).

4. Perils not covered

Cargo insurance all risks cover and limited cover, both list some perils not included. According to no. 2.4.1 DTV Cargo 2000 cover is not provided for the following perils:

- war, civil war or similar hostilities as well as perils which – whether war be declared or not – arise out of the hostile use of weapons of war and from the existence of derelict weapons of war as a result of one of these perils;
- strikes, lock-outs, industrial unrest, acts of violence by terrorist or political groups – regardless of the number of people involved – riots and other civil commotions;
- confiscation, deprivation of possession or other acts of authorities;
- the use of chemical, biological, biochemical substances or electromagnetic waves as weapons which constitute a public danger (so called "dirty bombs"[39]), irrespective of other contributory causes;
- nuclear energy or other ionising radiation;
- insolvency or financial default of the ship owner, charterer or operator, or in respect of any other financial dispute involving the above parties.

The reason why cargo insurance does not provide cover for the risk of war is closely linked to the basic principles of insurance. The insurer must always be able to predict and calculate the risks he accepts; otherwise the functioning of insurance would be threatened. To calculate the risk of war is simply not possible.[40] However, no. 2.4.2 DTV Cargo 2000 offers the opportunity to agree upon additional insurance terms and refers to the respective DTV clauses. Those clauses may be agreed upon in addition to the main insurance contract. In this manner it is possible to get cover for risks excluded from cargo insurance in general. The risk of war may be covered by the DTV War Clause. Cover is only provided for marine transport and carriage by air, whereas land carriage is excluded with the exemption of postal sendings and courier services. The risks are regarded calculable just in these limited cases.[41] Besides, the insurer is authorized to cancel the insurance contract at any time, provided written notice is given two days prior to the commencement of the insured transport. This enables the insurer to rapidly react to new developments in war. For the same reasons the risk of derelict weapons of war is not covered by cargo insurance in general, but may be insured by the DTV Derelict Weapons of War Clause.

The risk of strike is not covered for the said reasons as well.[42] It is possible to cover by the DTV Strikes, Riots and Civil Commotions Clause. It authorizes the insurer to cancel the contract at any time, provided written notice is given two days prior to the attachment of the insurance. Thus, he is able to react in case the risk gets incalculable.

The DTV Confiscation Clause faces the problem of incalculable risks of confiscation by setting out obligations for the insured. Those relate to typical reasons for confiscation and attempt to avoid these. If the insured breaches one of the obligations, the insurer will not be obliged to indemnify.

In contrast to the previous risks, the risk of dirty bombs is considered to be absolutely uninsurable. Therefore it is not possible to cover by an additional insurance clause. Moreover the DTV War Clause and the DTV Derelict Weapons of War Clause explicitly state that cover is not provided.

Nuclear energy is mainly regarded as an incalculable risk because of the accident at the nuclear reactor of Chernobyl.[43] This view probably strengthened after the incident of Fukushima. Supplementary cover is available under the DTV Radioactive Isotopes Clause just for damages by radioactive isotopes as far as such isotopes are being prepared, transported, stored or used for commercial, agricultural, medical, scientific or other similar peaceful purposes.

The reason behind the exclusion of insolvency or financial default of the ship owner, charterer or operator is rather simple. In the insurers view these risks were not included under the all risks cover, until the BGH decided differently.[44] From then on, cargo insurance conditions explicitly excluded the risks. It has to be noted that the insured can prove that he exercised the diligence of a prudent businessman in choosing the ship owner, charterer, operator or the responsible forwarding agent and would not lose cover. If the insured or assured is the buyer and, under the terms of the sales contract, had no control over the choice of persons involved in the transport of the goods, cover is neither excluded.

Pursuant to no. 4, 5, 6 and 7 ICC, the insurance does not cover loss, damage or expense attributable to/ caused by/ or arising from

- willful misconduct of the assured;
- ordinary leakage, ordinary loss in weight or volume, or ordinary wear and tear of the subject-matter insured;
- insufficiency or unsuitability of packing or preparation of the subject-matter insured
- inherent vice or nature of the subject-matter insured,
- delay, even though the delay be caused by a risk insured against;
- insolvency or financial default of the owners managers charterers or operators of the vessel,
- deliberate damage to or deliberate destruction of the subject-matter insured or any part thereof by the wrongful act of any person or persons (ICC (B), ICC (C));
- the use of any weapon of war employing atomic or nuclear fission and/or fusion or other like reaction or radioactive force or matter,
- unseaworthiness of vessel or craft, unfitness of vessel craft conveyance container or liftvan for the safe carriage of the subject-matter insured, where the assured or their servants are privy to such unseaworthiness or unfitness, at the time the subject-matter insured is loaded therein;
- war, civil war, revolution, rebellion, insurrection or civil strife arising therefrom, or any hostile act by or against a belligerent power;
- capture, seizure, arrest, restraint or detainment (piracy excepted) and the consequences thereof or any attempt thereat;
- derelict mines, torpedoes, bombs or other derelict weapons of war;
- strikers, locked-out workmen, or persons taking part in labour disturbances, riots or civil commotions;
- any terrorist or any person acting from a political motive.

The risks of war and strike may be covered by an additional Agreement on the Institute War Clauses and/or the Institute Strike Clauses. The ICC use different terms to express the connection between risk and loss. In particular the expressions "caused by", "arising from", "resulting from", "attributable to" and "reasonably attributable to" are used. The first three phrases require the risk to be the proximate cause, whereas it sufficient for the last two, that it is just a cause.[45]

5. EXCLUSION OF LOSSES AND DAMAGES

Cover is not provided for all possible losses of or damages to the goods. According to no. 2.5 DTV Cargo 2000 the insurer is not liable for losses and damages arising from:

- a delay in the transport;
- inherent vice or the nature of the goods;
- customary differences or losses in number, weight or measure of the goods, unless a deductible has been agreed;
- ordinary humidity or fluctuations in temperature;
- inappropriate and inadequate packaging or incorrect stowage insofar as the insured acted wilfully or with gross negligence;
- indirect loss or damage in whatever form.

Damage arising from delay in transport and indirect loss or damage is not necessary cargo damage but which is subject matter to cargo insurance.[46] Therefore, consequential damage or pure financial losses are excluded. Both may be insured by the DTV Pure Financial Losses Clause and the DTV Consequential Losses Clause.

The ICC do not distinguish between the exclusion of risks and losses/damages. Both are laid down in the General Exclusion Clause, no. 4 ICC.

III. DURATION OF THE INSURANCE

Both, the German and the English policy, provide cover from warehouse to warehouse.

Under the terms of the former edition of the ICC, cover is provided from the time the goods leave the warehouse or place of storage at the place named herein for the commencement of the transit. The ICC in the edition of 2009 refer to the time the subject-matter insured is first moved in the warehouse or at the place of storage (at the place named in the contract of insurance) for the purpose of the immediate loading into or onto the carrying vehicle or other conveyance for the commencement of transit which is more precise. The DTV- Cargo 2000/2011 cover alike commences in the moment the goods are removed from the place of storage for immediate transport. Transport needs to begin immediately which means that e.g. in-house operations are not included.[47] The place of dispatch does not refer to the geographical place but may be production sites, packaging areas and points of delivery, storage warehouses or consignment stocks.[48] With regard to the buyer's cargo insurance, the time the risk passes to the buyer is relevant for the insurance's beginning.[49] Under the Incoterm FOB e.g. the insurance commences when the goods have passed the ship's rail at the named port of shipment.

Depending on which occurs first, the cover terminates in the events listed in no. 8.2 DTV Cargo 2000 and no. 8.1.1–8.1.4 ICC. As a matter of course, the insurance ends in the moment the goods arrive at the place of final delivery named in the contract of insurance.

In case the goods are forwarded after discharge at the port of destination to a place of delivery not named in the policy, the insurance only terminates if this change aggravates the risk. Usually the modification of the place of delivery rearranges transport to such an extent, that cover is not provided any longer.[50] The DTV Cargo 2000 in contrast, require an increased risk, depending on the particular case. According to no. 8.2 ICC the insurance terminates in the moment the subject-matter insured is first moved for the purpose of the commencement of transit to such other destination.

Insurance may as well terminate on expiry of a period after the goods have been discharged from the means of transport at the place of destination. The precise number of days depends on the agreement and is to be filled in the gap provided for this purpose in the DTV Cargo 2000 as far as the German terms are concerned. The ICC establish a period of 60 days after completion of discharge. As far as the insured's own interest is involved, the German policy will not terminate at the end of the period agreed, if the delay of the insured voyage after discharge of the goods was caused by an insured peril and the insured reported the delay immediately. This is for instance the case of an accident involving the means of transport. In return, the insurer is due a reasonable additional premium that is to be agreed. For goods discharged of other means of transport than ocean-going vessels or airplanes, cover is not temporally limited. Though, delay is considered as an aggravation of risk so that the insured needs to inform the insurer who is subsequently due an additional premium, no. 5.2–5.5 DTV Cargo 2000 and no. 10 ICC. The ICC will not terminate in case delay is beyond the control of the assured, during any deviation, forced discharge, reshipment or transshipment and during any variation of the voyage arising from the exercise of a liberty granted to carriers under the contract of carriage, no. 8.3.

Apart from that, the insurance terminates when the goods are stowed on board of an ocean-going vessel if transported as per Incoterms FOB or CFR, no. 8.2.4 DVT Cargo 2000/2011. This is the time the buyer bears all risks either way. By the means of this clause, conflicts between buyer and seller about the time the risk transfers can be avoided.[51] If both covered by insurance admittedly double insurance may result.[52]

If the goods are sold due to an insured peril, the insurance ends when risk is passed, no. 8.2.5 DVT Cargo 2000/2011 and no. 9.1 ICC. Regarding the exact point of time, Incoterms can be relevant again, when agreed.

In case goods are temporarily stored by order of the insured, the insurance terminates upon expiry of the period agreed in no. 8.2.6, 9.1 DTV Cargo 2000 and no. 8.1.2 ICC.

IV. INSURANCE POLICY AND CERTIFICATE

The policy is often mentioned in the context of insurance. Often the term is not used to mention the insurance contract itself but the certificate documenting the contract, like e.g. in no. 11.1 DTV Cargo 2000 or section 22 MIA 1906. It has to give information about the contracting parties and the contract's content.[53]

The term policy is also used in connection with open cover (open policy) as opposed to individual cargo insurance. Open policy relates to the English Institute Cargo Clauses and was first established in the German insurance market by the means of the ADS 1973.[54] The former ADS and the DTV Cargo Insurance Conditions are designed for single transports in the first instance. In practise, open policy is quite common due to economic circumstances.[55]The open policy constitutes a framework for cargo insurance between insurer and insured. According to no. 1.1 DTV Cargo Insurance Conditions – Open Policy 2000/2011, the insurance covers all kinds of goods or all goods of the class designated in the policy which the insured is bound, in accordance with accepted commercial principles, to insure either for his own or for another's account.[56] The insured is obliged to declare any transport and storage named in the policy, either by means of individual declaration or summarised declaration (so-called turnover policy). Summarised declaration allows easier handling since the insured does not need to report every single transport.[57] He discloses his insured turnover in said transactions on a monthly, quarterly, half-yearly or yearly basis at the end of the respective period[58]

Open policy is not considered to be a policy in the sense of no. 11.1 DTV Cargo 2000 which has a certificate in mind. The insurer is rather obliged to issue certificates for single transports on demand of the insured, no. 6.2 DTV Cargo – Open Policy 2000/2011. These are equivalent to the policy mentioned in the DTV Clauses for single transports.

The policy in the meaning of no. 11.1 DTV Cargo 2000 has three main features. It serves as a documentary of proof (§371 BGB), as a promissory note (§925 BGB) and as a paper of identity. According to no. 11.2 DTV Cargo 2000, the payment to the holder of the policy discharges the insurer from further liability. In turn the insurer is entitled to request the policy's submission to make sure payment is authorised.

V. Burden of proof

The burden of proof lies with the assured as far as all risks cover is concerned.[59] The insurer may then establish that loss of or damage to the goods result from a peril not covered.[60] Under a named perils cover the insured has to proof that the damage was caused by an insured peril.[61] The onus of proof then shifts to the insurer to establish e.g. that an exclusion clause is applicable.[62]

F. Carrier's Liability Insurance

Carrier's liability insurance is considered liability insurance in legal terms.[63] The insurance indemnifies the insured against the risk of liability under a transport contract. Cover is only provided for liability under contracts of carriage via road, forwarding contracts and storage contracts if the insured is the carrier, forwarder or stockist. Carrier's liability under contracts of carriage by see, rail or air is not covered.[64] According to no. 1.4 DTV-CL 2003/2011 this includes transports performed by the forwarder as a carrier.

I. Insurable interest

Subject-matter of carrier's liability insurance is not the interest in the goods carried, but the interest not to bear the liability under the contract of transport.[65] Moreover the legitimate interest in the proceedings is part of the insurance, no. 4.1 DTV-CL 2003/2011. Only legal interests may be insured, otherwise cover will not be provided.[66]

II. Scope of cover

The insurance covers compensation of justified claims and protection against unjustified claims, no. 4.1 DTV-CL 2003/2011. Cover is only provided for liability for damages, e.g. for loss of or damage to the goods.[67] In addition the insurer indemnifies several other expenses and costs, listed in no. 4.2–4.5 DTV-CL 2003/2011. Those are basically reasonable costs of mitigation, general average contributions, additional transportation costs in case of misallocation arising to avoid damages covered by the insurance and statutory expenses arising out of salvage, destruction or disposal of damaged goods in case of damages the insurer is liable to pay compensation for.

The DTV CL 2003/2011 provide a flexible modular system of insurance. The scope of cover as well as the exclusions may be chosen corresponding to the individual needs of the carrier.

1. LIABILITY COVERED

No. 3 DTV-CL 2003/2011 lists the various bases of liability which may be covered. In practise, the whole list is incorporated into the contracts of insurance.[68] The Insurance indemnifies the insured from liability under:

- the German Commercial Code or the German Law of torts,
- terms and conditions of the insured, provided the insurer has agreed,
- the Convention on the Contract for the International Carriage of Goods by Road (CMR),
- the respective legal provisions of member states of the European Economic Area (EEA),
- the Convention concerning International Carriage by Rail (COTIF) and the Uniform Rules concerning the Contract of International Carriage of Goods by Rail (CIM),
- the Convention for the Unification of Certain Rules for International Carriage by Air (Montreal Convention),
- the Convention for the Unification of Certain Rules relating to International Carriage by Air (Warsaw Convention),
- the Hague Rules/ Hague-Visby Rules/ Hamburg Rules,
- the provisions of a FIATA Combined Bill of Lading (FBL) or Through Bill of Lading (TBL),
- a House Airway Bill (HAWB), a House Bill of Lading (House B/L) or other documents of the insured, provided the insurer has agreed,
- and the respective legal provisions of other states unless the insured cannot profitably claim that the previous provisions apply.

Even though carrier's liability under contracts of carriage by see, rail or air is not covered, the DTV-CL 2003/2011 refer to several liability conventions that deal with this topic. The reason behind is that, under German law, the liability of the forwarder under the forwarding contract may follow these rules.[69]

2. Exclusions

No. 6 DTV-CL 2003/2011 provides a list of typical exclusion clauses. Some were already discussed in the context of cargo insurance (e.g. natural disasters, war, strike, dirty bombs and nuclear energy, confiscation, deprivation of possession or other acts of authorities). Inter alia, carrier's liability insurance additionally exempts claims that are commonly subject to other kinds of insurance, like insurance for business, product, environment, water pollution, motor vehicle, personal liability or credit, no. 6.9 DTV-CL 2003/2011. Those risks shall not be subject to carrier's liability insurance, no matter whether they are in fact insured.[70] Claims that are already subject to other carrier's liability insurances are alike excluded, no. 6.10 DTV-CL 2003/2011. The exclusion underlines the difference between business liability insurance in general and carrier's liability insurance.[71] The latter only covers risk specifically linked to transport.[72]

Further exclusions refer to punitive damages, e.g. financial penalties and administrative fines, as well as related costs, no. 6.13, 6.17 DTV-CL 2003/2011. Besides, cover is not provided if the insured or his representative intentionally causes the insured event.

3. Business description

Further restrictions come along with the business description required by the insurer.[73] The insured needs to provide detailed information about business activities, possible bases of liability, crafts and counting. The business description constitutes the bases for risk assessment and the calculation of the insurance's premium.[74] As business activities might change quite rapidly, no. 1.3 DTV-CL 2003/2011 contains a precautionary insurance.[75] New activities not yet included in the business description are covered, provided activities and related risks are common to the transportation sector. The cover is then limited to the amount agreed on in the insurance contract.

III. Principle of "All-or-Nothing"

The DTV Carrier's Liability Conditions no. 7 sets out several obligations of the insured before and after the insured event occurred. First of all, the insured has to take care that the crafts and other tools used for transport are suitable for the respective purpose and in proper condition. This includes e.g. several measures for protection against theft. Moreover he has to carry out and document interface checks and carefully select and monitor his employees as well as subcontractors. Any changes concerning the carrier's liability need to be reported immediately. After the insured event has occurred, the insured is basically obliged to report the event of loss or damage immediately and to take action to prevent or to minimize the loss or damage. Legal proceedings need to be reported as well and if necessary the insured is obliged to entrust the insurer with the conduct of the case.

Any breach of obligation releases the insurer from his own obligation to pay, no. 7.3 DTV-CL 2003/2011. The principle of "All-or-Nothing" applies which means that the insurer has to pay the full amount of compensation for damages in case the insured acted only slightly negligent and is released completely in the event of gross negligence.[76] The provisions of the German Insurance Act in contrast, only release the insurer per rate depending on the insured's fault.

IV. DURATION OF THE INSURANCE

The term for carrier's liability insurance is usually about one year. It will frequently extend unless the contract is cancelled.[77] After the insured event occurred, both parties are entitled to terminate the contract extraordinarily under the rules of no. 13.2 DTV-CL 2003/2011. Contracts of transport that were concluded prior to the insurance contracts'cancellation stay covered.

G. CURRENT DEVELOPMENTS AND PERSPECTIVES

Although the commercial marine market currently faces unprecedented capacity, it is very unlikely that insurers release splendid new products to get a leg up on the competition. Marine insurance has been around for a long time, and has evolved and developed over that time. Within the main categories, hull, liability and cargo, there are upgrades to existing products, and there are ways and means of improving upon pricing. But new products are pretty rare.

That doesn't mean, however, commercial marine is immune to change. Like every insurance market, it will develop new products to respond to exposures as they arise. There are a number of emerging risks marine insurance will face in the near future.

Larger vessels. We are living in a world where economies of scale are very important. Container ships have grown bigger, better and faster over the last decade and are becoming more technically sophisticated. Today the world's largest container ships have a cargo carrying capacity of over 20,000 TEU (twenty foot equivalent unit). And it doesn't stop there. This is largely due to the creation of the shipping container itself, which allows transporting cargo to be more efficient and create cost savings. On the other hand, these large vessels bring a whole new set of exposures, like the wake damage they can create if they are maneuvered incorrectly. Furthermore, with the potential cargo on these larger vessels this presents a significant risk to marine insurers. Higher concentration of risk means that not only is a total loss considered but also the effects which a partial loss will have. For instance if there is an issue with a container, the ship will need to be unloaded. If only some ports able to accommodate these large vessels, questions arise such as where does it happen and how much will it cost.

Also fires on these vessels this size are an increasing concern. Finding, locating and containing a fire on a large vessel are extremely difficult. In remote locations and on the open sea, it can often be hours or even days after a fire has broken out before external assistance arrives. As a rule, only seagoing tugs carry the necessary equipment for effective fire fighting. Until they arrive, the crew has to rely on its own resources, and the fire can spread extensively. As a result, as with the *MSC Flaminia*, it can take weeks to bring the fire under control and, thus, result in a total loss of both, the vessel and the cargo.

Cyber. A big concern for more modern vessels is the use computerized equipment. The shipping industry has always factored risk into its daily business activities having sought to offset the risks posed by natural disasters, regulatory changes, and piracy and technology changes. So it is strange that it should now look the other way when faced with this new type of risk. Cyber-security may not be the first item on the agenda of ship owners and shipping companies, but as the risks mount, it can no longer avoid this problem.

People who want to do harm can hack into the systems and create havoc with the navigation and communication systems. Considering a large refrigeration vessel that carries fish, fruit or frozen products, a cyber attack could mess with the refrigeration systems, which are controlled by computers. The range of possible losses arising from a cyber incident is broad and can include damage to physical property, bodily injury and reputational damage –

as well as more obvious types of loss such as loss of data and business interruption.

Moreover, when ships eventually begin to follow the lead of driverless cars, cyber will become an even bigger concern. A possible shift in the future to unmanned vessels will create its own set of problems. Therefore, the increasing threats of cyber-security demands a new way of thinking by insurers and those calculating the risks, pricing models and potential coverage available to clients.

Risk accumulation. The problem of accumulation continues to receive far too little attention. Transport capacities by sea, land and air are increasing throughout the world and both port logistics and speed of transshipment is keeping pace with this development. Though marine risks are normally mobile, goods can easily remain in one place for a longer period of time. This results in higher value concentrations and consequently higher insured values. It is also considered that the risk of accumulation losses will increase due to climate change. As ambient temperatures rise all over the world, the increasing incidence of extreme weather events associated with climate change has become a global concern, posing challenges to logistics and shipping companies. Besides the loss of the cargo and pollution damage to the, environment, floating containers pose a threat to marine pleasure craft such as yachts and commercial vessels, and also increase the potential for passenger and third-party liability claims to marine insurers. The increased accumulation risk associated with climate change have given rise to a greater need for insurers to re-evaluate the risk associated with maritime shipping, and to invest in technology to detect the risk and develop the underwriting skills and knowledge to mitigate it.

LITERATURE

Abele, Erwin, DTV-Verkehrshaftungsversicherungs-Bedingungen für die laufende Versicherung für Frachtführer, Spediteure und Lagerhalter 2003/2011 (DTV-VHV laufende Versicherung 2003/2011), in: Baumann/Beckmann/Johannsen/Johannsen/Koch, Versicherungsvertragsgesetz, 9th Edition 2016, vol. 6 part 1, p. 237–339

Dunt, John, International Cargo Insurance, 2015

Ehlers, Henning C., AVB-Güterversicherung, in: Thume/Ehlers (eds.), Transportversicherungsrecht, 2nd Edition 2011, p. 169–339

Ehlers, Henning C., DTV-Güterversicherungsbedingungen 2000 (DTV-Güter 2000), 2nd Edition 2003

Ehlers, Henning C./Steinborn, Dominic/Wege, Christoph, Transportversicherung, in: van Bühren (ed.), Handbuch Versicherungsrecht, 6th Edition 2014, p. 2067–2154

Ehlers, Henning C., Transportversicherung – Güterversicherung – Versicherung politischer Gefahren, Transportrecht, TranspR 2006, vol 1, p. 7–15

Enge, Hans-Christoph/Schwampe, Dieter, Transportversicherung. Recht und Praxis, 4th Edition 2012

Goodacre, J. Kenneth, Marine Insurance Claims, 3rd Edition 1996

Hudson, N. Geoffrey/Madge, Tim/Sturges, Keith, Marine Insurance Clauses, 5th Edition 2012

Jaeger, Jens, Die Verkehrshaftungsversicherung, in: Hartenstein/Reuschle (eds.), Handbuch des Fachanwalts Transport- und Speditionsrecht, 3rd Edition 2015, p. 611–632

Kollatz, Peter, AVB-Verkehrshaftungs-Bedingungen, in: Thume/Ehlers (eds.), Transportversicherungsrecht, 2nd Edition 2011, p. 653–681

Koller, Ingo, DTV-Güterversicherungsbedingungen (DTV-Güter 2000/2011) -Volle Deckung-, in: Prölss/Martin (eds.), Versicherungsvertragsgesetz, 29th Edition 2015, p. 2663–2698

Riemer, Jens-Berghe, DTV-Güterversicherungsbedingungen 2000/2011 (DTV-Güter 2000/2011), in: Baumann/Beckmann/Johannsen/Johannsen/Koch, Versicherungsvertragsgesetz, 9th Edition 2016, vol. 6 part 1, p. 113–236

Rose, Francis, Marine Insurance. Law and Practice, 2nd Edition 2012

Steinborn, Dominic, Güterversicherung, in: Hartenstein/Reuschle (eds.), Handbuch des Fachanwalts Transport- und Speditionsrecht, 3rd Edition 2015, p. 585–609

Thume, Karl-Heinz, Einführung: Transportversicherung, in: Thume/Ehlers (eds.), Transportversicherungsrecht, 2nd Edition 2011, p. 6

Thume, Karl-Heinz, Rechtsgrundlagen der Transportversicherung, in: Thume/Ehlers (eds.), Transportversicherungsrecht, 2nd Edition 2011, p. 13–15

Thume, Karl-Heinz/de la Motte, Harald, Geschichte der Transportversicherungen, in: Thume/Ehlers (eds.), Transportversicherungsrecht, 2nd Edition 2011, p. 7–12

Thume, Karl-Heinz, Versicherungen des Transports – Einführung, Transportrecht – TranspR 2006, vol 1, p. 1–6

NOTES

* The author wants to thank *Carina Lutter* for her valuable support.

1 Enge/Schwampe (2012), p. 13.

2 Ehlers/Steinborn/Wege, in: van Bühren (2014), p. 2071, para. 2, 4; Thume, in: Thume/Ehlers (2011) p. 6, para. 22; Enge/Schwampe (2012), p. 15.

3 Dunt (2015), p. 1.

4 Enge/Schwampe (2012), p. 18.

[5] Attempts were made at the Buffalo Conference of the International Law Association of 1899, at the United Nations Conference on Trade and Development of 1964, within the European Union and through the work of the Comité Maritime International (CMI). For a detailed review see Dunt (2015), p. 6 et seq.

[6] Enge/Schwampe (2012), p. 18.

[7] Enge/Schwampe (2012), p. 19.

[8] Enge/Schwampe (2012), p. 18.

[9] Enge/Schwampe (2012), p. 47.

[10] Steinborn, in: Hartenstein/Reuschle (2015), p. 588, para. 12; Ehlers/Steinborn/Wege, in: van Bühren (2014), p. 2075, para. 22.

[11] Thume, in: Thume/Ehlers (2011) p. 15, para. 59; Steinborn, in: Hartenstein/Reuschle (2015), p. 591, para. 20; Enge/Schwampe (2012), p. 18 et seq.

[12] Thume/de la Motte, in: Thume/Ehlers (2011), p. 10, para. 43; Thume, TranspR 2006, p. 2.

[13] Thume/de la Motte, in: Thume/Ehlers (2011), p. 10, para. 43.

[14] Thume/de la Motte, in: Thume/Ehlers (2011), p. 10, para. 43.

[15] Jaeger, in: Hartenstein/Reuschle (2015), p. 612, para. 1; Kollatz, in: Thume/Ehlers (2011), p. 653, para 1.

[16] Riemer, in: Baumann et al. (2016), p. 130, para. 7; Steinborn, in: Hartenstein/Reuschle (2015), p. 591, para. 22; Ehlers (2003), p. 31, para. 2.

[17] Thume, TranspR 2006, p. 3.

[18] Rose (2012), p. 41; Ehlers/Steinborn/Wege, in: van Bühren (2014), p. 2079, para. 31; Ehlers (2003), p. 33, para. 6; Koller, in: Prölss/Martin (2015), p. 2663, para. 1.

[19] International Commercial Terms are pre-defined commercial terms published by the International Chamber of Commerce.

[20] Ehlers/Steinborn/Wege, in: van Bühren (2014), p. 2079 et seq, para. 32; Enge/Schwampe (2012), p. 52; Ehlers (2003), p. 34, para. 10; Thume, TranspR 2006, p. 5.

[21] Ehlers (2003), p. 34 et seq, para. 14.

[22] Dunt (2015), p. 57.

[23] Sanction Limitation an Exclusion Clause, Joint Cargo Committee JC 2010/014 of 11 August 2010.

[24] Ehlers, in: Thume/Ehlers (2011) p. 176, para. 35; Ehlers/Steinborn/Wege, in: van Bühren (2014), p. 2081, para. 39.

[25] Ehlers/Steinborn/Wege, in: van Bühren (2014), p. 2081, para. 39.; Ehlers (2003), p. 36, para. 2.

[26] Ehlers/Steinborn/Wege, in: van Bühren (2014), p. 2081, para. 39.; Ehlers, in: Thume/Ehlers (2011) p. 176, para. 35; Ehlers, TranspR 2006, p. 11.

[27] Riemer, in: Baumann et al. (2016), p. 137, para. 2; Ehlers (2003), p. 52, para. 18.; Ehlers, in: Thume/Ehlers (2011) p. 176, para. 36; Enge/Schwampe (2012), p. 59; Ehlers/Steinborn/Wege, in: van Bühren (2014), p. 2081, para. 40.

[28] Riemer, in: Baumann et al. (2016), p. 137, para. 2; Ehlers (2003), p. 52, para. 18; Ehlers/Steinborn/Wege, in: van Bühren (2014), p. 2081, para. 40; Ehlers, in: Thume/Ehlers (2011) p. 176, para. 36; Enge/Schwampe (2012), p. 59.

[29] Enge/Schwampe (2012), p. 59; Ehlers (2003), p. 52, para. 18; Riemer, in: Baumann et al. (2016), p. 137, para. 2; Ehlers, in: Thume/Ehlers (2011) p. 176, para. 36; Ehlers/Steinborn/Wege, in: van Bühren (2014), p. 2081, para. 40.

[30] Enge/Schwampe (2012), p. 59; Hudson/Madge/Sturges (2012), p. 13.

[31] Enge/Schwampe (2012), p. 153.

[32] The YAR are currently available in the edition of 2016. Further rules for general average exist in national law e.g. in §§588 ff. HGB. In respect of inland navigation the Rhine Rules (IVR) may apply.

[33] Ehlers (2003), p. 62, para. 51; Ehlers/Steinborn/Wege, in: van Bühren (2014), p. 2082, para. 45; Ehlers, in: Thume/Ehlers (2011) p. 180, para. 55.

[34] Ehlers (2003), p. 63 et seq, para. 55, 57; Ehlers/Steinborn/Wege, in: van Bühren (2014), p. 2082, para. 45; Ehlers, in: Thume/Ehlers (2011) p. 180, para. 58.

[35] Ehlers (2003), p. 63, para. 55.

[36] Ehlers (2003), p. 64, para. 58; Ehlers, in: Thume/Ehlers (2011) p. 181, para. 63; Ehlers, TranspR 2006, p. 12.

[37] Goodacre (1996), p. 311; Riemer, in: Baumann et al. (2016), p. 139, para. 14; Ehlers, in: Thume/Ehlers (2011) p. 181, para. 67.

[38] Ehlers, in: Thume/Ehlers (2011) p. 181, para. 67; Goodacre (1996), p. 311; Ehlers/Steinborn/Wege, in: van Bühren (2014), p. 2083, para. 49; Ehlers, TranspR 2006, p. 13.

[39] Ehlers/Steinborn/Wege, in: van Bühren (2014), p. 2088, para. 74.; Ehlers, in: Thume/Ehlers (2011) p. 193, para. 140.

[40] Ehlers (2003), p. 89, para. 148; Ehlers, in: Thume/Ehlers (2011) p. 188, para. 113.

[41] Ehlers (2003), p. 94, para. 165; Ehlers/Steinborn/Wege, in: van Bühren (2014), p. 2086, para. 62.

[42] Ehlers (2003), p. 95, para. 171.

[43] Ehlers, in: Thume/Ehlers (2011) p. 193, para. 140; Ehlers/Steinborn/Wege, in: van Bühren (2014), p. 2088, para. 75.

[44] Ehlers, in: Thume/Ehlers (2011) p. 193 f., para. 142 et seq.

[45] Dunt (2015), p. 65 et seq; Hudson/Madge/Sturges (2012), p. 19, 40.

[46] Riemer, in: Baumann et al. (2016), p. 150, para. 77; Ehlers (2003), p. 105, para. 212; Steinborn, in: Hartenstein/Reuschle (2015), p. 592 et seq, para. 25; Ehlers/Steinborn/Wege, in: van Bühren (2014), p. 2088, para. 78.

[47] Ehlers/Steinborn/Wege, in: van Bühren (2014), p. 2093, para. 98; Dunt (2015), p. 85.

[48] Ehlers/Steinborn/Wege, in: van Bühren (2014), p. 2093, para. 97.

[49] Ehlers (2003), p. 159, para. 7.

[50] Ehlers (2003), p. 161, para. 17; Koller, in: Prölss/Martin (2015), p. 2672, para. 2.

[51] Ehlers (2003), p. 165, para. 34.

[52] Ehlers (2003), p. 165, para. 34.

[53] Ehlers (2003), p. 181 et seq, para. 2; Ehlers, in: Thume/Ehlers (2011) p. 225, para. 318.
[54] Steinborn, in: Hartenstein/Reuschle (2015), p. 590, para. 18.
[55] Dunt (2015), p. 59; Rose (2012), p. 131.
[56] See no. 15 ICC.
[57] Dunt (2015), p. 6 et seq.
[58] No. 3.2.1. DTV Cargo – Open Policy 2000/2011; Rose (2012), pp. 131.
[59] Steinborn, in: Hartenstein/Reuschle (2015), pp. 591, para. 23; Dunt (2015), p. 91; Hudson/Madge/Sturges (2012), p. 13.
[60] Steinborn, in: Hartenstein/Reuschle (2015), pp. 591, para. 23; Rose (2012), p. 379.
[61] Goodacre (1996), p. 262, Enge/Schwampe (2012), p. 69.
[62] Goodacre (1996), p. 262.
[63] Steinborn, in: Hartenstein/Reuschle (2015), p. 585, para. 2; Jaeger, in: Hartenstein/Reuschle (2015), p. 612, para. 2; Abele, in: Baumann et al. (2016), p. 242, para. 3; Thume, TranspR 2006, p. 4.
[64] Abele, in: Baumann et al. (2016), p. 271, para. 40; Jaeger, in: Hartenstein/Reuschle (2015), p. 614, para. 11; Kollatz, in: Thume/Ehlers (2011), p. 655, para. 7.
[65] Thume/de la Motte, in: Thume/Ehlers (2011) p. 11, para. 44; Abele, in: Baumann et al. (2016), p. 242, para. 3, p. 243, para. 5.
[66] Thume, TranspR 2006, p. 5.
[67] Jaeger, in: Hartenstein/Reuschle (2015), p. 614, para. 9.
[68] Abele, in: Baumann et al. (2016), p. 288, para. 95.
[69] Jaeger, in: Hartenstein/Reuschle (2015), p. 616, para. 19.
[70] Kollatz, in: Thume/Ehlers (2011), p. 668, para. 86, 87.
[71] Abele, TranspR 2009, p. 63.
[72] Abele, TranspR 2009, p. 63.
[73] Abele, in: Baumann et al. (2016), p. 273, para. 43 et seq; Jaeger, in: Hartenstein/Reuschle (2015), pp. 614, para. 13; Kollatz, in: Thume/Ehlers (2011), p. 656, para. 11.
[74] Abele, in: Baumann et al. (2016), p. 273, para. 44.
[75] Jaeger, in: Hartenstein/Reuschle (2015), p. 615, para. 14; Abele, in: Baumann et al. (2016), p. 275, para. 53.
[76] Jaeger, in: Hartenstein/Reuschle (2015), p. 630, para. 89.
[77] Abele, in: Baumann et al. (2016), p. 334, para. 227.

CHAPTER XV

THE PORT PACKAGE III: A EUROPEAN FRAMEWORK FOR THE PROVISION OF PORT SERVICES AND COMMON RULES ON THE FINANCIAL TRANSPARENCY OF PORTS

Kai-Dieter CLASSEN

A. INTRODUCTION

Ports are the focal points of worldwide logistic chains, the entry- and exit-gates of national economies as well as whole economic areas in globalized trade and inevitable pre-condition for the maritime economy. They are highly complex agglomerations of infrastructure and home to a huge variety of companies at the interface of land and water. Ports constitute a functional unit, however, the term "port" suggests a concreteness of the object under scrutiny that does not exist. In fact, at closer inspection a port dissolves into a multiplicity of independent, yet functionally interacting stakeholders – depending on the port governance model and the level of liberalization.

Public international law deals with ports mostly regarding specific questions, for example a vessel's right of entry to a port or matters of port state control. As ports, being domestic institutions, do not have a particular status in international law and only few conventions deal with them, no systematic legal regime for ports has emerged on a global level yet.[1] European Union (EU) Law has a broader coverage of ports and a higher density of regulation. With its market freedoms, competition law and provisions on common transport policy and Trans-European Network infrastructure, there are several influential and far reaching EU policy areas which have generated a decision practice and secondary law that target ports either directly or at least affect them to a larger or lesser extent. The Regulation 2017/352 or 'Port Package III' – as it is often dubbed in the context of its legislative history – now constitutes the nucleus of European Port Law. Its adoption in January 2017 marks the keystone in a controversial regulatory project that, overall, has a history of 16 years and harmonizes the rules for European ports, as compared to their counterparts in the rest of the world, in a remarkable fashion.

B. SETTING THE SCENE – BACKGROUND AND CONTEXT OF THE PORT PACKAGE III

The Regulation that now has come into force and will apply from 24 March 2019 has a history consisting mainly of the enforcement of general European Law and failed regulatory attempts.

I. INDIVIDUAL COURT CASES

The series of case-by-case decisions which staked off the application of primary law to the port sector started in 1974 with the *French Seamen's case* in which the European Court of Justice (ECJ) confirmed that sea and air transport are subject to the general rules of the treaty, in particular the rules on competition.[2] Especially in the 1990ies, this finding was enforced in a series of port-related decisions by the Commission and the Court. The ECJ's 1991 decision in the first *Port of Genoa* ruling[3] illustrated exemplary what went wrong in some European ports: With respect to cargo handling services in the port of Genoa the Court found that their monopolistic and clientelistic organization based on different Italian laws violated Art. 90 EECT on public undertakings in conjunction with Art. 86 EECT on the abuse of a dominant position (now Art. 106(1) and Art. 102 TFEU), Art. 48 EECT on the freedom of movement for workers (now Art. 45 TFEU) and Art. 30 EECT on the prohibition of quantitative restrictions (now Art. 34 TFEU). The freedom of establishment, which was most likely affected as well, was not part of the ECJ's assessment as it was not included in the Italian court's request for a preliminary ruling.[4] Another example is the *GT-Link case*. Here, the Court ruled in 1997 that the system of duties to be paid to the operator of the Danish port of Gedser by ferry companies calling at the port violated the treaty rules on public undertakings and the abuse of a dominant position in so far as it favored the port operator's own ferry services and reciprocally those of some of its trading partners whereas it discriminated against others.[5]

II. FAILED REGULATORY ATTEMPTS

While other sectors of transport gradually became subject to EU regulation, most notably the airport sector which is often viewed as kin to the port sector, ports and port services remained uncharted territory on the map of EU secondary law until now – although the Commission had launched the debate on the regulation of the port sector already in 1997 with its Green Paper on Sea Ports and Maritime Infrastructure[6]. The Green Paper highlighted the vital role of sea ports for Europe both in terms of trade and transport and illuminated the function of ports with respect to specific aspects of the Common Transport Policy. It discussed the financing of ports and the charging for ports and maritime infrastructure in an increasingly competitive environment, and finally evaluated the organization and market access of port services. The Commission concluded inter alia that, complementary to the then case-by-case approach, a framework should be developed aiming at a more systematic liberalization of the port service market. Further, the Commission suggested that a coherent framework for port charging should be developed, taking into account the user-pays principle, and that such a framework should be complemented by transparency of public port funding and the development of port-specific state aid rules.[7]

In 2001 the Commission made the first attempt to regulate ports, presenting a proposal for a Directive on market access to port services and a corresponding Communication, the 'Port Package I'[8]. With a view to the growing trade volumes, the Commission argued that there were too many de-facto monopolies in ports causing inter alia a lack of performance, disproportionally high costs and altogether a situation of disparate competition between ports.[9] The legislative procedure came to a spectacular halt, when – under the pressure of port workers, unions and industry lobbyists – the Plenary of the Parliament rejected a compromise version in November 2003 by a majority of only 20 votes. Only one year later, the same Commission, while still in office, renewed its initiative vis-à-vis a freshly elected Parliament. In the explanatory memorandum of this 'Port Package II'[10], the Commission held that the previous legislative initiative's doctrine and general principles remained intact and all arguments were still valid.[11] This political move united the Parliament beyond expectation: The Committee on Transport and Tourism (TRAN) and afterwards the Plenary dismissed the renewed proposal as well – this time by a 392 votes majority. In both initiatives in particular the liberal rules on self-provision of services and the temporal restriction of the service providers' right to operate caused a controversial debate and stirred up sometimes violent protests of port workers.[12] In the aftermath the Commission published a simple 'Communication on a European Ports Policy'.[13]

C. THE ANAMNESIS OF A REGULATION

I. COMMISSION PROPOSAL

Case closed? By no means.[14] According to the results of a Commission-initiated study on the enhancement of port services presented in September 2012, the overwhelming majority of port users stated that, despite different legal limitations to competition or the de facto absence of competition with respect to certain services, they predominantly did not encounter any challenges related to port services ("no-problem"-ratings ranging from 71% for pilotage to 89% for ice breaking).[15] Notwithstanding such comforting results, the Commission presented a new proposal in May 2013 for establishing a framework on market access to port services and financial transparency[16], now in the form of a directly applicable Regulation, and published a corresponding Communication 'Ports: an engine for growth'[17], the 'Port Package III' (PPIII).[18]

As a justification for the new initiative the Commission referred to alleged weak competitive pressure on certain port services due to market access restrictions and monopolistic or oligopolistic structures potentially leading to market abuses. As the main problem, the Commission identified a structural performance gap in some TEN-T seaports, a problem that would be exacerbated by the need to adapt ports to new transport and logistics requirements at a moment of scarce public funding. This situation would potentially create risks of congestion and put at risk an efficient, interconnected and sustainable Trans-European Network and therefore the functioning of the internal market.[19]

To tackle the problems mentioned, the draft covered the following services: bunkering, cargo handling, dredging, mooring, passenger services, port reception facilities, pilotage and towage. The first major part explicitly applied the EU market freedom to provide services to the port service providers. The draft subsequently defined rules for the establishment of minimum requirements for the provision of port services, limitations on the number of service providers, public service obligations and the provision of port services by means of internal operators. Presumably as an act of appeasement, the draft explicitly excluded cargo handling and passenger services from the market access chapter and contained additional measures to safeguard employees' rights. Remarkably, the rules on the procedure for the limitation of the number of providers extended rules of the Concessions Directive 2014/23/EU[20] to port service contracts, even if they do not qualify as concessions in the strict legal sense of the Directive.

The second major part contained provisions on the transparency of financial relations between public authorities and the port, and the setting of certain port service as well as port infrastructure charges. Additionally, the Commission included the power to adopt delegated acts with respect to the infrastructure charge. These provisions correlated with the application of state aid law to ports, a practice that was then in a state of flux, as illustrated by the consultation on the extension of the General Block Exemption Regulation (GBER)[21] to ports and many case-by-case decisions. The third major chapter contained provisions inter alia on the consultation of port users and other stakeholders, the establishment of independent supervisory bodies and appeal procedures, thus adding additional structures and procedures to the bureaucracy already in place.

Given the heterogeneous nature of the European port sector with its varying commercial and organizational models, the proposal affected a complex muddle of interests and interdependencies of the stakeholders covered. What the Commission did not reflect upon was the fact that the market conditions for port operators, port service providers and the shipping lines had changed significantly as compared to the times of the Green Paper and the first and second Port Package. The growth that was common before the crisis of 2008 had collapsed and from then on cargo handling developed only moderately. At the same time EU ports have been building significant capacities and shipping lines have been going through an unprecedented process of consolidation and concentration. Achieving high utilization rates of the new built infrastructure became the paramount goal of ports' commercial strategies, boosting the inter-port competition in the battle for increasingly powerful shipping lines as customers. At the same time, this competition produces inward-directed pressure on the local port service providers concerning their efficiency and cost-attractiveness. Their performance constitutes an integral functional part of a port's service package as a whole and its competitiveness on the hard-fought market. Thus, it can be doubted whether the Commission's diagnostic findings, which it now intended to remedy, where fully accurate for all EU ports.

II. THE POSITIONS OF THE EUROPEAN COUNCIL AND THE TRAN COMMITTEE

The TRAN Committee did not conclude its deliberations before the election in May 2014. The members decided that there was too little time to finalize the compromises and that the interrelation with state aid law was too unclear to proceed. Instead, it was the Council under Italian Presidency that agreed on a general approach in October 2014[22] rather swiftly. Recalling the strong opposition that had initially come from many Member States such as France, Poland, Latvia, Sweden, Spain – and ironically even Italy, this was quite surprising. The Council naturally focused on provisions affecting Member States' established structures and adopted a rather restrictive position: The proposed supervisory bodies and user consultation mechanisms were slashed, the legal basis for delegated acts was removed and the autonomy of ports was significantly limited. In the first chapters, the Council induced fewer changes. In particular, it removed dredging from the scope of the draft, introduced the option for a national derogation regarding pilotage and kept certain hedged references to the Concessions Directive.

After the elections, the TRAN Committee again entrusted the matter to its previous rapporteur, Knut Fleckenstein (Socialists & Democrats). The 'Fleckenstein-Report'[23] contained 136 amendments and the members of the TRAN-Committee tabled more than 600 additional amendments. Most notably, in the report approved as amended the Committee removed dredging almost completely from the draft and exempted pilotage just like cargo handling and passenger services. In addition, it replaced the provision on the applicability of the freedom to provide services with a generic clause on the organization of port services. Furthermore, the Committee recognized the special situation of privatized ports and small and outermost ports, and, instead of borrowing rules from the Concessions Directive, it incorporated general procedural requirements regarding non-discrimination and transparency. The report strengthened workers' rights, underpinned the commercial freedom and autonomy of ports and did no longer contain a legal basis for delegated acts. Regarding the consultation mechanism and supervisory bodies, the Committee reduced the bureaucratic impact but did not go as far as the Council. The concluding trilog-negotiation rounds were driven at high pace. The final text[24] was approved by the plenary of the Parliament on 14 December 2016 with broad majority, and by the Council on 23 January 2017, against the sole vote of the United Kingdom.

D. CONTENT OF THE PORT PACKAGE III

I. SCOPE (ART. 1)

The PPIII[25] applies to all core and comprehensive maritime ports of the Trans-European Transport Network (TEN-T), as listed in Annex II to the TEN-T Regulation[26]. Member States may exempt comprehensive ports located in the outermost regions as defined in Art. 349 TFEU[27]; at the same time, they are free to apply the PPIII to ports which are originally not covered by the Regulation. A 'maritime port' is defined in Art. 2 No. 16 as "an area of land and water made up of such infrastructure and equipment so as to permit, principally, the reception of waterborne vessels, their loading and unloading, the storage of goods, the receipt and delivery of those goods and the embarkation and disembarkation of passengers, crew and other persons and any other infrastructure necessary for transport operators within the port area." This definition[28] is purely functional. Qualitative requirements are not included and can, at the most, be integrated only by way of the requirements for TEN-T ports as set up in the Regulation 1315/2013. The definition also lacks any geographical aspect, leaving it to the Member States to define the exact delimitation of the port area. Port boundaries, however, are often the result of historical developments which not necessarily reflect functionality. In some cases, the port area's definition is based on urban planning law, since many ports in densely populated Europe are embedded in urban areas.[29] The monetary provisions of the PPIII even extend its geographical applicability in a hidden way, by means of the definition of 'port infrastructure charge' which is to be levied from port users (Art. 13 and Art. 2 No. 9). This charge becomes due not only for the use of the port but also for the use of the 'waterway access *to* the port', that is port approaches, fairways, rivers, sea canals and fjords, as long as this access falls within the competence of the managing body of the port (Art. 2 No. 18). This confinement is essential if one considers that such accesses often fall under the administration of different bodies, for example in the case of Antwerp in Belgium, parts of the river Scheldt are under the administration of the Netherlands.

The PPIII applies according to Art. 1(2) to: bunkering, cargo-handling, mooring, passenger services, collection of ship-generated waste and cargo residues, pilotage and towage. Dredging was removed from the scope and appears only in Art. 11(2) on the transparency of financial relations between public authorities and a managing body of a port in case the managing body in receipt of public funds provides dredging itself. The list of services covered looks more comprehensive than it is: Cargo-handling and passenger services, as well as pilotage, are exempted from Chapter II on the organization of port services by Art. 10. The decision to exclude pilotage was eventually made to avoid potential conflicts of interests between the public interest functions of pilotage on the one hand and commercial considerations on the other. Member States, however, may submit pilotage to the rules of Chapter II, making use of the "opt in" clause contained in Art. 10(2) solely for pilotage.

II. Provision of Port Services

Chapter II on the provision of port services (formerly named 'Market Access') contains a set of rules on how and to what extent port services may be submitted to regulation. Thus, this chapter defines a common standard for market organization and liberalization. The freedom to provide services according to Art. 56 TFEU is not explicitly expanded to port services (Art. 58(1), Art. 100(2) TFEU). Recital 11, however, seems to presume exactly such applicability by stating that "in accordance with the general principles set out in the Treaties, providers of port services should be free to provide their services in maritime ports covered by this Regulation." The freedom of establishment (Art. 49 TFEU) is not subject to a reservation regarding its applicability to the transport sector and thus fully applies.

Member States are not permitted to regulate port services stricter than designated by the PPIII. However, they are free to liberalize further, for example by imposing only a few or even no minimum requirements (Art. 3(2) PPIII). As a general rule, the terms of access to the facilities, installations and equipment of the port must be fair, reasonable and non-discriminatory (Art. 3(3) PPIII). This general principle corresponds to key requirements from the application of Art. 102 TFEU on the abuse of a dominant position to cases where the entity authorized to dispose of a facility holds a monopoly position[30]. In essence, it can also be distilled from the fundamental rules of the TFEU, the principles of non-discrimination on grounds of nationality and equal treatment, and also the obligation of transparency thereunder.[31]

1. Minimum Requirements (Art. 4 and Art. 5)

Providers of port services may be required to comply with certain minimum requirements to be permitted to offer a corresponding service in a port. Art. 4 PPIII contains an exhaustive list of such requirements, inter alia (1) the professional qualifications of the provider of port services, (2) the financial capacity of the provider, (3) the equipment needed to provide the relevant port service in normal and safe conditions, (4) the availability of the relevant port service to all users, at all berths and without interruptions, day and night, throughout the year, (5) compliance with requirements on maritime safety or the safety and security of the port or access to it, environmental requirements, and obligations in the field of social and labor law, and (6) the good repute of the provider, as determined in accordance with applicable national law. Minimum requirements must be publicized appropriately. They shall be objective, non-discriminatory, proportionate, and relevant to the type of the port service concerned. Art. 5 contains additional procedures regarding compliance with the minimum requirements.[32]

In the context of the market liberalization aimed at by the PPIII, Art. 4(3) constitutes a remarkable oddity: A Member State may impose a flag requirement for vessels predominantly used for towage or mooring operations in its ports where it considers it necessary to ensure full compliance with the applicable obligations in the field of social and labor law. While this provision originates from the deliberations in the TRAN Committee – and found a strong supporter in France, its background can be traced to a treaty infringement procedure against the Hellenic Republic: The court came to the conclusion that the flag requirement imposed by Greece for towage services on open sea did not violate the freedom to provide services, because the transport service in question was subject to the reservation of Art. 51(1) EC (Art. 58(1) TFEU) and did not fall within the scope of Regulation 3577/92 on maritime cabotage[33] based on Art. 80(2) EC (Art. 100(2) TFEU). However, the court felt it necessary to point out, that the Commission based its application only on the complaint of infringement of Regulation 3577/92 and the freedom to provide services and that the court may not hand out a ruling that goes beyond the Commission's application under Art. 258 TFEU.[34] The compatibility of the flag requirement with the general principle of non-discrimination enshrined in Art. 18 TFEU and the freedom of establishment according to Art. 49 TFEU hence remains doubtful.

2. LIMITATIONS ON THE NUMBER OF PROVIDERS OF PORT SERVICES (ART. 6)

Art. 6 PPIII permits limitations on the number of providers of port services and contains an exhaustive list of acceptable reasons for such a restriction of competition: (1) the scarcity or reserved use of land or waterside space, provided that the limitation is in accordance with the decisions or plans agreed by the managing body of the port or any other public authority competent, (2) the absence of such a limitation would obstruct the performance of public service obligations as provided for in Art. 7, (3) the absence of such a limitation runs counter to the need to ensure safe, secure or environmentally sustainable port operations, (4) the characteristics of the port infrastructure or the nature of the port traffic are such that the operations of multiple providers of port services in the port would not be possible, and (5) a port sector or subsector, together with its port services, within a Member State carries out an activity that is directly exposed to competition[35]. It remains unclear whether Art. 6 only applies in cases of deliberate interference with competition or covers also cases of restrictions because natural conditions, such as limited resources within the boundaries of the port. If all appropriate locations are completely occupied, an interested port service provider cannot enter the market, even though no outspoken limitation exists.

A broad divide opened in the negotiations with respect to the proposed adoption of procedural requirements from the Concessions Directive[36] also for the selection of operators in cases of limitation of the number of providers of port services. It contains strict rules on the maximum duration of concessions and their alterability. During the negotiation of the Concessions Directive, its potential application to public domain and land lease contracts in ports was highly controversial. The outcome was recital 15 of the Directive which clarifies the scope of the directive. "Simple" public domain and land lease contracts are not covered by it unless the state or public entity is using them to procure specific works or services. Pasting procedural requirements from the Concessions Directive into the Port Package irrespective of the legal character of the contract to be concluded would have widened the scope of the Directive and thus extended the application of procurement law outside the Directive itself. This fault line saw several northern European Member States pitted against the Commission and several southern European Member States, with the Members of the Parliament backing both sides to a certain degree. The background to this controversy was that northern Member States traditionally use standard land lease contracts governed by the basic rules of civil law[37], whereas southern Member States traditionally use concession models of varying complexity due to the Romanic concept of public domain (usus publicus). Different legal traditions regarding the administration of state-owned properties were suddenly – and in a quite misplaced context – disputed with respect to the scope of public procurement law; and this dispute was charged with a political rallying cry for a "level playing field". The Commission was essentially interested in installing a uniform set of rules for contracts in ports. It obviously favored the harmonized EU rules for public procurement over fragmented and diverse legal concepts and rules in the Member States. This debate had also a future-oriented aspect: The possible inclusion of cargo handling and passenger services after a revision of the regulation, which is likely to be due after 2023, would increase the practical relevance of this question significantly.

The result of this debate was Art. 6(4) which contains only general procedural requirements. These are inspired by the Commission's own interpretative communication on the Community law applicable to contract awards not or not fully subject to the provisions of the Public Procurement Directives[38]. Such an approach is appropriate. In case the contract to be concluded falls within the scope of EU procurement law, the rules of the Concessions Directive apply anyway; if that is not the case, there is no justification for an extensive application of strict procurement law to cases where no procurement takes place. The distinction depends on the content of the contract to be concluded and not its formal designation as a 'concession'.

3. Public Service Obligations (Art. 7) and Internal Operators (Art. 8)

Member States may, according to Art. 7 PPIII, decide to impose public service obligations on providers of port services. The right to impose such obligations may be entrusted to either the managing body of the port, or to the competent authority. A public service obligation shall ensure at least one of the following goals: (1) the availability of the port service to all port users, at all berths, without interruption, day and night, throughout the year, (2) the availability of the service to all users on equal terms, (3) the affordability of the service for certain categories of users, (4) the safety, security or environmental sustainability of port operations, (5) the provision of adequate transport services to the public, and (6) territorial cohesion. According to Art. 11(7), public funds paid as compensation for a public service obligation shall be shown separately in the relevant accounts and may not be transferred to any other service or business activity.

This legal instrument, established in the transport sector to justify deviations from competition law and the market freedoms, is based on Art. 14 TFEU and Protocol 26. In the case of land transport its direct legal basis can be found in Art. 93 TFEU[39]. For maritime transport services, and consequentially their ancillary port services, the *lex generalis* of Art. 106(2) TFEU applies, implemented exemplary by Art. 4 Regulation 3577/92 on maritime cabotage[40]. Parallel to that, the EU's regime on services of general economic interest (SGEI) is applicable only to a limited extent.[41]

The right of a port to provide a port service itself or through a subsidiary remains for the most part untouched by the Regulation according to Art. 8 PPIII. The provision clarifies that Art. 4 on minimum requirements must apply equally to internal operators and their commercial competitors. Certain safeguards for maintaining effective competition are contained in cases of limitations on the number of providers pursuant to Art. 6. Finally, the managing body of a port in receipt of public funds has to keep the account of its internal operator separate from the account for its other activities according to Art. 11(2) PPIII.

4. Safeguarding Employees' Rights (Art. 9)

While the exemption of cargo handling and passenger services from Chapter II helped to mitigate the skepticism of the terminal operators towards the Commission's renewed regulatory initiative, Art. 9 on the safeguarding of employees' rights intends to do the same with respect to port workers and their unions. The provision has to be seen in connection with the sectoral social dialog between the Commission and European workers and industry associations. According to Art. 9(1) the managing body of a port, or the competent authority, shall require the service providers to comply with their obligations in the field of social and labor law and with social standards as set out in EU law, national law or collective agreements. That way, Art. 9(1) turns port authorities into agents for the legal compliance of others. Art. 9(2) goes far beyond that: It offers the possibility to extend the scope of Directive 2001/23/EC relating to the safeguarding of employees' rights in the event of transfers of undertakings[42] to cases where a mere change of the provider of port services occurs, e.g. because of the award of a concession or land lease contract. The decision whether the rights and obligations are to be transferred to the new provider is left to the discretion of the managing body of the port or competent authority ("may require"). However, this legally foreseen possibility will certainly whet the appetite of workers and unions and put pressure on port administrations to actually make use of it. A similar provision was already included in Art. 4(5) of Regulation 1370/2007[43], nevertheless such a requirement constitutes uncharted territory in the field of port regulation. It certainly improves the security of employment in a port's limited labor market, but at the same time protects incumbent operators by creating a market entrance barrier for newcomers because they are not free in organizing their own business operations.

5. Port Service Contracts (Art. 21)

Chapter II on the provision of port services must be seen in connection with Art. 21 PPIII on transitional measures regarding "port service contracts". The reach of this provision remains quite unclear. It states that "this Regulation shall not apply to port service contracts which were concluded before 15 February 2017 and are limited in time. Port service contracts concluded before 15 February 2017 which are not limited in time, or have similar effects, shall be amended in order to comply with this Regulation by 1 July 2025." In a roundabout way, this provision suggests, that any port service contract concluded has to be limited in time. Such a requirement, in connection with the selection procedure designated by Art. 6 on limitations on the number of service providers, bears a certain resemblance to the concept of temporal licenses for operations contained in the first two Port Packages. In the PPIII, the application of this limitation hinges on the meaning of the term "port service contract". The Regulation defines the term "port service contract" in Art. 2 No. 12 as "a formal and legally binding agreement or an act of equivalent legal effect between a provider of port services and a managing body of the port, or a competent authority, having as its subject-matter the provision of one or more port services, without prejudice to the form of designating providers of port services." It remains silent, however, on when and under what circumstances such a contract is concluded. The Commission's original proposal was clearer in that respect, stipulating that a port service contract must be concluded in cases of a limitation of the number of providers of port services.[44] This confinement of the use of port service contracts was given up in the legislative process, leaving it to the Member States to figure out whether they have contracts in their ports which qualify as port service contracts according to the now wider definition.

Based on a strict interpretation of the law, the act in question would have to be *bilateral* in order to qualify as an "agreement" or "contract", which is concluded between two parties. Consequently, this characteristic would also have to apply to an "act of equivalent legal effect". *Unilateral* acts, such as licenses or permits to operate a port service, e.g. implementing minimum requirements, would not qualify as an agreement or act of equivalent legal effect. Such acts are typically administrative decisions and an expression of the sovereign power of the public administration. They are typically issued on application. Agreements, on the other hand, are usually concluded by parties with a joint intent to be legally bound. The parties enter negotiations on equal footing without one party resorting to its sovereign power. When considering the "equivalence of the legal effect", these differences cannot be neglected.

Further, the agreement shall have as its subject matter the provision of one or more port services. A concession contract according to the Concessions Directive 2014/23/EU might qualify as such. A land lease contract, on the other hand, has as its subject matter the terms and conditions for the lease[45] and not the terms and conditions for the provision of the port service. Overall, the scope of Art. 21 PPIII does not seem to be all-embracing.

6. SELF-PROVISION OF PORT SERVICES

Given the past controversies, the PPIII does not contain a single word on self-provision of port services. The Commission's proposal at least touched upon the subject in a recital. It highlighted that several Member States regulated this issue for safety and social reasons and that the matter should be left, at this stage, in the Member States' sphere.[46] Even this declaratory statement was removed in the legislative process, leaving the legal status quo in all Member States unaltered.[47]

III. FINANCIAL TRANSPARENCY AND AUTONOMY

1. TRANSPARENCY OF FINANCIAL RELATIONS (ART. 11)

Art. 11(1) in Chapter III of the Regulation obliges public authorities and a managing body of a port in receipt of public funds to make sure that the financial relations between them are reflected in a transparent way in the accounting system in order to clearly show (1) public funds made available directly by public authorities to the managing bodies of the port concerned, (2) public funds made available by public authorities through the intermediary of public undertakings or public financial institutions, and (3) the use for which those public funds have been attributed.[48]

The provision further includes a definition of public funds (Art. 11(3)), an obligation to store all relevant information concerning the financial relations for at least five years (Art. 11(4)) and an obligation to disclose the financial information referred to in Sec. 1 and 2 in the event of a formal complaint and upon request to assess compliance with this Regulation in accordance with competition rules (Art. 11(5)).

This demand for financial transparency was controversial only in detail but not in general. It supports the *ratio legis* of Directive 2006/111/EG on the transparency of financial relations between Member States and public undertakings[49], facilitates state aid investigations of the Commission – based on own initiative or a competitor's complaint, and thus helps to maintain a level playing field. In the last stages of the negotiations, a heated dispute emerged pertaining to the application of state aid law to ports by the Commission, a practice that many perceived as too far reaching. Some ports, Member States and Members of Parliament tried to anchor a 'state aid guidance clause' in the PPIII, which was supposed to impose a more restrictive interpretation and application of Art. 107(1) TFEU on the Commission, placing more port infrastructures outside the scope of state aid law. Other Member States, however, which apply a more commercialized business model to their ports and/or are not willing or able to provide public funds, remained very skeptical towards linking the negotiations of the Port Package to state aid law practice. This conflict escalated to a point where the rapporteur of the Parliament threatened to stall the legislative procedure until the Commission adopts a generous framework for public financing of port infrastructure in the GBER; the amendment to the GBER regarding ports was in the consultation process coincidentally.[50] The Commission, in turn, was severely galled and denounced this move as political blackmailing. In the end, a political appeal was included in Recital 45 and the Parliament gave up its resistance.

2. Port Service Charges and Port Infrastructure Charges (Art. 12 and Art. 13)

Art. 12 addresses port service providers which operate under non-market conditions, such as internal operators under a public service obligation, pilotage services that are not exposed to effective competition, and port services operating under a limitation of providers according to Art. 6(1)(b). The charges of such services shall be set in a transparent, objective and non-discriminatory way, and shall be proportionate to the cost of the service provided.

Art. 13 contains a complex set of rules on how port infrastructure charges may be determined. Leaving aside the basic provisions in the first two sections, the criteria relevant for determining infrastructure charges are dispersed over the following three sections.

Under Art. 13(3), the "structure and the level of port infrastructure charges shall be determined according to the port's own commercial strategy and investment plans". This clause emphasizes the central role of ports and their nature as undertakings. The subsequent requirement of compliance with competition rules[51] is therefore not surprising. Pursuant to Art. 13(4), the charges determined on such a basis may vary "in accordance with the port's own economic strategy and its spatial planning policy". This Section, again, emphasizes the determining role of the port and its strategy regarding the design of infrastructure charges. What follows is a non-exhaustive list of permissible variations, "inter alia, certain categories of users, or in order to promote a more efficient use of the port infrastructure, short sea shipping or a high environmental performance, energy efficiency or carbon efficiency of transport operations." The criteria used for such variations must be objective and non-discriminatory and must be published appropriately to meet the transparency requirement. Reiterating Art. 13(3), the criteria must be "consistent with competition law, including rules on State aid". After having defined this rather straight jacket, the legislator then introduces an escape clause which allows the infrastructure charge to be varied "depending on commercial practices". While the first part of this Section with its list of permissible cases of variations suggests that the infrastructure charges can or should be used as a tool for incentive-based soft regulation, this last clause once again puts emphasis on the character of ports as undertakings operating in a market-based environment. Pursuing both approaches, however, seems to be inconsistent.

Finally, according to Art. 13(5), the "managing body of the port, or the competent authority, shall not be required to disclose differentiations in the charges that are the result of individual negotiations." This provision once more underlines the character of ports as undertakings, presupposing that – despite all the guard rails set up in Art. 13(3) and (4) – differentiations based on individual negotiations remain allowed. This is reaffirmed by Recital 48, which states that the rules of the port package should not affect the rights of the ports and their customers to agree commercially confidential discounts. Commercial departments of port authorities are left puzzled when they try to determine legally compliant port infrastructure charges. Are they too cheap, they might be considered illegal state aid in the sense of Art. 107 TFEU. Are the charges too high, the port authority, having a natural monopoly, might be accused of abusing a dominant position according to Art. 102(a) TFEU. If the port authority applies variations or determines the charge based on individual negotiations, it might be accused of abusing a dominant position according to Art. 102(c) TFEU.

The provisions cited above suggest that the power to determine the structure and level of the infrastructure charge falls into the competence of the port and its managing body. The Commission's initial proposal was straight forward about this question by pointing out that "the structure and the level of port infrastructure charges shall be defined in an autonomous way by the managing body of the port (. . .)".[52] But the term "autonomous" faced rigid resistance of Member States with a centralistic administration of ports; accepting such an autonomy, they feared, might lead to a significant loss of influence for the central governments and would impact on their respective legal orders, potentially including the constitutional allocation of competencies. Under this pressure the wording in Art. 13(3) was changed to "the (. . .) charges shall be determined according to the port's own commercial strategy and investment plans, (. . .). Where relevant, such charges shall also respect the general requirements set within the framework of the general ports policy of the Member State concerned". The Section now avoids the term "autonomous" as well as a precise determination of who shall have the power to define the charges. Instead, it adds a cloudy reference to Member State's ports policy. One should not overlook, however, that Chapter III, which includes Art. 13, is still labelled "Financial Transparency and *Autonomy*". In the end, a holistic look at the text of Art. 13 and the corresponding recitals suggests that, despite the changes to Art. 13 induced in the legislative procedure, it is nevertheless the ports which have the right and responsibility to determine the charges. It is them who negotiate with the customers on discounts and who define their commercial strategy and investment plans. That ports, in doing so, have to respect the framework of the general ports policy of the respective Member State should go without saying. Insofar, the dispute over the (non-)use of the term "autonomous" seemed exaggerated and becomes understandable only against the background of the tensions existing between central governments and regions in some Member States, for example Spain.

Ironically, Art. 13 on port infrastructure charges was hard-fought territory for yet another reason: While granting ports autonomy, the Commission had intended at the same time to include a legal basis for delegated acts, allowing it to define inter alia common charging principles. On this frontline, ports, Member States and the Parliament stood united against the Commission's approach and all legal fragments concerning this enabling clause were removed.

IV. General and Final Provisions

The general and final provisions in Chapter IV contain some surprising and potentially far reaching obligations. As part of the social aspects of the PPIII, Art. 14 obligates port service providers to provide training opportunities for the staff. The mandatory consultation of port users and "other stakeholders", introduced by Art. 15 PPIII, shall comprise the management body's charging policy (vis-à-vis port users only) and "essential matters within its competence", such as the coordination of port services, hinterland connections, efficiency and simplification of administrative procedures, environmental matters, spatial planning, and measures to ensure safety in the port area. The effect of this requirement of mandatory consultations is mitigated to some extent by the reservation that consultations have to be held "in accordance with applicable national law", giving the member States significant discretion for the implementation of a consultation mechanism. According to Art. 16 Member States shall ensure that an effective procedure is in place to handle complaints arising from the application of the PPIII. This flexible procedural safeguard replaced the bureaucratic original Commission proposal which had required the introduction of "independent supervisory bodies" as new institutions. In addition to the complaint procedure, any party with a legitimate interest shall, pursuant to Art. 18, have the right to appeal against the decisions or individual measures taken under this Regulation by the managing body of the port, the competent authority, or any other relevant national authority. This right of appeal guarantees a review according to judicial or quasi-judicial standards as appeal bodies shall be independent of the parties involved and may be courts. Art. 19, finally, requires the Member States to enact penalties applicable to infringements of this Regulation. The implementation of this provision seems difficult in cases where the perpetrator is a Member State acting as a legislator, for example regulating port services in a non-PPIII-compliant way, or a public entity resorting to its sovereign powers. In such cases, the rules on legal remedies and government liability seem sufficient and more consistent with established doctrine and practices in public law than administrative penalties.

E. Evaluation

The liberalization[53] and standardization of port services shall tackle the alleged performance gap in some TEN-T ports and increase the efficiency of the services and thus of the European ports in their entirety. However, prescribing the cure of 'more market' increases the exposure of port service providers to the forces of the market significantly. And these market forces have changed radically compared to 2001, when the first attempt to liberalize port services was made. In fact, in the recent past the process of consolidation, concentration and cooperation in the sector of maritime transport services has reached an unprecedented dynamic. The once diverse world of shipping lines is now dominated by a handful of carriers. They possess huge bargaining power which they make use of vis-à-vis ports and port service providers. Hence, it is the shipping sector benefitting most from Chapter II of the Port Package. From a Hamburg or northern European perspective, the PPIII brings little added value with respect to port performance.[54] Here, the by far biggest performance driver is the intense competition between the ports, forcing the port service providers in each port to be innovative and efficient. The existing tools of competition law prove to be sufficient as the recent case of the successful joint cartel investigations against towage companies in Hamburg and Rotterdam illustrates.[55] The Chapter III provisions on transparency of financial relations have to be welcomed as they support an effective application of state aid law, and thus strengthen the level playing field between ports. The rules on port infrastructure charges, however, are complex, sometimes cloudy and difficult to handle in practice. They appear to be inconsistent to a certain degree, as ports on the one hand seem to be acknowledged as business undertakings, but then on the other hand are sometimes treated as agents of the state, utilizable for the implementation of environmental and transport policies. While some ports welcomed the legal prescription of consultation and complaint procedures in Chapter IV, hoping that such provisions in a directly applicable EU regulation would strengthen their administration and the application as well as the execution of the law, other ports and Member States were very critical and regarded the proposed rules as an unnecessary and even counterproductive interference. They add a layer of European red tape to areas where either – under the angle of reasonable port stakeholder management – no legal regulation is needed, or where ports in Member States governed by the rule of law and bound by procedural fundamental rights should have respective procedures and legal remedies in place anyway. In such ports, there will be no efficiency gains and added value for port users coming from the PPIII's Chapter IV.

As claimed by the Commission, the PPIII does not force ports into a "one size fits all straight jacket", since it offers sufficient flexibility for Member States to regulate the services according to characteristics of their respective ports. The Commission needed to handle the ports pragmatically, given their diversity. All in all, after 16 years of political struggle ports find themselves with a somewhat ambivalent regulation, that clarifies many questions but also raises new ones. For some ports, it may bring an actual improvement, forcing the liberalization of most port services, setting common standards for their regulation, bringing light into sometimes arcane port financing and installing administrative procedures and legal remedies which enhance enforceability and legality of the regulation of ports. For others, the biggest added value might lay in the fact that this long and controversial political debate has finally come to an end. Whether the degree of political and legal certainty delivered is sufficient remains to be seen: According to the systematics of EU Law, secondary law enjoys primacy in application over the primary law of the TFEU in a sphere which has been the subject of exhaustive harmonization at Union level. National measures in such a sphere must be assessed in the light of the provisions of the harmonizing measure and not those of the Treaty.[56] It seems doubtful, whether the PPIII as secondary law can be considered an exhaustive harmonization of the port sector, given its sometimes restricted scope (exclusion of certain services and respective references to general principles set out in the case-law of the ECJ)[57] and broad references to the competition rules of the TFEU in Art. 13. In the end, identifying the applicable law will remain a case-by-case exercise.

Although the Port Service Regulation is binding in its entirety and directly applicable in all Member States according to Art. 288 TFEU, the German Federal Government and the coastal German states decided to initiate a review and implementation process. This process takes place within the framework of the permanent working group of the Federal Government and the coastal states. The background to this approach is that the content of the PPIII corresponds to some extent with federal legislative competences, to a much larger extent with legislative competences of the states and in some cases with rights and obligations of the port service providers. The goal is to come to a common understanding of the content and meaning of the Regulation, to review existing German federal and state law with respect to its compatibility with the Regulation, and implement the Regulation wherever necessary by either amending existing laws or adopting fresh rules; sometimes contracts with port service providers have to be brought in line with the standards of the PPIII as well. That way, conflicts between German and European law shall be avoided and legal certainty shall be increased.

LITERATURE

Adamopoulos, Anastassios, Europe's port services shake-up to create losers as well as winners, Lloyd's List – The Intelligence – LL Int, January/February 2017, p. 32–33

Classen, Kai-Dieter, The updated General Block Exemption Regulation – Facilitating public investments in ports, Baltic Transport Journal – BTJ, 2017, vol 3–4, p. 42–43

Gasche, Solveig, Das Port Package III – eine Kompromisslösung als Herausforderung des Verhältnismäßigkeitsgrundsatzes nach Art. 5 IV EUV für die Hierarchie der europäischen Rechtsakte, Recht der Transportwirtschaft – RdTW 2017, p. 401–410

Lagoni, Rainer, Ports, in: Max Planck Encyclopedia for Public International Law (MPEPIL), last amended April 2011, opil.ouplaw.com/home/EPIL

Liu, Hongyan, Access to the Market of Port Services – the European Port Package II, in: Ehlers/Lagoni (eds.), Maritime Policy of the European Union and Law of the Sea, 2008, p. 247–280

Parashu, Dimitrios, Der sekundärrechtliche Ansatz der EU zur Rahmensetzung von Hafendiensten, Europäisches Wirtschafts- und Steuerrecht – EWS 2017, p. 329–333

Paschke, Marian/Pottschmidt, Günter, Folgenabschätzung des Vorschlags für eine Richtlinie des Europäischen Parlaments und des Rates über Marktzugang für Hafendienste (Port Package II), Studie im Auftrag des Bundesministeriums für Verkehr und digitale Infrastruktur, 2005

Van Hooydonk, Eric, The European Port Service Directive: the good or the last try?, Journal of International Maritime Law – JIMR, 2005 (11), p. 188–220

Van Hooydonk, Eric, The Regime of Port Authorities under European Law (including an analysis of the Port Services Directive), in: Van Hooydonk et al. (eds.), European Seaports Law, 2003, p. 79–185

Verhoeven, Patrick, Fifty Years of Debate on EU Ports Policy, in: Wareham (ed.), Competition Law and Shipping, 2010, p. 193–206

NOTES

1 A concise overview is given by Lagoni, Ports, in: MPEPIL (2011).

2 ECJ Case 167/73, Commission v. French Republic, para. 17 et seqq.

3 ECJ Case C-179/90, Merci Convenzionali Porto di Genova.

4 In the Spanish Port Labor Pool Case the ECJ confirmed that mandatory labor pools for companies offering port services can violate their freedom of establishment according to Art. 49 TFEU, ECJ Case C-576/13, Commission v. Spain, para. 36 et seqq.

5 ECJ Case C-242/95, GT-Link / De Danske Statsbaner, para. 28 et seqq.

[6] COM(1997) 678 final.

[7] See COM(1997) 678 final, para. 98 et seqq. and para. 50 et seqq.

[8] COM(2001) 35 final; for the text of the proposed Directive see also OJ 2001 C 154E/290.

[9] A comprehensive analysis is offered by Van Hooydonk, in: Van Hooydonk et al. (2003), p. 79, 91 et seqq.

[10] Proposal for a Directive of the European Parliament and of the Council on market access to port services, COM(2004) 654 final.

[11] See Liu, in: Ehlers/Lagoni (2008), p. 247 et seqq.; Van Hooydonk, JIML 2005, p. 188; Paschke/Pottschmidt (2005), p. 1.

[12] See Verhoeven, in: Wareham (2010), p. 193 et seqq.

[13] COM(2007) 616 final.

[14] The Commission indicated an intention for a new regulatory attempt in its Communication 'Single Market Act II – Together for new growth', COM(2012) 573 final, para. 2.1. (p. 8).

[15] Study by PWC/Panteia, European Ports Policy: 'Unlocking the growth potential' IA Study on Enhancement of Port Services – Preliminary Survey Results, Sept. 2012, p. 13.

[16] COM(2013) 296. The Commission based its proposal on Art. 100(2) TFEU; some voices suggest Art. 91(2) TFEU as an additional legal basis, see Gasche, RdTW 2017, p. 401.

[17] COM(2013) 295.

[18] On the necessity and quality of the regulation as well as the chosen legal instrument (regulation instead of directive) see Gasche, RdTW 2017, p. 401, 408 et seqq.

[19] SWD(2013) 181 final, Commission Staff Working Document Impact Assessment, para. 3.

[20] OJ 2014 L 94/1.

[21] Commission Regulation (EU) 651/2014 of 17 June 2014 declaring certain categories of aid compatible with the internal market in application of Articles 107 and 108 of the Treaty, OJ 2014 L 187/1.

[22] ST 14652/14.

[23] European Parliament, 17.2.2016, A8–0023/2016.

[24] Regulation 2017/352 of the European Parliament and of the Council of 15 February 2017 establishing a framework for the provision of port services and common rules on the financial transparency of ports, OJ 2017 L 57/1.

[25] A summary of the content is provided by Parashu, EWS 2017, p. 329, 330 et seqq.; Gasche, RdTW 2017, p. 401, 403 et seqq.

[26] Regulation 1315/2013 on Union guidelines for the development of the Trans-European Transport Network, OJ 2013 L 348/1.

[27] Exemptions for small comprehensive ports (Art. 20(2)(b) Regulation 1315/2013) are possible according to Art. 6(7) and Art. 11(8) PPIII.

[28] It has been adopted in State Aid Law by Art. 2 No. 154 and 155 Regulation 2017/1084 amending the General Block Exemption Regulation 651/2014 as regards aid for port and airport infrastructure, OJ 2017 L 156/1.

[29] See e.g. Section 2 of the Hamburg Port Development Act, Hamburg Law Gazette [HmbGVBl.] 1982, p. 19, last amended on 21 November 2017 (Hamburg Law Gazette, p. 359).

[30] See e.g. Commission decision of 21.12.1993, IV/34.689, SC v. Sealink (Holyhead II), OJ 1994 L 15/8, para. 66 et seqq.; Commission decision of 21.12.1993, 94/119/EG, Port of Rödby, OJ 1994 L 55/52, para. 12 et seqq.; see also Section 19(2) No. 4 German Act against Restraints of Competition.

[31] ECJ Case C-221/12, Belgacom, para. 25 et seqq.; ECJ Case C-324/98, Teleaustria, para. 60 et seqq.; COM(2007) 616 final, p. 10.

[32] In Hamburg, port services are already liberalized to a high degree, notably cargo handling, passenger services, mooring, towage, port reception facilities and bunkering. Only pilotage is highly regulated, due to a traditional safety and security approach, upheld in German river ports like Hamburg and Bremen / Bremerhaven. Minimum requirements are in place for almost all services. E.g. the Ordinance on towage in Hamburg requires the towage company to have a license for the operation in the port and defines requirements for the qualification of the skipper and technical requirements for the tugs, see Seeschiffsassistenzverordnung of 11.03.1997, Hamburg Law Gazette [HmbGVBl.] 1997, p. 65; last amended 28 July 2009 (Hamburg Law Gazette 2009, p. 315, 318).

[33] Regulation 3577/92 applying the principle of freedom to provide services to maritime transport within Member States (maritime cabotage), OJ 1992 L 364/7.

[34] ECJ Case C-251/04, Commission v. Hellenic Republic, para 27.

[35] This has to be established pursuant to Art. 35 of Directive 2014/25/EU on procurement by entities operating in the water, energy, transport and postal services sectors, OJ 2014 L 94/243.

[36] Directive 2014/23/EU on the award of concession contracts, OJ 2014 L 94/1.

[37] Such as Sec. 535 et seqq. of the German Civil Code – Bürgerliches Gesetzbuch (BGB). A translation into English is available under http://www.gesetze-im-internet.de/englisch_bgb/.

[38] OJ 2006 C 179/02.

[39] Implemented mainly by means of Regulation 1370/2007 of the European Parliament and of the Council of 23 October 2007 on public passenger transport services by rail and by road, OJ 2007 L 315/1.

[40] OJ 1992 L 364/7; further explanations of the concept of public service obligations can be found in the communication from the Commission on the interpretation of Council Regulation 3577/92, COM(2014) 232 final, para. 5.

[41] See Recital 32 and Art. 2 of the Commission Decision of 20 December 2011 on the application of Article 106(2) TFEU to state aid in the form of public service compensation granted to certain undertakings entrusted with the operation of services of general economic interest, OJ 2012 L 7/3; Communication from

the Commission 'European Union framework for state aid in the form of public service compensation', OJ 2012 C 8/15, para. 6 and 7.

42 OJ 2001 L 82/16.

43 Regulation 1370/2007 of the European Parliament and of the Council of 23 October 2007 on public passenger transport services by rail and by road, OJ 2007 L 315/1. See also the implementation in Sec. 131 GWB – German Competition Act.

44 COM(2013) 296 final, Art. 7(4) and Art. 2 No. 12.

45 E.g. terms concerning entry into possession by the tenant, the use to which the property is to be put, the obligations of the landlord and tenant regarding the maintenance of the property, the duration of the lease and the giving up of possession to the landlord, the rent and the incidental charges to be paid by the tenant, see ECJ Case 241/83, Erich Rösler gegen Horst Rottwinkel, para. 27.

46 COM(2013) 296 final, Recital 6.

47 On an international level, self-provision of port services is affected under the aspect of organizational and occupational safety by the IMO's Code of Safe Practice for Cargo Stowage and Securing (CSS Code), Resolution A.714(17) of November 1991 and the International Management Code for the Safe Operation of Ships and for Pollution Prevention (ISM Code), Resolution A.741(18) of November 1993, contained in chapter IX of the International Convention for the Safety of Life at Sea (SOLAS). In Germany, the issue of self-provision of port services is not subject of specific regulation, the general rules on occupational safety apply.

48 Art. 11(2) contains a similar provision for internal operators and dredging services.

49 OJ 2006 L 318/17.

50 In the end the amendment to the GBER regarding ports was generous, see Commission Regulation (EU) 2017/1084 of 14 June 2017 amending Regulation (EU) 651/2014 as regards aid for port and airport infrastructure, OJ 2017 L 156/1; Classen, BTJ 2017 (3–4), p. 42.

51 This term refers to Title VII Chapter 1 "Competition Rules", Art. 101 – 109 TFEU.

52 COM(2013) 296 final, Art. 14(3).

53 Despite certain (politically motivated) voices, there is a liberalizing effect of the PPIII through its Chapter II. The extent of this effect depends on the way, port services are currently regulated by the Member States.

54 A political evaluation is offered by Adamopoulos, LL Int Jan/Feb 2017, p. 32.

55 See press release of the Bundeskartellamt, the German Competition Authority, of 18 December 2017, www.bundeskartellamt.de/SharedDocs/Meldung/EN/Pressemitteilungen/2017/18_12_2017_Hafenschlepper.html?nn=3591286, and the corresponding press release of the Dutch Authority for Consumers and Markets of the same day, https://www.acm.nl/en/publications/collaboration-between-bundeskartellamt-and-acm-leads-fines-towage-sector (both accessed on 28 March 2018).

[56] From the established case law see e.g. EJC Case C-322/01, Deutscher Apothekerverband, para. 64.
[57] Recital 38 of Regulation 2017/352.

CHAPTER XVI

THE WTO LEGAL FRAMEWORK FOR EXPORT TRANSACTIONS

Marian PASCHKE

A. WTO LAW AS LEGAL ORDER OF GLOBAL EXPORT BUSINESS

With the globalization of trade relations, the export business has changed dramatically. Goods and services are increasingly global in nature. The export industry is thus constantly faced with the challenge of having to adapt to very different legal environments and regulations. Different rules on market access and treatment of foreign goods in domestic markets create serious difficulties for the exporter in initiating and executing transactions. In view of this, a global, single legal framework has been created at the level of international law with WTO law.

Against this background, the World Trade Organization (WTO), founded on April 15, 1994, embodies the attempt to create and enforce international rules on cross-border trade, which should steer global trade with all its risks into more predictable ways than any other international organization.[1] Due to the fact that nearly all of the world's major trading nations are members of the WTO, the WTO (and thus WTO law) is of paramount importance for international trade, and especially for export. After China and Russia have also joined the WTO, the WTO has created a unique alliance that, with its legal norms, has standardized rules for its member states. Today, about 95% of global trade in goods and services is handled between the Member States of the WTO.

B. THE AGREEMENTS UNDER THE UMBRELLA OF THE WTO

The WTO was founded under the Agreement Establishing the World Trade Organization (WTO-AE); it came into force on 1 January 1995. The WTO emerged from the 1947 General Agreement on Tariffs and Trade (GATT). The GATT was originally intended to form an agreement under the umbrella of the International Trade Organization (ITO), but has gradually been treated as a de facto International Organization due to the failure of the ITO to resist the US Congress.[2] However, this situation has always been unsatisfactory, in particular with regard to the imperfect institutional structure of the GATT and the less effective dispute resolution mechanisms. These weaknesses should be overcome with the establishment of the WTO as a entity of International Trade and International Trade Law.

For the most part, all WTO members subscribe to all WTO agreements. However, there remained four agreements, which had a narrower group of signatories and are known as "plurilateral agreements".

The agreements fall into a structure with six main parts:

- an umbrella agreement – the Agreement Establishing the WTO (AE-WTO)
- agreements for each of the three broad areas of trade that the WTO covers (goods, services and intellectual property)
- dispute settlement – Dispute Settlement Understanding (DSU) and
- reviews of governments' trade policies.

The agreements for the two largest areas – goods and services – start with broad principles: the General Agreement on Tariffs and Trade (GATT) (for goods), and the General Agreement on Trade in Services (GATS). The third area, Trade-Related Aspects of Intellectual Property Rights (TRIPS), also falls into this category although at present it has no additional parts. Then comes extra agreements and annexes dealing with the special requirements of specific sectors or issues. Finally, there are the detailed and lengthy lists (schedules) of commitments made by individual countries allowing specific foreign products or service-providers access to their markets. For GATT, these take the form of binding commitments on tariffs for goods in general, and combinations of tariffs and quotas for some agricultural goods. For GATS, the commitments state how much access foreign service providers are allowed for specific sectors, and they include lists of types of services where individual countries say they are not applying the "most-favored-nation" (MFN) principle of non-discrimination.

C. TASKS AND GOALS OF THE WTO

The role of the WTO as an international organization is to provide a single institutional framework at the global level for the conduct of trade relations among the majority of all states.[3] It also aims to facilitate the implementation and management of the various agreements under its umbrella.[4] In addition, the WTO serves as a negotiating forum for individual Member States on their multilateral trade relations and has the task of settling disputes among them.[5] For this purpose, the DSU has established a differentiated dispute settlement procedure.

The goals set by the WTO go far beyond the mere administration of the respective agreements. The preamble to the WTO-AE first emphasizes the common ground of the contracting parties, when it says

"that their relations in the field of trade and economic endeavour should be conducted with a view to raising standards of living, ensuring full employment and a large and steadily growing volume of real income and effective demand, and expanding the production of and trade in goods and services, while allowing for the optimal use of the world's resources in accordance with the objective of sustainable development, seeking both to protect and preserve the environment and to enhance the means for doing so in a manner consistent with their respective needs and concerns at different levels of economic development"

and

"that there is need for positive efforts designed to ensure that developing countries, and especially the least developed among them, secure a share in the growth in international trade commensurate with the needs of their economic development".

D. THE STRUCTURE AND ORGANIZATION OF WTO

The highest body of the WTO is the Ministerial Conference, which meets every two years and is basically responsible for the tasks of the WTO.[6] Since the WTO was founded, the ministerial conferences have repeatedly been shaped by the differing interests of industrialized and developing countries. In addition to the general allocation of Art. IV: 1, the WTO-AE assigns a number of specific tasks to the Ministerial Conference. It reserves virtually all landmark decisions within the WTO. Of paramount importance is the power of the Ministerial Conference to grant the so-called waiver.[7] Waivers suspend a member from complying with certain obligations resulting from the WTO-AE or the Multilateral Trade Agreement; waivers are exemptions to certain conduct that in itself violates WTO law.

In the intervals between meetings of the Ministerial Conference, its functions shall be conducted by the General Council, to which all Member States send a representative (Art. IV: 2 WTO-AE). It shall meet as appropriate. The General Council also manages the special councils set up for the various agreements (GATT, GATS, etc.),[8] such as the Council for Trade in Goods, the Council for Trade in Services and the Council for Trade-Related Aspects of Intellectual Property Rights.

The Ministerial Conference and the WTO General Council are supported by the WTO Secretariat based in Geneva (Switzerland), which is headed by a Director-General.[9] The task of the Secretariat is, among other things, to prepare the conferences and negotiations within the framework of the WTO, to carry out general documentation duties and to organize the dispute settlement procedures.

The structure can be sketched as follows:

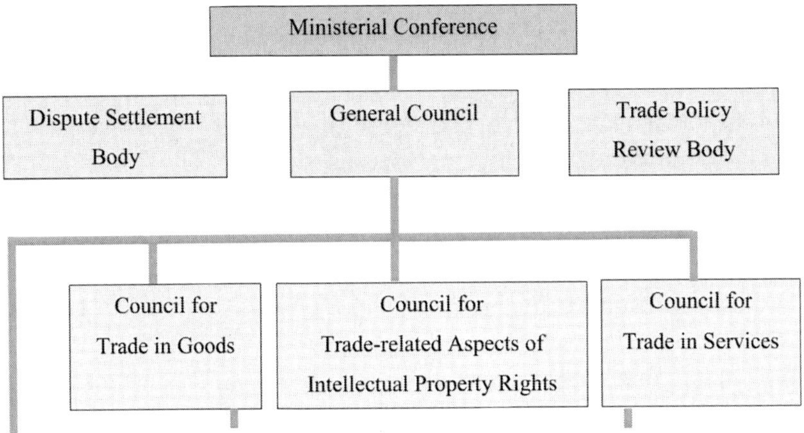

Committees on	**Committees on**	**Committees on**
- Trade and Environment	- Market Access	- Trade in Financial Services Specific Commitments
- Trade and Development	- Agriculture	
- Regional Trade Agreements	- Sanitary and Phytosanitary Measures	**Working Parties on** - Domestic Regulation
- Balance of Payments Restrictions	- Technical Barriers to Trade - Subsidies and Countervailing Measures	- GATS Rules
- Budget, Finance and Administration	- Anti-Dumping Practices - Customs Valuation	
	- Rules of Origin	
Working Parties on	- Import Licensing	
- Accession	- Trade-Related Investment Measures - Safeguards	
Working groups on		
- Trade, debt and finance	**Working party on** - State-Trading Enterprises	
- Trade and technology transfer		

Decisions are always taken in accordance with the principle of consensus, ie a decision is deemed to have been adopted if no formal objection to the proposal in question is lodged. At first there is no vote.[10] But if no consensus can be established, ie if an objection has been raised by a Member State, a vote will take place which, depending on the subject matter, will require different majorities.[11]

E. THE ENFORCEMENT OF WTO LAW

I. DISPUTE SETTLEMENT

The dispute resolution takes place according to the rules of the Dispute Settlement Understanding (DSU). The aim of the DSU is to guarantee security and predictability in the multilateral trading system.[12] The implementation of these aims is to ensure two instances: once the Dispute Settlement Body (DSB) and the Standing Appellate Body (AB) as the review instance. Essentially, the DSB is staffed as the WTO General Council and the DSB is responsible for setting up the so-called panels. This is a group of experts of at least three persons who draw up a report on the relevant dispute, which includes a description of the contentious issue and a decision recommendation. For each dispute brought before the DSB, a new panel will be set up.

The DSU procedure is characterized by several phases: if one member considers that the behavior of another member affects his legal position as warranted by International Trade Law, mutual negotiations are started (so-called consultation phase). In principle, there is an obligation of the infringing member to respond to the request of the injured member within ten days and to start consultations within 30 days; already these processes are to be indicated to the DSB.[13] If the consultations fail to settle a dispute within 60 days after the date of receipt of the request for consultations, the complaining party may request the establishment of a panel.[14] In order to make the procedures more efficient, the period in which the panel shall conduct its examination, from the date that the composition and terms of reference of the panel have been agreed upon until the date the final report is issued to the parties to the dispute, shall, as a general rule, not exceed six months.[15] The report will then be submitted to the DSB for approval. The decision is made in the so-called negative consensus, i.e. only if all members agree that the report should be rejected, will it be deemed accepted to the DSB for adoption.[16] The losing party may file an appeal against the report with the Appellate Body, which, however, is limited to issues of law covered in the panel report and legal interpretations developed by the panel.[17] The report must also be adopted by the DSB, again by way of a negative consensus. If this happens, the parties are irrevocably bound to its content and must comply with this without delay.[18]

In the individual proceedings issues of tariff dismantling play a subordinate role. This is due to the fact that great success has been achieved in this field. On the other hand, there were a number of cases dealing with the issue of equal treatment of foreign and domestic goods. Of even greater importance are questions of so-called cross-sectional areas (environmental protection, etc.). For example, several panels have dealt with issues related to restricting trade for reasons of health, environmental and consumer protection.

II. DECENTRALIZED ENFORCEMENT BY THE PRIVATE SECTOR

As the private sector shapes international trade, it often has an interest in enforcing WTO law: the WTO trade agreements favor them insofar as they regulate the trade policy instruments of the states, which in turn govern international economic relations between private individuals. As a result, private actors are the actual beneficiaries of WTO law, even if it only regulates the rights and obligations of the contracting parties, so that the benefit is predominantly a legal reflex.[19] The WTO Dispute Settlement Mechanism is not available to the private sector for the purpose of enforcing its interests; it can only be initiated by members of the WTO. The private sector, in so far as it intends to take action against the relevant trade barriers which are incompatible with WTO law, is therefore decentralized, ie domestic, enforcement mechanisms. It is important to distinguish whether to act against trade barriers in their home state or in a third country.

With regard to the removal of third-country trade barriers, ie the opening-up of third markets to export-oriented companies, the European Union and the United States, in particular, have developed mechanisms in their national law which allow the private sector to seek action by their home countries against these obstacles to trade. This approach may lead to the initiation of a WTO dispute settlement procedure. The EU adopted the Trade Barrier Regulation on 22.12.1994.[20] It sets up an investigation procedure at the request of EU Member States, business associations and individual companies, which fear disadvantages due to trade barriers from third countries. Applications submitted to the European Commission may be submitted in the event of breaches of international trade rules, including WTO law, which have an impact either on the EU market or on the market of a third country and have adverse effects on the EU economy. In the US, the relevant procedure is based on Section 301 US Trade Act 1974.

Private sector actors can sue in the courts of these states to tackle trade barriers of non-EU countries that are incompatible with WTO law, as well as those of their home country. However, the legal systems of almost all major WTO members fundamentally reject the direct applicability of WTO law. In the EU, for example, in the dispute over the GATT Council's contravention of the Common Organization of the Market in Bananas[21] German banana importers are not relying on the GATT to challenge the regulation.[22] However, under a recognized exception, the right to rely on WTO law for the private sector is possible when the EUC implements a specific commitment made under the WTO.[23]

F. WTO RULES ON TRADE IN GOODS (GATT)

The substantive WTO law on trade in goods is predominantly laid down in the GATT and the corresponding supplementary agreements. The GATT regulates both measures of the WTO members, which are concerned with the trade in goods and are accordingly applied by the customs authorities of a country at the border crossing of goods (import, export and transit), as well as domestic measures, which concern the market entry and the sales of imported goods in their respective markets. The main substantive principles here are the principle of most favored nation treatment[24], the prohibition of quantitative and other restrictions[25] and the binding of customs duties under Article II GATT. National measures are subject to the national equal treatment requirement of Article III GATT. Furthermore, the GATT and its additional agreements contain provisions on trade defense instruments that allow WTO members to levy anti-dumping, countervailing or protective duties on imports.

I. IMPORT AND EXPORT RULES

1. THE TARIFFS-ONLY PRINCIPLE

According to Art. XI: 1 GATT no prohibitions or restrictions other than duties, taxes or other charges, whether made effective through quotas, import or export licenses or other measures, shall be instituted or maintained by any contracting party on the importation of any product of the territory of any other contracting party or on the exportation or sale for export of any product destined for the territory of any other contracting party. Thus, Art. XI: 1 prohibits GATT in principle quantitative restrictions and quotas (for example so-called import quotas). In contrast, tariffs do not have to be completely abolished, but to be lowered. WTO members are thus obliged to abolish non-tariff trade barriers; but they can replace them with customs duties. The GATT thus recognizes in principle only tariffs as a legitimate state instrument for directly influencing the flow of goods at the border. This restriction on tariff barriers is based on the assumption that customs duties are comparatively transparent and less trade distorting measures.

In addition to the quotas and import and export licenses expressly mentioned, Art. XI: 1 GATT also extends to "other measures". This concept is widely interpreted in dispute settlement practice, so that Article XI: 1 of the GATT provides not only for a prohibition of quantitative restrictions but for all trade restrictive measures at the border crossing of a good. By contrast (and unlike EU law), GATT does not extend to measures having equivalent effect to quantitative restrictions applicable to domestic and foreign products, without distinction.

The GATT provides for a whole series of exceptions to this prohibition, for example in Article XI: 2 and Article XII GATT. According to Article XI: 2 (a) GATT, the prohibition of Article XI: 1 GATT does not apply, in particular, to export bans or export restrictions imposed in order to prevent or remedy a critical shortage of foodstuffs or other essential goods. However, the appropriate measures may only be temporary. Art. XI: 2 (b) and (c) GATT contain comparable exemptions for standards and regulations on the classification, grading or marketing of commodities (b) or for imports of agricultural or fishery products (c). In addition, Article XII of the GATT permits certain restrictions to safeguard national balance of payments. However, both the exemptions under Article XI: 2 GATT and those under Article XII GATT must always comply with the special most favored nation obligation of Article XIII GATT, which implies that the quantitative restrictions permitted under Article XI: 2 and Article XII GATT may not discriminate.

As regards non-tariff measures, WTO law contains provisions on technical barriers to trade and sanitary and phytosanitary measures. The Agreement on Technical Barriers to Trade (TBT) is intended to avoid creating unnecessary barriers to international trade through technical regulations, standards and conformity assessment procedures. However, WTO members have the right to take appropriate measures, provided they serve a legitimate purpose such as the protection of health and safety or the environment. Technical regulations and standards must not in principle lead to discrimination between domestic goods and similar imported goods. The Agreement on Sanitary and Phytosanitary Measures (SPS), on the other hand, applies to all measures necessary for the protection of the life or health of humans, animals and plants and that may directly or indirectly affect international trade. WTO members have the right to take sanitary and phytosanitary measures based on scientific principles. However, such measures should not discriminate against imported goods.

Finally, the GATT contains special rules for trade in agricultural products. Art. XI: 2 lit. (a) – (c) GATT, on the one hand, provides for exceptions to the ban on quantitative import and export regulations; Art. XVI: 3 GATT is merely an avoidance obligation for export subsidies in this area.

2. THE PRINCIPLE OF MOST-FAVORED-NATION TREATMENT

The principle of most-favored-nation treatment (MFN) is legally defined in Art. I GATT. Under the agreement, WTO members are obliged to immediately, unconditionally and unconditionally grant benefits, privileges, privileges or exemptions granted to another party to a good for any similar or comparable product originating in or destined for the territory of the other contracting parties are. These advantages may consist in particular in lower duties and the reduction of burdens of all kinds. The most-favored-nation (MFN) principle applies provided that these benefits are granted on imports or exports of like or comparable products. Similar legal definitions can also be found in GATS for cross-border services (Article II GATS) and in TRIPS for intellectual property (Article 4 TRIPS). At its core, this principle ensures that all WTO members are treated equally in terms of granted privileges. Here it becomes clear that the MFN principle is closely intertwined with the theory of comparative cost advantages, because the advantages resulting from these principles should not, as far as possible, be reduced by artificial trade barriers.

The scope of application of the MFN principle extends to all customs duties and customs duties which are bound in the concession lists under Article II GATT, to all other charges which impose import or export, measures to levy customs duties or other charges incurred when goods cross the border be collected. In addition, all tariff and non-tariff measures listed in Art. III: 2, 4 GATT are covered (Art. I: 1 GATT). Although Art. I GATT prohibits a difference in treatment on the basis of the origin of goods differentiations based on product characteristics are permitted. However, if a difference in treatment, which is in itself permissible, results in de facto discrimination on the basis of the nature of the product, it is also prohibited.[26]

The MFN principle can only be applied within the WTO to foreign goods and services; a privilege of domestic goods is not recorded. Furthermore, the principle does not apply to privileges that are agreed under free trade zones or a customs union (e.g. within the EU or MERCOSUR). The MFN principle should not work in such a way that the further development of regional integration projects is inhibited.

At the same time, the most favored nation principle indicates how liberalization of the world trade order is to be achieved: neither the GATT nor the GATS or TRIPS contain provisions that oblige members directly to open up national markets. Rather, this function should be achieved via the MFN principle.

3. TARIFFS

The outstanding goal of the WTO is to allow restrictions on trade in goods only through tariffs. Customs duties are defined as all taxes on goods levied solely on the basis of the border crossing of goods at a customs duty fixed in a customs tariff. WTO law does not prohibit tariffs, but recognizes them as a legitimate measure, in contrast to non-tariff trade barriers.[27]

Customs duties can also considerably restrict international trade. Therefore, Art. XXVIII bis: 1 GATT obliges the members to conduct tariff negotiations in order to achieve a reduction in the general level of customs. The result of these tariff negotiations should be the concessions of the individual members, which include the obligation not to exceed a certain customs level for certain goods. The concessions are summarized in country-specific schedules of concessions and are an integral part of the GATT.[28] The customs duties listed in these schedules represent maximum customs duties which may not be exceeded, but may be fallen below. The goods listed in the country-specific schedules are not only exempted from the customs duties which exceed the maximum rate laid down, but in principle also from all new customs-related charges.[29]

In principle, customs duties and duties equivalent to the most-favored-nation duty are subject to Art. I: 1 GATT. Thereof, however, according to Art. XXIV: 3 GATT exists an exception for free trade zones and customs unions: The reduction or abolition of internal customs duties there does not have to be passed on to third WTO members, provided that the conditions set out in Art. XXIV GATT are met. Also, with the help of the enabling clause developing countries, a reduced tariff can be granted under a generalized system of preferences.

4. RULES OF ORIGIN

On the basis of rules of origin, a product is assigned a specific origin – an origin. This allocation is complicated nowadays because of the international division of labor, since goods are often just the end product of a chain of processing that has taken place in different countries. Nevertheless, such an allocation of origin is important because it is only on the basis of that allocation that goods can be treated at a tariff level, in particular with regard to import duties and anti-dumping duties. Also, rules of origin serve to distinguish between goods that can be imported under low-tariff trade agreements and those that are not subject to a privileged agreement. Rules of origin should be technical, objective and thus ultimately non-political rules. In practice, however, they are also often used as trading instruments to enforce a particular trade policy.

As regards rules of origin, a distinction must be made between non-preferential and preferential rules: non-preferential rules of origin apply to cases which are not subject to a preferential trade agreement, while the preferential ones apply precisely to such agreements. In the case of non-preferential rules of origin, it depends on whether foreign products have been used for the production of a product or whether processing or processing has taken place outside the country of manufacture. If no foreign products have been used for the production of a product and no processing or processing has taken place abroad (wholly produced / wholly obtained), the product originates in the country of manufacture. If this is not the case, then the criterion of substantial transformation applies. This grants a wide judgment margin. In contrast, preferential trade agreements often contain special rules of origin to prevent the use of this privileging agreement by third countries.

In the Agreement on Rules of Origin (ARO), WTO law contains legal rules on rules of origin. However, the Convention itself does not establish an internationally harmonized system of rules of origin, but merely constitutes a legal framework within which such should be negotiated. However, until the achievement of this objective, certain transitional provisions apply. The ARO only applies to non-preferential rules of origin. For rules of origin in preferential systems, and thus for around 50% of world trade, the Convention gives only some guidance in its Annex II.

The aim of the agreement is to harmonize the national rules of origin, which should take into account the objectives of Art. 9 ARO. In this way, a uniform system of rules of origin should be created for all areas mentioned in Art. 1 ARO, according to which national rules on rules of origin must be aligned. In particular, Article 9 ARO requires that the rules of origin be objective, understandable and predictable and not used as a means of trade policy or distort trade.

5. FREEDOM OF TRANSIT

Pursuant to Art. V: 2 GATT, there is freedom of transit through the territory of each contracting party for the transit traffic to and from the territory of the other contracting parties using the means of international transit. However, each Contracting Party may require that transit be notified to the competent customs office. Transit traffic may not be delayed unnecessarily. In addition, it is exempt from customs duties as well as all transit or other taxes or charges, with the exception of levies, which correspond to the administrative expenses incurred by transit and the cost of the services.[30] Transit freedom acc. Art. V: 2 GATT does not apply to aircraft in transit; however, it applies to the transit of goods by air (including baggage).[31]

II. NATIONAL TREATMENT

The principle of national treatment acc. Article III of GATT seeks to ensure that goods that have once entered a foreign market are treated in the same way as equivalent, substitutable or directly competitive domestic products. Behind this is the realization that it is of little use to gain access to foreign markets if the distribution of the products is significantly impeded by national regulations.

The national treatment requirement presupposes that the trade deals with like products or directly competitive / directly substitutable products. Similar domestic and foreign goods are subject to an absolute prohibition of discrimination (Art. III: 2–1 GATT), while acc. to Art. III: 2–2 GATT for substitutable or competing goods the conditions of Art. III: 1 GATT apply.

The national treatment requirement covers – subject to certain areas of exceptions[32] – all imported products as far as they have passed the customs. Its scope therefore includes domestic fiscal measures: Imported goods should therefore not be subject, directly or indirectly, to higher taxes or duties than to comparable domestic products.[33] In addition, all laws and regulations governing the sale, supply, purchase, transport, distribution or use of domestic products must be applied in such a way that imported goods are not treated worse than domestic ones. Finally, domestic quantitative restrictions which stipulate that a certain proportion of the products must come from domestic production are also prohibited.[34] Like the MFN principle, Article III of the GATT prohibits both de jure and de facto discrimination.

III. GENERAL EXCEPTIONS

The GATT's derogations are aimed at giving WTO members a degree of freedom to protect their *ordre public*. Within this space, they should be able to pursue meaningful political and social goals, even if they contradict the WTO principles and regulations on free trade. In addition to the general exceptions of Art. XX GATT and to the security policy exceptions of Art. XXI GATT, there is the possibility of waiving a GATT obligation by waiver altogether.

Article XX GATT contains as justification reasons non-economic objectives that a WTO member may pursue. Their test needs a two-step test developed by the Appellate Body in the Gasoline case[35]: First of all, it is checked whether the measure belongs to one of the Art. XX lit. (a) to (j) GATT listed objectives and the particular conditions of this objective are met. Then the means chosen must meet the requirements of the "chapeau".[36] The "chapeau" is an expression of the principle of good faith recognized by international law and qualifies the admissibility of exceptions in two ways: they must not be applied in such a way that they lead to arbitrary or unjustifiable discrimination. In addition, they must not lead to a disguised restriction on international trade.

IV. PROTECTIVE MEASURES

In addition to the general principles of law mentioned above, WTO law also provides a legal framework for Member States' protective instruments, which apply in particular to anti-dumping measures and subsidy payments as well as to all other general protective measures that can be adopted theoretically.

1. DUMPING

Dumping occurs when the export price of a product is lower than its normal value. The difference between the dumped export price and the normal price is called the dumping margin. The normal value is the average selling price in the exporting State or a constructed value including the cost of production plus a reasonable profit margin.

The rules under WTO law on dumping are set out in Article VI: 1 GATT and in the Anti-Dumping Agreement (ADA).[37] WTO law condemns dumping if it results in material injury to the export market. However, WTO members are not required to intervene against such commercial practices of their exporters. On the other hand, the targeted promotion of exports through export subsidies is prohibited.[38] Art. VI: 2 GATT also allows the importing country to levy an anti-dumping duty for compensation.

According to Art. 1 and Art. 18.1 ADA, an anti-dumping duty may be levied only in the circumstances described in Art. VI GATT and after an investigation in accordance with the ADA. The substantive conditions for imposing an anti-dumping duty are the existence of dumping, injury to a domestic industry producing like products, causality between dumping and damage and the interest in imposing the anti-dumping duty.[39]

2. SUBSIDIES

WTO law contains provisions on subsidies in Article XVI GATT and in the Agreement on Subsidies and Counter-measures Measures (SCM). For the purpose of this Agreement, a subsidy shall be deemed to exist if:

"(a) (1) there is a financial contribution by a government or any public body within the territory of a Member (referred to in this Agreement as "government"), i.e. where:

(i) a government practice involves a direct transfer of funds (e.g. grants, loans, and equity infusion), potential direct transfers of funds or liabilities (e.g. loan guarantees);

(ii) government revenue that is otherwise due is foregone or not collected (e.g. fiscal incentives such as tax credits);

(iii) a government provides goods or services other than general infrastructure, or purchases goods;

(iv) a government makes payments to a funding mechanism, or entrusts or directs a private body to carry out one or more of the type of functions illustrated in (i) to (iii) above which would normally be vested in the government and the practice, in no real sense, differs from practices normally followed by governments;

or

(a)(2) there is any form of income or price support in the sense of Article XVI of GATT 1994."

If a state measure is subject to this subsidy concept, then in order for the regulations of the SCM to be applied, specificity must be ensured, Art. 2 SCM. The specificity feature is intended to separate publicly available subsidies from those that distort competition. It is necessary to distinguish between the irrefutable presumption of specificity, for example in export subsidies[40], and the separate determination of specificity according to Art. 2.1. SCM.

The SCM distinguishes between prohibited, contestable and permitted subsidies. Unlike EU law, there is no comprehensive ban on any subsidy with a duty to eliminate it in case of infringement. Only all subsidies listed in Article 3 SCM, namely export subsidies, are prohibited. According to Art. 5, 6 SCM, subsidies that are specific within the meaning of Art. 2 SCM and have a detrimental effect on the interests of another WTO member are considered countervailable. On the other hand, subsidies listed in Art. 8 SCM are permitted.

There are two options for banned and countervailable subsidies. First of all, using the dispute settlement procedure, with the SCM incorporating certain procedural modifications, it is up to the WTO to decide that another member must withdraw subsidies. On the other hand, a WTO member can, at the request of the private sector, autonomously impose countervailing import duties on subsidized imports by means of its internal anti-subsidy legislation, which must comply with Article 10 et seq.

3. General protective measures

The Agreement on Safeguards (AoS) in conjunction with Article XIX GATT is another trade defense instrument allowing WTO members to impose protective tariffs on imports. These protective duties are different from anti-dumping or anti-subsidy duties against legitimate commercial practices. The material conditions for the imposition of protective duties are, according to Articles 2 and 4 AoS, the sharp rise in imports, which leads to serious damage to a domestic industry. The increase in imports must be causal for the injury.

The adoption of protective measures requires an investigation in accordance with Art. 3 AoS. Protective measures may only be issued to the extent and within the timeframe necessary to remedy the damage. In contrast to anti-dumping or anti-subsidy duties, in the case of safeguard measures, the WTO members concerned can demand compensation for the trade restriction and, after unsuccessful consultations, suspend the application of substantially equivalent concessions or other obligations under GATT 1994, Article 8.2 AoS.

G. Trade in Services (GATS)

The GATS is a multilateral legal framework for cross-border trade in services.[41] Its main purpose is a comprehensive liberalization of trade in services, which is to be realized with a similar instrument as the GATT. This Agreement applies to measures by Members affecting trade in services.[42] "Services" includes any service in any sector except services supplied in the exercise of governmental authority, especially the production, distribution, marketing, sale and provision of a service.[43]

GATS regulations distinguish between areas for which the members have made liberalization concessions and areas without concessions. Concessions are made by the fact that the respective member lists the service sectors and respective activities (schedules), in which it binds itself to the special rules of the GATS and thus wants to open the market. While there is basically only the general MFN principle in service-sectors without commitments,[44] in sectors where market-access commitments are undertaken, above all, the requirement of national treatment and the prohibition of quantitative restrictions are added.[45]

H. TRADE-RELATED ASPECTS OF INTELLECTUAL PROPERTY RIGHTS (TRIPS)

The protection of intellectual property is governed by the Agreement on Trade-Related Aspects of Intellectual Property (TRIPS). TRIPS covers the protection of copyright, trademarks, geographical indications, industrial designs and patents. The Agreement knows about mechanisms that should help to effectively enforce or protect industrial property rights.[46] Like the GATT and GATS, TRIPS knows the imperative of national treatment and the most-favoured-nation principle.[47] The substantive requirements for the protection to be granted by the WTO Member States are set out in Articles 9–40 TRIPS; they are quite broad.[48] Articles 9 – 14 govern copyrights and related rights, Articles 15 to 21 regulate the protection of trade marks, Articles 22 to 24 Geographical Indications, Articles 25 and 26 Industrial designs, Articles 27 to 34 Patents and Art. 35 to 38 topographies of integrated circuits.

LITERATURE

Bronckers, Enforcing WTI Law through the EC Trade Barriers Regulation, 3 TRL (1997), p. 76

Grossmann/Horn, Why the WTO), in: Horn/Mavroidis (eds.), Legal and economic principles of world trade law (2013), p. 9 et seq.

Horlick/Shea, The World Trade Organization Antidumping Agreement, 29 Journal of World Trade (1995), p. 1
Jackson, Restructuring the GATT System (1990)
Petersmann, Why Rational Choice Theory Requires a Multilevel Constitutional Approach to International Economic Law, Illinois Law Review 2008, p. 359
Taubmann/Wager/Wald (ed.), A Handbook on the WTO TRIPS Agreement (2013)
Van Grassek, The History and Future of the WTO (2013)
Weiss, The General Agreement on Trade in Services 1994, 32 CMLRev. (1995), p. 1177

NOTES

1 Cf. Van Grassek, The History and Future of the WTO (2013); Grossmann/Horn, Why the WTO), in: Horn/Mavroidis (eds.), Legal and economic principles of world trade law (2013), p. 9 et seq.
2 Cf. Jackson, Restructuring the GATT System (1990).
3 Art. II:1 WTO-AE.
4 Art. III:1 WTO-AE.
5 Art. III:3 WTO-AE.
6 Art. IV:1 WTO-AE.
7 Cf. Art. IX:3 WTO-AE.
8 Article IV:5 WTO-AE
9 Cf. Art. VI:1 AE-WTO.
10 Art. IX: 1 WTO-AE.
11 Art. IX and Art. X WTO-AE.
12 Art. 3.2. DSU.
13 Cf. Art. 4 DSU.
14 Artt. 4.7., 4.3. and 5.3. DSU.
15 Art. 12.8. DSU. In cases of urgency, the panel shall aim to issue its report to the parties to the dispute within three months.
16 Art. 16.4. DSU.
17 Art. 17.6. DSU.
18 Art. 21.1. DSU.
19 Petersmann, Illinois Law Review 2008, p. 359.
20 See Bronckers, 3 TRL (1997), p. 76.
21 Council Regulation (EEC) No 404/93 of 13 February 1993, OJ 1993 L 47, p. 1.
22 ECJ, C-307/99, OGT Fruchthandelsgesellschaft, 2001, I-3159.
23 ECJ, C-69/89, Nakajima, 1991, I-2069 (31).
24 Art. I GATT.
25 Art. XI GATT.
26 Cf. Canada – Automotive Industry, WT/DS139, 142/AB/R.
27 Cf. Art. XI:1 GATT.
28 See Art. II:7 GATT.

[29] Cf. Art. II:1 lit. b S. 2 GATT.
[30] Art. V:3 GATT.
[31] Art. VII GATT.
[32] Exceptions exist for cinemamovies (Art. III:10 GATT), public procurement (Art. III:8 lit. a GATT), and subsidies Art. III:8 lit b GATT).
[33] Art. III:2 GATT.
[34] Art. III:1 GATT.
[35] US-Gasoline, WT/DS2/AB/R.
[36] Cf. the case US-Shrimp, WT/DS58/AB/R.
[37] Agreement on Implementation of Article VI of GATT 1994.
[38] Cf. Art. 3.1 Agreement on Subsidies and Countervailing Measures.
[39] Horlick/Shea, 29 Journal of World Trade (1995), p. 1.
[40] See Art. 2.3, Art. 3 SCM.
[41] Weiss, CMLRev. 32 (1995), p. 1177.
[42] Art. I: 2 GATS.
[43] Art. XXVIII lit. (b) GATS.
[44] Art. II:1 GATS.
[45] Art. XVI, XVII GATS.
[46] Art. 40 ff. TRIPS.
[47] Art. 3 und Art. 4 TRIPS.
[48] Cf. Taubmann/Wager/Wald (ed.), A Handbook on the WTO TRIPS Agreement (2013).

CHAPTER XVII

THE EU LEGAL FRAMEWORK FOR EXPORT TRANSACTIONS

Marian PASCHKE

EU law does not know a self-contained codification for export transactions. Rather, the legal situation is characterized by rules that differentiate whether an export transaction within the EU is carried out (see under A.) or whether it is related to non-EU states. In the case of the latter, a distinction must be made between exports from the EU to so-called third countries and imports into the EU from third countries. The following presentation is based on this very distinction (see under B. and C.) and additionally takes up legal issues of legal protection in foreign trade (see under D.).

A. EXPORT TRANSACTIONS WITHIN THE EU

Exports within the EU are significantly characterized by a far-reaching grant of freedom. Accordingly, the rules governing the free movement of goods governing imports and exports in the internal market must not be subject to any tariffs or other restrictions, but, in addition, can the other fundamental freedoms and competition law also play an important role in export activities. These guarantees of freedom can usually be enforced by means of effective legal protection instruments, which is of particular interest to companies active in the export sector.

I. THE FREE MOVEMENT OF GOODS

The free movement of goods within the internal market is first guaranteed by the Customs Union, the essential element of which is the prohibition of internal customs duties and charges having equivalent effect, Article 30 TFEU. he abolition of all restrictions is also ensured by the prohibition of quantitative restrictions and measures having equivalent effect, Article 34 TFEU.

1. THE PROHIBITION OF INTERNAL CUSTOMS DUTIES AND CHARGES HAVING EQUIVALENT EFFECT

Article 28 TFEU establishes a customs union covering the entire exchange of goods and the collection of import duties, export duties and customs duties between Member States. Article 30 TFEU also prohibits charges having equivalent effect. In addition, a Common Customs Tariff will be introduced to third countries. Due to these regulations, tariffs no longer play a role in trade within the EU, but only in the EU's common external tariff. Furthermore, since January 1993, controls on the movement of goods within the internal market have been abolished.

However, charges of equivalent effect may still cause problems. This term covers all financial charges incurred by Member States as a result of the border crossing. Such charges are as well as domestic duties according to Articles 28, 30 TFEU without exception prohibited. The delineation of domestic levies on products imported from other Member States on the occasion of the border crossing in accordance with Article 110 TFEU is problematic. The difference here is that the prohibited duties having equivalent effect are levied solely on the imported product as such, while the allowable domestic taxes under Article 110 TFEU apply equally to domestic and foreign products under objective domestic criteria, under a general system of domestic taxation or to offset the tax burden on domestic and foreign products.

2. THE PROHIBITION OF QUANTITATIVE RESTRICTIONS AND MEASURES HAVING EQUIVALENT EFFECT – THE FREE MOVEMENT OF GOODS

Although the abolition of customs duties has strongly favored trade in goods within the Union, which accounts for a large part of the total imports and exports of Member States, other barriers to trade aside from customs duties may restrict the free movement of goods within the internal market (so-called non-tariff barriers). In order to reduce those restrictions as well, quantitative restrictions on imports and exports and all measures having equivalent effect between Member States are prohibited under Articles 34 and 35 TFEU. This prohibition is directly applicable, ie the individual can rely on it before national courts. Quantitative import or export provisions (for example, quotas or quotas) are virtually eliminated between Member States, so that only measures having equivalent effect in the area of trade in goods are relevant.

As a measure having equivalent effect, the European Court of Justice recognizes any State trade regime which is capable of hindering, directly or indirectly, actually or potentially, intra-Community trade. The very broad scope of the free movement of goods, which has ultimately developed from a prohibition of discrimination to a restriction prohibition, restricts the ECJ since the early 1990s through the so-called Keck formula. According to this case-law, a distinction must be made between so-called product-related and sales-related modalities: national provisions which restrict or prohibit certain aspects of the distribution of a product and which do not discriminate directly or indirectly against foreign products are not covered by Article 34 TFEU. An example of such sales-related modalities is shop opening hours or another on restrictions on the hours of work of sales personnel. On the other hand, product-related rules continue to fall under the prohibition of Article 34 TFEU.

Trade restrictions within the meaning of Article 34 TFEU are not absolutely prohibited. Such measures can in many cases be justified by the exception of Article 36 TFEU or by the unwritten justification of overriding requirements in the general public interest, provided that they comply with the principle of proportionality. Article 36 TFEU cites public morals, order and safety, the protection of the health and life of humans, animals or plants, the protection of national treasures or the protection of industrial and commercial property as justifications for import, export and transit bans or restrictions commercial property.

As unwritten justifications, which however do not apply in the case of direct discrimination, the ECJ has so far recognized, for example, consumer protection, the fairness of trade and the protection of employees. In addition, fundamental rights of the Union and, with the entry into force of the previously legally non-binding Charter of Fundamental Rights, the fundamental rights set out therein may justify restrictions on the free movement of goods.[1]

The free movement of goods also gives Member States the obligation to intervene against disabilities by private individuals.[2] It is controversial and has not yet been clearly decided by the ECJ whether the principle of free movement of goods, in addition to other fundamental freedoms,[3] has a direct third-party effect in the form that it is directly applicable to private persons. However, the fundamental convergence of basic freedoms, which is to be seen in principle, argues in favor of such a third-party effect even within the scope of the free movement of goods.

II. OTHER FUNDAMENTAL FREEDOMS

The European internal market not only aims for an unrestricted exchange of goods between the Member States but also pursues a comprehensive approach to freedom of movement for services (Article 56 et seq. TFEU), the establishment of legal or natural persons (Article 49 et seq. TFEU), the free movement of workers (Article 45 TFEU) and capital and payments (Article 63 TFEU). Like the free movement of goods, these fundamental freedoms are directly applicable. Also in this regard, the enforcement of the internal market is of paramount importance.

The freedom to provide services (Art. 56 et seq. TFEU) comprises according to Art. Article 57 (1) TFEU any service normally provided for remuneration, unless it is subject to the rules on the free movement of goods and capital and on the free movement of persons. In contrast to the freedom of establishment, temporary self-employment is important. The ECJ has developed the freedom to provide services from a prohibition of discrimination to a restriction prohibition. However, a restriction is permissible if there are written or unwritten justifications.[4]

In principle, the freedom to provide services also includes the free export of services, that is, the Member States are not allowed to restrict the export of services from their territory, although in contrast to the free movement of goods, under Article 35 TFEU an explicit prohibition on restrictions on the export of goods applies. A prohibition of restrictions on the export of services is not expressly regulated in the EU Treaties. However, the ECJ requires that companies can also rely on the freedom to provide services in the provision of cross-border services to their country of residence.[5] Thus, in particular those measures which are likely to hinder the access of services to the market of another Member State are in particular prohibited.[6]

Under Article 49 TFEU, restrictions on the freedom of establishment of nationals of one EU Member State in the territory of another Member State are in principle prohibited. First of all, every EU citizen has the right to settle in another Member State, with Article 51 TFEU containing a derogation from that principle for activities involving the exercise of official authority in a Member State. Article 52 TFEU also allows derogations by Member States on grounds of public policy, public security, public health or public health. Under Article 54 TFEU, the freedom of establishment extends to companies incorporated under the legislation of a Member State having their registered office, head office or principal place of business within the Union.

The freedom of establishment grants a total of a right of residence for self-employed, a right to national equal treatment and a restriction prohibition.

In order to ensure the mobility of workers essential for market integration, the TFEU requires Member States to progressively establish the free movement of workers within the EU (Article 45 TFEU). The core of the freedom of movement for workers is the right of EU foreigners to be allowed to work and to work in the host Member State on the same conditions as nationals (Article 45 (2), (3) (c) TFEU). This employment-related national equality claim has been strengthened in the case-law of the Court of Justice to an almost universal prohibition of discrimination in favor of the foreign worker.

Finally, under Article 63 TFEU, all restrictions on capital movements and payments are prohibited. Unlike the other fundamental freedoms, it also covers trade with third countries, which plays a role in particular for export to the European Union. National rules restricting capital and payment transactions and affecting business operations outside the EU are prohibited, as are regulations that only affect trade within the EU.

III. EUROPEAN COMPETITION LAW

European competition law is laid down in Articles 101–109 TFEU and in a number of regulations, which mainly concern the procedure. From a theoretical perspective, it is clear that the creation of an internal market in which state interventions and obstacles should be kept to a minimum by means of the fundamental freedoms not only needs to have positive sides, but sometimes also facilitates cross-border restraints on the competitive process by private individuals. In the context of European integration, European competition law has the function of preventing these restrictions and thus guaranteeing a functioning and competitive economic system. The freedom offered by the European internal market should therefore be protected from private and public interference with competition, to put it in a nutshell. Competition law thus forms a functional unit with the fundamental freedoms.

Accordingly, Article 101 TFEU contains a general prohibition on cartel prohibiting restrictive measures between undertakings and associations of undertakings. The agreements under the prohibition are according to Article 101 (2) TFEU void. Finally, Article 101 (3) TFEU provides, under certain conditions, for the possibility of exempting from the prohibition agreements that are 'in itself' covered by the prohibition of competition (exemption). The corresponding antitrust proceedings are governed by the Antitrust Regulation,[7] in which the legal exception system in particular has been established.

In view of the fact that even a single undertaking, provided it has some market power, can harm competition, Article 102 TFEU seeks to prevent such conduct by prohibiting the abuse of a dominant position. In addition, mergers of companies may restrict competition. Accordingly, such concentrations are reviewed on the basis of the Merger Regulation.[8]

Article 106 TFEU regulates the principle of equal treatment of public and private undertakings, with certain exceptions. Finally, Article 107 TFEU prohibits Member States from influencing competition by means of subsidies (subsidies); The prohibition of aid laid down in Article 107 (1) TFEU is of particular interest in the context of the current economic crisis and the problem of export subsidies. With regard to export subsidies, it should be noted that they are in principle incompatible with the internal market in respect of exports to other Member States or to the EEA.[9]

IV. LEGAL PROTECTION FOR EXPORT MEASURES WITHIN THE EU

Where private operators, in particular export-oriented firms, are hindered in the internal market by the Member States in the exercise of their freedoms guaranteed by EU law, they have first and foremost legal protection before national courts. They must directly apply EU law, in particular fundamental freedoms, and moreover, give precedence over conflicting national law. In the event that the national courts have questions as to the interpretation or validity of applicable Union law, they have the preliminary ruling procedure under Article 267 TFEU at their disposal. Under this procedure, they can submit questions about the interpretation or validity of secondary EU law to the ECJ. With regard to validity issues, there is a duty of submission for all national courts. Interpretation questions, on the other hand, must be brought before national courts exclusively at the last instance. In the final instance, there are those courts against whose decision no appeal is possible. All other courts nevertheless have the right to call the ECJ. The decision of the ECJ is binding on the referring court.

Moreover, in the event of a Member State's injury to a European Union law which causes harm, a claim for damages against the Member State concerned may be made. The basis here is the judicature of the European Union created by the ECJ judicially. The condition for this is that the Member State infringes in a sufficiently qualified manner against a Union law providing individual rights to individuals and that there is causality between the infringement and the damage involved.[10]

If, on the other hand, acts of the European Union prevent private actors from carrying out their activities in the internal market, they are entitled, under the conditions laid down in Article 263 (4) TFEU, to bring proceedings for annulment of the ECJ. Accordingly, any natural or legal person may bring an action against the decisions addressed to him and against those decisions which, although issued as a regulation or as a decision addressed to another person, are of direct and individual concern to them.

The actions of other companies that infringe the competition law (eg by cartel agreements or the abuse of a dominant position) can be pursued by means of a civil dispute. In addition, the initiation of an administrative procedure can be requested from the competent antitrust authority.

B. EXPORTS FROM THE EU TO THIRD COUNTRIES

Another element of the EU's legal framework for export is the EU's export regulations in third countries. In this regard, primary EU law contains only a few regulations. Article 35 TFEU, which prohibits restrictions on exports expressis verbis, applies only in trade between Member States, but not in relation to export from the EU. But here too, EU law is based on a comprehensive guarantee of freedom: due to the principle of so-called export freedom, restrictions on exports from the European Union are only possible under strict conditions.

I. THE PRINCIPLE OF EXPORT FREEDOM

The principle of export or export freedom is not expressly laid down in primary EU law. It arises, on the one hand, from Article 206 TFEU, which reflects a commitment to a liberal trade policy, and, on the other hand, from various constitutional guarantees at Union level, in particular freedom of occupation, trade and business.

In secondary legislation, however, export freedom is expressly laid down in Article 1 of Regulation (EU) 2015/479 establishing a common export regime, the so-called Export Regulation.[11] According to Article 1 of the Exporting Regulation, exports by the European Community to third countries are free, that is to say, they are not subject to any quantitative restrictions. Under the Export Regulation, this freedom can be intervened by the Community and the Member States only under strict conditions. Export means the removal of goods from the territory of the Union to third countries. Third countries are in principle all states that are not member states of the EU within the meaning of Art. 52 TEU, 355 TFEU. European Union law prohibits not only quantitative restrictions on exports but, as in the case of fundamental freedoms, all measures having equivalent effect.[12]

II. PROTECTIVE MEASURES

The export freedom does not apply without exception.

1. PROTECTIVE MEASURES BASED ON EXPORT REGULATION (EU) 2015/479

Article 5 of the Export Regulation already provides:

"In order to prevent a critical situation from arising on account of a shortage of essential products, or to remedy such a situation, and where Union interests call for immediate intervention, the Commission, acting at the request of a Member State or on its own initiative, and taking account of the nature of the products and of the other particular features of the transactions in question, may make the export of a product subject to the production of an export authorisation, the granting of which shall be governed by such provisions and subject to such limits as the Commission shall lay down in accordance with the examination procedure referred to in Article 3(2), or, in cases of urgency, in accordance with Article 3(3)."

Excluded are initially goods that are subject to the EURATOM Treaty, as well as so-called dual-use goods. Where the interests of the Union so require, the Commission may, acting in accordance with the examination procedure referred to in Article 3(2), adopt appropriate measures:

"(a) to prevent a critical situation from arising owing to a shortage of essential products, or to remedy such a situation;

(b) to allow international undertakings entered into by the Union or all the Member States to be fulfilled, in particular those relating to trade in primary products."

According to the same regulation the measures "may be limited to exports to certain countries or to exports from certain regions of the Union. They shall not affect products already on their way to the Union frontier", Art. 6 (2) Export Regulation.

When quantitative restrictions on exports are introduced, account shall be taken, according to Art. 6 Export Regulation, in particular of:

"(a) the volume of goods exported under contracts concluded on normal terms and conditions before the entry into force of a protective measure within the meaning of this Chapter and notified by the Member State concerned to the Commission in conformity with its national laws; and

(b) the need to avoid jeopardising the achievement of the aim pursued in introducing quantitative restrictions."

In addition, international agreements concluded by the EU with third countries to restrict their exports or to remove quantitative restrictions have priority over export. Furthermore, export freedom can be restricted by EU economic sanctions within the meaning of Article 215 TFEU.

2. THE DUAL-USE-GOODS-REGULATION

The freedom to export is limited by the Council Regulation (EC) No 428/2009 on a regime for the control of exports of dual-use items and technology.[13] Dual-use goods are goods, including data processing programs and technologies that can be used for both civilian and military purposes. The export of dual-use items listed in the Annex to the Regulation requires an export license valid throughout the European Union. The approval is granted subject to substantive considerations such as considerations of national foreign and security policy and aspects of intended end use (Article 12 of Regulation No 428/2009).

For certain product groups listed in the Annex to the Dual-Use Goods Regulation, a general Union-wide export authorization is granted for Australia, Canada, the USA, Japan, Norway, New Zealand and Switzerland. All other exports subject to authorization shall be authorized by the competent authorities of the Member State in which the exporter is established. In doing so, Member States must respect the obligations stemming from the international non-proliferation agreements and the positions of the European Union, the OSCE or the United Nations.

For the export of dual-use items not listed in the Annex to the Regulation, it is necessary to submit an export license if the exporter has been informed by the competent authorities that the goods in question are intended for the development, manufacture, handling, operation, maintenance, storage, location, identification or distribution of chemical, biological or nuclear weapons or means of delivery of such weapons or could be used.

3. The regulation on the export of cultural goods

Certain cultural goods are subject to export restrictions under the Regulation on the export of cultural goods.[14] In contrast to dual-use goods, however, there is basically an authorization requirement of the respective exporter, unless certain conditions preclude – mainly national legislation for the protection of artistic or archaeological objects.[15] Article 1 of the Regulation refers to the Annex for the list of cultural goods, in which they are exhaustively listed. Art. 2 VO No. 116/2009 establishes the permit requirement and describes the approval procedure.

4. Restriction of export freedom through economic sanctions of the EU

Since the nature of EU economic sanctions, and therefore their legal basis, has long been controversial, Article 215 TFEU now contains a provision in this regard. Accordingly, common positions or joint actions may provide for action by the European Union to suspend economic and financial relations with third countries. The measures must be adopted unanimously according to Articles 28, 31 TEU. The measures will then be adopted by the Council, acting by a joint proposal from the High Representative of the Union for Foreign Affairs and Security Policy and the Commission, acting by a qualified majority.

In practice, a so-called embargo regulation is enacted, which can in principle constitute a (permissible) restriction of foreign trade freedom, for example by providing for a ban on the export of goods to a particular country. The respective regulations are based directly on Article 215 TFEU. However, as far as anti-terrorism measures relating to capital movements and payments are concerned, the special provision of Article 75 TFEU applies. The sometimes serious consequences of such sanctions have repeatedly challenged the ECJ in recent years.

5. Harmonization of export credit insurance systems

Each Member State has its own export credit insurance programs, whose guarantee arrangements, premiums and cover policies are significantly different. These differences can lead to significant distortions of competition within the EU and thus have a significant impact on exports. These differences can ultimately be at the expense of export freedom.

In order to reduce these distortions, the EC has adopted Directive 98/29/EC harmonizing the main provisions on export credit insurance to cover medium and long-term business. The Directive applies to transactions covering the export of goods and/or services originating in a Member State, provided that such assistance is granted, directly or indirectly, on behalf of or with the assistance of one or more Member States and the risk duration, ie the repayment period, is finally, the manufacturing time is at least two years in total (Article 1 (1) of Directive 98/29/EC). It shall not apply to the coverage of bidding guarantees, the reimbursement of advance payments, the proper execution, retention or covering of risks for equipment and equipment for public works used for the execution of the commercial contract (Art. 1 (2) Directive 98/29/EC).

Member States shall ensure that insurers act in accordance with the provisions of the Directive or its Annex in the insurance of transactions related to the export of goods and/or services. This applies to insurers providing cover, directly or indirectly, on behalf of or with the assistance of a Member State in the form of export credit insurance or guarantees or refinancing loans. It is also assumed that these transactions are addressed to countries outside the EU and that financing is provided by order or supplier credit or cash (Article 2 Directive 98/29/EC). The Annex to the Directive contains principles that have to be made applicable to export credit insurance, covering coverage (Chapter I), applicable premiums (Chapter II) and country coverage (Chapter III). In addition, notification rules are provided to increase transparency (Chapter IV).

C. IMPORTS FROM THIRD COUNTRIES

The EU not only guarantees its companies the freedom to export goods, but, in return, to import goods from third countries free of restrictions. The limits of this freedom are laid down in the Regulation on the common rules for imports.[16] In addition, tariffs and safeguard measures based on the common commercial policy play a major role here.

I. PRINCIPLE OF IMPORT FREEDOM

The importation of goods from third countries is subject to the principle of import freedom. This principle is expressly set out in Article 1 (2) of Regulation (EC) No 260/2009 on common rules for imports. The Regulation has established a common import regime of the EU. However, the primary legal anchoring should again result from the liberal basic attitude of the EU in Article 206 TFEU in conjunction with various fundamental rights of the Union. In addition to the principle of import freedom, the Regulation sets out procedures by which the EU may apply the necessary monitoring and safeguard measures with regard to imports in order to protect its interests.

The Regulation applies in principle to all imports of products originating in third countries. Exemptions exist for textile products[17] for which there is a specific import regime and for goods from certain third countries[18] which also have a specific common import regime.

II. RESTRICTIONS

Although the Council Regulation No 260/2009 prescribes the principle of the importation of goods originating in third countries, it provides for the possibility of any safeguard measures that may be adopted in accordance with the WTO law. The Regulation establishes a special consultation procedure (Articles 3 and 4) between the Commission and the Member States, which investigates whether third country products threaten to harm producers within the Community. If this is the case, monitoring measures can be established which subject both imports to statistical registrations (Article 11) and make them subject to the presentation of an import document (Article 12).

As an actual protective measure, imports may also be subject to genuine authorizations (Article 16 (1) (b)), the result of which being quantitative restrictions on imports by quotas. For these quotas, the material condition is that there must be an increased volume of imports of the specific product and / or that producers of like or directly competing products are significantly damaged or threatened with such injury. In relation to WTO members, under the WTO Agreement on Safeguard Measures, import restrictions are only possible if both conditions are met, ie there must be an increased import volume and injury.

In addition, Regulation (EC) No 1225/2009[19] and Regulation (EC) No 597/2009[20] provide for the possibility of imposing anti-dumping or countervailing duties in order to protect against the dumping of dumped or subsidized products from third countries. These regulations are based on the Anti-Dumping Agreement[21] and the Agreement on Subsidies and Countervailing Measures[22] of the WTO. The anti-dumping or countervailing investigation procedure may be carried out ex officio; it may also be requested by legal persons and natural persons acting on behalf of an EU industry who consider themselves harmed or threatened by dumped or subsidized imports from third countries. In the event of other illicit commercial practices by third countries, such persons may request the Commission to initiate a review procedure.

III. CUSTOMS DUTIES

Another instrument for controlling imports is customs duties, which are now the exclusive competence of the EU (Article 3 (a) TFEU). According to Article 28 TFEU, the Customs Union covers the entire exchange of goods between Member States. Article 31 TFEU empowers the EU accordingly to introduce a Common Customs Tariff (CCT), ie a common external tariff, vis-à-vis third countries. The basis of the Common Customs Tariff is provided by Regulation (EEC) No 2658/87[23] on the tariff and statistical nomenclature and on the Common Customs Tariff.

If goods from third countries cross the border of the Customs Union and customs duties are to be levied, their amount shall be determined by reference to their nature in a position of the CCT. Tariff rates are assigned to CCT headings, usually in the form of ad valorem duty rates, specifying what percentage of the value of the imported good is to be charged as duty.

In addition to ad valorem rates, there are so-called specific tariffs and mixed duties. In addition to rates of duty, the CCT also includes the combined nomenclature, a list systematically classifying the different categories of goods and thus allowing them to be classified at customs rates, and TARIC, which collects Community measures such as tariff suspensions or quotas.

Since the application of the CCT required the harmonization of customs and procedural law throughout the Community, 1992 adopted the Customs Code, Regulation (EEC) No 2913/92, which summarized the customs legislation previously scattered in numerous regulations.[24] The Customs Code defined the single customs territory, which consists essentially of all the territories of the Member States (with some historical exceptions, such as Helgoland, but including small European states, such as Andorra and Monaco). In addition, the Customs Code contained procedural rules on customs decisions, information and the customs examination, the determination of the origin and customs value of goods, the declaration of goods before their arrival and the customs debt.

In 2008, the Modernized Customs Code (MCC) was published, which should be applied from 2013. The entry into force of the Treaty of Lisbon on 1 December 2009 and delays in the development of EU-wide IT systems required a framework for further transitional solutions. The European

Commission agreed with the Council and Parliament in 2013 on the Union Customs Code,[25] which will apply from 1 May 2016. On 31 December 2020, the transitional period for the adaptation of IT systems will end.

IV. THE COMMON COMMERCIAL POLICY

The common commercial policy is set out in Art. 3 (1) lit. c TFEU and Art. 206 et seq. TFEU defines and deals with the external economic policy of the European Union. The scope of the common commercial policy initially covers trade in goods with non-member countries whose legislation is undisputedly an exclusive competence of the EU. With regard to the agricultural sector, agreements with third countries are part of the common commercial policy, while agricultural trade by autonomous measures falls exclusively under Article 43 TFEU. Production of and trade in weapons, ammunition and war material are according to Article 346 (1) TFEU subject to a special regulatory regime, whereby for dual-use goods the relevant regulation is relevant. As services and trade aspects of intellectual property were initially excluded from the common commercial policy, they were included in this area by the Treaty of Nice, but as mixed competences. With the entry into force of the Treaty of Lisbon, the entire common commercial policy, including services and trade-related aspects of intellectual property, has become the exclusive competence of the EU, Article 207 (1) TFEU.

As instruments of the common commercial policy, autonomous measures, that are one-sided by the EU, are initially available. In addition to amendments to the Common Customs Tariff, these may consist of import and export regulations and trade defense measures, such as anti-dumping duties, etc. Moreover, in the context of the common commercial policy, the EU can conclude bilateral and multilateral treaties with third countries in order to shape its external trade policy. These contracts are concluded by the Council pursuant to Article 218 in conjunction with Article 207 (3) TFEU, after negotiation by the Commission. Trade agreements, like other international treaties, are "integral parts of the Community legal order" and, pursuant to Article 216 (2) TFEU, bind the institutions of the Union and the Member States.

Insofar as the standards of these contracts are considered to be directly applicable (self-executing), EU citizens and third-country nationals can also rely directly on those standards. However, such direct applicability is denied, in particular by WTO law, in settled case-law by the ECJ.

Export subsidies are also part of the common commercial policy. In accordance with Article 207 (1) TFEU, national export aid systems are designed according to uniform principles. Apart from their compatibility with WTO law (namely the Agreement on Subsidies and Countervailing Measures), the problems with such export subsidies are the repercussions on the internal market and thus their compatibility with the EU state aid law, which is affirmed by the European Court of Justice on export subsidies.[26] Finally, as part of the common commercial policy, national protective measures should also be harmonized.

D. PROTECTIVE MEASURES IN FOREIGN TRADE

Due to the Union's extensive external trade and direct enforcement of most European Union trade law standards by the EU institutions, legal protection in foreign trade is usually directed against its actions, which is automatically the responsibility of the Union judicature and not the courts of the Member States.

In order to tackle restrictions on EU export freedom, exporters from Member States and third country importers may first lodge complaints with the Commission. Insofar as an EU or a Member State institution should indeed infringe provisions of EU law, it is conceivable that the Commission or the Member States might initiate infringement proceedings under Articles 258 and 259 TFEU.

In addition, individual natural and legal persons are subject to the action for annulment. Article 263 (4) TFEU. The subject-matter of the action may be, however, only those measures of the Union which were adopted as a decision against the applicant or those which, although issued as a regulation or as a decision addressed to another person, directly and individually concern the applicant. However, direct concern must be rejected if the EU merely authorizes a Member State to adopt measures restricting exports; then it must be brought directly before the courts of the Member States. The compensation for damages caused by unlawful acts of the Union can be claimed by means of an official liability action pursuant to Article 340 (2) TFEU in so far as an EU institution has acted. Legal protection against export restrictions through measures of the Member States must in principle be sought before national courts.

As regards import restrictions, in particular in anti-dumping and anti-subsidy legislation and in the framework of the Trade Barriers Regulation extensive legal protection exists for affected exporters, importers and Union producers. In this case, the ECJ affirms individual and direct concern for those persons to whom certain rights, such as various application or hearing rights, are entitled in the proceedings or which are otherwise affected by the investigation procedure. In the area of other import regulations and protective measures in accordance with Regulation No 3285/94, however, legal protection is limited, since there are generally measures of general application that usually exclude individual legal actions.

In contrast to legal protection in the internal market, it should also be borne in mind that the standard of review may be limited: as already mentioned, EU acts are, as a rule, not subject to WTO law review. However, this does not apply to anti-dumping and countervailing duties levied by the EU. These customs duties imposed by regulations can be challenged by natural and legal persons by way of action for annulment for breach of WTO law.

E. OUTLOOK

If one looks at the EU legal framework for exports in intra-EU trade, it is striking that the ECJ's case-law on fundamental freedoms limits state intervention to a minimum. Essentially, here is to refer to various exceptions and the immanent limits of fundamental freedoms. The Union's import and export regime with regard to third countries is also bound by this liberal approach. Its limits are defined by the so-called "export freedom" in a series of special regulations, for example the Dual-Use-Goods Regulation. However, exceptions are essentially only possible for a limited period of time, are subject to a strict procedure and must comply with the principle of proportionality. Ultimately, the EU law reveals a liberal profile that has remained untouched since the founding of the EC. Whether there will be restrictions on this freedom as a result of the global financial and sovereign debt crises and the recent criticism of free world trade is not yet decided.

NOTES

1 Cf. ECJ, Case C-112/00, *Schmidberger,* http://curia.europa.eu/juris/showPdf.jsf?text=&docid=47920&pageIndex=0&doclang=en&mode=lst&dir=&occ=first&part=1&cid=936763; ECJ Case C-36/02, *Omega,* http://curia.europa.eu/juris/showPdf.jsf?text=&docid=49221&pageIndex=0&doclang=en&mode=lst&dir=&occ=first&part=1&cid=937073

[2] Cf. ECJ, Case C-265/95, Commission/France, https://eur-lex.europa.eu/legal-content/EN/TXT/PDF/?uri=CELEX:61995CJ0265&from=EN

[3] Cf. ECJ Case 415/93, Bosman (freedom of movement for workers), https://eur-lex.europa.eu/legal-content/EN/TXT/PDF/?uri=CELEX:61993CJ0415&from=DE; ECJ Case C-341/05, Laval (freedom to provide services), https://eur-lex.europa.eu/legal-content/EN/TXT/PDF/?uri=CELEX:62005CJ0341&from=EN

[4] Cf. ECJ Case C-55/94, Gebhard, https://eur-lex.europa.eu/legal-content/EN/TXT/PDF/?uri=CELEX:61994CJ0055&from=DE.

[5] Cf. ECJ Case C-18/93, Corsica Ferries Italia, https://eur-lex.europa.eu/legal-content/EN/TXT/PDF/?uri=CELEX:61993CJ0018&from=EN.

[6] Cf. ECJ Case C-384/93, Alpine Investments, https://eur-lex.europa.eu/legal-content/EN/TXT/PDF/?uri=CELEX:61993CJ0384&from=DE.

[7] Council Regulation (EC) No 1/2003 of 16 December 2002 on the implementation of the rules on competition laid down in Articles 81 and 82 of the Treaty, Official Journal L 1, 04.01.2003, p. 1 et seq.

[8] Council Regulation (EC) No 139/2004 of 20 January 2004 on the control of concentrations between undertakings (the EC Merger Regulation)

[9] Cf. ECJ Case 6/69, France/Commission, https://eur-lex.europa.eu/legal-content/EN/TXT/PDF/?uri=CELEX:61969CJ0006&from=EL.

[10] Cf. ECJ joined Cases C-6 and 9/90, Francovich, https://eur-lex.europa.eu/resource.html?uri=cellar:7a76ea3f-a919--475c-8cbe-29e0b260ebc4.0002.03/DOC_1&format=PDF.

[11] Regulation (EU) 2015/479 of the European Parliament and of the Council of 11 March 2015 on common rules for exports, OJ L 83, 27.3.2015, p. 34

[12] Cf. ECJ Case C-70/94, Werner, https://eur-lex.europa.eu/legal-content/EN/TXT/PDF/?uri=CELEX:61994CJ0070&from=CS.

[13] Council Regulation (EC) No 428/2009 of 5 May 2009 setting up a Community regime for the control of exports, transfer, brokering and transit of dual-use items, OJ L 134, 29.5.2009, p. 1 et seq.

[14] Council Regulation (EC) No 116/2009 of 18 December 2008 on the export of cultural goods, OJ L 39, p. 1 et seq.

[15] Art. 2 (2) Regulation (EC) No 116/2009.

[16] Council Regulation No 260/2009 of 26 February 2009 on the common rules for imports, OJ L 84, 31.3.2009, p. 1 et seq. amended by Regulation (EU) No 37/2014 of the European Parliament and of the Council of 15 January 2014. OJ L 18, p. 1 et seq.

[17] Regulation (EU) 2015/936 of the European Parliament and of the Council of 9 June 2015 on common rules for imports of textile products from certain third countries not covered by bilateral agreements, protocols or other arrangements, or by other specific Union import rules, OJ L 160, 25.6.2015, p. 1 et seq.

[18] Counvil Regulation (EC) No 625/2009 of 7 July 2009 on common rules for imports from certain third countries, OJ L 185, 17.7.2009, p. 1 et seq.

[19] Council Regulation (EC) No 1225/2009 of 30 November 2009 on protection against dumped imports from countries not members of the European Community, OJ L 343, 22.12.2009, p. 51.

[20] Council Regulation (EC) No 597/2009 of 11 June 2009 on protection against subsidised imports from countries not members of the European Community, OJ L 188, 18.7.2009, p. 93.

[21] Agreement On Implementation Of Article VI of the General Agreement On Tariffs And Trade 1994, https://www.wto.org/english/docs_e/legal_e/19-adp.pdf.

[22] Agreement On Subsidies And Countervailing Measures, https://www.wto.org/english/docs_e/legal_e/24-scm.pdf

[23] Council Regulation (EEC) No 2658/87 of 23 July 1987 on the tariff and statistical nomenclature and on the Common Customs Tariff, OJ L 256, 7.9.1987, p. 1.

[24] Council Regulation (EEC) No 2913/92 of 12 October 1992 establishing the Community Customs Code, OJ L 302, 19.10.1992, p. 1.

[25] Regulation (EU) No 952/2013 of the European Parliament and of the Council of 9 October 2013 laying down the Union Customs Code, OJ L 269, 10.10.2013, p. 1.

[26] ECJ Case 142/87, Belgium/Commission, https://eur-lex.europa.eu/resource.html?uri=cellar:605288d7--0516--492a-a443-f54d63b62961.0002.03/DOC_1&format=PDF.

CHAPTER XVIII

LIABILITY RISKS FOR SHIPPING COMPANIES IN EUROPEAN CUSTOMS LAW

Lothar HARINGS*

A. INTRODUCTION

By transporting numerous containers on their vessels every year shipping companies handle a large part of the international trade in goods. Even though they transport these goods on behalf of their clients, it is the shipping companies that physically bring the goods across borders and into or out of customs territories.

European customs law focuses – among other things – on the person transporting the goods, i.e. on the person who has actual power of disposal over those goods. When import duties are incurred customs authorities therefore often consider shipping companies the customs debtors and issue notices of assessment against them charging them not only with customs duties but also with import turnover or excise tax. Shipping companies are thus confronted with various liability risks resulting from customs law.

B. RELEVANT LEGAL PROVISIONS

An integral part of the European Union is the establishment of a market without internal frontiers allowing free movement of goods, persons, services and capital between the Member States and therefore simplifying trade between the countries.[1] Free movement of goods is ensured by the implementation of a customs Union.[2] The Treaty on the Functioning of the European Union (TFEU) explicitly prohibits customs duties on imports and exports between Member States.[3]

The legal basis for the customs Union is a European regulation – the Customs Code. The Community Customs Code (CCC)[4] – which was in effect for almost 24 years – and its implementing regulation were replaced by the Union Customs Code (UCC)[5]. The UCC as well as its implementing regulation[6] and its delegated regulation[7] have been in full effect since 1st May 2016.[8] The UCC lays down the substantive rules on European customs law, like the Union's customs territory, the incurrence of customs debts including provisions for the determination of the customs value or for (special) customs procedures. Procedural aspects of customs law, for instance the competence of national authorities or the procedural provisions for contesting decisions of the customs authorities are laid down in national regulations – in Germany in the Abgabenordnung (AO), the Zollverwaltungsgesetz (ZollVG) and the Zollverordnung (ZollV).

C. INCURRENCE OF CUSTOMS DEBTS ON IMPORT

Customs debts on import in the European Union are generally incurred when the goods are released for free circulation.[9] The customs debtor is the declarant of the goods.

Customs debts on import, however, can also incur through non-compliance with the provisions of the UCC. Any person whose actions are connected to the import and therefore to the non-compliance can potentially be considered the customs debtor. This poses a high liability risk for shipping companies. As they physically transport the goods into the customs territory of the Union, there is always a causal connections between their actions and potential non-compliance with import provisions.

D. ENTRY OF GOODS INTO THE CUSTOMS TERRITORY – PROVISIONS AND OBLIGATIONS

When non-Union goods are brought into the customs territory, there are several obligations to fulfill. One of them is to provide the customs authorities with information on the transported goods prior to their arrival.

The obligation to provide information about the transported goods before they reach the European Union's territory has always been an essential part of the customs law system. The Revised Kyoto Convention of 1999 by the World Customs Organization stipulates in Standard 3.25 that "*National legislation shall make provision for the lodging and registering or checking of the Goods declaration and supporting documents prior to the arrival of the goods*".

This information is used to identify "high-risk cargo" and differentiate it from cargo that poses low security risks. Since the year 2001 and the terror attacks of 9/11 security measures have been of ever growing importance. There has been a heightened awareness of potential threats for public safety and security. Trade in goods and the international supply chain have been identified as potential delivery mechanisms for terrorists if not controlled and supervised. As a reaction to these events, new national security strategies were implemented. The U.S.A. have created a security program in 2001- "Customs-Trade Partnership against terrorism (C-TPAT) – establishing new security standards for international trade. The World Customs Organization (WCO) has even deemed these developments a "customs supply chain security paradigm"[10]. The Council of the Word Customs Organization has adopted a Framework of Standard to Secure and Facilitate Global Trade (Framework SAFE) which includes the obligation to lodge an entry summary declaration and forms the basis for the introduction of the Authorised Economic Operator ("AEO") in EU Customs Law.

I. ENTRY SUMMARY DECLARATION

When bringing goods into the customs territory the carrier of the goods is obliged to lodge an entry summary declaration.[11] This declaration is meant to provide the authorities with enough information to allow them to carry out a risk analysis and take the necessary measures before the goods have even arrived in the European Union.

The entry summary declaration has to be lodged by the carrier of the goods, i.e. the operator of the vessel on which the goods are transported. Depending on the port of departure, the entry summary declaration has to be lodged within a period of 24 hours before the containerized cargo is loaded onto the vessel, latest up to 2 hours before the arrival of the vessel at the first port of entry into the customs territory of the Union.[12]

II. PRESENTATION OF GOODS

After the goods are brought into the Union's customs territory they have to be presented to customs.[13] The person who physically brought the goods into the Union's customs territory, i.e. the shipping company[14], is responsible for presenting them at the port where they are unloaded or transshipped. When presenting the goods a reference to the entry summary declaration shall be made.

III. Temporary storage

If non-Union goods that were presented to the customs authorities are not immediately placed under a special procedure, i.e. transit, storage, specific use and inward or outward processing, or are released for free circulation they have to be declared for temporary storage. This declaration has to be lodged at the time of the presentation of the goods to customs and has to include a reference to the entry summary declaration.[15]

E. Incurrence of customs debt – Liability risks for shipping companies

If no entry summary declaration or no temporary storage declaration are lodged or if said declarations are faulty or lodged too late not all obligations relating to the introduction of goods to the customs territory of the Union are fulfilled. This constitutes a case of *non-compliance* with the relevant provisions of the UCC. Therefore, an import duty debt is incurred pursuant to Art. 79 para 1 lit. a) UCC.[16]

I. Missing summary declaration

As outlined before the carrier of the goods is in general obliged to lodge the entry summary declaration for all the goods transported on the vessels in order to fulfill the requirements of the regulations on the presentation of goods. Only if there is no obligation to present the goods an entry summary declaration is not necessary.

This constitutes a problem for shipping companies in different scenarios:

When a vessel arrives at a port within the European Union which is not the port of destination for the transported goods, containers may be unloaded for a brief period of time without lodging an entry summary declaration or presenting them to the customs authorities.

1. Unloading of containers

The containers may be unloaded for various reasons:

a) Planned unloading by scheduled re-stowing

The containers may be unloaded to enable the loading or unloading of other goods. Afterwards they will be loaded back onto the same vessel. The unloading is then planned and the customs authorities are usually informed about the procedure ("scheduled re-stowing"). Art. 139 para 2 UCC stipulates explicitly that when the goods are*unloaded and reloaded onto the same means of transport during its voyage in order to enable the unloading or loading of other goods*, there is no obligation to present the goods to the authorities. Without the obligation to present the goods neither is there an obligation to lodge an entry summary declaration. In these cases a customs debt is not incurred.

b) UNPLANNED UNLOADING

There are, however, cases in which containers have to be unloaded without prior notice to customs:

- If there are goods to be shipped that require an uninterrupted cold chain, containers with a cooling function have to be used. If these cooling containers ("reefers") are defective, they are unloaded to the dock to be repaired ("Reefer with malfunction"-cases). Depending on how much time is required for the repair of the reefers they cannot be reloaded onto the same vessel they have been transported on before.
- Containers may be unloaded due to safety reasons because of low water level or bad weather conditions. The decision of whether or not to unload the containers is made by the captain of the vessel after a risk analysis of the situation. The containers may then remain onshore while the vessel continues to its port of destination ("Cut-and-run"-cases). If a container cannot be re-stowed onto the same vessel or the repair of a reefer with malfunction takes longer, they can also become "cut-and-run"-cases.
- The unloading might be due to errors in the IT-systems: There may be wrong data of the shipped goods or problems with the IT-system so that a wrong port of destination is assigned to the goods in the data processing system, whereas the freight list contains the correct port of destination. In this case a container might be unloaded without lodging an entry summary declaration and without presenting it to the authorities.

In these scenarios the containers are not scheduled to be re-stowed to enable loading or unloading of other goods. Customs authorities do not consider the requirements of Art. 139 para 2 UCC met and issue notices of assessment against those who were obliged to lodge customs declarations, i.e. against the shipping companies as carriers.

2. LEGAL DEFENSES

The incurrence of import duties in the case of unplanned unloadings burdens the container carriers financially; even more so as the financial risk cannot be calculated in cases of unplanned unloadings due to IT-errors or in emergency situations. The notices issued by customs can be contested on different grounds:

a) DEFENSES UNDER CCC

The UCC has been in effect since 1st May 2016. There are, however, still numerous cases pending before the financial courts that are judged according to the substantive provisions of the CCC. Whereas procedural rules generally apply to all administrative or court proceedings pending at the time when they enter into force, according to settled case-law of the Court of Justice of the European Union (CJEU) substantive rules do not apply to situations existing before their entry into force.[17]

Under the CCC there were only limited options to contest the position as debtor: A relief from import duties could be granted if the goods were actually Union-goods[18] which had been exported from the Union and later returned to that territory within a period of three years ("returned goods", Art. 185 CCC). For all other goods, i.e. non-Union goods, there was no such possibility of granting a relief from import duties.

Another option was to apply for remission or repayment of import duties for equitable reasons.[19] However, custom authorities are not bound to grant remission or repayment – Art. 239 para 1 CCC stipulates that duties "*may*" be repaid or remitted for equitable reasons whereas in other cases they "*shall*" be repaid.[20]

b) DEFENSES UNDER UCC

The UCC also contains provisions on returned goods as well as on remission or repayment of import duties for equitable reasons. Additionally, it provides the container carriers with new options. Customs debts can not only be remitted or repaid but also extinguished. The possibility of extinguishing import duties has already existed under the CCC[21]. However, under the UCC the provisions on the extinguishment of customs debts have obtained an extended scope of application:

Firstly, import debts arising from unlawful introduction of goods "*shall*" be extinguished if the failure which led to the incurrence of a customs debt had no significant effect on the correct operation of the customs procedure concerned and did not constitute an attempt at deception.[22] Furthermore, all of the formalities necessary to regularize the situation of the goods have to be subsequently carried out.

There was a comparable provision under the CCC: A customs debt was not incurred if the failure had no significant effect on the correct operation of the temporary storage or customs procedure.[23] The question of whether the specific failure had a significant effect on the customs procedure, however, is answered differently under the CCC and the UCC. Under the UCC only the intention to deceive rules out extinguishment of the customs debt, whereas under the CCC also gross negligence already precluded the possibility of extinguishment.

More importantly, the delegated regulation for the UCC includes a provision which could significantly reduce the liability risk of shipping companies: Pursuant to Art. 103 lit e) UCC-DA it is generally considered a failure without significant effect on the correct operation of a customs procedure if the authorities are informed about the non-compliance before the customs debt has been notified or a control is announced.

Therefore, in cases of unplanned unloading of containers due to emergencies, bad weather conditions or necessary repairs shipping companies could inform the authorities about the unloading and profit from the new provisions on the extinguishments of duties.

Another option is provided by the UCC: An import duty which is incurred because of non-compliance with the provisions of the UCC on the import of goods shall also be extinguished if evidence is provided that the goods have not been used or consumed and have been taken out of the customs territory of the Union. Thus, if containers are unloaded and later transported to a port of destination outside the European Union, shipping companies may invoke Art. 124 para 1 lit. k) UCC.

In accordance with the settled case-law of the CJEU on the application of substantive provisions the German Bundesfinanzhof (BFH) has recently ruled that Art. 124 para 1 lit. k) UCC is a substantive provision and can therefore not be applied retrospectively, i.e. to situations existing before their entry into force.[24]

3. CONCLUSION

The unplanned unloading of containers still poses a liability risk for shipping companies as under the CCC as well as the UCC import duties are incurred.

It is to be expected, though, that under the UCC shipping companies have more effective means of defense against the collection of import duties.

II. Smuggling of excisable goods

Apart from the unplanned unloading of containers, there are other situations that pose a liability risk for shipping companies. One of these situations is the smuggling of excisable goods like tobacco products.

As outlined above, the carrier of the goods has to lodge an entry summary declaration and possibly a summary declaration for temporary storage for all goods they transport on their vessels into the customs territory of the Union. If there are no declarations at all, import duties can be incurred. If, however, summary declarations are lodged but do not cover all goods or if goods are wrongly designated in the declarations, customs authorities also consider this a case of non-compliance resulting in the incurrence of customs debts.

1. Smuggling and non-compliance with customs law provisions

Shipping companies usually acquire the necessary information on the transported goods from the Bill of Lading. The information contained in the Bill of Lading is provided by the consignor of the goods. Due to the processes of modern container traffic this information cannot be verified by the shipping companies. Especially if containers are transported FCL ("Full container load") shipping companies have no means of verifying the data of the Bill of Lading as the container is loaded and sealed before it is handed over to them. Therefore, they have to rely on the information provided by their customer.

Customs authorities randomly check the content of containers after their arrival. If they find for instance cigarettes or other tobacco products hidden behind other goods the tobacco products are usually seized and subsequently destroyed. Customs authorities have been holding shipping companies responsible for the smuggling and issuing notices of assessment against them.

With these notices the authorities usually do not levy customs duties; however, shipping companies are held liable for tobacco and import turnover tax. The incurrence of these excise taxes is closely connected to the incurrence of customs duties.[25] It is doubtful, though, whether shipping companies should really pay excise duties for smuggled goods.

2. No incurrence of import duties

A first line of defense – arguing that import duties are not incurred – is opposed by the settled case law of the CJEU. In 2005[26] the CJEU has ruled in that a customs debt is incurred because the smuggled goods have been wrongly designated in the declaration and are therefore unlawfully introduced into the customs territory of the Union.[27]

The CJEU's judgement directly applies to cases under the CCC. The equivalent provision of the UCC, Art. 79 para 1 lit. a) UCC, is phrased differently referring to *non-compliance* with *"one of the obligations laid down in the customs legislation concerning the introduction of non-Union goods into the customs territory of the Union"*. As Art. 79 para 1 lit. a) UCC is the successor to Art. 202 para 1 lit a) CCC it can be expected that the customs authorities will invoke the CJEU's judgement also in cases to which the UCC applies.

3. Wrong debtor

It can be argued, however, that while import duties are incurred, the shipping company transporting the container with the smuggled goods is not the debtor of the duties.

According to the CCC[28] the debtor of the import duties *shall be* the (natural or legal) person who introduced the goods unlawfully, i.e. the person who *"can be regarded as having been by his actions responsible for the unlawful introduction of the goods"*.[29]

The question is what this "responsibility" for the unlawful introduction can be based on: A mere causal connection of the actions of the persons involved regardless of whether or not they knew about the existence of these goods or even regardless of whether they had the possibility to know about them? If so, then shipping companies would be responsible insofar as their transporting the containers with the smuggled goods and lodging summary declarations that do not cover these smuggled goods have contributed to their unlawful introduction. The CJEU, however, is of the opinion that *"it is for the national court to establish, in the light of the circumstances of the main proceedings, whether the person who lodged the summary declaration or the customs declaration was, because he stated an incorrect designation, responsible for the unlawful introduction of the goods."*[30]

It can be argued that the circumstances of the smuggling cases usually speak against a responsibility of the shipping companies. As outlined above, shipping companies use the information provided by their customers when lodging summary declarations. In addition, they have no means of verifying this information.

This is, firstly, due to their contractual obligations: When goods are transported FCL the container is loaded and then sealed only to be opened again by the consignee of the goods. Shipping companies are not authorized to open the containers during the transport or after their arrival at the port of destination.

Secondly, it is virtually impossible for shipping companies to inspect every container. There is neither enough time for such inspections nor do shipping companies have enough staff at their disposal. In fact, if shipping companies were expected to perform these inspections they could no longer work cost-efficiently.

There are still cases pending before the German Financial Courts to which the substantive provisions of the CCC are applied. Whether or not the courts follow these arguments has to be awaited.

4. Extinguishment of customs debt under UCC

This argument can probably only be used in cases to which the CCC applies. The wording of the UCC differs from that of the CCC stating that the debtor of the customs duty shall be *"any person who was required to fulfill the obligations concerned"*[31]. As the shipping companies are the carriers of the goods they are obliged to lodge the summary declarations. If these declarations do not cover all goods or the goods are wrongly designated the obligation is not fulfilled. Under the UCC the status of the shipping companies as debtors of the incurred import duties may therefore be more difficult to contest.

However, under the UCC the provisions on the extinguishment of customs debts have a broader scope of application than the corresponding provisions of the CCC. A customs debt shall for example be extinguished *where goods liable to import or export duty are destroyed under customs supervision.*[32] If the customs authorities destroy the smuggled tobacco products this may lead to the extinguishment of the customs debt.

5. Levying of tobacco tax: Defeating the purpose of excise taxes

Import turnover tax and tobacco tax however, are not automatically extinguished. Yet, it can be argued that the taxation of excise duties in these cases would defeat the very purpose of excise taxes: Excise duties are indirect taxes on the consumption of certain products or goods.[33] Therefore, if these goods are not consumed but rather verifiably destroyed there is no need and therefore no justification for levying excise tax. They never entered into the Union's economic circuit and after their destruction there is no danger of them being consumed[34]. The relevant Directive thus states explicitly that "*since excise duty is a tax on the consumption of certain goods, duty should not be charged in respect of excise goods which, under certain circumstances, have been destroyed or irretrievably lost*"[35].

F. CONCLUSION

Shipping companies are confronted with various liability risks resulting from customs law when transporting goods across the borders of the European Union's customs territory. This is due to the fact that customs law provisions on the incurrence of customs debts do not take into account subjective elements like the knowledge of the carrier of goods of the non-compliance with customs law provisions. They focus solely on the safety and security of the international supply chain. However, custom authorities ought to find a way to ensure a high level of safety and security without burdening economic operators like shipping companies with import duties in situations where they conducted themselves lawfully.

NOTES

* The author thanks Franziska Zegula, Attorney at Law at GvW Graf von Westphalen, for valuable support.

1 Art. 26 TFEU.

2 Art. 28 TFEU.

3 Art. 30 TFEU.

4 Council Regulation No. 2913/92 of 12th October 1992 establishing the Community Customs Code.

5 Regulation (EU) No 952/2013 of 9th October 2013 laying down the Union Customs Code.

6 Commission implementing regulation (EU) 2015/2447 of 24th November 2015 laying down detailed rules for implementing certain provisions of Regulation (EU) No 952/2013 of the European Parliament and of the Council laying down the Union Customs Code (UCC-IA).

7 Commission delegated regulation (EU) 2015/2446 of 28th July 2015 supplementing Regulation (EU) No 952/2013 of the European Parliament and of the Coun-

cil as regards detailed rules concerning certain provisions of the Union Customs Code (UCC-DA).

8 Few specific provisions of the UCC have been applied since 30th October 2013, Art. 288 UCC.

9 See Art. 77 para 1 lit. a) UCC and Art. 201 para 1 lit. a) CCC.

10 See f. ex. Robert Ireland, WCO Research Paper No. 18, The Customs Supply Chain Security Paradigm and 9/11: Ten years on and Beyond, September 2011. http://www.wcoomd.org/en/topics/research/~/~/media/2498A32A98FB4A0792EE4D66C8D68383.ashx.

11 Art. 5 No 9, Art. 127 et subs. UCC; Art. 36a to 36c CCC.

12 Art. 105 UCC-DA.

13 If they are not already under a transit procedure, Art. 139 UCC.

14 Art. 139 No. 1 lit. a) UCC. The person in whose name the goods have been brought and the person who assumed responsibility for carriage of the goods after they were brought may be responsible for presenting the goods as well.

15 Art. 145 UCC.

16 The corresponding Art. 202 para 1 lit. a) CCC refers to an *unlawful introduction* of the goods into the customs territory of the Community essentially covering the same scenarios as Art. 79 para 1 lit. a) UCC.

17 CJEU, Judgment of 23rd February 2006, Case *Molenbergnatie*, C-201/04, para 32.

18 See Art. 5 No 23 UCC: a) goods wholly obtained in the customs territory of the Union and not incorporating goods imported from countries or territories outside the customs territory of the Union; or b) goods brought into the customs territory of the Union from countries or territories outside that territory and released for free circulation; or goods obtained or produced in the customs territory of the Union, either solely from goods referred to in point (b) or from goods referred to in points (a) and (b).

19 Pursuant to Art. 239 CCC.

20 See for example Art. 236 para 1 CCC for cases where it is established that the amount of duties was not legally owned.

21 Art. 233 CCC.

22 Art. 124 para 1 lit. h) UCC.

23 Art. 204 para 1 CCC and Art. 859 of the Implementing Regulation for the CCC (Commission Regulation (EEC) No 2454/93 of 2nd July 1993.

24 BFH, order of 24th July 2017, VII B 165/16.

25 See §21 para 1 and 2 Umsatzsteuergesetz (UStG), §19 Tabaksteuergesetz (TabStG).

26 CJEU, Judgment of 3rd March 2005, Case *Papismedov*, C-195/03, ECLI:EU:C:2005:131.

27 Art. 202 para 1 lit. a) CCC.

28 Art. 202 para 3 indent 1 CCC.

29 CJEU, Judgment of 23rd September 2004, Case *Spedition Ulustrans*, C-414/02, ECLI:EU:C:2004:551, para 26.

[30] CJEU, Judgment of 3rd March 2005, Case *Papismedov,* C- 195/03, ECLI:EU:C:2005:131, para 41.

[31] Art. 79 para. 3 indent 1 UCC.

[32] Art. 124 para 1 lit. f) UCC.

[33] Art. 1 para 1 of the Council Directive 2008/118/EC of 16th December 2008 concerning the general arrangement for excise duty and repealing Directive 92/12/EEC.

[34] Cf. CJEU, judgment of 2nd June 2016, joint cases C-226/14 and C-228/14 – Eurogate, para 67 et seq.

[35] Council Directive 2008/118/EC of 16th December 2008 concerning the general arrangement for excise duty and repealing Directive 92/12/EEC, recital No 9.

CHAPTER XIX

MARITIME ARBITRATION

Jan WÖLPER

A. HISTORY OF MARITIME ARBITRATION

Arbitration in general has a long history. Arbitration was already the favoured means for dispute resolution more than 2,000 years ago and long before any state court jurisdiction was established.[1] Also maritime arbitration dates back probably as long as shipping exists. London Maritime Arbitration traces its origins back at least to the birth of the Baltic exchange at the Virginia and Baltick Coffee House in 1744 and arguably much earlier.[2] The numerous rules of maritime arbitration changed over the centuries. The London Maritime Arbitrators' Association (LMAA) founded in 1960 has changed its rules frequently and most recently with effect from May 2017. The German Maritime Arbitration Association (GMAA) founded in 1983 has also adapted its rules to the demands of the market on a regular basis. And all associations will have to update their rules to Industry 4.0 requirements.

B. ADR ALTERNATIVES

1.1 Arbitration is not the only alternative to State Court jurisdiction. It is one of many means of Alternative Dispute Resolution (ADR). One form of ADR is not necessarily better than the other. They all serve a certain purpose, and in each individual case a decision needs to be made with regard to the most appropriate form of ADR.

1.2 Every dispute resolution should start with negotiations. Although this is not called ADR, it should always be the first step. Many modern dispute resolution clauses provide that negotiations shall take place to solve a dispute before any third party is involved. It is not unusual for such clauses to provide for two or even three layers, starting with negotiations between the operational teams, then if these fail referring the matter to the middle management, and if this fails referring the matter to the CEOs of the companies. The author has been advised by counsels at major German companies that the pure fear of involving upper management encourages early settlement at lower levels.

1.3 In many cases the parties only disagree on one or two technical issues which do not require a full scale trial or arbitration. For that type of dispute the proper way is to jointly appoint an expert to issue an opinion with binding effect for the parties just on the limited point.[3]

1.4 In huge building projects disputes tend to arise rather frequently, none of which may lead to a delay of the project as a whole so that decisions are required much faster than arbitration can deliver. For that purpose, project adjudication is the choice in the course of which jointly appointed experts decide very quickly what should be done. The respective adjudication clauses often provide that such decisions may be challenged later on.

1.5 Mediation has probably become the most modern form of ADR. It was developed in the US. For a number of years it has also been used in London, Germany and probably all over the world. The mediator is again a jointly appointed person who purely assists the parties in negotiating a settlement of their own.[4]

1.6 The next step to arbitration is conciliation. The conciliator assists the parties in reaching an agreement. If they do not, he is requested to make a settlement proposal of his own which, however, the parties may reject.[5] In particular in highly political matters conciliation is, nonetheless, very efficient.

1.7 One step closer to Court State litigation is arbitration. The arbitral tribunal is also appointed by the parties and decides the case with binding effect, as state courts do. Further details of arbitration will be explained here below.

1.8 And if nothing is agreed, there will always be one or more state courts competent to decide on a dispute.

C. INSTITUTIONAL ARBITRATION VS. AD HOC ARBITRATION

1.1 There is not just one kind of arbitration. Whereas many national arbitration regulations are based on the UNCITRAL Model Law on International Commercial Arbitration of 1985[6], the organisation of arbitration varies a lot.

There are arbitration institutions such as the International Court of Arbitration of the International Chamber of Commerce (ICC)[7]. The ICC not only offers a full set of arbitration regulations but also administers arbitration for the parties and the tribunal. To some extent the ICC may even check an arbitration award before it is released to the parties. Ad hoc arbitration, as for example provided for by the GMAA rules[8], is a non-administered arbitration the organisation of which is completely in the hands of the arbitral tribunal.

1.2 Again one cannot say that one form is better than the other. A party should check carefully before entering into an arbitration agreement whether the countries in which an award may have to be enforced accept arbitration awards of one or the other kind only. Such restrictions exist for example in China.

D. DIFFERENCES IN RULES OF PROCEDURE

1.1 The rules for maritime arbitration vary considerably internationally as arbitration rules even vary considerably within individual countries. And again there is no good or bad. All the rules have their advantages and disadvantages so that the parties agreeing on an arbitration clause should at least know the major differences.

1.2 A major difference between Anglo-American arbitration regulations and many continental European arbitration regulations is that the former provides for disclosure or discovery, i.e. the full release of all potentially relevant documents, whereas under the latter the parties normally have to prove the case with the documents they have at hand with limited rights to request an order for release of certain documents by the opposing party. Some say that the former procedure provides for higher probability of an arbitration being based on all relevant facts. However, disclosure or discovery can be disproportionately expensive and time consuming,[9] in particular as nowadays disclosure or discovery tend to include each and every electronic message once sent in relation to the matter at stake.

For example, in English court proceedings the parties must disclose all documents in their possession or control, even where they may be detrimental or have no relevance to their own case.[10] The LMAA terms deviate slightly from the traditional procedure by requesting submissions and documents attached thereto, entitling the parties to ask each other for missing documentation and to apply to the tribunal for an order on requiring disclosure of documents in case of need.[11] The GMAA has chosen a different route inasmuch as the arbitrators themselves may request the disclosure of documents if they find that this is needed to provide a profound basis for their decision.[12] In this context, the parties may, of course, try to guide the tribunal in one or the other direction, but, in the end, the decision is at the discretion of the tribunal.

E. HOW TO REACH AN ARBITRATION AGREEMENT

1.1 There is no arbitration without an arbitration agreement. Arbitration is contractually agreed ADR which cannot be forced upon the parties by either of them or by any third party. In line with the generally accepted freedom of contracts the parties also have a wide freedom in respect of arbitration agreements, both in respect of the wording for arbitration clauses and in respect of the chosen institutions and regulations.[13] There are only some areas which are not arbitrable under most national laws, such as criminal law and some family-related issues.

1.2 The arbitration agreement, although generally merely one clause of many in a contract, is considered a contract of its own which does not necessarily share the fate of the rest of the contract. If a contract clause is void because it is in breach of mandatory provisions, even if this renders the contract void[14] as a whole, the arbitration agreement usually survives this invalidity, i.e. the arbitral tribunal remains in charge of deciding amongst other things whether or not the contract is void[15].

1.3 Whereas complex arbitration clauses are used in some industries, including various layers of negotiations and ADR before arbitration may be commenced as the final step, the shipping community is used to rather brief standardized arbitration agreements. Such are laid down in particular in many of the BIMCO forms.[16] It is even sufficient to just agree on "GMAA" which is a sufficiently clear reference to arbitration in accordance with the GMAA regulations as valid at the time of commencement of the proceedings.[17]

1.4 Aforesaid freedom of contract is, of course, often a rather one-sided freedom. The party with the stronger bargaining power may also determine whether and what kind of ADR shall be used in the event of a dispute and dictates the respective ADR clause. But in the maritime world it is much more common to rely on generally accepted arbitration clauses and institutions such as those shown on BIMCO forms.

F. ADVANTAGES OF ARBITRATION

1.1 One major advantage of arbitration is that the parties can choose arbitrators who are, in general, familiar with the topic of the dispute. The parties may appoint a commercial shipping businessman/agent, a marine engineer if the focus of the dispute is of more of a technical nature, or a lawyer or judge with experience in maritime matters. If the parties can agree accordingly, a combination of two or even three of such experts is perfect to make sure that the arbitral tribunal can answer all or most of the relevant questions without the need of experts assisting the tribunal. Whereas state courts usually offer some specialized chambers e.g. on construction disputes or family affairs, actions in commercial matters often end up on the desk of the judge whose turn it is, no matter whether he or she has ever dealt with a dispute of the type at stake before.

1.2 Another advantage of arbitration is the general freedom to choose the forum. The parties may choose a neutral place which neither party has a closer link to than the other. Moreover, they can choose a tribunal which decides the case independently of the nationalities or other characteristics of the parties. Some state courts are said to have a tendency to decide in favour of nationals of that state, in particular if state-owned entities are concerned.

1.3 There is no unanimous view on whether it is another advantage of arbitration that arbitrators are usually not bound by state court decisions. Frequently, the arbitration is chosen to have disputes decided in line with the parties' understandings of a particular market and market usage which state courts may not be familiar with. For example, German arbitrators are said to be less likely to follow the strict rulings of the German Federal Supreme Court on general terms and conditions than state courts do. State courts often apply basically the same standards to general terms and conditions agreed between consumers on the one hand and business people on the other, although in most cases business people never thought of and do not want such drastic consequences when general terms and conditions of either party or even just proposed by either party are at stake.

1.4 Another advantage of arbitration is the freedom to choose the language or even languages of the arbitration. Obviously, this only works if the arbitrators are likewise familiar with the language. Whereas in German state court proceedings it is still the rule that all documents have to be submitted in the German language,[18] most maritime arbitration regulations provide that proceedings including submissions and exhibits may be pursued and presented in English as the language of the shipping world.[19] The use of the language of the specific trade not only saves the cost of translation but avoids uncertainty resulting from translations of documents or witness statements.

1.5 Whereas arbitrators are requested to apply the relevant contract terms and law correctly, in particular the interpretation of contract clauses quite often is not a matter of black or white. In particular arbitrators chosen from the community of maritime arbitrators are likely to take a more commercial approach to contract clauses than state court judges. Likewise, the latter may not be familiar with the market and might be more guided by the words of a clause than by the commercial background. Different to state court judges, arbitrators may even decide outside strict legal frameworks ex aequo et bono, however, only if the parties explicitly agree so.[20]

1.6 Another reason for parties choosing arbitration instead of state court proceedings is that the latter tend to be open to the public[21] whereas arbitration is usually private and confidential in the sense that only the parties and their representatives may attend the hearings.[22] And under many regulations the arbitral awards as such are confidential, too, and may not be published unless both parties explicitly agree to or do not oppose the publication.[23] Confidentiality is of particular importance in a rather small community like the shipping world where most players know each other and do not wish that any third party finds out that for whatever reason a dispute exists under a particular contract or in respect of a particular vessel.

Whereas in England it is generally considered an implied term of the arbitration agreement between the parties and the arbitrators that the latter have to treat the arbitration entirely confidentially,[24] it is not likewise clear to what extent the parties have to treat the arbitration as confidential. The LMAA rules are silent on this point, except as regards confidentiality of privileged reasons[25] and disclosure of documents to third parties in concurrent hearings.[26] However, under English law it is accepted that there is a general duty of confidentiality in relation to arbitral proceedings.[27] What exactly this comprises is, nonetheless, not entirely clear.[28] The GMAA rules are also as good as silent on confidentiality, save for a provision on the publication of awards.[29] There is no statutory provision and only a few court decisions concerning the issue.[30] As in many other jurisdictions, there is general consensus in Germany that arbitrators are bound by a duty of confidentiality towards the parties[31] and the respective duty covers all information that the arbitrators have obtained in their capacity.[32] Whether or not the parties to arbitral proceedings are subject to an obligation of confidentiality is, however, the most contentious aspect of confidentiality in Germany.[33] The prevailing view seems to be that, in the absence of a clear agreement on confidentiality, no broad confidentiality obligations exist.[34] Thus, the parties to an arbitration agreement are well advised to agree specifically on confidentiality if they consider this to be of paramount importance.

1.7 There is again no unanimous view whether or not it is an advantage of arbitration that, usually, there is no second instance in the sense of a regular appeal. Whereas under all national laws arbitral awards can be appealed in the event of severe procedural mistakes, e.g. by issuing an arbitral award without an underlying arbitration agreement or without having given both parties fair opportunities to present their case,[35] it is a general rule that state courts are not competent to revise a decision of an arbitral tribunal as far as the merits are concerned, not even if the arbitrators' decision is entirely wrong.[36] One exception to this rule can be found in Sec. 69 of the English Arbitration Act permitting an appeal to the state courts to correct some errors in law but in exceptional cases only.[37] The LMAA terms, unlike institutional rules such as those of the LCIA or the ICC, do not exclude the right of appeal, save under the small claims procedure.[38]

1.8 The final but also decisive advantage of arbitration is that in most countries arbitral awards are more easily enforceable than state court decisions. The enforcement of arbitral awards is in particular governed by the Convention on the Recognition and Enforcement of Foreign Arbitral Awards of 1958 (New York Convention)[39] which altogether 157 nations have signed. The Convention lays down uniform rules according to which a rather limited number of conditions has to be complied with to enforce an arbitral award in any of the member states. State court decisions, however, are only enforceable if corresponding treaties or conventions exist, as for example within the EU[40] or individual contracts between individual states. Some countries also accept state court decisions from other states as long as acceptance is done on reciprocity.[41] As an example, it is uncertain if Russian court decisions are enforceable in Germany and vice versa[42] whereas both countries are members of the New York Convention and therefore do accept arbitral awards issued in one of the two states or in other New York Convention member states.

G. DISADVANTAGES OF ARBITRATION

1.1 One disadvantage of arbitration is that either party can abuse it to some extent. Whereas arbitrators should, of course, act absolutely neutrally since they are obliged to serve both parties equally and fairly, most arbitration regulations do not impose any limits on the choice of arbitrators. Sometimes parties intentionally select an arbitrator whom they know or at least have reason to hope that he or she will rather decide in favour of the party appointing the arbitrator than in favour of the other party although such one-sided activity would clearly be in breach of all existing arbitration regulations. Another way to abuse arbitration is to simply appoint an arbitrator of whom the appointing party knows that he or she is so busy that any real activity by the tribunal may not be expected before at least a year or more has elapsed. In particular a respondent is not necessarily interested in an arbitration being efficient if the true cause for the dispute is not a legal argument but unwillingness or inability to perform the contract. Whereas all arbitration regulations provide for answers to such problems, e.g. the dismissal of an arbitrator because of bias[43] or the cancellation of the arbitration agreement, these means are hardly ever used. A reason for this is often that the outcome of such legal remedy is uncertain and the party seeking the remedy does not want to end up with a tribunal which it has attacked but is still hoping will decide in its favour.

1.2 Another disadvantage of arbitration is that it does not, as a rule, allow the enforcement of third-party participation as is the case in state court proceedings by means of a third party notice.[44] Thus, a party which has lost an arbitration and wishes to take recourse against a third party in a chain of transportation agreements often cannot just turn around and take recourse based upon the arbitral award. The third party will usually be free to argue that the decision of the arbitral tribunal was wrong and that it is not bound by the arbitral tribunal's findings since it had no influence on the arbitration proceedings. Therefore, if parties wish to agree on arbitration in a chain of contracts, they must make sure that all contracts are governed by identical arbitration clauses allowing and accepting third-party notice. In reality this is hardly ever done.

H. GMAA

1.1 The GMAA is one of many maritime arbitration associations offering arbitration rules to the maritime community which the founders and the members of the GMAA consider adequate for solving maritime disputes. The GMAA regulations are not completely unique but they provide for some specialities which clearly distinguish them from other German arbitration regulations and in particular arbitration rules tailored in line with Anglo-American ideals.

1.2 One speciality of GMAA is that, as a rule, an arbitral tribunal consists of two arbitrators only who only appoint a third person if they disagree on one point or another. The idea behind this concept is to save costs for the parties. And the system works. It rarely happens that a third person needs to be involved. And an award unanimously made by two arbitrators may be more convincing, in particular for the unsuccessful party, than an award from a three-party tribunal in which one does not know if one of the arbitrators may have had a dissenting view but was overruled by the other two.

1.3 Another huge advantage, at least from a German or continental European perspective, is in comparison to London or US arbitration that GMAA arbitrators, like German state court judges, under GMAA rules are requested to consider at every stage of the proceedings the possibility of an amicable settlement of the dispute or of particular issues in the dispute and, if they consider it expedient to do so, to suggest such settlement to the parties.[45] Whereas no statistics exist on arbitrations settled after corresponding proposals by GMAA arbitrators, it is probably correct to say that at least 50 % of GMAA arbitrations are settled at the latest during or after the first hearing. Some very experienced GMAA arbitrators say that they manage to make the parties settle in even 80 % or more of the proceedings under their guidance. Such settlement is not only more cost efficient than a full-scale arbitration taken to the very end but settlements protect possible long-standing commercial relationships which, however, may suffer seriously from a full-scale arbitration which probably ends with an award usually more favourable to one party than to the other.

1.4 A further speciality of GMAA arbitration is that the costs of the tribunal can be calculated in advance[46] and are fully recoverable. The same applies to the winning party's attorneys' fees up to the limits for attorneys acting in state court appeal proceedings.[47]

I. THE FUTURE OF MARITIME ARBITRATION

1.1 In Europe and North America, but also in some areas of the Far East, maritime arbitration has a long history. But new arbitration centres also offering maritime arbitration have been set up across most of the world over the last 10 years and have gained great acceptance. In particular Singapore has found its way into BIMCO standard forms for maritime contracts. All this, combined with the ever increasing level of shipping activity across the world and existing uncertainty in respect of some jurisdictions, seems to justify the assumption that maritime arbitration is still a growing business.

1.2 However, industry 4.0 and in particular web-based services likewise provide great opportunities and risks for the more traditional shipping community and maritime arbitration. There are risks for all those who do not move with the times. Fully electronic web-based arbitration is likely to be the future. Again, Singapore seems to be far ahead for example of London as far as web-based arbitration is concerned. It is unlikely that modern shipping companies which not only have contracts with partners from all over the world but also tend to have branches of their own all over the world, will accept that maritime arbitration in future will still be in the hands of solicitors and barristers all dealing with masses of paper for a subsequent meeting in a brick building in London or anywhere else and arguing for a week or more over a case, with all the costs that implies.

The future lies in arbitration institutions offering a fully electronic exchange of submissions, maybe even decisions based on artificial intelligence for standard questions, hearings by video conference or other modern means, and all this to avoid time-consuming and costly hearings far away from any of the parties' place of residence. In some states, the state court systems have already undergone modernization steps to different extents. The maritime arbitration community is well advised to realize that nothing that constitutes constant and steady business to date will survive if maritime arbitration does not closely follow the development of the maritime industry as such.

LITERATURE

Ambrose/Maxwel/Collett, London Maritime Arbitration, 4th Edition 2018

Baumbach/Lauterbach/Albers/Hartmann (BLAH), Zivilprozessordnung, 76th Edition 2018

Haas, Ulrich/Kahlert, Heiner, Privacy and Confidentiality, in: Böckstiegel/Kröll/Nacimiento, Arbitration in Germany, 2015

Palandt, Bürgerliches Gesetzbuch, 76th Edition 2017

Sparka, Felix, Jurisdiction and Arbitration Clauses in Maritime Transport Documents, 2009

Wolaver, Earl S., The Historical Background of Commercial Arbitration, in: 83 University of Pennsylvania Law Review (U.PA.L.REV.) 132, 1934, page 132

Wölper, Jan, Maritime Arbitration in: Böckstiegel/Kröll/Nacimiento, Arbitration in Germany, 2015

Zöller, Zivilprozessordnung, 31st Edition 2016

NOTES

1 Wolaver, U.PA.L.REV. 1934, p. 132; Wölper in Böckstiegel/Kröll/Nacimiento (2015), p. 787, marginal note 1.
2 Ambrose/Maxwel/Collett (2018), para. 1.4.
3 Cf. GMAA Rules on Expert Opinion, www.gmaa.de.
4 Cf. GMAA Mediation Rules.
5 Cf. GMAA Conciliation Rules.
6 www.uncitral.org with amendments as adopted in 2006.
7 www.iccwbo.org.
8 www.gmaa.de.
9 Ambrose/Maxwel/Collett (2017), para. 12.42.
10 Ambrose/Maxwel/Collett (2017), para. 12.42.
11 Ambrose/Maxwel/Collett (2017), para. 12.43.
12 §10.4.b. GMAA.
13 For a general overview: Sparka (2009).
14 §139 German Civil Code (BGB).
15 Ellenberger in: Palandt (2017), §139 BGB, marginal note 15 with further evidence.
16 www.bimco.org – BIMCO Contracts, e.g. NYPE 2015, Clause 54 Law and Arbitration.
17 §1.1 GMAA.
18 §184 Court Constitution Act (GVG).
19 §1045 para. 1 German Code of Civil Procedure (ZPO); §10.2 GMAA.
20 §1051 para. 3 ZPO; §12.3 GMAA.
21 §169 GVG.
22 Ambrose/Maxwel/Collett (2018), para. 13.1.; Haas/Kahlert in: Böckstiegel/Kröll/Nacimiento (2015), p. 964, marginal notes 1 and 21.
23 §14.6 GMAA; LMAA §28.
24 Ambrose/Maxwel/Collett (2018), para. 13.6.
25 LMAA, para. 24(d).
26 LMAA, para. 16(b).
27 Ambrose/Maxwel/Collett (2018), para. 13.2.
28 Ambrose/Maxwel/Collett (2018), para. 13.213.6 with further references.
29 § 14.6 GMAA.
30 Haas/Kahlert (2015), p. 964, marginal note 4.
31 Haas/Kahlert (2015), p. 964, marginal note 9.
32 Haas/Kahlert (2015), p. 964, marginal note 11.
33 Haas/Kahlert (2015), p. 964, marginal note 21.
34 Haas/Kahlert (2015), p. 964, marginal note 23.
35 §1059 ZPO.
36 Zöller (2016), §1059, marginal note 47; Ambrose/Maxwel/Collett (2018), para. 22.12.
37 Ambrose/Maxwel/Collett (2018), para. 22.3 et seq.

[38] Ambrose/Maxwel/Collett (2018), para. 22.3.
[39] www.newyorkconvention.org – Contracting States.
[40] Regulation (EU) No. 1215/2012 of the European Parliament and of the Council of 12 December 2012 on jurisdiction and the recognition and enforcement of judgments in civil and commercial matters (EuGVVO).
[41] §328 para. 1 no. 5 ZPO; BLAH (2018), Appendix §328.
[42] BLAH (2018), Appendix § 328, marginal note 17.
[43] §6.1.d. GMAA.
[44] §72 ZPO.
[45] §13.1 GMAA; §278 para. 1 ZPO.
[46] §7.2 GMAA; Rules on Remuneration of the Arbitral Tribunal.
[47] §7.5 GMAA.

CHAPTER XX

LAW OF CLASSIFICATION SOCIETIES

Felix GOEBEL

A. INTRODUCTION

Why play classification societies such a key role in international maritime safety law, although flag states are responsible for the safety of their merchant fleet under the United Nations Convention of the Law of the Sea (UNCLOS)? Classification societies provide the technical expertise to evaluate the actual condition of the ship by assessing the construction and design of ships. Flag States face the challenge to oversee their merchant fleet on a transnational level. Technical ship inspections are regularly not carried out in the territory of the ship's flag State. Usually, flag States do not have sovereign powers to conduct ship inspections outside their national boundaries. Classification societies can perform this task by providing ship surveyors all around the globe. One calls this service conducted on behalf of the flag State: public statutory certification.[1]

In addition to the public statutory certification, classification societies develop and continuously update privately developed structural, mechanical and electrical requirements for ships (classification rules). Classification is an intermediary function, which makes it possible for maritime stakeholders to determine the value (condition) of the ship. Information of the ship's condition is important to negotiate the contracts with the shipowner, such as the charter party or insurance contract. Interestingly, the International Convention for the Safety of Life at Sea (SOLAS) even stipulates that a ship must be built and maintained following the technical rules of a classification society.[2]

If one is looking for a uniform law of classification societies, one will only find a large number of distributed international, supranational and national public and private regulations. The following chapter provides an overview of the laws that most visibly regulate the private classification and public statutory certification markets.[3]

B. Public Maritime Safety Law

As classification societies play such a significant role for the ship's safety by simultaneously providing their services in various jurisdictions, extensive regulatory measures have been placed at the international level to ensure that the societies perform their business with due care. The International Maritime Organization (IMO) developed the most relevant public laws, in the form of conventions and IMO resolutions. While these laws primarily focus on the societies' public statutory certification services, it is the EU's approach to extend its regulation to the private classification business.

I. Public Statutory Certification at the Level of International Law

If one is looking for the legal bases regulating public statutory certification at the international level, one starts best with a dive into the UNCLOS convention. Article 94 UNCLOS obliges flag States to ensure the safety at sea concerning the construction, equipment, manning and seaworthiness of ships. UNCLOS concretises that a qualified surveyor shall survey each ship before registration and after that at appropriate intervals. As national authorities cannot typically perform all these tasks by themselves, IMO[4] conventions explicitly refer to so-called recognised organisations, which can be entitled to issue public statutory certificates on behalf of flag States.[5] Often, but not exclusively, classification societies act as recognised organisations.

1. MARPOL, TONNAGE, SOLAS, and Load Lines Conventions

The most relevant maritime conventions, which regulate the issuing of public statutory certificates, are the MARPOL, TONNAGE, SOLAS, and Load Lines conventions. All these conventions specify the flag State's and recognised organisation's responsibilities to ensure the safety at sea under Article 94 UNCLOS.

The International Convention for the Prevention of Pollution from Ships (MARPOL) mainly regulates the prevention of maritime pollution by ships. Every ship covered by MARPOL must hold a certificate stating that it fulfils the criteria listed in the convention. The link with the classification societies – in their role as recognised organisations – is that flag States usually delegate the inspections and issuing of MARPOL certificates to recognised organisations.[6]

The International Convention on Tonnage Measurement of Ships (TONNAGE) introduced a universal system for the determination of the tonnage of ships on international voyages. According to Article 6, the determination of gross and net tonnages shall be carried out by the flag State administration or its recognised organisations (classification societies).

SOLAS is the primary framework convention regulating the safety of ships. Currently, SOLAS contains over 200 pages divided into twelve chapters according to which flag States have to determine the seaworthiness of their merchant fleet. However, SOLAS and the protocols are not conclusive in practice. SOLAS does not describe the technical requirements for the ship's safety down to the last component of a ship. Classification societies, (must) use these framework requirements to develop their own private classification rules, which regulate partly on more than 4000 pages the construction and operation of ships. Here, the private classification service – issuing the classification certificate –, and the public statutory service – issuing the SOLAS certificate on behalf of the flag State – overlap to a certain degree. Classification societies play a dual role in this respect.[7]

The same situation can be found with the International Convention on Load Lines. The draught to which a ship may be loaded contributes significantly to its safety. On the one hand, the convention reflects the public statutory need to regulate the limits of loading in the form of freeboards, as well as the conditions for a weather-proof and watertight integrity of ships' hull below freeboard deck. According to Article 13, recognised organisations can be entrusted to survey and mark ships. On the other hand, classification societies specify the Load Lines convention with their private classification rules. The 1988 Protocol even connected the private classification with the statutory measurement of the ship's strength. The flag State can accept a ship's level of strength if the ship is designed, constructed, and maintained in compliance with the classification requirements of a recognised organisation.[8]

2. IMO III AND RO CODES

Further regulation of classification societies took place at the IMO in 2012/13. It turned out that the quality of flag State's monitoring of their recognised organisations differs internationally. The IMO has therefore introduced a uniform monitoring mechanism. It approved the Instruments Implementation Code (III Code)[9] and the new consolidated IMO Code on Recognised Organisations (RO Code).[10] These two Codes now directly and indirectly – through specific requirements for flag States on how to authorise their recognised organisations – regulate the delegation of public statutory certification at an international IMO level.

The IMO even adopted with the III Code[11] a key tool for assessing member states' performance in meeting their obligations and responsibilities as flag, port and coastal States. It provides the framework for an IMO Member State Audit Scheme. Its purpose is to enhance global maritime safety and protection of the marine environment. The III Code assists states to implement the IMO conventions[12]: SOLAS, MARPOL, COLREG[13], Load Lines, STCW[14], and TONNAGE. Due to IMO's limited jurisdiction, the III Code is not itself binding. Thus, the code has been incorporated into the above IMO Conventions to make it mandatory for member states.

The III Code directly affects the work of classification societies in their role as recognised organisations working on behalf of flag States. The III Code shall promote the development of policies, legislation and administrative procedures for the "selection, recognition, authorisation, empowerment and monitoring of recognised organisations [...] and nominated surveyors."[15]

Besides the III Code, the IMO acknowledged the need for a common code – the RO Code[16] –, which now provides a standard tool for all flag States in meeting their responsibilities in recognising, authorising and monitoring recognised organisations.[17]

The RO Code applies to all flag States which intend to delegate specific responsibilities regarding the public statutory certification of ships to recognised organisations under the IMO instruments, in particular, the SOLAS, MARPOL, Load Lines and TONNAGE conventions. It shall set the common quality standard for audits by recognised organisations.[18] In part 1, the Code establishes mandatory requirements for such organisations, which intend to be recognised by a flag State. Part 2 introduces mandatory requirements that recognised organisations shall fulfil when performing public statutory certification services on behalf of a flag State, as well as mandatory requirements that flag States should adhere to when authorising recognised organisations. The last part provides guidelines for flag States to monitor their recognised organisations. The appendix 1 lists the minimum quality standards for training and qualification of recognised organisation's technical staff. Those minimum conditions are also part of Annex I to the European Commission Regulation No. 391/2009 (see below).

3. OTHER IMO INSTRUMENTS

Beside the above conventions and codes, the IMO adopted several more instruments relating to classification societies, such as the HSSC Guidelines and Goal-based standards.

Since 2000, the Harmonised System for Survey and Certification (HSSC Guidelines)[19] provides a technical framework upon which flag States shall base their arrangements for carrying out surveys. Classification societies use the HSSC Guidelines as international standards to perform public statutory services on behalf of flag States. The guidelines are directly incorporated to SOLAS, Load Lines, and MARPOL, as well as to the IBC and IGC Codes[20].

In 2005, the IMO developed goal-based standards (GBS). GBS are as standards and procedures that are to be met through regulations, rules and standards for ships. GBS are comprised of at least one goal, functional requirement(s) associated with that goal, and verification of conformity that rules/regulations meet the functional requirements including goals. To meet the goals and functional requirements, classification societies – acting as recognised organisations – and flag States shall develop the rules and regulations accordingly.[21]

IMO's idea behind the implementation of a GBS system was that it recognised that an utterly free classification market could not ensure the economically desired level of ship safety. It has been argued at the IMO[22] the classification societies have difficulties to perform high-quality classification services if they are subject to economic pressure. One suggested that one should remove competition at all between classification societies to achieve a higher level of ship safety. However, this proposal has – rightly – not been accepted. Instead that, the IMO – as the United Nations body of flag States – concluded that it should play a more significant role in determining the standards to which new ships are built and maintained. Despite the stipulations of Article 94 UNCLOS, this role rested traditionally with classification societies and shipyards. The IMO pursued to the goal that the flag States themselves can only specify an economically desirable level of ship safety (as already required by Article 94 UNCLOS). However, as prescribed-based regulations proved to be of limited practical use to cope with the challenges of new types of ships, the IMO took action and incorporated the goal-based philosophy into the technical regulations of SOLAS. The GBS shall, on the one hand, reflect the need for competition on innovative designs and, on the other hand, ensure that ships are constructed in such a manner that, if properly maintained, remain safe throughout their whole economic lives.[23]

II. PUBLIC STATUTORY CERTIFICATION AND PRIVATE CLASSIFICATION AT THE LEVEL OF EUROPEAN LAW

Before 1994, EU legislation was criticised for shortcomings regarding the safety of ships calling European harbours. Both, the monitoring of ships and the international safety rules themselves have been considered revisable.[24] The reason was (and still is) that coastal and port States – such as member states of the European Union – face the actual risk of substandard shipping. Notably, environmental disasters as the sinking of the oil tankers *Prestige* and *Erika* off the European coast increased the public pressure on the European Commission to counteract. However, the EU cannot merely adopt higher safety standards for ships by issuing stricter European ship safety laws. The problem lies in the internationalism of shipping. Flag States are responsible for assuring the safety of their merchant fleet under the international maritime law (Article 94 UNCLOS). This responsibility includes the right to impose sanctions if a ship is unsafe. However, the consequence is also that coastal and port States can only scrutinise whether a ship fulfils the prevailing international standards (through port State control).

If coastal and port States develop higher safety standards for foreign ships, they violate the sovereign rights of flag states. Thus, they are bound to regulate new risks at the international level. As changes of international laws can be slow, it may take some time until new, so far unregulated risks are added to the international laws. From the European Union's point of view, this is a very unsatisfactory result. It cannot guarantee a comprehensive protection of the European Territories in this way. As the EU is already entitled to regulate safety issues of all other European transport modes – rail, road, air, inland waterway –[25], it searched for solutions to improve the safety of all ships calling European harbours. Because the EU cannot introduce stricter rules for flag State's public statutory certification schemes (Article 94 UNCLOS), it used some back door. As flag State's public statutory certification is primarily based on the more specific classification rules, the EU decided to regulate the private classification market. As a result, the EU has promised itself that the requirements of public statutory certification will indirectly increase, as well.[26]

Briefly, the European Commission has implemented a recognition scheme according to which a classification society must be recognised if it desires to participate in the European single market. As the presence on the European single market is crucial for a globally acting classification society, it has a definite incentive to fulfil the requirements for recognition.

1. EU'S RECOGNITION SCHEME

In 1994, Directive 94/57/EC[27] established the present system for the community-wide recognition of classification societies. The Directive was amended by Directive 97/58/EC[28] and Directive 2001/105/EC. It was finally revised by Directive 2009/15/EC[29] and Regulation (EC) 391/2009[30]. These legislative acts together now form a coherent piece of legislation that regulates the activities of recognised organisations under European law.

Motivated by the perception that flag State's public statutory certification was often not upon European standard, with Directive 94/57/EC the EU implemented common minimum criteria for classification societies conducting surveys and inspections on behalf of EU member states. These minimum criteria were derived from the membership criteria of the International Association of Classification Societies (IACS). The idea was that only the organisations recognised by European Commission could be authorised by member states. It should achieve a uniform standard for the delegation of public tasks to privately acting classification societies.

Presently (2018), eleven classification societies have been recognised. Through such recognition and periodic monitoring, the EU exerts control over the major classification societies.[31] With a system of state recognition, the European Commission can now impose specific minimum standards on the classification societies' business structure, which shall indirectly increase the safety of non-EU ships. Without EU recognition, classification societies would risk losing significant market share. It incentivises the classification societies to have an economic interest in maintaining high professionalism in their classification activities.

In practice, the assessment and periodic monitoring are carried out by EU officials who frequently travel to the headquarters and branches of all recognised organisations (worldwide). The criteria according to which the EU Commission decides whether the performance of an organisation acting on behalf of a flag State should be considered an unacceptable threat to the safety and the environment are laid down in Commission Decision 2009/491/EC.[32]

Five years later, after the EU Commission introduced the European recognition scheme of classification societies, in 1999, the oil tanker *Erika* encountered a severe gale in the Bay of Biscay. She broke in two, sank and released thousands of tons of oil into the sea, causing exceptionally high damages to the environment. In the aftermath, the EU Commission adopted the so-called legislative packages Erika I, II and III, which have further strengthened the safety along the European coasts. The Erika I package – especially Directive 2001/105/EC[33] – has been of particular concern to classification societies.

Since the adoption of the community-wide recognition of classification societies, some further developments have occurred in the relevant legislation at Community and international level requiring adjustments of Directive 94/57/EC by Directive 2001/105/EC. For the societies' legal situation, the primary revisions have been,[34] firstly, the implementation of a stricter monitoring system of recognised organisations.[35] Secondly, applicant classification societies can now only receive recognition if they demonstrate a proper safety and pollution prevention performance record of the whole fleet they have certified.[36] Thirdly, the Directive implemented additional obligations for recognised organisations, such as the duty to provide any relevant information about the fleet they classed, irrespective of flag, to the member states' authorities.[37] Fourthly, specific new requirements were implemented regarding the procedures to be applied when the shipowner transfers a ship from one society to another, as well as requirements on the increased exchange of information between classification societies and port State control. Scholars and practitioners realised that an unregulated transfer of ships from one class to the class of another class society increases economic pressure on the societies. Shipowner can use forum shopping to obtain temporary exemptions from class if the ship is not able to obtain class under normal circumstances. The policy goal was thus to minimise forum shopping to the detriment of the ship's safety.

However, the most controversial concern about Directive 2001/105/EC surrounds the specific requirements on the sharing of the financial liability between the flag State and its classification society in cases where the flag State is held liable, but the cause is linked to the public statutory survey of the classification society.[38] The divergence in the financial regimes of the member states represented a difficulty in the proper implementation of Directive 94/57/EC.

It was seen appropriate to bring about a degree of harmonisation at the Community level of the liability arising out of any incident caused by recognised organisations. The revised provision of Article 6 of Directive 94/57/EC now provides a uniform unlimited liability for the classification societies if the damage was caused by their wilful acts, omissions or gross negligence, and a limited liability up to EUR 4 million for negligence and recklessness. While the European Parliament endorsed this approach, the Council opined that the societies' liability should perhaps be unlimited even in the latter case.[39]

In this context, it seems appropriate to point out a much more severe challenge regarding state liability. The EU now regulates the liability arising out of any incident, if the liability is finally imposed on the flag State administration by a court of law. However, often a ship sails under the flag of a non-EU flag State. If a European court rules that a foreign non-EU flag State administration be liable for damage than it risks to breach the sovereign rights of the flag State. Under the international law's principle of state immunity, in principle, no foreign state may sue the state authorities of another state. The consequence is not only that European courts may not sue non-EU flag state administrations for violating ship's safety. In the proceedings of the cases *Erika* and *Al-Salam Boccaccio 98*, the parties also discussed whether the classification society is protected by state immunity if it carries out public statutory certification on behalf of the flag State. Without having taken a final decision on this in the proceedings, the question of immunity with regard to public statutory certification is likely to be affirmed. However, the private classification service is unlikely to be protected by state immunity.[40]

Lastly, Directive 2001/105/EC enhanced the EU Commission's competence to withdraw recognition, which shall put economic pressure on poorly performing classification societies. It modified the existing *all or nothing* principle by implementing a more flexible principle of suspending recognition. The EU Commission is now authorised to suspend recognition for one year, during which time any shortcomings must be rectified, or recognition will be withdrawn.[41]

In 2009, the EU adopted the latest Erika III package, introducing some new legislation, such as the currently existing Directive 2009/15/EC and Regulation (EC) 391/2009 on common rules and standards for ship inspection and survey organisations.[42] Since further amendments were to be made, the EU decided to recast Directive 94/57/EC in the interests of clarity. While the Directive 2009/15/EC directly addresses the member states. The Regulation (EC) 391/2009 now provides a framework for the recognition and periodic assessment of the recognised organisations without differentiating according to the ship's flag. Regulation (EC) 391/2009 established further measures to be followed by the recognised organisations entrusted with the inspection, survey and certification of ships.[43] The Regulation aims to save navigators and other people aboard from harm and aims to offer a competitive market for survey organisations while guaranteeing equal levels of safety and environmental protection.[44]

Motivated by its inability to adequately sanction the recognised organisations that had certified the capsized *MT Erika* and *MT Prestige*, the EU Commission was determined to make the system of penalties more flexible and efficient.[45] Regulation (EC) 391/2009 amended the only available penalty thus far (suspension/withdrawal) and instead empowered the EU Commission also to impose individual fines and periodic penalty payments until the required action is entirely carried out.[46] The aggregate amount of fines and imposed periodic penalty payments is limited to 5% of the recognised organisation's total average turnover. With the possibility to impose fines and periodic payments on recognised organisations, the EU Commission has (now) a powerful tool to influence the market-behaviour of recognised organisations.

In this context, the EU Commission developed a new Regulation (EC) 788/2014[47] in 2014, which laid down detailed rules of procedure to impose fines and periodic penalty payments and to withdraw the recognition of recognised organisations under Articles 6 and 7 of Regulation (EC) 391/2009. To identify any infringements, the EU Commission must now prove that an infringement under Article 6 of Regulation (EC) 391/2009 is attributable to the severe or repeated failure by a recognised organisation to fulfil one of the minimum criteria of Annex I of Regulation (EC) 391/2009 or failure to fulfil its obligations under Articles 8, 9, 10 and 11 of that Regulation.[48]

2. Potential Conflict Between EU and IMO Law

The introduction of the IMO III and RO Codes at the international level made it necessary to adopt EU law in 2014. Directive 2014/111/EU[49] and Regulation (EU) 1355/2014[50] amended the two above described EU acts – Directive 2009/15/EC and Regulation (EC) 391/2009 – dealing with the formal role of recognised organisations. The Directive and Regulation essentially clarify that several provisions within the new IMO instruments would contradict European law if the member states fully ratify the new RO and III Codes. The underlying problem is that the EU introduced with the Community-wide recognition of recognised organisations, a scheme which is applicable to all recognised organisations. EU's scheme is not limited recognised organisations which conduct services on behalf of EU flag State administrations but covers all classification societies which provide services on the European internal market.

Directive 2014/111/EU and Regulation (EU) 1355/2014 stipulate that[51] the III Code provides a minimum list of resources and processes for flag

States to establish administrative instructions of ship classification, which shall demonstrate the compliance with the structural, mechanical, and electrical requirements of an international convention.[52] If Union law incorporates the provision of the III Code, it would restrict the application of criterion A.3 in Annex I of Regulation (EC) 391/2009 to the recognised organisation's performance with regard only to ships flying the flag of member states.

Furthermore, the Directive 2014/111/EU and Regulation (EU) 1355/2014[53] emphasise that the RO Code[54] defines public statutory certification as a single category of activities that a recognised organisation is entitled to perform on behalf of the flag State, including the issuance of both public statutory *and* classification requirements. By contrast, the definitions set out in Regulation (EC) 391/2009[55] draw a clear distinction between public statutory certification and classification.

Lastly, Directive 2014/111/EU and Regulation (EU) 1355/2014[56] clarify that the RO Code[57] provides a mechanism of cooperation between recognised organisations under the sole framework established by the flag State to standardise processes concerning public statutory certification services.[58] Under Union law, cooperation between recognised organisations is governed by Article 10(1) of Regulation (EC) 391/2009. It requires that recognised organisations consult with each other to maintaining equivalence and aiming for harmonisation of their rules and procedures. The EU argues that the cooperation processes under Article 10(1) pertain solely to the private activities of the classification societies. They apply irrespective of a ship's flag. The cooperation mechanisms in the RO Code would, therefore, limit the scope of the cooperation framework established by Article 10(1) of Regulation (EC) 391/2009, which is not limited to ships flying the flag of an EU member state.

To sum up briefly, EU Commission's legal policy is that nothing in the III Code or RO Code should restrict the Union's capacity to lay down appropriate (stricter) conditions for the granting of recognition to organisations seeking authorisation from EU member states. All this shall achieve the Union's objective: enhancing maritime safety and environmental protection.[59]

3. TECHNICAL SAFETY REQUIREMENTS

Besides the formal standards and procedures of how to receive and maintain the recognised status in the EU, there are several technical safety requirements in EU law according to which ships must be built and operated. Classification societies use these laws and the conventions to perform their public statutory certification and classification services. These laws reflect the technical safety requirements, which are developed at the IMO and incorporated in the SOLAS, TONNAGE, Load Lines, and MARPOL conventions. However, European member states have for the most part themselves incorporated the IMO conventions into national law, such as the German legislator for SOLAS with the Federal Ship Safety Act (Schiffssicherheitsgesetz)[60]. Currently, the most relevant EU Directives and Regulations covering technical safety requirements are:

- Directive 2014/90/EU on marine equipment
- Regulation (EU) No 530/2012 on the accelerated phasing-in of double hull or equivalent design requirements for single-hull oil tankers
- Directive 2001/96/EC establishing harmonised equipment and procedures for the safe loading and unloading of bulk carriers amended by Directive 2002/84/EC and Regulation (EC) No 1137/2008
- Council Regulation (EC) No 2978/94 on the implementation of IMO resolution A.747(18) on the application of tonnage measurement of ballast spaces in segregated ballast oil tankers amended by Regulation (EC) No 2099/2002 and Regulation (EC) No 1882/2003
- Council Directive 97/70/EC setting up a harmonised safety regime for fishing vessels of 24 meters in length and over amended by Commission Directive 1999/19/EC, Commission Directive 2002/35/EC, Directive 2002/84/EC and Regulation (EC) No 219/2009
- Council Decision of 17 February 2014 authorising Member States to sign, ratify or accede to the Cape Town Agreement of 2012 on the Implementation of the Provisions of the Torremolinos Protocol of 1993 relating to the Torremolinos International Convention for the Safety of Fishing Vessels, 1977 (2014/195/EU)
- Regulation (EC) 336/2006 on the implementation of the International Safety Management Code within the Community amended by Commission Regulation (EC) No 540/2008 and Regulation 1137/2008

4. POLLUTION PREVENTION

UNCLOS grants coastal and port States additional rights to adopt stricter regulations on the reduction and control of pollution from ships. Such additional laws may relate to discharges or navigational practices but shall not require foreign vessels to observe design, construction, manning or equipment standards other than generally accepted international rules and standards (Article 211 UNCLOS). The EU has made use of this right. In 2005, it implemented Directive 2005/35/EC, amended by Directive 2009/123/EC on ship-source pollution and introduced penalties for infringements.[61]

The EU realised that neither the international regime for the civil liability and compensation of oil pollution nor that relating to pollution by other hazardous or noxious substances provides sufficient dissuasive effects of discouraging the parties from engaging in substandard practices. Common rules on criminal penalties shall make it possible to use more efficient methods of investigation and capable cooperation within and between the member states. The Directive stipulates that penalties should apply to any party causing or contributing to marine pollution. The Preamble of the Directive expressly mentions classification societies.[62]

C. CIVIL LIABILITY OF CLASSIFICATION SOCIETIES

Besides the International and European public maritime law which shall regulate the market behaviour of classification societies, the societies also face the risk to be held liable under civil law. Some recent court decisions, most prominently *Erika*[63] and *Prestige*[64], rekindled the discussions on the liability of classification societies among scholars[65] and at the CMI conferences in Dublin (2013)[66] and Hamburg (2014)[67].

There is especially no international third-party liability regime for classification societies. Liability law is subject to national jurisdiction. Scholars and courts widely agree that classification societies can limit their contractual liability concerning their clients. Meanwhile, the more critical question is whether classification societies can be held liable for third-party damages and whether they are or should be entitled to limiting their liability towards third parties.[68]

I. RECENT JUDGEMENTS

Some recent court decisions and related legal publications[69] have discussed whether classification societies can be held liable towards third parties, both in common and civil law jurisdictions.

The *Erika* case (French law)[70] and the *Al-Salam Boccaccio 98* case (Italian law)[71] revolved around the controversial discussed question whether classification societies are immune from jurisdiction in any state other than the flag State when performing statutory services on behalf of the flag State or (even) when providing private classification services.[72] In the *Prestige* (United States law)[73], *Erika* and *Al-Salam Boccaccio 98* cases, it was disputed whether classification societies could be held liable towards third parties for negligently conducted classification surveys. In the *Al-Salam Boccaccio 98* case, the plaintiffs argued that liability should derive not only from the negligent classification surveys but also from the insufficient classification rules the society had developed. In the *Erika* and *Prestige* cases, the courts had moreover to discuss whether classification societies fall under the Convention on Civil Liability for Oil Pollution Damage of 1992, potentially limiting their liability. In the *Redwood* case (Italian law)[74], the court ruled on the question as to what extent a grossly negligent classification society is liable towards a third-party.

II. Third-Party Liability

Third-party liability of classification societies has been predominately analysed by scholars concerning US, English, German, and Scandinavian law.[75] The following section shall not reiterate existing findings but selectively describe whether the most prominent court decisions in *Erika* and *Prestige* may have any diverging impact on the existing third-party liability regimes.

To pre-empt the answer, it seems that the decisions will not have a significant diverging impact on the different third-party liability regimes. Instead, the analysis of such prominent decisions by scholars of different jurisdictions contributes to making the fragmented civil liability law more predictable for classification societies.

In *Erika* and *Prestige*, one of the questions was whether coastal States could claim compensation from classification societies even though the states are unaware of the ship's classification. Such claims may be for lost or damaged property or economic loss. None of those mentioned above jurisdictions provides protection against economic loss unless the state explicitly relied on the representations made by the society. However, under specific prerequisites damages to property can be compensated. This property interest is unlikely to be protected under English law. Though US law provides a mechanism to protect property in §311 and §552 Restatement (Second) of Torts, in *Prestige* the court decided that coastal States cannot claim damages. Under German law, a legal doctrine so-called contract with protective effects towards third parties (Vertrag mit Schutzwirkung Dritter) also does not afford coastal States to be compensated for oil pollution. The state is neither in the proximity to the performance of the classification contract, and its protection is not in the interest of the contractual creditor (shipowner), nor is the risk foreseeable for the classification society. However, a negligent classification society can be held liable for damages to property under §823 German Civil Code.[76] To claim non-physical damages under the Scandinavian law – such as economic loss – scholars suggest that claimants must prove three qualified foreseeability prerequisites: relevant interests, closeness, and predictability of the actual loss. Especially, closeness and predictability of the loss for the classification society would seem very difficult to prove for a coastal State.[77]

III. LIMITATION OF THIRD-PARTY LIABILITY

In *Erika* and *Prestige*, the defendants also objected that classification society's liability is limited. An unlimited liability – in comparison to the liability caps of shipowners – would only lead to a shift of liability, which is seen as an imbalanced and unfair liability regime in shipping.[78]

In brief, the reasoning behind the existing concepts of liability limitation in shipping is that historically shipowners had limited opportunities to forecast weather conditions and other maritime risks, which had compromised safe navigation. In those days (as today), cargo was typically worth more than the ship that carried it, meaning that the value of the ship would not suffice as security in case the cargo owner sued the shipowner for the total loss of the cargo. While the maritime industry faced the risk of a shipowner's bankruptcy, it developed mechanisms to distribute the losses, such as marine insurance and general average contributions.[79] It had also been the legal opinion that classification societies perform quasi-governmental functions for which they cannot be held directly liable. For the private classification service, this view has changed during the last decades. Nowadays it is the prevailing legal opinion that classification societies can be held liable under civil, as well as criminal law.

The question arises whether the maritime liability conventions can also limit the liability of classification societies. Despite *Lord Steyn's* leading opinion in the precedent English case *Nicolas H.*[80] to the effect that a limitation of liability for classification is *fair, just, and reasonable* according to English policy considerations, international court decisions are ambiguous as to whether classification societies fall under the scope of the existing limitation conventions. Clear is that classification societies are explicitly not mentioned in the different IMO conventions on the limitation of liability. In *Erika* and *Prestige*, the courts have also been reluctant to recognise a gap in the conventions that needed to be filled in. Scholars, therefore, focus on the question of whether it is a legitimate policy goal to limit the liability and – if one answers the question in the affirmative – how one could implement the limitation best.[81]

It seems that most scholars support a limitation of liability to establish a balance between shipowners' liability caps and the unlimited liability of classification societies.[82] One can also find first legal and economic discussions to modify the traditionally grown liability caps of the shipowner to unlimited liability in shipping. Scholars point out that insurers are even able to reinsure an unlimited liability risk resulting from nuclear fallouts.[83] There is no more the risk that shipowners would stop its activity in shipping because of a risk of bankruptcy in the case of a maritime casualty. Unlimited liability means that insurers can adjust their insurance premiums accordingly to the overall risk resulting from the activity (shipping). However, it is unlikely that politics will change an over decades filigree developed international regime of shipowner's liability soon.[84]

D. OUTLOOK

Giving an outlook on the future of the classification market can barely be more than a glimpse into the glass sphere. An anniversary publication nevertheless tempts a junior scholar to think about the upcoming decades of classification. Fortunately, it can be left to the next anniversary publication to deal with the accuracy of the predictions.

I. REGULATION AND COMPETITION OF CLASSIFICATION SOCIETIES

Smith predicts that classification societies will increasingly replace all forms of public statutory regulation in shipping. The role of transportation regulation will change to one of policy-making, with the limited role of administrations to oversight the classification market.[85] One can already observe this trend. Administrations increasingly rely on the performance of classification societies not only in their role as recognised organisations but also as classification society. The policy consideration behind the implementation of the GBS standards underlines this indication.

Smith furthermore anticipates that there will be little market growth for non-IACS classification societies.[86] Smaller competitors indeed face higher barriers to entry the classification market.[87] Newcomers must incur higher sunk costs to build up a competitive amount of reputation. Besides reputation, the classification system heavily relies on network effects. The value of a classification increases with the number of other classifications carried out according to the same set of classification rules. It strengthens the presumption that non-IACS societies will find it hard to grow.[88]

Smith also emphasises that competition among the classification societies will increase, and the businesses will continue to expand across technical standards, safety systems and management consulting.[89] The traditional classification market depends on the growth of the global ship fleet. During a shipping crisis, the societies have strong incentives to expand their activities into new market segments. Indeed, already today, the classification societies are increasingly expanding into further testing, inspection and certification market segments (TIC markets) to overcome the mature structure of the classification market.[90] Otherwise, they would risk that competitors use the first-mover advantage. This effect can also cross-subsidise the classification segment, which reduces the costs of classification. One can already observe cross-subsidisation in the classification of new ships. Some classification societies offer lower prices for the first classification, expecting to refinance the losses with future classifications of the ship.[91] Similar to Maersk Line's decision to concentrate predominately on liner shipping, it is also not unlikely that the classification societies will continue to specialise in individual market segments, such as the bulk carrier or cruising ship segment.

II. Competitive Market Model and Dual Role of Classification Societies

De Bruyne raised another competition policy issue, questioning whether the dual role of classification societies (on the one hand, private classification and advisory services for shipowners and on the other hand, public statutory services on behalf of the flag State) is still politically desirable in the light of potential conflicts of interest.[92] Such policy considerations would significantly change the classification market. However, an efficient reputation mechanism can minimise such concerns, and administrations should instead continue to concentrate on disclosing such potential dependencies. Transparency and market forces can keep the risks at bay.[93] Similar discussions on potential conflicts of interest were made in the aftermath of the financial crisis 2007/08 regarding the big four players in the financial auditing markets and the credit rating markets.

De Bruyne's concerns, however, indirectly point to a problem that seems to be potentially much more severe for classification societies. In addition to the financial – but insurable – burden of unlimited liability in the event of a medial general average, think of the *Costa Concordia*, a public debate could arise on whether the current competitive-oriented system of classification should continue to exist at all. The question is: can a competitive classification market guarantee safe shipping, in which flag States (only) set goal-based standards? Without finally answering the question, it should be noted that today's private classification and public statutory certification systems are the most efficient systems in the history of shipping.[94]

III. BLOCKCHAIN TECHNOLOGY

It is clear that classification societies will face new competition in the next century due to the increasingly digitalised world. Already today, the actual condition of a ship is continuously monitored by a large set of data. Digital data of the ship's condition leads to the development of new information technologies. The interesting question is to ask whether new technologies might have the potential to compete with the core task of classification: the trustworthy intermediation of information between two or more stakeholders, such as the insurer and shipowner. While negotiating the contracts, rational stakeholders do not trust each other that the ship is in the alleged condition, even though the shipowner provides the data. Too high transaction costs prevent that the shipowner's contractual partner evaluate the data. Classification society's reputation vanquishes the lack of trust in their contractual relationship.[95]

Also, banks intermediate financial transactions between two parties, which do not trust each other. Excessive transaction costs prevent that the parties carry out their financial transaction without the involvement of a bank. Today, a so-called blockchain technology starts challenging the business model of banks. Technological experts point out that a blockchain algorithm can retrieve a lack of trust between two stakeholders, which can then enter into a financial transaction without interposing an intermediating bank. The blockchain technology is currently used for crypto currencies, such bitcoin and etherium. However, the technology is also arrived in the maritime industry. Maersk and IBM recently started a blockchain project to optimize their liner shipping. The technology shall devise an end-to-end shipping solution giving all parties involved in global trade a single view of where cargo is and it shall allow authorities to give electronic approval for its movement.

Also, a start-up project called WAVE uses a blockchain to revolutionise the transfer of bill of ladings.

The public statutory certification and private classification consist of a development of classification rules, the physical fitness-check of the ship's condition according to the rules and the inspection of the documents on board the ship. One can think of smart contracts – based on a blockchain – which could provide a strong digital technology to substitute the manual inspection of documents in the near term. In smart contracts each traditional contractual clause has a digitalised counterpart in the form of an algorithm. This shall make the contract self-enforcing. For example, a breach of a contractual duty can automatically unblock the legal consequence – punitive damage, which the algorithm directly transfers from one contractual partner to the other.

Already today, intelligent on-board systems transmit data information about the ship's condition directly to shore. DNV GL recently even published a project in which it uses drones to check the condition of remote structural components. The technology shall have the potential to reduce survey times and staging costs significantly.[96] Such information could be embedded directly in smart contracts in the future.

Generally, digitalised classification offers immense opportunities to optimise the whole classification system and even its core task: intermediation. This can significantly increase the ship's safety in the next century. It, nevertheless, seems unlikely that a blockchain technology – or similar digital development – will remove an intermediating classification society in long term. The societies asset still lies in the actual evaluation of the ship's fitness. However, similar to Maersk and IBM's developments for the liner shipping market, the use of blockchain technologies has the potential to revolutionise the current classification market.

IV. SHARING OF INFORMATION ON INNOVATIVE PRODUCTS

A final comment deserves the provision of information among the classification societies. The policy adopted by IACS and endorsed by the EU Commission – exchanging information on innovative products between the classification societies – should be viewed with precaution. The economic consequence is that classification societies, which invest in research and development, are forced to make information available to its competitor free of charge. This practice can distort the price of a classification service and impede safety relevant innovation. The socially desirable investments in research and development – which enhance ship safety – must then be cross-subsidised, such as through competition on the market of type-approval certification.[97]

LITERATURE

Basedow, J., and Wurmnest, W., Third-Party Liability of Classification Societies – A Comparative Perspective, 2005

Billah, M. M., Effects of Insurance on Maritime Liability Law – A Legal and Economic Analysis, 2014

De Bruyne, J., and Vanleenhove, C., An EU Perspective on the Liability of Classification Societies: Selected Court Issues and Private International Law Aspects, Journal of International Maritime Law (2014), pp. 103–120

De Bruyne, J., Liability of Classification Societies: Cases, Challenges and Future Perspectives, Journal of Maritime Law & Commerce, Vol. 45 (2014), pp. 181–232

Clyne, R.G., and Saville, Jr., J.A., Classification Societies and Limitation of Liability, Tulane Law Review, Vol. 81 (2006–2007), pp. 1399–1431

Daniel, B.D., Potential Liability of Marine Classification Societies to Non-Contracting Parties, U.S.F. Maritime Law Journal, Vol. 19 (2006–2007), pp. 183–296

Galiano, E., In the Wake of the PRESTIGE Disaster: Is an Earlier Phase-out of Single-Hulled Oil Tankers the Answer?, Tul. Mar. L.J., Vol. 28 (2004), pp. 113–133

Goebel, F., Classification Societies – Competition and Regulation of Maritime Information Intermediaries, 2017

Jessen, H., The Liability of Classification Societies – Some Practical Issues, CMI Yearbook 2014 (2014), pp. 275–281

Jessen, H., Mutual Recognition Within Ship Classification – Fundamentals and Some Possible Future Problems of Art. 10 Regulation EC/391/2009, RdTW, Vol. 10 (2015), pp. 368–374

Jessen, H., Dritthaftung von Klassifikationsgesellschaften, RdTW, Vol. 4 (2015), p. 160

Jessen, H., Commentary on Regulation EC/391/2009 on Common Rules and Standards for Ship Inspection and Survey Organizations and Directive 2009/15/EC on Common Rules and Standards for Ship Inspection and Survey Organizations and for the Relevant Activities of Maritime Administrations, in: Jessen and Werner, Brussels Commentary on EU Maritime Transport Law, Baden-Baden (2016), pp. 713–855

Kröger, B., Presentation on Behalf of the German Shipowners' Association and of the Maritime Law Committee of ICS, CMI Yearbook 1997 (1997), pp. 185–192

Lagoni, N, The Liability of Classification Societies, 2007

Micallef, A., A Legal Analysis of the Limitation of Classification Societies, presented paper at the CMI Annual Symposium, Dublin 29 Sept – 1 Oct 2013, (accessible at http://www.cmi2013dublin.com, last accessed 08 October 2015), pp. 1–26

Reuß, M., and Pichon, J., The European Union's Exercise of Jurisdiction over Classification Societies, ZaöRV, Vol. 67 (2007), pp. 119–144

Ringbom, H., The Erika Accident and its Effects on EU Maritime Regulation, in: Current Marine Environmental Issues and the International Tribunal for the Law of the Sea, ed. by Nordquist and Moore, London (2001), pp. 265–290

Siccardi, B., Immunity from Jurisdiction are CS Entitled to it (a) as Recognized Organizations acting for Flag States (b) when Performing Class Services, in: Classification Societies Regulatory Regime and Current issues on Liability, London Shipping Law Center (2013)

Skou, A. W., Presentation on behalf of IACS to the Centenary Conference of the CMI, CMI Yearbook 1997 (1997), pp. 180–185

Smith, J. J., On a flood tide: Classification Societies and Canada's marine industry in 2020, (2011), (accessible at http://www.dieselduck.info/library/01%20articles/2011-Class%20Society%20-%20JJ%20Smith.pdf, last accessed 08 October 2015)

Somers, E, and Gonsaeles, G., Consequences of the Sinking of the M/S ERIKA in European Waters Towards a Total Loss of International Shipping Law, J. Mar. L. & Com., Vol. 41 (2010), pp. 57–84

NOTES

1 Such as the MARPOL, SOLAS, Load Lines Certificates.

2 E.g. II-1 Part A-1 Regulation 3–1 of SOLAS Convention of 1974.

3 For more detailed information see Goebel (2017), p. 61 et seq.

4 International Maritime Organisation.

5 See Regulation I/6 of SOLAS 1974, Article 13 of Load Lines 66, Regulation 6 of MARPOL Annex I, Regulation 8 of MARPOL Annex II, and Article 6 of TONNAGE 69; Cf. Clause 8.1 RO Code, Res. MSC.349(92).

6 See, e.g. Regulation 7 para. 3.1 of MARPOL 73/78 Annex 1.

7 Goebel (2017), p. 42 et seq.

8 Annex 1, Reg. 1 (2) of the Protocol of 1988 to Load Lines.

9 Approved by the IMO Marine Environment Protection Committee's 65th session and the IMO Maritime Safety Committee's 91st session. Adopted by the IMO Assembly in December 2013 (28th session), IMO Resolution A.1070(28).

10 Adopted by the IMO Marine Environment Protection Committee's 65th session and the IMO Maritime Safety Committee's 92nd session.

11 The III Code was initially developed in 2005 by A.973(24) and revised in 2011 by A.1054(27).

[12] IMO Assembly adopts mandatory audit scheme, 4 December 2013, (accessible at www.imo.org/MediaCentre/PressBriefings/Pages/A-28-ends-.aspx#.VKQSxYqG9y4, last accessed 30 November 2017).

[13] Convention on the International Regulations for Preventing Collisions at Sea, 1972, as amended (COLREG 1972).

[14] International Convention on Standards of Training, Certification and Watchkeeping for Seafarers, 1978 (STCW).

[15] Article 7.7 IMO Resolution A.1070(28).

[16] IMO Resolution MSC.349(92).

[17] Cf. Preamble to Resolution MSC.349(92).

[18] See MSC 92, 2 July 2013, p. 2.

[19] For a list of the amendments to SOLAS, Load Lines, MARPOL, and the mandatory IMO Codes, see Annexes 1–4 of IMO Resolution A.1053(27), amended by IMO Res.1076(28).

[20] IBC Code = International Code for the Construction and Equipment of Ships Carrying Dangerous Chemicals in Bulk; IGC Code = International Code for the Construction and Equipment of Ships Carrying Liquefied Gases in Bulk.

[21] Cf. IMO.org, available at http://www.imo.org/en/OurWork/safety/safetytopics/pages/goal-basedstandards.aspx, last retrieved 03.01.2018.

[22] Cf. IMO C 89/12/1 of 8 October 2002.

[23] Ibid.

[24] Cf. Ringbom in: Nordquist/Moore (2001), p. 269.

[25] According to Article 100 Treaty on the Functioning of the European Union.

[26] A detailed list of current Union Legislation on Maritime Safety can be found here: https://ec.europa.eu/transport/sites/transport/files/union_legislation_on_maritime_safety_0.pdf, last retrieved 07.01.2018.

[27] Council Directive 94/57/EC of 22 November 1994 on common rules and standards for ship inspection and survey organisations and the relevant activities of maritime administrations.

[28] Commission Directive 97/58/EC of 26 September 1997 amending Council Directive 94/57/EC on common rules and standards for ship inspection and survey organisations and the relevant activities of maritime administrations.

[29] Directive 2009/15/EC of the European Parliament and of the Council of 23 April 2009 on common rules and standards for ship inspection and survey organisations and the relevant activities of maritime administrations.

[30] Regulation (EC) No 391/2009 of the European Parliament and of the Council of 23 April 2009 on common rules and standards for ship inspection and survey organisations.

[31] Cf. Ringbom in: Nordquist/Moore (2001), p. 269.

[32] Commission Decision 2009/491/EC of 16 June 2009 on criteria, to be followed in order o decide when the performance of an organisation acting on behalf of a flag state can be considered an unacceptable threat to the safety and the environment, notified under document number.

[33] Directive 2001/105/EC of the European Parliament and of the Council of 19 December 2001, amending Council Directive 94/57/EC on common rules and standards for ship inspection and survey organisations and the relevant activities of maritime administrations.

[34] See also Reuß/Pichon, ZaöRV 2007, pp. 127–128.

[35] Articles 9 and 10 of Directive 94/57/EC.

[36] Ibid., Article 9(2).

[37] Ibid., Article 15(3).

[38] Ringbom in: Nordquist/Moore (2001), p. 270.

[39] First Reading Report of the European Parliament PE R5–0534/2000 of 30 November 2000 and Council's Common Position No. 14/2001 of 26 February 2001, OJ 2001, C 101,1.

[40] See for a comprehensive discussion: Goebel (2017), p. 330 et seq.

[41] Ringbom in: Nordquist/Moore (2001), p. 270.

[42] Comprehensive Commentary: Jessen in: Jessen/Werner (2016), pp. 713–855.

[43] Cf. Article 1 of Reg. (EC) No. 391/2009.

[44] See Recital 3 of the Preamble to Regulation (EC) No. 391/2009.

[45] Reuß/Pichon, ZaöRV 2007, p. 130.

[46] Article 6 of Regulation 391/2009.

[47] Commission Regulation (EU) No 788/2014 of 18 July 2014. It lays down detailed rules for the imposition of fines and periodic penalty payments and the withdrawal of recognition of ship inspection and survey organisations under Articles 6 and 7 of Regulation (EC) No 391/2009.

[48] See regarding Article 10 (Mutual Recognition): Jessen, RdTW 2015, pp. 368–374; Goebel (2017), pp. 407–422.

[49] Commission Implementing Directive 2014/111/EU of 17 December 2014 amending Directive 2009/15/EC with regard tot he adoption by the International Maritime Organization (IMO) of specific Codes and related amendments to certain conventions and protocols.

[50] Commission Implementing Regulation (EU) No 1355/2014 of 17 December 2014 amending Regulation (EC) No 391/2009 concerning the adoption by the International Maritime Organization (IMO) of specific Codes and related amendments to certain conventions and protocols Text with EEA relevance.

[51] Cf. Recital 17 of Directive 2014/111 and Regulation 1355/2014.

[52] Paragraph 16.1 of Part 2 of the III Code.

[53] Cf. Recital 21 of Directive 2014/111 and Regulation 1355/2014.

[54] Section 1.3 of Part 2 of the RO Code.

[55] Article 2(g) and (i) of Regulation (EC) No 391/2009.

[56] Cf. Recital 22 of the Directive 2014/111 and Regulation 1355/2014.

[57] Section 3.9.3.1 of Part 2 of the RO Code.

[58] Section 3.9.3.2 of Part 2 of the RO Code.

[59] Cf. Recital 24 of the Preambles to Directive 2014/111/EU and Regulation EU (No) 1355/2014.

[60] http://www.gesetze-im-internet.de/schsg/, last retrieved 08.01.2018.

[61] Directive 2005/35/EC of the European Parliament and of the Council of 7 September 2005 on ship-source pollution and the introduction of penalties for infringements.

[62] Preamble No. 7 of EU Directive 2005/35/EC.

[63] Cour de Cassation, Judgment of 25 September 2012; Tradewinds, Erika ruling pushes liability in spill cases, 28 September 2012.

[64] Reino de España v. American Bureau of Shipping, Inc., 691 F.3d461, 476, 2012 AMC 2113, 2136 (2d Cir. 2012), 29 August 2012.

[65] See, e.g. Jessen, CMI Yearbook 2014, pp. 275–281; de Bruyne/Vanleenhove, Journal of International Maritime Law 2014, p. 103 et seq; de Bruyne, Journal of Maritime Law & Commerce 2014, pp. 181–232.

[66] Micallef, CMI Annual Symposium, Dublin 29 Sept – 1 Oct 2013 (accessible at www.cmi2013dublin.com, last accessed 22 November 2017), pp. 1–26.

[67] Presentations of Hare and Jessen (accessible at www.cmi2014hamburg.org/down-loadcenter/documents, last retrieved 22 November 2017).

[68] For a discussion of Belgian law, see de Bruyne, Journal of Maritime Law & Commerce 2014; for French, New Zealand, and Australian law, see: Basedow/Wurmnest (2005).

[69] Wurmnest/Basedow (2005), Lagoni (2007), Goebel (2017).

[70] See e.g. Somers/Gonsaeles, J. Mar. L. & Com. 2010, pp. 59–60; Goebel (2017), p. 319.

[71] De Bruyne, Journal of Maritime Law & Commerce 2014, p. 217 et seq; Goebel (2017), p. 326.

[72] See, e.g. Siccardi, in London Shipping Law Center (2013).

[73] Galiano, Tul. Mar. L.J. 2004, pp. 113–114; de Bruyne, Journal of Maritime Law & Commerce 2014, p. 213 et seq; Goebel (2017), p. 323.

[74] Corte di Appello di Genova, 18 July 2014 – Sentenza n. 993/2014 publ. Il 18/072014, RG n. 650/2010, Repert. N. 1129/2014; Jessen, RdTW 2015, p. 160; Goebel (2017), p. 328.

[75] Basedow/Wurmnest (2005); see also Daniel, U.S.F. Maritime Law Journal 2006–2007, pp. 183–296; Lagoni (2007); Goebel (2017), pp. 330–356.

[76] Cf. Lagoni (2007), p. 234.

[77] Cf. Goebel (2017), pp. 337–350 with further references.

[78] Cf. Clyne/Saville, Tulane Law Review 2006–2007, p. 1399; Boisson, Are classification societies above the law?, (accessible at www.maritimeadvocate.com/classification/are_classification_societies_above_the_law.htm, last retrieved 22 November 2017); see also Micallef, CMI Annual Symposium, Dublin 29 Sept – 1 Oct 2013, p. 10 et seq.; Skou, CMI Yearbook 1997, pp. 181–183; Kröger, CMI Yearbook 1997, pp. 187–188.

[79] Cf. Micallef, CMI Annual Symposium, Dublin 29 Sept – 1 Oct 2013, p. 6; see also Billah (2014), p. 19 et seq.

[80] Marc Rich & Co. AG v Bishop Rock Marine Co. Ltd and ClassNK ('The Nicolas H.'), [1992] 2 Lloyd's Rep. 481 (Q.B.Comm.), [1994] 1 Lloyd's Rep. 492 (C. A.), [1995] 2 Lloyd's Rep. 299 (H.L.).

[81] See Jessen, CMI Yearbook 2014, p. 280 et seq.; de Bruyne, Journal of Maritime Law & Commerce 2014, p. 231 et seq.; Micallef, CMI Annual Symposium, Dublin 29 Sept – 1 Oct 2013, p. 10 et seq.; see also Lagoni (2007), p. 316 et seq.

[82] Goebel (2017), p. 354 with further references.

[83] Billah (2014), see also Goebel (2017), pp. 359–406.

[84] Regarding the question whether the policy consideration – to align the liability of shipowner and classification societies – might already be achieved by national liability law without changing the liability conventions: see (forthcoming) Goebel, Limited Third-Party Liability of Classification Societies – Land Ahoy? A Comparative Analysis of the gestörte Gesamtschuld Under German and English law, (2018).

[85] Cf. Smith, On a flood tide, 2011, p. 16 et seq.

[86] Ibid., p. 16.

[87] Goebel (2017), p. 212 et seq.

[88] Goebel (2017), p. 431.

[89] Cf. Smith, On a flood tide, 2011, p. 16 and p. 18.

[90] Cf. SDNV/Germanischer Lloyd, Case No COMP/M.6885, 15 July 2013, p. 8.

[91] Goebel (2017), p. 432.

[92] De Bruyne, Journal of Maritime Law & Commerce 2014, p. 232.

[93] Goebel (2017), pp. 432–433.

[94] Some basic research on this issue can be found in Goebel (2017), p. 131 et seq.

[95] Goebel (2017), p. 151.

[96] DNV GL, Droning in the deep, DNV GL publications for the maritime industry, 01/2016, pp. 13–15, available at https://www.dnvgl.com/maritime/publications/magazines.html, last retrieved 08.01.2018.

[97] Type-approval certification: one final classification certificate consists of thousands of type-approval certificates issued by the classification society to the manufacturer of marine components. The final classification certificate will only be issued if the classification society has certified all components in advance, see also Goebel (2017), p. 408 et seq.

Contributing Authors

Kai-Dieter Classen
Dr. Kai-Dieter Classen, LL.M. (Berkeley), Deputy Director of the External Affairs Division of the Hamburg Port Authority

Kai Holger Drews
Attorney, Dr. iur. Kai Holger Drews, Senior Consultant at Aurigon Advisors

Peter Ehlers
Prof. Dr. Dr. h.c. Peter Ehlers, President of the Federal Maritime and Hydrographic Agency (ret.), Institute for Law of the Sea and Maritime Law, Universität Hamburg

Felix Goebel
Attorney, Dr. iur., LL.M. in Maritime Law (Oslo), fellow of the Institute for Maritime Law and the Law of the Sea at the University of Hamburg (2013–2017)

Vladimir Golitsyn
H.E. Judge, President of the International Tribunal for the Law of the Sea

Lothar Harings
Attorney, Dr. iur., partner GvW Graf von Westphalen; founder and managing director of Hamburger Zollakademie ("Hamburg Customs Academy"); chairman European Forum for Foreign Trade, Customs and Exercise (EFA)

Jens Jaeger
Gesamtverband der Deutschen Versicherungswirtschaft e.V. (GDV)

Henning Jessen
Dr. iur., LL.M. (Tulane), Associate Professor for Maritime Law & Policy at the World Maritime University (WMU), Malmö, Sweden; Member of the Institute for Maritime Law and the Law of the Sea at the University of Hamburg (2012–2016)

Carina Lutter
Assistant at the Institute for the Law of the Sea and Maritime Law, Universität Hamburg

Marilena Mroß
Assistant at the Institute for the Law of the Sea and Maritime Law, Universität Hamburg

Nico Nolte
Dr. iur., Head of Management of the Sea Department, Federal Maritime and Hydrographic Agency, Lecturer at the Institute for Law of the Sea and Maritime Law, Universität Hamburg

Marian Paschke
Professor Dr. iur. Dr. h.c.; Full Professor for Private Law, Commercial and Business Law at the Universität Hamburg; Director of the Institute for the Law of the Sea and Maritime Law

Klaus Ramming
Attorney, Dr. iur.; Master Mariner; Senior Lecturer at the Universität Hamburg; Co-Chairman of the German Maritime Association

Katherina Reiling
Dr. iur.; formerly interim professor for the international law of the sea at the University of Hamburg; currently Research Assistant at the University of Konstanz

Stefan Rindfleisch
Attorney, partner, Dr. iur., lecturer at the University of Hamburg, Maritime Commercial Law

Dieter Schwampe
Prof. Dr. iur., Attorney, partner; Senior Lecturer at the Universität Hamburg; Co-Chairman of the German Maritime Association

Suzette V. Suarez
Dr. iur. (Hamburg), LLM (Dalhousie), LLB (Univ of the Phils), BA (Lebanon Valley); currently Vertretungsprofessorin at the Faculty of Law, University of Hamburg

Jan Wölper
Attorney, partner, Chairman of the German Maritime Arbitration Association